TIME IT WAS

TIME IT WAS

American Stories from the Sixties

Karen Manners Smith

Emporia State University, Emporia, Kansas

Tim Koster

Search Systems, Newbury Park, California

PEARSON

Prentice
Hall

Upper Saddle River, New Jersey 07458

Library of Congress Cataloging-in-Publication Data

Smith, Karen Manners.
    Time it was : American stories from the sixties / Karen Manners Smith and Tim Koster.
        p.   cm.
    ISBN-13: 978-0-13-184077-5 (alk. paper)
    ISBN-10: 0-13-184077-0 (alk. paper)
    1. United States—History—1961–1969—Anecdotes.   2. United States—History—1961–1969—Biography.
3. United States—Social conditions—1960–1980—Anecdotes.   4. Social problems—United States—
History—20th century—Anecdotes.   5. Social justice—United States—History—20th century—Anecdotes.
6. Vietnam War, 1961–1975—Social aspects—Anecdotes.   7. Vietnam War, 1961–1975—
United States—Anecdotes.   8. Vietnam War, 1961–1975—Personal narratives, American.
9. Nineteen sixties—Anecdotes.   I. Koster, Tim.   II. Title.

    E838.3.S64 2008
    973.923—dc22

                                                                        2007010492

Editorial Director: Charlyce Jones-Owen
Editorial Assistant: Maureen Diana
Senior Marketing Manager: Kate Mitchell
Marketing Assistant: Jennifer Lang
Production Liaison: Marianne Peters-Riordan
Manufacturing Buyer: Ben Smith
Cover Art Director: Jayne Conte
Cover Design: Bruce Kenselaar
Cover Art: Gina Flanagan / Tim Koster
Director, Image Resource Center: Melinda Patelli

Manager, Rights and Permissions: Zina Arabia
Manager, Visual Research: Beth Brenzel
Manager, Cover Visual Research &
  Permissions: Karen Sanatar
Image Permission Coordinator: Kathy Gavilanes
Composition/Full-Service Project Management:
  Shiny Rajesh / Integra Software Services
Printer/Binder: Courier Companies, Inc.
Cover Printer: Phoenix Color Corp.

Credits and acknowledgments borrowed from other sources and reproduced, with permission, in this textbook appear on appropriate page within text.

Pearson Education LTD.
Pearson Education Singapore, Pte. Ltd
Pearson Education, Canada, Ltd
Pearson Education—Japan
Pearson Education Australia PTY, Limited

Pearson Education North Asia Ltd
Pearson Educación de Mexico, S.A. de C.V.
Pearson Education Malaysia, Pte. Ltd
Pearson Education, Upper Saddle River, New Jersey

10 9 8 7 6 5 4 3 2 1
ISBN-13: 978-0-13-184077-5
ISBN-10:   0-13-184077-0

Dedication

To our spouses, Prudence Koster and Chris O'Carroll; to Darryl, Dana, Noah, and Abraham, who were the inspiration; and to the memory of R. Thomas Collins, Jr., Steve Diamond, Paul Plato, and Leann Flynn.

Time it was, and what a time it was, it was
A time of innocence, a time of confidences
Long ago, it must be, I have a photograph
Preserve your memories, they're all that's left you.

Paul Simon

Contents

Preface

HOW THIS BOOK CAME TO BE: A NOTE FROM THE EDITORS

We owe the genesis of *Time It Was: American Stories from the Sixties* to an e-mail. In the summer of 2001, Tim was searching online for some friends he had lost touch with over the years. One of these people was Karen, whom he had known at Boston University summer school in 1968. He found her e-mail address on her faculty web page at Emporia State University and wrote to her. Delighted to hear a voice from the past, she wrote back.

The first question we asked each other was, "What happened to you?" Tim explained that he "won" the first draft lottery held in 1969, was drafted, fought the draft, and was deferred as a conscientious objector. Karen revealed that she had dropped out of graduate school and spent five years with a religious cult.

In subsequent correspondence, we began to wonder what other Sixties stories might be out there, stories of people now leading "ordinary lives" who had done something brave or principled or adventurous or stupid in those days, or who had been caught up in one of the memorable events or movements of the period. We decided that a collection of such stories would make a great book for college students.

It has been our experience as parents, and Karen's as both a parent and a university professor, that today's college students, the offspring of baby boomers, have little understanding of their parents' young lives. Partly, this has happened because the parents themselves may feel that their colorful pasts have little to do with the lives they lead in the present. But the generation/knowledge gap has also occurred because of the culture wars of the last 25 years and a generalized disapproval of some aspects of Sixties youth activity. Many people who have great stories from the Sixties have been reluctant to tell them to their children.

Further, these children are confused by the very mystique of the 1960s that they have inherited. Whereas schools may have taught them the historical existence of a Vietnam War and a Civil Rights Movement, they see the Sixties, largely though the lens of the media, as a hazy mass of sex-and-drugs-and-psychedelic-music clichés, instead of the complex period of political and social experimentation that it was. Even those who can see beyond the montage of cultural imagery may assume that all the Sixties-era battles about race, class, gender, and sexuality have already been won. Few are aware that much of the twenty-first-century American culture they inhabit grew out of a mixture of Sixties initiatives and a reaction against the social upheaval of that era.

Whether students vaguely idealize the Sixties or despise the period as a national "wrong turn," few today see avenues for meaningful involvement in social or political issues larger than themselves. We wanted to create a book that would help correct stereotypes by presenting detailed and vivid stories of individuals and, at the same time, demonstrate through personal narrative what young people— many of them very ordinary—can and did do. We wanted stories that would both enrich the historical narrative and provide examples of commitment and personal growth. We hoped that students would see something of themselves in these stories, and that they would begin to think about how individuals make history, and how they might become historical actors themselves.

We began a search for contributors, looking for people who would write their own stories. We wanted stories that had never been published before, and we wanted writers who were not necessarily famous for their Sixties experiences. We looked for individuals whose lives had been affected by the Vietnam War and for participants in Sixties social and political movements and Sixties culture— representative people whose stories would communicate what it felt like to be young in that exciting historical period and what it felt like to make choices among the options then available to young people. We found that some of our writers identified themselves as leaders. Others remembered themselves as foot soldiers or observers in civil rights or antiwar or conservative youth movements, yet turned out to have been leaders and innovators when all was said and done. We found other writers who felt that they had had little choice or control over their lives during the period, and that history or fate had pushed them in the direction they eventually followed. In every case, it was clear that our writers' Sixties experiences, both positive and negative, shaped what they did with the rest of their lives.

Our goal was a topically organized story collection covering as many aspects of sixties culture and experience as could fit into a single book. Inevitably, we were not able to get "all" the stories, if it were even possible to determine what "all" the stories are. We connected with some of our writers through personal acquaintance and others through academic and professional contacts, through their published work, or through topical searches. We received a few stories that, unfortunately, we were not able to include. And there were stories we very much wanted that never materialized. We will pursue those for a subsequent edition.

It took us four years to gather all these memoirs. In the end, we had 23 original stories, one previously published, and three based on interviews. Between them, the stories span the years from the mid-1940s to the late 1970s, though they all center on the Sixties era, a period that cannot be contained in a single decade. Readers can learn more about each of the contributors in the brief biographies included at the end of the book.

Acknowledgments

A project that casts a net this wide cannot happen without a lot of help. We would like to thank the following for their assistance, encouragement, and patience: First of all, our contributors; our spouses and our families—Chris O'Carroll, Prudence Koster, Noah Smith, Abraham Smith, Amanda Atkinson, Darryl and Jane Koster, Dana Koster, Chris Wolowiec; our editors and editorial staff at Prentice Hall: Charlyce Jones-Owen and Charles Cavaliere, Maureen Diana, Emsal Hassan, Paul Hightower, Marianne Peters-Riordan, Shiny Rajesh, and the historians who reviewed the manuscript; Max Helix, our transcriber; Justin Souza; Lily Haggerty; librarians at Kent State University and Western Reserve Academy; Mary Beth Sigado at the Swarthmore College Peace Collection; Wendy Notsinneh, in Jackie Goldberg's office; Margaret Cox Smith, Cherie Rankin, Gregory Schneider, Terry Anderson, Jameson Campaigne, Phyllis Jackson, Rob Okun, Ann Withorn, Robert and June Coe, Judy Coe, Haley Coe, Chris Wilson, Sean Dickson, Jerry Mooers, Tom Fels, Michael Dover, Jane Whiteside, Janet Brown Ruhl, Joyce and Len Berkman, and Ann and Michael Meeropol.

Karen Manners Smith
Tim Koster
February, 2007

Introduction

APPROACHING THIS BOOK

The stories in this book are personal memoirs covering a period from the 1940s to the late 1970s, though the focus of each is on an activity, event, or experience of the Sixties era. The chapters are organized in a series of topical clusters, each with an introduction providing historical background, introducing the individual stories, and indicating ways those stories relate to the cluster theme. It will be readily apparent that historical themes cannot be contained neatly in clusters, and that certain issues, trends, and events appear in multiple places throughout the book. The memoirs can be read alone and they can also be read and examined in relation to each other. Questions following each chapter are designed to offer students a chance to discuss stories individually or to compare them with each other.

The first section of the book deals with the Vietnam War, a looming presence that spanned almost the entire historical period. Stories in this section cover military life, women's support services, draft resistance, and the war's impact on the Vietnamese people themselves. The second section deals with a wide variety of the period's social problems and social justice campaigns, including the Civil Rights Movement, the American Indian Movement, and women's and gay liberation movements. One story provides a picture of southern race relations prior to the Sixties. The third section of the book presents a variety of Sixties youth pursuits, some in government-sponsored New Frontier and Great Society programs and others both less formal and less orthodox, including drug experimentation, going "back to the land," and joining a religious cult. The fourth section contains a variety of stories from young conservatives, participants in a growing movement compounded of anti-Communism, traditionalism, and libertarianism that would have its major political successes in a later era, during the administration of Ronald Reagan. The fifth section tells the stories of participants in some of the era's landmark events: urban riots, the Chicago Democratic Convention of 1968, Woodstock, and Kent State. The final section includes three leadership stories from the Berkeley Free Speech Movement, the United Farm Workers grape boycott, and the anti-nuclear power movement of the early 1970s.

We anticipate that this book will be used as a course reader, a supplement to a Sixties or post-1945 textbook, and to lectures by the course instructor. However, the cluster introductions are designed to provide the historical overview necessary to understand the stories in the cluster and to place them in context. We recommend that students read the introductions before approaching the stories.

A WORD ABOUT MEMOIRS

Memoirs are primary documents written by eyewitnesses to history. As the word implies, "memoir" is based on memory. It is a form of storytelling that places the narrator inside an historical episode or period—usually something experienced in an earlier phase of the storyteller's life. Memoirs do not necessarily offer an objective view of the past. Instead, memoirs, like oral history, and like letters and diaries, offer vivid pictures of the past; they infuse the past with a sense of immediacy, and they make historical people seem more human and understandable. When memoirists tell us what they were feeling when they stepped into a particular moment of history, they give us access to the emotional side of historical experience. We believe that the memoirs we have selected for this book will contribute evocative, detailed narratives to the documentary history of the Sixties era, and that students will find that they enrich and humanize the historical picture.

Something students may want to be aware of as they respond to the stories in this book is that writers of memoirs are engaged in representing themselves to their readers, a process which also shapes the "history" being related. Inevitably, when we tell our own stories, we become characters in those stories and present ourselves in a particular light. We choose the self we want others to see—a heroic self, a modest self, a decisive self, a bewildered self, and so on. Further, people who write memoirs may have political or social biases, or they may be protective of their own or other people's reputations. For all these reasons, we encourage readers to explore the rich layering of these memoirs and to think not only about the historical episodes they cover but also about the storytellers' craft, the representational and rhetorical strategies they use to achieve their effects, and the tone and impact of the stories.

Vietnam

Introduction

For the United States, the Vietnam War (1961–1975) was the single most devastating episode of the larger Cold War, the near half-century of political and ideological tensions between the East and the West that reverberated around the globe from 1945 to 1991. It has also been said that the Vietnam War was the most divisive event in U.S. history since the Civil War, pitting Americans on the home front against each other in support of the war or in angry opposition to it. Along with the Civil Rights Movement, the war in Vietnam—and responses to it—shaped much of what we have come to think of as the history of the 1960s. The Vietnam War is still fresh in many minds; its validity and meaning are still contested and still politically sensitive. Veterans, survivors, and their families in both the United States and Vietnam still live with the after-effects.

The stories in this section illustrate multiple aspects of the war and its long aftermath. Two are written by American combat soldiers, one by a Red Cross volunteer, and another by a draft resister who became a conscientious objector. The author of the final story is a former Vietnamese national, forced to flee his own country, who came to the United States as a refugee in the late 1970s.

In the Vietnam War, more than 58,000 Americans were killed or classified as missing in action and more than 153,000 were wounded. Nearly two million Vietnamese soldiers and civilians on both sides of the conflict lost their lives. Hundreds of thousands more were injured and maimed. There were also casualties among American allies from

South Korea, Australia, New Zealand, and the Philippines. Agent Orange defoliated vast tracts of Vietnam and much of the country's environment was poisoned by toxins used during the war. Both the Americans and the North Vietnamese planted mines throughout the landscape and along the coastal waters. In the end, the United States removed its military from South Vietnam, and the victorious North Vietnamese Army forcibly unified the country under Communist leaders. Thousands of war refugees fled Vietnam, seeking asylum throughout the world but mostly in the United States.

The United States first became involved in the life and politics of Vietnam in the 1950s, while trying to help the French sustain their colonial empire in Southeast Asia. After a disastrous defeat at Dien Bien Phu in 1954, the French withdrew, leaving a revolutionary Communist-leaning government on the north side of a Demilitarized Zone (DMZ). Vietnam was divided pending reunification elections but those elections never occurred. From 1954 onward, U.S. presidents sent civilian and military "advisors" to help train South Vietnamese soldiers; all U.S. policy decisions were based on the perceived need to maintain a Western presence in Vietnam to halt the spread of Communism throughout Southeast Asia. However, insurgent Communists formed a "National Liberation Front" in South Vietnam in 1960. The insurgents, later known by the name "Viet Cong," waged guerilla warfare throughout the south in support of the efforts of the North Vietnamese Army and the Communist government of North Vietnam.

In late 1963, the government of South Vietnamese premier Ngo Dinh Diem was toppled in a coup that had the covert support of the U.S. government (U.S. leaders felt Diem's government was ineffectual in halting the spread of Communism). The following August, North Vietnamese torpedo boats allegedly attacked U.S. destroyers in the Gulf of Tonkin, an event which precipitated President Johnson's order for retaliatory air strikes against North Vietnam. Passing the Gulf of Tonkin Resolution in 1964, Congress gave Johnson full authority to "take all necessary measures to repel any armed attack against forces of the United States and to prevent further aggression." From this point on, the war expanded, drawing more and more American military into what turned out to be a quagmire, a war of attrition in which neither side gained territory and the only assessments of progress were body counts. The U.S. Congress never officially declared war.

Lyndon Johnson had committed the country to a war it could neither win nor withdraw from without—as he saw it—appearing weak and defeated to the rest of the world. Johnson's presidency foundered as the Vietnam War grew increasingly unpopular at home and abroad. By 1968, the year of the Tet Offensive, the My Lai Massacre, and massive anti-war demonstrations in the United States, nearly half a million American men were in Vietnam and Republican presidential candidate Richard Nixon was promising the electorate that he would bring peace with honor.

During Nixon's first term, gradual troop withdrawals began. Nixon's stated program was to remove all the Americans and turn the fighting entirely over to the South Vietnamese. But in 1970, Nixon ordered the invasion of Cambodia and made incursions into Laos. Protests erupted on campuses all across the United States and unarmed student demonstrators were shot and killed by National Guard units and police at Kent State and Jackson State Universities.

At the Paris Peace Talks in 1973, both sides agreed to a cease-fire and the last American troops departed in March. But the war in Vietnam dragged on until the South Vietnamese government surrendered to North Vietnam. In April 1975, the last Americans—embassy staff, marine guards, civilian workers, and their dependents— along with South Vietnamese loyalists, were hastily evacuated by plane and heli- copter. The Provisional Revolutionary Government took control on June 6, 1975. Vietnam and the United States did not normalize diplomatic relationships until the 1990s.

Vietnam left a bitter memory in the minds of most Americans. People had lost friends and family members; veterans returned scarred and traumatized. Other young men had fled the country, never (they assumed) to return. There were no gains from the Vietnam War, only losses. Had it been worthwhile, Americans asked each other, or had it been a terrible mistake? Did the government ever tell us the truth about what was actually going on in Vietnam? The questions are still being asked. Issues connected with Vietnam continue to affect presidential elections and policy-making to this day. Like so many people whose lives were touched in some way by the Vietnam War, the contributors to this section feel that the war influenced who they became and who they are today.

Brothers Wayne and Paul Coe were born in the late 1940s to a devout Mormon family living in California. Their father was a career Naval officer who had served in World War II. Wayne, the older brother, went directly from high school graduation into an Army flight school, where he earned the rank of Warrant Officer and learned to fly helicopters, fulfilling an ambition that had been growing since his childhood.

In 1967, when Wayne Coe's story begins, the price of that ambition was a year's service in Vietnam. Assigned to the Blackhawks, the 187th Assault Helicopter Company based in Tay Ninh, Coe became an aircraft commander with the call sign "Blackhawk 54." He flew supply and medical evacuation (Medevac) missions from Tay Ninh and other American bases of operation. Frequently under fire, especially when extracting wounded soldiers from live battlefields, Coe was shot down seven times, sustained several injuries, but managed to survive the war. Versions of the sto- ries he tells here first appeared on the Blackhawks' Vietnam veterans website, where Coe crafted narratives from memories, good and bad, that continue to haunt him more than three decades after the war.

Like most American soldiers in Vietnam, Coe only occasionally interacted with the Vietnamese themselves. Like most soldiers, he trusted individual leaders while remaining skeptical about the military command as a whole, and he decided to inter- pret the meaning of the conflict for himself. Like many of the young men sent to fight a baffling and perhaps unwinnable war, he focused his heart and his energies on his friends and on saving the lives of his brothers in arms.

Wayne Coe was decorated for his helicopter rescues, but he left the Army as soon as he could after his tour in Vietnam and spent a number of years as a commer- cial pilot. Now retired, he stays connected with his former comrades in the Blackhawks and commits much of his time to helping other Vietnam veterans find the services they need to cope with war-related illnesses and post-traumatic stress disorder (PTSD).

Unlike his father and his brother, Paul Coe had no military ambitions. A bright and lighthearted California teenager, Paul decided on college and attended the University of California at Berkeley. He sympathized with the anti-war protestors he met at college, even though his brother was serving in Vietnam. As a practicing Mormon, Paul did not drink, smoke, or take drugs. However, after attending a fraternity party where the campus police found some marijuana seeds, he and several other students were expelled from the university. Paul lost his student deferment. In April of 1969, he found himself drafted into the U.S. Army. His letters home from boot camp reveal a gentle, ironic sense of humor, a strong religious faith, and a powerful sense of duty. They also reveal his deep internal conflict about being trained to kill.

Because desertion was not in his character, even though he thought about it, Paul Coe decided to stick with the Army. Following a brief interlude of leave, during which he married his college sweetheart, he was sent to Vietnam. Initially assigned to an office job, Paul grew impatient with the Army's wartime bureaucracy and infuriated by the incompetence and complacency of the "lifers." He requested a field posting to an instant reconnaissance team.

There is no accurate count of the number of American women who worked in Vietnam during the conflict, but estimates exceed 7,000. In that period, decades before women could be assigned to combat units, they were able to participate in a variety of ways. Women served in all branches of the military as professional nurses and physical and occupational therapists. There were women air traffic controllers, intelligence and language specialists, and administrators. Civilian women worked in Vietnam in the Red Cross, the U.S. Agency for International Development (USAID), and the U.S. Health Service, as well as in other government agencies. There were also American women journalists in Vietnam, as well as a number of women who volunteered to work as missionaries and social service workers with churches and humanitarian organizations.

Fresh out of college, Leah O'Leary decided that she wanted to see for herself what the war in Vietnam was about. She was also looking for an adventure. In 1968 she joined the Red Cross's Supplemental Recreation Activities Overseas (SRAO) program and became a "Donut Dollie," a nickname she explains in her story.

Donut Dollies wore light blue cotton uniforms with knee-length skirts and black loafers or light blue sneakers. They ran recreation centers on bases, but they also visited groups of soldiers anywhere they were standing down or providing support services to troops in the field. Donut Dollies worked 10- to 12-hour days, usually six days a week, and traveled long distances by helicopter or in military vehicles over mined roads. Sometimes they lived in tents, and, even in places where they had plumbing, they most often had to use outhouses. Surrounded in a strange land by people with whom they could not speak and with whom they had little direct contact, heavily protected by military guards, hedged in by strict rules governing their conduct, and aware that danger was always nearby, Donut Dollies nevertheless found ways to make their jobs in Vietnam meaningful to themselves and to the young enlisted men they were assigned to entertain.

Initially skeptical about the utility of conducting recreation programs in a war zone, O'Leary later saw value in her low-key, friendly interaction with young

American men sent halfway around the world to fight in a war that terrified and threatened to dehumanize them. Although O'Leary's story minimizes the heat and the hard work of wartime service in Vietnam, she does not hesitate to discuss her feelings of cultural isolation or her emotionally charged encounters with young men living constantly on the edge of death. Donut Dollies were kept away from combat areas; they did not nurse or even visit with casualties right off the field. Yet, as O'Leary tells us, they felt and understood what was going on all around them. Donut Dollies suffered from PTSD in the years following their tours in Vietnam, as did soldiers and nurses. Today, Leah O'Leary continues to process her memories and to dedicate her life to international service. She runs A Red Thread Adoption Services, Inc., an agency specializing in foreign adoptions.

While Wayne Coe and Leah O'Leary chose to go to Vietnam, and Paul Coe went because he was drafted, there were others whose hatred of war, and particularly the war in Vietnam, led them to resist the draft in a variety of ways. Tim Koster, born in the Midwest, a former high school football player, had just turned 20 and was attending Boston University. However, before starting college he had worked in a warehouse to earn money for tuition, so he was not enrolled in enough total hours to maintain his student deferment. He was reclassified I-A, becoming eligible for service just before the first draft lottery drawing in December 1969. Koster's story tells about his journey from youthful naiveté to political awareness through his educational and social encounters in Boston—a national center of the anti-war and draft resistance movements during the 1960s and 1970s—and his surprising and creative response to being drafted to fight in a war he could not support.

The United States has used the system of a draft—the enforced conscription of able-bodied men to fight the country's wars—off and on since the nineteenth century. In 1940, the Selective Training and Service Act created the country's first peacetime draft and made the Selective Service System an independent federal agency. During World War II, the agency used a lottery system, and after the war, whether the United States was at peace or at war, all men between 18 and 26 had to register for the draft and any number could be called up to fill vacancies in the armed forces that had not been filled through voluntary enlistments. Draft deferments in the 1960s were available to full-time students, men involved in occupations considered vital to the country, those physically unable to serve, and those with serious hardships, prior service, or any one of several other classifications. The draft-eligible were classed I-A, full-time students were II-S, conscientious objectors, I-AO, I-O, or I-W, and those physically unable to serve were IV-F.

The first draft lottery of the Vietnam War was held on December 1, 1969. All the dates of the year, enclosed in blue plastic capsules in a giant glass bowl, were drawn one by one and matched to lottery numbers 1 to 366. The first date picked was September 14 and the last was June 8. That meant that all men born on September 14 in any year between 1944 and 1950, if not otherwise exempt, would be the first to be drafted for the year 1970. It was generally considered that if your birth date fell among the first 100 to 120 numbers drawn, you were headed for military service. If you were born on June 8 (lottery number 366), you could relax. The active draft ended in 1973, though draft registration is still in place.

In 1969, when Tim Koster's number came up, his life and all his plans were transformed beyond anything he could have foreseen. He was confronted with a set of unappealing choices: he could join one of the military services or be drafted into the Army; he could refuse the draft and go to prison; he could leave the country, never able to return, and eventually sacrifice his American citizenship. He could file for status as a conscientious objector—an official pacifist—although it was almost impossible to be classified as a CO because many draft boards required the applicant to demonstrate a lifetime of religious or ethical commitment to pacifism. If, however, a young man were to be reclassified CO, he could either work as a medic in the Army or be assigned in the United States to a service job that contributed to the national safety, welfare, or health. One thing Koster could not do was continue with the life he had planned. He decided to seek the advice of draft counselors and make himself familiar with the activities of the draft resistance movement being organized by his peers. When he received his draft notice, he left the country to give himself more time to plan his response.

Most draft resisters, contrary to some historical accounts, were highly principled young men who opposed the war in Vietnam and refused to participate in it. They organized protests, picketed draft boards, and published pamphlets and newsletters. They counseled each other on ways to avoid the draft by deliberately failing the physical exam, or finding exempt employment, or leaving the country, most often for Canada, which had no legal provisions for extraditing young men seeking immigrant status simply because they were draft-eligible in their country of origin. Some resisters publicly burned their draft cards. Failure to carry one's draft card at all times was a crime, so burning a draft card was not an idle gesture. Vietnam veterans who opposed the war joined protests or staged their own. Some turned in their medals and, in at least one Washington, D.C., protest, some hurled ribbons and medals at the Capitol building. As the war moved into the 1970s, acts in opposition to the draft became angrier and more dramatic. Radicals burned or vandalized draft board files, sometimes pouring blood on the files as a symbolic act.

Draft resistance was part of the anti-war movement in the United States. Around the country, draft resisters encountered both support and hatred. How Americans felt about draft resisters tended to coincide with how they felt about the war in Vietnam. Those who thought the war was a mistake wanted the United States to withdraw from Vietnam and bring the troops home. They tended to sympathize with young men taking action to avoid the draft. Others felt the draft resisters were cowards and coined the term "draft dodger" as an insult, an attempt to assign them a permanent badge of dishonor. Competing visions of patriotism were at work, as they are in every war. One side felt patriotism meant supporting all of the country's policies, including wars, and making sure its warriors did not feel they were dying in vain or in a dubious cause. The other side felt patriotism consisted in demanding accountability from the government, declaring publicly that the war was a mistake, and insisting that the troops be brought home before more men died.

When the war finally ended with the fall of Saigon in April 1975, it left chaos in its wake. South Vietnamese loyalists, those who had fought the North Vietnamese or worked for the Americans in any capacity, anti-Communists, and other political or religious dissidents fled the country in fear for their lives. More than 125,000 left Vietnam in the first few weeks; another quarter of a million followed in later months. These first refugees and their families traveled by plane or ship, their escapes facilitated by the Americans, who felt obligated to former allies. Many of these refugees were settled in the United States. Policies of the new Communist government in Vietnam brought massive relocations, redistribution of land, and further repression for former South Vietnamese soldiers, intellectuals, and religious leaders, as well as their families. Many were incarcerated in brutal "re-education" camps, such as the one Huỳnh Quang Ngọc describes in his story.

The camps were designed not only to punish but also to engineer political and cultural conversion. Repression created a new wave of refugees, ethnic minorities as well as Vietnamese, who began to escape Vietnam in 1977, this time without assistance. Carrying small children and household goods, many walked hundreds of miles through jungles and mountains to cross the border into another country. Others spent their life savings for passage in overcrowded and unseaworthy boats. These vessels attempted to sail to nearby countries—Thailand, Hong Kong, the Philippines, Indonesia, Malaysia, and Singapore—where temporary refugee camps were set up. Many boatloads of Vietnamese refugees were lost at sea or became victims of robbery, rape, and sometimes murder at the hands of pirates. By 1981, however, nearly 400,000 Vietnamese had escaped the country. From refugee camps, they gradually made their way to countries around the world that would grant them asylum and allow them to apply for citizenship. The United Nations High Commission for Refugees and the U.S. Refugee Act of 1980 facilitated entry into the United States. The U.S. commitment to family reunification gave priority to refugees who had relatives already living in America.

Huỳnh Quang Ngọc's journey began at the end of the Vietnam War, when he was a university student in Saigon. The son of a farmer, outspoken and idealistic, he was arrested and sent to a re-education camp where he nearly starved to death. In "A Life in Flight," he tells the story of his idyllic rural childhood, his arrest, his life in a prison camp, his repeated attempts to escape from Vietnam, and his subsequent life as a refugee in the United States. Huỳnh's chapter is a short version of his 1994 memoir, *South Wind Changing*, which was named a *Time* magazine Best Non-Fiction Book of the Year and was nominated for the National Book Award.

Huỳnh was not among the first wave of Vietnamese refugees who received resettlement assistance from American sponsors. As a "boat person" from the second wave, he gained access to the United States because a brother was already living there, but he started his American life with empty pockets and almost no English. A thirst for education and a gift for writing enabled his extraordinary adaptation to his new home. With degrees from Bennington College and Brown University, Huỳnh is now a professor of creative writing, the author of two novels, and the co-editor of an oral history collection about Vietnamese boat people.

BLACKHAWK 54
Wayne "Crash" Coe

"Crash"

The Blackhawks are doing a combat assault close to the Cambodian border in an area known for hot landing zones. Capt. Rock Lungarella is the flight leader for the first platoon. Flight leader means the first one in the formation, first one to land in the LZ (Landing Zone). I'm two weeks in Vietnam and this is my first mission.

A month before I had wings I already had orders sending me to the Blackhawks (187th Assault Helicopter Company, Tay Ninh, Vietnam). I knew that it would be rough being a new guy; in fact the term for new guy was FNG or Fucking New Guy. No one wanted to know someone with so few flying skills that he could be dead tomorrow; they would rather use the time-honored Army Aviation way of having you earn your way into the Aircraft Commander's seat. Up until that point you would just be a peter pilot (copilot), the worst type of peter pilot, an FNG peter pilot.

Peter pilots are passed around, so they get a chance to fly with every aircraft commander in the unit. I was the new peter pilot fresh from flight school and Capt. Rock was a seasoned veteran of the air war. An Airborne Ranger, Rock was one of the original Dirty Dozen, troublemakers from all the other units sent to the Blackhawks when they arrived in country. He was thick, muscular, covered in black hair, always a smile on his face. The first thing he said to me when I got into the helicopter was that helicopters are Italian because they go wop, wop, wop, all day long. Then he laughed and we all laughed with him.

We pick up the combat troops and start for the landing zone. Rock is chatting away on the radio, alternating with the intercom. I'm scared, having never seen that many helicopters in the air at once. The gunships and artillery are all pounding the landing zone right in front of us. Rock instructs me to put my hands on the controls to follow him through the control moves; in case he gets hit I can take the controls immediately. Rock is calm, almost amused as we descend into the landing zone.

Cobra gunships on the right side, Air Force fast movers shooting up the trees with their twenty-millimeter guns and Rock singing along with the Armed Forces Radio over the intercom. "People who need people, are the luckiest people in the world." Streisand at her best, while out of the windshield all hell is breaking loose.

We drop the troops off and we are taking fire from the tree line as we depart the landing zone. Our helicopter is hit bad, we are going down. Rock at the controls, we make it across the river and autorotate to a field. We jump out of the helicopter, scramble for the nearest cover, and watch the Viet Cong running from the tree line to get a better shot. I don't have a weapon; I have left everything behind in the shot-down helicopter. This will be the last time I make this mistake; I get an M-16 rifle from the gunner and start shooting. First come our Rat Pack gunships fast and low. They start shooting up the tree lines with a loud roar, coming right over our heads, the ping of spent brass hitting the helicopter sitting silent on the ground.

Then low level over the tree line Warrant Officer Sam Bose going like a bat out of hell. He brings his helicopter in with a big sideways flair and he's beside us with a strained smile on his face. We grab the radios and run as fast as we can for the open door of that beautiful Huey.

The feelings I have when I look up and see that rescue ship would be hard to describe to anybody. We are not out of trouble, but we are being picked up by one of our brothers. There is no doubt about it, Sam is putting his life and the lives of his crew on the line for us. At that moment he has a running helicopter and it's the ride home we desperately need. We are taking heavy automatic fire; it's obvious Sam Bose could care less. Sam gets out of there the way he came in.

(I can vividly recall the feeling of being alive as the helicopter went up and up and the air started to cool down. I knew I was going to live and was overcome with joy.)

Rock is plugged into the intercom of our rescue helicopter and so am I. Rock is still smiling and says to Sam Bose and his crew, "They say that when you get to where you really love the combat flying, you are changed forever, and God I love this shit."

I am in the Blackhawks two weeks and I get shot down the first time out, which makes me a survivor and acceptable to my pilot buddies who are already starting to call me "Crash."

***

I grew up in California in a pretty typical American family. I thought my parents were the best anyone could have. My hippie brother, Paul, with his long blond hair and handlebar mustache, was 13 months younger and my best friend. My sister Jane was growing up fast, and the baby of our family, Keith, was getting taller every minute I wasn't there to watch.

All of us in my family were practicing Mormons. I always went to church on Sunday and came home to a huge meal my mother would prepare. I thought my mother, June, was the best cook in the whole world, and while I enjoyed flying for the Army, I missed my mom's cooking.

My father, Robert T. Coe, had gone into the Navy when he was sixteen, after being orphaned. He became a Navy Chief before World War II started—at age 21. He spent twenty years in the Navy, retiring as an E-8 Chief Petty Officer. He witnessed the painting of the battleships from white to gray and was at sea from the Japanese attack on Pearl Harbor to the dropping of the atomic bombs on Hiroshima and Nagasaki. I was proud of my father all dressed up in his uniform, covered with battle ribbons and other cool things I knew nothing about.

Dad's best friend and fishing buddy was a Navy Chief Pilot. He took a direct commission during WWII so he could continue flying. But in his heart he was always a Chief Radioman. He had a tattoo of his Navy wings across his back, the result of a bet during a drunken spree in the Philippines. I remember very clearly my father taking me to the airport and the two of us climbing into the mosquito sprayer and going for a ride with Dad's friend to see the Navy base from a different angle. I never wanted to do anything else but be a pilot after that. I was hooked at an early age.

I graduated from high school in 1965 and Paul the year after. I wanted to go to college, but once I found out that I could fly an Army helicopter right out of high school, I made application and was accepted to the Army's Rotary Wing Warrant Officer Candidate School. I arrived in Texas at the ripe old age of eighteen to start flight school.

Army flight school was an officer prep school and a flight school together. That made it possible for the Army to put the maximum pressure on all the men to see who was good enough to wear a pair of wings. Of the 400 men who started out in my class, 114 graduated with wings on April 11th, 1967.

I loved it. I was an eighteen year old who loved speed, power, and danger. They should have called it Disneyland instead of flight school.

As a young Warrant Officer with pilot wings on your chest, there was only one destination you would consider and that was Vietnam. I wanted to fly and Vietnam was the only place in the world that a nineteen year old could be the Aircraft Commander of a $400K machine, and they would give you all the fuel and bullets you wanted. I was going direct to a line aviation outfit, the Blackhawks.

I arrived in Vietnam April 24th of 1967. Two weeks later, I was "Crash."

Smells

Did I sleep last night? I must have. I am here on my cot under the mosquito net, just like I have been every night since I arrived at Tay Ninh. Wide-awake at 0400, I know it is flying time again. I can hear all six Warrant Officers farting and moving around in my GP (General Purpose) medium tent mounted precariously on a plywood platform. Time for the morning shit, the line forms quickly at the four-holer near the showers; funny they would call it a shower, when it's just a tank with cold water running out through some shower heads mounted on a crossbeam. You even get some adrenaline in the shower when the cold water hits your grimy skin.

The prevailing wind in our area comes from over the jungle to the west of Tay Ninh. I am up-wind of the JP-4 (jet fuel) powered crappers. Downwind, this particular crapper had a plume of stink coming off of it that was identifiable over a half mile away out on the flight line. When it's my turn to enter the torture chamber, I first take several deep breaths of the perfumed air coming from the jungle. Then, as my father had instructed me years ago when I was learning to free dive, I enter the mental state of a deep diver holding my breath. Total time spent is less than two minutes. I manage to not inhale any of the air, therefore eliminating a major source of nausea in the early morning.

I have a pile of clean clothing washed by the Vietnamese down at the river. I pull on the jungle fatigues and inhale the brown slimy river that is all over my shirt. I liked the smell of body odor better. The river-washed shirts always itched my skin; later I would take the whole pile to the hospital next door and have it cleaned there—one of the side benefits of having a nurse girlfriend and flying so much Medevac.

Any meal in Tay Ninh was an experience. Breakfast was particularly nauseating. Today my shirt smells like a duck pond, and the smell being pumped out of the mess hall by the big electric fan in the door strikes my olfactory senses like a mallet. The slightly sour smell of the garbage, body odor, cigarettes, and coffee, no way. I make a 180 and head back to the tent for my flying gear. C-rations for breakfast, no problem for me.

I look for my maps and notes from last night's briefing in the dark of my tent. I grab my clean guns and my camera, time to go to the flight line, Captain Lungarella would be at the aircraft ready to go right now. He loved to fly and would never be late.

On the way to the helicopter I stop at the Operations tent to pick up my survival radio. I am home again, the smell of the radios and batteries is just like the radio shop my father worked in. The smell of the hot lead solder is unmistakable. I sign for the survival radio, say hi to the radio tech, and I am off to the flight line.

Captain Rock is untied and starting to light the fire, always impatient. I loved to fly with the Ranger Rock. I am barely plugged into the intercom and Rock is picking up to a hover and calling for takeoff: full power south departure. We are off Tay Ninh at 0450 out into the beginning day, hell it is still dark. I get my shoulder harness and lap belts hooked up, the plate on the seat moved forward, and look over at Rock; he is laughing at me. "So what took you so long?" He was always fucking with my mind. We were airborne 10 minutes early. I was not late, he was early.

Rock's first command of the day, "Let's get some tunes on the ADF, see if you can get armed forces radio from here." Rock pulls some pitch and we go up in search of a clear signal. The sun is just coloring the horizon, its sixty-five degrees outside of the cockpit at 2,000 feet AGL, and we are rocking and rolling singing along with the radio. Life was good when you were a helicopter pilot.

Our first mission of the day is in support of an ARVN (Army of the Republic of Vietnam) unit south and east of Saigon in an area Captain Lungarella has worked many times before. We near Saigon as the sun is just coming over the horizon. It illuminates the plumes of smoke coming off of cooking fires in the thousands of small grass houses that dot the countryside. The air is still, no movement.

One of our Fire Support Bases is firing in our direction; we either have to go to 16,000 feet or low level. Low level, my favorite. Streaking along at over 100 knots, cyclic climbing over the trees, every garden has its own perfume, its own beautiful smell. Some smell like jasmine, and some smell like gardenia, some just smell new and exotic. A Vietnamese villager spends his whole life growing a beautiful garden to surround his home and we fly through at 100 knots sniffing and singing on the radio. I am getting paid to do this.

The smell starts to change as we near the built-up areas. No more perfumed gardens in the countryside, now it is pigs, people, and black rivers. The stench of garbage and sewage forces us up a few hundred feet as we cross over into the Delta south of Saigon. Rock is on the radio, doing all the flying and I am left with my own thoughts as we streak south in the morning calm, gaining altitude as we head out into the Viet Cong-held Mekong Delta.

"Pop smoke," Rock calls on the FM radio to the U.S. Advisors on the ground. I can't see a thing. It all looks dark to me. We are 1,500 feet in the air with the breaking day flooding in the windshield, I can't see a fucking thing. Rock keys his mike "Tally ho! Goofy Grape!" and starts a screaming approach to the black void as they roger our identification. I can just make out the camp and can see the smoke coming up. We make our approach to the smoke grenade. The purple smoke is choking and it swirls around the helicopter and covers everything with its acrid thick purple dust. Smells like sulfur everywhere.

Rock lights up a smoke and turns to me, "Shut her down." Rock jumps out shaking hands and patting every one on the back, wearing his big smile. Rock finds out just what they want us to do today over a cup of coffee and another cigarette, sitting with friends in the middle of nowhere. Watching Rock work made it enjoyable just to be out there.

Quiet takes on a new meaning out in the Mekong Delta early in the morning. I pull my helmet off and get out of the helicopter. We have landed in the middle of an ARVN night defensive position, and they are all up and cooking breakfast. Their food smells good mingled with the smell of tobacco and cooking fires. I am offered a bowl of rice. I accept, handing over a box of C-rats in trade. Just before the little Vietnamese cook hands me the bowl, he gives it a small shot of Nuoc Mam from an old black bottle. The fermented herring sauce tastes salty and good, but it smells worse than any thing else in Vietnam. They claim that the buzzards drop dead when they fly over the factory on the coast, just from the smell. They layer salt and herrings and leave the whole thing in the sun until black juice drips out of the mess. I eat my rice holding my nose, and in a few minutes we light up the chopper and haul troops and supplies around for most of the morning, taking time out only to refuel.

We get released early from the ARVN advisors and Rock heads for Tan Son Nhut Airbase in Saigon. Lunch in Saigon with Rock is a real experience. He knows all the good places to go. Within minutes of leaving Hotel-3 helipad in a Renault taxi, we are at a Chinese restaurant in Cholon sitting down to a feast. Rock orders seafood. "Just keep it coming," Rock calls into the kitchen. They bring us huge tiger shrimps on a stick, and soup with unidentifiable sea creatures all smelling so good and tasting wonderful. I think my favorite is the coconut milk and curried shrimp, with the jasmine-scented rice. Smells like flowers, tastes like rice. I have eaten enough to feed a small family.

My belly is so full I can hardly take a breath. We are packed into a little taxi and head off full speed to the airbase; we can hardly see where we are going, the air is full of blue smoke from all of the two-cycle engines running wide open all around us. Fires burning, people cooking, three-wheeled Lambretta scooters belching smoke, and enough Honda 50-cc motorcycles to make the roads impassable and the air unbreathable. It's fun tearing across town in a taxi, Rock telling stories and smoking cigarettes out in the blue smoky air of the city streets. But I would be happy to be airborne and breathing clear, clean air again.

Traffic in and out of Hotel-3 is always heavy. We are running on the refueling pad waiting our turn for take off. Everywhere around us are helicopters landing, taking off, and hovering around. The burning jet fuel from all the turbine engines gives off an overpowering smell of JP-4 and it's wonderful. It seemed I had always wanted to be a helicopter pilot; I had dreamed about this moment. We are holding next to go after an H-4 on short final. As their rotor wash hits our helicopter, I can smell the distinctive odor of 115/145 gasoline feeding that old round engine. Gasoline, another of my favorites, one of the smells from the flight school days. Only months in the past, it seemed like forever ago.

"Blackhawk 69 Tan Son Nhut tower, say again your destination."

Rock picks up his own number, "Tan Son Nhut tower Blackhawk 69, we are en route Tay Ninh, over."

"Roger Blackhawk 69. Hover to the VIP pad and hold. How much room do you have? We have the new Donut Dollies fresh from the world needing a ride to Cu Chi."

Rock does not skip a beat and answers the tower, "Blackhawk 69 has room for all of them, send them out."

We set down on the VIP pad and went to flight idle. Out of the Operations building came 10 round-eye women each carrying identical luggage and dressed in the same light blue dress. They all had wide eyes and had never been on a helicopter before. And the smell. I could smell them thru the rotor wash and the JP-4, I could smell them almost before I could see them. Rock had sent the Crew Chief and Gunner to assist the girls, but they came with handlers and we loaded them with no problem, just a few blown up skirts from Rock holding a little pitch in the blades to help circulate the air. The big sliding doors slammed shut and for the first time in the whole day Rock stepped on the floor button and said, "You got it."

My turn to fly, I call the tower, and make a smooth full-power take off and start up the right side of the highway climbing fast to get to cool air. Rock already knows all of their names and hometowns. I love working with Rock, he is relentless. One of the Donut Dollies is from New York; Rock is out of the seat and in the back, holding her close, screaming in her ear. I ask him once why he did not give them helmets to wear; he grins as he answers, it is only an excuse to hold them close and smell their smell. I will probably never see her again, but I will remember what she feels and smells like forever. I'm getting instructions on life from the master himself.

"Blackhawk 69 Cu Chi tower on Guard." I switch to Guard and answer for Rock, still in the back. "Ah, Blackhawk 69 go ahead. Blackhawk 69 change frequency to Cu Chi tower frequency and contact Cu Chi tower immediately."

I have the Cu Chi tower in a preset channel and switch to them immediately, and key the mike. "Blackhawk 69, Cu Chi tower," and I get an animated voice on the radio inquiring about how many girls are on board and how many seconds until we would be landing. Then they make sure I knew where to land. A Major will be there to greet them. I turn to Rock and give him my best puzzled look. He climbs back into his seat, buckles up and says have fun in the back, the one from New York needs a flying lesson. I help her get in my seat, thread up the shoulder straps, and the smell of the perfume and the big smile as I reach to help with her lap belt has to be experienced to be believed.

Rock drops the nose and we free fall down to extreme low level. We are going like a rocket. I am in the middle of 9 Donut Dollies all holding onto me as Rock flies between the trees sideways and generally lets it all hang out. The girls scream. I am trying to figure out which one is from California while they are all hanging onto me for dear life, their terror plainly visible on their contorted faces. Rock is making sure their first flight in a helicopter is a memorable one. I cannot see a thing in the back, Rock makes huge flair and we are there. He sets the helicopter down and we are besieged by all the special services REMF (rear echelon mother fuckers) and in one fast movement we are empty and on our way to Tay Ninh. Rock is laughing. The girls are so glad to be away from the helicopter insanity they do not look back.

Cu Chi to Tay Ninh is a short hop. Rock has flown it so many times before he lets me practice flying low level, directing me left and right as we go from rice paddies to banana trees to the triple canopy jungle. The smell changes from mud to perfume as we near our Area of Operation. Rock is talking to the crew and I am madly flying along. Rock keys his mike, "I've got it." We cyclic climb up, up, up, and Rock calls for smoke. I hear both smoke grenade caps pop. Rock is lined up with the Cau Dai temple and does a mock strafing run on the temple, pulling up to skim over the top of the building. Life is good when you are the top link in the food chain.

1 January 68—Fire Support Base Burt

As an aircraft commander my call sign was "Blackhawk 54." WO (Warrant Officer) David Webster was my co-pilot, SP4 (Specialist 4) James Holston was the gunner on the UH-1 D model aircraft #64-13817, and SP4 M. Martin "Magnet Ass" Jansen was the crew chief (we called him "Magnet Ass" because he'd been shot so many times).

I loved the view from the top of Nui Ba Dinh, Black Lady Mountain. You could see the lights from the far away cities. And I loved the challenge of a perfect pinnacle landing—especially in the early evening just as the sun drops below the horizon. It was my last stop on New Year's Eve. I could go back to Tay Ninh for the night's festivities at the club. It was amazing how fast they could get the cases of champagne off my helicopter.

Tonight would be great fun, Captain David R. "Doc" Warden, our Group Flight Surgeon, would be on the courier from Cu Chi and would be staying in the guest quarters. I loved flying with Doc and we had flown a lot of missions together. Doc was the greatest storyteller of all time, and tonight I would get a double dose as we stayed up late for New Year's stand-down.

I was the last bird in that night and after fueling and a quick stop at the arming pits for some linked 7.62 mm ammunition for the M-60's, I put my D-model in the revetments, and started the hike to the Operations tent, walking right past the mortar watch ships. WO Bill Britt was saying that something is cooking down at Fire Support Base Burt, and they were on alert.

I found Doc and we started cooking a steak out on the grill set up behind the Officers' Club. I liked it when the Army made an attempt during the holidays. Almost anything was better than C-rations. The party had started before Doc and I got there and seemed to be in full swing by the time we sat down to eat our steak. WO Jim Conde could get anything and these steaks were proof. Jim was a Special Forces type who went to flight school. He could speak the local language and he knew people in low places, if you know what I mean.

The party was a success, we watched a movie, heard and told some great stories (all true of course). As a practicing Mormon I didn't drink any of the champagne, and at the end of the festivities I headed off for bed, wishing the tent had cooled down enough to allow me to sleep. I walked over with Doc to find him a cot in the tent we kept for visiting crews, and on my way back was stopped by the on-duty orderly.

"Mr. Coe, find your Doctor friend and get to Operations now." I thought, "What kind of silly bullshit is being pulled now by one of my more than slightly inebriated flying buddies?" So rather than wake up Doc, I walked over to the Operations tent and a very serious Major Bauman looked up and said "Where is your Flight Surgeon?"

"Well," I started to speak and he cut me off.

"Get him now, and get back here as fast as you can. Your crew has been sent for, hurry."

Doc was still awake. He jumped into his boots and grabbed his gear and was out the tent flap in one move. For a huge airborne ranger, Doc moved so well, the word would be graceful, if not applied to 250 pounds of raw muscle and brains. My flying gear was in my tent and we both double-timed over to it and double-timed to the Operations tent.

Major Bauman looked very unhappy. He was gruff even when he was happy and tonight he looked sinister. "Men, I have a bad job for you two tonight. Mr. Coe you are my only sober pilot, and Captain Warden, I have to send you as the co-pilot, I have no one else to send."

I looked at Doc and he smiled at me. I knew he was up to it whatever it was.

We were taken to the revetment by jeep and my crew had the bird untied and ready to rock and roll. We were airborne in minutes, first stopping by the ammo bunkers and taking a full load of ordnance. As my heavy helicopter staggered for some altitude, I noticed just how black it could be in Vietnam, and started to fly on my instruments, tuning my radios to the Ground FM, the FAC (Forward Air Controller) on VHF and my company UHF. "Blackhawk 54 inbound with a load of ordnance, where do you want it? Over."

No response. We must be too far out for them to hear us, and I pulled a little more pitch and grabbed some more altitude to help with the radio.

I was busy flying, I could hear the gunships on Victor (VHF) and I could hear fast movers on Uniform (UHF), but no grunts on Fox-trot. Doc keyed his mike, "Good night! Look at the fire fight going on out there." In the inky darkness was a fountain of horror, a full-fledged fire fight, tracers coming in, tracers going out, explosions, fire, it looked like a real mess down there. Bullets were ricocheting at every angle. I knew our 25th Infantry 2/22, the Triple Deuce Mechanized men, were fighting for their lives down there, and they would be needing our ammo and Medevac now.

I ask the FAC for the ground frequency and he gives it to me.

"Ground control Blackhawk 54 over."

I can hear the din of battle behind a voice on the radio. "Blackhawk 54, we are under heavy attack and are requesting you stand by, say again: Ordnance on board?"

"Roger Ground, I have 105 Beehive and a doctor."

After a moment of silence, Ground comes back on the radio, "It is too hot to land now, but we urgently need your load."

I don't hear the Rat Pack, so I call the Stinger gunships, "Stinger lead, Blackhawk 54, over."

"Stinger, go ahead."

"I have 105 Beehive and a doctor on board can you get us in?"

"If you want to go in there we will escort you in, what is your location?"

"Blackhawk 54 is north west 5 miles out."

"Roger Blackhawk. Come to the south end of Burt, we will pick you up and escort you in, but there is a lot of fire down there so make it a fast approach."

We fly south of Burt and I can see the Stingers coming out to escort us. I start the 120 knot approach, at first going past the gun cover, but then as I start to flair they are by my side, mini guns roaring, low level insanity. I can't see a fucking thing with all the smoke and flares competing with the tracers. I see a lone trooper standing with his arms over his head, guiding me in, exposing himself. The bravery of the men on the ground chokes me up.

I am guided to a spot with wounded men, Doc is out of his seat on the ground, doing the much-needed triage, so we can take the worst-hit out and hope to save them. Men come from the dark and take the ammo off. The volume of fire in the perimeter is intense and I am taking hits. It will only be a matter of time and this helicopter will never fly again, Doc has his load and is back in the right seat, I call coming out, and look up to see a pair of gunships covering my ass coming out.

We are low level in the dark with a load of men, all severely wounded. Doc says, "I had better get busy," and jumps over the console and starts taking care of the men in the back. I fly directly to the 12th Evac pad in Cu Chi. I call, "Golden Umpire, Blackhawk 54, inbound with eight wounded about 10 minutes out."

The calm voice of Big Bill Giles on the radio comes back, "Late night 54, you are our only chopper right now, land on pad one." It's nice to hear a familiar voice on the radio. I wonder if he ever sleeps, he's always there when I need him. He and his crew will expedite the unloading of our wounded. Bill Giles, best Hospital Pad Man in Vietnam.

Cu Chi tower clears me direct to the Medevac pad and I come in hot, flaring sideways to clear the tail boom. I am almost down and on jumps Big Bill Giles and he takes charge. Bill strips off the loaded weapons and explosive devices, gently lifting the men onto stretchers waiting by the open doors. Bill does his work like a madman, but every move is practiced. Nobody speaks. The noise of the chopper overwhelms every sound. Bam, Bill hits me on top of my helmet to tell me he is jumping off and I can pull pitch. Total time on the pad is maybe two minutes, but probably less.

We lift to a high hover and ask tower for permission to go to the ammo bunkers, and they clear us direct. The ammo lumpers know what is going on and have our load waiting; we watch them put it on the aircraft, then a quick call to the tower and we are staggering into the air again. We have enough fuel, and I would like to be light going in, to help with the control of the aircraft down low behind the perimeter of Burt.

Doc and I start to hear the radios first, things are bad, looks like one of the Stinger gunships has been shot down in the dark. I see the fast movers laying down Napalm, lights things up, kind of pretty and deadly at the same time. I cannot see

FIGURE 1.1 Soldiers of the U.S. 1st Cavalry Division carry a slain comrade to a medical evacuation helicopter during the battle of the Ia Drang Valley, Vietnam, November, 1965. Throughout the Vietnam War, the Army flew helicopters into firefights to drop off troops and ammunition and help evacuate the wounded. Pilots and crewmen continually risked their lives and their aircraft to remove wounded soldiers under fire, earning themselves reputations and decorations for bravery. The Army's general-purpose helicopter was the Bell Series UH-1 "Huey," pictured here.

Source: AP Wide World Photos

Burt yet, but the fireworks are spectacular coming from a concentrated spot on the horizon. As we get nearer we call the ground and ask for status. They wave us off, too hot. Now fuel is a problem. It takes a few minutes to find a gun team. They had one of their own down and were pissed off big time; I think they would have escorted me into hell if I had asked. They call the fire and I make the approach, we turn this one around in seconds, not one mistake, in and out.

I call Big Bill on the radio and Doc Warden goes to work on the men in the back of the helicopter.

Doc and I fly all night, and in the morning we land by the shot-down burned Stinger gunship so Captain David Royal Warden Jr. MC can perform his duties as a Flight Surgeon and issue a Cause of Death for the crew. The men in the Stinger gunship have been burned very badly by the fire. I know it's a shock to Doc, his whole demeanor changes. Fight hard all night and then in the morning perform autopsies on the men who have been covering your ass that night is a tough one. Doc has to load each still-hot crewman in a body bag, after figuring out who they are. Doc says, "Some smells are with you for life."

Doc Warden and I flew into Burt numerous times that night, New Year's Eve, but what we really remember are the aviators we lost, not the men we saved.

Graves Registration

0400, O-dark-thirty, the tent flap parts and in steps Captain Lungarella and in a loud voice he asks, "Where is Coe?"

I was right in front of him on my cot.

"I am right here sir." My weak sleepy answer seemed good enough for now.

Rock growled, "I want to be in the air in ten minutes. I will be waiting for you on the pad in front of operations."

Getting dressed in the dark is no sweat. I had speed laces in my boots and hit the JP–4 powered four-hole crapper and still made the operations pad before Captain Lungarella. I could hear a UH-1 crank up out in the revetments as I scurried along towards the operations pad. It was the only one cranking up and I knew it was my ride for the day. I had on my flak vest, chicken board, 45 caliber, crotch protector, camera, and helmet. I was ready to fly. Rock brought the helicopter in with a sideways flair onto the operations pad and I jumped in my seat.

"Tay Ninh Tower, Blackhawk Six Niner on the Blackhawk operations pad for take off to the north. Over."

"Six Niner, Tay Ninh Tower, we have no traffic and no north firing artillery, you are clear to take off to the north. Good day."

Double click from Rock and we were pulling pitch. I watched as the lights of the compound faded and the predawn darkness covered everything from our view but the dim, red glow of the instruments.

"Bad mission today." Rock was speaking to no one in particular, just keying his mike and talking to his crew. "We have to fly bodies to Graves Registration today. I do not know how many, but I do know it will be several loads. This is the aftermath of the big fight they have been having north of Cu Chi. I am sure Major Bauman hates me and must not like you very well either." Rock laughed and we flew on our instruments while we watched the eastern horizon start to color up. Soon we would have enough light to land and start our grisly business.

It was a long flight up and we started hearing our own Rat Pack guns on the company frequency. "Rat One Eight, Blackhawk Six Niner, over." It was our first contact.

"Go ahead Six Niner."

"We are inbound looking for a load to go to Graves Registration. Is it still hot down there? Over."

"Six Niner the LZ is cold, we are just mopping up after last night's attack. Call Manchu on their Fox Mike." CW2 (Chief Warrant Officer 2) Art Cline overhead with his fire team would assure a quiet Landing Zone.

The sun was still behind the horizon but the predawn bright sky made everything glow on the ground. We circled the Landing Zone and called the ground frequency to get them to pop smoke so we would know where to land.

We could all see the bright yellow smoke plume coming up from the landing zone in the still morning air. Rock brought the helicopter down right in front of the smoke grenade, making a light yellow windstorm, blowing the poncho liners off the row of dead bodies. In the dim light with all the yellow smoke swirling around, the gray faces, some contorted in death, were only a few feet away from my perch in the Huey. I could not stop looking at them. The taste of cordite in my mouth from the smoke grenade made it all like a dream with all my senses running wild. Some of the dead looked like they were just sleeping, others were more a collection of parts than a body.

The supply line with the body bags had not made it here to the battle zone, so with stretchers made from tree limbs and poncho liners they loaded our aircraft. Rock was out of his seat and busy supervising the loading of our dead soldiers. Rock made sure they were shoulder to shoulder, wrapped tightly in their ponchos. When the floor was covered with bodies Rock put one more on the seat. When they tried to load more Rock would not let them.

Stone faced, Rock climbed in and buckled up. I started adding throttle to the turbine engine and in seconds we were ready to go.

Rock picked up to a hover and then started our takeoff right over the top of the dug-in troops. The grunts could see our load, they all knew what we were hauling. They were mostly face up into the rotor wash watching their dead being taken on the first leg to home. Some waved and in the middle of hell hauling bodies a young trooper flashed me the peace sign in a hundred-knot dusty rotor wash.

Even at one hundred knots the smell of the bodies that had been lying in the tropical heat for who knows how long started to make us all sick. Rock had the gunner and crew chief come forward and hold on to the seatbacks for the ride to Graves Registration.

The Army had put Graves Registration next to a soccer field. We landed right in front of the front door and Rock jumped out to supervise the unloading of the dead.

The sun was now fully in the sky, the tropical heat was breathtaking. The men at Graves Registration would unload each body onto a stainless steel gurney and then wheel it into the large refer box (refrigerated truck) that was being used as a receiving area.

Things were not going fast enough for Rock and after they had taken about half of the bodies we had on board, no one came back out. There seemed to be a break in the action. Rock grabbed a gurney and with the aid of our crew loaded it and then loaded two more. With Rock in the lead each of the crewmen pushed his loaded cart up the ramp and through the door.

I was sitting in the helicopter at flight idle. I watched our crew disappear into the Graves Registration double doors and they were gone for some time. The doors flew open and Rock and the rest of the crew ran down the ramp and jumped on the helicopter and I hovered forward to the water trailer so we could rinse out the helicopter. Our crew chief got the water pump motor started and we hosed off the floor and the seats.

We had more bodies to haul and so as soon as we could we were off looking for fuel, then back to the landing zone to get the rest of the dead.

Each time we would land to the smoke and Rock would jump out and make sure every body was wrapped tightly and placed shoulder to shoulder in the aircraft.

We flew in complete silence. Rock never let me touch the controls.

It was early in the afternoon when we were finally finished hauling bodies. We all helped clean the helicopter and she was wet inside with water running out the back door when Rock picked her up and headed home.

Rock flew without speaking about half way home, then he keyed his mike and started talking about the day, "It was a good thing you never went into Graves Registration," he said to me. "I have never seen anything like it in my life—black men in aprons and bodies everywhere, the cold fog of the refrigerator, cold air blowing the smell of death around so you could see it. I hope I never ever have to go back there again as long as I live."

Both our crewmen started to talk at once. Just the descriptions over the intercom made the hair on my neck stand at attention. I was glad to have been stuck in the helicopter.

I flew way too many trips to Graves Registration in my tour of duty, but I was never ever curious enough to look inside.

Relocation

It was very common in III Corps to relocate villages from an area controlled by the Viet Cong to an area controlled by the South Vietnamese.

It takes a coordinated effort to move a whole village. Animals, people, and supplies of every kind were moved by helicopter to a new village already built in a strange, controlled place.

This is not a good time for the villagers, as they have never lived anywhere else. Chances are that their families have lived there for several hundred years. Their ancestors are buried outside of the farms in small raised grave plots. These Vietnamese people did not want to leave their land and go to a strange place, no matter what the South Vietnamese were offering, or how safe it was. These farmers thought in generational terms, governments would come and go, but the land would always be there and they would be with it.

Flames from the straw houses burning in the midday sun reached far into the cloudless sky and the smoke from the fire went straight up and up in the hot-humid air making the LZ easy to find from many miles away. ARVN Grunts armed to the teeth were herding the people and animals away from the burning farm houses and on to the CH-47 cargo planes and the UH-1s coming and going from the makeshift Landing Zone—a harvested rice paddy.

We hovered up to take our load of Vietnamese, just like we had been doing since 0700. This load looked different. The men were not wearing black pajamas, they had on very nice European clothing, and the women all had on Oriental-style dresses, not the Ao Dai or traditional long flowing dress worn by most of the village women.

One of the women stood out from the rest. She did not appear to be frightened by the helicopter like the rest of the passengers. She did not smile or frown and she looked me right in the eye when I looked back to watch them load.

She had a large intricately woven straw purse she clutched to her chest. She was dressed in dark blue silk, which contrasted against the pale straw of her handbag and conical hat. She sat down in the middle of the bench seat, putting her hat under the seat and winding her hair into a bun. She moved gracefully and I was taken by her beauty. Not the vigorous beauty of youth, but the beauty that comes with time, the beauty that comes from within.

Our artillery was pounding one side of the village to discourage participation in the move by the Viet Cong. We would have to climb over the village to stay away from artillery rounds coming in from all the firebases in the area. It is always fun to slowly make circles under full power while gaining altitude like an elevator in a bad dream.

"Mr. Coe, the lady in blue is trying to get out of her seat," said my crew chief, and I turned around in time to see her run and jump out of the door. I slammed the collective down and kicked full anti-torque as I laid that old D model on her side. The woman floated down just past the tip-path plane of my rotor blades. She was tracking very well. With her arms folded over her chest and her silk skirt adding stability to her body, she fell like a lawn dart.

I followed her down far enough to have to worry about pulling out of a serious over-the-redline free fall.

She hit a rice paddy filled with water and made a small muddy spot where she disappeared underground completely out of sight except for a small piece of her blue silk dress marking the spot.

I hovered over the discolored water spot wondering what would be a fitting marker for someone who refused to live if that meant being told what to do and where to live.

There was no one to call, no reason to dig her out right now. I started making circles in the air, gaining altitude so I could deliver my load and go back for another.

She was a middle-aged Vietnamese woman not willing to part with the past. Who knows what she was leaving behind in that small village. It did not matter now as it was on fire. It was stunning to me to realize that the village had been there in that little bend in the river since before recorded time. And some dickhead in Saigon ordered them loaded in a chopper and moved to a refugee camp. What was fair about that?

I was certain the Vietnamese woman did not die frightened; she looked me in the eye when she boarded and she looked me in the eye while she was falling. I was a conduit for her self-destructive actions, her final gesture at a government that would never be sympathetic with the needs of the human on the land.

All of the other passengers were crying when we delivered them to the resettlement village. I wondered who she was, our Lady in Blue Silk. Someone's daughter for sure, but she was probably someone's mother and someone's wife. She was most likely someone's sister and someone else's mentor. She was obviously loved by many.

I thought of my own mother, and what it would be like for her to be removed from her house at gunpoint and all of the things she had acquired over a lifetime were torched while she watched.

Thu Douc

Major Bill Bauman was sending his helicopters into a Landing Zone where there had been no artillery fire or gunship prep. While the flight was still on base, the Rat Pack reported seeing troops in uniform and asked if they were ARVN. The answer was no.

We were to insert a combo force of U.S. and ARVN troops across from Phu Loi, beside a river. As typical of ARVN insertions, it was to be a cold LZ. We were told there would be no suppression by our guns.

As the gunships made their flyover prior to our landing, they started taking heavy fire from dug-in emplacements. (Later Jansen heard one of the gunship crewmen say he had seen a boat with a large caliber gun set up on it.) The Rat Pack informed Maj. Bauman of the heavy fire. The ground commander in the C&C (Command & Control) ship again stated, "No suppression by any aircraft." The gunships continued taking heavy fire and Maj. Bauman called for everyone to return fire, which was the Bauman I knew. We were all extremely nervous and the troops we were carrying were silent. We were observing radio silence, so even the radio was quiet. The formation was so tight—every pilot straining to keep his helicopter full of troops in the correct chock (position)—that there were only a few feet separating each helicopter in my flight of Blackhawks. Our orders were to insert our load of troops into the right side of the Landing Zone as far to the front as we could get. As we got closer to the LZ it looked like we were in for some serious trouble.

As we started our approach we could see the fight unfold in front of us. They opened up from their foxholes and tracers were coming up in a huge volume. Our gunners were shooting out the side of the aircraft and the formation was spewing 7.62 out of 16 machine-guns at a horrendous rate. As I started to cross my UH-1D over the tree line into the landing zone on final, the entire world seemed to erupt. The NVA crawled out of their foxholes and started to shoot at the low flying helicopters. I was trying to be as smooth as possible, but all hell was breaking loose, and aircraft in the formation started taking hits and calling mayday, mayday, mayday chock four, wounded Pilot on board, breaking off, mayday, mayday, mayday, trail is going in, mayday, mayday, mayday chock two has wounded, breaking out. Six of my formation were shot up and two were still in the Landing Zone all shot to pieces, the grunts were taking heavy casualties and we could not suppress the small arms fire coming from the tree line.

The Rat Pack above us threw everything they had at the tree line. The sound of the rockets whooshing past the flight and the serious roar of the mini-guns working let us know we were not in the fight alone. When we unloaded the troops, an ARVN Radio Telephone Operator refused to get off our helicopter. Gunner Jim Holston and Martin Jansen tried to throw him off, but he got behind the pilots' center console where they could not reach him.

After we lifted off, Maj. Bauman asked Captain Presson if another insertion attempt was unwise. He replied that the troops needed the additional support. Captain Billie Presson, all heart and balls.

We had four ships left to insert the next lift.

Chalk eight, aircraft 66-926 with Aircraft Commander WO1 John M. Yirak and Pilot CW2 William J. Koch were cleared for a one-time flight to Phu Loi with numerous bullet holes throughout the aircraft. The Flight Leader, Capt. Presson, reported that there were four flyable aircraft in the PZ (Pickup Zone) and that they were loaded with troops. Aircraft 66-932 with AC Captain Jerry T. Wagner and Pilot WO Robert L. Pinckney had now joined the flight as the fourth aircraft. Blackhawk "6" was monitoring the ground commander's frequency and asked him what the situation was on the ground at Phu Loi. He replied that the ground forces had not received fire for more than thirty minutes and that he considered it safe to bring in the next lift.

We left the PZ with our load of troops and headed for the LZ. We all were sweating heavily. Maj. Bauman let us shoot out of the right side of the helicopter. Just as I brought the helicopter to a hover, an NVA-uniformed soldier stepped from the bamboo tree line just past the end of my rotor blades and shot an entire clip from his AK-47 through the windshield of my helicopter. I thought I was dead. I had been hit but did not know how bad. My co-pilot was slumped in his seat. The windshield was full of holes and most of the instrument panel was blown to shreds with electrical sparking and smoke everywhere. I pulled pitch and went right up and over the NVA soldier putting a new clip in his AK-47. The transmission was screaming like a woman in pain from all the rounds in it. We tried to call mayday, but none of the radios would work. I switched to hot mike and guard, but still nothing would transmit.

At an altitude of about 200 feet and out over the river my aircraft was hit by a fifty caliber antiaircraft weapon. The entire tail boom came apart. My crew chief could see the tail rotor not spinning, just hanging. The tail boom, wrinkled and bent, started to come off the aircraft. Over the intercom my gunner said the fuel cell was burning and his smoke grenades were going off.

The torque of the engine started the helicopter spinning and the gyroscopic precession flipped the helicopter up on its side and then over. I slammed the collective down and rolled the throttle off. We were completely out of control now and starting to spin in the other direction but not as violently. It is hard to know just how many times the helicopter flipped over in the air.

As my burning shot-to-shit helicopter neared the ground, I knew I had little cyclic control and only the pitch and throttle to get me on the ground. I waited and waited and waited for what seemed to be a lifetime while my crippled ship fell out of the sky. At the last possible second I tried to level the helicopter and rolled on the throttle and pulled pitch. The helicopter stopped spinning and I got it close to the rice paddy. The forward motion and the attitude of the helicopter caused one of the rotor blades to hit the ground. The helicopter beat itself to death right beside the river.

I was in the left seat and was wet from the water in the flooded rice paddy. I could not breathe. In the violence of the crash I had the wind knocked out of me and I was struggling to find the harness release somewhere in the muddy water. I was starting to panic. I calmed my screaming mind and found and pulled the release on the harness and started to climb out of the burning helicopter. The fire was in the back and spreading so I tried to climb out the co-pilot's door above me. I was so weak and beat up I could not climb out of the helicopter. My crew chief M. Martin "Magnet Ass" Jansen was standing on the side of the burning helicopter. He grabbed me by the edges of my helmet and dragged me out of the wreckage. I was his second rescue. First he had freed the leg of the gunner who had been trapped in the mud under the weight of the burning helicopter. The gunner's seat belt mounts had pulled out of the bulkhead on impact and thrown him into the butterfly handles of his M-60, breaking his nose. Jansen went back in twice to get us all out. He remembers looking up at the sky while we were spinning out of control and seeing ammo boxes flying around thinking that they were going to hurt when they hit him.

When I hit the rice paddy, I looked around and all four of us who had left that morning from Can Tho were still alive. We were cut up from the flying Plexiglas and shrapnel, thrashed and broken from the experience, but still alive.

I pulled out my survival radio to call for a ride home, but before I could key the mike there was a 118th AHC Thunderbird shooting an approach to us. They were in the area and they saw us tumbling out of the sky without a tail boom. They followed us down and were happy to see four survivors. There was a chaplain on the rescue helicopter and he was shooting out of the door with his carbine, just like the rest of us. One of the Crew was a Texan and commented on the Texas flag Jansen had on his helmet. Texans bonding with each other wherever they go. It must be a sickness.

The 118th rescue ship took us to the hospital and the doctors started pulling pieces of Plexiglas out of all of us. They kept my gunner for the night.

After the trip to the hospital, Major Bauman put me in a different helicopter with another crew. I do not remember the tail number, but I am certain that it was not a Blackhawk aircraft. I had never met the crew or the peter pilot. I do remember very clearly the peter pilot telling me that he had just been released from the hospital after being shot through both legs with one bullet, a large caliber round, on a combat assault. He had some horrible scars he showed me, and it was his first time in a helicopter since the hospital in Japan. I thought it was odd when this stranger dropped his pants and showed me his mangled legs. The scars were still bright pink and angry looking. It was obvious he had been through hell and back.

Many people had been hit on the ground at Phu Loi and ammo was being expended at a huge rate, so we were sent back to the Landing Zone by Major Bauman to take in ammo and take out the wounded.

I started my single-ship hot approach to the Landing Zone while looking for the wounded grunts. There was so much shooting going on, and people in desperate trouble calling on all three of my radios, my new co-pilot completely freaked out and started to fight me for the controls of the helicopter. He did not want to go into the Landing Zone. It was not a pretty picture with all the tracers coming up at us, and the medics calling for Medevac on all the radios. The crew chief came to my aid by pulling the seat release and harness, pulling the screaming out-of-control peter pilot away from the controls, so I kept coming hot and fast and at the last possible second flared and came to a hover right beside our load of wounded. We kicked out the ammo we had on board, loaded as fast as we could, and pulled pitch and went out the way we had come in.

The trip to the hospital with the wounded and the flipped-out pilot only took a few minutes. I had called the hospital and advised them of the nature of the injuries and the crazy co-pilot.

On the hospital pad, my crew and I checked out the helicopter and made sure it was safe to fly. I installed my crew chief as peter pilot and we went back to the Landing Zone to haul ammo in and wounded out. We kept taking hits and one of them hit a hydraulic line. Helicopters are hard to fly when everything works perfectly, and they are dangerously difficult with no hydraulics. My crew chief/peter pilot and I made it to the hospital pad with our load of wounded, but that helicopter never flew again. They dragged it off the pad with a jeep and some wheels. I never saw that aircraft again. It was a total loss for someone.

My first crew chief Martin Jansen received a DFC (Distinguished Flying Cross). He deserved more. I still do not know who the second crew chief was, I did not know then. He was the real hero, saved all our lives. I don't think he got anything more than a pat on the back and the satisfaction of a job well done.

I got on a Medevac helicopter at the hospital and went to Saigon, and from there took a courier from Hotel-3 back to Tay Ninh. When I got there, I was the first to return. It was a quiet evening waiting for the Blackhawks to return. They came back in the morning and performed a 360 degree overhead maneuver with smoke. All of the pilots and crew ran to the flight line to cheer them back. It brings tears to my eyes to remember how we closed ranks after a fight. The 187th Assault Helicopter Company stood down for a few days. General Senif flew in and pinned on a Silver Star for me, and DFCs for the rest of the crew. I still do not know who the other crew was or what company they were from. And I owe my life to an unknown man.

***

After I flew one year in Vietnam it was time for me to go home. The Army only made us spend a year at a time in Vietnam.

The flight from Saigon was uneventful, we landed at Travis AFB near San Francisco, California, not forty miles from my parents' house, so when the military let me go, I hopped in a taxi and headed home.

It was early on a summer morning that the cab pulled into the driveway of my father's house in Clayton. It had only been a year since I had gone to fly in Vietnam, but I felt different, rummaging around under the doormat for the key.

I let myself into the dark house, put my bags down in the living room, and grabbed a shower. By the time I was out of the shower the whole family was up and they were glad to see me home from the war.

Everything at my mother's table was just as I had left it, but I had changed.

How could they sit there and pass the toast with a smile on their faces while there were men dying in the rice paddies fourteen hours away by jet airliner? I was just there!

My first encounter with my brother Paul he called me a baby killer. I listened for a few seconds before I wrestled him to the ground, I hissed in his ear, "Don't ever call me that, ever again! You can only imagine the death I have had to deal with every day and yes some of them were children."

Paul did not know what he was saying; it was something he had heard them chant at one of the numerous anti-war demonstrations that were being held all over the San Francisco Bay area.

I only stayed in the Army as long as I had to. I got my early out to go to Brigham Young University and left the U.S. Army with four years under my belt and the desire to get as far away from the Army and all it stood for as fast as I could.

In March of 1969 Paul's draft board sent him his Notice of Induction into the Army.

QUESTIONS FOR DISCUSSION

1. Wayne Coe's story is divided into six vignettes or subsections. How would you characterize the sections called "Crash," "1 January 68—Fire Support Base Burt," and "Thu Douc?" What is the tone of these sections? What seem to be Coe's main concerns? What is the effect of Coe's language and his use of profanity?

2. Why do you think Coe included "Smells," "Graves Registration," and "Relocation?" How do these stories add to your knowledge of the soldiers' life in Vietnam? Who is the Wayne Coe that emerges from these stories and how is he different from the Wayne Coe of the other stories?

3. Is Coe ever critical of the way the war is being run? How do you think he feels about being a part of the war in Vietnam? How does he regard the Vietnamese people he encounters? Do those feelings change over the course of the stories?

4. Does Wayne Coe resemble your previous notion of a Vietnam-era U.S. serviceman? How is he different? How would you compare Coe to American soldiers you have seen in films?

5. Many Vietnam veterans consider Wayne Coe a true hero for risking his life to save theirs. Yet Coe lost his brother, who was also his best friend, and many other friends in the Vietnam War, and suffers today from PTSD. What do these apparently contradictory situations tell you about the life of a soldier and the nature of warfare?

6. By 1968, the Vietnam War was becoming increasingly unpopular in the United States and a number of Vietnam veterans joined the anti-war protests. Soldiers still in Vietnam became distrustful of the high command and discouraged by the lack of success in the war they were fighting. Does Coe's story provide any clues about what motivated American servicemen to continue to conduct missions and obey orders despite their doubts about the war as a whole?

LETTERS HOME
Paul Thomas Coe

SELECTIVE SERVICE SYSTEM
ORDER TO REPORT FOR INDUCTION

The President of the United States   March 17, 1969
To: Paul T. Coe
GREETINGS:
You are hereby ordered for induction into the Armed Forces of the United States, and
to report to: Local Board No. 31 on April 16, 1969, Wednesday at 6:00 A.M. (morning)
for forwarding to an Armed Forces Induction Station.

Basic Training

4/24/1969
Loving Parents & Assorted Siblings:
    This is the first chance since I've been here that I've been able to write at all. All
spare time comes in 5–10 minute parcels.
    It's really been fun and kisses so far. But I've decided not to make my Army
career 20 years as planned but will get out in 724 more days instead.
    You're all probably sick with suspense wondering what I did yesterday, ok I'll let
'cha know: 15 hours (long sickening hours) of kitchen patrol, in Army jargon that's
#%&*ing K.P. Not a punishment, just duty. We were supposed to be relieved after lunch.
Ha! But nobody laughed. Got up at 3:30, at the mess by 4:00 AM, and worked till
7:00 PM without a break or in other words on our feet except for 5 minutes to eat 3 times.
    There's one other Latter Day Saints boy named Willy in the platoon. He's a con-
vert from the Fair Oaks ward. We were gonna go to services last Sunday but both
pulled K.P. instead; oh joy.
    Called Barb when I got here. She sure is fine. Guess I'll marry her when my
hitch is up. But PLEASE don't tell anyone cuz nobody knows or will know for a long
while & that includes Barb. OK? I'm heading straight for Portland my first leave.
Have no desire to see anyone else.
    I've been recommended for photography school. Nobody will guarantee it so
I don't know what chance there is but if I get anything it will be that. Just pray for me.
I pray for two things each night (hope for a dozen more). I pray to remain an individual
and to keep my temper. I was doing fine until this stupid 19 year old PFC cook was bawl-
ing me out for something I didn't do. I didn't do anything really wrong. We were both
scared, he was scared I was gonna punch him & I was scared cuz I knew the stockade
was a bad place. But there were no repercussions except he didn't get on me anymore &
I vowed to be careful. Since then I've taken more crap & not even flinched (much).
    Seems there are about 3 guys out of the 45 in my platoon that don't have a
prison record. The platoon leader was up for attempted murder. Oh well, I've been in
worse company. There are 3 graduate students and one master's degree here also.

I'm assistant squad leader. The Drill Sergeant, 5'6" with an 8th grade education (honest!), picked the biggest and dumbest for squad leaders & platoon guide, and put some of us as assistants to tell them which is right & which is left. Time for dinner must split.

Peace

P.T.

***

Friday Evening

Been trying to get time to mail this for a while, they keep us going 24 hrs. a day. Got your letter today, thanks for the fine mail father, they really are an inspiring impetus to get my life in order. Maybe some day I'll grow up to the way you are. I'm not really wicked, but I'll bet I'm a lot closer to the heat than St. Peter's Gate.

Lots of strange things going on here. Ft. Lewis is an open post & people (scuttlebutt sez S.D.S. & Black Panthers) have been coming in and stealing weapons and ammo. Guards have been tripled and officers carry 45's. CQ [Charge of Quarters—the officer in charge at night] carries a loaded M-14 rifle. The roaming guards carry baseball bats with orders to hit first ask later. They just installed 2 more (now 4) overnight guards in the weapons building. One guard must be awake at all times with a loaded M-4. One member of the platoon has been selected to run his weapon to the D.S. [Drill Sergeant] in case of field attack. The D.S.s don't carry weapons, just ammo. Starting tonight the armored cavalry [tanks] will be patrolling the hills surrounding the post. They've tried to keep it under cover. I'm sure the press doesn't know, but hundreds of weapons and 1000's of rounds have been taken. Sooo, keep yer nose to the wind. Fired the M-16 today, shot expert. . . .

Really didn't have time to write this so I'd better go. Love to all and happy Father's Day Dad.

P.T.

***

Good morning—

It's 3:30 AM, so if you can't read this it's because I can't see: 1) since there's no light, and 2) I couldn't see anything at this hour if there was.

There has to be someone awake in the barracks 24 hours a day so we go in hour shifts and take an hour shift a night for each floor. My hour is nearly up.

Thanks so much for the kind letters. Basic is such a poor place that letters are really a boost. Yesterday was our first day at the rifle range. They taught us quick kill which is the spontaneous reaction to a surprise target. You don't use the sights. They made us start with approximately 90 Rounds with air rifles, then in the afternoon we graduated to the M-14 rifle. We shot discs thrown in the air and standing body-shaped targets at varying distances.

I shot a $1\frac{1}{2}$ inch disk 10 out of 11 tries, and I also shot a penny. The M-14 was a little more difficult, but I didn't do too badly. As long as I'm told to shoot TARGETS the Army & I will get along just fine. . . .

I miss you all, and appreciate your letters very much. I'll write again soon. Maybe we'll have time after inspection tomorrow.

Love to all

P.T.

***

Oh you lucky people—

2 letters in one day! The first letter is OK so I'm mailing it anyway.

We had that inspection this morn. The company has competition each week based on inspections (daily and the big one) to see who is going to be the honor platoon. We came in second this week 1 point (out of 500) behind. Honor platoon has no K.P. or details and gets to watch T.V. and play pool on Sunday in the day room.

I really miss my peaceful friends at home. Everyone here is soooo violent. They gave a blanket party to (beat up) some poor guy who walked on a waxed floor when he was told not to. I sat on my bunk, and got really uptight, and wished I was someplace far away.

I've never been one to cringe at profanity but, goodness gracious, land of Goshen, leapin' lizards, I just haven't heard a sentence longer than 3 words that hasn't been obscene since I've been here. Our D.S. can do more things with the colloquial of intercourse than the cooks can do with hamburger. Maybe it wouldn't bother me as much if I didn't find it so easy to emulate.

We've been called to fall out. Love to all, I'll write again when the opportunity is present.

Love and peace from P.T.

***

Back again after 2 days.

Not much happening except we had a big inspection this morning by the C.O. and my bunk mate went AWOL last night. He isn't back yet but scuttlebutt has it that he's been caught already. My ankle was swollen last night so it's Sick Call tomorrow morning. Told the D.S. I was going to sick bay & he looked at me weird & told me I was in the Army now.

Really wish I was away from this place. I look at myself in formation & say P.T. what are you doing here? Hating it. I don't mind marching but I HATE to be told that I must march. I know why Wayne is so messy, for 1/2 a chance I'd throw all my belongings into a pile, burrow into the middle and live.

Really don't think I'll graduate from Basic with the honors I'd hoped for. Got tired of smiling at the D.S. & getting a snarl in return, so now I glare at him & he smiles back. You see he's really small so he picked a few of us taller people to pick on. He'll tell us to do something & then jumps on us for doing it. I haven't really screwed up yet but he's trying. At this time I wish I was small & inconspicuous. . .

Nothing like the Army to show you the bad side of people & the human race in general. I knew Basic was going to be bad but I figured—once I got out it would be OK, but now I want no part of it at all.

All leaves have been permanently cancelled because of Meningitis. I won't go any further into that for fear of saying something NASTY, OBSCENE, MALICIOUS, PROFANE, CRUDE, BASE, GROSS, BOORISH, or un nice and like Mom says if you can't say anything nice, don't, Right?

They've been teaching us how to properly kill & destroy the enemy. I figure they better not teach me too good because as of now they're the only enemies I've got. Last night the D.S. got drunk & came back to post & told me to do something with my weapon, but his clouded mind made it come out weird so I just laughed at him. He started to get uptight but realized what I'd do to him if he tried anything (like turn him into the CO with 54 witnesses) so he started laughing also. I wasn't laughing because he was funny but because I wanted to jump up and down on his empty little head. . .

Oh, guess what—I lost the cap to my tooth. The Army won't replace it until after Basic so I have $1\frac{1}{2}$ front teeth. Am I beautiful!

Have to fall out again bye love and of course Peace.

P.T.

***

Father:

It is Sunday the 4th of May and I'm the most popular man in my squad. Everyone was arguing over who was to stand next to me in line. Not because of my stimulating conversation, because we're disallowed talking. Not because I'm so pretty, I only have $1\frac{1}{2}$ front teeth. But because today is fast Sunday & the people next to me get my meal.

You are probably the most important person in my development as a person, and whatever I am now it's because of your influence. Although I pretend to have a mind of my own, I fear that it is little else than a carbon copy of yours.

Because of the heavy influence you've had on me, I want to thank you and tell you how much I love and appreciate you for teaching me of the things like church and marriage that I find daily more important. For I believe that if you were anything but the great spirit you are I would have sandy foundations on which to build my life.

You know that you're the major reason that I went into the Army. You know how strongly I feel about killing and hate. But I knew you wanted me to accept my responsibilities honestly, and you raised me to believe in this country. So a combination of my desire to serve my country coupled with the knowledge of how you would feel if I tucked my beliefs under my arm and took that 2 year step. But fortunately the lord has fixed a way for me to stay in the Army out of jail and out of combat at the same time—my bad Achilles tendon. If you know the myth of Achilles you can really see the irony in it.

So thank you father for giving me a future and being so strong and honest with me. I realize more each day all the things you've done for me. Thanks Dad. Like the poet once said "There is a great bit of thee in me." Even if you are a stubborn old reprobate.

Peace father, your son,

Paul C.

***

25 May 69

Only 28 days left of Basic:

'Twill be a happy day to be sure. Having a wonderful time here. Don't let my letters fool you, I'm just looking for sympathy.

Been having a real smash every day at the rifle range. Nothing more fun than handling, manipulating, and cuddling man's favorite implement of destruction. Am both proud and ashamed to say that I shot expert the last few days of training. Record fire is Monday, don't know how I'll do, don't really care. But who in the name of Aristotle wants to be proficient at killing things? Even targets?

HA! I didn't go to church today. Steeped in sin this kid is. I know I'll regret it tomorrow but I just knew if I went I'd fall asleep (some excuse eh?). The devil took momentary control and convinced me that I shouldn't go. So there my guilt is expunged. I confessed.

The D.S. got mad at me last week. We had pugil stick training. Supposed to simulate bayonet battle. Two guys fight with fiberglass gunstocks, as long and heavy as our M-14 with a bayonet on it, and padded on each end. I had to fight with Niehaus, a guy with his masters in Geology. He won the first bout by stabbing me in the neck. The second bout I clouted him along side the head and knocked him down and pierced his heart. Whereupon I threw down my pugil stick, flashed a peace sign and said "Peace." Everyone thought it was funny but the D.S. called me a meathead. He's too slow to catch most of my cynical witticisms. He doesn't pick on me much anymore because when he leaves me alone I leave him alone. . . .

How kind of you to ask of Barb. I only have one worry as far as she's concerned. How am I gonna pay the phone bill?. . . She sent some fudge and some sunflower seeds last week. She writes every day or so and writes interesting compassionate letters. It was kind of you to say mother that you'll be happy to welcome Barbara as a daughter-in-law in another two years. BUT!! If I do marry that chick it'll be bunches sooner than 2 years. Do you think that if I love a woman enough to marry her that I'm gonna wait 2 years to do it? We won't get married immediately or even for a while, but if we do it will be within the next 6 or 8 months. She's not gonna want to wait another 2 years. She says she would but I doubt it. When I get my first long leave after she's back from Europe we're gonna blast over to your house and have a good time. . .

Thanks for the newspaper clippings Mom. I have an idea—from now on put the clippings in a coffee can to cushion the cookies you send. Love to you all.

Peace always,

P.T.

***

It seems once again that I'm calling upon you to share my burden. I'm not asking for help, there is none you can give me. What I'm stumbling over in this paragraph is that I'm down folks, really down and I'm telling you about it because it will make me feel better. Maybe a little by habit, you've always been kind enough to accept my problems as your own. I'd tell Barbara also, but she's leaving for

Europe tomorrow, and I want her to have the best time possible; knowing that I'm going to infantry AIT [Advanced Individual Training] certainly won't help that.

The drill sergeant told several of us in the platoon that we probably have infantry. Nothing is official yet.

I guess it's a culmination of many things. The reasons don't really matter but I'm a rather discouraged young man this evening. Disappointed, disgusted, and confused, tired of the whole hassle and looking for an end, and that's elusive and seems nowhere in sight.

I'm tired of trying to rationalize things in my mind. All my beliefs seem to form a giant paradox. There is no room in my heart to justify killing, I can't ever justify the training to kill, and yet I can't justify copping out. I can't justify desertion although that seems the only logical course of action. I know inside that a time is drawing near when our families will need to draw together and the world will be in an uproar, so leaving for another country is out. The church speaks so loudly against breaking the law, and so loudly for supporting our constituted way of life that I can't justify refusing my orders. I want to do what is called of me for my country, but I can't justify the senseless loss of life.

I was hoping to be sheltered from this decision or series of decisions but it doesn't seem fit for the Lord I suppose.

I will go to infantry AIT, although I'm sure it will be as detestable as this. I sure hope they don't order me to Vietnam.

It all seems so strange that I could be here. The reality of it seems to float above my head only to drop down every once in a while to remind me that this really isn't a game and all these people so filled with hate are really people.

But with every day I become more conscious of the ominous power we've given the military, and hate it so much more. Hate is such an overused word and I see it more than I hear it here. But just the same I'd prefer being a part of something else, where people smile at you and the only power is in love.

It is an easy mold to fit into. I blame many things on the Army that I should blame on myself. I had hoped I wouldn't be so susceptible, but my temper is short these days. My patience has been replaced with something else, something that doesn't taste nearly as sweet. The pessimist in me has found lush pastures to graze on, and this letter is a shining example.

We have a forced march tomorrow—12 miles in 3 hours with full packs. I'll call you when my orders are official. Love to all.

Peace on Earth

P.T.

***

On Leave

Just sitting here on a rickety old front porch in the sun, no people, no traffic, no hassle just music from inside the house.

You would like our house, it is so very fine. The walls are ready to fall down, my bride Barbi jumped on the bed and put the bed post through the floor, and it's so hard to keep clean. But I'd live here forever.

I wish I could express all the joy in my heart as there is more than happiness. I lose reality and the Army here. The sun shines warm, the wood smells old, and acres of unharmed land surround our little island home. But probably most of all it's Barb. She's the perfect thing that gives reason and purpose to the confused world. As she walks with me through the brown fields past birds and rabbits amid a dozen dogs it seems that it was all made for her. She doesn't fit the environment, she's a part of it. If I could only show you the movies of her that are in my mind. Yesterday she made her own bread from scratch in that rickety old stove. She makes everything here beautiful and groovy. I more than love her. I live for her, and I don't know how I lived so long without her. The moments of greatest happiness in my life have been with her. If I could only convey . . . the importance of losing yourself in another. I would hate to think of marrying someone you don't love, or letting sex or infatuation blind you. Marrying someone in the church is so much better, all the things you've been preaching for so long. I only hope Wayne is as blessed as I. We thank God every night for each other and our love. It's like we've got a secret and Wayne & Jane & Keith can know too when they marry. We can tell them and they still wouldn't know. It's love. We can explain for hours and they wouldn't even begin to comprehend man's capability to love.

Plan to drive through Vegas to the Southern coast and driving up the coast till we get near Big Sur, Carmel & Monterey. Then we'll be looking for a place for the month leave I have. Should see you the end or middle of January. Have a merry Christmas and New Years, we'll be thinking of you.

If there can't be peace between men, then let there be an inner peace for men.

P.T.

***

For Barb

When I look at a tree I see
A sky, a field, and the world behind it.
When I look upon the moon I can see
The black night, shining stars, and clouds.
When I see a flower I see leaves
And grass and butterflies too. But
When I see you that's all I can see
The world is hidden behind you
Maybe because you're so close.
If I touch a tree I touch the
Bark the leaves a moth or whatever is on it
If I touch a flower I feel also
The cool breeze, the dirt on my feet.
If I feel the sun I feel more too

The shirt on my back, the wind and
Air around me. But
If I touch you that is all I feel, everything
Is hidden behind you
Maybe because you're so close.

***

Vietnam

Apr. 5, 1970

Never thought I'd be anxious to leave for Vietnam, but after months of apprehension, I'm ready to get through this thing. We're in a huge building full of beds, and the beds are full of GI's smoking. I hope I keep this journal, it makes me think. There are many things I could write about Barb but I won't. It's too early for that.

After leaving Wake Island I fell asleep. I don't know where we are or when we are. We're making this flight in an old Trans International Airlines DC 8. It's pretty cramped, which doesn't help the poor stewardesses. I feel very much like a sheep being herded to market. Everyone is nice but I feel like there's some conspiracy here. I also feel like I've just made a very big decision and I'm just finding out that it was a mistake.

I miss Barb. I missed her especially in Hawaii where I'd feel her in the wind and saw her walking my way a dozen times.

***

Apr. 8, 1970 in country

Left the sympathetic smiles of the stewardesses and stepped out of the womb into Vietnam. I sensed rust and mildew and looked at my arms to see if they were as wet as they felt, but they weren't. We're assigned to 90th Replacement here at Bien Hoa. Terribly apprehensive, I feel alone in a building with at least 1,500 people in it. At least a hundred fans push the weighted dank air around so that it won't cling to you.

Camp Evans is about 5 miles from the DMZ [Demilitarized Zone]. We hear artillery every night. It's weird to be awake at night in a different land of different people, listening to the sounds that death makes as casually as listening to barking dogs.

P.T.

***

8 PM Apr. 8

Getting used to this place isn't going to be easy. I was a bit dizzy out in the sun today. Met a fellow who plans to be here 25 months before he goes home. I asked why he would want to do that. He replied that there were things here he couldn't get in the outside world like grass and 3 dollar whores. Then he asked what there was in the world that he couldn't find here. I said freedom.

P.T.

***

10:50 PM Apr. 9

Finally got my assignment, received orders for the 101st Airborne at Phu Bai, which is approximately 50 miles south of the DMZ. I'll ship sometime tonight or early tomorrow. Will have just missed the monsoon. They've put us in filthy barracks for tonight with no dinner. My mattress is filthy, so I'm going to just sleep on springs. I learned pinochle tonight, won my first game. I'll sleep now, Barb is too heavy on my mind to stay awake.

***

Nite of April 20th
Dearest Civilians:

Oh thou who are fortunate, tonight is the eve of great rejoicing, gnashing of the jaws and rending of sandals.

For it is said so it is written that mine supplications have been acknowledged. My fondest dream has been granted.

In one brilliant flash some divinely inspired clerk at Fort Evans or wherever out of nowhere picked my name out of beaucoup others and said in reverence: "Him I will save from the clutches of death in the darkest of jungles; HE yes HE and only HE will I put to work in his M.O.S." [Military Occupation Specialty]. And so it came to pass that good ol' P.T. ended up with a rear echelon job in an air-conditioned underground TOC [Tactical Operations Center] exempt of details, wearing starched jungle fatigues and expectorate-shined boots. I work with 2 majors, 4 or more captains, even more lieutenants, 2 colonels (one full), 2 E8's, 1 E6 & 2 other E-5's. I work 12 hours off 12 on, so my newly acquired tan will surely fade as I go to work at 8 AM or so & get off at 8 PM or so. It is such a brassy outfit everyone smokes big cigars and is clean shaven. My first hour in the compound I was told to shave my mustache 5 times. The general hates them, the colonels can't stand them and the major is murder on them. They just ruined a Sergeant Major's career and sent him to the boonies in some useless function because he'd refused to shave the mustache he'd had for 32 years. When I heard this in conjunction with the word Boonies I smiled brilliantly and ran, not trod, but Ran to the nearest razor and shaved and neatly tucked my wire rimmed glasses away for later use like about a year later. Today the General noticed me and introduced himself. He's from Texas, so you can imagine what a gala occasion introductions are. I was lucky to get away with my right hand and wrist. He also noticed my pale upper lip. Going thru the proper channels he inquired of the 1st Lieutenant who replied that it was due to the recent eradication of the mustache. Whereby we did a routine not unlike the introduction scene, except the latter was more of a good riddance thing, and a congratulations back to the human race. The crowning glory was a shouted AIRBORNE!! and a backslap. I gave him a humble-yet-proud two-toned smile and nodded my affirmations that yes it certainly feels better.

P.T.

***

11 September
June Ol'Kid

Certainly was nice to hear you talking again, I really didn't have that much to say but only wanted to know if everyone is alive and well. Had I checked the time I would have known Barb would be at work. But I just went over to buy some Coke (they have a cooler), and they were talking on the radio, so I told them to make a call for me & they did. Don't really like the calls cuz people don't sound human & you really can't say anything, but they always make me happy.

You know I'll bet I could be an outasight police dispatcher, I mean I've dispatched just about everything imaginable. If I can get a million dollars worth of bombs and B52's where they're wanted I could manipulate 2 cops in a Ford no sweat. Especially since I have to memorize a complete set of call signs, frequencies, and designators every month or less & police signs and frequencies stay the same. It does really matter here if the bad guys know all our codes. The brass really get mad when Nguyen Van Bad Guy talks on my radio & we have to change it all around again.

This salt mine is really getting me down. I wanna come home to Mama and my wife. There really isn't that much I can tell you. Rain has begun and the monsoons will be here soon. The hole in my roof keeps me company. I'm gonna get it fixed though cuz sometimes I go away & forget to put my wash basin under it & come back to a flood.

I'm gonna run over to the mess & see if I can get something to eat. Another thing, the chow is sorry. I mean ungood food & I'm sick of dried up burnt gristly cold roast beef, nearly every day. You'd think they'd at least learn how to cook that one thing if that's all they cook, but no not them. By the way have you taught Barb to make decent gravy yet?

Miss you Mom. Give love to all.

Paul

***

24 Sept. 70
Unpardonably fortunate brother & deserving wife:

Good day my friends may benevolence and good fortune grace your hearth till 6 new moons.

It is my most sincere wish that this missile finds you in good humor. Actually the main reason for my writing is to tell kin what's up with P.T.

As telling Barb would only worry her day & night; same with parents, they can't keep a secret anyway. Here's hoping you can.

I feel some sort of compulsion to write someone referring to what I've done; am now doing, in that if some misdeed does befall my stout heart, at least you will be able to tell them what I'm doing.

The job I had at TOC was the most trying thing I've ever done and the strain was beginning to show after 12–14 hrs a day, 7 days a week for six months. It was bearable at first cuz it's a critical job with beaucoup responsibility & I didn't want Barb to worry, so I stayed in the rear and hassled with the lifers. Well most of the old staff DEROSed [end of overseas duty], and their replacements are incompetent; spineless, yes-men. The few that were not were efficiently removed. It started getting on my nerves, then the lifer B.S. got to the point where P.T. said it's time to dash. So I told 'em 6 months was 5½ months too long: relieve me, remove me, that I wanted the heck out.

Rather than go out with some battalion Recon [reconnaissance] team and sit in the rain, I joined what is called the 3rd Brigade Air Cavalry. It's an instant Recon team. They insert us into trouble spots for a day or two & then extract us. If a Bird gets shot down they rappel us in to secure it, things like that. You may see more Sierra Hotel India Tango but you can take anything when you know they're gonna pull you out in 2 days.

Just got back from a 3-day mission directly west of Hue about 3 ridgelines east of the A Shau Valley. We were sent in there to investigate enemy supply routes into the 101st's A.O. [Area of Operation]. Found 6 bad guys, brought an armed LOH [Light Observation Helicopter] team in on 'em, turned up a hooch (hut), put a t.o.t. [time on target—artillery barrage] of 155's on that, definitely brought that hooch a dam-damn. I think it was about then that our position was compromised but nobody knew it. We were still up on the ridgeline & had to check out the Rao Lao river [Rao Lao Asap River]. I realize you can't imagine this cuz the only mountain down south was a knoll called Nui Ba Dinh [Black Virgin Mountain]. Anyway, we were inserted somewhere above 900 m. according to my map. River level was about 200 m. which means we walked down for a little over a day through thick jungle. I was wearing special Vietnamese camouflaged fatigues [called Tiger Fatigues] and they ripped up the back from the knee up the crotch to the belt. Realize of course that in the jungle nobody wears any type of underwear. Truly an uncomfortable position since unfortunately one cannot be medevaced out for air-conditioned pants. I was definitely ready to go back. I wore my right buttock down to the mesoderm and other tender parts of the physiology rather raw, and got rather painfully insect bitten as well. I finally fashioned a loin cloth out of the rag I had been using to clean my weapon. Really felt weird unbuttoning the front to pee when there was no behind.

After walking & sliding with 60 lbs. of rucksack, plus ammo, claymores, etc. DOWN for 8 years we finally reached the Rao Lao river to find negative activity, except we were being escorted. We would just catch a glimpse of one or two not enough to fire at but enough to know they were there. Then we discovered we were too far down in a valley for radio communication, so if they had decided to hit us we'd definitely been in a bind.

Then we found that the LZ [Landing Zone] we were supposed to go to was ¾ up the Ridge and washed out, so nobody could get up to it. About this time they sent a bird [helicopter] looking for us cuz we had negative communication & they thought we'd been bushwhacked. We told them our problem and the pilot found a wide spot in the river about a mile away. So we dashed for it about waist deep in water. We got there but found a burning campfire en route. We knew we were gonna get ambushed with no place to hide and high ground all around us. Eeeech, the pucker factor was about sky high. We made it to the LZ & the Birds were beautiful. After circling for 10 minutes they figured how to get in, but they didn't like it either because there was high ground all around. But they came in anyway about 10 feet off the water. Our bird came in at about 60 knots and I thought he was gonna run me down. Then he just stopped and hovered over my head, so I threw my weapon in, grabbed that skid, pulled myself to a boulder and jumped in. Felt good. Let my legs dangle out the door all the way back. Felt real good. So now I'm back & my story is told.

Thanks, I feel better having told it. I'll be off again until our next mission. I hope for a few days for all the cuts and bruises to go away. I feel like one big scab today.

But if anyone asks I'm still in the T.O.C. I'll still get my mail there, so nobody except you & me will know.

Regards to all be seeing you in 120 days or less. If you know anyone with a neat house or apt. near BYU [Brigham Young University] for cheap let me know. If there's anything you need here let me know.

Paul

***

DEPARTMENT OF THE ARMY
Headquarters and Headquarters Company
3d Brigade, 101st Airborne Division (Airmobile)
APO San Francisco 96383

08 DEC 1970

Dear Mr. and Mrs. Coe,

By this time I am sure that you have been notified of the death of your son, Paul T. Coe. I want you to know that Paul's death came as a tragic shock to me and to all the men who knew him. On behalf of the entire company, I extend our deepest and most sincere sympathy.

On 14 November 1970, Paul was a member of a daylight patrol in the vicinity of Camp Evans, with the Headquarters Reconnaissance Platoon, when the patrol hit a booby trapped area. Your son was killed by multiple fragmentation wounds when one of the hostile booby traps exploded. I hope that it may be of some comfort to you to know that Paul died instantly and did not suffer.

The Brigade Chaplain conducted a memorial service in honor of Paul on Monday, 16 November 1970. The service was attended by all the members of Paul's unit.

Once again, personally and for the men of Headquarters Company, please accept this letter as a symbol of our deepest sympathy.

Sincerely,
FRANK A. LIGHTLE
Captain, Infantry
Commanding Officer

FIGURE 1.2 Visitors reach out to touch the names inscribed on the Vietnam Veterans Memorial in Washington, D.C. The memorial was created in 1982 by a group of veterans who successfully lobbied Congress for a site near the National Mall. A Yale architecture student, Maya Lin, won a national competition for her design featuring two intersecting granite walls that slope away from a central apex. The walls' polished surface is engraved with the names of all the men and women who died in the armed services during the course of the Vietnam War or died of their wounds sometime later. Lin said she kept the design simple to avoid evoking the political dissension of the war era and to allow everyone to "respond and remember . . . the veterans, their service, and their lives." The memorial receives 3,000,000 visitors every year.

Source: Tim Koster photo, April 2002

Paul Thomas Coe's name is on the Vietnam Veterans Memorial Wall at Panel 06W, Line 58.
　　—Editors.

QUESTIONS FOR DISCUSSION

1. How is Paul Coe different from his brother, Wayne? How do the tone and language of Paul's letters differ from the tone and language in Wayne's stories? Which brother do you identify with? Why?

2. In what ways do the two brothers symbolize the divisions in the United States during the Vietnam War?

3. A certain picture of the U.S. Army emerges from Paul Coe's letters. What do we learn about the general educational level and background of draftees of the Vietnam era? Why do you think are there so few educated men in Paul Coe's basic training group? Who predominantly got drafted during the Vietnam War?

4. Why would Paul Coe and others suspect that the weapons and ammunition missing from Ft. Lewis were stolen by members of SDS or the Black Panthers? How is such a suspicion a clue to the stresses in American society in this period?

5. Paul Coe doesn't hesitate to voice his criticism of the war, of his commanding officers, and of killing in general, and these letters are not censored. Does this free expression surprise you? Compare Paul's attitude to that of his brother. What kinds of people or situations do the brothers find funny or ironic or exasperating in basic training or in the thick of war? Why does Paul become disenchanted with the officers in Vietnam?

6. Look back through the letters in Paul Coe's chapter to see if you can understand why Paul does not resist the draft, even though he opposes the war and opposes killing and even being trained to kill. Why doesn't he desert when he considers doing so, and why does he ask for the combat assignment that leads to his death? What are the influences that create such a strong sense of responsibility in this young man?

THE G.I.s CALLED US DONUT DOLLIES
Leah O'Leary

I'm a Libra. I was born on October 13, 1946. The symbol for Libra is the scales, always balancing two opposing options. Libra sees both sides of a question so well that it sometimes has difficulty deciding which option to choose. When you know someone is a Libra, you don't ask them to help you pick out a prom dress. When I was expressing frustration with this quality in myself on one occasion, a friend relieved me of the burden by saying, "Oh, that's because you're a Libra." Finally, it wasn't my fault.

So, in 1968, when so many people had concluded that the war in Vietnam was evil, I was still struggling with uncertainty. I had a passionate need to resolve this terrible conflict inside me about the war. So, I went to Vietnam to see for myself. I joined the American Red Cross as a Recreation Worker and went to play recreational games with G.I.s in combat settings and rear support areas in the middle of the war. The guys called us "Donut Dollies." This all made perfect sense to me at the time.

In the life of my family, 1957 had been an important year. My parents bought a restaurant on Cape Cod in the town of Dennis. The property included frontage on Scargo Lake in Dennis and a dock with a diving board. About a month after the restaurant opened, my older brother Ralph dove off the diving board into Scargo Lake and broke his neck. Ralph spent the rest of his life as a quadriplegic. Ralph died in 1991. He lived a heroic life and had many lessons of hope, courage, and resilience for us all.

I think partly because of what had happened to Ralph and the resulting pathos in my family life, I was having trouble believing in a God during my high school years. I had been raised as a Catholic. My Irish father was Catholic. My mother was raised Catholic as a child but her anti-Papist Italian immigrant father had taken the whole family out of the Church.

The Church and God were big issues for me. I couldn't understand how God could have let such a terrible life befall my brother. The chaos in my family as a result of the accident was a very powerful backdrop to my teen years.

Outside the family, the world also seemed upside down. I remember following the Civil Rights marches in the south. The Democratic convention of 1960. The election of John Kennedy. And of course, Kennedy's assassination. Kennedy's assassination felt a little like Ralph's accident—in another arena, in a sense, the world turned upside down. Certainly, for those of us growing up in Irish Catholic Norwood, Massachusetts, Kennedy represented the best of who we were and he called on all of us to give our best for larger social goals and aspirations. I don't know if the '60s would have played out in the same way if it had not been for his expectations about who we were and what we were supposed to do.

College

When the time came to pick a college, I decided to go to Trinity College in Washington, D.C., an all-women's college operated by the Sisters of Notre Dame. I wanted to give the faith of my father a "last try" before I decided I didn't believe.

In the meantime, I hung on to Albert Camus and his writings for a framework that helped me get through the night on bad days: *The Plague, The Myth of Sisyphus.* Trinity gave us a sense of the Church's possibilities in the wake of Vatican II. We actually read Protestant theologians like Harvey Cox as part of Theology class!

Being at Trinity between 1964 and 1968 put me in Washington, D.C., during so many important events. I remember Johnson's War on Poverty and his Great Society. I remember the impact of Michael Harrington's *The Other America* on shaping the War on Poverty. (I still cannot believe it when graduate social work students have never heard of this book!) As a political science major in a conservative political science department, I studied with Edna Fluegel and Jeanne Kirkpatrick, later Nixon's Ambassador to the United Nations. Both women had razor sharp minds. Both were dedicated teachers who students respected. Emilia Goven, another teacher in the department, provided a more liberal viewpoint.

However, as a Catholic women's college, Trinity was definitely not "where the action was." Heavily protected by the Wackenhut Security Police, we used to sit around and complain about what an insular environment we were in. Our contemporaries at other campuses were discovering marijuana and LSD. If you merely had too much to drink at Trinity you had to report yourself to the student judiciary as dictated by the Honor Code on campus. The biggest taboo, it seemed at Trinity, was losing one's virginity.

I spent the summer between my freshman and sophomore years in Honduras with 17 other college students from Trinity. I was stationed with three other students in La Lima, which, at the time, was the headquarters of the United Fruit Company, and also a kind of suburban slum about 10 miles outside of San Pedro Sula, the second largest city in the country. There were fields of bananas all over the place.

Our job was to help distribute surplus food from the United States—we would break down 50 lb. bags of flour and other foodstuffs into 5 and 10 pound bags for distribution around the community. It was not unusual to open a bag and discover maggots, larvae, and other bugs, but the need was so desperate that most of that got handed out too. The images of those slums are still very vivid in my mind. The dwellings were made up of corrugated sheets of metal and heavy cardboard somehow attached. Dirt floors. The poverty was dire. I remember the children and adults who would pick through the neighborhood dump, looking for food, building material, any kind of material to support life in this neighborhood.

Going back to college in the fall of 1965, I felt like all the action was going on somewhere else, but I became very active in student government, becoming president of my class for junior and senior years.

Despite the school's protected environment, we could not escape race issues any more than anyone else in the Sixties. As a rule, Trinity attracted a population of very bright, socially conservative, white Catholic women from the upper middle class. The school was predominantly residential. While I was there, the College started a scholarship program for women of color from the Washington, D.C., area. By the time I was a junior, I was noticing that the women of color hung out in the lounge for commuters, and that there was not a lot of mixing taking place between the residential community and the day hops, as all commuters were called. I decided that we should do something to initiate some form of dialogue. I did not know what we should talk about, but felt we should do something.

I announced the formation of an Interracial Book Discussion Group for residential students and day hops. The idea was for folks to get together and agree on books dealing with race issues or related topics, and use the readings as a way to explore race and comparative cultural themes. We had about three or four meetings. I could not persuade my white college classmates to go to the meetings. "What was there to talk about?" they asked. I was told that there was no difference between the white day hops and the day hops of color—no need to have special meetings. I can't say that I really understood myself why it was so important, but I just had a sense that there was something wrong with having all the students of color in one lounge and the rest of the college going its own way without some kind of dialogue.

The first few meetings, I showed up with one or two white friends. It seemed like all the students of color showed up. They really showed up. I apologized and said I would have to work harder to get more white kids. By the third or fourth meeting, the black students stopped trying. I think there were two of us white students showing up at this point. That day, the black students politely, calmly, and with some amount of clarity announced the formation of the Trinity College Black Power student group on campus. They also indicated that, although they really appreciated everything I had done on a personal level, they had to organize their own group and that there was no room for white students. They talked to me about things that Stokely Carmichael was saying and about the need for black people to find their own way, and about Black Power. They said I would have to leave, but there was nothing personal in this development.

I'll never forget what it was like walking away from the social hall in which we had met. I felt I had utterly failed in a very important cause. I had been operating on a hunch that something was wrong, a vague sense that we needed to do more but I had not been able to make the compelling argument for action or even to conceptualize the chasm that we needed to bridge. I felt stupid, inarticulate, and a total failure at something that was very important.

As I walked away from the meeting, the head of the psychology department, Sr. Mary Margaret (students called her Sr. Psych.) came up beside me. She talked to me about what had just happened in the social hall and she told me that everything that had just happened might be what needed to happen. She explained that groups go through different stages in their development and that sometimes they needed to be by themselves as part of a process.

What happened in that group was an important lesson for me. Looking back, I'm amazed that Sr. Psych was there in that moment that felt like total despair. I am so grateful for the insight she shared in this brief exchange in the hallway as I walked away from the meeting I had organized and then been kicked out of. As the years have passed, I have even felt a twinge of pride at having been the student leader who helped develop the Black Power movement at Trinity College. I also have carried with me the importance of helping create the "frame" for understanding situations.

By my senior year at Trinity, I was up for an adventure. At another time, I would have joined the Peace Corps. In 1968, however, the biggest issue of my era was the war in Vietnam. I had the information, but I couldn't choose sides. Our country was being torn apart by the divisions being created by the war. I couldn't believe our country's policies could be as wrong as the anti-war protesters argued. I was pretty confused and was jealous of all the folks in my generation who had such a clear idea of right and wrong. I would, therefore, go see for myself.

It's a little embarrassing to share some of the influences that led me on this adventure. I was very taken by the notion of being a witness to the great events of my times. I had read *Witness* by Whittaker Chambers (not unusual reading in a political science department in the '60s, where I was taught by teachers who had developed their world views in the '40s and '50s). Then there were the books by Thomas Dooley, a medical doctor who ministered in Vietnam and Laos and who died at an early age—books like *Deliver Us from Evil, The Edge of Tomorrow,* and *The Night They Burned the Mountain.* These books were inspiring and they were consistent with the ethos that John Kennedy had helped create with his inaugural speech: "Ask not what your country can do for you, ask what you can do for your country." I had pictures in my head of doing great things and saving a lot of people like Dr. Dooley or being in a critical vantage point to witness the great events of my era, like Whittaker Chambers.

There was another book. If I had been writing this piece in my twenties or thirties, or even forties, I would be too embarrassed to admit that the other book that helped form my belief that a woman ought to have an adventure in her early twenties was *Our Hearts Were Young and Gay,* by Cornelia Otis Skinner and Emily Kimbrough. It is a delightful story of two adventurous young women and their exploits on their first trip to Europe in the 1920s. As it turned out, the adventures of women volunteers in Vietnam could not have been more different.

The Red Cross

After I decided to go to Vietnam I researched all the non-profit humanitarian agencies that were working there. I applied to 12 non-profits—from USAID (United States Agency for International Development), to the American Friends Service Committee, a Quaker organization. I even applied to the American Leprosy Mission. But none of the humanitarian agencies were sending women to what had become a much riskier war zone since February 1968—the time of the Tet Offensive. One door after another closed. The Peace Corps was not sending volunteers to Vietnam because of the war. The last two organizations I tried were the American Red Cross, which operated a recreation program for American servicemen stationed in Vietnam, and the U.S. Army. I was accepted to both. The Army, however, would not assure me that they would send me to Vietnam; the Red Cross did. I signed up with the Red Cross. I went to see Sam Krakow, head of the International Division of the American Red Cross. He was a wonderful man who did the kind of work I wanted to do—relieving world suffering by helping organize disaster relief around the globe. Mr. Krakow sent a referral slip over to Mary Louise Dowling, the head of the Supplemental Recreational Activities Overseas (SRAO) program of the Red Cross. Part of me thought the whole idea of "recreational activities"—board games, quiz competitions, etc.—was crazy, but, hey, if this was the only way to get there, I'd go play games.

My hometown newspaper, the Norwood (Massachusetts) *Messenger,* decided my adventure deserved a little article. They wrote it using a press release issued by the American Red Cross in October 1968.

Miss Leah C. O'Leary, daughter of Mr. and Mrs. Dennis P. O'Leary, 269 Walpole Street, Norwood, Massachusetts, has joined the American Red Cross as a Recreation Aide in the Supplemental Recreation Activities Overseas program.

As a worker Miss O'Leary will conduct recreation programs for American servicemen in South Vietnam. Clubmobile women may operate from a fixed center, where garrison type military installations are located, or from mobile units which travel to remote outposts near the front lines. In the latter case the women often travel by jeep or helicopter and set up their fast-paced audience-participation programs in unit mess tents, motor pools or anywhere they can find adequate space.

Clubmobile women must be in perfect health and are usually between the ages of 21 and 24 when first employed.

At present 110 recreation workers are operating Center-units at 20 locations in South Vietnam, including Da Nang, Nha Trang, Bien Hoa, and Di An. All centers are located on U.S. military bases.

The Red Cross recreation programs in South Vietnam and Korea encourage active soldier participation in activities that provide a relaxing break in the routine and help keep young Americans in touch with home.

In September, 1968, I reported to the national headquarters of the American Red Cross in Washington for a two-week orientation for the job I would do in Vietnam. I was part of a class of 20 or 30 young women, mostly recent college graduates. The Red Cross put us up at the Hotel Washington near the Red Cross Headquarters and gave us a daily allowance for food. We were treated very nicely. There was a genteel quality about the program and the way we were treated. As I recall, they called us "ladies" a lot.

A number of memories stick out about those two weeks in Washington. We were fitted for uniforms, had shots including gamma globulin for hepatitis and the like, and a lot of lectures about the Red Cross and the military. We had lectures about the history of the Red Cross, and the different programs operated by the Red Cross, including the disaster program, the blood program, services to military families, and the international program. Because we were going to be important and very visible ambassadors of the agency, we had to be able to answer questions. They taught us about the Red Cross during World War II and assured us that Red Cross women had never sold donuts during the war, contrary to "the lies and rumors" that still prevailed. The implication that Red Cross women volunteers had been low-level war profiteers, charging soldiers for what they were supposed to be distributing for free, was highly insulting. In fact the first time I heard the words "Donut Dolly," I almost changed my mind and didn't apply. In training we were told that in Vietnam we provided Kool-Aid and coffee but never sold drinks to soldiers. This was a very important lesson for us to get right.

There was a lot of information provided about the Red Cross's relationship with the U.S. military. When all was said and done, it seemed that they were trying to describe an organization separate from the military establishment but a part of it at the same time. Some of the distinctions escaped me. It seemed to me that we were the recreational and social services component of the U.S. military. But we were "separate" from the military. Still, we needed to learn the different ranking systems for the various branches of the armed services. I was left with the impression that these ranking systems were very important and you had to understand who was over and under whom. Some of the Red Cross girls were from military backgrounds and had the ranking systems down pat. Coming from a civilian background, I found the whole discussion about how many stripes there were on a soldier's sleeve just didn't interest me. So, there were parts of this training where I felt like an alien in a strange land. There were a lot of southerners in the group, too. So, between ribbons, stripes, southern drawls, and whether we had sold coffee in World War II, there was definitely an air of unreality to the whole two weeks for me. I think I stood out in the group, too, because I cracked a lot of jokes.

In addition to the immunizations and a stern warning about taking your malaria pills (which no one took), they showed us a slide show on the health problems women needed to be aware of in a damp, hot climate. Many of us had all we could do not to barf as they showed slides of the vaginal fungi and bacteria that one could acquire. Now, about sleeping around, or having sex with any of the men, the message was clear: Sleep around and you got sent home immediately. The training emphasized that we were there for all the men, so all "special relationships" were discouraged. When we got to Vietnam we would discover that the real way the Red Cross dealt with this issue was to move us around from one unit to another to prevent "special relationships" from forming—with men or with women. This approach to "sleeping-around prevention" made for a lonely year; you no sooner became comfortable with the other women and men in a location and they moved you to another location. I was stationed in three different units during my year in-country.

A recently returned veteran Donut Dolly taught us the format for a standard program that recreation workers delivered on "clubmobile runs." Each program was created around a theme, such as "Sports," "Movies," "T.V. Programs," "Famous People." The first activity was a warm-up activity, such as flash cards. Then we'd have the main game in which the group was divided typically into two teams—perhaps the "red team and the blue team." The game might be built around a Jeopardy, Tic Tac Toe, or Concentration board theme. Fellows from each team would compete to guess the correct answers to questions that were hidden behind the game board grid squares. After the game was over and one of the teams was determined to be the winner, we would leave pen and pencil games behind—word mazes, crossword puzzles, things like that.

I remember the lesson. The veteran Donut Dolly was telling us how to make up the games, assuring us that units were generally well stocked with multicolored sheets of cardboard and magic markers and all the equipment necessary to put board games together. She showed photos of women "programming" to groups of G.I.s in-country—in motor pools, aircraft hangers, offices, and at firebases with the board games leaning up against the heavy artillery guns. I thought the whole thing was hysterical. I couldn't believe we were really being trained to go to a war zone and play games with soldiers. I couldn't believe that I was really doing this. I mean, half of American womanhood were burning their bras and finding their feminist voices, the other half were out on the picket lines and marching in anti-war demonstrations, while I was going off to play games and "skits" with G.I.s in Vietnam.

My friend in training, Misty, who was a dear and was very supportive to me while I questioned what the hell was I doing here helped me keep my muzzle on long enough to get through the orientation.

Part of the selection process during the training was a final interview. It took everything in me to sidestep the questions. I was committed to going, but thought this whole scene was crazy. I mean, really, the revolution was at hand around the country, and we were getting instructions in how to refute the "donut selling scandal" from World War II. While my motivation for going was not about supporting the war, I did feel that young men being drafted and sent over were victims in this whole war. Playing games with G.I.s in a war zone did present some incongruity with what other members of my generation were doing, nevertheless, you couldn't beat it as a grand adventure. It might have been a silly thing to do, but my conscience was clear. In my own mind, my role would not make a difference in the execution of the war effort, one way or another, but at least it was compassionate.

The last memory that really sticks out is the stack of IDs we were all given, seven in all if I recall correctly. We received a Red Cross identification card, an ID from the Department of Defense as a civilian worker, and some other ID card in duplicate that identified the holder as a person in a non-combative status. The veteran recreation worker explained, all bright eyed and bushy tailed, that those were the ID cards you needed if captured by the Viet Cong ("V.C."). She went on to explain that if you were captured by the V.C. you kept one copy and gave the other to the V.C. The V.C., according to the rumors in-country, then nailed the other copy to your forehead.

Vietnam, 1968–1969

The Red Cross flew us over on commercial aircraft, just like the Army did with G.I.s. I wrote to my folks about my arrival in-country:

Friday, September 27, 1968. Saigon:

"I don't know where to begin describing the kaleidoscope of impressions I've experienced since Wednesday when we arrived around 5:00 p.m. Saigon time. First of all, I made a very graceful entrance onto Vietnamese soil. I tripped on the gangplank off the plane, fell, and landed upon my knees. I wasn't hurt—not even a scratch—but it wasn't the mental image I had had of the momentous occasion of my arrival.

"Since it's the monsoon season in Saigon, it isn't as hot or as humid as I thought it would be. Let me put it this way—the weather was more uncomfortable in Washington in July than Saigon is now. It rains quite a bit—but only three or four hours a day—as far I can tell from the short time I've been here.

"Saigon has the potential of being a very beautiful city. I say potential because with this weather, it takes some amount of upkeep to maintain houses and public buildings. Because of the war, little or no attention has been given to this upkeep, of course, but you can still see why Saigon used to be known as the "Paris of the

Orient." I don't really feel that I'm in the Orient. The French and American influence is so strong in this city, and there are so many Americans, it's hard to realize that this is Southeast Asia.

"They are keeping us pretty busy with more briefings and orientation. We're up at 6:30 or 7:00—bus picks us up at 7:30 and brings us to Red Cross headquarters, which is located at MACV—Military Assistance Command Vietnam—headquarters for the military effort. This is where Gen. Abrams and all the VIPs of the military are. We're staying at the Hotel Ambassador—accommodations are clean and quite adequate—rooms are $1.00 every night.

"We're finished every day around 4:30, the bus brings us back to the hotel and we're free until 10:00 p.m. when the curfew for Saigon necessitates an early return to the hotel.

"How do I like Saigon? That's a difficult question. I feel very distant from the Vietnamese people. As we ride to and from headquarters every day we pass crowds of people—there are thousands of Hondas (small motorbikes) and people milling around on the streets—I try to read the faces of the Vietnamese for some indication of how they feel about our being here. We look at them and they look at us. I'm sure that the presence of half a million American G.I.s in Vietnam is a corrupting influence. Last night I went to two bars where the prostitutes hang out. An American Samoan who owns a half interest in the first one we went to knew one of the fellows with whom we had come. He was quite proud of the going business he had. He gave us quite a run down on the prostitution business and later took us to one of the after-hours places in Saigon—illegal but condoned—where the prostitutes work for the hotel. Anyway, you get a feeling for what the U.S. presence in Saigon is doing to the local culture. You get the same impression walking through the shops. Everyone's trying to sell you (the rich American) something. Two newsboys cheated me out of a quarter between them. I knew what they were doing but it didn't seem worth the trouble to say anything.

"Anyway, it is difficult being an American in Saigon—especially knowing no Vietnamese. I feel like the ugly American—I don't belong here. Maybe I'm just reacting to the inscrutable Orient.

"My very short stay in Saigon hasn't been all bad. It hasn't been bad at all, in fact. I hate leaving this place on Sunday, because there is so much to learn from these people. After Sunday my contact with the native population will be almost non-existent."

Danang

My first assignment was I Corps, Danang, MACV Marine Headquarters. The guys called it the "crotch of the war." That's because some of the fiercest battles and skirmishes were in I Corps. Military lingo, in so many situations, considered the crotch to be the center of all the action. (The U.S. Military divided South Vietnam into four sectors: I Corps, II Corps, III Corps and IV Corps. "I Corps" is pronounced like "eye corps." Folks had a funny way of talking about everything over there.) When I was in Vietnam, there were 525,000 G.I.s in-country. There were 110–125 Red Cross girls, some USO women, some special services women, and military nurses. With so few women and so many sex-starved G.I.s, a lot of experiences were sexualized.

More than once, we would laugh about being a "Donut in the crotch of the war." It was funny at the time.

With 12 women assigned to Danang, it was one of the largest of the Red Cross Recreation units. When we flew into the Danang airport, the whole unit came out to greet and pick up the new recruits. It was a little overwhelming. They were all smiling, happy, welcoming. Some of them were holding poster boards with homemade welcome signs. I thought they were a little weird. Some of my reaction to the welcome I later came to see as representing a cultural divide between my reserved New England background, and the natural warmth that is more comfortably expressed in other parts of the U.S.

I was still trying to figure out what I had gotten myself into. We all climbed into a red bus for the ride from the airport to the house the Marines had rented for us in the civilian part of the city. I was so nervous, I remember asking Jackie Hill, the Unit Director of Danang, if she knew what the political structure of the civilian Vietnamese government was. I never heard the end of that question. I was forever known as the new recruit who asked about the Vietnamese government upon arrival. If that wasn't bad enough, within a week or two, I managed to walk into an open sewer ditch that was overflowing with monsoon rainwater on the way to breakfast one morning. I forget the nickname I got after that—"Leah the sewer rat," or something like that. The harassment was brutal after that. But it did serve to take the edge off my Boston pretentiousness and stiffness.

Eloise Spell was my first roommate in-country. She had short black hair, and a turned up nose and hailed from a small town called Hot Coffee, Mississippi. Talk about a cultural divide. When I first realized that she and I had been matched as roommates, I did not know if I would survive the experience. I was intense, pretentious, intellectual, and not sure what the hell I was doing playing games in Vietnam. She was spunky, spontaneous, funny, and totally committed to the men we were there to serve. Her Mississippi twang still rings in my ears: "I tay you whot," she would say in this sing song cadence, "I ain't thinkin' about it, I ain't pick'd a day ta think about it, I ain't thinkin' about pickin' a day to think about it," in her Mississippi drawl. She was one of the naturally funniest people I've ever met. That's how I felt when I left Danang. When I first got there, however, I didn't know if I could survive the roommate arrangement with a person who was one of the strangest people I had ever met in my life.

In the end I came to see all the women who went over as a rare breed. Across the board, they were bright, creative, determined, and, above all, independent. Jackie Hill, from Kansas, was the Unit Director and, at age 24, was a little older than some of the women; she was a charismatic leader. Jiggie Brickner from Hawaii was the Program Director for the Unit. She was a beautiful Hawaiian woman; the guys went nuts over her. Georgette DesRoche, from New Jersey, and I got along pretty well. As two northerners, we understood one another. She had a wry sense of humor and played a wonderful version of Bob Dylan's "Tambourine Man" on her ukulele.

It was a solitary experience in some ways. The program incorporated a number of group work components to help build and maintain unit morale, but nevertheless, you went over alone and kept moving from place to place alone. We worked in teams, but the team member you worked with changed every day. No special relationships of any kind was the rule.

The way the SRAO program worked, the senior command of a major military unit would request a unit of recreation workers and support the unit through arranging billeting, drivers and vehicles, helicopter transportation for runs to forward areas, and access to officers' mess for meals. Women were stationed in groups of four to twelve or so throughout the country. Recreation services were provided through the operation of recreation centers and through "clubmobile runs." In a clubmobile run, two women would conduct one-hour recreation programs to 5 or 6 groups of men a day ranging in size from 5 or 6 men to over a hundred men. Sometimes a team would have no idea how many men they would see in a day.

In Danang, we operated a recreation center on Hill 327, or Freedom Hill. Freedom Hill was like a shopping plaza for Marine infantry in from wherever the front was in I Corps. There was a USO Club, a PX, Post Office, Red Cross Center, and several other operations, including a beer garden! Every morning, our assigned driver would pick us up at our house in the city and drive us the 15–20 minutes to the Center. The Center was a large building. As you walked in the front door, there was a check-in room manned by our Vietnamese staff who checked all weapons on G.I.s coming into the Center. Turn left into a large room with pool tables and a few ping-pong tables. Turn right into a room with a lot of tables, chairs, and a table with coffee and Kool-Aid that was re-filled all day. The Center had a sound system that pumped the music of the '60s throughout the building.

Shortly after being assigned to Danang, I wrote my folks describing daily life and trying to reassure them that I felt quite safe.

Tuesday, October 1, 1968:

"Our house in Danang is located in a very nice residential suburban area of the city. It's not luxurious but it certainly is more than adequate. Did I write you about our maids? Over here they call them 'mamasans'—they do everything from laundry to shine your shoes! Two Vietnamese guards are posted at our billet (the house) 24 hours a day. The reason for the guards is not so much the V.C. as our own American 'boys' from back home. The Volkswagen bus picks us up every day at 7:30 a.m. so we're up sometime between 6:30 and 7:00. (Today I got up at 7:20 and was ready to go by 7:30.) We're back in the billet by 6:00–7:00, depending upon how much cleaning there is to do. . . . There are 12 girls in the Danang unit. . . On a regular day, two girls are in the Club, one in a smaller center, six girls might be making three separate clubmobile runs, and one is usually in the office working on a program or doing administrative work. That girl is usually either the unit director or program director.

"Yesterday I went out on a run to the flight deck (I think that's what it's called) where we served Kool-Aid. Today we went out on a program run and made four 55-minute stops at various Army 1st Cavalry platoons. On the whole, it appears to me that most of the guys enjoy these stupid little games. Tomorrow I go out with another girl—we make three stops in the morning and then visit the 95th Evac. hospital in the afternoon.

"If I don't sound very enthusiastic about my work, it's just because I'm still not quite sure of what I'm doing and the job is quite different from anything I've ever done before. These girls have surprised me with the professionalism with which they go about their jobs.

"There is some amount of fighting going on around the Danang area; however, it is quite possible to forget about the war—to know very little about what is really going on over here. Although a helicopter ride of 10 minutes from where we are may be the scene of some real tough fighting, everything goes on quite nonchalantly around here. The fighting occurs outside the area that I am restricted to. I explain all this because you both may read in the paper or hear on radio and T.V. that 'Danang was hit very badly' or that the fighting is very serious at one time or another. The reports may or may not be true—if they are there is little cause for alarm. I say this quite honestly, Mom and Dad, because I know how disconcerting some news reports may be to you both. I can only say that I feel safer here than I did in Washington. I haven't been here long but I've been here long enough to realize one or two misconceptions about the war: (1) There really are areas that are safer than others. After hearing so much about 'Charlie can be and is everywhere' I think I expected every street to have a regular sniper. This is not true. (2) The Tet Offensive was a real exception to the normal course of this war. The only reason that I am writing all this is that one of the girls recommended that I do so. Apparently, her mother read some reports and got quite upset—the girl didn't even know that a 'big attack' had occurred. As I said, in many ways it is possible to forget that the war is going on—especially as close as it is. This is one thing that I had not at all anticipated.

"The first thing I'm going to buy when I get my monthly 'hardship allowance' is a good camera and then take some snaps so you can get some idea of what this area is like. In many ways, being over here is not at all what I had expected. . . ."

I did get the camera. In fact, that year we all bought state-of-the-art photography and sound system equipment. I bought my Canon 35 mm, Sansui 5,000 tuner/receiver, Pioneer 88 speakers (the bigger the better), and a Sony reel to reel tape recorder. I earned $5,200 for the year. I didn't come home with much in the bank. But I had the best camera and stereo equipment on the block.

It's funny, really. When we were there no one talked about whether we should be in Vietnam. We talked about where we were from, how long we'd been in 'Nam, when we were returning to "the world," and what camera you were shooting with. For me, I think I experienced my year through the lens of my Canon. When you photograph an event, like a wedding, or a year in Vietnam, you really aren't in the situation as much as you are without the camera and lens between you and the situation. The camera provides a layer between you and whatever it is. In Vietnam, we all ran around with a 35mm in front of our faces.

The city streets in Danang were full of bicycles, pedicabs, military vehicles, and little automobiles. A lot of dust in the air. Exotic smells from mamasans cooking food for sale on the sidewalks. They wore sandals, black pajama pants, white blouses, and conical hats. Their faces were heavily lined; their teeth totally blackened from chewing betel nuts all day. Young Vietnamese women—slim, elegant in the traditional white Ao Dai—they were just beautiful with their long black hair, walking in groups on their way back and forth to school or work. Children played games on the sidewalks. Stores opened onto the sidewalks with displays of pirated American products. Little kids hawking American cigarettes. "Cigarettes? You want cigarettes?" as they held out a package of Marlboros. Seemed strange. This kid trying to sell me Marlboros. Anyway, I smoked Kents. On the next block, a little kid trying to hawk his sister to some fellows up ahead: "My sister. You need a girl, mista? My sister. Number One Boom Boom. You want, G.I.?"

It was hard not to be the center of attention wherever we went. There were about half a million American servicemen in-country at the time, hundreds of nurses in uniform, but only a little over 100 American Recreation Workers and a smattering of women in USO and other support positions. For me, I think it was worse because I not only had white skin and round eyes, I also had bright red hair. The old Vietnamese women on the sidewalk would put their hands in front of their mouths to giggle something to each other (what, did they think I was going to lip read what they were saying?), point to me and have a hearty laugh. They were very tiny. I felt very big next to them. They had a way of sitting on the calves of their legs while they tended the food over an open fire. We had been fully prepared in Washington— I never ate anything from the street. I only ate at military messes or a few restaurants in Danang and Saigon.

The Marines, or grunts, were a great group of fellows. They had the least amount of worldly comforts and they worked under the worst of circumstances. With these fellows, they had so little that they were triply appreciative of anything you gave them or did for them. A few of them we saw come through the Center had been in the field and away from civilization for too long. A colleague of mine went to pour a cup of coffee for this huge bruiser of a grunt, a little rough around the edges. She asked him if he'd like a little cream or sugar with that. He grabbed her by the left breast, squeezed, and said "I'll just take a little milk with that coffee instead, ma'am." A little too long in the bush. Jackie talked about the Marine she had to kick out of the Center because he was sitting along the side of the room masturbating in full view as he watched the Donut Dollies walk back and forth.

I was lucky the whole year. I didn't lose anyone really close or see anything really horrible. The horrible stuff was more like a presence I was aware of out of the periphery of my vision. Like the day a few of my colleagues were talking about the Marine who'd been in the Center that day showing folks the human ear he had in a box, a trophy he'd taken from a firefight in the bush.

Being in Vietnam at the height of the build-up, with the soldiers under tremendous tension, was an experience of being sexually harassed in one form or another every day and sometimes several times a day. Sex was everywhere. All conversations had a sexual subtext. I learned not to start a program on a clubmobile run with "How're you doing, fellows?" because I learned the answer was going to be, with some assurance, a loud, resounding "WITHOUT!" We all knew what they meant. We were standing up there as a reminder of what they were without.

Most of the time, though, there was a nice give and take. Most of the time, we'd show up to a work group, by jeep or by chopper, and use the recreation program as a vehicle for connecting with the fellows. In most situations, with most groups, they were happy to see the "Donuts," simply for the break in routine. "Here come the Donut Dollies," would typically go up whenever we would pull into a unit. The guys would clear a space for the program materials, pushing desks away if it was an office setting, or pulling a vehicle out of the motor pool in a transportation company. The typical group of guys were just like the guys we went to high school or college with.

FIGURE 1.3 Leah O'Leary, the author of "The G.I.s Called Us Donut Dollies," drinks coffee with some G.I.s from the motor pool during a break in a "Clubmobile" recreational program. Donut Dollies were Red Cross volunteers who ran recreation centers on major military bases in Vietnam and conducted audience-participation recreation programs, playing board games and sharing conversation and refreshments with servicemen in remote areas behind the lines. Clubmobile workers, traveling by jeep, truck, and helicopter, visited with about 280,000 servicemen a month. They shared many of the privations of the war while attempting to fulfill the American Red Cross' mandate to help sustain morale.

Source: Leah O'Leary photo

It was interesting visiting 5 or 6 different groups a day from a group dynamics perspective. The unit head was key in setting the whole tone of unit. Some units had sergeants or lieutenants who were angry and they took their anger out on us. It was not the typical unit, but it was there. But even in those situations, there were fellows who wanted us there and were laughing with us. In the end, I finally came to understand that it didn't matter if the guys were laughing with us or at us; we still represented a diversion for their attention from the war, from the boredom, and, in some cases, from the horror.

There was one exception to this in my experience. I forget where he was. I think I just crossed paths with this soldier—maybe it was at the PX or at the Post Office. He was in from the bush, in full infantry uniform and equipment. As we crossed paths, he looked at me in my Red Cross uniform, hem just above knee, and he gave me such a look of hatred, I've never forgotten it. It was scary. I think he could have murdered me. I don't know what seeing me triggered in him—whether it was that he really needed to be with a woman and knew he couldn't—whether my very presence said in his mind, "Look but don't touch;" whether he had just been involved in a gruesome firefight with horrible images of body parts and suffering and whether coming upon me in that moment was so incongruous to his recent reality—I don't know—I've wondered a lot about what it was.

One of my most poignant memories of Danang involves the first time I was propositioned. I was having a cup of coffee with a G.I. right out of the bush. He was an 18- or 19-year-old kid from farm country in Idaho or Iowa or one of those farm states. Twenty minutes into the conversation I understood that for the whole time we had been talking, he was trying to proposition me for $65.00, which was what the rumor mill had was our going rate. (Sixty-five dollars was the equivalent of a month's combat pay in those days.) It took him 20 minutes to get clear enough for me to understand and it took me 20 minutes to understand that that was what he was trying to do. I recall that gentle conversation as a kind of "dance of innocents." His unit had told him that the Red Cross girls could be had for a going rate and he was simply following instructions. When I realized what he was suggesting, I gently clarified the rules of the game and he was very embarrassed and asked forgiveness for any offense he might have made. He was a real dear.

Tuy Hoa

After five months at Danang, I requested a transfer to a different unit. I was getting stale and feeling that it was time to move on. I went from a unit of 12 women to a unit of four women. I had the chance to work with Linda Sullivan and Dorset Hoagland. Linda was and is one of the most talented persons I know. She was an artist with pen and ink, a song writer, guitar player, writer, punster, and all around solid person. Dorset was a vivacious, playful, very funny woman who could make you laugh. Tuy Hoa was a relief to me.

March 10, 1969—to Dad:
"My schedule tomorrow includes flying out to an artillery support firebase in the morning—get back around 2:00 p.m. Then, tomorrow evening I'll ride around part of the perimeter of Tuy Hoa with another girl (same one as in the morning) and we'll just stop to say hello at the various watchtowers and bunkers."

March 13, 1969—to [my sister] Martha:
"Must cut this short. Have a bit of flying via chopper tomorrow—go out and see a few artillery support firebases. A few days ago I was out and visited a Special Forces camp (green berets and all that stuff). Five Americans advising a S. Vietnamese force of about 700–800 men. While we were there a fellow came running in saying that one of their patrols had just killed 3 NVA (North Vietnamese Army regulars) about

3 miles away. I just gulped—but that's not dangerous for me. 3 miles is all the difference in the world—I've learned since being over here."

March 17, 1969—to [my brother] Dennis:
"When asked what the hell your kid sister is doing in the Nam, your response should be—'Just spreading joy and mirth in the villages and hamlets—on the runways and firebases of Vietnam—wherever our boys are to be found.' "

March 22, 1969—to Martha:
"Also, received my dresses—thanks. Now I won't feel embarrassed when I go to a party, if you know what I mean. I'm making a few friends here at Tuy Hoa so, of course, I'm beginning to like the place more and more. So far, the fellow whose company I enjoy the most is a married man—a Major, no less. So, what's new? No, I'm not in love, no crush—he's just a friend. I've got lots of male friends, now-a-days, you know!"

Tuy Hoa was the gentlemen's war. It was an Air Force Base located about 60 miles north of Cam Ranh Bay on the ocean. At Tuy Hoa 5,000 men supported a few hundred F-4 fighters and fighter pilots. The fighter pilots were the prima donnas of the social system. A lot of them were nice guys.

It was a little weird, even then in the moment, to sit and chat with them over breakfast and hear them joke about their assignment to fly over Never-Never Land that day, then to get together with them that evening over a cookout with steaks and drinks. One unit of flyers had pilot jump suits made for all the Donut Dollies in the unit. I still have mine. The rest of the men never came into contact with the war. They went about their technical support roles in helping maintain the fighter jets, personnel, intelligence, housing, food management, etc. Five thousand men to support a few hundred fighter pilots. I recall that, even then, it was said that it took 9 or 10 military personnel in support roles to support each combat soldier. It really came home to me one day when I was talking to an Airman who was complaining to me that the soldiers at Tuy Hoa were so far from the war that he was going to go home without seeing any action. I pointed out a flare in the distant sky, and he was very grateful because seeing the flare was the closest he had come to the war.

Donut Dolly billets at Tuy Hoa were air-conditioned trailers, which we shared. I had one half, Linda had the other half and there was a bathroom in the middle. The housing accommodations were very comfortable; the food was good. And the war seemed pretty far away.

We operated a recreation center with ping-pong tables, card tables, pool tables, and ran a weekly schedule of recreation activities. We shared our space with the air base radio station. The radio disc jockeys were a wonderful, funny, and very bright group of guys. Unlike Danang, at Tuy Hoa we had a chance to form friendships with one another and with the men.

So, from a recreation point of view, we were working with a pretty stable population and boredom and lack of meaning were the biggest problems facing the men. My answer to the situation was to start a literary journal for the Tuy Hoa Airbase. We called it *The Concrete Crier*. We actually had a lot of submissions and put out an edition of a base journal with poems, short articles of thoughts and feelings of guys stationed there.

I thought the first issue of the journal was going over pretty well with the men, when I was called to appear before the Commanding Officer of the Base. As I stood in his office in front of his desk, I noticed how perfectly ironed his nice, neat uniform was with the row of military medals and bars on his shirt. He had a copy of the journal on his desk. After he cleared his throat, he told me that we couldn't use the front cover symbol, it just wouldn't do. I had used a modified peace symbol on the front cover. I asked him what the problem was, and he said that it just wasn't appropriate for a publication sponsored by the air base. But, I pointed out, weren't we here in Vietnam fighting for peace in the world? Indeed, wasn't the peace symbol the best way to communicate the highest aspirations of our presence in Vietnam? The commanding officer just shook his head and said that it just wouldn't do and that we just couldn't use it again. I was feeling a little exasperated with this dolt. He just didn't get it, from the way I looked at the world. I looked down at the journal and a light bulb went off in my mind. I hadn't seen before the mistake the fellow who designed the cover had made when he drew the peace symbol. He had left off the bottom half of the vertical bar on the peace symbol. I hadn't realized before that instant. I looked up at the commanding officer and said, "There's really no problem here. If you just look at the symbol, it's really the logo for the Mercedes Benz automobile company. See, there's really no problem using it, right?" He didn't even think I was funny. We were out of his office in about 20 more seconds with firm instructions not to use whatever the symbol was. I thought it was hysterical. But there was something about the censorship this guy exerted. It took the fun out of the effort and we didn't come out with a second issue.

Coming Home

In my year in Vietnam, I served 5 months in Danang, 5 months in Tuy Hoa, and 2 months in Lai Khe.

I wish they had talked to us in orientation about losing your memory in war. When my year was up, I stopped in San Francisco on the way home and stayed with friends for a few days. They showed me around San Francisco. It must have been a wonderful time because San Francisco is such a beautiful city and it was definitely an "in" place to be in the 60s. But I have no memory of the visit. These friends came to see me in the mid-1980s and started talking about my stay with them—I had no memory of the three or four days I spent with them. I still don't.

My family and friends were ecstatic when I first got home. My family draped a huge sign "Welcome Home, Leah" with a big Red Cross painted on it and hung it from the front of the house. I think my parents were relieved that I was home safely. Now that I am a parent, I can't believe the stress and worry that I put them through.

After the first few days and weeks, I made a point to go to Washington and visit the national Red Cross headquarters and my teachers and friends from Trinity.

One of the strangest conversations I had when I got back occurred in my visit to Washington. I called Sam Krakow, the head of the International Division of the American Red Cross who had helped me get into the SRAO program. He took me out to lunch. It was so great to see him. He did the kind of work I wanted to do. He was really a mentor and role model for me. We had a pleasant lunch. He asked me a lot of questions about what we did in Vietnam and how we did it. He seemed very interested. Then, he leaned forward across the table and, in a slightly lowered voice asked, "But really, Leah, wouldn't a thousand camp followers done the job just as well?"

Camp followers. The time-honored nickname for prostitutes who attached themselves to armies in the field. Well, it's hard to describe the impact his words had on me. It was like a prize fighter had taken aim and thrust a full knockout punch to the center of my stomach. I was speechless and breathless, like someone had knocked the wind out of me.

When I started to respond, the words came haltingly at first but then I seemed to find my footing and my voice. "No, Sam, I don't think that a thousand camp followers would have been just as good. It may sound silly that you have a hundred or so women running around playing games in Vietnam. But it works. It doesn't matter if they're laughing with us or at us. But we were a reminder of the world they came from and that people cared. We were their sisters, their girl friends, their daughters, their friends. These guys, they're just kids. They're just young kids. We didn't make a difference to everyone, Sam, but for some, it was important that we were there."

I think the hardest time in my life was those first six months after I came home from Vietnam. I was relatively fortunate. It took me only 6 months to get a job and begin to re-enter "the world," as we called home in "the Nam." It was much harder coming home than surviving over there. Doors closed on you when you were looking for a job and told people that you just got home from Vietnam. The voice at the other end of the phone would bristle and you'd find yourself holding the phone because there was no one on the other end. And I wasn't even a grunt from the front line. They had it much worse. I get angry when I think what we put these guys through. Most of the men who served were drafted and had no choice. Then we blamed these men when they got back.

It took a long time for me to feel comfortable with the American flag again. I'd heard so much hype—hype and patriotic slogans that sent our guys into war and then broke faith with them when they came home. When my first child joined the Boy Scouts, his troop had a ceremony at the end of the school year where all the Boy Scouts marched into the church hall to patriotic music and holding 2 or 3 flags including Old Glory. I almost freaked out. I was afraid for my son. I was so relieved when he dropped out and picked up the violin instead. I was afraid for him. They were starting to get him ready already to "serve his country." I felt in La La Land again. Like in Vietnam.

In the end, I took back the flag. We fly it in front of our home. In the end, I think it's important that I fight to define what it stands for. I'm not going to let the other side define its meaning. There can't be an assumption that you fly the flag, you go along with whatever the hype is that's being connected to it. No, it's my flag too, but I have my own ideas about its meaning.

I don't think that I really "came home" to my year in Vietnam until the dedication of the Women's Vietnam Memorial in November, 1993. Forty percent of all the women who served as Red Cross Recreation Workers in Vietnam came together in a number of ceremonies and gatherings over a period of several days. It was an amazing experience to talk to women I had been with over twenty years before. They had continued to be a remarkable group of women. They had gone on to live interesting lives and we were able to start conversations and be with one another as though we had been together the day before.

On the actual day of the dedication there was the annual, traditional Veteran's Day Parade in Washington, D.C., that ended at the Vietnam Memorial and culminated in the dedication of the Women's Memorial. The whole contingent of "Donut Dollies" participated in the parade. As we were lining up, one of my friends asked if I had ever marched in a Veteran's Day parade before—identified as a "Donut Dolly." I answered that, no, I had never done it before. "Wait till you see how the guys react when they see you," she said. I had no idea what she meant.

I don't remember how many of us marched in the parade—a hundred or so— we were all wearing blue teeshirts with big red crosses and "Donut Dolly" written across them.

As we marched through the streets, the Vietnam Veterans on the sidelines went crazy when they saw us. It was like being on stage when the curtain comes up on the cast of a great play or rock concert—the guys went crazy—hooting and hollering—one guy yelled out to me, "Thanks for the pencil and paper puzzles." I couldn't believe they even remembered such simple gestures that we had extended to them over twenty years before. I couldn't believe the response of these guys over twenty years later. As we marched, guys would run out of the crowd to shake our hands and give us hugs. It was very touching and very humbling. I felt in a way—like I had never felt before— connected to these guys in a drama that had been so much bigger than any of us, even all of us together, and that it had really been an honor to have been there with them. Here we were in our 40's, yet for a moment, again, we were in our early 20's and they were in their late teens, jumping up with the enthusiasm of kids just out of high school.

I went back to the Wall and the Women's Memorial the next day with a couple of friends. I was amused by the historical inaccuracy depicted by the statue. The sculpture has one of the women holding a wounded soldier—almost in a Pieta pose—while another woman soldier—presumably a second nurse—is scanning the skies for a helicopter. The statue is inaccurate because all the nurses were in Medevac units in the rear; they wouldn't have been in the front line calling in the choppers. Still, the motif is powerful and the drama of the wounded soldier embraced by the woman is very compelling and evocative.

I sauntered over to the Wall and started reading the letters left behind by the side of the wall. The ground running alongside the Wall was covered by letters written by wives to the husbands they lost, children to the fathers they never knew, G.I.s to the buddies they had lost on patrol—by their sides in some cases. Letters, pictures, medals, hats, badges, memorabilia. It was overwhelming.

I wandered back to the Women's Memorial and stared at the faces on the figures. All of a sudden a wave of sadness like I had never felt before welled up from the bottom of my torso. I was overcome with a grief I didn't even know was there. I staggered to the side and leaned against a tree sobbing from a place deep, deep inside. The next thing I knew there were these arms that circled around my shoulders and embraced me. I looked up and there was this guy in fatigues and a beret. He nodded. There was a complete knowing between us. I let my head rest on his chest, and just sobbed, and sobbed, and sobbed, my body shuddering with the sobs in a way I had never experienced. I absolutely surrendered to the moment, and to this place, and to this sadness, and to this stranger who knew.

When it was over, and I had stopped sobbing, I stepped back and thanked him. He nodded and stepped back. We parted without talking further. I think he had been a volunteer assigned to the Wall. I've heard they have fellows stationed at the Wall for folks. I cannot write or speak of this moment without tears still.

Epilogue

I was one of the lucky ones coming out of Vietnam. In the early 1990s, I participated in a support group for women who had served in the war. All the other women had been nurses. I was the only Donut Dolly in the group. I had to leave the group because their stories traumatized me. They had seen the carnage of the war on a daily basis. Their descriptions of the G.I.s coming through the Medevac units were gruesome. As a group, these women were struggling—in their 40's—with sleep problems, intrusive thoughts, needing to sleep with the lights on, and other symptoms of post-traumatic stress disorder (PTSD). I had had a taste of PTSD, which took me completely by surprise. I woke up one morning clutching my pillow, hearing the explosions from the ammo dump going up in Danang, experiencing the horror of that moment for the first time at age 42, 20 years after the event.

These women were incredible. I listened to their stories of service and love to these wonderful, wounded, and oftentimes, dying guys. These nurses' service to our men in Vietnam was inspiring. I couldn't listen to their stories any more. They urged me to stay in the group and deal with "my Vietnam stuff." It took still another 10 years—I'm a slow learner—to figure out why I was having a different experience sorting out my experience from others I knew.

I think for those who went to Vietnam sure of what they were doing—in whatever role they played—they eventually ended up having to question what they did and to rework the meaning the experience had for them. And, of course, they had to deal with the trauma they were exposed to.

For me, it was different. I had thrown myself into a situation full of doubts about what I was doing. From the beginning, I consciously sought for some shred of meaning for this crazy idea of playing games with soldiers in a war zone. I think the experience in-country was harder for me than for the women I served with because there was such a struggle for meaning inside myself. It took a lot of psychic energy just to function over there.

Now, looking back, I have no regrets, no second-guessing about what I did. Instead, when I look back, I smile at the kaleidoscope of memories and images that come to mind. I love those guys I worked with. They were such wonderful kids. I remember the proposition from that Idaho farm boy; I remember serving at the chow line in some unit on Christmas day offering the guys a choice of chicken breasts or chicken legs but saying to them, "Do you want 'this' or 'that' " to avert the inevitable wise crack; I remember the special Donut Dolly outhouse the men fixed up for us at one of the firebases outside Lai Khe.

I remember the moments of simple friendship, connection with fellows far away from home and the appreciation they showed to any small kindness or words of friendship. I think it helped that we were there. I think that we helped remind them of who they were at their best in a situation that was structured to allow the worst.

The story of my year in Vietnam was about my internal struggle to find meaning in this crazy job I'd agreed to do in exchange for the chance to witness history and to have my adventure.

This search for meaning is a theme that has continued through my life. I'm now 60. I've had a lot of jobs in the years since Vietnam. Every time I'm sure about what I'm doing, I end up in a crisis of questioning. When I first got back from Vietnam, I became a welfare worker to help distribute money and food to poor people, only to realize that I was an instrument of the capitalist system helping maintain the marginal poor working class as a disposable labor resource. I then worked in child protection, helping "save" children from abusive parents, who, I came to understand, were folks in need of all kinds of help but who were not being served and protected by a social contract that only served the wealthy in this country. I now operate an adoption agency and help find homes for children in orphanages around the world who need families. I am clear, though, that the real issue is the inequitable distribution of wealth around the world, and I seek ways every day to find openings to act on the local level. I look for ways to help poor families in poor countries take care of their own children.

Libra. Always the scales. I can't get away from this balancing act. When all is said and done, I have come to know that I'm okay when I'm not entirely sure of what I'm doing; and I start to worry when I think I've got the answer.

QUESTIONS FOR DISCUSSION

1. Leah O'Leary describes herself as naïve and confused about the war, yet she deliberately seeks an opportunity to go to Vietnam. What is her motivation? Is it patriotism, idealism, or something more complex? What is the influence of her education? What military or auxiliary service options were available for women in the 1960s? What options are available now?

2. Initially skeptical about her job as a recreation volunteer in a war zone, O'Leary comes to see her service as valuable. Why does she feel that what she did in Vietnam was worthwhile?

3. Compare the tone of Leah O'Leary's story with that of Wayne Coe's story, "Blackhawk 54." Contrast the two writers' self-presentations. Compare their descriptions of Vietnam and the Vietnamese people they meet. Finally, contrast O'Leary's picture of G.I. life in Vietnam with that provided by Wayne Coe. How might you account for the differences in their views?

4. Leah O'Leary encounters an almost constant stream of sexual innuendo from American G.I.s. Compare her descriptions with the scene in Wayne Coe's story where he and Captain Lungarella fly a group of newly arrived Donut Dollies to their first assignment. Do you think the men's behavior and the women's responses can be attributed solely to the tensions of war? How does O'Leary deal with the wisecracks she hears, and with being propositioned? How might women in such situations be treated today? What has changed?

5. What do you think is the cause of O'Leary's emotional collapse at the Vietnam Women's Memorial in 1993? What has she realized? What has she allowed herself to feel?

6. Leah O'Leary took a detour from the life course she might have expected to follow as a college graduate. Given a similar opportunity to participate in a momentous event, or to offer some kind of service, would you make a similar choice or would you stick to your plans? Do you think people in your generation are more reluctant or less reluctant to experiment with life detours than the people in O'Leary's generation? Why?

UNITED STATES BLUES
Tim Koster

I was born four years after the atomic bomb dropped at Nagasaki.

At grade school, we were subjected to regular "duck and cover" drills: in case of nuclear attack, we were supposed to duck under our desks and cover our heads with our arms, which was supposed to save us from the blast of a thousand suns. We'd seen films of atomic explosions on TV and in the movies. Duck and cover. They really thought we were stupid. We all knew that we'd be fried when the bombs dropped.

On Saturdays, my older brother Todd and I would go to the Beach Cliff theater and watch science fiction movies like *Them!* (gigantic desert ants), *Attack of the Crab Monsters* (gigantic tropical island crabs), and of course *Godzilla, King of the Monsters* (gigantic Japanese lizard). They always had the same theme: atomic fallout would create huge monsters from normally benign creatures. The monsters would kill lots of people in a bloodless manner while suspenseful music played, and then the human heroes would find some creative but bloodless way to kill the monsters.

We knew about the Cold War. The crazy Russians developed the atomic and then the hydrogen bomb. Then they put the *Sputnik* satellite into space and those bombs could suddenly be on our doorstep. We put our own satellites up and it was a "space race," but it didn't take a lot to figure out that the race wasn't really to the moon. It was who could drop a hydrogen bomb on whose house faster. They called it "mutually assured destruction." If either side attacked, both would be destroyed. We were constantly reminded of it.

The only family political discussion I remember during the fifties was the Nixon–Kennedy election. My father and his family were Catholic, but staunch Republicans. Kennedy may have been a Catholic, but he was still a Democrat and therefore not somebody they would vote for. In sixth grade we had a mock election and only two of us voted for Kennedy. Kelly Curran did because she was Irish Catholic. I did because I watched the Nixon–Kennedy debate and thought that Nixon looked creepy.

I don't remember much discussion about race in our family. We lived in a white Republican suburb west of Cleveland. "Colored" people lived near downtown, mostly the Hough area on the East Side. A friend whose father was a policeman bragged that "colored" people were met at the Rocky River Bridge and escorted out of town. They certainly couldn't live or work in our conservative town.

In 1962 the engineering company that my father worked for transferred us to France. We moved into a house in Montmorency, just north of Paris. The second day there my father showed Todd and me how to get to Paris and use the Metro subway. He explained to us how to buy Metro tickets and read the map, then gave us 25 francs (5 dollars, a fortune) and told us to be back at his office at the end of the day. Todd was 14, I was 12 and we hadn't been allowed to go to Cleveland by ourselves, but we were on our own in Paris! We couldn't get enough.

After a month at school, the Monsignor finally tired of trying to rein us in and told us that we didn't have to come back—that we'd learn as much or more in the city. That was the last he saw of us. We raced to the top of the Eiffel Tower, explored the parks, museums, Notre Dame, and a knife shop where a three-fingered man sold us switchblades. We watched butchers pour vats of blood into the gutters at Les Halles marketplace and stood on the steps of Sacré Coeur Cathedral with mouths open as the sun and parallel shadows of streaming clouds turned the hills of Paris from three to two dimensions and created God's Best Diorama.

I fell in love with Paris: The ghostly echo of an accordion playing soulful French love songs in the Metro. That curious aroma of the Paris streets—like aged cheese soaked in wine. Sublime hot chocolate at an island restaurant in the Bois du Boulogne. Who puts a restaurant on an island accessible only by rowboat? Parisians. It was definitely not Cleveland.

Algeria was fighting France for independence and French soldiers with machine guns routinely stopped us. The rules that control the police don't seem to apply to armed soldiers on a city street and I remember the steel taste of fear. I think that was the effect they were trying to achieve.

How could all that not transform me? How could I come back and even try to explain what I'd seen and how I'd changed? My world was no longer the small closed pattern of a Midwestern town. I'd been taken beyond the shores of Cleveland, Ohio, America, and became part of a greater world.

I was never the same again.

My freshman year of high school I was a skinny bookworm. I'd played clarinet since grade school and had dreams of being in the school band. I made the mistake of telling Todd and he informed me that band was not acceptable. Football was the only option, and that first year playing football my mantra was, "I won't hit you hard if you won't hit me hard."

The next year (1964) my father was transferred to a New Jersey town about twenty miles outside of New York City. The school was picked partly for its academic standards, but mostly because they had one of the best football teams in the area. Band was forgotten.

Football practice started in the summer and it was brutally hot. That year I grew to football size, but couldn't run fast, catch, or throw. I became a "Guard," whose entire job is to knock people down.

Coach scared the hell out of me. He subjected us to two practices per scorching day. Mornings were skill drills and exercise—sprints, blocking assignments, pushups, sit-ups, more sprints, reaction drills, and sprints again. We never knew how many 50-yard sprints we'd have to do and that made it torture. He'd simply run us until it looked like we would collapse. You couldn't save your energy because if he caught someone lagging he would use that as an excuse to add on more sprints. You simply went full-out every time with no idea of when it would stop.

Afternoons we practiced in full pads and helmets—blocking drills, tackling, and lots of just plain running into each other. By the end of the first week my arms were a mass of cuts and bruises and I'd lost ten pounds.

Coach was the drill sergeant. His job was to make us tough. We weren't allowed water during practice, no matter how brutal the heat. After practice we'd sprint for the locker room, bypassing the single dribbling water fountain. We never even took the time to drop our pads—just spun the showerheads off and let the cold stream pour down our throats. It seemed impossible to get enough.

Word got back to one of the parents, and soon the school doctor showed up and forced Coach to give us water during practice. That really pissed him off, but he got us back. He arranged for our water to be dispensed out of dish-soap squeeze bottles, and made sure that there was still plenty of soap in them. We were desperate for water, but the concoction was horrible. When we spit it out, I remember Coach smiling at the doctor and saying, "See, they weren't that thirsty."

The goal in football is to acquire territory—move your squad forward and the enemy's squad back. But Coach had an additional strategy: our job was to move the football AND hurt people because hurt people were intimidated and injured players couldn't play. Fewer opposing players increased our chances for success.

I accepted this because it was expected of me. My family expected me to play football and Coach expected me to hurt people. He made it clear that if a runner was set up and ready to go down but hadn't gone down yet, you were expected to hit him as hard as you could. Full speed. Helmet first. Hurt them if you can. They are the enemy.

I got pulled out of a game once because Coach saw me ease up on a runner whose legs were pinned but still hadn't gone down. If I had hit at full speed I would have broken a leg or an ankle. I couldn't do it. So he pulled me out of the game to make an example of me.

The summer before my senior year I lifted weights, ran distances and finished up the runs with my own sprints on the football field. I got big, muscular, fast, learned to like to hit, and could run forever. The first practice of that summer a skinny sophomore looked across the line at me and said, "I won't hit you hard if you won't hit me hard."

BOOM!

"Welcome to football with the first-string," I said as I stood over him. No mercy.

One great thing about football was that everyone was equal. In our uniforms we all looked alike. It didn't matter if you were White, Black, Irish, Italian, or Catholic. Coach gave everyone the same treatment. It was there that I found that inside we're all the same. Something I might have never discovered in Rocky River.

That was the year that I noticed my first anti-war protest. A dozen or so fellow students and their parents stood in the rain and picketed outside the public library with "STOP THE WAR" and "U.S. OUT OF VIETNAM" signs. I didn't understand what it was all about. Why would we want to get out of Vietnam? And what was so wrong with the war that these people would stand in the rain to protest? It just didn't seem right.

I finally escaped high school in the summer of '67. In July my younger brother Bart asked me to drive him into New York City to see the "Young Rascals" play in Central Park. (The Young Rascals were a typical upbeat mid-Sixties strum 'n sing pop band.) I agreed if he paid for the tickets. First came the warm-up band just arrived in the United States from Europe: Jimi Hendrix. His music exploded around us. Nobody had played like that before. He cranked the volume up, crashed the strings of his guitar and then held it up to the wired-up amplifier and blasted sounds at the audience that just blew us away. We loved it! It wasn't just noise. It was a primal sound brought forward by the miracle of electricity and we all recognized what it was: the end of music as we knew it. Shit. It was the end of the world as we knew it.

After the Hendrix set the Rascals came on and people just started filing out. There was no point in staying.

I worked that summer, but for a few weeks two foreign exchange students came to stay with us. One was from Australia, the other from New Zealand and they were both surfers. We spent much of that time zooming back and forth to the Jersey shore with borrowed boards wedged into the back seat of my mother's old convertible.

They wanted to see the "Real America" and Todd and I wanted to show it to them. One evening in July we decided to drive the freeway through Newark into New York City to spend the evening at clubs in Greenwich Village. We had all heard about the Newark riots that were raging at the time and wanted a glimpse of the fires. We did see some, but they were far enough away to be no more than flickers. On the way back Todd decided to get a better look and veered off at an exit. The exchange students didn't know what they were getting into and I knew it was pointless to try to dissuade Todd. He'd always sought danger. The city was aflame and he was the moth.

It wasn't hard to figure out the riot's causes. White prejudice kept the black residents from buying homes or getting jobs outside of the city just as it had in Cleveland. Throw a hot summer and the right incident into the mix and the eruption became inevitable. Cleveland had blown the summer before and now it was Newark's turn.

It was surreal. Buildings still burned and every few blocks we saw police cars stocked full with helmeted police. With the exception of the driver, each rigidly held a shotgun in front of himself. These flag-bearers from some bizarre parade never glanced at us.

The air smelled like scorched brick and cinders and smoke hung low over the city. It was clearly not the place to be and we convinced Todd to find a way out—only to discover that all the side streets were blocked off. All we could do was drive back and forth through the devastation in the hope that we'd find our way back onto the freeway.

We came to a set of barriers and were forced to turn onto a side street. We found ourselves nose to nose with a tank. Todd slammed on the brakes. I held my breath as the tank's turret slowly turned, and the gun pointed directly at me. I grabbed at the door handle and as I looked out the window saw that armed National Guardsmen lined the street on both sides. They grabbed us and pulled us out of the car to inspect the interior. One shouted, "Open up the trunk!" My father's car had a trunk release in the glove compartment, so I reached in to flip the little door up to press the button. Todd was spread-eagled on the other side of the car and I heard him say "Tim, make sure you move very, very slowly." At that moment I felt the barrel of a rifle at the back of my head and heard the *ka-chunk* of the bolt action as a bullet was fed into the chamber. I slowly and gently pushed the button before they shoved me to the ground and stepped on me. There was that steel taste of fear again: soldiers on our streets.

They searched the trunk for weapons since they assumed that we were white supremacists looking for targets. I guess it was hard to grasp that we were just a bunch of stupid kids with an adrenaline junkie at the wheel.

They let us go and directed us back onto the road home. As we headed up the on-ramp, Todd turned his head, grinned at the students in back and said, "Welcome to America!"

Summer ended and I had to decide what to do next. I hadn't spent much time studying in high school so I had no chance of getting into a good college. I didn't even make applications. My family was being transferred back to Europe and I had to do something, so I followed Todd up to Boston, where he was starting his second year at Boston University (BU).

I paid $40 per month to share an apartment near Central Square in Cambridge and got a job with Jordan Marsh, a Boston department store. At the interview they didn't think I was bright enough to handle paperwork or meet with the public, so they placed me in their Cambridge warehouse to run the auxiliary freight elevator.

I discovered that I didn't need to make an application to go to evening classes at BU. I could take whatever courses I felt I could handle as long as I paid the tuition. Over the next year I took as many night and summer classes as I could and kept up a 4.0 average. I also found that it was easier to get into the College of Business Administration than Liberal Arts. I had done well on the college boards, so I applied to BU with a letter admitting that I screwed up in high school but I had seen the light. I told them that I had finally found a challenge at their school and my BU night school grades proved that I could do the work and would make them proud. Then I tracked down the names of the administrators who would consider my application and called a different one each day to find out if I was admitted yet.

While I was at the warehouse my best friend was Tony, who had just returned from a tour of duty in Vietnam. We would walk across the truck lots to Washington Park where we would sit on the berm, eat lunch, and Tony would tell me about fighting in Vietnam.

He never said whether the Vietnam War was right or not. He received his draft notice and went because that was what his government wanted from him. And when he came back he knew he'd changed.

He told me about the fear of being point man on patrol—where every bullet and booby-trap seemed to be meant for him and him alone; about the failure time and again of his M-16 rifle when it got wet or overheated, and how he always had to keep it out of sand or dirt for fear it would get jammed; and he told me about the insanity of riding a helicopter to a brutal deadly fight for a piece of land, winning the battle, counting the bodies, and taking the helicopter ride back to base—giving the land back.

I heard about how hard it was to kill a man for the first time and then how easy it became over time. And I learned about the pain that comes from watching a friend, a brother, bleed to death next to you.

The way the war was run there was no conquering Vietnam. During the day the land belonged to the U.S. military and the South Vietnamese. The night belonged to the Viet Cong. All that mattered to the military and the politicians was the body count. We were winning as long as more of them were killed than us. Both sides poured their young men into the battle and the loser would be whoever finally said "enough."

So Tony and I would sit by the Revolutionary War cannons of Washington Park and Tony would tell me about what fighting the war in Vietnam was like, the stupidity of the men running the war, the pride he had in the other American soldiers, how hard they fought, and how much their brotherhood meant to him. The irony was that we were sitting by George Washington's cannons, the ones he used to fire across the

Charles River to bombard the British in 1776 and force them finally to leave Boston. It was from this fort that the British found how difficult it was to subdue a land that didn't want you.

BU admitted me in the fall to the College of Business Administration with what had to have been the lowest high school GPA in the school's history. All those calls to the admissions committee had paid off.

I immediately applied for and received a II-S student deferment from the draft.

After my conversations with Tony I was strongly against the war in Vietnam. It just seemed crazy to assume that one side or the other would finally think that enough of their young men had been killed and would give up. Neither side was going to blink.

I went to anti-war rallies. It was guys my age who were getting killed in Vietnam, yet we weren't old enough to vote (the voting age then was 21). They could send us to war, but we had no political voice. So we took to the streets to get them to listen to us.

FIGURE 1.4 In October, 1969, more than 250,000 anti-war demonstrators gathered at the Mall in Washington, D.C., under the shadow of the Washington Monument to declare a "moratorium" to end the war in Vietnam. Elsewhere in the nation, thousands of others held protest rallies in their own cities on the same day, demonstrating growing popular support for an end to the war. A month later, on November 15, 1969, when this picture was taken, 500,000 war protestors again rallied at the Mall and in front of the White House, where they staged a demonstration with speeches and music.

Source: Peter Simon Photo

I wasn't against the soldiers in Vietnam—I wanted to bring them home. I just didn't want any more to die.

1968 was a disaster, starting with the Tet Offensive. The My Lai massacre was in March. On April 4th Martin Luther King, Jr. was murdered. On June 5th, Bobby Kennedy was shot and killed. In August, Russian tanks crushed Prague Spring and the hope of a free Czechoslovakia. Also in August, I watched on TV as others like me gathered at the Democratic National Convention in Chicago to protest the War. Mayor Daley called out almost 20,000 police and the National Guard to control a few thousand demonstrators. The worst battles were on Michigan Avenue, not far from the convention headquarters. We watched in horror as police and guardsmen pushed back the crowds and indiscriminately clubbed anyone within reach. "Chicago 68" was later described as a police riot, but at the time much of America celebrated the event as a triumph of Law and Order. That year there were an average of 1,200 U.S. soldiers killed in Vietnam each month. In November Richard Nixon was elected President on the promise of a "secret" plan to end the war.

The world was changing and I was trying to keep up. At a party I met a cute girl dressed in blue jeans and a flannel shirt. She explained to me that she was a "radical lesbian feminist." The only word I recognized was "radical," which was cool, so I spent the rest of the evening trying to get her to date me. I was either naïve or the world was moving ahead too fast for me. Most likely it was both.

1969 was the year that I discovered that I hated the smell of patchouli oil, but loved the advent of the "braless" look. I let my hair grow, bought my clothes at Army Surplus stores because they were the cheapest source for blue jeans and pocket t-shirts (the "uniform"), and spent $100 on a VW bus—not because it was a symbol but because it was cheap and disposable transportation. I painted "Magic Bus" on the front, but with a top speed of just over 50 MPH it didn't feel very magic.

We organized a food-buying co-op in the neighborhood so that people could pool their money and get better food at better prices at the Farmers' Market. Often the food was of that heavy, earnest, stodgy kind (fresh ground peanut butter, swimming in oil—you'd spend fifteen minutes kneading it to cream to make a sandwich and the next time you went to use it, there it would be, all oil again); bread that weighed pounds, chewed like taffy, and tasted like cotton because it had been earnestly and sincerely made entirely without salt. You get the picture.

FM radio was still new and definitely cool and the "alternative rock" stations were commercial free (a welcome relief from the same 10 bubble-gum songs played over and over on AM radio). Long hair on guys was very cool. The length of your hair was a measure of how long you'd been cool. Coors was the beer to drink if you knew someone who was traveling through Colorado (the only place we knew you could buy it). We stopped buying Coors when we found out about Adolph Coors' stand against environmental and labor laws and his treatment of minorities.

Beards and moustaches were in—but sideburns by themselves were for wannabe cool insurance salesmen who topped the look off with big-lapel, light-colored polyester suits and wide ties.

The peace sign—two fingers raised in a "V"—now that was cool and a true sign that you belonged.

The summer of '69 I painted houses with a friend to earn money for school and took an August trip to visit my parents, who had been transferred to Italy. I missed Woodstock, but Todd and some of our friends went. Todd (motto: what's mine is mine, what's yours is mine) took the hand-made quilt that my mother's friend gave me for college. It was ugly—cream colored with a flowered pattern and a wide bright pink border—but it was a gift and it kept me warm. At Woodstock it rained and the quilt got soaked. Todd left it in the mud, Nick Ercoline and his girlfriend Bobbie picked it up, wrapped it around themselves, and the photograph of that moment became the cover of the Woodstock album.

In late November I got a letter from my draft board in New Jersey. They determined that I hadn't earned enough college credits after high school and took away my student deferment. That made me I-A (eligible for the draft).

The first draft lottery was coming up. If my birth date was a high number I'd be safe.

December 1, 1969, came and Congressman Alexander Pirnie (R-NY) of the House Armed Services Committee came on TV to pick the capsule with the birth date that would become "Number One" in that first draft lottery of the Vietnam War.

Todd had the twisted idea to have a "draft" party so we could cringe or cheer as each fortune was revealed. Our neighbor "Sergeant Rock" didn't care—he'd already fought in Vietnam more than one tour with the Marines and was there to drink beer and laugh at us.

As the first capsule was drawn I walked out to the kitchen to get a beer. I'd never won anything in my life—so what were the chances of winning this? Then a roar came from the other room. "Tim! Hey Tim! You won the lottery! It's September 14th, your birthday!"

Shit.

Number one. My birthday came up number one. I was stunned. I was already opposed to U.S. involvement in the war, and I knew that I didn't want to be part of it. I'd thought hard about it and knew from my football experience that I didn't have the will to resist once I was in. I hadn't wanted to hurt people in football yet I did because I was trained for it and it was expected of me. If I accepted the draft the Army would train me to kill. I might get good at it like Rock, who knew ten ways to kill a man with his bare hands in less than ten seconds. I might find over time that I liked it.

I had to do something.

I called the *Boston Globe* immediately and asked if they would be interested in talking to me, the "Number One" draft pick. Bill Davis and a photographer showed up in less than a half hour. I told them that I would refuse induction, that I was opposed to violence and war, and that I had considered emigrating to Canada but rejected the idea of permanent exile. Bill told me that the average sentence for refusing induction was two to three years. I answered that in that case Canada didn't seem like such a bad idea.

The next day the lottery was headline news and the story included my picture and interview.

Within a week I received and ignored both my "Notice to Report for Physical" and the dreaded "GREETINGS" from my draft board. I had been drafted and if I reported I would be on my way to Vietnam. I had no time left. I didn't want to go to

Canada and I certainly didn't want to go to prison. I was running out of options. My only hope was to get help.

I went to the American Friends Service Committee office. They told me that I could apply for a conscientious objector (CO) deferment and it would stop the draft process. Technically, if you were opposed to war on moral or religious grounds you could apply. Realistically, though, the deferments were only being awarded to those with proven religious objections. I couldn't remember anyone ever calling the Catholic Church a pacifist organization.

The Army couldn't take me away until a final decision was made about my deferment. If my local Draft Board denied it I could appeal to the State Board. If the State Board turned me down I could appeal to the National Board, who had the final decision. Each appeal took six months, so the entire process could delay the Army for a year and a half. I read the rules carefully and found that if you made a deferment application from outside of the country your appeal time was doubled. That would give me three years. It seemed like a lifetime. In three years the war might be over.

A few days later I was at my parents' door in Paris (they'd been transferred again).

What did they think? On the day I learned how to ride a bike my father taught me how to repair a flat tire and told me, "If you're old enough to ride it you're old enough to fix it." That was how my parents thought. More than anything they wanted us to be independent.

I had no job and was living in an unheated attic room in my parents' building. Paris is a hard place in winter. If it isn't raining, it's drizzling. If it isn't drizzling, it's misting. If it isn't misting, it's threatening. And when that icy rain comes it doesn't come from above, it hurtles at you from some point on the horizon, forces you to brace your weight against it and use your umbrella as a shield. I already had a cloud over my head and the rain just wore me down.

I wrote to my draft board and asked for an application for a CO deferment.

In the meantime I tried to make sense of how I felt. I was confused. I felt a responsibility and loyalty to my country, but at the same time thought that the war in Vietnam was a never-ending disaster. The "light at the end of the tunnel" metaphor for the end of the war that Lyndon Johnson kept seeing was the rear light of a subway train moving away from us. There wasn't anything noble about this war—it was ill conceived by politicians. Both sides threw their brave young men into battle with huge losses on both sides and both hoped that the other would finally say, "Enough young men have died, you win."

How could I be the person to take some father, son, brother, or husband from his family forever? And why—simply because that's what my government told me to do? Wasn't the government there to represent us and our will? Who were they to treat me like a cog in some gigantic machine? And didn't our founding fathers give me the right to question that government—wasn't that my duty?

And so as I waited for my CO application I read Camus. I also read *Homage to Catalonia* by George Orwell, *Man's Fate* by André Malraux, *The Prince* by Machiavelli, "Civil Disobedience" by Thoreau, "A Mystery of Heroism" by Stephen Crane, *Arms and the Man* by George Bernard Shaw, and an essay by William James written just before his death in 1910 called "The Moral Equivalent of War."

I was being forced to look at myself and determine my place in the world. What made me different? Did I have a right to refuse the draft? Was it war in general that I was against, or was it this war that I felt was unjust, or was I just a coward looking for a way out? I felt ill prepared for these issues. Jeez. I was just a boy from the Midwest.

The draft board's questionnaire came back and I filled it out as best I could. Nothing I had read could really help me—all I could do was tell them what was in my heart. I sent it back to them along with some personal references, one of which was a poignant letter of support from my mother.

They wrote back with the news that they had reviewed my application and that they wouldn't draft me until they had made a final decision on my CO status. I was invited back to the United States for a formal interview.

When I got back to Boston in early March the snows that had been beautiful, soft, and white in December now crunched under my feet and were as gritty-gray as the late-winter skies. And back at the apartment I found out that the FBI had been around the neighborhood asking questions about me.

I'd met Erika from Amsterdam on the flight back and she convinced me to hitchhike to California with her for what might be my last view of America. We got our first ride with two salesmen returning to Albany. The second ride was from Neal, who was on his way home to Berkeley in his VW bus and needed help with gas and driving.

All through the Midwest we saw cars with "America, Love it or Leave it!" bumper stickers. I was back in the Midwest, but it didn't look very friendly.

Outside of Chicago we stopped at a diner and were refused service because Neal and I had long hair. We drove on to Freeport, Illinois, hoping to stay the night with Erika's sister and her physician husband. Erika was told that only she was welcome. Neal and I would have to sleep in the bus out among the farms, as they didn't want any of their neighbors to see that they had let "our kind" into their home. Erika simply got back in the bus and said "DRIVE!"

That was my first glimpse of what it was like to be on that side of prejudice. Neal and I were white and educated (i.e. privileged), but our jeans and long hair made us members of an underclass not fit to be served food or made comfortable on a cold night. All we had to do was cut our hair and we'd be white and privileged again.

We battled a snowstorm in Iowa and tripped our way across Nebraska. In Colorado we took Route 40 into the mountains for a day of spectacular vistas. Utah gave us the endless white horizon of the Great Salt Lake desert. In Nevada dust devils twirled across the landscape and tumbleweeds blew across the road. California was warm, fragrant, and green.

In San Francisco perfect strangers gave us food, comfortable beds, and made us feel welcome. I'd never been to California before but it felt like coming home.

We explored the Berkeley campus, Chinatown, the Presidio, walked the Golden Gate Bridge, and sat in every park we could find—just to feel the grass and smell the flowers and eucalyptus. We visited a ranch in Castro Valley, where I climbed a hill to sit beneath an oak tree. From the ranch below came the sound of the Grateful Dead, and above me two hawks rode the perfect air. After a week I called Todd in Boston to let him know that I wanted to stay and he reminded me that I'd promised to be the best man at his wedding in April.

Before starting back we decided to buy some blue jeans, as it was still winter back east. I looked up the address of the nearest Army Surplus store and we hitch-hiked over. The neighborhood was Black and as we walked the last blocks to the store there was an odd paranoia on the streets. Small groups of men would huddle and stare at us. Two men paced us on the other side of the street, joined later by three more. There were men on the street—except wherever we walked. When we reached the store we found that it was a burned-out shell. As we turned around to head back I was startled to find a young man standing in our way. He asked, "Have you read the latest Black Panther newspaper?" I told him, "No, but thanks man." He looked me in the eye, smiled, and said, "You should really buy this paper, it's just a quarter." As I paid him, he placed the paper in my hand and winked at me.

On the way back the neighborhood was transformed. Gone were the paranoia and the threatening knots of young men. Women and children were on the street now and everywhere we looked there were smiles and waves for us, and questions about how we liked this or that article. We had become welcome guests.

The next day we started back on the road to Boston. We spent hours in San Francisco waiting for a ride and were finally picked up by a stubbly-gray-bearded man driving a primer-gray 1950s Dodge pickup. He was already halfway through a quart of cheap gin and the free-play on the steering wheel took an entire turn. As we headed to Reno he didn't drive the road into the mountains, he tacked. He would let the truck drift across the traffic lanes until two wheels were on the shoulder and then whip the wheel around until it caught and nudged the truck in the other direction. We'd drift back across the road and make the same maneuver on the other side. Every dozen or so tacks he'd reach under the seat and take another swig of gin. When we got to Reno he left us outside of town where Erika and I spread our sleeping bags and slept under the stars among the sagebrush.

Twenty or so more rides and we were back in Boston. We survived the trip (including a frigid night in an Iowa shed and a night on the floor of a gas station bathroom in New York). But our relationship didn't. It was like a lot of relationships back then, young men and women spinning quickly through life, forming tenuous, easily broken bonds, and then rushing on towards the next promise of contentment or even love. I found that in April when I met Ginger, a feminist who, like me, came from the Midwest and shared a passion to find a way to end the war.

On April 30th, Richard Nixon (who had been elected on a "secret" plan to end the Vietnam War) announced on national TV that he had ordered U.S. troops to invade Cambodia. As he stood next to the huge map of Southeast Asia he briefly lost his place in his notes. At that moment he looked so confused that I almost felt sorry for him.

The local response to the invasion was immediate and overwhelming. Students from around the Boston Area closed down the colleges and filled the streets in protest. The city was paralyzed for days.

In Ohio, National Guardsmen fired on the protesting Kent State students and killed four. Ten days later two more students were killed at Jackson State in Mississippi. This was the beginning of the end of the protest era and was to me the end of the Sixties—shot through the heart. Those who had stood up to protest the war now knew that steel taste of fear of soldiers on our streets.

I turned my attention to my draft board interview scheduled for July. If I wanted to get out of this madness with a CO deferment I was going to have to convince them of my religious objections to war.

I didn't know that the Supreme Court was at that moment helping to decide my fate. During the Vietnam War they had heard two cases that incrementally expanded the definition of religions that were sufficiently pacifist for their members to be considered for a CO deferment. Then on June 15th in *Welsh V. United States 398 U.S. 333 (1970)*, they ruled 4-3 that objectors could qualify for a CO deferment based on moral or philosophical objections to war.

I had a chance.

A month later I sat before the members of the Plainfield, New Jersey, draft board and tried to answer their questions:

"Why didn't you become a CO until you were drafted?"

"What would you do if a criminal threatened to kill your family? Would you protect them?"

"Why won't you prevent evil from happening to others?"

"Should we let the Communists take over Vietnam?"

"You say you object to killing, but aren't you just afraid of being killed?"

"Don't you think that this makes you a coward?"

"Don't you have any duty to your country?"

"By refusing to fight, aren't you helping North Vietnam?"

"How do you feel about living a comfortable life while others risk their lives fighting for you?"

I remember the room, the men, the questions, and the feeling like I was struggling against quicksand, but the curious thing is that I don't remember my answers. And I wish I could say that they were impressed, but I was nervous and scared and the looks on their faces told me that they were not thinking, "Wow, this kid is brilliant."

The last question was "Have you ever made your views known publicly?"

I handed them the *Boston Globe* article. Each man read it carefully and nodded.

Slowly it dawned on me. They were a local draft board that reported to a state board that answered to a national board. It was a gigantic bureaucracy and the local board members would have to justify any decision they made to the bureaucratic layers above them. By giving them published proof of my convictions I had removed any risk that they might have of being criticized. If anyone questioned their decision they could hand my press clippings to them and say, "Here, he made his views known to the world, why should we doubt him?"

All the tension and doubt left the room and without any further discussion they simply told me that they would grant my deferment application. Stunned, I slipped out the door and drove back to Boston.

What next? The requirement of a CO deferment is two years of alternative service—work that the draft board considered of "national importance." I got a job at Massachusetts General Hospital and they put me to work as a janitor for a retired Army Colonel who told me that I was "shit and piss" and that was all I was going to see for the next two years. He put me on a shift that required me to get up at 3 AM and gave me literally every job in the hospital that had to do with human waste. If the job involved toilets, bedpans, lavatories, spills, diarrhea, or incontinence he had me there to clean it up. No one likes those smells, but they're worse in a hospital and I never got used to it.

That was my first lesson to keep my mouth shut about my deferment. To most people, COs aren't heroes—they're just the opposite. If you want to get spit on, become an Objector.

I quit my job, married Ginger, moved to Minnesota and did my full two years of alternative service at St. Joseph's hospital in St. Paul. They were happy to have me work there and placed me in the purchasing department. After three weeks they promoted me to supervisor. Good thing I'd cut my hair.

In 1971, Daniel Ellsberg, a Pentagon analyst, released what has become known as the "Pentagon Papers." These secret documents showed that the Pentagon knew in 1966 that the war in Vietnam was unwinnable. Our government had lied to us and in spite of what they knew, continued to send our young men to their deaths.

I still think about whether I made the right decision. It would have been easy to just accept the draft, report for induction, put myself in the Army's hands and leave the rest to fate. I consider the questions they asked me that night in New Jersey. Was I a coward just looking for a way out? What about my duty to my government—regardless of whether it lied to me or not? And what would I do in another war—the Korean War, World War II, the Civil War, or even the Revolutionary War? Was it my core beliefs that led me to that decision to become a CO or was it just a reaction to the insanity of the war that we were in?

I still don't have the answers.

QUESTIONS FOR DISCUSSION

1. Tim Koster spends the first part of his story describing events that happened to him growing up. Consider his Cold War childhood, the impact of his year in Paris, his visit to the riot-torn streets of Newark, and his lunch-hour conversations with Tony, the Vietnam veteran. What does he learn from being trained to play football? How does each of these experiences contribute to his self-awareness and the decision he has to make at the age of 20?

2. What does Koster initially think about the Vietnam War? What changes his mind? What do you think about that war now that more than 30 years have passed since it ended? How would you say American society, in general, views that war today?

3. Koster says that it would have been easy to accept the draft—do you think that is true? He seems adept at using the "rules" to his advantage; how does this help him in his quest to resist the draft? What do you think happened to others who were eligible for the Vietnam-era draft and didn't have Koster's advantages? Was that fair?

4. Koster is dealing with the draft but he mentions race and racial incidents in his story. Why does he include these? What do they tell you about the country's racial and social

climate in the late 1960s? Can you see any connection between racial tensions and concerns about the draft and the war in Vietnam?

5. While Koster is preparing to make his application for a CO deferment, he reads books, plays, and essays. Why do you think he chooses that particular list? Is there a common thread or theme in his choices?

6. Looking back, Koster asks a number of questions of himself: What would he do in another war? What about his duty to his government? Was he at heart a conscientious objector or was he just looking for a way out of the Vietnam War? Was he a coward? Try to answer some of these questions about Koster. How do you think members of your family or community would answer them?

7. What do you think about the decisions that Koster made? He says early on that he always did what was expected of him. This time he didn't. What changed him? What about you—do you always do what is expected of you? Would you have made the same decisions? Would you have taken a different path?

A LIFE IN FLIGHT
Huỳnh Quang Ngọc

According to the zodiac, I was born in the Year of the Rooster, 1957. I grew up in Tan An, a rural village in the Mekong Delta in South Vietnam. Ours was a large family, with seventeen children. I was number eleven, a middle child. We were poor but we took care of each other; my big brother cared for me and I took care of my sister and my sister cared for her little brother. And that's how we lived. My parents were married through a traditional arranged marriage when my mother was only seventeen. She was from Hoa Loc, Dinh Tuong, on the other side of the Mekong River. Although my grandfather on my father's side was a rich landowner he didn't help my father at all. Sometimes we didn't have enough clothes to wear and that was including my parents. They had to share a pair of satin pants between them when they received guests. One talked with the guests while the other was hiding in a corner of the room.

Aside from fulfilling his duties as a son to my grandparents, my father worked very hard. At one point he borrowed money from his aunt, with interest, to plant an orange orchard. Eventually he prospered.

We lived in a Ba Gian house constructed with a tile roof supported by a few mahogany pillars. Inside, everything was very simple. There were no dividing walls for our privacy. There was an ancestor altar placed in the middle of the house and a table with long benches where we ate our meals. There were bamboo beds scattered around the house where we slept. The house was boarded with bamboo walls to stop the howling wind from blowing through. However, it was so empty that I could feel the chill in the night where we cuddled each other to sleep during the monsoon season. The wind was not the only thing that could go through the house. People or animals could too, since there was no door to stop them.

My father cultivated oranges, mangos, bananas, and rice, while my mother took care of the whole family. She cooked, cleaned, did laundry, and any other household chores a third world countrywoman could endure. Sometimes she had to tend the cows and pigs as well as our ducks and chickens. She had to pay her duties as a daughter-in-law to my grandparents, and my aunts and uncles made her life a living hell, playing cruel tricks to test her housekeeping or cooking skills, making sure she was blamed for all the porcelain dishes they broke, and trying time and again to make her look bad in the eyes of her mother-in-law. I watched her cry many times but she never complained. She was as gentle as a cloud and as flexible as bamboo. She sacrificed for all of her children and I wondered if I would ever have a chance to pay it back. If I were a Nobel Prize judge I would give my mother the Prize for Humanity. She held us after we had been spanked by our father and she fanned us at night when we could not sleep because it was humid, or because mosquitoes had got inside in our nets. She reassured herself that we had a good night's sleep. She seemed never to have a full night's sleep herself and never had a break. She sometimes gave me a sweet when I returned home from school and told her that I was ranked at the top of my class. She would stop cooking and would hold my face in her sweaty palms and look into my eyes with her own eyes filled with tears, "You're a good boy.

You're going to have a better future when you grow up." Then she would kiss me on the cheek and wipe the sweat off my face. "Now go and play with your sister." She would feed the fire and return to her frying bananas, which were sizzling in the boiling oil wok. My heart was as warm as the fire. My mother's kisses, and her tears, were better than any sweets.

My village was peaceful, bordered by a road that followed the river in a giant, gentle curve and surrounded by rice paddies spread to the end of the horizon. Dikes divided the fields and formed hundreds of shapes carpeted with green rice stalks. When the rice stalks turned a golden color, farmers called each other to harvest the crops. The scent of the ripening rice rose in the air and the breeze carried it beyond the village no one knew where. When the sun set and the buffalo boys marched home from the fields, they sang, "Ai Bao Chan Trau La Kho"—"Who says tending buffaloes is a hard life?"—while waiting for their supper. Their voices blended with the water and the water carried the music up and downstream like the current babbling on the banks of the river. Smoke from stoves in the village rose and wrapped around the areca and coconut trees as if it dressed them up for a feast—the feast of a rice harvest and of family and neighbors getting together to share the spring season. The sky was clear blue and hot. Children played in the courtyards and dogs barked in the distance. Oil lamps lit up and the night advanced. The moon would spill over the garden as if it was my own happiness. I slept well within the love and protection of my family.

This environment nurtured me until the Tet Offensive of 1968, when war mowed through my village, taking the life of my younger sister Luoi. On Mung Ba, the third day of Tet, I had been forced to transport wounded Viet Cong soldiers to the end of the village and when I returned home, an American helicopter, pursuing Viet Cong, shot off the roof of the house and the temple. Luoi was hit and trapped and died. I remember her fat cheeks and how peaceful she was asleep. Without seeing the blood pouring out I would never have thought she had died. I didn't have a chance to cry for my sister but a part of me died with her that day, the first day of Tet Mau Than. I was twelve then, and I had been hit by shrapnel myself. I carry small pieces of it in me to this day.

On the fourth day we evacuated from the village to the city of Vinh Long to avoid the battle. On our way, American helicopters from the nearby air base chased after us and shot at us as if they had gone mad. I didn't know what to think of the Americans, whether I liked or hated them. I was sure I hated the Viet Cong since they had brought destruction to my village during the New Year and they had no respect for our ancestors and didn't honor our traditions.

It seemed as if corpses from all the villages in South Vietnam piled up and turned into mounds, into hills, and became mountains. Blood spilled down from the mountains onto the hills, the villages, and the rivers, and blended in the water. The water spilled over the dikes and into the rice fields to fertilize the rice stalks. Every drop of blood grew into a bud and bloomed into flowers and turned into grains of rice. The rice fed me and I grew to learn of love and hate. Love and hatred soaked our soil all at once in full force and I was caught in the middle. What was I supposed to think? How could I speak? How could I breathe? The aroma of rice cooking in the afternoon, the smell of smoke from a stove, and the freshness of the rice paddies no longer existed. They had yielded to the smell of burning flesh and decayed bodies, the stench of blood, and the burning smell of gun powder. My gentle world had ended along with my happy childhood. My family was broken apart and the feast was gone. Villagers were killed and disappeared. The peace had evaporated into thin air, although dogs still barked and roosters still crowed at dawn as if they were calling their owners to come back. Was there anything to return to?

My family moved back to the village after the Tet, but I stayed in Vinh Long, in a small house my father had bought for me and my brothers and sisters to live in while we attended school. I took an entrance exam to compete among 20,000 students for 1,500 sixth grade places at Thu Khoa Huan High School. I got in at 108. I studied hard and later on moved to Tong Phuoc Hiep, a coed school. Here I met Hanh, a crippled boy who had had polio, who became my good buddy. We talked about our future and dreamed what we wanted to do with our lives. While studying, we still helped out our parents in the village with farming. I didn't do well with farming since I was fragile and skinny.

The war intensified, especially in the central part of Vietnam, and the draft circulated. I was seventeen and was about to be drafted but I was not included since I was attending school and doing well. Every time I returned to the village I witnessed funerals. It got to the point that only elderly men, women, and children were left. Many young men my age who never attended school but had gone on farming were being drafted into the Army. They received a few months training then were sent to fight. Many of my childhood friends died during the blistering summer of 1972 in Lao (Ha Lao 719).

The village became emptier. The VC infiltrated the streets and houses at night and withdrew when the South Vietnamese Army moved in during the day. The cat and mouse game went on and the war went on like a chronic disease.

I took both national and university exams and passed. In the fall of 1974, I moved to Saigon to attend Saigon University. Before I left home my mother cooked a big meal for us to celebrate my new journey, the journey all my own, with a destination and a future I didn't know. We gathered at the dining table and ate. Mama kept filling up my bowl and I ate till I could not walk and till I could not laugh anymore. "Son, you have to eat regularly so you can stay healthy. Mama won't be around to take care of you. If you need money or anything ask your aunt. And whatever you do remember to pray to Buddha every night." She reminded me again and again. We talked and shared. It was wonderful to be a part of my big family. I went to bed while Mama packed my clothes and necessities, including the bottle of green oil to use for Cao Gio healing rituals, or to rub on my temples or stomach when I was sick. When I left in the morning Mama sat at the wooden divan and pretended to talk with my sibling but her eyes were directed at me and at the front door. Even now, more than thirty years later, I have not forgotten her look. She didn't want to say goodbye to me; but later on when I was on the bus passing through the street in front of the house she stood there in the courtyard and searched the passing cars.

I stayed with my aunt's family in Saigon, missing my own family terribly. Saigon was a big capital and very crowded. They called it the city of light in Asia. Cars, trucks, buses, cabs, motorcycles, vespas, mopeds, bikes, and cyclos (bicycle taxi-cabs) ran like mad and I didn't know how to get across the street. I often got lost and it took me a while to get used to the city. Saigon seemed to me to have the biggest shopping centers, cinemas, theaters, churches, temples, and libraries in the world. But the most striking thing was that the city never went to sleep. The lively time was after 5 pm when it really came to life. The war went on every day but it seemed no one in Saigon noticed there was a war. I was totally shocked.

At the university it was different. I barely had a chance to study or to get to know my teachers except for talking about what was going on in politics, who was going to replace President Thieu, and what would be the outcome of the American withdrawal. I wondered what my future would be after that, and I started to become disillusioned about my study of Literature and Law.

I went home for the New Year, 1975, and when I returned to the University the situation had changed drastically. No one paid any attention to study but everyone engaged in a heated debate about what our country would become very soon. Many of my classmates had left the school for France or the U.S. and other foreign countries. The atmosphere was intense and serious. The war drew closer to the capital and the news changed so fast I could not keep up. We felt the urge to go and yet feared what we would lose. My class divided into two groups. One group wanted to stay and fight the North Vietnamese invasion, and another group tried to find a way out of the country. The second group reasoned that they could return and fight if they were well equipped. I chose the second group.

It was the 30th of April 1975 when the North Vietnamese marched into Saigon Capital. I went to the dock at Ben Bach Dang in downtown Saigon, to Tan Son Nhut Airport, to Vung Tau 135 kilometers north of Saigon, which had been a tourist destination for fishing and drinking. I went any place I had heard was evacuating people, but I could not get out. I was stuck in Saigon.

The conquering government employed what I saw as Nazi tactics on the southerners: to the world they propagandized them as their brothers and sisters, but the yellow-uniformed policemen began to implement mass arrests. They confiscated books, tapes, films, and any intellectual properties of the South Vietnamese and burned them and the whole civilization of the Republic of Vietnam. Without warrants, they seized businesses, private property, and currencies. They could take anyone in without giving a reason and put him on the execution line for a firing squad. Sometimes the police executed people on the spot; no questions asked.

The new regime used the poor to denounce the rich; the illiterate to denounce the intellectuals. It was a Cultural Revolution—fascist and totalitarian style. They bulldozed the southern national cemetery and any other cemetery that had a few South Vietnamese soldiers who were resting in peace. They left the dead to rot a second time. This was no policy, except to revenge themselves on the southern people whose only crime had been to prosper and enrich themselves on all fronts, from education to medicine, from humanities to arts. The new regime sucked resources from the South and took them to the North. Whatever they did they would do in the dark of the night. They could pull an Army truck up to a house and load up whatever materials they had spotted earlier and be gone within an hour. No one saw the residents or the head of that household any time after that. The Government changed the currency, set a limit on how much the local residents could exchange, and wiped out private enterprises. The only businesses that existed were state-owned. The black market was rampant. Every family had to register with the government and report to the police any new faces in the community. Travel became very limited.

I returned to the University and tried to pick up what was left under a new Vietnamese Communist Government. But I found that at all levels the only things being taught were the doctrines of Ho Chi Minh and the Vietnamese Communist Party. It was a major subject for everyday life.

I was outspoken about my resentment of the new regime. One day, running an errand, I was picked up by the police at a flea market, arrested, and sent to a "re-education camp" at Ha Tien near the Cambodian border in the middle of the jungle in the middle of nowhere. Hundreds and thousands of former South Vietnamese soldiers, policemen, security officers, intellectuals, teachers, religious leaders, and anyone related to the former government ended up at these concentration camps, which had been hastily assembled throughout the South. Hard labor, tortures, starvation, and execution were common in the camps.

We worked clearing the jungle for farming from 5 am to 6 pm, then studied about the Communist Party and Ho Chi Minh until 11 pm. We wrote confessions and self-criticism and if there was something missing from our reports, the Viet Cong would interrogate us. We were required to disclose our family trees and list exactly what everyone on them had been doing during the war and how they had related to the former government.

Re-education was a misleading name for these camps, because there was nothing to re-educate us for, except that we learned to live in a state of fear, hopelessness, anguish, humiliation, and pain. We learned to expect nothing at all except a slow death. A cold, a small cut, anything that happened to you here could lead to your death. I was so starving that I caught crickets and lizards and ate them alive. I could feel them still moving inside my stomach sometimes, since I hadn't chewed them fast enough or had just swallowed them straight. I ate leaves when I was at work. Other inmates and I stole vegetables and roots at night to eat. We would face execution if we were caught.

The guards who controlled the camp were mostly Viet Cong, with a few veterans from the Northern Vietnam Army. All of them were fanatic, uneducated, parroting propaganda machines. To us they were not people, since they had no conscience and no soul. I did manage to befriend one southerner VC, a man named Chu Tu, but I also tried to create conflict between the Northern and Southern guards so we could benefit from their quarrels and inattention. I knew I could not make it out alive. All I could hope for was to die quickly without pain.

And then, one day, I found a chance. During a battle between the Khmer Rouge and the Viet Cong, Chu Tu was wounded. I was allowed to help him to a hospital outside the camp, and once he was under care, I slipped out through a side door and disappeared into the city.

I made my way to Sa Dec, a city about 35 miles from Vinh Long where my old friend Hanh was living with his parents. I could not go home. The government had seized my parents' property in Vinh Long and kicked them back to the village. I had begun the life of a fugitive and I knew my identity would soon be uncovered. I had no money and no possessions. I had no choice but to look for a way out. Escaping from the country seemed to be imminent. Hanh and my aunts became my sponsors. The passage price to escape by boat was 3 bars of gold for each adult or the equivalent. Hanh managed to steal some of the gold for me; the rest of the money I borrowed from my aunts.

We finally found a rickety boat in Rach Gia. With 124 other people I departed for Thailand, but luck was not on our side and we were pushed back because of a storm. The Viet Cong navy captured our boat and towed it back. I did not want to end up in the concentration camp again, and I was not ready to be dead, so I grasped a plastic container and slipped into the open ocean when the boat approached the land. The wind washed me up on Hon Khoai Island and an old fisherman saved me. I lived there in paradise for a few weeks and came back to Sa Dec again. Here I was reunited with my older brother Lan.

I continued my quest to get out of Vietnam and, after I failed five times, Hanh decided to get involved. He and Lan and I outfitted an old river boat owned by Hanh's cousin. We gathered 22 other passengers, many of them members of Hanh's family, and set sail to the South China Sea. We sailed smoothly for two days till the blue water got darker and the salt got saltier. We were in the middle of nowhere except the sky and open ocean. Black clouds gathered; the wind picked up speed; the waves became more intense. The rain poured and engulfed our boat. Lan and I scooped out the water non-stop while Hanh and the captain struggled to steer the boat. Children were crying; women called out to them and said their prayers. I never saw waves so big in my life and I was certain this was my last minute. I thought of my mother and father, my brothers and sisters, and prayed to Buddha to let me go peacefully.

"The engine is broke!" Hanh yelled to me. Then his voice was swallowed by the storm. The boat drifted and the waves pushed it up and down. It vibrated as if it was about to break into pieces. Water streamed in from every crack in the wood. I understood now why our boat could not withstand the violent storm: it had been designed only to travel on rivers. Had it been worth it to escape on a rickety boat? A twister wave slammed down on us and filled the boat half full of water. Lan and I scooped faster. Everyone got seasick and vomited on each other and held onto whatever they could put their hands on. The whole sky became dark, as if we had sailed into the mouth of a giant whale or fallen into an abyss. I closed my eyes and waited for my death.

I didn't know how long the storm lasted, but when I couldn't hear the violent wind or the pounding waves any longer I opened my eyes. Everything was calm again as if nothing had happened earlier, there was not even a trace of the storm except the crippled boat with its helpless refugees. We gathered ourselves and salvaged what we had left and helped one another to keep our hopes alive.

We traveled for three days and three nights after the storm. We ran out of food and water. We even drank each other's urine. A Thai fishing boat spotted us and saved us with some supplies, but we were still at sea. The next Thais we met were not so friendly. They were pirates, who robbed us of what little we had and raped some of the women who were with us. They also tried to crush our boat. In the end we survived, and we landed at a coastal town called Sattahip, where Thai police detained our boat. We lived on the local people's mercy and went to a temple to beg for food. In March of 1978, about a month after we set sail, other refugees started to land at Sattahip, so we decided to move on. We eluded the Thai police and,

FIGURE 1.5   Thousands of refugees ("boat people") fled Vietnam during the decade following the end of the war. Many, including the author of "A Life in Flight," set sail in dangerous, ramshackle craft, like the boat pictured here, seeking political asylum. Those who were not intercepted and returned to Vietnam, captured and killed by pirates, or lost at sea, headed for refugee camps in Thailand or Hong Kong. There they hoped family members who had already escaped or agents from the United Nations High Commission for Refugees would help them find new homes in the West or in other Asian countries.

Source: AP Wide World Photos

on April 1, 1978, presented ourselves at the Leam Sing Refugee camp. At last, I said to myself, I was no longer in Vietnam.

Life in the refugee camp was harsh but it was nothing compared to the concentration camp. Hanh and I and my brother Lan lived in a rough shelter on top of an old cemetery that was part of the refugee camp. We felt a little like wandering ghosts ourselves. We were waiting for the United Nations High Commissioner for Refugees to process our paperwork to go to Canada. After several months Hanh went to Italy. Then I received a letter and money from my older brother Tuong, a pilot for the South Vietnamese Air Force, who had escaped in 1975. He lived in a trailer park in Corinth, Mississippi, with his wife and four children. I asked him to find a way to let our family in Vietnam know that Lan and I were alive.

At the end of November 1978, we were allowed to go. Lan and I left the refugee camp and flew to Memphis, Tennessee, to meet Tuong. He drove us to his trailer in Mississippi. I was so happy to see him and his family. We all cried. I got drunk that day and passed out in the bathroom. We talked about our family in Vietnam and our escape and he told me how he was faring in the new land. He and his wife, To Lan, both had jobs with IT&T.

Tuong took us to the supermarket to buy groceries. I was shocked to see what was in the store. Such abundance! Enough meat to fill the house, enough to feed the whole village; and everything all together, food, nail clippers, everything. The supermarket was huge, and it was so cold! (I had a lot to learn about air conditioning). Tuong told me to watch out for thieves of the poor and thieves of the children because he was caught once when his family shopped for groceries. His wife left her purse in a cart and asked her son Long, four years old, to stay with the cart while she went to get a box of Cheerios. When she returned the purse was gone while Long played on the floor. My brother had just cashed a $60 check for two weeks of work and it was gone. They put all the groceries from the cart back onto the shelf and hurried home. They scraped pots and pans for a whole week for whatever was left to stay alive and waited for the next check. I wondered if the thief ever saw the faces of my hungry nephews or the faces of their parents when they told the children they had no food to feed them. My heart sank and I wondered what my life would be here.

I played with my nephews and got to know them. We chased wild rabbits and flew a kite and ventured into the woods. I experienced my first snowfall in my entire life and it was such a spectacular sight.

I had arrived in Corinth without any money except a pocket full of English "Hello, how are you? What is your name?" I was twenty-two years old and it was hard for me to learn a new language and surely I never spoke perfect English. I only found minimal employment, often faced discrimination, and was taken advantage of for my labor.

After six months Lan moved to San Jose, California, to find better opportunities, while I continued to work at McDonalds for $1.90 an hour. There was no future in Corinth for me but at least I had my family. Both my brother and sister-in-law had jobs, though we knew their meager income could not make a better life for all of us. I hesitated to relocate and yet my happiness to be with my brother's family had not filled up an emptiness in me. Should I risk the unknown, or stay with what's familiar? Finally, I followed Lan. I signed up for the Job Corps when I arrived in San Jose and later found employment as a machine operator in Santa Clara.

I often thought of my family in Vietnam, and all that I left behind, and I blamed myself for my selfishness in fleeing because fleeing was an easy way out. What would I have done if I stayed? Would I have been able to help my family or would I have just made more trouble for them with the government authorities? I missed my parents, brothers, and sisters in Vietnam terribly.

In 1981 my two younger brothers, Minh and Nhut, my sister Kha, and a nephew, Phong, escaped from Vietnam and came to me in San Jose. By then, I had saved up some money and was able to help them a little. In 1983, I quit my job, took out $1,000 from my savings, and closed my account. I threw sleeping bags, clothes, and dried food into the trunk of my 1967 Pontiac Firebird and took my two brothers and nephew with me for an adventure. Kha stayed behind with Lan in San Jose. I wanted to find a place to call home and raise the young boys the way my parents had done for me.

I didn't know where to go but simply drove eastward. We visited Nevada, Utah, Colorado, Nebraska, Iowa, then Chicago, Indiana, Michigan, Ohio, Pennsylvania, and New York. We stopped in every state to discover how we liked it. We talked to local people at laundromats, churches, and schools. Nothing felt quite right, though. Vermont, New Hampshire and Maine would be my last stops. I was anxious and nervous but I didn't show it or let my brothers and nephew know of my feelings. What would I do? There was Canada and then there was the Atlantic Ocean. I wondered if I might have to start all over again from the refugee camp since Lan and I had originally signed up to immigrate to Canada.

We drove into Bennington, Vermont, and my car broke down. I discovered Bennington was a nice little place. Why not settle? Besides, I had run out of money and I had run out of places to go. I rented a shabby apartment and moved us in. I signed up for English lessons at the Bennington Tutorial Center and took a couple of classes at the Community College of Vermont. I applied for welfare for my brothers and nephew, then brought them to Mt. Anthony High School to register them. At Mt. Anthony I met Joan Costin, a counselor who helped us as if we were her own family.

"What do you want to do for your life, Jade?" Joan asked. "Your brothers and nephew have their own lives, you must have yours."

"I love to go to school," I answered.

"Why not apply for colleges?" Joan said, smiling.

Joan gathered applications and helped me to fill them out and sent them off. Bennington College extended a full scholarship for me to start in the Fall of 1984. I studied American and English Literature and Creative Writing with Arturo Vivante, Joe McGinniss, Edward Hoagland, Susan Daitch, and Wayne Hoffman Ogier, among others. I wrote the first part of my Vietnam memoir as my senior thesis and graduated in December 1987. I met Maxine Swayze, the Vermont woman who would become my wife.

The boys grew up. Minh returned to California and got married to his sweetheart and found a job at Apple Computer Company in Cupertino. Nhut and Phong graduated from high school. Nhut got married soon after and Phong went to Pomona College in California.

While I taught part time for the Community College of Vermont, I worked for a nonprofit Lutheran Church Refugee Community Center in Manchester, New Hampshire. As Director there for two years, I assisted and settled refugees from around the world. I tried to help them build bridges to their newfound American culture and language and to ease their culture shock. I was bombarded with harrowing refugee stories on top of my own. I began to feel I must find a way to tell these stories and reach out to others so that people could understand about the refugee flight, the displaced people.

In 1990, I applied to the creative writing graduate program at Brown University. Brown gave me a full fellowship and I took up the challenge. I studied with Meredith Steinbach, Edmond White, Keith Waldrop, and Nuruddin Farah. During the year at Brown, I received news that Joan Costin had died in a car accident and I returned to Bennington for her funeral.

I felt lost again, like I was back on the boat without a compass. I listened to Joan's husband speaking about her up on the hill at Bennington cemetery and I wanted to do my own eulogy for Joan. But I just stood still and numb in the cold November afternoon. My feet were heavy, my breath was short, and my heart ached. I was speechless and my tears became dry. It was too much. There had been so much crying during the Vietnam War and afterwards. I felt no longer human. I was floating instead.

I went back to Brown and completed the second part of my memoir and Joe McGinniss told me to send it to his agent. I graduated with an MFA in May 1992. Maxine was happy for me, but I didn't celebrate my accomplishment much since I had none of my Vietnamese family to share it with. There were no parents and no relatives. I felt sad and told myself I would get over it. It was not a big deal. I had made it through Bennington College without them. I managed to contain myself, but my heart sank deeper when I met my classmates' parents, aunts, uncles, and their siblings who came to Brown for the commencement. What was the point for me to do all of this? Would it be just for me, or would it be, someday, for my children? Or for whom? I certainly didn't know.

To answer my question, my wife gave birth to a gorgeous baby girl in 1992. We named her Alexandra. She brought warm sunshine to my life and I felt as if I was reborn again. My memoir, *South Wind Changing* was published by Graywolf Press in 1994 and became a *Time* magazine "Best Book" of the year. It was shortlisted for the National Book Award. In August 1995, I joined the English Department at Appalachian State University in Boone, North Carolina, as an Assistant Professor of English. I spent five wonderful years there. I won a National Endowment for the Arts Fellowship for Literature.

I was happy, but there was even better news. The Vietnamese government let my parents leave the country and come to the States to visit all of us. They stayed with my sister in Austin, Texas, where we could all take turns visiting them. I drove my family down to see them.

On the drive down, I seemed calm but I was feeling overwhelmed because I had always wanted to see my parents before they passed away and my dream was becoming a reality. There was no joy I could compare to my feelings, and I had no words to describe it. My wife and Alexandra didn't really see it, but they noticed that I drove nonstop and I was always in a hurry whenever we stopped for food.

We arrived at night and I ran to my parents' room. I embraced my father and he looked at me and called me, "Nhut."

"No, Baba. I'm Ngọc not Nhut. I am not your youngest son, Baba. He's coming soon." I said.

My father released me and looked at me again, smiling.

"I can't recognize you. You look different, younger."

"I am a big boy now, Baba."

Then my mother stepped into the room. I reached for her. I felt her warm tears on my face.

"How long have you been away, son? " she finally burst out.

"Twenty five years, Mama" I cried out. "It has been so long."

Her chest heaved up and down and she became silent. She held me tight as if she were afraid of losing me.

"You've grown, son."

She released me and kissed me on the cheek then hugged me again.

I introduced my wife and Alexandra. My parents reached for Alexandra and talked to her in Vietnamese. Alexandra was shy and I told her to kiss them.

Together we walked out of the room to the dining table. My mother asked my sister to bring the food out and we ate the meal together as if we were recycling the day before I went to college in Saigon. I talked to my mother throughout the night about our relatives, my former teachers, our friends, about the temple, the garden, the rice paddies and how they were all faring back home. I was nostalgic and time seemed to stop for me.

After a month, I returned home to my job, and only visited my parents once again during the two and a half years they stayed in Austin. I felt so guilty for not being with them as much as I could because of my economic circumstances. They went back to Vietnam in 2001. They were in their eighties. I wondered if we would ever have another reunion in our own home in Vietnam.

Please Buddha look after them for me.

QUESTIONS FOR DISCUSSION

1. Consider the writing style of "A Life in Flight." Can you tell that the writer's first language is not English? How does the simplicity of the prose help to tell the story? There are multiple tones used in this story. At which point does Huỳnh Quang Ngọc seem the happiest? At which, the most somber? What do these high and low points tell you about Huỳnh's current understanding of his experiences?

2. How many times and under what hardships does Huỳnh attempt to escape from Vietnam in the course of his story? What does his need to escape, even though it means abandoning his education and leaving his family behind, tell us about the post-war political situation in the former Republic of South Vietnam? Who is safe there? Who is not? Take another look at Huỳnh's description of post-war Vietnam.

3. Huỳnh time spent in the concentration camp and his meeting with Joan Costin are both huge turning points in his life. What are some other turning points in this story? What effect do these turning points have on Huỳnh's life as seen in the story?

4. Does the author take sides in the conflict between North and South Vietnam? Which side is he on? Trade and diplomatic relations between the United States and Vietnam have been "normalized" for some years now. However, some Vietnamese exiles, particularly those who worked for the Americans or were outspokenly critical of the post-war regime, fear they might never be able to go back to Vietnam without being arrested. What does this tell you about the nature of war and memory?

5. Discuss the problems Huỳnh encounters as a new immigrant to the United States. How does he experience culture shock? What other kinds of culture shock might an Asian immigrant have encountered in the 1970s? How is he treated by his employers? Why do you think many Vietnamese refugees ended up in places like Corinth, Mississippi, or Oklahoma City instead of on the west coast, where most Asian immigrants clustered in the nineteenth century?

6. What constitutes fulfillment for Huỳnh? What is his version of the American Dream? What is missing for him, and when does he start to find it? Consider the central importance of family in Asian culture, as we see it in this story.

Struggles for Social Justice

Introduction

The stories in this section span a period from the 1940s to the late 1970s. They deal with the lives of African Americans before and during the Civil Rights Movement, and with the work of women's liberationists and gay and lesbian activists. The final selection tells the story of a young man's life in the American Indian Movement.

Gwendolyn Zoharah Simmons ("Mama Told Me Not to Go") was born Gwendolyn Robinson in Memphis, Tennessee, in 1944. Her great grandmother had been a slave. As Simmons explains in her story, she was raised to be a lady but she also expected to become an educated professional, even though the pervasive racism of the South in the 1950s made achieving such goals nearly impossible for an African American girl. Rebelling against her family, the conservative black community of her childhood, and her highly respectable all-women's college, she joined the Civil Rights Movement as a member of the Student Non-Violent Coordinating Committee (SNCC). At the end of her sophomore year in college, Simmons volunteered for field-work in Mississippi.

This was the summer of 1964. Following half a decade of Freedom Rides, lunch counter sit-ins, and voter registration drives in a number of southern states, the student branch of the Civil Rights Movement had decided to launch Freedom Summer, a nonviolent assault on key elements of racial discrimination in the Deep South. The focus would be Mississippi, where African Americans had the lowest rate of voter registration in the country and threats of violence routinely kept black citizens away from the polls in local, state, and national elections. Many families lived in poverty. Black children attended segregated schools that were desperately under-funded and provided little in the way of effective or relevant education. Rigid segregation laws and customs, as well as threats and acts of violence by whites, had all but extinguished hope for economic advancement or social justice among many of Mississippi's African Americans.

However, when nearly a thousand white and black college students of SNCC and the Council of Federated Organizations (COFO) arrived in Mississippi to open freedom schools and register black voters, they met a movement already in progress. As Simmons relates, African Americans had been organizing in southern churches and communities and in older civil rights groups such as the National Association for the Advancement of Colored People (NAACP) and the Congress of Racial Equality (CORE) long before the students came to Mississippi. They had been in the struggle a long, long time. Working together during the summer of 1964, residents and students combined existing civil rights networks within communities and churches with the fresh energy and inspiration of the young newcomers to initiate real change in the hardcore segregationist South. By summer's end, more than 160,000 African Americans, although denied access to white-controlled official voter registries, voted for the first time in their lives, creating a "Mississippi Freedom Democratic Party" and challenging the all-white Mississippi Democratic Party delegation at that year's national convention. All across the state, Freedom Schools like the one Simmons started in Laurel taught more than 3,000 children and adults basic literacy, civics, and African American history.

During the summer, six civil rights workers were killed in Mississippi and scores were injured. There were more than a thousand arrests. Angry white vigilantes destroyed black-owned businesses and burned 30 African American churches. There were 35 shooting incidents, 30 bombings, and more than 80 beatings. As Simmons' story makes clear, all the participants in Freedom Summer were risking their lives in a lethal battle and yet, like Simmons, they were motivated by a passion for justice and concern for one another that bolstered their courage and enabled them to keep working. For many of the volunteers and the Mississippians who worked with them, the movement became the "beloved community."

Unlike the majority of the SNCC volunteers who returned to their college campuses for the fall 1964 semester, Simmons stayed on in Mississippi for another 16 months, unwilling to abandon programs she had started and people who had come to trust her leadership. In 1965, she left Laurel and returned to work for SNCC in New York and Atlanta. In later years, Simmons joined the Nation of Islam and took the name Zoharah. Eventually, she completed college and graduate school and became a professor of world religions.

About a decade older than Zoharah Simmons, Ray Hubbard ("Deep in the Heart") was a child of the Depression. He grew up in San Antonio, Texas, deep in the heart of the segregated South. Like many African Americans of the period—a time when southern agriculture was becoming increasingly mechanized and throwing laborers off the land—Hubbard's parents had migrated to an urban area in search of opportunities. They lived with their four sons in an all-black housing project, drank from separate water fountains, ate in separate restaurants—when they could afford it—and had to step to the back of the bus—when they could afford bus fare. The

Hubbard children attended segregated schools. Hubbard's father, who had served in the Army during World War II, worked odd jobs as a hauler; his mother cleaned white folks' houses. The whole family felt themselves infinitely more fortunate than relatives who were sharecroppers in the cotton belt.

Hubbard's story tells us what it was like to grow up black in America before the Civil Rights Movement and federal intervention changed laws, customs, and, eventually—though not completely—attitudes about race. Starting with his naïve and happy childhood, Hubbard describes his growing awareness of the distance between his family and neighbors and the whites who shared his city but kept the best parts for themselves—the good housing and schools, good jobs, better public facilities, and opportunities for advancement. When it came to making choices for his own life, Hubbard saw education and a trip through military service as his ticket to a better future.

Hubbard's brief participation in civil rights activity did not lead him to join the movement, though he was fully sympathetic. Like many other African Americans of his generation, he felt he had to make his life a success entirely on his own, and one of his priorities became getting out of the South. Hubbard's personal trajectory provides a contrast with the militancy and collectivist strategies we see in Zoharah Simmons' story: He stresses self-reliance and his ability to defy the odds against black men in the 1960s through his own persistence and determination. Hubbard's mathematical skills eventually led him to California and a professional career in technology, from which he just recently retired.

The Civil Rights Movement modeled courage, strategy, and social awareness for other groups seeking equality in 1960s America. The largest and ultimately the most effective of its followers was the movement for women's liberation. As historian Sara Evans has pointed out in her books *Personal Politics* (1980) and *Tidal Wave: How Women Changed America at Century's End* (2003), women working within the Civil Rights Movement discovered their own oppression as women by comparing their situation relative to men with that of African Americans relative to whites. They carried their awareness into the anti-war movement, where they found themselves treated as inferiors by male leaders and began to wonder if the movement's touted commitment to participatory democracy actually included women.

Through consciousness-raising, organizing, marching, and the publication of thousands of articles, women's liberationists began to arrive at an understanding of women's historic subordination to men and to formulate approaches for change. Their work was sometimes painful, always intense, and often exciting. They were trying to unravel centuries of assumptions about women's "natural" inferiority that had become so ingrained in daily life that most people never questioned them. For example, to most 1960s Americans it seemed perfectly reasonable that women received less pay than men for equal work, that they were excluded from most of the high-paying professions and professional schools, did all the housework, surrendered all the major decision making to their husbands, and, in most states, lacked any legal protection from spousal abuse.

Women's liberationists were mostly white and middle class when their movement began. They had to confront their own attitudes about race and sexuality when pushed to respond to women of color and lesbians, who insisted that their specific concerns be understood and included. Working alongside and sometimes with the more mainstream women's rights movement of the same period, women's liberationists helped to enact legislation that outlawed discrimination against women in every economic and civil rights area of American life. More radically, they promoted the transformation of relations between men and women, working toward a future of mutual understanding and full gender equality.

In "Not my Mother's Path," Sara Evans recounts her initial encounter with women's liberation and the profound changes it made in her thinking and in her life. A white southern-born minister's daughter, Evans realized while growing up that her own gifted, intellectual mother lived a frustrated life as a housewife. She vowed not to follow her mother's path.

Evans began her search for social justice in the Civil Rights Movement. Her feminist activism started in Chicago, a center of the women's movement from its beginnings in the late 1960s. When her career took her back to the South, she and a cohort of women activists focused on child care and gender equality in child raising. A lifelong activist, Evans became a historian of the modern women's movement and is today one of the foremost women's historians in the United States. She maintains regular contact with her friends and colleagues from the heady days of women's liberation.

Inspired by Civil Rights and women's liberation movements, gay and lesbian liberation movements emerged in the 1970s, politicizing the formerly private issue of sexual orientation and giving a voice to a silent minority. Among revolutionary activists, "gay pride" and "gay power" replaced gay shame and energized the movement to end discrimination against gay men and lesbians in employment, social relations, and the law.

Toby Marotta ("Students of Stonewall") has written extensively about gay culture and politics. In the early 1980s, he published *The Politics of Homosexuality* (1981) and *Sons of Harvard: Gay Men from the Class of 1967* (1982). Most recently, he created "The Community Roots Archive," an online digital exhibition honoring the Stonewall Era. He also conducted social research on AIDS during the worst years of the epidemic in the United States. In "Students of Stonewall," Marotta tells his own story of coming to terms not just with his homosexuality but with the militant gay liberation movement.

From early adolescence, Marotta had quietly acknowledged and understood his own sexual orientation. Like many elite and middle-class gay men of his generation, Harvard-educated Marotta initially decided to live his life as a closeted gay man. While attending graduate school and after meeting his life partner, he became involved in a number of campus causes, though he remained largely an observer of gay activism until he decided to study gay political culture for his doctoral dissertation.

Marotta's research led him to encounter gay liberation in the aftermath of the violent and exhilarating Stonewall Riots of June 1969, a two-day uprising in New York's Greenwich Village that is now considered the watershed event in the modern gay rights movement. As Marotta discovered, gay people had been organizing for equal treatment in society and law for many years before Stonewall, but the vast majority had continued to hide their sexual orientation in the face of society's fierce condemnation of sexual difference. After Stonewall, gay activists became outspoken, defiant, sexually uninhibited, and visible. New leaders emerged; the Gay Liberation Front, the Gay Activists Alliance, and scores of small branches of these groups took up the cause of gay liberation, staging demonstrations, street dances, and gay liberation marches. They lobbied for protective ordinances in major cities, successfully persuaded the American Psychiatric Association to stop labeling homosexuality as a mental disease, and began the long, uphill battle for full civil rights protection for sexual orientation. Colorful and frequently confrontational, the gay liberation movement was a shock to the American system. Marotta himself—cautious, conservative, and committed to a monogamous relationship—was apprehensive at the prospect of encountering militant gays. His story describes how he eventually came to acknowledge their courage and their importance in his own life.

Yolanda Retter ("Sisterhood is Possible"), the daughter of a Peruvian mother and a North American father, is the author and co-author of several works on gay and lesbian history, including *Gay and Lesbian Rights in the United States: A Documentary History* (2003) and "On the Side of Angels: Lesbian Activism in Los Angeles, 1970–1990."

After a childhood in which she firmly established her Latina identity, Retter began her adolescence in search of something else, some authority that would tell her more about who she was and help to explain her feelings. She found that little was known about lesbianism in the 1950s and 1960s, and much less spoken. Initially, she didn't even have a word for it. While a teenager in the early 1960s, she managed to connect with lesbian subculture, which at that point was confined to single-sex urban bars and clubs. After making this important connection, Retter still took several years to emerge publicly as a lesbian, experimenting with a number of issues and ideas before joining the Lesbian Feminists and committing her life to the lesbian community and lesbian activism.

Like other writers for this book, Retter is concerned to situate her memoir in the context of the larger Sixties-era history, noting popular music, the assassinations of John and Robert Kennedy and Martin Luther King, Jr., and her brief encounters with Vietnam veterans, Haight Ashbury, drugs, and the counterculture. Predominantly, though, hers is the story of a search for a movement that would become a community. Still in the movement today, Retter embraces activism of many kinds but remains clear about her priorities as a lesbian woman of color and a separatist. Although she is deeply motivated to help society's casualties, she is nevertheless uneasy with movement "alliances" that either denigrate lesbians or fail to reciprocate lesbians' support for their causes. Retter works as a professional archivist, social worker, and historian.

Native Americans in the 1960s had some of the oldest and deepest grievances of any people in the United States. Those who lived on reservations had the lowest incomes, the highest rates of disease and alcoholism, and the lowest life expectancies of any ethnic group in the country. Their housing and educational facilities were decades behind even the most minimal American standards. Urban Indians suffered from high rates of unemployment and police harassment. Native Americans everywhere were angry at the nation that had broken so many treaties over the years and they hated the paternalistic Bureau of Indian Affairs, which had run the reservations and their lives since the nineteenth century. Sporadic protests around the country throughout the 1960s highlighted the loss of ancient fishing rights, the illegal sale of Indian lands, and other encroachments on tribal sovereignty and traditions.

A movement for "Red Power" coalesced in Minneapolis in 1968 as the American Indian Movement, or AIM. Initially organized to help urban Indians gain funding for anti-poverty programs and establish the Indian equivalent of "freedom schools," AIM gained popularity and adherents throughout the country and began to tackle major issues of importance to Native Americans nationwide. AIM members became primarily concerned with publicizing grievances and demanding change. They took their cue and their confrontational stance from the rising militancy of the Civil Rights Movement, as embodied in Black Power, and from the more radical elements of the student anti-war movement. Some of AIM's tactics—particularly the armed occupation of Wounded Knee, South Dakota, in 1973—remain controversial to this day, but there is no doubt that the sustained and dramatic protests of AIM pressured the government to address Native American problems and won greater respect for Indian culture. AIM continues to exist, focusing its energies today on youth programs and job training and sponsoring the National Coalition on Racism in Sports and the Media.

Johnny Flynn's story, "Something in the Wind," starts with his childhood as the son of a Potawatomi Indian mother and an Irish-American father. In 1972, Flynn left college to join the American Indian Movement. He became a foot soldier in AIM and threw himself into it heart and soul. Today, he claims that he was unimportant in the movement, but he appears to have been on the spot wherever AIM was in action, and he had the bruises to prove it. Beginning with a small protest against the Boy Scouts in Topeka, Kansas, Flynn and his fellow foot soldiers, both men and women, joined AIM leaders in ever larger and more daring protests, culminating in the occupation of the Bureau of Indian Affairs building in Washington, D.C., and the siege of Wounded Knee. Arrests became a part of Flynn's life; violence, property destruction, and narrow escapes were frequent occurrences. It all happened very fast—between Topeka and the surrender at Wounded Knee, only about a year elapsed. Flynn continued working with AIM for several years but left to pursue other goals, eventually becoming a professor of comparative religion and Native American spirituality, a folklorist, and a historic performer. He has remained an activist and an advocate for Indian rights through all the years since his involvement in AIM.

Flynn addresses his memoir to his children, who have frequently asked him to tell them about his days in AIM, but he brackets his activist adventures within the larger story of his own development and his growing sense of responsibility for the preservation of Indian people and the reanimation of Indian spiritual traditions.

MAMA TOLD ME NOT TO GO
Gwendolyn Zoharah Simmons (a.k.a. Gwendolyn Robinson)

The Beginnings: Memphis, Tennessee

My parents named me Gwendolyn Delores Robinson. I am a southerner from birth. I grew up in Memphis, Tennessee, during the 1950s and experienced firsthand all of the indignities of being black in the South: the "White Only" signs at all the downtown restaurants, the public library, the Memphis Art Gallery, and the front doors of the theaters. There were the same signs on the "good" water fountains (the ones that had cold water) and the clean toilets. And of course there was that yellow line across the middle of the bus with the "White Only" on the front of it and "Colored Only" on the back of the line. You know, "separate but equal."

Of course, given the apartheid system under which we lived in the South—the Jim Crow system—I lived in an all-black neighborhood, attended an all-black school and spent all day on Sunday and a few hours on other days in an all-black church. I knew intimately what Lillian Smith called the "peculiar system" and I knew my "place" in it from a very young age. My grandmother, Rhoda Bell Temple-Robinson-Hudson-Douglas (she was married three times and outlived them all), reared me from the age of three (so she was "Mama" to me and that's what I called her). She told me a lot about the ways of the world for a black girl-child in the heart of the Deep South.

My grandmother had been raised by her own grandmother, Lucy Temple, and Lucy had spent her youth and early adulthood in slavery. Grandma Lucy was the offspring of her white "master" and an enslaved African-American mother. She was blonde and blue-eyed (hard to believe if you saw my grandmother or me). Grandma Lucy hated the color of her skin because of all the suffering it had caused her. When she was eleven or twelve years old, her slave master/father gave her as a wedding gift to her half-sister, his white daughter. This sister hated Lucy immensely, presumably because she knew that her father was Lucy's father too. The punishment the new "mistress" meted out to her half-sister for any infractions of her draconian codes included lashing her with a buggy whip and, most cruel of all, jabbing long darning needles between her fingernails and nail beds. Lucy would bleed profusely, begging for mercy.

Grandma Lucy told my grandmother the stories of slavery as she grew up, and my grandmother then told them to me. I have told them to my daughter, Aishah Shahidah Simmons. May the chain be unbroken!

Mama was a great storyteller. She had many stories to share and she loved to share them. She warned me often about the pitfalls of being a black female. She told me about the harsh realities she had faced under the sharecropping system as a girl in the early years of the twentieth century. She and her family were trying to eke out a meager living from the soil from year to year in the face of harrowing racism and an economic system stacked against them and in favor of the landowner. She had spent all of her early life moving with her family from farm to farm in Arkansas. While the conditions in each place she lived were none too good, she said that she always gave thanks for not living in Mississippi, which in her opinion was the worst hell-hole in the whole wide world for black folks.

I can remember being terrified by the stories she told about "Negroes" still living at that time under a virtual form of slavery in Mississippi. She would say that she knew people who had recently escaped from Mississippi plantations where they had been held for years at gunpoint due to "indebtedness" to their white landowners under the sharecropping system. She said that she thanked God every day that she had not had to set foot into the state of Mississippi and she warned me never to land in that "hell-hole of a place" if I knew what was good for me. "If anything," I thought, "I am going to New York, or Chicago, or L.A. when I grow up, where 'Negroes' are treated decently!" I wouldn't even think of going to a place which was even worse than Memphis. After all, folks in my neighborhood used to say, "The Mississippi Delta begins on the Main street of Memphis, Tennessee." Memphis was bad enough and I certainly didn't want it any worse. Mississippi would not be a destination for me under any circumstances, or so I thought.

For the most part, growing up was joyful. I lived happily in my all-black world, surrounded by a loving family and wonderful teachers and church members who showered me with tender care, support, and encouragement to reach the highest goals that I could imagine, in spite of the obstacles of race and gender. Mama was a happy person by nature, kind and loving and full of the joy of life. I guess our temperaments and personalities meshed well together and life with my grandparents was a happy one. Also, my mother (Juanita Cranford-Robinson-Watson) and father (Major Lewis Robinson) were loving and affirming and were actively involved in my life. I spent many weekends with my sweet mother, who was more like a big sister to me. My father lived in the house with my grandparents and me for most of my growing up. While he wasn't one to express much verbal affection, he clearly loved me and as I grew up to be a leader at school and at church, he was visibly proud. And then there were my Aunt Jessie (Jessie Neal Hudson) and Aunt Ollie Bee (Ollie B. Smith), both of whom took great interest in me and encouraged me to excel. These were both strong women who took their destiny into their own hands and carved out rich and wonderful lives for themselves and all who were around them.

My Aunt Jessie was especially attractive, lived in Chicago, and boasted a wardrobe and colognes that I thought only movie stars owned. On her bi-yearly treks home to Memphis, she regaled me with stories of her life in the "windy city." Her arrival made our house, the extended family, and my whole community come to life in a big way. Aunt Jessie brought presents for many of the kids in the neighborhood, or she baked cookies, cakes, or pies for everyone. There was music and dancing in the house when she came. She taught me how to dance. And the clothes that she brought or sent me twice a year made my eyes bug out. She was all of my friends' "Aunt Jessie" too. She was bold, audacious, daring, and a pioneering spirit. With her high school diploma in hand, she had migrated to Chicago in about 1939, as so many Memphians did, and pushed her way into the white preserve of retail window design. It was through her that I learned that while the North did offer more opportunities to blacks than the South, it was still no Promised Land!

I was blessed in my formative years with many excellent women role models. There was Miss Willa McWilliams-Walker—my second-grade teacher—who was the first black person to run for the Memphis School Board. She remained a close friend throughout my school years in Memphis. At my church, there were Dr. Clara Brawner, the first black woman doctor I ever saw, her sister, Alpha Brawner, a world renowned opera singer, and Ophelia Little, another opera singer on the world's stage, just to name the more famous ones.[1] Additionally, there were many good teachers at my school and mentors at my church who made special efforts to help me develop my humanity and leadership potential. At my church home, there were Mrs. Edna Haywood, Mrs. Mary Webster, Mrs. Mamie Cartwright, Miss Ernestine Peoples, Miss Fannie Crawford-Smith. By and large, it was these women-folk who made indelible impressions on me during my developing years. They told me constantly that I should reach for the stars because they were truly attainable for those who really tried. I believed them. I studied hard, played hard, did well in school, and set my sights upon attaining a full tuition scholarship to either Howard University in Washington, D.C., or Spelman College in Atlanta, Georgia, two of the most prestigious traditional black colleges in the U.S.

Yes, I was subjected to the daily indignities common to all blacks at that time and in that place. But, for the most part, these things were the grey background to the technicolor life that I was busily leading at the time. Segregation and racism only minimally intruded upon my busy, event-filled, and purposeful life.

Awakening to the Reality of Racism

At the end of my junior year in high school, I was clear that I had to get a job and begin saving up the money to help with my college expenses. A number of my peers, particularly the boys, had begun working during the summers long before me. Many of them worked in the cotton fields nearby, weeding and picking cotton where they were paid by the pound. I had been spared this back-breaking work by my grand-mother, who said, "I have picked enough cotton for the both of us and I don't want any grandchild of mine picking cotton in the broiling sun."

Our family could afford to live without my adding to the family's income. This was not the case for many of my chums, whose families had many more mouths to feed than mine did, with only me, my dad, grandmother, and grandfather. Plus, both of the men in the house were working. My father worked in a furniture factory. My granddad, Henry (Lev) Douglas, had a "good" job at a whiskey distillery. It was even unionized, and my granddad was proud to be a union man. In spite of our relative financial security, there wasn't a lot of excess money. And even if there was, that summer I decided that I had to make some "real" money, my "own" money. I had new clothes and school supplies to buy and I would need a nest egg to help out with college costs not covered by the scholarship I was so sure that I was going to receive.

For some reason I got it into my head that I wanted a "nice" job (a white folks type job), working in an office or as a clerk in a department store. I began reading the

---

[1]This is an example of the unintended benefits of segregation: African Americans of all classes and educational status lived and worshipped together, enabling poor children like me to rub shoulders with highly educated, professional, middle-class women and men. These persons would show through their life stories that escaping poverty and ignorance and achieving greatness, even in a highly racialized society, was possible if one was willing to persevere in the pursuit of excellence.

classified ads in the major dailies looking for job openings. I went to several of the establishments to answer their want ads, only to be told by the irate and anxious clerks that this was not a job for a "colored girl." After several such turndowns, I began to feel a bit depressed about my prospects. On one particular day in early June, I was again rebuffed due to my race. I was in mid-town Memphis' commercial district. It was hot and the air was thick and humid. I was standing outside an office building wondering if I should answer some of the other ads I had circled in the paper or just call it quits for the day. Quite suddenly, a violent thunderstorm blew up. It took me by surprise, and before I could collect myself, I was caught in torrential rains with thunder and lightning flashing around. Having been raised to fear thunder and lightning, I was quite disturbed about being caught out in the open in a thunderstorm with no shelter. All around me were glass and concrete buildings and whites standing in the windows looking out at the storm and me in it.

I was seized by the feeling of being stranded in an alien land. I was in my "home-land," yet, somehow, I did not know the place. I stood there on the street, soaked to my skin, with thunder and lightning playing all around. I began to cry as I looked at all the cold buildings with their white inhabitants surrounding me. There was no shelter for me in this storm. I felt foreign and alone. For the first time I think I realized what it meant to be a black person in the American South. Mama and all the loving ones who had shielded me from the harsh realities of being black in Memphis were not there. This was the real South for a black girl. I was afraid and angry. The scales fell from my eyes in a flash. For the first time, I felt hatred for the white South and all the white southerners in it. Dripping wet and seething with a feeling I had not known before, an unknown rage, I made my way to the bus that would take me back to my part of town.

I was steaming and mad as hell. I glared at the white bus driver, dropped my coins into the fare box, and sat down on the front seat across from him. Rivulets of water dripped from the hem of my skirt onto the floor and water seeped out from my squishy shoes. The driver, obviously shocked, looked at me and said, "Gal, I don't want no trouble; you better git on to the back where you belong." I responded with a stony silence and a hate-filled gaze. There were no white passengers on the bus but there were a scattering of blacks seated in the extreme rear. They were quite agitated by my actions. Several of them began hissing at me to get my attention. When I looked their way, they began to gesture in exaggerated movements, beckoning and urging me to "come on to the back" and "not to start any trouble." There was both fear for themselves and concern for my safety in their expressions. I looked away from them, unmoved, and stared straight ahead. I had no plan. There were no rational thoughts. I did not know what I was going to do. All that I knew was that I was not going to give up my seat without a struggle. I didn't know how far I was prepared to go. I was a human being, not a dog. I was somebody in spite of my humiliation in those stores and businesses where I experienced the cold and harsh reality of the Jim Crow system in a situation that really mattered to me. Gone were all the sheltering adults who had done their best to protect me from the harsh realities of being black and female in the Jim Crow South. Here, it was just me and them. I was an "uppity nigger" at that moment and it felt good. "Who the hell did white people think they were?" I thought. I didn't give a damn what the next moment would bring. All I knew was that I was a "nigger" to be reckoned with!

I was lucky that day in 1961. They say that God looks after fools and angels. Clearly, I committed a dangerous act and did not have to pay for it. The driver didn't call the police or physically throw me off the bus, as he could have. The few whites who boarded that No 31 cross-town bus didn't insist on their "skin privilege" that day. They cursed and muttered mostly under their breath and stood in anger over me, as the rule was that "no white person should sit behind a black person on any public conveyance." I think a few even sat down on the opposite side of the bus, glaring menacingly at me all the while. I returned their glares with equally menacing ones. The blacks in the back looked on in fear and astonishment at the scene and seemed to breathe sighs of relief when their stops approached and they got off. I reached my destination and got off heavily. The bus sped away, glad to be rid of its angry black cargo.

I didn't try to find a job in white Memphis after that. A dear neighbor, Mrs. Alberta Simpson, got me a summer job at a Harlem House, one of a chain of hamburger joints scattered across black Memphis. I washed dishes until my hands became raw and, when I was lucky, and the regular waitress didn't come in or was on her break, I got to flip burgers.

I didn't pull off any other daring acts of courage in Memphis. I did become a member of the NAACP youth organization and engaged in their meetings and joined the youth choir. Things were pretty tame in Memphis at that time compared to what was going on in other parts of the Tennessee and across the South. In Greensboro, North Carolina, in 1960, black students had exploded across the headlines with their sit-ins at all-white lunch counters. Students were sitting in and demonstrating in Nashville. Also, the Freedom Riders had begun challenging the segregation on interstate transportation. This was of course long after the 1955 Montgomery Bus Boycott had occurred. No doubt about it, change was in the air; no black person with breath in their bodies was unaware of the rising tide of resistance surging through black America. Nonetheless, the white Memphis fathers, in collusion with the city's so-called black leadership, had kept the lid on. "Gradualism" was the watchword in Memphis. The few crumbs and concessions handed down from the "master's table" were enough, for the moment, to appease Memphis's black religious and business leaders and cause them to discourage and undermine any attempts to change the Jim Crow system in our city. It was pretty disgusting and some of the youth in the NAACP group were champing at the bit to get something going in Memphis.

College Bound: A Dream Come True

I did get that scholarship to Spelman College that I had dreamed about earlier. I also received offers from Bennett, another black women's college, from Morgan State University, and from a small white college in the Midwest that was integrating its campus. I chose Spelman. In my mind, it was the most prestigious. Several of my role models—Clara and Alpha Brawner, as well as Mrs. Paula Epps, my pastor's wife—were graduates. In June 1962, I graduated third in my high school class of over 320, and beamed with pride when my name was called and my lists of scholarships and honors were read. I was really on my way. I had reached for the stars and they were coming closer.

My grandmother was so proud of me. Of course, everyone in my family, my school, and my church were, too. But this was so special for Mama as she had wanted to go off to boarding school when she was a girl so long ago in Arkansas. I was living out her dream. Her long-held desire to get an education and to go to college would be experienced through me. Mama, my mother, my stepfather (Rev. Granville Watson), and my uncle (Wesley Cranford) drove me to the campus in Atlanta. I was thrilled as we pulled into the beautiful tree-lined campus with all of its old stately buildings. I had to pinch myself to see if I was dreaming or if it was all real. I was assigned to a room in Packard Hall, one of the older buildings on campus. It was like heaven to me, and a long, long way from the four-room shotgun house in which I had grown up. Everything was spotless; the beautiful wooden floors and magnificent wooden trimming shone like burnished brass. My dream had come true; I was a freshman at Spelman College.

My folks stayed a couple of days for the parents' orientation. I could see in Mama's eyes how thrilled she was for me and herself. I promised her that I would do good for her, that I would be good, study hard, and not let anything or anyone come between me and my studies. Her parting words were for me to not get into any trouble with boys and not to let anything pull me away from my schoolwork. I promised!

I was so thoroughly caught up in my new life on campus that it was some while before I really noticed that there was a movement going on right outside the tall brick walls which separated Spelman from the housing project at its gates and from the reality of Jim Crow Atlanta. Outside of my Spelman utopia was the same ugly reality I had experienced all of my life in Memphis. In this city "too busy to hate"[2] was the same Jim Crow system: the same white and colored water fountains, segregated toilets, hotels, and buses. Movie theaters had separate seating, the nice restaurants were for whites, and even the hamburger joints were segregated. Public libraries were segregated! Downtown Atlanta was all white except for menial laborers; the maids and trash collectors, the porters, and the messengers were African Americans.

The headquarters of the Student Non-Violent Coordinating Committee (SNCC) and the Southern Christian Leadership Council (SCLC) were there in Atlanta. Both groups were actively working to destroy legal racism in the city and make the white fathers live up to the city's motto. The Spelman administrators warned us "Spelman women" to stay clear of any involvement with "The Movement." We were there, we were told often, to "get an education" and not to get involved in demonstrations and protests. They made it pretty clear that any young ladies who got involved could be summarily dismissed, especially those of us who were on scholarships. I heard that! I certainly had no intention of getting involved. I had my priorities straight. This was the opportunity of a lifetime for me; I was certainly not going to blow it.

---

[2]Atlanta's motto at that time.

The Conflict

As fate would have it, I was selected through some random method to be assigned to an experimental course that combined history and American literature. The two faculty, Dr. Staughton Lynd and Ms. Esther Seaton, were northern white liberals who were well acquainted with the African-American struggle for freedom from 1619 onwards. They both understood and taught convincingly that in this centuries-old struggle lay the roots of the Civil Rights Movement that was swirling across the Southland at that very moment. They set out to awaken us, their charges, to that incredible history through both the literary and historical documents of that great struggle. As I look back on those classes, I smile and say to myself that my being placed in that class was fate. Over those four months of my first semester, I learned about books and events that I had never heard of. I became acquainted with the history and protest writing of my people. A part of me that I had never known was awakened. I felt pride in my people and their long struggle for justice. In addition to what was happening in that classroom, I met several other persons who fanned the flame of black pride and identity so newly ignited. Two of those persons were Dr. Vincent and Rosemary Freeny Harding, who were co-directors of the Mennonite House in Atlanta. There was also Dr. Howard Zinn, who was head of Spelman's History Department at that time. I was privileged to hear many of Dr. Zinn's lectures on the African-American contribution to the expansion of democracy in the U.S. His radical interpretation of American history was illuminating.

Another very important factor in my burgeoning transformation was my membership in the West Hunter Street Baptist Church. Following my grandmother's orders to join a church, I had joined the Rev. Ralph Abernathy's church without knowing of its significance to the Civil Rights Movement nor of Rev. Abernathy's relationship to Dr. King, Jr. and the Southern Christian Leadership Conference (SCLC). Rev. Abernathy's sister-in-law was in my class at Spelman, and she had invited me to attend her sister's church with her. It seemed like a nice congregation and reminded me somewhat of my own church back in Memphis, the Gospel Temple Baptist. Plus, it was just a few blocks from the campus. Staying true to my upbringing, I went every Sunday and joined the choir, something that I knew Mama would approve of; plus, I loved to sing.

I was totally unaware of it, but, clearly, the stage was being set for what was to occur. The convergence of what I was learning in my classes with what I was hearing in church on Sundays about the demonstrations and mass meetings began to erode the defense I had constructed against anything that would come between me and my precious, long-awaited college education. I even had the opportunity to see and hear eloquent sermons from Dr. Martin Luther King, Jr., himself in my new church. Added to all this were the regular visits to the campus by recruiters from SNCC, who would cajole us to join in the particular demonstration or sit-in planned for that day. Alternatively, they would lambaste us for not joining. They loved to say that we were the next generation of "handkerchief head Negroes"[3] who, with all of our college

---

[3] "Handkerchief head Negroes" was a term used in the black community to describe blacks who were considered "traitors" to the race. It was used interchangeably with terms like "Uncle Tom" and "Aunt Thomasina."

degrees, would still be bowing and scraping to "Mr. Charlie" saying, "Yassir boss," and "Nawsu boss," following the white man's orders till the day we died. The SNCC workers would ask rhetorical questions like "What is a black man with a Ph.D.?" and answer "A nigger." They had some real effective recruiters. One of the best amongst them was Willie Ricks, sometimes called Rev. Willie Ricks. He'd stand on the campus in his denim overalls (his uniform) and talk about how the SNCC folks were "making" history while we studied it!

Many of these barbs hit their target with me. The more I learned about this great "River of Black Protest" which began on the African Continent as our foreparents fought against European and Arab slavers, and was continuing at that moment right outside the walled campus, the more I yearned to become involved.

It wasn't an overnight change that I went through. It was gradual. First, I went against Spelman's rules and dared to visit SNCC's headquarters at 8½ Raymond Street. It was in walking distance of the campus, just two blocks from my church home, and not very impressive, rather cluttered and chaotic. But boy, was the place jumping! There was James (Jim) Forman, SNCC's Executive Secretary, who I later learned was the brains of the organization. He was truly one of the unsung heroes of the Movement. Always frantically working, it seemed, was Ruby Doris Smith, a powerhouse of a woman who brought talent, energy, leadership, and commitment to her job as Jim's assistant. She had put her college education on hold to work full time in the student movement. And, of course, there was dear (Rev.) John Lewis, who was chairman of SNCC at that time. He was so pious, so committed, and really very shy. Even in those early days, he had been jailed many times and had faced all manner of danger as one of the student leaders in the first sit-ins and Freedom Rides. He had dropped out of theology school to work full time. Mildred Forman, Jim's first wife, was there, a quiet and calm force in the storm. Mark Suckle, a Jewish student from the North, was somebody else who had put his studies aside to join this momentous movement.

To my amazement, there were two Japanese Americans working in the office at the time, Ed Nakawatase and Tom Wakayama. I couldn't believe my eyes when I first saw them. They were the first Asians I had ever met. Early on in my furtive and clandestine visits to the SNCC office, I asked them what they were doing working in a black people's movement. This was when I learned about the Japanese Concentration Camps during World War II and the internment of thousands of Japanese in the American West, plus the seizure of their property and wealth. I could not believe it. I had never heard of it in school. It had been completely written out of our history books! I bonded with both of them early on during my secret forays to the SNCC headquarters.

There were many others: Jack Minnis, an older white leftist who was in charge of SNCC's Research 5 Center; Casey Hayden, a white southerner from Texas; and Mary King, another white southern woman who looked the part of an Agnes Scott coed with her mohair sweaters, penny loafers, soft perm, and just right make-up. I was truly shocked to see these white "ladies" fraternizing with black men in the Deep South. Boy, did I admire them and all the rest of the SNCC gang who were defying all the southern norms and building a movement.

At first, I just offered my services as a volunteer to type press releases, stuff envelopes, help mimeograph the flyers about upcoming demos or mass meetings.

I tried to pick work which was useful but out of the limelight and definitely away from any news cameras or police wagons. I consoled my fearful heart by assuring myself that I was just going to do a little "support work, nothing heavy," which might cause me to be discovered by Spelman or, even worse, Mama. I convinced myself that I would never participate in any demos or marches and that I would study doubly hard to make sure that I kept my grades up and did not endanger my scholarship, lest I be sent home in disgrace.

This worked for the most part during the second semester of my freshman year. I did not demonstrate; I kept my involvement secret from my family and the school. I kept my grades up so that my scholarship was renewed. I didn't do so well, however, during my second year. I was returning to Atlanta in the fall of 63, after the great March on Washington (August 28). I had watched every televised moment of the March and read everything I could get my hands on which described the event. I had been lifted to unbelievable heights as I listened to the soaring rhetoric of Dr. King, John Lewis, and many others during that historic event. I had wanted to go so badly. There were buses going from Memphis, but Mama would not let me go. We were one of the few families on our little street with a TV, so our living room was filled with adults and children watching the March together. I took this occasion to brag about the fact that I had met Dr. King and shaken his hand, and that I had even been to his house and met Mrs. King. Boy, did that get me some brownie points that day! Everybody kept saying, "You've met Dr. King?" "You've been to Ebenezer Baptist Church?" "You've been to his house?" I beamed with pride but was careful about what I told and did not tell. I didn't want Mama to know that I was getting "mixed up" in the Movement.

Upon my arrival back at school in the fall of 1963, I resumed my SNCC volunteer work. I also started quietly trying to recruit other Spelman women to work as volunteers at the SNCC office, and I was successful in getting a few. I also was elected to be the representative to SNCC's regional coordinating committee for the Atlanta University Complex, which was made up of the six traditional black colleges in Atlanta: Atlanta University, Clark, Morehouse, Morris Brown, and Spelman Colleges and ITC (the Interdenominational Theological Center). A part of me knew that I should not have run for that office as it would be hard to keep my deepening involvement with SNCC a secret from the school and, by extension, Mama. My growing commitment to SNCC and my pride at being selected by my peers got the best of me and I accepted the nomination as well as the results of the election.

A Secret No Longer

In many ways you could say that this was the beginning of my new life. I did my best to balance my school work with my new duties as a member of the committee, which was a decision-making body composed of college and high school student representatives from across the South. It was becoming harder not to participate in the demonstrations, which were increasing in number and growing in intensity as SNCC targeted several downtown restaurants for its desegregation activities. Among these were the Shoney's Big Boy Restaurant, "Axe Handle" Lester Maddox's restaurant, the Pickerick Cafeteria, and the Krystals hamburger joints, which were dotted all over downtown Atlanta. When I first decided to join "the line" (term for demonstrations) along with several of my Spelman sisters, we marched triumphantly singing, "Ain't gonna let nobody turn me around," through the Atlanta University Center and the black neighborhoods along Hunter Street to the Hunter Street bridge, which was the gateway into commercial, "white dominated" Atlanta.

I calmed my fears by promising myself that I would not get arrested, no matter what. I convinced myself that if the police ordered to us to leave the restaurant or be arrested, I would quietly excuse myself without guilt, as my future hinged on Spelman not becoming aware of my involvement. I was committed, but I wasn't crazy! "No one should expect me to give up my future," I angrily told myself. Irritated that fate had put me into such a bind in the first place, I thought, "Why do white people put other human beings who happen to be of a different skin hue into this predicament? Why are they so mean and low down? Why do they hate Negroes who have always been so loyal to them and this country?" At that moment and for many more as my involvement deepened, I hated them—at least some of them—for what they were doing to me and to my people. It was such a dilemma because the Spelman women who had joined me on the demonstration included three white exchange students, Pam Parker and Karen Haberstrom from Carlton College in Minnesota, and Marci Walker from the Connecticut College for Women. It was all so damn complicated; my head hurt just trying to think about the contradictions.

My strategy worked for a while but, alas, I was not able to extricate myself from one of the demos in front of Lester Maddox's restaurant. A bunch of us were arrested, including several other Spelman women. Those of us arrested from Spelman included my good friend, Barbara Simon, a wild black Spelman woman who feared no one and nothing! Well, I thought, this is it! But I didn't give a damn at that moment. I had stood up to those cops with their German shepherds, to "Ax Handle" Maddox and to the "white Atlanta" fathers. We blacks were going to get our "freedom," our "rights," our "dignity," no matter what! "What the hell if I lost the scholarship and got thrown out of school? Sometimes a woman has got to take a stand and do what she's got to do!" I was consoling myself as I looked through the bars of the paddy wagon that was transporting me and my cohorts to jail. "I'm going to jail. I'm going to jail," I thought—this, too, would be a first in my family, first in college, and now first in jail. The paddy wagon literally shook with our clapping, stomping, and singing: "Oh Freedom, Oh Freedom, Oh Freedom over me. And before I'll be a slave, I'll be buried in my grave, and go home to my Lord and be free." The white cops snarled: "You niggers better keep it down back there before we give you something to shout about." Undaunted, we sang even louder. For the moment it was fun.

We arrived at the jail and were ushered in none too politely. We were told to shut up or else. One by one, we were booked, photographed, fingerprinted, and led off to the "bull pen" to join the other "ladies." This was a sobering sight. There were prostitutes, drunks, pickpockets, and women arrested for fighting. They were all black because, of course, the whites and blacks were separated in jail just as in all other aspects of Atlanta life. Some of them seemed hardened beyond reach, sullen and dangerous. Boy, was I glad that there were several of us black women demonstrators in there together. I think I would have died from fright if I had been in there alone. We sang freedom songs, told jokes, smoked cigarettes, and huddled together for safety throughout the long night as we waited word from SNCC's lawyer.

As best I can remember, we Spelman women were locked up just overnight before attorney Howard Moore's lovely, smiling face appeared. He was carrying the papers that secured our release. Boy, was I glad to see him! Now came the really scary part, returning to the campus to face the music there. Howard grinningly told us that we had made the front page of the *Atlanta Constitution* that morning: "Spelman Girls Arrested for Disorderly Conduct in Desegregation Attempt at Local Restaurant." He said, "You're famous!" I groaned in disbelief. This was definitely not good news.

As expected, there was trouble. I was called into the Dean's office and asked why I had left the campus without permission, lied on the dorm sign-out sheet, and disobeyed the school's regulations regarding participating in civil rights demonstrations. She reminded me that I was there on scholarship, which I was putting into serious jeopardy. Last, but certainly not least, she said that she had called my grandmother and told her of my arrest. She told me that my record would be reviewed and that I would be informed about my status later. In the meantime, I was to call home immediately.

Making that call was one of the worst moments of my life. Of course, Mama read the riot act over the phone, saying how I had disgraced the family, that I was the first person in our family to be arrested. She sounded so pained. Her voice was low and husky. It was the same tone she had used all my life just before she would go out back and cut a strong branch from the peach tree in preparation for giving me a whipping. Thank God there were over 400 miles between us. She said that the Dean had told her that I could lose my scholarship and be expelled from school. She said that if the school didn't kick me out and send me home in disgrace I had better mend my ways and stay clear of those marches and this "SNICK" organization (she said it with such venom), whatever it was.

Clearly, my wee hope that Mama would be proud of me for going to jail for "Negroes'" rights was dashed. After all, I had seen her stand up to some white policemen (with a shotgun across her forearm) who were roaming around in our backyard late one night "looking for a suspect" without authorization. Hadn't she told me the stories about Grandma Lucy during slavery and her own struggles as a sharecropper with unscrupulous white landowners? Hadn't she told me all my life "White people are dirty; they'll kill a Negro just as soon as look at them?" Why wasn't she proud that I was standing up to them and fighting for what was rightfully ours? I knew if my grandmother didn't support me that my mother and father, who had questioned my going away to school in the first place, certainly would not understand. I was broken hearted. I went to my room, got into my bed, and cried and cried until my pillow was wet. When I went to dinner at Chadwick, my legs felt like lead and my heart was quivering with fear and anxiety over being thrown off campus and forced to go back home to Memphis and Mama in disgrace.

No one can imagine my joy and surprise when many of my Spelman mates stood up and cheered as I entered the dining hall. They started singing, "For She's a Jolly Good Fellow." "Speech! Speech!" they shouted. Now I knew why my roommate, Smith Tuggle, had made me get out of bed and go to dinner instead of bringing my meal to me as I hid away in my room awaiting news of my fate. I felt better knowing that many of my friends as well as others whom I only knew slightly thought that I had done a good thing.

By the grace of God, I was spared. The administration put me on probation for lying and bringing dishonor to the college. From then on, I really tried to hide my civil rights activities. But I had been bitten by the bug of resistance. There was really no turning back for me, though I still wanted to finish college and make "something" of myself. If anything, the conflict was worse than ever. For the most part, I went to the demos but stayed out of jail, back to my old strategy. But later, this too changed. Several of us, Spelman women, the same ones I worked with earlier, decided that we were going to launch our own campaign against the three or four Krystals hamburger joints in downtown Atlanta during spring break. We talked it over with Jim Forman and others at SNCC, who thought it was a good plan. At this point in the Atlanta struggle to desegregate public accommodations, the restaurants had begun to close up as soon as blacks went in and asked for service. They would put a "Closed" sign in the window and even lock the doors so that no person could enter. Krystals had been using this tactic. Our strategy was to go from Krystals to Krystals, black and white women together, sit at the counter and ask for service. After they would close, we would leave and go to another one and do the same. We would repeat this all day long, beginning early in the morning right through the lunch hour, when they had most of their business. The plan was to hurt them financially and to hurt them badly, putting pressure on the chain's national headquarters to give up their segregationist policies in the South. It was the same strategy used for the Woolworth's chain. Jim had assigned two or three of SNCC's local male regulars to accompany us at a distance to offer protection in case we were attacked.

We were in our third day of this campaign. We had been able to keep three of the Krystals closed for most of the day on the two previous days. On this day, when we went in, sat down, and asked for a cup of coffee and a hamburger, they announced as usual, "We are closed. Please pay the cashier for your purchases and leave as quickly as possible." The waitresses were so angry, they were livid. So was the manager, a skinny little man who went immediately to the door and locked it. The "Closed" sign went up, also as usual. What was different was that they steamed the windows so that no one could see into the all-glass front and we could not see out either. The waitresses turned on us with a "cat that swallowed the canary" look. All of a sudden, several youngish white men came running in from the back room with sticks and clubs in their hands. They attacked us with a fury. Before we knew it, we were being beaten. The manager and the waitresses joined in the fray. Before I could think, I had jumped across the counter trying to get away from one of the male attackers, only to be jumped by one of the waitresses. She and I began to wrestle. She grabbed one of my arms and embedded her fingernails into my flesh with such fury that I started bleeding. At which point, I punched her with all my might and shoved her off of me. I then began throwing cups, saucers, and dishes at the attackers, trying to keep them away. My sisters were trying to defend themselves too. Suddenly, there was a loud crash and the three SNCC guys who were assigned to us were bursting in through the plate glass door and beating the men who were beating us. The place was in shambles and a bloody row was in progress when "Atlanta's Finest" came in, stopped the fracas, and arrested all of us. None of our attackers were arrested. It seems that the official version was that we had attacked them!

It came as no surprise that we were charged with a number of crimes, including "inciting to riot," "rioting," "disorderly conduct," "assault and battery," and "destruction of private property." This had been a frightening experience. I had been only slightly injured but I felt as if I was going to have a heart attack right there in the paddy wagon, waiting with my Spelman sisters to be taken to jail. I knew that this was really it. I couldn't imagine what the headlines would read this time, or rather I could! I knew that it was really going to be "*Sayonara* Spelman" this time.

Howard Moore really had to struggle hard to get some of the charges against us dropped and our initial bail reduced. He also had to call upon the Spelman

FIGURE 2.1   Angry whites pour ketchup, sugar, and mustard on civil rights activists attempting to desegregate a Woolworth's lunch counter in Jackson, Mississippi, in May, 1963. Lunch-counter sit-ins, which gave rise to the student wing of the Civil Rights Movement, started in Greensboro, North Carolina, in February, 1960, when four African American students from North Carolina Agricultural and Technical State University sat down at a "whites-only" Woolworth's lunch counter and asked to be served. Their action launched a wave of student sit-ins and protests in cities and towns across the South, and sympathy pickets and boycotts in the North. Some protestors at the sit-in pictured here were attacked with fists, boots, brass knuckles, lit cigarettes, and broken glass. They sat unresisting for three hours.

Source: AP Wide World Photos

administration to intervene on our behalf. We languished for three days in jail while these negotiations were in process. It seemed like a life-time, sleeping on the iron slabs with no mattresses and no blankets. Carrying out our bodily functions in full view of all the others in the pen and trying to stay clear of the amorous advances of some of the other inmates was a trying experience. We survived on half-rotten bologna-on-white-bread sandwiches and Kool-Aid. We were unable to shower and we had no change of clothes, so we were very rank when we were released and finally tumbled out of those dank quarters into the bright Atlanta sunlight.

Somehow, I had kept my mind off of the fate that I knew awaited me. My earlier probationary period had ended without incident and here I was in trouble all over again, big trouble. Plus, I had been getting some unwanted attention already from Spelman's administration due to the rallies I had been helping to promote on campus in an effort to get more campus freedoms. (We were kept on a very tight leash in those days. Up until Junior year, coeds could only sign out to the library or another dorm after six p.m. during weekdays, and only to a social event on Morehouse's or Spelman's campus or to the one neighborhood movie theater on weekends. You had to get special permission to do anything else!)

So—tired, smelly, and scared, my comrades and I arrived back on campus and I went right to my room, but not before seeing that look of disapproval on the face of our housemother, Mrs. Gordon. We had of course made the newspapers again. You would have thought that we had been caught trying to rob a bank from the way the story was written.

At least they did let me have a good night's rest before I was hauled in before both the Dean and the President. Ironically, Spelman's President Manley, a distinguished looking black man, asked me if I was a communist and if I had been sent to foment dissent and chaos on the campus. A communist? I hardly knew what that was. A paid instigator? Boy, I was as poor as "Job's turkey" (an old black southern saying) with hardly a penny to my name; I wished that somebody was paying me to catch the hell that I was catching. It was left to the Dean to tell me that my scholarship had been suspended and that I would need to start packing my things. Her office would call my parents to inform them that I would be asked to leave the campus and to find out if they would be able to pick me up. While I expected the worst, hearing it for real caused me unimaginable pain. A part of me wanted to throw myself at the Dean's feet sobbing and begging for another chance. Another part, however, wouldn't let me grovel. That part won out and so I rose slowly when dismissed, mumbling something unintelligible as I left her office. I hardly remember making it back to my room. I felt numb, hollow, frightened. The tears fell in torrents once I was safely in my room with only Smithy to hear my sobs.

Word spread like wildfire and, unbeknown to me, Smithy and some of my friends and associates began planning a protest march and demonstration demanding that my scholarship and my status as a student be reinstated, along with those of the other Spelman women who had been arrested. The next day during the lunch period, a number of students and SNCC workers marched to the President's house and held a rally. They sang Freedom Songs and made speeches about the importance of the student movement, the bravery of those of us who had demonstrated, been attacked, and then arrested and falsely charged for trying to exercise our civil rights.

They declared that they would organize a boycott of classes and that they would get their brothers over at Morehouse College to do the same. In fact, a number of Morehouse men joined the rally and quite a number of SNCC organizers participated. The SNCC folks included Willie Ricks, Mark Suckle, Ed Nakawatase, and Tom Wakayama, who declared that they would turn the campus out if something wasn't done to rectify the situation for me and Barbara Simon. The exchange students from the northern universities were not in the same kind of trouble as we were. In fact, they would most likely have been seen as heroes on their liberal campuses. Some of the folks sat in on the President's lawn and vowed to stay until an answer was given. Somebody burned President Manley's effigy. It was a hell of a time on the "*ole*" campus.

I was overjoyed; I could hardly believe what I was seeing and hearing. My sisters and friends had come to my defense, and, in the case of the Spelman women, they were endangering themselves! While I didn't think I would be reinstated, I was so proud of my sisters and my SNCC folks. What was more, Jim Forman phoned to assure me that I did not have to go home if I didn't want to. I was 19 and I could stay and work with SNCC and move into the "Freedom House." Miraculously, the protest worked! Barbara and I were permitted to stay but under strict probation. My friends saved the day for us both.

The Big Decision

Something bigger was on the horizon for me, though I was only faintly aware of it. During the months I had served on SNCC's regional coordinating committee, a plan was being finalized for the Mississippi Freedom Summer Project scheduled for the summer of 1964. The plan was largely developed by SNCC's Mississippi staff in concert with the local black Mississippi leadership. It is very important to highlight the local black Mississippi leadership to set the record straight. Contrary to the portrayals in later films like *Mississippi Burning* and *Ghosts of Mississippi,* black Mississippians had been organizing and fighting the gross injustices they faced in their state long before SNCC came into existence. When SNCC's Mississippi Field Director Robert (Bob) Moses went into the state, he connected with the black leaders he found working there against the forces of tyranny and injustice. Let the names be called: Amzie Moore, Annie Devine, Susie Ruffin, Vernon Dahmer, Victoria Gray, Aaron Henry, Eunita Blackwell, and many more. These heroic men and women were not then, nor were they ever, waiting for the FBI or even the SNCC staff to come and save them. They provided leadership to us and faced incredible odds in the struggle to bring democracy to the state of Mississippi. There were also a number of young black men and women who joined with Bob Moses and the older black leadership. Their names should be called too: James and Willie Peacock, Hollis Watkins, Jesse Morris, Jesse Harris, Joyce and Dorie Ladner, John Handy, Ben Hartfield, and Ulysses Everett, just to name a few.

The Mississippi Freedom Summer Project was sponsored by COFO (the Council of Federated Organizations), which was made up of the NAACP, CORE (the Congress of Racial Equality), SCLC and SNCC. The plan was to recruit 1000 college-age young people from across the nation to spend their summer vacation in Mississippi working on voter registration and the development of an alternative political party that would focus on civil rights issues. They were also to work on developing Freedom Schools across the state, which would offer classes in African and African American history, civics, and basic literacy. They also proposed to train people in both the theory and practice of nonviolent resistance.

The plan called for at least 80 to 90% of the volunteers to be white Americans. The organizers understood the high value placed on white life as opposed to the value placed on black life in America. Whites had been killing blacks with impunity in the South for decades, and basically the national government did not give a damn. Often, the local and state governments were either involved in the actual murders or were duplicitous in the cover-ups. The murder of the three Mississippi civil rights workers, which would occur that summer, is a famous case in point. Medgar Evers' 1963 murder is another one. It was thought that bringing 800-plus white young men and women to Mississippi and placing them in harm's way of the white suprema- cists—who ruthlessly ruled the state and had no compunctions against killing any- one who tried to change the "racial arrangements"—would force the nation to confront the ugly reality of Mississippi. They knew that the parents of these children could possibly look the other way when blacks were slaughtered but could not do so if it were their own sons and daughters. Those middle- and upper-middle-class white parents would demand that their Congressional representatives and senators protect their children from the "rednecks" in Mississippi. Also, their children's pres- ence in the state would bring in the news media en masse, and the ugly underside of America would be further exposed to the world. The fact that there were millions of "citizens" living in the southern bastion of "democracy" without the right to vote or participate in the democratic process would be known to the world, finally.

The strategy included the following: since blacks were prevented from register- ing to vote as well as from the voting itself, COFO would set up parallel voter registra- tion centers all across the state and organize to get blacks to register at these centers. This was of course intended to refute the lie propagated by the state of Mississippi that "blacks did not want to register to vote." A "Mississippi Freedom Democratic Party," a rival to the state's regular, white-supremacist Democratic Party, was also to be organized with branches all across the state. On primary election day, black Mississippians would cast their votes at parallel voting stations also set up across the state, selecting delegates for the Freedom Democratic Party and casting votes for the U.S. President, Vice President, Congressional Representatives and the two Senators from the state. The culmination of all this work was to occur in August at the 1964 National Democratic Convention in Atlantic City, New Jersey, where the Freedom Democrats would challenge the regular Mississippi delegation for their seats.

I was so excited about the project. In my joint history/English class, which con- tinued into my sophomore year, Dr. Lynd was working on developing some of the curricula for the Freedom Schools. I had an opportunity to help with this both in class and out. Dr. Lynd wrote a primer for the freedom school classes, which ended up being used everywhere. We wanted to teach African American history, but knew we would also have to teach basic skills. The plan was for me to be a Freedom School director, teaching the basics—math, reading, and writing—as well as African American history. Voter education and voter registration were to be linked.

I knew that I wanted to go, to be one of the few black college students who were likely to participate. Actually, I was terrified at the prospect of spending three months in Mississippi. Hanging over my head were the horror stories about Mississippi from my childhood. I could visualize being caught by some "rednecks," raped, and tortured before being shot and thrown into a creek tied to a bale of cotton to keep my body from floating to the top. My thoughts and dreams were haunted by childhood memories of those gruesome pictures I had seen of Emmett Till in *JET* magazine's centerfold. (Emmett Till was a northern black teenager who was visiting relatives in Mississippi in August 1955, when he was seized and murdered by white men for allegedly insulting a white woman in a grocery store. Published pictures of Till's mutilated face and body helped fuel national outrage. Till's murder was one of several events that launched the Civil Rights Movement.)

I tried to figure out how I could persuade Mama to let me go. I talked to Vincent Harding, Staughton Lynd, and some of the Spelman women who were also thinking of going—Barbara Walker, Barbara Simon, and Pam Parker. I also talked to SNCC's Mississippi staff about the conditions in the state and how they survived. In my heart, I knew that I had to go, even though my rational mind was still objecting and my fear was great. I needed people whom I trusted to convince me that I should go. I needed them to tell me that it was going to be one of the greatest events in my life-time, and in the history of black people, and in the struggle for the expansion of democracy in America. They all told me. Jim Forman, Vincent and Rosemary Harding, Staughton Lynd, Ruby Doris Smith Robinson, and many others whom I loved and trusted encouraged me to go. I was convinced.

The next challenge was getting Mama to let me go. After much thought, I decided that she would never agree to it given her fear and hatred of Mississippi. I was 19, and I didn't really need her permission. I talked to SNCC folks about it and they said that I could stay at the SNCC Freedom House or with one of the staff after my spring term exams and go with the crew to the orientation session in Ohio, where I would be assigned to a project for the summer, after which I could go home safe and sound and all would be forgiven. "Yes," I thought, "all would be forgiven," and "there is a tooth fairy." But I queasily agreed that this was what I would do. I shared my plans with my SNCC pals and some of my good friends on campus, swearing everyone to secrecy when I told them. My plans were all made. I filled out the application forms for Summer Project participants and was soon informed of my acceptance. Yes! I would be a part of this history-making event. I reassured myself that I would just stay for the summer and would be back at school in time for the fall 1964 semester.

The Big Break

Somehow, I got through the remainder of my second semester, prepared for and took my exams while running over to the SNCC office every chance I had to keep abreast of the plans and preparations for the Summer Project. Things were really jumping and they needed all the volunteer help they could get with every conceivable task. I helped out a lot with typing, mimeographing (this was before the days of the photocopier), and working in the print shop helping with the binding of all the pamphlets, ballot forms, registration forms, Freedom School Primers, Mississippi Freedom Democratic Posters, signs, etc. It was totally exhilarating to be a part of this important part of history in the making. 8½ Raymond Street was "Command Central," and I was there helping to make it happen.

After my exams, I had begun to pack my trunk and suitcases in preparation for moving in with some SNCC friends. Early one morning before Smithy and I were out of bed, there was a knock on our dorm door. It was Mrs. Gordon. "Miss Robinson, Miss Robinson get up and get dressed; you have guests." I couldn't imagine. Then a voice I knew only too well called out: "Gwen, it's Mama. Your mother and Rev. Watson and I have come to pick you up and take you home. Hurry up and get dressed!" My heart began to race. What on earth are they doing here? I was supposed to take the bus home. I meekly said, "Yessum, I'm coming." I was fighting back the tears. Everything was ruined. They must have found out—but how could they? Oh my God, what could I do? I had to tell the folks at SNCC. But how could I? There were no phones in the rooms. The only phone in the dorm was in Mrs. Gordon's office, and she would be guarding that like a hawk. My only recourse was to hurriedly write a few notes and leave them for Smithy to deliver. One was to Jim Forman and the other was to Dr. Lynd. I had to let them know what had happened and that I still wanted to go but I didn't know how. I would write to them from Memphis to see what could be worked out.

Fighting tears and humiliation, I finished packing my things, got dressed, and met Mama and the others in the office. They were all somber. Mama told me that the Dean had learned of my plans and had alerted them, advising them to come and get me. She told me how ashamed she was that I was planning to run off with these "SNICK" people to "godawful Mississippi!" She couldn't believe it. She said she thought that those "SNICK" Negroes had hypnotized me; possibly they had put something into my food to make me go crazy. "Thank God," she said, "the Dean found out and alerted us. We were able to catch you and bring you home before you take your fool self off to Mississippi and get killed trying to get Negroes to vote! Don't you know that those Mississippi 'crackers' are going to kill up a bunch of you crazy kids?" she asked, her voice screeching out of control. I rolled my eyes and said nothing. I rode all the way back to Memphis in stony silence. Mama threatened to beat me when we got home, saying that I still wasn't too big to get a beating!!!! She assured me that when I looked back on this day down the road, I would thank her for saving me from those Mississippi "peckerwoods" (another black southern derogatory term for whites).

I was kept a prisoner when we got home. Mama intercepted all my mail and monitored all my phone calls. I had one girl friend, Geraldine Shaw, who had her own phone and her own car. As I was practically penniless, I had no money for long distance calls. She let me use her phone to call the SNCC office and Staughton Lynd. It was agreed that SNCC would send a money order to cover the cost of bus fare and a little pocket money to grab something to eat en route. It was sent to me at home and Mama got it, opened it, and saw that it was from SNCC. She destroyed the money order and later told me about it. I was really angry now. Tension had been building in the house since our return from Atlanta. I had been sulking the whole time and saying very little. I called Dr. Lynd, told him what had happened, and asked if he could send another money order, but this one was to go to Geraldine's house. That money order came; I got it and cashed it. I told Mama that I was over 18 yrs of age and that she could not stop me from going. She called my mother over and got my dad into the room and they all threatened, begged, and pleaded with me not to go. But Mama and my mother cried. My dad was more angry than I could remember. His position was to let me go. "She'll see," he said. "She has a hard head. Two years of college have turned her into a fool; she has to learn the hard way." Mama said that I would be raped and killed. She continued to cry. Both my mom and my dad blamed my grandmother, saying she had no business letting me go off to college. In their opinion, I should have stayed right there at home and gone to LeMoyne College.

When Geraldine came to pick me up to take me to the bus station, Mama said that if I left, I shouldn't ever come back. This was it as far as she was concerned; she would wash her hands of me. With a heavy heart, I put my bags in Geraldine's car. I looked back at the angry and sad faces of Mama, my mother, and my dad as we drove off.

That was one miserable bus ride for me. While I had "stuck to my guns" at the house, once en route to the Greyhound bus station, all of my bravado began to come apart. My imagination took over and I began envisioning all of the horrible things that most likely would await me. After purchasing my bus ticket, I would have a little under $10 left. Ten dollars between me and the cold world, without the love and support of my family. Doubt assailed me from all sides. I cried all the way to Atlanta. Clearly, I had embarked upon a major new phase in my life. I wondered where the future would take me.

Dr. and Mrs. Lynd met me at the Atlanta bus station and warmly welcomed me to their home for the interim period before the Freedom Summer Orientation, which was going to take place at Western Women's College (now part of Miami University) in Ohio. I quickly got in the swing of things again at the SNCC office. Only now, I went there freely and put in long days working on the preparations for the Project.

I drove to the Orientation with Dr. Lynd and some other Project-related people. For the next two weeks, the beautiful campus would be swarming with young people, the majority of whom were white, being trained for their summer sojourn in Mississippi. There were 500 volunteers being trained for each of the two weeks. As SNCC staff, I was given a job as an assistant trainer and therefore stayed for both sessions of training. The curriculum included lessons on the disenfranchisement of blacks in the state, the philosophy of nonviolent resistance, and its strategic use in the Civil Rights Movement. The volunteers also learned what to do when stopped by a law enforcement official, how to use walkie-talkies, what to do if physically attacked, and on and on. The SNCC organizers were dead serious and tried to convey the seriousness of the mission to all the participants. But many of the participants, especially the white students, couldn't really believe that they would be in any danger. Several of them asked, "How bad can it be? This is still America." Our evenings were filled with cookouts, song fests, and all-night parties, and during the workshop breaks we lay out on the lawns, getting to know one another as we absorbed the Ohio sun.

In June the first group set off for Mississippi with their assignments, duties, and orientation packets in hand. James Chaney, Andrew Goodman, and Michael Schwerner were in that first group to take off. I had met Chaney and his mother and sister at the first week's orientation but not Goodman or Schwerner. Around the second or third day of the second orientation, we were pulled away from our scheduled workshops and training and called into the largest auditorium for a special plenary. Some of the leaders—I remember Bob Moses, Vincent Harding, and James Forman in particular—were on the stage with very grim expressions as they called the session to order. They told us that three of the civil rights workers had disappeared in the state. They said that Chaney, Goodman, and Schwerner were known to have been arrested in Philadelphia, Mississippi. The sheriff, we were told, claimed that he had arrested them but that he had also released them. I remember Bob, speaking barely above a whisper, telling us that this was highly unlikely. Chaney was from Mississippi and Schwerner had worked in the state before. "They knew the deal. If they have been released, they would have contacted the office immediately," he said. If they were missing, we were told, it was most likely they were dead. The room became deathly still. The shock of what Bob said sent all of us reeling. Oh my God, many of us had just seen them, watched them pull off, wished them well. They couldn't be dead! We all became extremely serious from that moment on. I imagine that the whites in the room could not believe that two white men had been killed by other white men for trying to help black folks get the vote! As they said earlier, "This is still America." Even I was shocked that they had killed white men! I remembered all the stories about Mississippi that I had learned from my grandmother. I was really afraid.

Bob and Jim and the others gave all of us the option to go home with no questions asked. After that session, many of us milled around talking about whether we should leave or continue on our mission. I felt that I didn't have an option. I couldn't go home after what Mama had said. I only know of one or two people who left. Almost everybody stayed.

Into the Fire

I was assigned to Laurel, Mississippi, along with James (Jimmy) Garrett, a black college student from Los Angeles, and Lester McKinney, a SNCC field secretary from Washington, D.C., who had worked in Laurel before. Only three of us were assigned to Laurel at the time and we were all black. The reason given was that Laurel, located in southeast Mississippi, was in Jones County, a stronghold for the Klan, with little to no Movement infrastructure. In fact, as we were to learn later, no groundwork had been laid in Laurel. This was none too assuring. We were told it was too dangerous to send whites in at the time, as they would attract too much attention. The whole idea, I had thought, was to bring in white students so as to open up the state and in some sense let them act as "human shields" between the violence of the state, the Klan, the White Citizen's Council—white individuals who thought nothing of taking a black life—and the black locals and activists in Mississippi. I couldn't believe that I was one of three persons going to work in an all-black project because it was "too dangerous for whites!!!" The prospects for the three of us did not look good.

That was one scary ride into the state. I sat in the back while Lester and Jimmy sat up front. I couldn't even drive a car at that time. My way of dealing with my terror at entering the state of Mississippi was to sleep most of the way. I would wake up and ask, "Are we there yet?" "Are we in Mississippi?" When we did cross into the state, I was surprised to see that the sky, the trees, the land looked the same as they did in other states. I fully expected a horror-show scenario where the trees would be gnarled and the sky threatening. I thought about the three workers who were still missing at the time we rolled into Mississippi. This must have been the most frightening experience of my life up until then.

Learning to Organize, Learning to Lead

Initially, we couldn't even stay in Laurel as no preliminary work had been done and no residents had agreed to house us. We had to sleep in Hattiesburg, 30 miles south, for the first two weeks, driving up to Laurel every day, scouting out the prospects for actually establishing a project there. We had two or three names of persons who had been active in the Laurel NAACP. They were Mrs. Suzie Ruffin, Mr. Richardson, and Mr. Simmons. We did contact them and began meeting secretly with them and a few others. There was interest. A number of blacks in Laurel wanted their city to be a part of the Summer Project.

I was given the address of a Mrs. Eberta Spinks, who was known to have an interest in securing civil rights for herself and other black people. I stepped up on her porch and knocked. When she came to the door, I introduced myself as one of the civil rights workers in the state assigned to work in Laurel. Mrs. Spinks opened her screen door and said, "Come on in. I have been waiting on you all of my life."

This was the big break we needed. After hearing our plans for the summer, she offered to take me in. She said that she thought that her neighbor across the street, Mrs. Carrie Clayton, would be willing to put up the two men at her house. These two brave women came forward and offered to house the three of us. Lester and Jim moved in with Mrs. Clayton and I moved in with Mrs. Spinks.

To Mrs. Spinks and Mrs. Clayton and other local activists, we SNCC workers were "leaders," people who brought a vision, people who brought resources, ideas, and materials that they wanted. At the same time, because of our youth, we were also children to them.

I had to obey Mrs. Spinks when it came to what time I could come in at night. I had to tell her where I was going and where I had been. If she said I had to go to church, I had to go. But at the same time, she and the others were willing to follow me into the jaws of the jail. It was a very interesting dynamic.

Without warning, just a few days after we moved to Laurel, Lester, who was project director, disappeared. Everyone in our fledgling group feared the worst. After some intervention by some of the black ministers, law officials admitted that they had picked Lester up on an old warrant. It seems that Lester had neglected to tell any of us that when he was last in Laurel he had been arrested and had jumped bail. Because he had jumped bail, the sheriff refused to let him out on a new bond. I was terribly upset for Lester and for the Project. Lester was the seasoned SNCC worker; Jimmy was a California college student with no southern organizing experience (of course, what he lacked in experience he more than made up for in creativity and grit), and what little I knew I had learned in Atlanta attempting to desegregate lunch counters. In my mind, neither of us could carry on the project without Lester or someone of his caliber. COFO sent in a lawyer to get Lester out of jail. The authorities said that Lester would do five years of hard labor if he didn't sign a statement saying he would not set foot in Jones County for five years. COFO's attorney thought that Lester would have to sign the pledge and leave the county or be locked up for a long time. And that's just what happened: Lester was barely given time to collect his belongings and bid us farewell. As it was, the sheriff trailed the lawyer and Lester all the way to the county line. He assured Lester that it would not be a pleasant experience if he were caught in Jones County again.

I kept calling COFO headquarters in Jackson and SNCC in Atlanta, asking them to send a replacement for Lester. I was told they did not have anyone to send, at that point, as everybody was already deployed. I was told that, therefore, I would have to assume the directorship of the Project until they could find someone else. I couldn't believe what I was hearing! They wanted me to act as interim project director. Jim Foreman kept assuring me that I could do it. I couldn't believe that I, a little Memphis girl with no field organizing experience, was told to run the Laurel Project. By the Grace of God and the support of many people, the job was done. And I guess I did do it, but not without a lot of fear and trepidation.

The first job was to stabilize the Project. That meant that Jimmy and I had to find a place for an office and a Freedom School. First, we got local contacts set up—names and phone numbers. We had a mimeograph machine and other equipment, which we left at Mrs. Clayton's for a while. We had a terrible time renting an office. Nobody wanted to rent to us; they were afraid of firebombing. But then a few local people began to say, "Yes, we want you here." They told us who to approach and who owned property. You had to have a local group willing to say, "Yes, we support it." Finally, we found an old nightclub that had been boarded up. It was owned by a black man. He offered to let us rent it for what was a lot of money in those days in that part of the world, but we took it. Local people paid some rent, bought some supplies, and repaired the place. We had large numbers of people with skills and we got that place up and running very quickly. It became the office and the site for the school as well. It came with a huge dance floor and a bar area, so we had room for a library. The books were donated. SNCC started sending books in as a part of Freedom School initiative. Eventually, we had two sites in Jones County, one in our center and another in another part of the city. This second site was the Freedom Day Care Center, which took children aged six months and older. At the main school, we had kids from 6 to high school, and at night the parents came for basic literacy.

That building was bombed and totally destroyed later that summer. We moved to a little shotgun house and that too was firebombed. The (all-white) Laurel Fire Dept. let it burn down. This second place had some of our people sleeping in it to protect it, plus it was part of a duplex with a whole family on the other side. What saved the two SNCC workers, Ben Hartfield and Ulysses Everett, and the family as well, was that the bomb was placed under the gas line outside. So instead of blowing up the structure, with a family in the adjacent building, it blew the line away from the building and nobody was injured, even though the building did burn down.

We began recruiting housing for additional volunteers and urging COFO and SNCC to send us more volunteers. And send them they did. More and more local people took our workers into their houses. All told, we had 23 volunteers over the summer. All of the volunteers but two were white, mostly college students from middle- and upper-middle-class families. There were also two older white adults, a Quaker woman and an Episcopal priest, who joined our ranks. We had two black college students assigned to Laurel besides Jimmy and me.

While handicapped in the beginning, the Laurel Project became one of the more successful projects in reaching COFO objectives for the summer. We established the schools and the child-care. We held successful mock voter registration campaigns in which we registered hundreds of black Laurelites. We also participated in the state-wide mock elections, had a good turnout, and selected the Democratic Presidential and Vice-Presidential nominees as well as their choice for Mississippi's Senators and the Congressional candidate for their area. We built a strong Laurel Chapter of the Mississippi Freedom Democratic Party and selected the delegates who would represent Laurel at the MFDP State Convention. One of the crowning achievements of the summer was the establishment of a 1500-plus volume public lending library. Unlike Laurel's Public Library, which was closed to blacks, our library was open to everyone. Children and adults from all over the county began to visit the library and to borrow books. For many adults, it was their first time ever being in a library.

Events picked up momentum as the summer progressed. Many local people who were afraid at first began coming out to the meetings. In the beginning, we held all these meetings in the smaller churches, as we did not have the support of the large churches at first. Ironically, those churches with the largest congregations and the most wealth were the most reluctant to open their doors to us. But as the fame of the Project grew and the people began participating in our educational and cultural activities, the larger churches were pushed by their members to let us in to use their facilities. COFO arranged for the widely acclaimed Free Southern Theater to visit a number of the Project sites across the state with their fantastic performances of "Purlie Victorious" and "Waiting for Godot." Laurel was one of the sites chosen for a presentation of the plays. I am fairly certain that this was a first for blacks in Laurel—to see real theater—and these wonderful artists performed to packed audiences several times during their stay. Our site was also chosen for performances by nationally known folk singers Lynn Chandler and Julius Lester. They, too, performed to packed houses.

I could hardly believe that the Laurel Project was not only surviving, it was flourishing! An incredibly dedicated group of volunteers were assigned to Laurel. I was amazed at the amount of work that we were able to do as a team with a relatively small amount of rancor and discord.

While I was not aware of the concept for many years to come, I now know that I naturally used a feminist style of leadership which was extremely democratic (sometimes to a fault: it could take us hours and, on at least a few occasions, days to make a decision by consensus) and included the whole staff in the decision making process. It was an incredible experience for me and I think for all of the volunteers who worked in Laurel. They encountered few top-down edicts from this director, which made for a very different experience from many of the COFO projects. As one of the few women project directors in the state, I was particularly sensitive to the high level of sexual harassment which occurred routinely within many of the

FIGURE 2.2   Local people along with white and African American volunteers from SNCC and COFO join hands to sing the anthem of the Civil Rights Movement, "We Shall Overcome," at the True Light Baptist Church in Hattiesburg, Mississippi, as part of Freedom Summer 1964. This photo was taken after a performance by the Free Southern Theater. Music and plays were among the many things that helped to forge community bonds during Freedom Summer, when volunteers and local activists taught Freedom Schools and risked life and safety to register voters and combat racial injustice in Mississippi.

Source: McCain Library and Archives

Projects. (Of course, we didn't even have this term for it then, but there was a lot of very aggressive male sexual posturing and pursuit of women that went on in those days.) One of my few non-negotiable edicts was to ban all forms of sexual harassment and particularly to declare all underage local women off limits to Project males. There would be one warning and one warning only for any infraction of this rule. If it happened again, out you went. Given the conservative nature of the community and our need to gain and maintain approval, I also insisted on a dress code of no shorts in the streets and generally modest dress. Since the church was such a strong and respected institution in the community, we all had to attend church regularly, generally with our host family.

I was just a girl myself, and I had to grow up real fast. I had to assume an air of authority, especially with the white male volunteers who could not believe that a black girl younger than themselves was the Project Director. Boy, did I learn a lot about the northern liberal brand of racism and about male sexism. I felt I had been thrown into the fire and I had to learn to escape with my skin intact. Difficult, but unbelievably rewarding!

There was a considerable amount of homegrown leadership in Laurel which came to the forefront during this Project. In actuality, they provided much of the leadership related to our recruitment efforts and the development of strategies to motivate more black Laurelites to become active participants in their Movement. Mrs. Spinks, Mrs. Ruffin, Mr. Richardson, Mr. Simmons, and Mr. and Mrs. Gore, among others, proved to be examples of the dynamic and powerful local leadership which existed in that community, as it did across the state. At one point, Mrs. Spinks proudly went to jail for integrating the restaurant at the Pinehurst Hotel.

Of course we were not able to organize and make the achievements that we did without encountering strong opposition from many whites in Laurel. Southeastern Mississippi was strong Klu Klux Klan territory and they certainly were not going to take "niggers" changing things lightly. One of the most devastating acts was their firebombing of our offices and beautiful 1500 volume library. Over the summer, crosses were burned on the lawns of local residents who were known to support the Project. Citizens had their jobs threatened and lost, and all of us were harassed and tormented by both the city and county officials. There were arrests and death threats. At one point during the summer, the threats were so intense that Mrs. Spinks began sitting up all night with her shotgun at the ready in case there was an attack upon the house.

The summer sped by and all of us who had come as volunteers had to decide whether we would go home and back to school or stay in Laurel to continue the work that we had begun. It was a difficult issue for all of us. I had spent many sleepless nights trying to decide what to do. When I looked into the eyes of my new friends in Laurel and thought of leaving them when our work was really just beginning, I felt terrible. I knew that the white reactionary forces were just waiting for the COFO volunteers to leave—especially the white ones—so that they could step up their reign of terror unfettered. While Mrs. Spinks, Mrs. Clayton, and all the others would not ask us to put our education on hold for their Movement, I could see in their eyes concern for a future without all the human and material resources that we had brought with us. I had begun to question much earlier how I could leave. I felt a real sense of commitment to this community and to this work that we had begun. Here again, I was torn to shreds inside.

And I really did have to make a choice. Staughton Lynd, who well knew my difficulties at Spelman and the probability that things would only get worse, had helped me to apply to transfer to Antioch University in Yellow Springs, Ohio. Mrs. Coretta Scott King, Dr. Martin Luther King's, wife, who was one of the first African American Antioch graduates, wrote a wonderful recommendation for me at Rev. Abernathy's request. In fact, she had invited me over to her home for an interview and to discuss my longing to have both a college education and the chance to be a civil rights activist. Antioch was well known for its radical academic environment and its support of student activism. I was accepted with a full scholarship. So here I was in Laurel, Mississippi, trying to decide whether I should avail myself of a full tuition and room and board scholarship to Antioch versus staying beyond the summer in Laurel to help keep the struggle going. With a heavy heart, I decided to stay in Laurel; I couldn't do otherwise. I told myself that it would just be for the fall '64 semester. I wrote to the Antioch administration, explained my dilemma, and asked for an extension. They readily granted it and said that they would see me in January of 1965.

Three of the summer volunteers decided to remain in Laurel: two of the white women volunteers, Marion Davidson from Pasadena, California, who was a Smith College graduate, and Linnel Barrett of Compton, California, and me. Ben Hartfield and Ulysses Everett, the two high schoolers from Hattiesburg, Mississippi, who had narrowly missed being blown up in the shotgun house, had been permanently expelled from school for their civil rights' activities. They joined our ranks. By fall, the five of us were the newly constituted Laurel Project. Somehow, I got the reputation of being an Amazon, which meant "She don't take no shit, especially off of men." Because of this, people in the Movement began to call the Laurel Project "The Amazon Project." Other than Ben and Ulysses, no other males would agree to join the Project. They did not want an "uppity" woman boss. Later, another Mississippi local, John Handy, joined the Project staff. The six of us would remain until the Project ended in December of 1965, some eighteen months after it began. There were more firebombings, more arrests, and many, many frightening events; some were life threatening. There were violent incidents and murders throughout Mississippi for months. After each brush with death, I thanked God for saving us all from what could have easily ended our days on this earth. We never again achieved the heights of the 1964 summer in our organizing activities, but we did deepen the foundation laid over that summer. And upon that foundation rested many of the dramatic changes which were to occur over the next ten years in Laurel and the rest of the state.

I stayed 18 months. When I left, I was about to break down. The breaker had been fifteen days in a makeshift jail in Jackson, Mississippi, in the heat of summer in 1965. Nearly 1000 of us had been at the statehouse on June 14, protesting the state's discriminatory voting laws. We were arrested and transported to the state fairgrounds in paddy wagons and garbage trucks. They locked us in livestock pens, treated us brutally, and we were there for more than two weeks. Reeling from that, I got back to Laurel and an outbreak of cross burnings. People were terrified, and many began to think the situation was intractable. I hung on into the winter, but Jim Foreman finally persuaded me to leave. "You won't do anybody any good if you fall apart," he told me. In December of 1965, I went to the New York SNCC office and worked there for some time, slowly healing. Part of my job was fundraising and part of it was working with student groups, telling my story of what it was like. Later, I went back to Atlanta to work on Julian Bond's election campaign, which became SNCC's first major urban project.

The "Amazon Project" was a title that I was proud of. It meant that I had "come through the fire" and was much the better for the experience. I had faced virulent racism and I had not backed down. I had proven that a woman could run a SNCC project in Mississippi and succeed. I had faced my fear of Mississippi and overcome that too. I had proven myself worthy of being called a SNCC Field Secretary and, more impressively, I had joined the ranks of those known as the Mississippi Field Staff, considered the "baddest organizers" in SNCC.

QUESTIONS FOR DISCUSSION

1. Gwendolyn Zoharah Simmons describes a sheltered childhood and a cruel awakening that made her aware of the depth of racism in the American South and her place as a black woman in that racist system. How was her childhood sheltered? What was the event that opened her eyes? How would you describe the attitudes and concerns of her family and neighbors: fearful or wise, experienced or conservative? Why would southern African Americans be opposed to the involvement of young black people in the Civil Rights Movement?

2. Why do you think Spelman College would hire professors to teach the truth about racism and yet prohibit its students from engaging in civil rights activity? How does the college's attitude reflect the perceived educational needs of black women in the South in the early 1960s?

3. Simmons makes a point of naming female role models and grass-roots women activists in Laurel, Mississippi. Did hearing about these people surprise you? What do these people contribute to the Civil Rights Movement? Why do you think they don't usually appear in the history books? What do they contribute to Simmons' awareness of the capabilities of women?

4. What is Simmons' attitude toward the position of women in SNCC? Why is Simmons proud that the Laurel project earns the name "Amazon Project?"

5. Simmons is frank about her fears of Mississippi and modest about her courage. How did the plan to "shield" black civil rights workers with the presence of white college kids work out in practice? After Chaney, Goodman, and Schwerner were killed, only a very few volunteers dropped out. If you had been a volunteer, would you have stayed or dropped out? Does your answer depend at all on whether you are black or white?

6. Do you think Freedom Summer was effective in the fight against racial discrimination in the South? What is your opinion of the effectiveness of the 1960s Civil Rights Movement overall? Do you see any race problems in the United States that remain to be solved?

DEEP IN THE HEART
Raymond Hubbard

From about 1942 or '43 to about 1951, our family—four boys and mother and father—lived in government housing ("the Projects") on the east side of town in San Antonio, Texas. America was still in a deep economic depression in the early '40s. Neither of my parents had a job with any reliable income. Mom, when she could find work, helped bring money into the household by doing domestic work and ironing clothes. Dad would occasionally find construction jobs, but for the most part he helped move or relocate people, usually within the city, and he hauled trash. Later on, after serving in WWII, he was able to buy a truck in which he continued moving and hauling to bring in income. During the summer months, he and my oldest brother and I would sell fruit—most of the time it was watermelons—off the back of his truck.

There were a couple of things I learned while helping sell watermelons. To cut their risks, customers would want you to "plug" the melon—that is, cut a triangular plug out of one of the melons to see if it was ripe or not. My dad, being the nice guy that he was, would accommodate them by plugging the melons. If, for whatever reason, the customer did not want the melon, we were stuck with it. Sometimes, the same customer who turned down the first plugged melon would ask my dad to plug another, and another, until they found one they liked. Needless to say, this was a bad business decision on my daddy's part. He was either stuck with melons that had been plugged or had to convince someone else to buy the plugged melon that the other person did not want, or reduce the selling price to get rid of the plugged melons. There were two things I learned from this experience. (1) Don't plug the melons. Let the customer, in this situation, share in the risk as Dad did when he bought the melons from his source. (2) People will gladly take advantage of you if you are willing to let them. Obviously, # 2 is a lifelong lesson.

Although we Hubbard kids were poor, we did not know we were. We didn't know what being poor meant, because our exposure to things outside of our immediate neighborhood was so limited. Our "project" consisted of concrete housing units of six families, three upstairs and three downstairs, each unit having its private entrance. The buildings covered over two full blocks for a total of about 200 families, all black, ranging from married adults with no kids to families with eight kids. Of course the housing unit's size for each family depended on the family's size, for the most part. Our unit was as large as they got, but, if I had to guess, I'd say our unit was less than 600 square feet; and there were many families much larger than ours.

During the 1940s, growing up in an all-black neighborhood was not something I gave much thought to. I just lived there. I don't think there were any differences in growing up in an all-black poor neighborhood than in any other poor ethnic neighborhood. We saw or heard about everything from missing bicycles to sex crimes, from illegal drugs to child abuse. Interestingly enough, I don't remember anyone's house being burglarized. Maybe that was because many women were not part of the workforce and stayed at home during day.

Most of the businesses in our neighborhood were black-owned. For example, the grocery store, cleaners, drug stores, restaurants, barber and beauty shops, and automobile repair shops were all black-owned. However, there were exceptions. The shoe repair shop was owned and operated by a Mexican-American; Chinese merchants owned the larger food stores, and a Jewish gentleman owned the used-items store. Of course, we referred to it as the "Junk Store" when we were away from the store.

This reminds me of other experiences. At about seven or so, I realized that there were all kinds of ways for a young boy to make money, especially during the war. Metals were needed to help make war materiel. We could gather scrap metals at various places around the area and redeem them for money; we could also redeem pop bottles, coat hangers, and a few other things. We took our collections to the used-items store, where the proprietor bought metals, iron, and tin in particular, for so much per pound. I don't recall exactly how much we were paid for metal items; however, I do remember that for coat hangers we were paid 1 cent per hanger. Occasionally we got as much as 2 cents per hanger. We would also go from door to door and ask the neighbors if they had any "spare bottles they did not need." Bottle money was used as seed money to (1) rent a lawn mower to mow neighbors' lawns, or (2) buy a stack of newspapers to sell in the local community. Usually we would try to save money from the previous week of selling papers in order to buy papers the next week. When we spent too much during the week, we went temporarily into the scrap metals and bottle businesses.

For the most part, we made our toys; that is, we would take an old roller skate and a 2 × 4 piece of lumber, and other scraps of lumber, and make a scooter that would rival anything being sold today in stores. Besides learning ingenuity, I remember other positives from my make-do childhood in the projects: one was the competitiveness I developed while playing sandlot games—there were no grassy ball fields in our neighborhood—and the other was the usefulness of this competitive spirit in becoming a "tougher" person, being able to deal with adverse situations. I'm not sure that these are not life experiences that many people had during those times; however, I do know my own kids did not have these toughening experiences.

During these early years, our parents were very committed to their religion. We were members of Blue Bonnet Church of God and Christ, a holiness church. Most of life's activities revolved around the church. A typical week usually meant that on Sunday we would get up early to attend Sunday School until around 10 or 11 a.m., followed by noon services which lasted usually until about 2:30 p.m. Then we would go home to have our family dinner, only to return to church in the late afternoon to attend youth services from about 5:30 to about 6 or 7. Then it was time for evening services that easily lasted until 10 at night. We also had Junior Choir rehearsal for about an hour or so one day a week in preparation for Sunday services. If there was a church revival during the week, of course, the Junior Choir had to attend. This was how my three brothers and I spent our time when we were not in school or playing with our friends.

I was the second of four boys born about 18 months apart. During the days we were growing up in public housing, the three oldest boys had numerous fistfights with each other; and today I still do not know why. Of course, we knew not to let our parents find out because that would mean additional punishment. In spite of all our confrontations, today my brothers and I are very close and get together whenever we can. Two of us live in California about 2 hours apart, the youngest lives in Maryland,

and our other brother still lives deep in the heart of Texas. My dad lived to the ripe old age of 89 and passed away in October 2000. My mom, as of the day I'm writing this, still lives in San Antonio at the age of 86, still drives her car, and, yes, is still very active in the church.

Although I never gave much thought to it when growing up, we never did many fun things together as a family and I attribute this to two things: (1) my parents' dedication to their religious beliefs (in the '40s and '50s, cards, dominoes, movies, dancing, etc. were seriously discouraged, though over the years this attitude softened); and (2) a lack of money in the household. Even for family picnics and other outings it takes a little money and fuel for your car, if you are lucky enough to have a car in the first place.

As I recall, our first car was very old—maybe from the 1920s—and little or no use. In order to start it, my dad had to hand-crank it. Those early cars did not have electric starters as cars do today. It was often an ordeal just to start the car. Later on in the 1940s we got another family car, a rusty, fading red 1940 or 1941 Chevrolet. I always wanted to have a newer, prettier car. However, after our dad got out of the service, he purchased an International truck that he used to earn a living. There were two occasions in which we got to ride in the bed of the truck: (1) to help dad in some work related travel (selling fruits, hauling trash, moving people to a new residence, etc.); and (2) going to and from church and participating in fundraising activities for the church, such as hayrides. We walked almost everywhere we went for personal errands: to the movies (if we were allowed to go!), to the grocery store, and downtown to pay bills. Yes, during these days, we paid bills in cash and we walked to the establishment to pay them. We only used city public transportation for very long trips.

My mom sent me and my brothers to nursery school until we were five years old. The nursery school was paid for by the state of Texas. The state support is a fact I never knew until recently. My mother remembers that we also received some form of public assistance as a family at some time. Given the state of the economy during this period, this was not surprising. At age five, I entered elementary school. Most of the students I became friends with were with me through high school. Our parents and our neighbors alike put a lot of emphasis on education. Many of them had very little formal education, but they were intelligent and full of common sense when it came to surviving, and they knew the value of education. Even though neither of my parents graduated from high school, which would have been quite an accomplishment for black Texas kids in their day, they always pushed us kids to finish high school. And we all did.

Until I finished high school, my life was school, church, and an occasional trip during the summer months. One summer, however, our parents did my brothers and me a great favor. They gave us a summer vacation by sending us to spend a few weeks with relatives in Reedville, about 50 miles outside San Antonio in the vicinity of San Marcos. This is where our parents had been born and raised, but, like many others, they had migrated to San Antonio to seek employment and a better standard of living. The problem was that the relatives, for the most part, were still earning their living by. . . . you guessed it, picking cotton. So my three brothers and I joined them picking cotton every day for five or six days a week. To date, that has to be the hardest work I have ever done—bar none.

A typical day of picking cotton entailed getting up very early in the morning to start while it was relatively cool (it could be 80 degrees at 8 in the morning). Also, the longer you were in the field, the more money you could make. Each person had his or her own cotton sack to fill because you got paid based on how much you picked, not on your hours. First, after getting a bag to fill you would enter one of the rows of cotton and begin to pick that row. The rows were so long that you could not see the end. The more experienced pickers would straddle a row and pick from three rows at a time. One could be very productive this way, with 1/3 the walking. My brothers and I were new to the heat and the pace of the work. We easily became dehydrated and, needless to say, we were not in the happiest mental state. Besides dehydration and extreme discomfort, there were occupational hazards that went with the job. Cotton has bolls, sort of like pods. The bolls open when the cotton is ripe for picking and the ends of the bolls are hard and sharp and stick into your fingers when you try to remove the cotton. A second hazard was rattlesnakes. Although none of us ever got bitten, the fear of having to watch for snakes and watch out for the bolls did not make for very productive days.

Almost equally demoralizing, when it was time to take your pickings up to be weighed, after having to drag the bag up and down the rows, you'd find out that you only had, at most, half as much cotton, weight-wise, as you thought you had. This was because, after having dragged that bag around for hours, you thought it was a lot heavier than it was. Of course, after several of these trips to weigh your bag before emptying it, it was very tempting to weigh the cotton down with a few rocks in your bag.

The days picking cotton were very long. Somehow, though, at the end of the day, if there was any daylight left, we kids would find the energy to play before having to turn in for the night. In this rural town, there were no streetlights, no electric lights. Kerosene lamps provided any lighting needed. Also, since you knew that there were no lights and the outhouse was located far behind the house, you tried to take care of these needs while it was still light enough to find your way there and back.

My summer picking cotton was a valuable motivation in my life. Although I have never asked my brothers the impact those summer experiences had on them, I'm sure it influenced them as well. It made me determined to find a better way of making a living, preferably by using my mind and not my back. This is not to say that using your back and hands is not an honorable way to make a living; just the opposite is true. But I wanted something different.

Another thing the summer experience did was to make me even more aware of the contrast in lifestyles of the haves and the have-nots. My relatives lacked the formal education and the skills to earn more money. If you are so busy trying to earn enough just to survive, then the connection between education and the ability to make more money is just not going to be in your mind and it wasn't, for those folks, in those days. Also, the opportunity was not there, and that was due to years of racial discrimination. There were few places, if any, where you could get enough social support to pull yourself up by your bootstraps in order to better yourself, especially not if you were black and poor and lived in rural Texas.

Age of Awareness

Off and on when I was little, my mother cleaned white folks' houses in order to help support the family. On one job, where she doubled as a nanny, she would sometimes take us to the house where she worked and we were able to see, firsthand, how the upper class lived. I don't remember feeling any resentment at all. Maybe it was because it was a new experience for us and we knew the environment was contributing to our livelihood.

Later on, maybe when I was about ten and I could venture out of my immediate neighborhood a little, I began to notice the differences in living standards between where we lived and how people on the "other side of the tracks" were living. By that I mean where the white people lived. The black doctors, dentists, college professors, and schoolteachers all lived in the same part of town as the rest of us, although they could afford to live in the "better" black neighborhoods. These "better" neighborhoods, with almost no exceptions, developed where whites had vacated because a colored family had moved in. Realtors played on this fear by finding someone who was willing to sell their house to a black, usually at an inflated price. Then watch the white flight begin! All the houses suddenly went on the market. Realtors made good commissions as long as it lasted and, of course, the last white people to sell out did not get such a good price. So, in most cases, panic would set in when the first black moved in. This sometimes led to bricks thrown through windows, cross burnings on lawns, anything to push the black family out.

Naturally, a little black kid, you began to wonder why things are the way they are. There was always some reminder that something was not adding up. On the other side of the tracks, the white folks seemed to be living much, much better. They always had pretty new cars, lived in nice homes. Their schools, from what we could see, were newer and better than our schools. Their churches were much more attractive, and so were their places to dine, compared to where most blacks ate, if you could afford to dine out in the first place. Also, when it came to jobs for the summer, white kids always got the better jobs and usually seemed to have them the first day following the close of school.

I got a real taste of envy when I got my first job. I answered an ad for a dishwasher at a restaurant and motel combination called The Westerner, located out on the Austin Highway. Sometimes I would double as a busboy, depending on how busy they were. If they were very busy, the restaurant would almost run out of dishes, so I had to help bus tables as soon as they became empty and then run back in the kitchen and get the dishes washed for those waiting on their meals.

Getting to my job required me to commute to work on the city bus that passed through what was at that time one of the more affluent parts of San Antonio. For all I know, it may still be today. I saw the beautiful homes, schools, churches, and restaurants up close. I was very impressed how the folks on the "other side of the tracks" could afford to live this lifestyle.

As I started observing things more closely it raised more questions. Why did I have to ride in the back of the city transit buses where all the diesel smoke always gave me a terrible headache? Why were there separate water fountains—one that read "Whites Only" and the other "Colored Only?" (In those days, we were "colored" and to call someone "black" were fighting words—even, or I should say especially, if you were called black by others of your race.) In this segregated situation you couldn't be sure who you were or where you fit in. Your self-esteem was so low you'd want to be anyone else except who you were. We had been brainwashed into believing that we, as a people, were not worthy of first-class citizenship. The signs of low self-esteem were everywhere. Some would try to straighten their hair or lighten their skins in order to be more white-like. Even blacks discriminated against other dark-skinned blacks; and to some degree, particularly in southern and eastern states, that kind of color discrimination still exists today.

I think this bias began because during the first part of the 20th century the "successful colored person" always had to be very light skinned. So the message we got was: in order to get ahead in life, you can't be too dark. There was a common saying when I was growing up: "If you are white, you are all right; if you are brown, you can hang around; if you are yellow you are mellow; but, if you are black stay back." Even some of our teachers in segregated public schools in San Antonio treated us based on the shade of our skin.

I became aware that not only were housing, schools, and sports events segregated, but so were the movies and even the field trips we took downtown to the Majesty Theater. I remembered going to the theater and sitting in the balcony with all of the other "colored kids." We were not allowed to sit downstairs. Also, there were the lunch counters that were not just "separate but equal," you could not eat there—period. The city had one amusement park called Playland Park. There was only one day a year that colored folks were allowed admission, the 19th of June or Juneteenth. For those who are not familiar with Juneteenth, here is how it came about. Abraham Lincoln's Emancipation Proclamation (January 1, 1863) was supposed to free all the slaves in the Confederate states. However, the slaves in Texas were not freed until months after the Civil War ended in April, 1865. So June 19, 1865, the day Union solders arrived in Galveston, Texas, became the day former slaves celebrated as their Independence Day. Down through the years this tradition of celebrating this day has taken on a life of its own, and Juneteenth is celebrated in many places.

So, on that one day of the year there were only colored attendees at Playland. Now, I don't know if whites were barred from attending on that day or if it was their personal choice not to attend, but in those days, in the South, whites would not be caught in a segregated setting with colored attendees. This kind of mixing, believe it or not, would have made the evening news and exposed those individuals to publicity that they dare not seek. It would have meant being ostracized by their race and, possibly, loss of their livelihoods.

It was also during my time of awakening and asking questions that I realized why a certain thing had happened to me when I was much younger. From my infancy, I had had a hernia and was in need of an operation but my family could not afford it. However, during WWII, my father, who had a wife and four kids to support, was drafted into the U.S. Army at the age of 33 or 34. That meant the whole family was entitled to medical care, which provided my parents the opportunity to get the hernia corrected.

I was admitted, around the age of 5, to Brooke Army Hospital at Fort Sam Houston, Texas, for corrective surgery for the hernia. There were three things that left a lasting impression on me: some of the nurses (all white women) were very mean spirited toward me and for what reason I did not know; the hospitalized white male soldiers were very friendly; and I appeared to be in a hospital in which I was the only kid. I later found out that, indeed, there were other children in the hospital. It was just that I did not have "the right paint job" to be admitted to the children's ward. But, it was ok for me to be admitted and share quarters with the white male soldiers, who could be pretty rowdy and foul-mouthed as they convalesced. The Army made sure that white children were protected from such exposure.

FIGURE 2.3   An African American man exits the "Colored" Waiting Room at the Trailways Bus Terminal in Jackson, Mississippi, in 1961. For more than 80 years, segregated public facilities had been standard in municipalities throughout the South. The facilities—drinking fountains, restrooms, theater seating, trains and buses and waiting rooms for public transportation, and all public schools—were supposed to be separate but equal. In practice, facilities for African Americans were always inferior. Among the first challenges to this "Jim Crow" segregation were boycotts, lunch-counter sit-ins, Freedom Rides (attempts to integrate interstate buses), and school integration campaigns.

Source: Corbis/Bettmann

I'm talking about these experiences to show how prevalent race prejudice was and how it could, if you let it, seep into every part of your life. As a child you tend to feel you are damaged goods—a situation over which you have no control. And you have no role models to emulate. For a young person whose dreams are all that he has, this can be devastating. During the '40s and early '50s, there were few African American heroes. People like Joe Louis, Jackie Robinson, Cab Calloway, and Jesse Owens were all in sports or entertainment; yet even many of the heroes ended up penniless and berated in the news for one reason or another.

So, as a child, I made these observations, but one thing that I could not under-stand in any logical, rational way was why? Why were things the way they were?

Why did we live where we lived? Why couldn't we or didn't we live in "nicer" neighborhoods? Why did we not own a good car? Why were the churches segregated if blacks and whites believed and worshipped the same God? Why didn't someone try to change this?

Fortunately, with youth comes a healthy dose of optimism. I tried to answer my own questions. It was not too much later that I became aware of "the trilogy"—really kind of a circle—that represented both hope and defeat. It went like this: Education is the key to it all, a better education means the potential for a better-paying job, and the job means you can live in better housing, which usually means a better neighborhood with better schools for your kids. But in order to get a good education, you needed money, and you needed a well paying job to get the money to get. . . . well, you know the song. Still, the only solution seemed to me to get an education somehow, some way. Short of doing something illegal or immoral to get money, education was the only real option.

However, I also knew that an education in itself was no sure ticket to the good life for a black man in America. I did not dwell on it, just accepted it. When you grow up in a totally segregated town from birth, you are making compromises and adjustments that you don't even know you are making. Sometimes you had to compromise standing up for your civil rights just in order to survive. For example, if you happened to be in an all-white community after dark, you had to be prepared to answer to the police why you were in that neighborhood. The only acceptable reason for your being there was that you worked close by and were on your way to or from work, or you had driven someone to work or were on your way to pick someone up from work. As far as the police were concerned, there were no other legitimate reasons for being there. If you were lucky and subservient enough, maybe you would get the opportunity to continue your journey. But, if you were a black male, it was not uncommon to be framed by the police, who would either plant illegal drugs on you or trump up some other charges against you and take you to jail. If they did not arrest you they would scare the hell out of you by hinting that you would want to avoid getting yourself in this situation again. No, this was not one or two bad cops—this was typical police behavior during this time. Although I never got arrested, I and everyone else knew that it was not too hard to be accused of some felony and have your young life ruined forever.

Somehow, in the back of the minds of whites was the fear that black males wanted to marry white women strictly because, somehow, everything was better because a woman was white. This paranoia about race mixing was what fueled most of the hatred and fears. There were many times, particularly in the South, when trumped-up charges in which a white woman and a black male were somehow involved in a sexual escapade were enough to get you jailed or killed without any proof. Sometimes, just the word of a white woman that you had raped her, looked at her, or whatever, was all it took. It happened much more than America would like to believe. I was not particularly afraid this would happen to me because I was not aware of it happening too often in the city where I lived. But everyone was aware of the possibility that it could happen.

Now even if you were a black kid fortunate enough to get a higher education, and you were branded a felon for some previous trumped-up charges, then all you accomplished would be for nothing, because you would never get the opportunity to get a better job, or the chance to live wherever you wanted. We knew that the same rules did not necessarily apply if you were white. Often, authorities or employers would look the other way and give you a chance.

I was not always preoccupied with the differences in opportunities for blacks vs. whites in the South. You cannot focus on the negatives because they will eat you alive. What you need to do is decide what it is that you do have control over, and what you can't control, you don't worry about. Once you take responsibility for yourself and what you can do, it takes away that victim mentality and gives you control. Easy? No, but it's essential that you get over it, in the overall scheme of things, regardless if you are white, black, Native American, or whatever.

Now, having said all of the above, did I continue to give these negative possibilities thought from time to time? Of course I did. But, like most experiences in life, how you react to situations depends on how you turn that unpleasant experience into something positive and grow from it.

After high school very few of the guys I knew went to college, probably because of a lack of funds and, too, I don't think most had been encouraged to seek a college education. I certainly feel my friends were capable of entering and finishing college. Mostly, we were encouraged during those days to join the military to learn a skill that would be useful later in life or go to a trade school to learn a trade to support ourselves. Two of my brothers went into the military service after high school.

Trade or the military: this was the primary thinking and planning for African American boys in the '40s and early '50s. Girls usually expected to get married before graduation or right out of high school and become homemakers. In practice, that didn't work out for most black women. In most black households there was so little money that, even after getting married, women had to do whatever work was available to help the family make ends meet. Oftentimes, they were the primary breadwinners in their families. Those who chose or had to work often found they could only get jobs as maids or waitresses. They were not welcomed in industry until WWII caused a shortage of men in the labor force. I remember that jobs in the Texas aerospace industry became available to women then, and for the first time they were paid comparatively decent salaries. However, after WWII, women were expected to go back to their "traditional roles" in the job market—waitress, maid, laundress—even though they had proven they could more than hold their own in the workplace.

Since education is the key to upward mobility, it must have been frustrating for black parents in the '40s and early '50s to encourage their children to aspire to a higher education after high school. This was because all around us we saw examples of people who had gotten higher education and were not able to better their standard of living. Discrimination was like a glass ceiling. It was easy to adopt a "what's the use?" attitude. By the mid-'50s, black high school graduates, boys and girls, started to think more about college. Exactly why it happened at this time I'm not sure, but it probably had something to do with the U.S. Supreme Court's emphasis on equality in education, which started with the Brown decision in 1954.

Separate but Equal Decision

As long as I could remember in the 1940s and the early 1950s, racial segregation in public schools was the norm throughout the South and in some other parts of the U.S. as well. The problem was that most "colored" schools were grossly inferior in their construction and in the quality of their education compared to their white counterparts. And I was painfully aware of the differences. In elementary school, we used the textbooks that the white schools had used the previous years. That's right. They got the new up-to-date textbooks and we got their used books. But, if separate but "equal" is the law of the land, in order to change things, timing and the right case had to be presented to change the law. Otherwise, depending on where you lived in the country, challenging this law could get you arrested or threatened with physical violence or, at a minimum, cause the loss of your livelihood.

So, in Topeka, Kansas, in 1951, a Mr. Oliver Brown, in conjunction with the NAACP, challenged the separate but equal law on behalf of his daughter. His case eventually ended up in the U.S. Supreme Court, which turned up the historic 1954 decision called *Brown v. Board of Education*, the beginning of the end for the separate but equal practice. Although Mr. Brown had filed in Kansas, by the time several pending lawsuits were combined, the Supreme Court's decision had widespread applications: i.e. it applied to all public schools.

This was only the beginning. It would soon become apparent that even a partial integration of schools was years away. This is because the will, political and otherwise, has to be there in order for any law to be enforced; and race issues in America were far from resolved. Of course, as a teenager, I was aware of the moral issues associated with racial discrimination, but maybe not of all the fears that white people had about what would happen if integration in public schools became the law of the land. Some whites' fears were about employment: a better-educated colored population would tend to provide more competition in the workplace, and hence, perhaps, fewer jobs for whites. Also, for years politicians used the threat of miscegenation—race mixing—particularly in southern states, as a means of scaring voters to keep things the way they were: segregated, with special privileges if you were white. I think as I matured and understood all the possible consequences of changing the law, I became aware of white people's fears.

The Brown decision in regard to schools did not change segregation practices in other areas of public life. Throughout the South, places such as restaurants, restrooms, swimming pools, and public parks continued to practice not just separate but equal policies, but, in many cases, refused services altogether to anyone who was not white. If a black family wanted to drive across several states to see relatives or take a vacation it required very coordinated planning. This is because, even during the '60s, the family could not stay in hotels or motels or eat a sit-down meal in most of the facilities en route to their destination. These facilities did not serve people of color. The choices you had were to drive straight through, that is stopping only to refuel, and continue your trip; or, you slept in your vehicle. For food, your choices were to carry enough with you until you reached your destination or locate a food establishment that was willing to serve you—to-go, at the rear door, of course.

After high school, I attempted to enroll in San Antonio Community College, which was a predominately all-white portion of the San Antonio junior college system. I was persuaded by the Superintendent to attend that "other" school, the traditionally black St. Phillip's College, which I did. It was just as well that I did. I got the close kind of faculty attention I needed, which prepared me for things to come.

After attending St. Philip's College for two years, I wanted to follow my friends to a senior college, Texas Southern University, about 200 highway miles away in Houston, Texas. However, I lacked money, and my parents pushed hard to discourage me from going to Houston without money or a job. So I dropped out. I needed a job quickly so that I could earn enough to at least get me to Houston for one semester. I saw a job opening in the local paper for a stockroom person. Because you had to receive stock from the deliverers, you needed the basic skills to add and multiply and reconcile the delivery list with the order. I was given a basic arithmetic test to determine if I could reconcile the deliveries. Needless to say, having had two years of college algebra and trigonometry, I aced the test. Then I almost did not get the job because of acing the test. The manager, who was from North or South Carolina (remember this was in 1957, in Texas), wanted to know who "helped" me with the test. I was shocked, on one hand, that he thought I could not have done it without someone helping me; on the other hand, I was pleased that maybe, just maybe, this would change his stereotypical attitude about black people and intelligence.

In about six months, just before the start of the spring semester, I gave my two-week notice. It became apparent that, over the months, I had won the manager over. He tried to talk me into staying. He offered me the opportunity to become the top stock person at the store with the potential of making $5000 a year. He said there was another colored stock boy in another branch of the store, and he was making $5000 per year. That, indeed, was a lot of money in those days. (I'm not sure he used "boy." Funny, though, I remember exactly the amount of dollars quoted.) He did not mention, as I noted at the age of 19, that there might be an opportunity to become a manager of one of the stores. I guess that was because, in his mind, a black manager was inconceivable. There are many signals one learns to read about people—racial biases and otherwise. Most people are not even aware that they send them out, in volumes.

Sit-in Movement

In January 1958, I left for Houston to attend school at Texas Southern University, which was one of America's historic black colleges. Education comes in all forms. By the spring of 1960, there were protests galore all over the U.S. Houston was no exception. Restaurants were still not serving us (I think we were still "colored" during this time) and young people all over the country were starting to protest the discrimination by politely "sitting in" at restaurants and lunch counters, even while being refused service. I had on several occasions the opportunity to participate in lunch counter sit-ins. The focus in Texas was on a chain of Woolworth-type stores named Weingarten's, whose restaurants did not have integrated facilities. I knew history was being made and I wanted, even in a small way, to be a part of it. While sitting at the counter, I don't mind admitting, I was frightened that violence would break out or maybe I'd get arrested. It's a very uncomfortable feeling not knowing what is going to happen next, and, in those days, the power structure did what they pleased. We had good reason to be scared.

Although I never got arrested for my participation, I felt good inside knowing that I was a party to these events. I don't think I have ever even mentioned this to my wife, kids, or grandkids. I did it for me, us, or whoever would benefit from my participation; not to do it to say one day "I was there."

Well, it did not take long for the sit-ins to reach the TV news and I remember my mom writing a letter to me, something on the order of "I hope you are studying and not striking" or "in the sit-ins." As remote as it seems today, if kids participated in behavior that, in the judgment of the white power structure, was anti-establishment, their parents could lose their jobs. And this was real. No paranoia here, it was simply a fact of southern life.

Even the president of the Texas Southern University, Dr. S.M. Nabrit, was under great pressure from the governor of Texas and the Texas legislature to quell the sit-ins. I remember Dr. Nabrit called a general assembly and, before a standing-room-only crowd, addressed the student body, telling us that powerful authorities had "requested" that he stop the public demonstrations. He told us that he and his wife could live comfortably the rest of their lives if he were asked to step down as president of the university. The way he said it made it clear that he had no intentions of asking us to stop demonstrating.

This decisive act by the university president went a long way in our lives, I'm sure. We saw him standing up for what he thought was right in spite of intense pressure from others in power. The message was "stand up for what you think is right," but, also, "be prepared to pay the price." I think who we are is portrayed by what we stand for and what price we are willing to pay.

I met my wife, Geneva (Gean), on a blind date in early 1964. She was living with an older sister at the time and had left Mississippi about a year and a half earlier. As everyone knows, Mississippi had a special reputation for violent acts against blacks. It seemed that whites there performed these acts with impunity. Therefore, civil rights demonstrations in Mississippi and other parts of the Deep South required real courage. Gean told me about several incidents, all pretty close to home for her and all of which played some part in the demise of flagrant discrimination in that part of the country.

One of Gean's brothers, Rudolph Coats, and an uncle were very active in civil rights in Mississippi. In Canton, Miss., during the late 1950s, Rudolph helped organize the boycotting of stores in an effort to break down various discriminatory practices in the town. Like many protesters, he was jailed on several occasions. In Belzoni, Miss., Gean's uncle, Gus Coats, along with a friend and others, was leading a campaign to register black voters. Gus Coats was shot for daring to attempt voter registration, but he survived and, after his recovery, left town for Chicago. His friend chose not to leave town and was eventually killed for his continued efforts to bring democracy to the town.

It's very difficult to describe the psyche of the average person of color during these times of changes in America. You always felt that you were being watched for the first misstep—something that would give the people in power a reason to put you back in your place. In my opinion, a healthy dose of paranoia was a necessary ingredient for surviving those times. To let your guard down even for a moment was potentially dangerous. Unfortunately, this paranoia could be unhealthy, too. Too much of "watch your step and don't make any waves" could carry over from generation to generation, prolonging a defeatist attitude.

Well, after taking jobs on campus as a part-time janitor and several other weekend jobs, I made it through school. I had enjoyed school enough to get a government loan in order to go to graduate school in mathematics. But I did run out of funds. I dropped out and was immediately drafted into the U.S. Army, since I had lost my student deferment. Although I did not know it at the time, joining the Army was part of the healing process for all of the negative programming I had received in my years growing up in Texas. To my surprise, looking back on it, the military added a lot of positives in my life and very few negatives.

This was my first time living in something other than a predominately all-black environment. I saw the way things were different from the South. For example, in the South you usually did not have to guess what you were dealing with in being denied opportunities or whatever. It was usually right up front for you to see. In this new environment, things were different. Acts of racial discrimination were done surreptitiously but were just as effective. That is, the biases had taken on a degree of sophistication that I had not noticed in my experiences before.

For example, given the opportunity for a job or a promotion, although I could clearly see I was better qualified than my white counterpart, and although an effort would be made to give the appearance that the selection process was unbiased, it was just window-dressing, just a façade. The white guy would get the job or promotion. That kind of experience just became another piece of the puzzle, helping me learn to deal with the real world.

After spending two years in the U.S. Army I went to California because, although it was the early 1960s, I knew that in order to find decent employment I would have to search in places other than Texas, search in a place where my performance and skills were what counted; not my paint job. This venture would be my first attempt to get into America's mainstream and compete with others for jobs, promotions, and all that goes with managing your career.

Although I was approaching 26 years old and had spent a couple of years in the military, I was quite naïve about life in general and the workforce in particular. I was lucky or blessed, however one would care to express it, in finding employment within two weeks of arriving in California. But, in all fairness, I had connections within the workforce; friends from college were already employed at what was called at that time North American Aviation, Inc., an aerospace company that had been awarded a piece of NASA's Apollo Manred Space Program. I was hired as a computer programmer and given the fancy title of Computing Engineer. I realized how fortunate I was to have taught myself a programming language while in the military service. This initial job was followed by other national high-profile projects at other companies. They were state-of-the-art technical jobs at that time.

I soon found out that even California was not the promised land I had anticipated. I had to learn to be a good judge of character without stereotyping; that is, judge each person based on his or her merits and deeds. During one sales meeting while I was working for IBM in Los Angeles a presenter made a point about how tradition played such an important part in the success of the company and how important tradition was. In the audience was one black employee who took offense at the use of the word "tradition." I knew exactly what the problem was because, having been raised in the South, I knew the word as a code for keeping things the way they were—the Confederate flag, racism, etc. In my opinion, that was not what the presenter intended. However, due to their different life experiences the word's connotation had different meanings for each person.

One of many things that really got us thinking well about ourselves was when we left being "colored" and became "black." A song by the Godfather of Soul— James Brown—came out in 1968 with the title "Say it Loud: I'm Black and I'm Proud." By singing it and saying it in our everyday conversation with each other, it helped change our opinion of ourselves, which is far more important than what someone else thinks of you. Having the benefit of this new attitude and elevated self-esteem affects all aspects of your life. Renewed self-confidence can be passed on to your kids and grandchildren. It's like magic in a bottle; it changes everything. Obviously, the song itself did not change attitudes—it was just a symbol—but it gave us the words. The political climate was changing as well. One could still get arrested or framed and sent to jail for trivial things. But now that there was hope that things could be changed, more people were willing to take the risks to help make things better. Trying for a better life did not seem to be in vain. And success feeds upon success.

In the mid-1960s, President Johnson helped pass the Voting Rights Act. The sit-ins, boycotts, etc. all added momentum to the changes going on in America. Fortunately, there were a lot of good people in America who were willing to lock arms with the civil rights protesters and go to jail if necessary. And Americans were able to see on the television news how police were treating demonstrators: setting vicious dogs on them, beating and kicking them, knocking them over, and hosing them down with fire hoses. It was real, it was on TV, and it raised America's moral conscience.

Even with increased hope, there was a perception by blacks in general that things were not changing fast enough to our satisfaction—and rightfully so. This frustration manifested itself as riots during the '60s. My family and I were living in Los Angeles during the 1965 riot. We lived in the curfew area. I was afraid for the family because I worked in Pasadena, at least an hour's drive from home, and could not get home quickly if there was a need to; and I was afraid for me because, having to drive through the curfew area, I was not sure if I was putting myself in harm's way either from the rioters or the police. There were other riots in other cities. Somehow, when you are going through these events, it's very difficult to know that positive change is also taking place.

Today, my wife and I have a very comfortable lifestyle here in southern California. Over the years, we have made various efforts to give back to "the community" in the inner cities of southern California as well to the community in which we currently live. Our primary aims are to continue to enjoy living and to make sure those in our immediate family get all the attention and encouragement they need to make a go in life. We hope we have been able to instill values in our children and that they will, in turn, pass those values down to our grandchildren.

In spite of all of the various experiences over the years and the ongoing negative (though subtle) messages about race that continue to permeate society in America, excuses are never reasons for not giving life your all. Parents need to try to minimize the heavy dosage of negativism that is potentially damaging to their children's self-esteem. And one does not have to be rich to make this work. Dedication, determination, and sacrifices will go a long way in getting the desired results for your children. After all, isn't this the ultimate measure of our success?

QUESTIONS FOR DISCUSSION

1. In what specific ways do both racism and poverty limit opportunities for Raymond Hubbard and his brothers when they are children in the 1940s and 1950s? How do they respond to the limitations of their lives in San Antonio? Are they resourceful? What actions do their parents take to support the children and give structure to their lives?

2. Why do Hubbard's parents send their sons to work in the cotton fields one summer? What lessons about race and society would an urban black child learn there? What was your response to Hubbard's description of living and working conditions in the rural South of the 1950s? Have you had any similar "boot camp" work experiences? What did you learn from them?

3. Hubbard says his childhood was relatively sheltered but that he slowly became aware of segregation and racial discrimination in the South of his youth. What are some of the places and occasions where Hubbard meets racism and discrimination? What else makes him realize that life is different for black and white people in the South? Hubbard attempts to describe the psychology of racism as it affects both black and white people. What are some aspects of the psychology of racism?

4. Hubbard briefly reviews civil rights legislation from the 1950–1960s. What is his view of the effect of legislative changes? How does he explain the slow pace of progress? What are his feelings about the Civil Rights Movement of the 1960s? Compare Hubbard's experiences with those of Gwendolyn Zoharah Simmons in the story, "Mama Told Me Not to Go." Hubbard seems to feel he must fight for a place in American life all on his own, whereas Simmons joins a movement to end discrimination. What do you think contributes to the differences between the two?

5. Hubbard tells us how he feels when faced with racial prejudice and discrimination. Assuming his experiences to be fairly typical of the time and place, what would you say contributes to the destruction of self-esteem that young black people experience in the 1940s and 1950s? To what political and cultural changes does Hubbard attribute a rebirth of self-esteem? Does Hubbard's story help you to understand what it felt like to be young and black in the South in this period?

6. Hubbard sees education as the key that unlocks all the doors in American life. But he remains cautious about asserting this because he is aware that doors for black people, even educated black people, may have double locks. What are some of the unique impediments to advancement for black men in the South in this period?

7. Why do Hubbard, his brothers, and so many of their friends choose the military? Why does Hubbard leave the South? Do you think his options for professional work would have been the same in the South of the early 1960s as they were in California? How would the southern racial climate be different now from the way it was in Hubbard's youth?

NOT MY MOTHER'S PATH

Sara M. Evans

Heather Booth gave me a ride to the meeting. I was new in town and had only the vaguest idea where we were going. I remember walking up dark stairs in a West Side Chicago apartment building. At least three locks clicked before the door opened and a young woman with horn-rimmed glasses[1] ushered us down the hall and into a living room furnished in non-descript second-hand furniture. Dull green is the color I remember, with the yellow glow of several floor lamps lighting the faces of a dozen or so young women sitting in a circle on couch, chairs, and floor. As I stepped from the dark hall into the room Sue Munaker, who had invited me, handed me a leaflet about a proposed action on abortion and a mimeographed article on sexism in the anti-draft movement. They were in the middle of a debate about how to initiate public action on the issue of abortion. Having never even thought about abortion, I gasped at their radicalism.

It was November 1967. Abortion was illegal. Married women could not get credit in their own names. Medical and law schools routinely imposed quotas as low as 2% on admissions of women students. Popular culture portrayed women as sex objects and housewives, little else. The women in this room, however, defined themselves as activists, their worldviews shaped by the Civil Rights Movement, by community organizing in the urban North and by campus activism against the war in Vietnam. Most of them had worked in Mississippi in 1964 and 1965, registering voters and teaching in Freedom Schools, under the constant threat of violence. I had never met a group of such brilliant, energetic, and sophisticated women. Their determination to mobilize women was driven in part by personal anger but even more by the realization that the movements to which they had committed their lives were blind when it came to women's subordination. After the discussion on abortion they moved on to analyze how the anti-draft movement framed women as passive supporters of men who refuse to be drafted, i.e., "girls say 'yes' to men who say 'no.' " Then they planned a women's workshop for an upcoming anti-war/draft resistance conference.

I was 23, going on 24, married for just a year and a half, and a recent migrant from North Carolina to Chicago. Like millions of American women, I was totally ripe for feminism. It was as if someone flicked a switch and all the connections already there suddenly lit up. Born and raised in South Carolina and Texas when racial segregation was still a way of life, I grew up knowing that my world was drastically immoral and unjust. My mother, who warned me that "they will tell you in school that slavery was not the cause of the Civil War, but they are wrong," subordinated her scientific passion for plants and animals to play the proper role of a minister's wife. I lived in the shadow of her anger and frustration as well as her gut-level

---

[1]This was Jo Freeman, veteran of the Berkeley Free Speech Movement in 1964 and the Mississippi Freedom Summer. Jo was then a freelance photographer and journalist, living like the rest of us on very little. She founded and edited the journal, *Voice of Women's Liberation,* and later became a major scholar of the movement. Her works include the classic essay "The Tyranny of Structurelessness" and *The Politics of Women's Liberation: A Case Study of an Emerging Movement and Its Relationship to the Policy Process* (1975), as well as *At Berkeley in the Sixties: The Education of an Activist* (2003).

egalitarianism. My deeply intellectual father, who could not imagine his own wife in any role but wife, delighted in my academic success and intellectual bent. I wanted to be like him, but in high school the only way I could fantasize my future was to imagine being the wife of (a doctor, a lawyer, a minister, a professor . . .).

When I went to Duke University in 1962, the burgeoning Civil Rights Movement offered an opportunity to act on values my parents had given me. My entry into activism wasn't instantaneous or without fear, but it was deeply liberating. Through the Methodist Student Center and the campus YWCA I stepped gingerly into service programs in black neighborhoods and gathered courage to jump into the protest movement. My first demonstration was a "pray-in" at the white First Baptist Church in Durham, NC, in the spring of 1963. Ushers stopped our integrated group on the church steps, refusing to let us join the service in progress. We stood outside in protest, reading the biblical passages assigned for the liturgy that day and forcing the parishioners to flow around us as they left. We looked at them. They averted their eyes.

That fall my history professor, Anne Firor Scott, said, "Read this book by Betty Friedan." From the moment I began to read *The Feminine Mystique* I knew that I did not have to follow my mother's path. I would not be angry and frustrated, I would do it all—marriage, family, and career. I went on to leadership in the campus YWCA, to union support work with nonacademic employees at the University, to a master's degree focused on African anti-colonial struggles, and to anti-war activism. Just before moving to Chicago, I spent the summer of 1967 as the North Carolina coordinator for Vietnam Summer, driving from town to town to set up groups that could sustain an ongoing anti-war presence. But I did not yet imagine that there needed to be a women's rights movement. Blissfully unaware of the obstacles most women face, I thought any woman could make a simple, individual decision to "do it all."

In Chicago, pride in my newly completed master's degree wilted as I discovered that the only jobs available to me were clerical. I ended up working as a secretary on the University of Chicago campus. Suddenly I was ready for feminism, to link my experience to broader patterns. The women in the West Side group brought up things I had never thought about—like abortion—and offered me opportunities to act on them. For example, I joined Heather Booth's underground abortion counseling service that linked incredibly desperate women (an amazing number of whom were married) to doctors willing to provide safe but illegal abortions.[2]

For the next seven months I went to every women's meeting I could find. I don't remember myself as a leader; I was a sponge, learning everything I could. I listened to Naomi Weisstein's horrific stories of graduate study in psychology at Harvard where they refused to let her work in a lab because "you might break something." Her rage, always leavened with wicked humor, and her amazing way with words left me in awe.

---

[2]Across the country, informal abortion counseling was a frequent part of women's liberation activism. The group in Chicago in subsequent years became increasingly structured, calling themselves "Jane," and ultimately began to provide the abortions themselves. See Laura Kaplan, *The Story of Jane: The Legendary Underground Feminist Abortion Service* (1996).

The group was not without tension. My closest friends, Heather Booth, Susan Munaker, Naomi Weisstein, Amy Kesselman, and Vivian Rothstein, had deep links to the student New Left. They knew (and some were married to) its leaders and had been closely involved with campus and community struggles sponsored by Students for a Democratic Society. They held a vision of a broad progressive movement that incorporated the struggles for civil rights, for working people, and for women. The thought of separating women from the rest of the left raised fears that women would fail to challenge the inequalities of race and class by seeking equality in a world otherwise unchanged. Other women, led by Jo Freeman, and perhaps (though I don't remember much about what she said) Leah Firestone, whose sister Shulamith had initiated a group in New York about the same time, were afire with conviction that women's rights represented the next big wave of activism and that our task was to create a women's movement without looking for approval to the rest of the left (and especially its male leadership). Women are half the population, Jo pointed out, and their struggle must incorporate all of those other issues.

The fact is, it wasn't up to us. Jo was right; women's liberation was explosive. We could light the fires but we could not control them. It took very little organizing skill to build the movement. Just call a meeting, go speak to a group (neighborhood, workplace, dorm room—anywhere), utter the words "women's liberation," and lights would go on. As one of the hubs of new left activism, Chicago was a key node for organizers across the country. I had been an activist in the South, relatively unaware of these national networks, so I was astonished by the visitors who showed up at our meetings from New York, Toronto, Washington, D.C., Berkeley, and Los Ageles, each with stories of newly forming groups and creative actions.

The big question was, what do we do now that we have identified the issue? How do we reach masses of women and mobilize them for change? Our activist arsenal included guerilla theater performances—women in a Laundromat loudly talk about their double duty and the fact that men assume little or no responsibility for household chores; women at a crowded subway stop or a construction site goose good-looking men and talk loudly about their shapely behinds. Other tactics included: subversive leafleting (stuff a leaflet detailing women's legal disabilities into every issue of *Ladies Home Journal* on a newsstand shelf); picketing employers known for their poor treatment of female employees; finding ways to combine underground abortion counseling with public actions to raise the issue; convening women's caucuses and workshops in community groups or conferences held on other issues; issuing mimeographed position papers that could be mailed across the country; and talking, talking, talking. For the moment it seemed that everything worked. The response was electric. As it dawned on us that a new movement was coming into being, we had a thrilling sense that we could, in fact, make history. Women's liberation provided a space where our yen to make the world a better place felt like it had no bounds. I returned to North Carolina in the summer of 1968 with missionary fervor to build the movement. Paula Goldsmid, who I had met in a Hyde Park women's group, also moved to N. Carolina that summer and we agreed to call a meeting once we were there.

When "Group 22" sputtered into being in Durham in 1968 it was the first women's liberation group in the state. We had no name at first, but, as new groups

FIGURE 2.4   Women's rights activists of all ages stand quietly on the steps of the U.S. Capitol building in Washington, D.C., wearing signs that demand equal rights. Demonstrations for women's equal rights—equal pay for equal work, equal access to higher education and the professions, equality of opportunity based upon reproductive freedom—characterized the activist heyday of the women's movement in the late 1960s and early 1970s. The demand for an Equal Rights Amendment to the Constitution gathered momentum in the 1970s, passed the House and Senate in 1972, but, ten years later, failed ratification as it did not win passage in the required 3/4 majority of the states.

Source: Corbis/Bettmann

quickly spun off or formed independently, labels like the "single women's group" or the "older women's group" seemed clumsy. So we decided to number ourselves—not hierarchically but randomly, choosing numbers that pleased us. Twenty-two was Paula's favorite number.

The early members of Group 22 were in many ways homogeneous, brought together through friendship, school, and work networks: white, college-educated, some of us veterans of civil rights and student movements. During 1968–69 many came to meetings only once or twice. Those of us who stayed found something there that changed our lives in ways we had been yearning for. Like my Chicago groups, and every other consciousness-raising (CR) group around the country, we searched for ways to ask, and answer, the "big questions." Why are women's choices so limited? How do they internalize a stereotyped view of themselves? Is it biology? How can we raise children without imposing limiting stereotypes? Is it possible to redefine relationships between women and men—marriage, sexuality, parenthood?

Some of these questions prompted action related to what quickly became a central theme of the group: how do we create new ways to raise children, for ourselves and for society? Three of us, who were pregnant when we met in the fall of 1968, planned and executed a childcare cooperative in which six parents, mothers and fathers alike, took turns caring for three infants between 8:30 and 5:30 every weekday. It only lasted one year, but that cooperative made it possible for me to begin graduate school. Several younger women split off to form their own CR group because they found our focus on childhood socialization not "relevant" to their immediate interests. But for Group 22, partly because most of us had, or were about to have, children and partly because we had a high concentration of sociologists, the ways that children "learn" to be female or male became the focus. In many other consciousness-raising groups, women talked about and thought through their own socializations. We, instead, were determined to find ways to do it differently and to make it possible to liberate children from the constraints of cultural prescription. Ultimately, the need to turn that concern into action led to the creation of Lollipop Power.

Before the first meeting, all of us had already embarked on life choices very different from those of our mothers' generation. Yet, more than twenty years later, participants remembered feeling that they were clueless about how to live those lives and how to deal with the internal and external criticism that seemed ubiquitous. Several described walking into their first Group 22 meeting and feeling "at home" immediately. They talked about relief at experiencing social support for their efforts to combine mothering with careers. Even more important, I suspect, was that their strong-minded, outspoken, quirky individualism received affirmation in Group 22 rather than placing them on the margins. Two women—both already mothers—immediately changed their married names back to their birth names. The rest of us did not, but we cheered Linda when she created quite a fuss by refusing to register at the Chapel Hill hospital where she had gone for surgery until they agreed to list her records under her own name rather than her husband's.

Group 22 was downright evangelical. Eager to spread the movement, we helped organize new groups, we published a newsletter so that multiplying groups could stay in touch, and we participated in regional gatherings and workshops. We wanted answers (imagining naively that they existed) and we plugged through a mixture of turgid sociological "sex role" literature and angry mimeographed pamphlets that circulated from group to group around the country. In the days before the Internet, the inexpensive mimeograph made it easy to disseminate ideas and essays. When we read communiqués from other women we joined a national conversation about just what this movement was, what kind of change it should advocate and possible strategies for getting there. Like our sisters across the country, we wanted to change things both in our own lives (renegotiating housework and childcare with male partners was a big item) and in the world. In true counterculture style, we looked for gaps where we could create "counter institutions."

In our discussions of early childhood socialization, we noticed that most media designed for children, from television to books, portrayed girls as passive observers while boys could be the heroic actors, the adventurers. No wonder girls grew up unable to imagine themselves actively changing the world or taking charge of their own lives. We toyed with the idea of creating a TV show but knew we did not have the resources or the skills to do that. Writing, however, was something we could do, so we named ourselves Lollipop Power and set out to write, edit, and publish our own books. The idea was that all of us would try our hands at writing books for young children and we would read and edit them collectively. I took the assignment seriously and sat down one morning during naptime at the childcare collective to write. Never before or since have I written a children's book, but that morning the words flowed. It was a simple story in which I up-ended gender expectations rather matter-of-factly. Here is what I wrote (expecting pictures to be added since I have no talent for that):

Once there was a girl named Jenny. She was five years old.

Jenny had a brother, Loren, who was three and a half, and he tried to go everywhere Jenny went.

But Jenny had a secret place under her mother's study desk.

It was a doorway into a magic land. In her magic land Jenny could climb trees that were taller than tall, and no grown-ups would tell her that she was going too high and must come down.

She could swing and play and eat candy that grew on the trees. And she was never too full, and she never would fall.

Best of all, she could ride a two-wheeled bicycle and even do tricks without having a wreck.

Whenever Jenny came back from her magic land, she wished and wished that she had a bike of her own.

One day . . . Jenny had a birthday. She was six years old. Her father, who was an especially good cook, made her a super-duper birthday cake to share with Loren and all her friends.

Then her parents said, "Come outside Jenny, we have a surprise for you."

And there was a beautiful, new two-wheeled bicycle, just like in Jenny's magic land.

Jenny jumped on and began to ride. At first she had a lot of wrecks, but soon she could go like the wind.

Her brother Loren cried because he could not go where she went anymore. Even on his tricycle, he was too slow.

Jenny remembered how sad she had felt when she could not do what she wanted to.

So she said to Loren, "I know a place where you can ride a two-wheel bicycle even when you aren't big enough. Whatever you wish for really hard, you can do there."

"It is right here in a secret place under Mommy's study desk." Can you guess what Jenny was talking about?

Of course, the magic land!

We all vividly remember that late night at the University of North Carolina campus YWCA when we, and many friends and supporters, printed, collated, and stapled *Jenny's Secret Place,* our first book. The next year we waged a campaign to force the University of North Carolina to provide day care for employees and students. When that failed (despite a "baby-in" in the administration building), we founded the Community School for People Under Six, still in operation after more than three decades. Lollipop Power, Inc., also persisted until the mid-1980s, long after most originators had moved away.

A look at the subjects of the first three Lollipop Power books[3] reveals that our feminism was not markedly different from that of any liberal feminist group, though most of us thought of ourselves as radicals.[4] In simple picture-book stories we scrambled sex roles—female heroines, moms who study, fathers who nurture—and conveyed a broad sense that girls (and boys) could do anything they chose. Paula Goldsmid wrote the second book, *Did You Ever,* which showed, in rhymed couplets, that whether you were girl or boy "you can do everything." Margrit Eichler (today a leading Canadian feminist and professor of sociology and women's studies at the University of Toronto) wrote *Martin's Father.* In it she described a single-parent family: a boy whose dad cooks, tucks him in bed, and takes him to day care. At first we had no prescriptions beyond our opposition to traditional sex roles.

We also knew that our experiences were not the same as those of all women, though we inevitably fell into language that presumed such commonality. Probably our greatest intolerance was towards the women we felt most judged by—those in earlier generations who, we believed, would accuse us of maternal failure for not choosing a life of total devotion to husband and children. Class difference was a major topic of discussion. We read Lee Rainwater and Mirra Komarovsky on the plight of poor and working class housewives and told each other stories from our own backgrounds (which were considerably more varied than our current statuses—ranging

---

[3]The first three books, all published in 1970, were Sara Evans Boyte, *Jenny's Secret Place;* Paula Goldsmid, *Did You Ever?* and Margrit Eichler, *Martin's Father.* At that time, Margrit was a graduate student in sociology. She and her husband were members of the childcare cooperative. Today, she is Professor of Sociology and Equity Studies in Education at the Ontario Institute for Studies in Education (OISE) at the University of Toronto and Director of the Institute for Women's Studies and Gender Studies (IWSGS) at the University of Toronto. Paula Goldsmid was at that time an assistant professor at the University of North Carolina School of Social Work. Subsequently, she was Associate Dean of Arts and Sciences (in charge of Women's Studies) and Associate Professor of Sociology and Anthropology at Oberlin College from 1974 to 1981, Dean of Faculty at Scripps College (Claremont, California) from 1981 to 1989, where she also taught gender role courses, and Director of the Center for Women and Gender Education at the University of California, Irvine, from 1990 to 2000, as well as Lecturer in Women's Studies during some of that time. Her current title is Graduate Fellowships/Medical Sciences Coordinator at Pomona College.

[4]Liberal feminists such as members of the National Organization for Women (NOW) and the National Women's Political Caucus worked for women's equality by lobbying for new laws and using the court system to sue for the enforcement of rights. Radicals argued that equality within the current system was not enough because genuine equality for women required cultural changes that could redefine our understandings of politics, family, work, and even "male" and "female."

from working class ethnic immigrant to professional middle class).[5] But the fact is there were many perspectives that we had few ways to imagine.[6] When the Community School for People Under Six opened its doors in the fall of 1970 in the basement of a black church, the issue of race also became increasingly salient, though, to be honest, in those Black Power years we were mostly waiting for black women to tell us what to think about them. Not surprisingly, by the second or third year, Lollipop Power stories had begun deliberately to challenge the stereotypes of race and class.

I did not stay in Lollipop Power beyond about 1972. At that point another off-shoot of the original Group 22 had begun to play a central role in my life. Many of us continued to struggle with the theoretical problem of women's subordination and tried to understand its relationship to oppressions of race and class. And we were still hard-pressed to figure out how we could go about mobilizing a massive move-ment of women that incorporated these concerns. We wanted to name a vision that included all these things, and we found that name: socialist-feminism.

My old friends in Chicago—Heather Booth, Vivian Rothstein, Naomi Weisstein, Amy Kesselman, and Day Piercy (who had gone to Chicago after some of our early meetings in N. Carolina)—were creating a thrilling new model for socialist-feminist organizing. Their position paper, which we read and debated over and over, made a compelling claim for the importance of a broadly inclusive vision which they then linked to a series of highly practical organizing strategies. Drawing on the thinking of Italian communist Antonio Gramsci and the organizing practices of Saul Alinsky, they made a strong case for the importance of small victories that could, incremen-tally, give people a greater sense of power and possibility. This was an apocalyptic time when too many people around us, in the name of socialism, were advocating violence, demanding total change and disdaining incremental reform. The Chicago Women's Liberation Union was a huge breath of fresh air. It solved the old dilemma of the women's movement's relationship to the left by saying that our project was centrally important to the broader hope for egalitarian social change and at the same time it was up to women to organize other women.

In Durham/Chapel Hill we formed a socialist-feminist group that named itself after Charlotte Perkins Gilman—probably because I was then in graduate school studying women's history and had been thrilled to discover this socialist-feminist foremother whose writings from the 1890s were still amazingly compelling. Gilman had pointed out, for example, that women's energies are wasted when each woman

---

[5]Lee Rainwater, Richard P. Coleman, and Gerald Handel, *Workingman's Wife: Her Personality, World and Life Style* (1959); Mirra Komarovsky, "Cultural Contradictions and Sex Roles," *American Journal of Sociology* (November 1946); Komarovsky, *Blue-Collar Marriage* (1964); and Komarovsky, *Women in the Modern World: Their Education and Their Dilemmas* (1953).

[6]My own work in 1968 and 1969 as a community organizer in the poor white community of Durham, North Carolina, was a constant reminder of such differences. My pregnancy was an immediate link to the women I worked with but they were astounded that this was my first child at the age of 25, as some of them were already grandmothers in their mid-30s. Their complicated familial and work histories involved work in textile and tobacco factories, welfare, and frequent household moves in response to divorce and changing economics.

performs all the household chores alone. Women could be liberated to pursue meaningful professions if much of that work were collectivized and professionalized: central kitchens, for example, rather than one in every home, and professionalized (well-paid) childcare.

We decided to become an all-woman chapter of the New American Movement, a newly formed national organization in which several of us were deeply involved, as were the men in our lives. The Gilman chapter, we hoped, would resolve for us that old debate about the relationship between the women's movement and the left. The earlier worry that the women's movement might be co-opted by the left carried little weight in the aftermath of a series of spectacularly self-destructive moves within the student movement as one organization after another exploded, dissolved, or caved in to manipulation by small sectarian groups. The left needed a new center, and no one questioned any longer that feminism would have to be fundamental. All the men we knew in the movement were deeply envious of our energy, solidarity, and sisterhood. Many of them had formed men's groups to learn how to offer each other support and to engage in their own version of "consciousness-raising" discussion about the cultural definitions of manhood.[7]

The Gilman chapter sent out a call to convene a socialist-feminist conference in Durham over Thanksgiving weekend, 1972. Our male allies agreed to provide childcare, and we prepared to house and feed attendees in the Presbyterian and Baptist Student Center buildings at Duke where we held our meetings. Over 200 women showed up, sleeping bags in hand. For three days we held workshops, watched films, ate peanut butter, granola, and vegetarian soup, and debated the links between women's oppression, the working class, and anti-colonial revolutions. And then we danced. It was a heady slumber party.

Truth be told, the Gilman chapter never did figure out how to organize in the ways we wanted to, largely because most of us were graduate students whose creative energies were absorbed in learning, researching, and writing. Our real contributions were ahead, in the intellectual work we were preparing to do, but the intense debates we had were a part of that preparation. We ran a series of "free schools" and cooperated with others in support work for unions and for day care. We also played together. For several years running, we rented a beach cabin and piled into an old Volkswagen bus for a weekend of sun, good food, and play.

One of the great things about involvement in women's liberation outside the large metropolitan areas was that we managed to avoid the worst of the splits for many years. As socialist-feminists we insisted we were fully a part of the separate movement and also deeply linked to class- and race-based movements for social justice. In our Gilman group meetings, we wrestled endlessly with the dynamics of social change. How could we make the world better? How could it be changed fundamentally?

---

[7]Many of the men in that group wrote essays reflecting some of the kinds of conversations that went on there. See Peter Filene (ed.), *Men in the Middle: Coping with the Problems of Work and Family in the Lives of Middle-Aged Men* (1981).

While we talked about macro systems, we also tried to find ways to live out our values in everyday life. What does freedom mean for women? Freedom to work? Freedom to choose motherhood or to reject it? Freedom from marriage? We really had no idea what truly free relationships would be like, and we seriously entertained the possibility that marriage was an inherently oppressive institution given its long patriarchal history. And what about monogamy? We were not sure. Some wanted to take the world in which we had been raised and turn it upside down, challenging every norm.

In these discussions, I was always just a bit on the margins. Once Group 22 evolved into other formats, and many of the original women with children had moved away, I found myself in a movement dominated by younger women who had yet to decide whether they would have children or not. I recall standing up at a regional conference in Atlanta in February 1969 during a discussion about the unavailability of birth control on college campuses. Waxing indignant, I said that at Duke University, women students could not get a prescription for birth control pills even if they were married. As the room erupted in laughter, I realized that my advanced state of pregnancy could be seen as an illustration of my point.

I never felt judged for my choices, though as a monogamous married mother, I was in fact a bit of a bystander to the sexual revolution that swirled around me. We talked about everything—orgasms, sexual preference, monogamy—and many experimented. Several members of the group established collective households in the hope that communal living might offer an alternative to the privatized households we had always known. Some of those collective households lasted a year or two.

My own personal struggle had to do with trying to live an egalitarian marriage, something for which neither my husband nor I had been trained. As soon as we married, we started the long process of figuring out how to share housework. First, I cooked and he cleaned the kitchen. I liked that, but he pointed out that I had all the creativity. Then we took turns, and whoever cooked did not have to clean. Problem: I clean as I cook. He dirtied every pot in the kitchen. We began to switch by week, all on or all off. Other household tasks, we realized, were far more visible to me than to him. So we made lists, divided the tasks, and posted them on the refrigerator. Whoever did the task did it their way to their standard of what is clean or tidy. When our son Craig came along, we tried hard to divide the childcare equally, though it was quickly clear that I was already socialized to take pleasure in caring for a newborn while my husband had to learn. Our weekly cooking schedule was perfect, as whoever was not the cook of the week would be in charge of bedtime, bath, stories, and songs. I think many of the younger women looked to us as models. I was lucky that Craig was a fabulous sleeper. He went with me to meetings night after night, sleeping anywhere and everywhere—in the portable crib I carried along in the first years, on beds or even pillows in the corner of the room.

During these years I began to take myself seriously as a historian, changing my name in 1974 back to the name I received at birth, both because I had always wanted to do that from the moment I realized that could be a choice and also because I wanted my scholarship to stand on its own rather than be seen as an extension of my husband's writing. I knew too many stories of academic couples in which that had happened. My dissertation research focused on the story of the emergence of women's liberation out of the Civil Rights and New Left movements. In the process of doing that research I followed networks I had learned about in Chicago to interview many of the members of the West Side Group as well as key activists in New York, Washington, and California. Everywhere I went, people housed and fed me and loaned me their cars, whether they knew me or not. In several weeks of travel in 1973 and 1974, I experienced again the fact that I was part of a national movement, even though it was changing rapidly. Some of the early activists from the Sixties were already burned out and had turned from group involvement to a focus on the personal. Some were damaged because of the fierceness with which leaders were accused of elitism and the intensity of battles over which version of feminism was correct. Some had pulled into an extreme form of separatism, trying to avoid any contact with men or even other women whose views were different. And some had adopted highly authoritarian versions of Marxist dogma, leaving the women's movement altogether to participate in small, sectarian radical groups, some of which advocated violence.

Only as a historian was I able later to reconstruct some of the broader social forces that were tearing us apart and feeding the vicious backlash against our movement. The mid-1970s were a hard time: a contracting economy began to destroy high paying blue collar jobs in massive numbers while the new right made cultural issues like abortion and affirmative action central to a politics that targeted women and minorities as scapegoats. I left North Carolina in 1976 to teach women's history at the University of Minnesota where I have been ever since.

In 1990, Group 22 held a reunion. The experience of reconnection was so powerful that we have continued to meet for a weekend every year or two since then. At our second reunion, at a small lake cottage in northern Ontario, we talked about the ways that Group 22 left a mark on the lives of all of its members. One founded the women's caucus of the American Statistical Association and co-founded the women's caucus of the American Public Health Association; another is a leading feminist scholar and activist in Canada; a third went on to direct the women's studies program at Oberlin and moved from there into collegiate administration; a fourth built her career founding and running day care centers. A quarter century later, several found little direct linkage between their feminism and their current work lives except that they treasured their own independence and believed in their right to meaningful work. Some later came out as lesbians (a topic Group 22 never got around to discussing, though its successor groups certainly did).

We reflected on our early commitment to raising a new, and different, generation, though we knew at the time that we were doing this without a compass. Sharing our stories two decades later, we acknowledged that we have all been humbled by the overwhelming power of culture. "Did your daughters get into Barbies? Did your sons play with guns?" we asked each other sheepishly. How did you get through the teen years? The answers were all over the map. It isn't that we thought we'd be doing this in a vacuum but that we simply had no inkling about how to think. Frankly, the stories we told were not so different from anybody else's kids raised with a strong emphasis on tolerance and respect for others. With a sobered recognition of the role of sheer good luck, we took pleasure in describing the good people our kids have become and comfort in sharing the hard bumps along the way.

At least one member of Group 22 spoke with some bitterness about the impact of feminism on her life. She plunged into professional school, convinced that she could "do anything," but the professional path she tried did not work out successfully. She finds herself now doing work that she does not love and finding pleasure in the details of private life. Our naive search for perfection became, for her, not only "you can" but "you should" and set a standard of expectation that was, finally, undermining. But, for most, the legacy of this group, as of thousands of others, is one of greater freedom and new possibility.

For me, the experience in Chicago followed by Group 22 and its successors, Lollipop Power and the Gilman group, became a springboard into my career as a historian. The questions raised in women's groups about the origins of female subordination, and the links between women's liberation and other social movements around labor, peace, and civil rights, led me to challenge the knowledge I had received as an undergraduate history major and a graduate student in political science. I recalled the single class in which women were acknowledged to have some historical agency: Anne Firor Scott drew on her research on southern white women to tell us about the importance of women in Progressive Era politics and their utter invisibility in existing historical accounts. Though at the time I had been too busy fighting other battles to think much about the implications, several years later that experience endowed me with an unshakeable belief that we could recover the stories of women in the past. Though there were no women teaching American history at the University of North Carolina in 1969 and no courses on women's history, several other students arrived with similar questions and we discovered that self-education was entirely possible simply by writing papers on women in connection with virtually any course. Little did we know that we were part of a cohort of several thousand across the country, collectively inventing women's history as a major field of historical inquiry and women's studies as a discipline. For more than three decades it has been my privilege to teach and write in this field, and my most recent work on the history of second wave feminism is dedicated to communicating to younger women the stories on which their struggles will build.

QUESTIONS FOR DISCUSSION

1. Sara Evans presents the status quo for women in 1967, the point when she first encountered the women's liberation movement: "Abortion was illegal. Married women could not get credit in their own names. Medical and law schools routinely imposed quotas as low as 2% on admissions of women students. Popular culture portrayed women as sex objects and housewives." Can you name other areas in which women lacked equality in the 1960s? What do you think has changed for women since then? What has not changed? What issues still remain controversial?

2. How does Evans view her mother's life? What does she initially expect will be her own future? What experiences are particularly important to her realization that her life need

not be limited to the roles of wife and mother—that she can aspire to a career as well? What is the effect of her education and her work in the Civil Rights Movement?

3. Evans describes her activities in the early women's liberation movement. Why does she think the movement was initially such a big success? How would you describe the feeling activist women had in those early days?

4. Evans and her women colleagues in North Carolina established the Lollipop Power group because they wanted to create a "counter-institution" for child raising, or "child socialization." What aspects of child raising were they hoping to change? What were some of their successes? Think of the books you encountered as a small child. How do these books represent the capabilities and personalities of little girls and little boys? What has changed?

5. Women's liberationists had many concerns about the subordination of women and the institution of marriage in American society. Evans describes her own efforts to live in an egalitarian marriage. Do couples still struggle with some of the work-sharing issues Evans faced? Think about the meaning of housework in our society. Is it valued? Respected? Why or why not? Why do you think housework remains a difficult issue for men and women?

6. What sources of controversy within the women's movement does Evans describe? Why did women's liberationists become embroiled in controversy with people in the anti-war movement? Evans states she became a socialist-feminist. What does she mean by that? What larger problems did Evans and others hope socialist-feminism would solve?

7. Sara Evans is one of several women scholars who developed the field of American women's history. How does she explain the need for such a field? Compare Evans' story with those by Gwendolyn Zoharah Simmons and Yolanda Retter. Each of these authors is discussing involvement in a historically important movement. How are the three stories different in tone and approach?

STUDENTS OF STONEWALL
Toby Marotta

Cautiousness kept me from giving in to the Sixties with ease. I had to take this decade's measure intellectually. I had to size up its effects on people I respected. Most of all, I had to come to terms with myself. Thanks to the impressive walls of Harvard College, I remained sheltered from what precocious leaders of my generation called "the real world" until I graduated in 1967. Civil rights and anti-war activity on campus did the most to alert me to the currents that were roiling around the country.

JFK's New Frontier and LBJ's Great Society had developed and popularized a number of models for solving social problems. I wanted to be part of the constructive agenda, so I followed college by enrolling in the Kennedy School of Government, also at Harvard. Midway through my first year, Uncle Sam's imposition of a military draft forced me to make a choice between what activists posed as the war in Vietnam vs. the war at home. The latter referred to public service that would improve our country. Choosing to fight in the war at home made me draft exempt. I spent a year teaching in an all-black junior high school in North Philadelphia, then moved to a poor white high school in Charlestown, Massachusetts—close to Harvard so that, when the time came, I could pick up where I had left off with my graduate work.

Yet the major theater of my education remained the real world. And the war that upset me most was closer to home than anyone knew.

"Batman & Robin"

It was 1970. The charming academy I had entered in the fall of 1963 was transformed. Gone was the gentility that for more than three centuries had encouraged Harvard students to look and to act like their cousins at Oxford and Cambridge in England. In place of coats and ties, any get-up was now acceptable in the undergraduate dining halls. Also abandoned were the limited afternoon hours in which "gentlemen" were permitted to entertain "ladies" in their "suites." Having swept over Harvard's walls, red brick and otherwise, those waves of change—dubbed the counterculture, the New Left, the sexual revolution, and the Movement—were now trying to democratize every aspect of life on campus.

The one realm that remained off limits for either discussion or study was sexuality. This taboo was impressed on one and all by the fact that Harvard's main library, the Widener, kept all of its materials pertaining to sex, including *Playboy* magazine, in a locked room devoted to the "X" category of its immense catalog. To sign something out, one had to convince a librarian that one's purposes were "legitimate." Since there were neither college courses nor on-campus groups concerned with sex-related issues, it wasn't clear what "legitimate" use could apply to, but the implication was clear. Intimate matters were to be dealt with in the proper British way, meaning privately. For those lacking confidence—or confidantes—there were therapists at the University Health Service. No matter that any kind of mental health record was the kiss of death for a career in public service.

Years earlier, while attending nearby Medford High School, I had sustained my success as a student leader by concealing my homosexual bond with an older student behind a heterosexual male façade of flirting, fawning, and religiously correct dating. In the spring of my junior year, after an admissions officer from Harvard College had come to interview me for early consideration, my assigned guidance counselor made his own prejudices clear: "You don't want to go to Harvard. It's full of queers. Try Holy Cross."

I still chose Harvard. Throughout my undergraduate years I spent a great deal of time and energy squelching my natural inclination to be intimate with others of my gender. It was easy to maintain my façade with fellow students but difficult to remain opaque in the presence of perceptive administrators. I resorted to the most telltale shield of all: objecting that any older "bachelor" who seemed too eager for student company was "queer."

Rusty Kothavala was Senior Tutor of Lowell House when I met him at the start of my junior year there. His real name was Rustam. His background and persona were as exotic as mine were square, and so were his looks. He was a Parsi from India, and he had inherited the idealism and integrity of the mythological Persian hero whose name he shared. In Rusty's case, proper British schooling had produced a dashing young frontiersman. Rusty was the toast of what newly cosmopolitan Harvard had to offer—something of a cross between James Bond and Zorba the Greek. While wearing several influential administrative hats, he taught a popular and pioneering natural sciences course that opened political eyes by extrapolating from geology to ecology. At the age of 35, he was awarded tenure.

By that time I was a 25-year-old graduate student, politicized by my experiences as an inner-city teacher and ready to tackle every troubling aspect of "the real world." As Rusty and I grew close, I became privy to the relevant local context, which was called the "gay" scene. It was Rusty who let me know that the sophisticated word for men who loved men wasn't "queer."

Long gone were the early-twentieth-century years in which Harvard's administration and its unofficial but powerful secret "court" had run homosexual students out of Cambridge. The days when disapproving deans could ostracize faculty members or fire administrators for being indiscreet about their homosexuality were over. By the late 1960s the popularization of psychology had ushered in the view that sexual matters raised issues of mental health and behavior rather than "morality." Yet the prevailing ethos about sexuality remained Victorian, often summed up with that era's adage about doing whatever you want so long as you don't frighten the horses: engage as you must and will, but in private. It was an early version of "Don't ask, don't tell."

Not once during my years as an undergraduate and graduate student did I encounter a Harvard man who went about life as a gay person with openness and pride. The idea of a same-sex couple operating as such was inconceivable. If there were such couples, they kept very quiet about it.

For want of alternatives or models, I projected popular American mythology onto my bond with Rusty to envision a partnership suited to my evolving sense of self and its politics. We were engaged in a number of campus issues. As allies in intramural skirmishes over tie-less dining, women in the dorms, and humanistic education, it was easy for us to work as student leader and leading teacher. When our causes became more consequential—Harvard's complicity in an escalating war in Southeast Asia and its unlimited encouragement of planet-despoiling development and consumerism—I was content to follow Rusty's lead. Once we resolved to give life a try as firebrand partners, however, I turned to comic book characters for respectable icons, fancying myself an American Robin for this intercontinental Batman.

Big were the dreams of students inspired by dream-spinning liberal leaders like Robert Kennedy and Martin Luther King, Jr. Batman's beat was the world. Robin would tackle the metropolis. For a start I would carry our fight for truth, justice, and daylight to the one turf that, for reasons I still couldn't fathom, our powerful University, supposed to be boundless in its pursuit of *veritas* (truth), seemed too cowed to address openly—the world of homosexuality.

Sizing Up Façades

Small signs on campus hinted that not all going on behind the impressive red brick facades was as healthy or as moral as the prevailing ethos presumed. As a resident proctor, and later as a Lowell House tutor, I counseled more than one freshman who complained about being solicited by a fellow student or seduced by a befriended benefactor. The administrators I turned to for advice in helping these students portrayed such incidents as manifestations of identity crises that were being worked out in private. But no one could offer a satisfactory explanation for the crude graffiti, or the blatant invitations and actual sexual encounters that took place in certain public men's rooms on campus, despite all manner of physical barriers and police surveillance. If these wily dimensions of male sexuality represented legitimate concerns in situational ethics and psychology, then why couldn't they be talked about openly?

I was also encountering more substantial student problems that seemed to be rooted in sexuality. They began with long-term consultations with psychiatrists, surprising relationship breakups, and sudden decisions to leave school, and ranged to hushed-up misdemeanors and shocking suicides. When I began hearing of similar problems among seemingly happy and respectable alumni I had even more questions about what was really going on behind the imposing walls of silence and conventionality.

During my two years as a public school teacher I had become accustomed to hearing about sex-related issues in the much less advantaged and far less protected precincts of the real world. But Harvard remained silent on such issues. True, the university had begun to respond to complaints that it lacked "social conscience" about the war in Vietnam and urban and environmental problems, and it had promised to share "relevant" knowledge with the community. But nothing was forthcoming about the sensitive subject of sexuality. Just the opposite, in fact: denial, resistance, dismissal.

In the fall of 1969, a student at M.I.T., following the lead of gay students at Columbia, NYU, and Cornell, organized a Boston chapter of the Student Homophile

League. His dean refused to let this fledgling SHL meet on university premises. Come spring of 1970, partly to lend support to this homeless gay group, John Boswell, then completing his Harvard Ph.D. in history, took the lead in organizing a Graduate Student Homophile Association at Harvard. Its membership remained miniscule, and Boswell, later to write the scholarly classics *Christianity, Social Tolerance, and Homosexuality* and *Same-Sex Unions in Premodern Europe,* left to teach at Yale.

During the following academic year, the Harvard-Radcliffe Gay Students Association, a first for local undergraduates, advertised its arrival in the "Harvard Crimson." Eugene Hightower, an African-American freshman from Berkeley, had mustered the required ten enrolled students and two faculty advisors necessary to officially charter this group. Both of the faculty advisors were heterosexual.

By this point I had moved on to write my doctoral dissertation in government and education under the supervision of a coterie of conservative professors in the Graduate School of Arts and Sciences. Once I announced that I was changing the topic of my dissertation from the politics of school desegregation to the politics of homosexuality, I was left to my own (de)vices. My official adviser met his obligations and was sympathetic, but warned that I was committing professional suicide because "gay lib" was a fad.

(Perhaps his view was widely shared. Certainly no former colleagues or professors from the university have ever turned to me for professional expertise about homosexuality, not even after AIDS arrived in America in 1981. By now, of course, the price of insistent silence and persisting ignorance has become undeniable suffering, enormous financial expenditure, uninformed political controversy, and unprecedented loss of life to a global pandemic.)

Slipping Over the Walls

In 1973, for lack of attention and support, the Homophile Union of Boston (HUB), then the oldest gay group in town, was folding. The organization's files were about to be dumped, but the retiring office manager urged me to salvage and save them for my research, which I did. I also needed to interview people involved in the politics of homosexuality, so I headed for the nearest center of action: New York City.

Still Harvard-style discreet about my relationship with Rusty and the evolution in my own personal life, I spent the weekend as a guest in the East Side home of a friend from college. He and his parents were traditional Democrats. On Monday morning, I took off by myself, walking across midtown, heading down to Greenwich Village. From HUB files I knew that this neighborhood of many cultural and political firsts had become home to the first gay bookstore in the world. Located at 15 Christopher Street, it turned out, poetically, to be directly across from the entrance to a short curving way named Gay Street.

The bookstore's façade was as welcoming as its location. Above a low rise of stairs stood a door that was a checkerboard of little wood-framed windows. You could see right in through the glass. To the left of this door hung a lantern-style light above an old-fashioned wooden sign. The name was embossed in gold paint on a white background: Oscar Wilde Memorial Bookshop.

Without knowing quite why, I was trembling. One at a time I took the stairs. Upon reaching the landing I looked in. It was a tiny room, maybe 15 feet wide and 20 feet long, and its three interior walls were lined with floor-to-ceiling shelves full of books. There was also a low table covered with piles of glossy bound volumes and magazines in the middle of the floor. The sight of this many books about homosexuality made my jaw drop.

Directly inside the door stood a checkout counter. I could see that its top half doubled as a glassed-in display case. But there was no one behind the counter, and not another soul visible in the store. I guessed that the curtained doorway in the far corner of the back wall led to a workroom and the proprietor. Without making a sound, I pushed in the door, stepped inside, and then carefully pulled the door back into place. I would demonstrate that I was a respectful newcomer by waiting at the counter.

The floor of the display case was bright with clusters of pin-on buttons that bore gay political slogans—something else that I had never seen before. Zeroing in on one of them sent a shiver down my spine. It was a pin the size of a half dollar. Its pinkish-purplish background bore a white graffiti-scrawl in the shape of a heart. Inside, also etched in white, lay the names of my comic-book heroes entwined—"Batman & Robin."

Class of '67

With a flap that sounded like a trailing cape, a short young man with a crew cut plunged through the rear curtain. He was wearing well-scuffed chinos and a white T-shirt streaked with dust. In his arms was still another stack of books. After dropping them onto the table, he whirled around, slipped behind the counter, and sized me up for the first time.

"Need help?" His voice was nasal, his look direct, but expressionless—all business. I had no idea how old he was, but he looked and acted like an off-duty teacher.

"I'm visiting from Boston. Is the 'Batman' button something new?"

"Old. See that tiny white button with the lavender equal sign? That's the first. The Batman and Robin came later."

"From where?"

"Randy Wicker made them."

"When?"

"'65, '66. When the militants won control of the Mattachine Society they wanted something up front. So we had Randy make a little number just like the Civil Rights button but with a lavender equal sign rather than a black one."

"Was Wicker one of the militants?"

"He's a lifer. But a loner. He started his button business after the Civil Rights Movement made political buttons popular. Opened a head shop to sell them in '66 or '67."

"'67?"

"That's when I opened 'Oscar Wilde.' "

I grinned. "So we're all members of the Class of '67."

He shrugged. "Guess we are if you are. Want buttons?"

"How much are they?"

"The oldies I'm trying to get rid of. The tiny ones go for a dime. The Batmans . . . you can have the whole box for five bucks."

"I'll take 'em all."

Still stone-faced, he counted aloud as he picked up the little ones and slipped them into a bag. "That's twenty-five for $2.50." Then he plopped a top on his box of "Batmans," added that to the bag, and exchanged it for the ten-dollar bill I held out, pivoting like a soldier to ring up the sale and produce my change.

"How about that 'Love the Mattachine' button?"

"That's a freebie. Their office is right down the street."

"So is the Mattachine still going strong?" From preliminary spadework at HUB I knew that the Mattachine Society of New York had been the most influential gay group in town since the middle of the 1950s.

"Going weak." His look remained opaque so I couldn't tell if my name-dropping had impressed him. "That's why they've moved down here where the action is."

"Maybe I should go down and check things out."

"It's on my side of Christopher, just before you reach Seventh Avenue. Right across the street from the park in Sheridan Square."

"I like the grid of windows in your door, by the way."

"They're easier to replace than plate glass."

It was my turn to stare.

"We still get our share of rock-throwing punks."

"Love the Mattachine"

By day, at least, this easternmost end of Christopher Street was crowded with pedestrians. They looked every bit as purposeful as other New Yorkers I had seen on my walk downtown, but more dramatic in their chosen looks and styles and with a denser population of what my traditional friend's mother referred to as long-hairs.

Several of the Oscar Wilde Bookstore's neighboring buildings also appeared to be brownstones that had been turned into shops. As I neared traffic-clogged Seventh Avenue, however, there was a line of apartment buildings followed by a string of commercial storefronts. Overhanging one boarded-up storefront was a sign in the shape of an upside-down T square that seemed to have been blackened by fire. The park lay right across from it, as if in a delta of auto-filled side streets.

The Mattachine Society advertised its presence with a small sign in its upstairs window. Its business card was discreetly located in a lineup of doorbells and mail-boxes on one side of a raised, open-air entryway. The moment I pushed the Mattachine's bell, a buzzer replied, unlocking the front door.

A balding, heavy-set gent, with a bowtie a moustache, stuck his head out of the first inside doorway. I replied that I had come from Boston to begin some field research on gay politics with a visit to Oscar Wilde and that its owner had sent me here.

"That's Craig for you."

"Is that his name?"

"Craig Rodwell."

"He said that you've just moved in." This was obvious from the stacks of cardboard file boxes that littered the office.

"What you see is 20 years worth of civil rights history which nobody gives a hoot about now. But the library is up."

"That's what I'd like to see." Here, too, there were floor-to-ceiling shelves stuffed with books.

During my decade at Harvard, I had encountered, and later read, but a single book on homosexuality: *The Homosexual in America* by Donald Webster Cory, published in 1951. Rusty included this volume in the large and varied collection of books he kept in the living room of his suite in Lowell House. It was his unimposing way of allowing those who cared to see know of his interest. Now I spotted a copy of this seminal publication with a lineup of related volumes by Cory, including *The Homosexual and His Society* and *The Lesbian in America,* along with what looked like several unpublished reports. There were also copies of Cory's original book in several foreign languages, apparently published abroad.

I turned back at my host and found him eyeing me. I stuck with the business at hand. "Is Donald Webster Cory involved with the Mattachine?"

He snorted. "Ed Sagarin hasn't been around since the militants beat his ticket in the 1965 elections."

"Edward Sagarin, the sociologist of deviance?"

"That came after he lost. It used to be Donald Webster Cory, father of the homophile movement. Now it's Edward Sagarin, professor of sociology. I think he's teaching at City College."

"Wow."

"What's your own angle, by the way?"

"My angle? Too soon to tell. It's a Ph.D. dissertation on the politics of homosexuality, and I know that Manhattan has always been the center of action in the East."

He raised a trimmed eyebrow. "Don't you mean country?"

"Probably. But I have to find out why. At HUB . . ."

"I hear they're in trouble, too."

"Uh-huh. Ex-group, really. Their officer manager gave me full access to their files and a lot of old periodicals. So I know that things kind of exploded after the Stonewall Riots in June of 1969."

"That's why we moved down here."

"Is the Gay Liberation Front still around?"

"GLF was over in a year. But the radicals it riled up, they're everywhere."

"And the Gay Activists Alliance?"

"GAA came next. They got the City Council going on a gay rights bill, something we've advocated for years. Then they took one to the New York state legislature. Now their publicity machine is headquartered in a renovated firehouse down on Wooster Street."

"How about the Stonewall Inn itself?"

"What about it?"

"Is the bar still open?"

He arched his eyebrows into peaked rooftops, then apologized with a sliver of a smile. "Wait a minute, I'll see."

He picked his way through the boxes, wound open a slatted window and leaned out. By the time I reached his side he was calling down to a passerby with long hair. "Hey, Starship. Any signs of life at the Stonewall?"

Without waiting for a reply he pulled his head in. "Nope. Doesn't look like it's recovered yet."

"You mean it's the boarded-up storefront next door?"

"With that thin, black bar of soap as its tombstone."

"Soap?"

"For the great unwashed."

"Patchwork Majority"

A year and a half later, I sublet an apartment on the Upper West Side and began a thorough bout of field research on the politics of homosexuality in New York City. For introductions to the local scene I relied on Craig Rodwell at the Oscar Wilde. I always made my visits to the bookstore at noon on Monday, sure that I'd catch him alone at work, all finished stocking up.

Even when he seemed happy to have my company Craig remained businesslike. My own routine was equally professional. I'd start by examining the piles of new books he had laid out on his centerpiece table. Then I'd pick my way through each set of shelves searching for new additions. Not until I was ready to make my purchases would I mosey up to his checkout counter and assess the state of his button collection, knowing that he would join me there.

Before ringing up my books, he was willing, in his shorthand way, to converse, especially if we focused on the buttons. As on the day we met, the mode of teaching he favored most was visual. I obtained the highlights of Mattachine history while buying my first gay buttons; I got an outline of post-Stonewall developments by purchasing more.

"Didn't the Gay Liberation Front have a pin?"

"GLF didn't work like an organization, but some of its people made pins and buttons," he replied as he opened the rear door of his display case and reached in.

Deftly, with his thick middle finger, he scooped half a dozen buttons into his palm, lifted them out, and lined them up on the top of the counter. Their slogans introduced his story: "Homosexuals for Peace." "Make Love Not War." "Sexual Revolution/Social Revolution." "Freaking Fag Revolutionary." "Gay Revolution."

"That sounds like GLF."

"GLF was started by Movement people. After Stonewall they believed that lots of other gays were ready to join them. But the rest of the Movement was as homophobic as everyone else. So they split up into little work groups and published a community newspaper and did lots of consciousness-raising."

"What are all those buttons with the upside down Y on them?"

"It's a lambda." I remembered that lambda was a letter in the Greek alphabet. With the same deft maneuver Craig laid out a second line of buttons. These lambda buttons were larger and flashier than the revolutionary ones, obviously commercial in origin, and there were many more of them. Some of their designs were simple: a

FIGURE 2.5   In the early 1970s, Toby Marotta, the author of "Students of Stonewall," collected these buttons from the Oscar Wilde Memorial Bookshop in New York's Greenwich Village, a center of the Gay Liberation Movement on the east coast. The messages on the buttons communicate self-assertion and gay and lesbian pride. Several buttons use the Greek symbol, lambda, which was adopted by the gay community; some display biological symbols, male with male and female with female; others assert claims to full social equality and equal protection under the law for gay men and lesbians.

Source: David Gilmore and Toby Marotta, Continuing-Cause Posters, Community Roots Archive Copyright Toby Marotta, used by permission

glowing orange lambda draped across a background of midnight blue; a white lambda on black; a green lambda with its tail rounded into what look like palm fronds.

A few in this set took advantage of the fact that the lambda resembled the letter A by including it in slogans: "Anything Goes," with the "A" a lambda. "Hold Hands," with the "a" represented by a lambda. But most of these buttons wove lambdas into tiny arrangements of initials, names, or slogans. Among the ones that stuck out was "GAB Puerto Rico," beneath a lambda grown into a palm tree. Also featuring the lambda was a button that read "Support Gay Teachers." Another said, " ' . . . and the Pursuit of

Happiness'—Gay Activists Alliance of N.Y." This last button was red, white and blue to highlight the most apropos phrase from the Declaration of Independence.

"So did GAA invent the lambda?" I asked Craig.

"Uh-huh."

"As their logo?"

"Uh-huh. It stands for energy."

"What's the GAB?"

"Gay Activists of Brooklyn. Once GAA got hot, they started chapters in Brooklyn and Queens. See the blue one with the little white crown next to its white lambda, that's Queens."

"So . . ."

"So GAA's goal was to bring us out as a powerful minority by publicizing political issues. They held all kinds of dramatic demonstrations to get into the newspapers. Zapped candidates with direct confrontations to make them speak out about gay rights. Sit-ins, everything. Lots of energy." He pointed to his coffee-table display. "Probably half those books are by people who got active in GAA."

"But most of them are about gay lifestyles."

"It's like black power, black pride. The founders were politicos. But they attracted a lot of people who believed we also need a decent, visible culture."

"No women?"

He glared at me. Then he scanned his case and pointed to a button that stood out because of its size and coloring. It looked like a big round badge assembled from six puzzle pieces, each a different color. The lavender block in the middle contained a silhouetted lambda. Its neighbor on top featured a black peace sign. The block below carried a black power fist. The other three pieces contained entwined sets of male and female symbols for gender: adjoining males, adjoining females, and the traditional male with female. Emblazoned across this pieced-together ensemble was the slogan "Patchwork Majority."

"GAA was started by GLFers who wanted to reform the system," he began. "They believed it would happen if activists from each oppressed minority organized their own people. Their women ended up organizing Lesbian Feminist Liberation, Inc."

"Wow. I've seen all of your lesbian books but I didn't know they had their own group."

In fact, to the extent that merchandise was evidence of patronage, it was clear the Oscar Wilde had already succeeded in assembling a patchwork of minorities. In addition to homophile literature, books, and pamphlets by radicals of every color and ideology, and both political and cultural offerings from GAAers, there was a whole wall devoted to books for and about women.

Later, when he was sure that my efforts were serious and he had become comfortable talking without the help of visual aids, Craig confided that his shop had always attracted almost as many women as men. "Rita Mae Brown used to hang out and buy books from me. So did a lot of the GLF Women and the Radicalesbians."

On my own I discovered how Craig's buttons could be organized to symbolize the origins of lesbian feminism. There was still a handful that touted the earlier women's rights movement: "I Love You Susan B. Anthony," "Women for Freedom for Women." But the drift toward women's liberation was clear. "Free Mothers."

"Sisterhood is Powerful." "Amazon." "A Woman without a Man is Like a Fish without a Bicycle."

Current efforts to promote feminism among lesbians predominated: "Lesbians Ignite." "Mother Nature is a Lesbian." "Dyke." "Stars & Dykes Forever."

Annual Reminders

By this time, I knew that the ultimate symbol of Craig's selfless leadership was something far grander and more consequential than his bookshop and its buttons. I had reached my conclusion after winning access to his personal papers.

From the start he had shrugged off my requests for a formal interview by saying that actions spoke louder than words. I felt the truth of what he meant in the most personal possible way after asking if I might see any movement papers he had saved. In this case he replied by handing me the key to his apartment as he said, "They're in the trunk."

He lived alone in a studio apartment in a nondescript building on Bleecker Street. The trunk did double duty as his coffee table. Despite his insightful Monday-morning button lessons, and the countless hours I had spent reading books from Oscar Wilde, it wasn't until I examined the trunk's haphazard contents that I realized what a crucial role Craig Rodwell had played in giving modern gay political activity its distinctive shape.

During the early part of the 1960s, when his ability to work with others had set him apart from an equally young and dedicated, but independent-minded, Randy Wicker, Craig had been a behind-the-scenes stalwart at the Mattachine Society of New York (MSNY). In the late spring and early summer of 1965, he had participated in the homophile-movement picket lines that Frank Kameny had staged in Washington D.C. When this spate of picketing was over, Craig had urged following up with an annual "reminder" in the form of a picket line in front of Independence Hall in Philadelphia to be held every year on the fourth of July.

Craig's papers gave me more of his own history, as well as some information on Kameny, whose ideas about tactics differed significantly from Craig's. During the 1950s, Franklin Kameny had gotten a Harvard Ph.D. in Astronomy, gone to work for the Army, and been dismissed on the basis of an earlier charge of an alleged public solicitation. In 1960, he had responded to outreach efforts from MSNY by starting the Mattachine Society of Washington, dubbed MSW.

From the outset, Kameny both advocated and embodied prevailing opinion that the homophile movement should work to show experts, officials, reporters, and members of the public that homosexuals were just as respectable as heterosexuals. His picket lines were single-file ovals in which all of the participants—wearing required coats and ties if they were men, regulation dresses, blouses, and skirts if they were women—carried signs that had been carefully printed out by the organizers. Early on, Craig had set himself apart from Kameny by urging that picketers be allowed to express themselves as and for what they wished.

The fifth annual Reminder at Independence Hall took place the weekend after the Stonewall Riots. Frank Kameny remained true to homophile form by forbidding the members of an openly affectionate lesbian couple to hold hands as they circled. Craig was deeply offended. Applying lessons learned from Stonewall, he concluded that a very different kind of annual reminder was needed to sustain the impassioned community action necessary to produce "gay power."

That November, at a meeting of the Eastern Regional Conference of Homophile Organizations, Craig engineered passage of a resolution to replace the July 4th Reminder with an annual Christopher Street Liberation Day. For the next seven months he used his bookshop to organize the first "Gay Pride Week" with a concluding Sunday march from Greenwich Village to Central Park. "Gay" organizations of every kind were invited to attend. "Gay" people were encouraged to dress, act, and advocate as they chose. On Sunday, June 28, 1970, there were sizable marches ending with "gay-ins" in Manhattan, Hollywood, and Chicago, plus scattered celebrations and a spontaneous walk down Polk Street in San Francisco. Ever since, the Stonewall Riots have been commemorated with end-of-June parades and festivals in cities throughout the world.

"Think Straight; Be Gay"

During 1977, having readied myself to write my dissertation by reviewing my extensive collection of interview notes, documents, and buttons, I made a trip back to Manhattan to cover the most obvious gap in my research. By then I had interviewed dozens of founders, leaders, and members of path-finding gay groups from New York City. Several of my respondents said that they had been patrons of the Stonewall Inn. A few recalled participating in the heady resistance that had erupted in front of this bar in the early morning hours of Saturday, June 28, 1969. Others said that they had been drawn into the more calculated melee that took place on the following night. I had managed to pull snatches of this story from Craig, but no one had been able to make me understand exactly who was involved in these riots, or why they had taken place, or how they had set the stage for the pivotal events in gay political activity that had followed.

I arrived on a Monday morning to find that Craig was celebrating his 10th year in business with a political button that seemed to speak directly to me. It said: "Think Straight; Be Gay." Naturally, I took it as an invitation to be straight with him. For the first time, I asked him tell me the whole story without the help of buttons or trunks— to share what he knew personally about the Stonewall Riots.

"Plenty. I was there for all of them."

"So would you tell me what happened?"

"Only because you're a lifer."

The rest of this session was a rapid-fire Q&A. He spoke with the intensity of an urban soldier-boy.

"How did you learn about them?"

"I was going home when I saw a little crowd across the street from the Stonewall."

"So you knew it was a raid?"

"Raids were common."

"Because gay bars were illegal?"

"Even after we got the state to declare that they weren't, the local precincts had to police them. Sometimes they'd raid to make news. You know, show people they were protecting public morality. But they'd also do it so that owners who wanted to stay open would pay bribes."

"Which forced gay bars into the hands of the Mafia."

"What kind of gay person could afford to play that game? Only Mafia ones."

"So the Stonewall was a Mafia-financed bar that was run by Mafia gays?"

"Uh-huh. Some of them were gay. But the bar was sleazy, filthy, oppressive, and unhealthy. Since the cops were pumping its owners for payoffs, they had to keep prices high and help at a minimum. They didn't even wash their glasses right."

I stared at him.

"When I arrived in New York I worked as a busboy."

"So tell me what happened on that Friday night."

"It was after midnight, and really hot so a lot of people were out. That's always a busy corner. The police were escorting some drag queens out to their van. Drag queens were used to being hassled by the cops. But now they had an audience."

He paused.

"So-o-o . . ."

"So the queens started playing to the crowd as they were escorted out, primping themselves and making smart-ass remarks. The police got rough. The queens snapped back."

"And this pissed off all the street people?"

"It wasn't just street people. Lots of college kids. Lots of older men. Couples. It was your typical Friday-night crowd in the Village."

"As opposed to a Stonewall crowd."

"The Stonewall drew the same mix. Without the straights, I mean, just the bi's, and only a few women. But when the police kept hassling the drag queens, the queens resisted, and their resistance gave everyone else backbone. A few hotheads started shouting 'pigs.' People threw pennies, pebbles from the park."

"Someone jumped out of the van and escaped. The crowd was really pissed off. Somebody lit a trashcan on fire. I think someone was walking around and bashing things with a parking meter. It was all this pent-up anger spilling out."

"So what did you do?"

"I was shouting 'gay power, gay power.' But no one picked up on it. There was too much chaos. But after Saturday night I went home and typed up a leaflet to hand out."

"What did it say?"

"A lot."

"But what was its headline?"

" 'Get the Mafia and the Police Out of Gay Bars.' "

"And did people take it?"

"Of course they did. By Friday night, word had spread, so it was a circus. The bar was trying to stay open but the show was outside. The police had set up barricades and were everywhere. The drag queens taunted them with kick lines. But Christopher Street was ours. It was, like, what do you call it—spontaneous assertion. People were writing gay power slogans on the boarded-up walls. Dancing in the streets. Holding hands and kissing. We felt like a community. We were free at last. Proud. Political."

"Is all of this coming from memory or are you basing it on things you've read?"

For the first time, ever, he looked like I had taken him by surprise. But he rattled on with emotion. "Well, I've talked to lots and lots of people who were there. But . . ." His face flushed red. "But now I'm going to be really straight with you, Toby."

"You always have been, in your way."

"Never went to college. Can't see words straight."

He waved a hand in the direction of the shelves, "Never read any of these books."

Dynamic of a Personal Liberation Movement

The genius of the post-Stonewall liberation movement that Craig Rodwell did so much to launch was that it encouraged everyone to contribute as they could and would. That's why a geometrically expanding number of people got involved. And this dynamic of exponential growth continues through this day, now a globe-spanning empowerment movement.

Craig had been right in pegging me as "a lifer." After producing and publishing my dissertation on "The Politics of Homosexuality," I wrote a collective coming-out chronicle called *Sons of Harvard*, then used its publication to organize a national gay alumni group for the university. Thereafter, in a project comparing the lives of middle-class gay men and lesbians with those of the less fortunate gays and lesbians, I worked as a federally funded action-anthropologist studying health problems of the homosexual underclass. Ultimately I conducted 15 years of behavioral research on AIDS while I was based in San Francisco, which allowed me to chronicle the course of the epidemic from its start in another pioneering capital of this new community.

In the middle of the 1990s, after residing in Cambridge, Massachusetts, and then the Bay Area, Rusty and I moved to Tucson, Arizona. Here we continue to lead lives inspired by the values I found personified in Craig Rodwell and the decade that brought him into his own.

QUESTIONS FOR DISCUSSION

1. Toby Marotta knew that he was gay from an early age. Why did he keep it a secret during his undergraduate years at Harvard? What elements of traditional campus attitudes toward homosexuality does Marotta describe in his story? When and how does the campus climate begin to change? What would you say are the attitudes toward gay people on American college campuses today?

2. Marotta describes coming to terms with his own sexual orientation and establishing a permanent relationship with another man in the early 1970s. The two men lead a variety of campus justice and environmental crusades, and Marotta announces his determination to write a doctoral dissertation on the politics of homosexuality. Yet Marotta does not openly identify himself as a gay activist. He describes himself as very nervous when approaching the gay culture center of Greenwich Village, New York. Why do you think he is nervous?

3. Marotta continues his research in New York through the mid-1970s. His story mirrors his discoveries of the history of the militant gay rights movement. How does Craig Rodwell, owner of the Oscar Wilde Bookshop, help Marotta in his research? What is Marotta's opinion of Rodwell?

4. What is Craig Rodwell's attitude toward gay rights organizations of the 1950s, the Mattachine Society, and the larger "homophile" movement? Does he feel those earlier movements were ineffectual? Why? According to Marotta's story, what causes disagreement

among leaders of the homophile and gay liberation movements? Do these disagreements resemble disagreements in the women's liberation movement, as described in the essay by Sara Evans? If so, how?

5. Marotta leaves Craig Rodwell's description of the June 1969 Stonewall Riots to the end of his story but describes post-Stonewall events in the section "Patchwork Majority." What is the effect of delaying the dramatic high point of the story?

6. Historians regard the Stonewall Riots as the turning point in the gay rights movement. How were things different for gay men and women after Stonewall? What was the effect of "gay pride" and gay activism?

7. Would you say life is different for gay men and lesbians in the United States since the advent of the gay liberation movement? Can you name some legal and social changes since then? What changes in American attitudes toward homosexuality are reflected in our culture today, particularly in the media? How do members of your family and community feel about gay rights?

SISTERHOOD IS POSSIBLE
Yolanda Retter

Introduction

My Peruvian mother, Yolanda, and my Wisconsin-born father, Henry, met in Lima, Peru, in the 1940s. My future parents fell in love while learning to fly airplanes and my mother earned a license to fly small planes, a rarity for a Peruvian woman in the 1940s. These mismatched romantics married and moved to New Haven, Connecticut, where I was born in 1947, while my father was getting a master's degree in architecture at Yale. My mother instilled in me a sense of pride about being Latina, and that stood me in good stead later on. My father instilled in me an interest in history, philosophy and travel, but he had his limitations when I questioned authority.

El Salvador

At the beginning of 1951, just after my brother Buddy was born, we moved to El Salvador, where my father worked for a State Department program. Later he owned his own architectural firm in partnership with one of his *compadres*. My father prospered and at Christmas time, when my four siblings and I made our lists for Santa Claus, we were allowed free rein in the Sears catalogue.

A number of my father's clients were members of the Salvadorian oligarchy and if I had stayed in El Salvador, I probably would have gone to jail (or worse) for opposing them during the civil war of the 1970s and '80s. I went to school with some of their children and they became my friends. Later, during the civil war, it would not be as easy for me as it was for progressives in the United States to choose sides. Most wars are conflicts between males, while women and children on both sides suffer.

At my Catholic school in San Salvador I was considered incorrigible and was given the nickname *La Tremenda* (meaning: a force to be reckoned with).

When I was six and in first grade I had my first crush on a girl. She was in second grade. During that time, two experiences made a deep impression on me. My father's profession gave us a level of economic privilege that we would not have had in the United States, and his clients, who were members of the ruling class, gave him access to people in power. If there was a problem with the bank, he called his client, the bank president; if it was a problem with the police, he called the chief of police and so on and they took care of the problem. My child's mind concluded that those in power used their power to help others. Since that time I expect (against the odds) that those with power and extensive resources will use them to help others . . .

The second influence came from Hollywood. During the 1950s, the studios made a series of movies about the Knights of the Round Table and variations thereof. The scripts combined history, adventure, good deeds, and romance. Most importantly, the knights stood up for the underdog. This role appealed to me. I wanted to be a knight traveling about the kingdom, saving the downtrodden and courting a lady. Service became a byword. One day a nun asked us what we wanted to be when we grew up. I had just seen a movie about Albert Schweitzer and was inspired by his life story. Schweitzer was a doctor in Africa (but he was no saint). He was religious, and my child's (Catholic) mind interpreted that as an inclination to be saintly. I told the nun that I wanted to be a doctor and a saint.

In 1954, there was a political crisis next door to El Salvador in Guatemala. My father (and *Time* magazine) asserted that Guatemala's President Jacobo Arbenz was a communist (synonym for bad person). A few weeks later the Arbenz government was overthrown and Arbenz was forced into exile. I didn't know that the CIA had colluded with Arbenz's enemies to get rid of him. Arbenz had been trying to redistribute Guatemala's land, to make land ownership more equitable. Five years later, Fidel Castro overthrew Cuban Dictator Fulgencio Batista. I liked Castro until his regime executed thousands of people. Later I learned that his regime was homophobic—another example of the oppressed becoming the oppressor.

When I was nine, I began reading *Time* magazine on a regular basis. Unaware of its right-wing sympathies, I learned about current events and the names of places and people who were making news around the world. One day, after I read in *Time* that the Russian government lied to its people, I had an unsettling thought—what if the United States government was lying to us? Later, I read portions of *The Ugly American* when it was serialized in a magazine. It was an expose of U.S. diplomatic arrogance and incompetence in Southeast Asia. My parents bought me the book and I avidly read my first book in English. The 1950s was also a time when the atom bomb began to haunt the collective conscious. I remember one day thinking about what would happen if there was an atomic war. Some people said they would rather die because the aftermath would be so horrible, but I remember thinking that I would rather survive so I could help rebuild what was left.

Connecticut

In 1959 we returned to the U.S. and moved to Westport, Connecticut. Much later I realized that few families of color lived in this affluent community. My brother and I soon noticed that people in Westport had stereotypes about us. Without testing us, the teachers placed my brother (third grade) and me (sixth grade) in the lowest reading groups. Within two weeks we were shifted to the highest reading groups. Classmates thought my earrings were exotic. When I looked at the section on Latin America in my social studies book, I cringed. The outdated photos focused on stereotypic locations and people. My classmates had their stereotypes, but I had my judgments. I saw my classmates as culturally deprived because they only spoke one language, had not lived in another country, and had not had the experiences we had in El Salvador.

In Westport, we had less privilege and money than we did in El Salvador but we adjusted. Good memories from those times include playing baseball-card games in the summer with the boys on our street. In the winter we sped down a big hill standing on our sleds, sailed over a ramp, and sometimes managed to end the trip in an upright position. Music was a constant companion via vinyl records and transistor radios. Countless songs between 1959 and 1985 provide a readymade soundtrack for my life. To this day, I can name the year a song came out by remembering who I had a crush on.

My mother loved John F. Kennedy and in 1960 we went to see him at a campaign stop in Connecticut. As he rode past us in a convertible, I thought, "I want to remember this moment." He was standing, waving in his diffident manner. His hair was rust color, which was new information to me since I had only seen him in black and white photographs. He moved slowly past us. Someone could have shot him then, since the car was open and there were multi-story buildings all around.

In junior high, my classmates Candy (Candace) and Ann were active in SANE, an organization working against nuclear proliferation. There were missile silos in Westport and some residents wanted them out. The graphic on the SANE buttons, which combined a missile with a peace sign, made a lasting impression on me. Candy and Ann invited me to a meeting at a synagogue and that is where I first heard and sang "We Shall Overcome." I wrote a letter to Khrushchev asking him to "give peace a chance" (as John Lennon would later put it). Khrushchev did not respond. When the Cuban missile crisis was in progress in the fall of 1962, we worried about being bombed and dying. Since we didn't have a bomb shelter, my sister Iliana and I put up bricks and insulation around the crawl space of our split-level house. That's where we planned to go in the event of a nuclear attack.

In ninth grade my friends Mary and Faith both had crushes on Miss Beck, the gym teacher, who we soon learned was lesbian. I had a crush on one of my friends. One night at a slumber party the song, "Bobby's Girl," was playing and my friend (ostensibly straight) reached over, patted my head, and said, "You be Bobby." I went to the school library to look up what I was feeling. All I found was Freud and that's how I learned that I was an "invert." I decided to keep my feelings to myself. Being in the closet was extremely stressful. Many LGBTI (Lesbian, Gay, Bisexual, Transgender, Intersex) people have felt "different" since they were children, so for them (me) it is not simply a "choice." In the bad old days, LGBTI people had few sources of support and gay and lesbian bars were one of the few spaces where they could be "out." My support network during those years was made up of friends and several kindly adults. In those days there were few malls and I spent a lot of time in the Westport Public Library. Once, when I ran away from home, I spent the day at a Boston library doing research on Anastasia, the youngest daughter of the last Czar of Russia.

Several years later, Faith and I borrowed her mother's car and drove to New York City. We had a plan. Armed with IDs that said we were old enough to go into New York bars, we waited on a street in Greenwich Village. When we saw a lesbian-like couple, we said, "Where are the bars where girls go?" They directed us to "Cookie's" and to the "Sea Colony." Going into my first lesbian bar was a rite of passage. One moment I was outside the door and the next moment I had passed through an ontological warp and was qualitatively different ever after. Faith immediately made friends with some of the regulars. One of them later invited us to a popular gay nightclub on 125th street. One of the songs that was playing was "I'm In with the In Crowd." In this Harlem nightclub, the "out" crowd was "in."

On November 22, 1963, I was in 10th grade homeroom when the principal announced that President Kennedy had been shot. My friend Mary and I, along with millions of people around the world, spent three days in front of black and white televisions, watching his funeral. "Chilly Winds" (Kingston Trio) is the song that reminds me of those days.

In high school I felt alienated from the intense heterosexual activity going on around me. Sports became my source of social support and self-esteem. Field hockey was my favorite. I was a wild center forward. Miss Parker, our coach, once made me write an essay on "finesse." When I was sixteen, I tore the ligaments in my right knee playing hockey and had an operation. While my knee was healing, I tied my crutches to my Honda 50 scooter (it had an automatic clutch) and rode to my part-time job at the phone company. My friends Bonney and Scotty, who were sisters (and lesbians), also worked at the phone company. In those days no one we knew was "out" at their job.

California

By the mid-Sixties my parents had separated; later they divorced, and my father remarried and it was altogether a difficult time for me. In 1966, I left Connecticut to attend Pitzer College in Claremont, California. Pitzer, one of the five Claremont Colleges, was only three years old and placed great emphasis on the concept and practice of "community." The concept of community has had a lasting influence on me. Pitzer started out as a women's college and I was in the last all-women's class that completed four years at the school before it went coed. Many of the professors were excited about "building" a new school. Two of the language professors (women) had been "friends" for decades and had been hired together. One woman was very butch, but since they were discreet, no one seemed to object.

At Pitzer I fell in love with several classmates but said nothing. Sometimes depression overtook me. It was a time when LGBTI people were still classified as sick, and the American Psychiatric Association officially considered homosexuality a mental disorder. One day, after our abnormal psychology class, my best friend (whom I had a crush on) said to me derisively: "You're a homosexual." This from a woman (ostensibly straight) who one day sat on her bed staring at me as she sang along with The Lovin' Spoonful: "A younger girl keeps a-rollin cross my mind!!"

Notwithstanding the *Sturm und Drang* related to being in the closet, I had a good time at Pitzer. My friend Marylynne Slayen (now Morgan Stewart) was Tom Sawyer to my Huckleberry Finn. She was a proper student and I was the opposite. Sometimes we stayed up all night writing songs and laughing. Later, in San Francisco, when we smoked pot, we would time travel, yes time travel. It was a more innocent time. Those were the days when dumping a bucket of water on a student who had reported some of us for drinking peach brandy in our dorm room was considered outrageous. One night I rode my Honda 50 through the lobby of one of the dorms, to the amusement of some and the consternation of others. Another time, some friends and I "borrowed" the school car and went to Tijuana (Mexico), where we met some U.S. soldiers. One of them decided he liked me and later wrote me letters from Vietnam. I had the feeling that it was important for him to be able to say that he was getting letters from home. I wrote to him for a while, but I don't know what happened to him.

In 1968 I was on leave from Pitzer and went to live in San Francisco. Haight Ashbury still exuded the energy and activity that made it famous: music, hippies, drugs, "free love," and good cheer. I worked the graveyard shift at the post office. We smoked pot to make the time pass as we sorted the endless stream of packages passing on a conveyor belt. At the time, a "lid" (an ounce) of grass/pot cost $15. I went to several concerts at Golden Gate Park where people in tie-dyed and brightly colored clothing danced, tripped, and exuded utopian aspirations. One night I went to a concert at the Fillmore Auditorium and watched the crowd of people. As I had in the park, I felt alienated from this heterosexual world.

Living in San Francisco exposed me to the New Age movement. I attended free classes at San Francisco State, including one taught by Steve Gaskin, before he became a patriarchal guru, and a yoga class taught by a nice guy from the Himalayan Academy, which was part of a Hindu organization, the Saiva Siddhanta Church. I started reading books on astrology, metaphysics, the Tarot, the Sufis, etc. Regardless of what critics think, there is something valuable and meaningful in this material. It politicized me spiritually. One afternoon as I was hitchhiking near Berkeley, a guy stopped to give me a ride and asked if I wanted to take acid (LSD). Such were the times (then) that I said okay. This was the first time that I had taken acid. I "tripped" all night in the Japanese Tea Garden in Golden Gate Park, while Stephen (an Aries) served as my guardian/guide. Later he told me he liked me, but I was not interested. During that time I began keeping a diary and have kept one off and on since then. I remember writing an entry when Bobby Kennedy was shot, lingered briefly in the hospital and then died. After Martin Luther King, Jr. and Bobby Kennedy were assassinated, some of the hope seemed to fade from those who believed that we could change the world.

In February of 1969 I was back at Pitzer. The new Ethnic Studies programs were recruiting faculty and students of diverse colors and economic backgrounds. On the campus, the BSU (Black Student Union) and MECHA (*Movimiento Estudiantil Chicano de Atzlán*) were vibrant. I did not join MECHA because the males were in charge and, in general, they were sexist and homophobic. Most of the girls went along lest they be accused of betraying *La Raza*, hating men, or—even worse—being lesbians. These same dynamics (sexism and homophobia) were at play in other social movements and in the anti-war movement.

Many Claremont Colleges students were against the war, including General Westmoreland's daughter who was a Pitzer student. The administration of the Claremont Colleges was smart. They seldom overreacted when students demonstrated and staged sit-ins. In the spring of 1970 Nixon invaded Cambodia and students were shot at Kent State and Jackson State. Outrage spread across the country. Students at campuses all over the United States prepared to descend on Washington. We hoped our presence in Washington would contribute to stopping the Nixon juggernaut. Since I was Chair of Community Council (the equivalent of Student Body president) someone suggested that I represent Pitzer in Washington. I did not feel I was politically savvy enough, but people were used to my speaking up and so they voted for me to go and I went.

In Washington, groups of us were herded into the offices of congress (men) and senators. I was in the group that met Senator Henry "Scoop" Jackson. The meetings were pro forma and meant to assuage our anger and concern. One of the Claremont administrators who escorted us to Washington had a membership in the Cosmos Club and arranged for us to go there for lunch. When we got to the entrance of the club, the African American doorman (ironically) informed us that the women had to go in through the side door. I argued and received no support. I went in through the side door and groused about it but the others remained passive. When we left, I walked out through the front door. The doorman watched, but did not try to stop me.

While I was not officially part of a social movement, my experiences at Pitzer and in San Francisco and the social movement activity going on on campus and on television began to politicize me. The Stonewall Riot in New York City (which gave rise to the gay liberation movement) took place in June 1969. I did not know about the riot, but the "vibes" must have traveled far and wide because, in August of 1969, I remember thinking, "I'm tired of being in the closet. Next time a mutually agreeable opportunity presents itself I'm going to come out." On October 15th, I came out with Vivian, who, for a while, was my girlfriend. More than thirty-five years later, we are still friends.

Lesbian Activism

In the spring of 1971, my friend Linda, a bisexual white woman who was active in campus politics and was having an affair with a male Black Studies professor, told me about a political lesbian group in Los Angeles and we decided to investigate. One Tuesday night we walked into a crowded room at the L.A. Women's Center. It was a meeting of the Lesbian Feminists, a radical lesbian group. Linda immediately plunged into the discussion. I was more circumspect. Linda soon lost interest, but I had finally found my movement. These women were smart and wanted to change the world. Great! This is where I first learned that "the personal is political."

Although lesbians and gays began actively organizing in the 1950s, it wasn't until 1969 that the radical gay liberation movement was born. In 1970 lesbians began to form their own movement, one that grew out of lesbian frustration with gay male sexism and drew inspiration from the new wave of feminism. Many members of Los Angeles Lesbian Feminists were in their early twenties. We had a lot of energy and time to invest in activism. Some of us had part-time jobs, some were students, others had trust funds, some were on disability, and a few had husbands who still paid the bills.

We participated in consciousness-raising groups and gay-straight dialogues, learned to march, make banners, publish newsletters, speak on talk shows, organize conferences, and organize support systems such as rape hotlines. We supported the causes—abortion rights and, later, AIDS—of those who often did not reciprocate by helping our causes. We also formed alliances with groups that at first were hesitant to accept us (the National Organization for Women, the anti-war movement, the United Farm Workers).

During its heyday in the 1970s the lesbian movement was made up of what I call "lesbian feminists" and "feminist lesbians." Although we did not use the latter term at the time, in retrospect, the difference between the two was significant. The former were women who were feminists first and then came out as lesbians. The latter (lifelong lesbians like me) were lesbians first and were later influenced by feminism. This difference in identity development paths led to lesbian civil wars over issues of monogamy, roles (butch/femme), and whether lesbians were born or socially constructed.

Internecine conflicts notwithstanding, the lesbian feminist movement spread across the United States. The movement created a national network whose key nodes were poorly-funded women's centers, women's bookstores, and women's (lesbian) music. All over the United States, many lesbians volunteered at women's centers, read the same books, and attended concerts featuring the same lesbian musicians. These activities generated common experiential reference points. One could travel from coast to coast and find a welcoming network of women's public spaces and private homes, as I did when in I traveled around the U.S. visiting women's land projects in 1975.

Researchers and commentators who were not there (or not paying attention) assert that the lesbian movement was middle-class and white. As an active participant in a number of lesbian and feminist groups, I can attest that while some of these groups had a middle-class agenda and their membership was very white, the membership of most grassroots groups was mixed in terms of class. Some may be conflating lesbian groups with NOW (the National Organization for Women), a feminist group that was generally white and had many middle-class women (and many lesbian) members. Like other social movements, the lesbian movement was complex in terms of membership, agendas, and dynamics.

Although white lesbians had separated from the gay male movement due to sexism, lesbians of color found it more difficult to separate from ethnic co-gender movements and groups. As a number of women of color have explained, women of color are ontologically located at the "intersection of oppressions." This may mean that they wrestle with multiple identity issues, such as race/ethnicity, class, gender, and sexual orientation, sometimes all at the same time. Thus, for most women of color there is no single root oppression to combat, and this influences their willingness and ability to choose gender or sexual orientation over race/ethnicity. However, by the mid-1970s, some lesbians of color had begun organizing their own groups. Examples include Salsa Soul Sisters in New York City and Latin American Lesbians in Los Angeles, both founded in 1974.

After I graduated from Pitzer, my first job was as a prison guard at the California Institution for Women (CIW) in Corona. The first time I went in for an interview at CIW, the interviewer asked me about homosexuality. I acknowledged that I was lesbian and was not hired. Several months passed and I went in for another interview. When they asked me the same question, I said, "It's a fact of life" and was hired. After I began challenging the prison status quo, my days at CIW were numbered. The prison administrative junta decided that I was a lesbian and too friendly with one of the prisoners who had a reputation for consorting with staff. They accused me of using "intellect rather than structure and control" to deal with the prisoners, who in general were cooperative with me. In my world, that was a compliment; in theirs it was grounds for dismissal. When I consulted an activist attorney who had made his name defending black activists, he said I wouldn't have a case.

Feeling traumatized, I moved to Los Angeles and continued my work with Lesbian Feminists. I became the manager of the Women's Liberation House, a kind of halfway house "crash pad" for women. Residents included women of diverse ages and economic and ethnic backgrounds: lesbians, lesbian "tourists," heterosexual women, women on disability, lesbians newly arrived in Los Angeles, and a few underage runaways. The house was a stately turn-of-the century building, owned by a tolerant judge who lived next door. The neighbors on the other side of the house hated us. They wrote a letter complaining about the noise and the "gaily colored rags" we used as curtains. They also called the health department, but by the time the inspectors arrived, the house was neat and clean and it seemed as if only a few people lived there. The Liberation House lasted for ten months. The songs "American Pie" and "Imagine" remind me of those days.

In 1972, I applied to the UCLA School of Social Work and in my application I mentioned my lesbian activism. Two lesbian friends (Jeanne and Del), who were students at the school (and in the closet), advocated for me. The head of Chicano recruitment told them that he did not want any lesbians in the program and rejected my application. So instead, I decided to learn cabinetmaking at L.A. Trade Tech, while my partner at the time studied to be an electrician and became one of the first women admitted to the electricians' union.

One day in 1972 I went to the Gay Community Services Center in Los Angeles. When I left, I drove my VW bug west on Wilshire Boulevard and stopped at a red light. There, I was surrounded by people demonstrating in front of the Nixon re-election headquarters. For some reason I looked to my right and saw a man gesture to another as if to say, "Let's go!" They ran in front of my car and into the crowd and I saw one of them knock a man out of his wheelchair. I thought, "That's chicken shit." A fight broke out, the light changed, and I drove away. Apparently the police arrived and there were arrests. Years later I realized that what I had probably witnessed was a government provocateur knocking anti-war activist Ron Kovic out of his wheelchair. The moment was later featured in Kovic's memoir, *Born on the Fourth of July,* and in the 1989 movie of that name starring Tom Cruise.

A few years later, Nixon's regime was unraveling. Impeachment proceedings against him were underway. Barbara Jordan, an African American congress-woman and closeted lesbian, was serving on the Impeachment Committee. She made several powerful speeches, including one where she asserted, "My faith in the Constitution is whole, it is complete, it is total. I am not going to sit here and be an idle spectator to the diminution, the subversion, the destruction of the Constitution."

While Nixon was waning, the lesbian movement was waxing. Jeanne Cordova, one of the UCLA social work students who had advocated for me, had become a full-time lesbian activist. She transformed the Los Angeles chapter newsletter of the Daughters of Bilitis (the first lesbian organization in the United States) into *The Lesbian Tide.* The *Tide* is arguably the newspaper of record for the heyday of lesbian activism (the 1970s). In 1973, Jeanne and friends also organized a national lesbian conference. They discreetly called it a "women's conference" when they reserved the site at UCLA. Sheila Kuehl, then an administrator at UCLA and now a California state senator, facilitated the reservation. Over 1500 women from 26 states and 4 other countries attended the weekend conference. There were the usual arguments about whether this should be a cultural or a political gathering, about allowing transsexuals (as they were then called) to attend, about socialists, and about class issues. At this conference lesbians of color made one of the first presentations on the issue of racism in the lesbian movement.

In 1977, four of us chipped in $15 each, and put together the first issue of the *L.A. Women's Yellow Pages,* a directory of women's businesses and services. By the time the first issue was ready, the other editors had disappeared and I inherited the publication, which I managed until I sold it in the 1980s.

In November of 1977, I was working as the Director of the Pasadena Rape Hotline and my supervisor offered to pay my airfare to the International Women's Year conference in Houston. Having served as the security person at many community events, I volunteered for the same job at Houston. This was a government-sponsored event and the government agents did not want me to work security because I was staying at what they referred to as a "lesbian hotel" and they thought I might be a provocateur. The lesbians in charge of security thought otherwise and assigned me to be a sergeant-at-arms, a position that allowed me to experience this historic conference from various vantage points.

The California and New York delegations had a strong lesbian presence and were instrumental in gaining support for a "pro-lesbian" resolution. The official who had not wanted me working security had heard a rumor that the lesbians would revolt if their measure did not pass. After I spoke with the "potentially revolting" lesbians, he seemed to accept my assurances that a riot was not part of their plan. Just before the vote, feminist icon Betty Friedan apologized for her lesbian-baiting of years past. In spite of opposition from conservative activist Phyllis Schlafly and friends, over two thousand (mostly heterosexual) women publicly voted to support their lesbian sisters. The resolution could not be enforced, but the gesture was a key moment in U.S. lesbian history. *Time* magazine published a photo of two women at the conference seemingly confronting each other. In reality this was a woman I knew who was trying to out-shout the Schlafly contingent, and I was asking her (yelling above the roar of the crowd) to let them speak, especially since they were hopelessly outnumbered! I wrote a letter to *Time* asking them to correct the caption, but they refused.

In early 1978, Jeanne Cordova decided to organize the National Lesbian Feminist Organization (NLFO). Few women of color were invited as delegates to the organizing conference and that caused a major commotion. The debate was settled when lesbians of color who were there as observers and staff (I was one of them) were recruited to be voting delegates. The NLFO set a precedent by adopting a policy that required that half the positions on decision-making committees be held by lesbians of color. Shortly after, a group called Lesbians of Color (LOC) formed in Los Angeles. Although differences based on class and ethnicity created intra-group friction, LOC held together long enough to organize the first National Lesbians of Color Conference in 1983. Over 200 women of color with differing political and cultural agendas attended. We discoursed and argued and celebrated women and for many it was a memorable event.

In 1977 former singer and orange juice queen Anita Bryant had inspired John Briggs, a small-time politician who wanted to be the governor of California, to place an Initiative (Proposition 6) before the voters that basically said that lesbian and gay teachers would be fired and anyone who supported lesbian and gay rights could also be fired. After years of leading separate political lives, many lesbians and gay males agreed to work together to defeat the so-called Briggs Amendment. They put on their three-piece suits and pantsuits and enlisted the help of politicians, Hollywood powerbrokers, the media, and the citizens of California and, in 1978, defeated the amendment. Even Governor (later President) Ronald Reagan—after being counseled by one of his gay aides—decided to oppose the measure. It was a major victory against homophobia. Shortly after, Harvey Milk, the first "out" gay man elected to the San Francisco Board of Supervisors, was assassinated, along with SF Mayor George Moscone, by a disaffected former supervisor.

In 1978, after managing the Rape Hotline for a year, I decided that I wanted to learn airplane mechanics and decided (horrors) to enlist in the Air Force Reserves. My activist friends signed off on my plans after I explained why. I figured that since I did not have confidence in my mechanical ability, I could probably succeed in a program tailored for enlisted personnel; plus, if I was going to criticize the military, why not find out firsthand what the "belly of the beast" was like? Finally, if there was ever a national emergency, the military and a few others would be the only ones allowed to leave their houses, the only ones in a position to help. When asked by the recruiter, I acknowledged lesbian experiences. He took this answer to an officer and the latter coached me to say that that had been in the past. I enlisted. In basic training, I survived a dysfunctional drill sergeant and a culture where beer was more important than a book. After basic training I reported for monthly duty to military bases where, usually, there were no planes to work on. One sergeant told us to go hang out at a bar and come back at 5 p.m.

Since I was above the age for compulsory four-year service, I asked for and received an honorable discharge. I enrolled in a junior college where one could get a Federal Aviation Administration A&P (airframe and powerplant) license for a fraction of what a private technical school was charging. For two years, I was the lone female in the A&P program. The males in my class displayed a variety of IQs, sexist behaviors, and attitudes. One of the proudest moments in my life was taking apart a broken airplane carburetor, drawing every part, fixing it, putting it into a WWII vintage plane, turning on the ignition, and holding my breath while I watched all the gauges climb to the right levels and remain there! I got my A&P license in 1981. I didn't work in the field, but have always loved what I learned and some of it has served me in good stead, especially when looking at a mechanical problem.

The 1970s ended with the first gay and lesbian march on Washington. The more mainstream gay organizations felt that the time was not right for a national march. Grassroots activists ignored these concerns and, at a meeting in Houston, Texas, they voted to have lesbians of color lead the march. The mainstream groups eventually endorsed the march and participated. Before the march, people of color came together for the First Third World Gay and Lesbian Conference. The energy was high because this was the first time LGBTI people of color had gathered for a conference of their own. There was also tension because Latinos and African Americans (who were in the majority) seemed to be ignoring issues of importance to Native Americans and Asian Americans. In spite of the differences, the people of color contingent marched together. For those of us who were old enough to remember the bad old days, marching in the midst of thousands of LGBTI people was a very emotional and inspiring experience.

After the defeat of the "Briggs Amendment" (1978), many lesbians had decided to work in co-gender projects, an inclination that gained momentum in the 1980s when the AIDS epidemic began to decimate the gay male community. Some lesbians had mixed feelings about this turn of events. After years spent at a distance from the sexism of gay males, lesbians were offering and being asked to dedicate time and resources to gay males while their own lesbian centers and projects were losing support and closing. Some lesbians (myself included) who publicly expressed their concerns were taken to task by segments of the LGBTI communities. Years later, when unsafe sex practices were increasing once again in the gay male community, lesbians

FIGURE 2.6 Lesbians at a Gay and Lesbian Pride march carry signs with portraits of lesbian "foremothers" and slogans proclaiming the marchers' open identification with lesbianism and feminism, as well as their desire to transform and embrace former slurs, such as the word "queer." Women carrying the large banner on the left are members of the Lesbian Herstory Archive, an organization founded in 1974 to collect and preserve letters, diaries, photographs, books, and other publications related to lesbian history and culture.

Source: Pearson Education/PH College

who had supported their gay brothers for more than fifteen years were angry. However, most were still reluctant to express their feelings in public.

The 1980s was also the decade when lesbians of color came into their own. They formed their own groups, published their own anthologies, and began to be included in generic lesbian anthologies and on feminist conference programs. It was also a time when more lesbians and gays appeared in the media. In 1988, three lesbian separatists (myself included) and four non-separatist lesbians appeared on Oprah. These were the days when Oprah used a "shooting gallery" format, where high drama was more important than education. We fielded the usual questions and hostile comments and then I asked, "Oprah, if six black activists came on the show they would probably not be asked 'Why do you hate white people?' So, why is it that the question we always get is, 'Why do you hate men?' " Oprah paused and then went to a commercial.

By 1990, the lesbian movement was in what sociologist Verta Taylor calls "abeyance mode." This is a state that movements go into when the cultural and political climate is sluggish or unfriendly. Many of the lesbians I know began to work for other causes, for example the environment. Some went back to school or decided to get "real" jobs, some started families and others grew tired and stayed home.

As we approached the millennium, I had earned library science and social work degrees from UCLA and a Doctorate in American Studies from the University of New Mexico. My dissertation topic was an insider account of lesbian activism in Los Angeles, 1970–1990. I began to work on behalf of lesbian history and visibility by volunteering in lesbian archives and creating a lesbian history web site. I also began to research the history of Peruvian photography and now maintain a web site on the subject.

Several years into the 21st century, I am in my late fifties. I am in a relationship with Leslie, a DCT (dream come true) femme who is a first-class hospice social worker. Many in my historical cohort (myself included) still feel like we are thirty-five (even though we used to say "Never trust anybody over 30!") and, for better or worse, we live at that pace. But we know that things are changing because now our conversations are peppered with comments about our health and our "senior moments" and a growing number of activists from our generation are gone.

In spite of our gradual graying, many Baby Boomers still participate in social justice causes. For example, women who once worked in the lesbian movement against sexism and homophobia have created lesbian retirement communities and senior lesbian groups and continue to fight for the rights of lesbians and women. I continue to be a gadfly on the body politic, raising issues of racism, sexism, and homophobia (sometimes at the same time), because too often, wherever I am, someone is being overlooked. I volunteer with the Red Cross during local disasters, often translating for Spanish speakers whose homes have been destroyed by fire. In one national disaster I worked with a Salvadorian family who lost their mother on one of the 9/11 planes. In 2001, I was in Peru on a research trip. After a fire in Lima killed more than 300 people, I volunteered with a Peruvian mental health group helping victims and their families. Sometimes I participate in marches against outrages such as the Iraq War and what I call the "Axis of Greed."

Like a number of activists, I am suffering from what I call "Activist PTSD" (post-traumatic stress disorder). One gets APTSD from too much exposure to the rough and tumble dynamics of social movements and causes and from visceral reactions to the increasing amounts of greed and violence in the world. If one is a member of despised or devalued groups, one can also get it by absorbing attacks from those who do not like those groups.

Yes, my generation is a bit tired, but it is unbowed. As the authors of the book *Generations* have suggested, the Baby Boomer generation has an "unfinished agenda," one that may have a second chance to make its dreams of peace and social and economic justice come true. I am a child of the Sixties, and for me hope springs eternal. As the song we learned in the Sixties taught us, "Deep in my heart, I do believe . . . we shall overcome some day."

QUESTIONS FOR DISCUSSION

1. Why does Yolanda Retter feel so lonely and unsure of herself as an adolescent? Why do you think it is difficult for her in the 1950s and early 1960s to find any information that will explain her sexual feelings? What would it feel like to learn that society regards people like you as abnormal, or as a member of a despised group? Why is her discovery of the lesbian bar so important to her?

2. What challenges does Retter face in her work and education that are directly related to her lesbianism? Is she uncompromising in proclaiming her sexual orientation in every situation or does she sometimes keep quiet? Do you feel that for the most part she is clear about who she is and true to herself?

3. Retter, whose mother was Latin American, describes herself as a lifelong Latina lesbian, feminist, and separatist. What does she mean by each of those terms? How would you describe Retter's character or personality? Her politics?

4. Retter freely uses parenthetical remarks and quoted words or phrases in her story. She frequently refers to famous events of the '60s and '70s and to popular songs of the period. What is the effect of these choices?

5. Yolanda Retter and Toby Marotta ("Students of Stonewall") share the experience of self discovery in relation to their sexual orientation and the growth of their political awareness. How would you compare Retter's experiences and the tone of her story with Marotta's story about the gay liberation movement?

6. Toward the end of her story, Retter discusses disagreements within the LGBTI community. What are the sources of some of those disagreements? Were you surprised to learn that the AIDS epidemic, which started in the United States among gay men, did not evoke sustained sympathy from some lesbians?

7. Compare the lesbian feminism of Retter's story with women's liberation in Sara Evans' "Not My Mother's Path." On what issues do they intersect? How do their priorities differ? What challenges do their groups and organizations share, especially with regard to their connections with the anti-war, civil rights, and gay liberation movements? Why do you think both groups experience fracturing or internal warfare? Why does Retter make a point of discussing the class and color of feminists of the period?

8. Retter's title, "Sisterhood Is Possible," is a pun on Susan B. Anthony's famous statement about the women's suffrage movement of the nineteenth and early twentieth centuries: "Failure is impossible." Can you think of any ways that Anthony, who didn't even have a word for lesbianism in her day, might nevertheless have understood the challenges Retter's movement faced?

SOMETHING IN THE WIND
Johnny Flynn

Dear Sam and Maria,

You have asked me many times about what it was like growing up in the 1960s and about my involvement in the American Indian Movement. I can't remember everything that happened, maybe not even most of what happened. What follows is some of what I remember. I will tell you the truth as I know it, but as I have told you many times, the truth is what people believe and it often has nothing to do with the facts.

I grew up in a small town, Ellinwood, Kansas, Irish on my father's side and American Indian on my mother's. How a Potawatomi/Sac and Fox/Dakotah Indian woman and an Irishman fell in love, created me, your uncles Mike and Wes, and aunt Celesta, and raised us on the central plains of Kansas is a long story. It is a story of the Great Depression. It is about the oil boom and bust in Oklahoma. It is about the oil boom in Kansas and how my Indian relatives couldn't find work in Oklahoma and had to follow the drilling rigs out of Oklahoma and into Kansas after WWII. And it is, finally, a story of the efforts of the federal government to "relocate" Indian people from allotted lands that were worthless after the oil was pumped from under them and salt water was pumped on them, and down the creeks where your ancestors and mine used to hunt and fish. I found out later that all these events, and others like them, were to play a part in the movement of Indian people around the country and would provide the seedbed from which the American Indian Movement would grow.

My mother's parents were Indians. Grandpa Bruno was a full-blooded Potawatomi Indian and Grandma Bruno, Potawatomi and Sac and Fox. The Sac and Fox were still eating dog when my Grandma was little. Whenever a dog turned up dead on Grandpa's place he would accuse her of putting it in the stew pot. It was a bone, pardon the pun, of contention between them. If you ever see the old photographs of Indians by Charles Curtis and others you won't see a single one of the images with a smiling face. But my Indian folks smiled and laughed all the time. Every Indian family I ran into through the years was serious about their jokes and powerful teasers. That's how I remember growing up Indian—laughter, jokes, and constant, sometimes biting, teasing.

Dad's folks, the Flynns, were Irish and a little German. My dad's maternal grandmother was a Fitzgerald and Grandma Flynn always said we were related to the Kennedys. Don't know if that is true but they were sure Irish. Like the Indians, the Flynns were storytellers. Your Grandpa Flynn—my father—was born and raised in Kentucky and that branch of the Flynns has been in America since the early 1700s. One of Dad's cousins did a family tree and found that a Flynn ancestor fought with Colonel Benjamin Logan during the French and Indian War. They fought a combined force of Shawnees, Potawatomis, and Sac and Foxes in Ohio in 1769 or so. When I told mom about it she said that is why she and my dad fought so much. It was likely Mom's ancestors and Dad's ancestors had looked at each other over the barrel of a gun.

I am named after both my grandpas: Edgar Preston Flynn and Johnnie Baptist Bruno. Maybe I was set on a spiritual path early on from having an interesting combination of Irish and Indian, both groups superstitious, both very spiritual instead of religious, and both struggling with their heritage and discrimination against that heritage.

Memory is a funny thing. I remember the summer before I turned five we took a trip to see my father's folks in Kentucky. He had been born at home and had no birth certificate so he had to go there and get affidavits from three people who were alive when he was born to certify he was born when he said he was so he could apply for Social Security. I guess Dad and them never thought about what would happen if they hauled a woman of color, my mother, through the South, but Mom sure did. Early in the trip we stopped at a gas station in Arkansas and Mom went in to use the bathroom. Maybe she didn't remember about Whites-Only bathrooms in the South. The man inside told her to use the "colored" bathroom out back. Color is a tricky thing for folks who are "colored." Indian people don't consider themselves to be colored folks, only white people do. I remember Mom's face when she got back in the car at that piss-ant gas station in Arkansas. It was like someone had slapped her in the face. "I'm not colored," she said. It was like a mantra, seemed like she said it over and over for a thousand miles. Maybe she said it only once and it echoed in my head. Maybe she never said it. Dad said later that she never said it so maybe she only said it in her mind. But I heard it and the night I sat with her body all night, I heard it again as I looked on that brown face in the casket. I remember on that trip that Mom pissed in the woods whenever she had to pee in the South. Does an Indian piss in the woods? In the 1950s in the Deep South they did.

What I remember most about growing up was the land. The Great Bend of the Arkansas River ran just south of Ellinwood and as early as I can remember we—my brothers and friends—lived on that river. We hunted in the trees along its banks and hand-fished the drifts and cut-banks for fifteen miles up and downriver of the town. It is, or at least we were told it was, legal for Indians to hand fish the rivers of Kansas and we learned the art from Grandpa Bruno.

He used to take us by the heels like Thetis dipping Achilles into the river Styx, and shove us under water into the cut banks so we would drive the fish into the shallows. He would tell us not to let our folks know, although Mom knew; she learned to noodle fish the same way.

Dad worked the oilfield when I was young and would leave town for days or weeks at a time. He did teach us to hunt early on and I don't remember a time or season that we were not on the river or in the woods. We had no television in my early years so we lived outside. Nights were times of stories and reading.

I graduated from Ellinwood High School in 1969, the first high school graduate on my mother's side of the family. My parents, their parents, and their grandparents had never graduated from high school so my graduation was an event. Although I was offered a drama scholarship to go to college, I was quite honestly sick of school at the time. I had worked many jobs through high school and the summers between school, mostly farming and associated jobs, so I went to work right away in a grain elevator. It was located just a few miles east of Ellinwood and I stayed there for a year and a half. One fall day in November 1970, a friend of mine fell from the top of the elevator and was killed. I was ready to do something else.

Indian School and AIM

Two of my cousins were accepted into the newly reorganized Haskell Indian School in Lawrence, Kansas, and eventually talked me into going, which I did in the spring semester of 1971.

Most of the Indian people I grew up with were relatives. Going to college with nearly one thousand Indians of all tribes was an experience. A sizeable number of the students at Haskell were urbanized, with tenuous connections to a tribal identity. Others were totally bureaucratized from attending Indian boarding schools all their lives. There were others who had grown up on distant reservations, attended reservation schools, and were going to Haskell as a way of escaping the grinding poverty of America's third world.

Divisions at the school were many. There were tribes, bands within tribes, and other allegiances based on reservations, states, experiences, intentions, and traditions. Then there were those of us who were on the verge of entering the cultural wasteland of America's mythical "melting pot." Like everyone at the school, I was divided also. I was a mixed up mongrel, drifting somewhere between being a Catholic who hated organized religion and an atheist, or at least an agnostic looking for something beyond religion qua religion.

Drugs versus alcohol was another division at the school. The drug culture was in full swing all over the country in the early 1970s and Haskell was no exception—although the drug of choice there was alcohol and plenty of it. There were those who drank, those who used drugs, and those who did both. I was in the latter category, so I had friends who only drank, friends who only used drugs, and friends who did both.

The attitude toward drugs at the time was interesting. We were questioning authority. Police, school administrators, dorm supervisors, and others in authority had no right, we felt, to decide how we chose to encounter obliviousness, which is the ultimate goal of alcohol and drug use. Alcohol made you stupid after a short period of bravado. Bravery among Indian people so bureaucratized was in short supply. Drugs, especially hallucinogens and marijuana, made one contemplative and secretive; being contemplative and secretive is how Indians survived as Indians in the face of the longest war in human history, the war against aboriginal peoples of the world.

I spent my first semester at Haskell getting a lot of my education outside the classrooms and was relieved to go back to Ellinwood. In academics, I learned almost nothing. In terms of myself, I learned a lot. I learned that there were other people out there like me. When I looked in the mirror at that age, 19, I saw someone who did not fit any category of classification common to a small town on the edge of the high plains of Kansas. In the common white parlance of the time I was/am a "half-breed." But at Haskell there were hundreds of folks just like me.

I also learned that the boarding school experience of my grandmother, my great-grandparents, my mother, and others of my relatives was a horrible caricature of other people's educational experiences. I know my experience was a pale shadow of theirs, and that things have changed since, but in 1971–72 we had bed check at eleven o'clock, had to be up when it was still dark-thirty, and had to make our beds, clean our rooms, iron our clothes, and work at some menial job in order to get the free education promised our ancestors in exchange for 99 percent of the land in the

United States. Haskell would slowly evolve into a regular college but when I was there it still had a serious boarding/government school hangover.

That summer I followed my dad out to California to work offshore on the oil platforms in the Santa Barbara Channel. I didn't go back to Haskell until spring semester. Things had gotten a little more interesting. What had been a whisper in the air became a speech when Dennis Banks, the National Director of the American Indian Movement, came to Haskell. He told us there was an AIM branch in Lawrence, just down the road. After his speech about Native American civil rights we were inspired. Some students reacted by taking over the administration building, a sit-in of sorts, which would pale in comparison to what happened around the country over the next few years.

We had a lot of Vietnam veterans in school that year. They were not taking shit from anybody. A few of the matrons got knocked on their butts when they tried to get them into bed at eleven or up at six. The single speech of Dennis Banks became a chorus of voices against what we believed were discriminatory practices by the administration. We became a voice heard but not understood, not even by ourselves.

I joined a drum group and started singing Indian songs, mostly pow-wow and round dance songs, but it gave me a sense of belonging to something more ancient than my own generation.

I started going to Native American church meetings that spring, up in Mayetta, Kansas, a place where my great-grandparents had been born before their removal to Oklahoma in the late 1860s. Some of the old people on the reservation remembered my grandfather and great-grandparents and many times I was the only young person at the meetings.

The Native American church is also called the peyote church because they use medicine in the ceremony. At that point I already had a certain familiarity with hallucinogens, but not the ceremonial aspects of the use of peyote. We entered a teepee at sundown and didn't come out until the next morning. The old people told me that there would come a time when the teepee poles would begin to sing and that happened one night. But I am getting ahead of myself.

At one peyote meeting there was the skeleton of an old sweat lodge* in the tree line. When I pointed it out one old man explained what it was. Later, I told Mom about it and she said her grandpa was known for using a sweat lodge for healing people down in the Sacred Heart area of Oklahoma. It was the first time I saw a sweat lodge and I connected with it in a way that I had not connected with the sacred since I was a little kid in Catholic church hearing the Latin prayers. I didn't go in the sweat lodge at that time, but I was captivated by the mystery of healing.

I got kicked out of Haskell that spring. I went to Ellinwood for spring break and when I came back, my stuff was packed. I moved into the AIM house up on Oread Hill just off the University of Kansas campus in Lawrence. They needed me. I could type, the result of getting kicked out of Old Man Carlson's shop class back in high school. When I found the stash of whiskey-soaked cigarettes Carlson used to smoke

---

*A sweat lodge is a small hut, roofed with boughs covered with hides or blankets, which is heated by steam from water poured over red-hot rocks. In Native American cultures, the sweat lodge is a ceremonial space, used for private or communal prayer, healing, and purification.

in the closet, I was given a choice of home economics or typing, which was no choice for a guy in those days. At least there were other shop class rejects in typing.

I typed proposals for AIM, and press releases and letters and so on. We had a four-story house with an attic where we sang on the drum especially during storms. There were about six or seven of us living in the house and we kept the partying to a minimum. I was going to peyote meetings every Saturday and making connections with other Indian activists from around the country who passed through either Lawrence or Mayetta. I met a bunch of AIM people including Vernon Bellecourt, and Carter Camp, who we asked to stay and run Kansas AIM.

We went to the first AIM convention at the Leech Lake Indian Reservation in Minnesota in May of 1972. We had the convention there because of the fishing rights controversy, which continues to this day. Although on the surface the issue appears to be subsistence (Indian) fishing, versus sport (white) fishing, it is about deep-seated resentment toward Indian treaty rights. We were shot at a few times and I remember feeling that even though I missed Vietnam, there was a battle brewing in America that was part of that longer war against Indians.

Indian history was not part of any curriculum I had experienced in any of the schools I attended. The Indian histories I heard from my mother and grandparents were tales of stolen land, broken treaties, trails of tears, and death. But at Leech Lake that spring, those stories were not just stories anymore. I could see with my own eyes the effects of America's longest war and it was not in Southeast Asia, but in Leech Lake and Mayetta and Oklahoma and Arizona. It had its own propaganda machine with outlets in Indian schools that did not teach Indians our own history and in public schools that did not teach non-Indians what the government did to Indians. The impact of seeing Indians fighting for fishing rights guaranteed by treaties older than state governments was empowering to me.

We came back to Kansas that summer with a new sense of mission. Not long after the AIM convention, the Topeka Indian Center called the AIM house and asked for our help. The Boy Scouts of America had (and still have) an Indian dance group called the Koshare dancers. It was not bad enough that they were named after sacred Pueblo spirit dancers, but they were being paid two thousand dollars to dance in Topeka. Up at Mayetta there was a dance group and a drum group composed of real Indians and they had never been asked to dance or offered any money.

The Topeka Indian Center people wanted to organize a protest against the Koshares. Now, opposing the Boy Scouts is not really the "American" thing to do, but we figured we were more American than the Boy Scouts: our ancestors inspired them. But we needed to get the AIM people out front on any issue that Indian people wanted to address. So we decided not only to organize a protest but also to try to break the drum. Several hundred people showed up for the protest. There were signs, marching, and real Indians singing from a drum with real Indians outside the theatre where the fake Indians were dancing. Five of us, AIM people, managed to slip past the squads of cops guarding the Boy Scouts and went for the stage. I made it to the second door of the auditorium before a half-dozen cops beat me to the floor. We didn't break the drum but we accomplished two things. We proved to the Indian people that we—the American Indian Movement—were going to put ourselves, our bodies, on the line. And we captured the imagination of the general public.

American Indians against Boy Scouts was embarrassing to the City of Topeka, who hired the Koshares. We also realized the power of non-violent protest coupled with direct political action which threatened violence. I am not sure what I would have done if I had made it to the stage. Our plan was to kick in the drum and stop the dance, not to hurt the scouts. I was just glad I didn't piss my pants when the first cop hit me in the back with his nightstick.

The image most people have of the American Indian Movement at the time, and even now, is one of violent protest, but few realize that, at least in the beginning, we were deeply interested in the welfare of Indian people in general. In early June of 1972, we heard on the news that a devastating flood had hit Rapid City, South Dakota. Within a few days the AIM chapter in Kansas organized a food drive. A private air freight company in Lawrence agreed to fly for free whatever we collected for flood relief. It was the first time I ever flew on a plane and it was a little puddle jumper loaded with food and clothing.

I had seen floods before but was not prepared for what I saw when we arrived at the Rapid City airport. Rapid Creek came into the city from the Black Hills to the northwest and wound through the streets of downtown Rapid City. Most times it was a shallow, rocky creek, but several days before we arrived there had been heavy rain in the mountains. An earthen dam spilled over and then broke apart and a wall of water thirty feet high rolled through Rapid City killing over two hundred people. Since living along Rapid Creek was what poor people did, nearly one hundred of the dead were Indian people and there were hundreds more who were left homeless. The devastation along the creek was unbelievable. Most of my time there I spent organizing and handing out supplies to people who had found some place to stay, or ferrying Indian families back to the reservations to the south and east to stay with relatives. I met dozens of Indian families and experienced my first sweat lodge. It was also my first look at the poorest county in America, Shannon County, on the Pine Ridge Indian reservation.

Like most Americans, I had not done much thinking about the Sioux people. I was proud of the fact that they whipped Custer. But I was not prepared for Pine Ridge. It was an island of absolute devastation amidst one of the most beautiful places on Earth. We have relatives there, from the Irish side, believe it or not. I was not to meet them until just before the liberation of Wounded Knee eight months later, but my heart fell the first time I saw Pine Ridge.

We spent three weeks in South Dakota working flood relief and making friends. The Lakota people told me that South Dakota was the "Red Man's Mississippi," and even though I have never been to Mississippi, before or since, they were right about racism in South Dakota toward the Indian people.

South Dakota was divided between whites, Indians, and mixed bloods. You must know that I use white not as a color, but a mindset. I believe that a full-blooded Indian can be white in their minds, and I believe in the opposite, that a full-blooded white person can be Indian, or black in their outlook. That attitude comes from what maybe I can see when society makes me put one foot each on both sides of America's line of color. I think in South Dakota I began to see how my mother felt that day outside of a small gas station in Arkansas. I was not born a colored man. I am not a colored man. I was, am, and will be, an Indian, an individual. The American Indian

Movement was for me at the time about finding out who we were, about establishing our place at the table of human beings being set elsewhere in the world of "colored people."

By this point in 1972 the American Indian Movement was four years old. The leadership had begun to think that non-violent protest and connections to the Sixties' Civil Rights Movement would not work for Indian people. We had been subjected to violence for generations and when our ancestors fought back with violence they captured the attention of the press and the people. We knew that it was a rule of thumb in the history of the Indian wars that the bigger the geographic distance between the non-Indian people and the war, the bigger the support for the Indian cause. Violent protest in the past had sometimes worked for Indians in ways that it did not work for other people. With hindsight, we seriously underestimated the amount of violence the U.S. government and its minions were willing to dish out to us. And we underestimated the power that agencies of the U.S. government had to manipulate docile tribal governments.

The AIM leadership also knew that the treaties of times past gave us legal traction that could not be matched by any other part of the Civil Rights Movement. We received a call that July from AIM people in Denver telling us that some of their people had been arrested in an action in Flagstaff, Arizona. Every year the businessmen of Flagstaff put on a "ceremonial" for tourists. They paid Indians to come and dance at the gateway to the Grand Canyon. In the midst of that year's ceremonial some AIM people had jumped up on stage, taken over the microphone and denounced the secularization for profit of the sacred dances of the Indian people. A month earlier I had written a successful grant proposal to the National Indian Lutheran Board, so the Kansas chapter of AIM finally had some cash in the bank. We were young and naïve and so we went to Flagstaff.

In the end we found ourselves cooling our heels at a campground in the Coconino National Forest while the AIM leadership negotiated a settlement with the city of Flagstaff. In trying to help we had blown several thousand dollars of the grant money from the Lutherans and all we were able to get were reduced charges against those who had attempted to grab the microphone. One thing we failed to learn, and which would later haunt us, was the fact that the people in power were willing to charge us with the most grievous of criminal charges for the smallest of infractions. Grabbing a microphone at a dance is at most disturbing the peace, but the Denver AIM people were initially charged with multiple felonies. And nothing changed with the Flagstaff ceremonial except that it was moved into an area where it was easier to provide police protection.

Back in May, during the AIM convention in Leech Lake, the leadership had decided to convene an All-Indian Grand Jury to solicit testimony from Indian people regarding mismanagement by local, state, and federal government agencies. When we left Flagstaff we hooked up with the All-Indian Grand Jury and went down to Ajo, Arizona, where I watched the AIM leadership learn a big lesson.

Phelps Dodge Corporation owned most of southern Arizona at the time. There were Pima and Papago Indians living in the long desert stretch from Tucson to the California border. Phelps Dodge was mining copper from the desert and it controlled the towns on, and adjacent to, the Indian reservations. Phillip Celaya was a young

Indian man who for some reason crossed paths one night with the local Ajo police. They shot him to death in the street.

There had already been some noise and protest over the shooting, but things began to get even hotter by the time we arrived in Ajo. The issue had grown beyond a police shooting. Now we began to confront Phelps Dodge's control of reservation towns and discrimination against Indian and Mexican workers. We organized a march of people through the town of Ajo and up to the gates of the Phelps Dodge mine. That is where it stalled. At the time I didn't have a lot of experience with protest marches and demonstrations, but when you march you have to be going somewhere. Going to a locked gate is not a destination, especially when the folks on the other side, the folks you want to confront and argue with, are looking at you from the windows and laughing. Somehow Dennis Banks had gotten hold of a Pima County Sheriff's bull horn. He yelled himself blue trying to get folks to climb the fence and break into the Phelps Dodge building, to no avail. We were part of a "coalition." And while some of us were willing to break down the gate and go to jail for certain, others were not so willing. It was a hard lesson the AIM leadership learned. Don't trust others to support the radical position we felt we had to take to get our message across. It was a lesson that we later would take to Washington, D.C., and on to Wounded Knee, South Dakota.

Republicans

When we were in Arizona a group of us hooked up with the Dennis Banks group. Some of us were recruited to go to Washington, D.C., and process the over 1500 complaints the All-Indian Grand Jury received from Indians all over the country. We spent about six weeks in Washington at the offices of Americans for Indian Opportunity putting the paperwork in order for submission to the United States Department of Justice. During that time, we received an invitation to go to the big demonstration scheduled for the Republican National Convention in Miami, Florida, in August of 1972.

I had been to anti-war demonstrations, but missed Woodstock and the Democratic Convention in Chicago in 1968. So the Florida Republican Convention was a big deal for me. Who invited the American Indian Movement to Florida, I don't remember.

The first morning after we arrived in Miami, we were joined by about thirty Seminoles in a half dozen cars and pickups. Together we went over to the convention center. On the way we taught everyone the AIM song and when we arrived we stretched out to make our little band look bigger and, with the drum in front, started off down the street. We made it into that week's *Time* magazine, but we didn't know that at the time.

After the little demonstration we organized a press conference for the next afternoon to be held in the lobby of the Fontainbleu Hotel. I typed up the press releases and put them in the in-boxes of every reporter in the basement press room of the hotel. The next afternoon, Dennis Banks and Ron Petite were in the lobby of the Fontainbleu for the press conference. Two reporters showed up. One of the things that had happened after the All-Indian Grand Jury wrapped up business was the drafting of a position paper called the Twenty Points. It was basically the American Indian Movement's stand on issues like sovereignty, treaty rights, health care, and so on. Dennis wanted to talk to reporters about this but with all the dignitaries and others floating through the hotel, a handful of Indians wanting to talk about Indian treaties got no attention.

Dennis called us over. "There is a bullhorn from the Pima County Sheriff's Office in the car. Go get it." My stomach started to ache. They were arresting so many people in the streets, if we caused trouble in the lobby of the hotel, in the belly of the beast itself, there was a good chance we were going to get our heads bashed in. Dennis was going to jump up on a table and start hollering through the bullhorn. Two of us went outside to the car, dragging our feet. By the time we got back into the hotel lobby, the place was full of Secret Service. Change of plans. Julie Nixon Eisenhower, President Nixon's daughter, was going to sign autographs in the lobby.

Dennis and Ron got in line with Dennis' two little girls. The Secret Service swarmed them. After telling the suits that he wanted autographs for his girls, they let him by, but stayed close.

When it was Dennis' turn, he gave Julie Eisenhower a copy of the 20 Points paper and said, "Give this to your dad." Eisenhower said she would. When that was over, there were a dozen reporters waiting to talk to the two Indians who had just spoken to the president's daughter. Nothing of substance was ever printed as far as I know.

One more Republican story. Around the first of September, after Miami, we started getting calls from Indians in Oklahoma about their kids being kicked out of school for having long hair. The Republican National Committee was doing minority voter registration drives. We wrote a proposal to the RNC to do voter registration in Oklahoma among the Indian people. We got the funding and were on our way to Oklahoma to help register Indian Republicans, if we could find them.

We set up shop in Pawnee, Oklahoma. It was my first taste of Oklahoma Indian politics and now, more than thirty years later, it is still ashes in my mouth.

Oklahoma is unique in Indian country because Indian lands are no longer considered reservations with identifiable boundaries. The Oklahoma Land Run in 1889 caused all kinds of problems with lands, deeds, and legalities regarding the difference between Indian lands and non-Indian lands. Pawnee was no exception. Built after the land run, Pawnee city had an ambivalent relationship with the Pawnee tribe. The immediate issue was that Indian children were being kicked out of district schools for having long hair. A secondary undercurrent was the fact that the school received federal funds based on the number of Indian kids in school. Even though the kids were not attending school because of their hair, they were still carried on the rolls because the money was used to supplement school district funds. That was the leverage we eventually used to get the kids back in school. Scratch the surface of any town in Oklahoma and you will find a long and involved history of theft of Indian lands and funds.

On September 13, 1972, my twenty-first birthday, we took over the Bureau of Indian Affairs office in Pawnee and basically held the BIA folks hostage until they agreed to act on behalf of the parents and withhold funds for Indian education until the district could prove that the kids were back in school.

The Pawnee people were great to us and we stayed through the end of October in and around Pawnee working on the school issues and generally dodging the Republican National Committee's effort to get progress reports on the number of Indians we were trying to register to vote. I should add that our net effort that fall was Republicans 0, Indians, radicalized.

There were a lot of issues to address that fall in Oklahoma. Indian students at Riverside Indian school took over the school. We, the AIMster gangsters, as we were dubbed in the press, had nothing to do with the takeover. We did go down and help with the negotiations. The *Lawton,* Oklahoma newspaper, called us "earringed toughies." Those of us who didn't have our ears pierced went out and had it done immediately. I had had mine done way earlier so I guess I was one of the people the newspaper was talking about.

The Bureau of Indian Affairs Takeover

By early that fall we were organizing in Oklahoma to go on the "Trail of Broken Treaties," the name someone in Minnesota had come up with back during the May AIM convention. The plans were to have at least three caravans of representatives of Native Nations starting from the west coast and traveling through Indian Country, picking up Indians all the way from one coast to the other. In Oklahoma, the southern caravan would go east and circle through the eastern Cherokees and the Lumbees living in North Carolina. Some of us left early to make arrangements for places for the people coming to Washington, D.C.

The caravans were set to arrive in Washington, D.C. during election week. What we were to do in Washington when all those people arrived we didn't have a clue. Wander the halls of Congress lobbying legislators was one idea bounced around. I was in Washington two weeks early and we had arranged for people to stay in the basement of a church near the downtown area. On November 1, early in the morning the caravans arrived. By my count there were close to fifteen hundred Indian people from around the country and when they went into the church they were nearly outnumbered by the rats in the basement. They were mad.

The day they arrived I was at the Americans for Indian Opportunity office trying to find food and lodging for the overflow of people. I knew that most of the people from the caravans were down at the Bureau of Indian Affairs office. About four o'clock in the afternoon I received a call from some friends down at the BIA building telling me to "get down here right away." It was only about a ten minute walk to go to the BIA building and as I approached I could see in the parking lot about thirty police in riot gear start into the back door.

I ran around to the front and some people I knew were holding the door open and I made a dive over some desks that had been moved to block the door. In the time it took me to run from the back to the front, the fight was over at the back door. One guy I knew from Kansas had been hit in the head with a nightstick and was bloody, but most of the people who drove the cops out seemed to be unharmed. The siege was on.

We stayed in the building for seven days, eating, sleeping, and generally tearing the place up. For the first couple of days the building sustained little damage but the third night several bus loads of police in riot gear pulled up in front of the building. They all got out, lined up and stood there for an hour not moving. We moved desks, chairs, and file cabinets to block the doors and waited. We had no weapons except a few hunting knives which were turned into spears. We did break up a bunch of very expensive wooden chairs and turned the legs into clubs. For the next three nights the buses loaded with cops pulled up to the building and unloaded in full view. Each time they did that, the building was torn up a little more.

Louis Bruce, who was Commissioner of Indian Affairs at the time, eventually joined us in the building. We had a team of people who were negotiating with officials of the Department of the Interior and representatives of the White House to keep them from coming into the building and throwing us out. We stayed busy reading the BIA files. There were a lot of FBI reports, background checks and so on, of people who were high level BIA or Interior people. They said later that we removed over a million files from the building and some of them made their way into the hands of Jack Anderson, the newspaper columnist. We also heard later through John Erlichman, President Nixon's domestic affairs advisor, that Nixon had told his people to "get them out of there but don't hurt any of them." On Election Day we decided to leave quietly, that is after they paid us sixty-five thousand dollars in cash.

The basement, where most of the Oklahoma people stayed, was pretty clean. The windows opened up to the parking lot so the night we were getting ready to leave we were going out the window carrying our stuff out to cars. It took several trips and when we came back in we would step down onto the window sill. On one of my trips back into the building I noticed that someone had drawn the curtains shut. When I stepped down and through the curtains I found several people in the room had drawn pistols and had them trained on me. Where they got the guns I don't know but there was sixty-five thousand dollars lying on the desk.

There were three caravans headed out of Washington so they divided the money up based on the number of people in each caravan and how far they had to go. I stayed in Washington for some time afterward. The feds were flying their favorite tribal leaders into D.C. to look at the damage we had done to the building. Later, they had a press conference where we were denounced. We went to the press conference too and argued with the tribal officials. It made for good news film.

In the course of the negotiations, the people from AIM kept insisting that the Twenty Points paper we had drafted over the summer be taken seriously. After we left the building, federal officials simply stopped talking to anyone from the American Indian Movement. The idea for the Trail of Broken Treaties had included other national Indian groups and most of them were pretty upset over what happened. There was no shortage of Indian "leaders" wanting to get national press after they toured the BIA building.

Wounded Knee

There was a lot of planning going on with the national leadership of the American Indian Movement. It was one thing to depend on a coalition of Indian groups to do a national action. The AIM people wanted to do one that would be bigger in terms of publicity than what happened at the BIA. Wounded Knee was not just a single event but there were a series of things that happened which led up to the takeover of that tiny town in the hills of South Dakota.

For many years in small towns all along the reservation borders in South Dakota, Indians were beaten up and murdered. Earlier in the year, Gordon, Nebraska, just off the Pine Ridge Reservation, had been the place where AIM people had protested the death of Raymond Yellow Thunder. At first no one was charged with Yellow Thunder's death, then AIM people took over the town with about five-hundred protesters and two men were finally charged with manslaughter. After the BIA occupation in D.C., another murder happened in Custer, South Dakota. Wesley Bad Heart Bull was stabbed to death and, again, no charges were filed. That murder was one of several things that led us to Wounded Knee in the late winter of 1973.

The chairman of the Pine Ridge reservation, Dick Wilson, was about as corrupt as any tribal chairman I have ever encountered and we knew among ourselves that the next action would be at Pine Ridge. I was back in Lawrence and, as quietly as I could, starting to call people together. I had to be cautious because we knew by this time that the feds had begun to infiltrate AIM, using Indians over whose heads they had some kind of dirt. Those problems would get worse after Wounded Knee was over, but for now we trusted and loved each other.

Late one night the phone rang and it was an old friend from Pine Ridge. He told me to stick by the phone. Thirty minutes later Carter Camp called me and said in a purely happy voice, "Guess where we are?" Without waiting for an answer, he added, "We took over Wounded Knee." (Wounded Knee, on the Pine Ridge reservation, had been chosen because, in 1890, it had been the site of the last armed Indian resistance to U.S. soldiers.) Carter told me to get on the phone and call all the press and give them the number where he was at. He told me he would phone me every thirty minutes. I got to work. When he called me later, he told me he couldn't even put the phone down without it ringing with press from all over the world. If you look at the first few days of press coverage out of Wounded Knee, all the quotes are from Carter. Apparently, the other leadership went to bed early that night. That fact caused considerable animosity later on but we thought it was funny.

An hour or so after the first call, I went down the street to get some cigarettes. There were two FBI cars parked conspicuously outside the door of the apartment. I made a quick trip to Lincoln, Nebraska, to meet up with a strong AIM chapter there. We were there for two days during which the local AIM chapter leader and I took a little drive so we could talk. We had driven five blocks from his house and we were surrounded by half a dozen police cars. The registration needed "checking at the station" they said. We cooled our heels for about an hour and one by one we were taken into a room where sat two FBI agents.

It was good cop, bad cop. "What are you doing in Lincoln?" "Visiting friends," I said. The fencing went on for about an hour. I said nothing. Bad cop, "Listen you little cock-sucker, you take one step north of Lincoln, Nebraska, and I will personally find the worst jail in Nebraska for you to die in." I stared at him.

I went back to Kansas and organized 135 people and several tons of supplies. When we left the Mayetta reservation we drove straight north through Lincoln. As we went by, I rolled down the window and gave Lincoln the finger. By the time we were north of Omaha, we had picked up a five-car escort behind us, unmarked, but feds. On the radio we heard that Archie Fire and a caravan from California had been busted in Nevada. We stopped and talked about it, and headed on north. Over the state line in South Dakota, our escort grew to ten cars—that we could see. When we pulled into Rosebud, the staging area for the Wounded Knee entry, they passed us on by and we gave them happy waves.

The camp at Rosebud, about a hundred or so miles from Wounded Knee, had almost three hundred people waiting to get into the Knee. We didn't know it at the time but there was some internal bickering inside the camp leadership and we cooled our heels there for about a week. Some of the people who came with me got antsy and left. I was just a peon, but I still felt some responsibility for taking care of the people who came with me.

At the camp, cars with Pine Ridge plates driven by mostly elder women, would pull into camp and load up supplies to take them to into Pine Ridge, where they were dropped off at safe houses close to Wounded Knee. At night, the folks in the Knee would walk out and fill their backpacks and walk back in all in the same night. One evening, after about a week of boredom at Rosebud, I saw two cars pull in. I knew one of the women from work during the flood relief. "I got room in the cars for five of you if you want to walk in tonight," she says. I rounded up four others and we were in the cars before the camp leadership could intervene.

We arrived at the Manderson drop about ten that evening. The guides, young Lakota men familiar with the trails in and out, had already left. Aaron Desersa, a Lakota activist, gave us the choice of waiting till the next night or making a go on our own. I had been to Wounded Knee several times but only during the day. Aaron drew us a map. "Down the road, two miles, haystack on the right, cornfield on the left." "Through the cornfield, down a ravine, it will be dry, up a little hill and you hit Wounded Knee Creek." "Follow its banks and six miles or so you will see the lights of Wounded Knee." "Feds are all over the hills so stick to gullies and ravines."

The elder ladies had an Indian car with no working speedometer or odometer. Two miles in enemy country was as far as two thousand. South Dakota is covered with haystacks and cornfields. We went maybe a mile, maybe a half mile. Haystack and cornfield. We piled out carrying packs full of food, at least fifty pounds apiece. No guns. Through the cornfield. Dark as pitch. Ravine. Mike Meyers from Canada has the map and a little pen light. Mike says, "Here's the ravine but it looks like it is full of water." I stepped around Mike to look at the map and stepped off into the creek, six feet down, in early March, three feet of water. Like a turtle on its back in freezing water. They fished me out and we wandered the hills for the next four hours. Lost.

We knew it would be getting light in an hour or so and we were trying to decide either to lay up for the day or take another direction. While we tried to decide, we heard an enormous explosion. We jumped up and followed the sound. We trailed up a dry ravine and as we got to the top, another big explosion. As we topped out the ridge we could see the lights of Wounded Knee. We slow crawled the next mile and we could see bunkers with men moving around. We thought they were feds. Every five minutes or so flares would go off. By crawling between the flashes of light we made to the old Catholic church on the hill. When we walked into the basement of the church there was a brother cleaning an old deer rifle. "What are you guys doing still up?" he says. I wanted to slap him. What I was carrying in my pack was oatmeal and flour. The water had made that

FIGURE 2.7   Stationed in front of an upside-down American flag, armed members of the American Indian Movement (AIM) guard the village of Wounded Knee, South Dakota, during the winter of 1973. AIM chose to seize and occupy the small town on the Pine Ridge Sioux Reservation because it had been the site of the last armed Indian resistance to U.S. government takeover in 1890. AIM's occupation was a public protest of the long history of broken treaties, the deplorable conditions of reservation life, and decades of mismanagement by the U.S. Bureau of Indian Affairs. Federal marshals besieged the occupied village until AIM surrendered in April after two members died in gun battles. The protest received national and international attention.

Source: Corbis/Bettmann

fifty pound pack weigh a hundred pounds and they had to throw most of it away. We also later found out that the explosions we heard were our own people planting old, very unstable dynamite close to the fed positions and setting it off. It had set off a firefight that night which had covered our movements through the federal positions.

What I did for the next several weeks was mostly walk in and out, carrying supplies. The feds had us pretty much surrounded but whenever it snowed or rained or was bitterly cold, we filed out of the Knee like ants on the move. We tried to carry as much food as we could on those nights but we were always hungry. The morale of the people inside was pretty good most of the time but when the food got low and bullets were whistling overhead it was easy to be scared. Bravery is being scared and still being able to do what one needs to do to save the lives of the people there and there were many, many brave people.

Toward the end of April, when we thought there would be a disarmament, we decided to take as many of the guns out as we could. The night before I was scheduled to leave the Knee, one of the best guides, Chris Westerman, the brother of the actor Floyd, was busted along with fifteen other people. It didn't do much for our confidence about our own chances. Two of us decided to go out anyway. We left long after dark and walked out the first five or six miles in the water of a creek that led north and east toward the small town of Porcupine. We could hear the feds walking the banks of the creek with guard dogs. It was near daybreak when we reached one of the safe houses and so we hid in a haystack for a couple of hours until the family stirred and we could see who it was. They got us out of there and into Rapid City.

Over the next couple of days, a lot happened. The negotiations being held in Washington, D.C., broke down and it was decided to try to get back in the Knee. By this time the weather was warmer and feds were getting braver at night when we were on the move. They kept insisting they could hear and see people moving through the ravines and crying late at night. We knew it was the spirits of those who were killed back in 1890, massacred by the Seventh Cavalry.

We went to a safe house outside of Denby, south and east of Wounded Knee. It was about a fifteen mile walk to get in and we left about ten that night, nine of us including the two young Lakota guides. We had gone about six miles when we came to a fence. We had been told to go through the fence instead of over it because the feds had been planting trip flares on the fences. Sure enough one of the young women with us put her hand on the barbed wire fence and there was a whoosh and a trip flare sailed two hundred feet in the air. We had just enough time to hit the ground when the sky lit up. We lay still for a few minutes until the flare went out. About one hundred yards down the hill, we could see a little red light wink on.

We lay still for a few more minutes and we heard an engine start up. It was an armored personnel carrier. It turned slowly in a circle shining its lights over the top of us. It finally turned back around and shut the engine down. We lay there in the dark whispering about what we should do when a couple hundred yards back to the west we could hear two cars roar up and doors slam. Even at that distance we could see and hear people get out with flashlights and start up the hill. We crawled back below the crest of the hill and hotfooted it back toward Denby.

When we got back to the safe house we decided to head back to Rosebud. The young guides chose to sit it out at the safe house in case we came back the next night. A few days later we ran into those guides and they told us that twenty minutes after we left, about thirty tribal police, goons we called them, hit the safe house and the two guides had to dash into the trees in order to get away.

The leadership outside Wounded Knee decided to send me and some others on a speaking tour of the eastern states in order to raise money. We were in St. Louis when the wire services reported the death of Buddy Lamont inside the Knee. They were also reporting that parts of the 82nd Airborne were on the alert to come in and take the place over. For the next couple of days we were in a panic, but eventually word came that a cease fire and stand-down was agreed to, and by May 7th, it was over.

A Political Movement Becomes Spiritual

While we were in the Knee, we had held two sweat lodges and often would hold other spiritual ceremonies. When everyone stood down, most of us left and were not arrested, though some were hunted down later. We were scattered, but we took with us a hunger for things spiritual. Most anthropologists and religionists have ignored this but a new religious movement came out of Wounded Knee. It is the sweat lodge religion.

In my research through the years I have found that many tribes had some form of sweat ceremony. By the early 20th century most traditional ceremonies of Indian people were banned and outlawed. Some tribes kept their ceremonies and performed them in secret. After Wounded Knee, like a dandelion blown to the wind, the seeds of this reborn purification ceremony scattered to the four directions.

I eventually left the movement. The leadership was in jail and those who came in later tried to reenact Wounded Knees in other places. Pine Ridge Reservation became an armed camp. Over the next three years there were almost eighty unsolved murders in Pine Ridge, most committed by the police who were armed by the FBI. It climaxed with the shootout with the FBI at the Jumping Bull compound near Oglala, S.D., in June of 1975. AIM folks all over Indian country were hunted down and jailed on petty charges and then committed "suicide" in jail.

When I moved to California in 1974, there were only one or two sweat lodges that I knew of in the whole state. By 1980, there were dozens. Indian people who had not done the ceremony for generations dusted off old songs by searching the memories of the elders and crawled back into the womb of the Mother Earth and purified themselves for a revival of Indian spirituality.

What did it all mean? Now more than thirty years later I can say these things. Our militancy during those years brought America face to face with a giant historical lie. There was no such thing as the Vanishing Indian. Each decade since the 1970 census the Indian population has increased by huge percentages. And each generation has redoubled the effort to bring the culture and tradition back to life.

By the 1980s, due to a new consciousness about Indian treaties and government promises, tribes began to enjoy a new sense of self-determination. While we never slew the multi-headed Bureau of Indian Affairs, we did start sub-contracting programs they had long mismanaged, and for some tribes this has led to a new sense of commitment to Indian progress in education, health care, and child care, and a realization that our languages and our culture have an intrinsic value to the American experience. We ourselves have started to realize that we have our own history.

Even though the issue seems trivial to most people, our anger about the use of derogatory names for sports teams has at least caused the American public to realize that we don't like to be called savages, redskins, braves, or squaws, or be the subject of caricature about our history and our contribution to American history. The founding documents of the American system of government were based in large part on the Indian way of government.

You, my dear sweet children, were given your Indian names at birth, and before your grandmother, my mother, died she named almost seventy of your relatives. I was twenty years old when I first crawled into a sweat lodge. Both of you were still inside your mother's belly when you came into the womb of the Mother Earth. Our militancy, our stridency, our willingness to stand up at the last possible moment to save our culture, gave you an option that many of our ancestors did not have.

Be proud of your Indian heritage. Fight to hold on to something that was torn from your grandfathers' and grandmothers' grasp. Fight to be able to pray in a language as old as this land. Indian activists of my generation were not noble, sometimes we were not even brave, most of the time we were damn naïve. But maybe we heard something on the wind, a lost song, a whispered prayer, an echo from a drum long ago silenced by racism and genocide. And all we did was strain to hear it, say it once again, and make the earth resonate with the heartbeat of a drum that is also the heartbeat of our people, your people.

Love, Dad

QUESTIONS FOR DISCUSSION

1. Johnny Flynn describes growing up as the son of an Irish American father and an American Indian mother. How do the events of his youth contribute to his awareness of his place in American life? What roles do his mother's family and his father's family play in his life? Can you compare any elements of Flynn's childhood to the childhood described by Ray Hubbard in "Deep in the Heart?" For example, how do Indians and African Americans experience racism while traveling?

2. What divisions among Native Americans does Flynn first encounter at the Haskell Indian School? How does this awareness affect him? Why does he resent the school? What is he looking for when he joins the drum group and the Native American church?

3. How does Flynn first become involved in the American Indian Movement? He talks about American Indian history as a "battle brewing" and a "longer war." What does he mean by the "longer war?" How is AIM a part of this longer war? How does the government react to AIM and how does that reaction affect the decisions that AIM and Flynn make? Do you feel the U.S. government could have handled its response to AIM differently?

4. Flynn says that the AIM leadership believed that the nonviolent protests and methods used by the Civil Rights Movement during the 1960s would not work for Indian people. Why does AIM choose militant confrontation? Are there other ways (besides confrontations) in which AIM tries to help Indian people?

5. Flynn takes part in a number of AIM actions: disrupting the Koshare dancers, protesting at Phelps Dodge, Rapid City flood relief, the Trail of Broken Treaties, and the occupations at the Bureau of Indian Affairs and Wounded Knee. Are some of these protests more effective in achieving AIM goals than others? Do you feel AIM members were justified in their occupation of the BIA and the town of Wounded Knee?

6. Compare Flynn's piece with Sara Evans' "Not my Mother's Path," a story of the women's liberation movement. Both are memoirs, both tell stories of Sixties-era liberation movements, yet they differ widely in tone and intent. Describe the "person" that emerges from each story. What is the effect on the reader of Flynn's framing device—the letter to his children—and the conclusion of his story?

7. Flynn counts spiritual renewal, starting with the sweat lodges and peyote ceremonies, as successful outcomes of the period of Native American activism that began with AIM. Do you think the place of Native Americans in American society has improved since the 1970s? What problems persist?

Pathways

Introduction

The Sixties provided unprecedented choices for young Americans who were searching for meaningful lives. Born as "war babies" and "baby boomers," they had grown up in the Cold War. They had seen African Americans fighting for civil rights and witnessed people their own age protesting social inequities at home and United States policies abroad, particularly the Vietnam War. Urged forward by the era's presidents, Kennedy and Johnson, and by their teachers and college professors, some young people who had been raised in middle-class comfort rejected what they saw as the materialism and complacency of their parents' generation and the careerism and conformity of industrialized society. The path through college to a career and a suburban house did not seem as attractive to them as it had seemed to the generation that had grown up during the Depression. Instead, they sought jobs or lifestyles that would make a difference either in the world or within themselves.

Many young Americans found meaning in service to their country, and the government provided a number of options in addition to the military. The Peace Corps was a service option created by John F. Kennedy, who planned the program while seeking election in 1960. At the time of its founding the following year, the Peace Corps embodied both the youthful idealism of the period and the desire of the United States to cultivate an international image of itself as something more than just a military and economic superpower. For more than a decade, the United States had been competing with the Soviet Union for influence in the developing nations of

Africa, Asia, and Latin America, employing a combination of economic assistance, military aid, and propaganda. The Peace Corps promised to send volunteers to many of those countries to work on a variety of educational, agricultural, and development projects, hoping thereby to cultivate pro-American goodwill and contribute to international communication and understanding.

More than 5,000 applicants vied for the first Peace Corps positions. Within a year, 750 volunteers were serving in more than a dozen countries. The agency expanded dramatically over the next several years, reaching its peak with 15,000 volunteers working around the world in 1966. In many cases, Peace Corps volunteers succeeded in combining life-changing personal experiences with genuine contributions to education, development, or social welfare in their host countries. They worked without salaries, drawing subsistence-level allowances that enabled them to live in approximately the same conditions as the people with whom they were working. They ate the local foods and spoke the local languages in their efforts to share as much as possible in the life experiences of their hosts. By the early years of the twenty-first century, more than 170,000 Peace Corps volunteers had served in more than 130 countries around the world.

Not long after Lyndon Johnson took office in 1963, he announced his intention to create a "Great Society," and he declared "War on Poverty." Working with a cooperative Congress, the Johnson administration created Medicaid and Medicare and established the National Endowments for the Arts and Humanities. Programs organized under the new Office of Economic Opportunity (OEO) focused on improving opportunities for the poor to help themselves. The agency's establishing legislation declared its intention to "eliminate the paradox of poverty in the midst of plenty in this Nation by opening to everyone the opportunity for education and training, the opportunity to work, and the opportunity to live in decency and dignity."

VISTA (Volunteers in Service to America) was created as a domestic version of the Peace Corps. The OEO also established the Job Corps, for training young men and women in skills they could use to gain decent jobs; Community Action Programs, where residents ran federally funded programs in their own impoverished neighborhoods; Head Start, for pre-schoolers from poor families; Upward Bound, to help bright, disadvantaged high school students go to college; and an astonishing variety of clinics, help centers, and social agencies. In some "Great Society" or "War on Poverty" programs, college-educated youth could help the urban or rural poor by working alongside members of the affected communities. All the programs represented a serious commitment of federal energies and tax dollars to fighting poverty and social problems on a national scale. Not surprisingly, the War on Poverty had critics as well as supporters, but a number of the programs proved their worth and still function in the country today.

Another pathway for young people not ready to embrace their parents' life choices was voluntary engagement in social and political protest, though, it must be said, the era's anti-war and liberation movements offered few opportunities for paid work. Almost by definition, activism was voluntary and sporadic. What was more, coalitions of young activists could be short-lived. Alliances on the left were fragile democracies, ideological battles were fierce, and groups often succumbed to factional fights. Even the Students for a Democratic Society (SDS), a large, inclusive group of college-age youth who led the anti-war movement on campuses around the nation, broke into factions during their annual meeting in 1969.

After the Tet Offensive (a shockwave of attacks by the Viet Cong in the winter and spring of 1968), followed by the additional commitment of American soldiers to the war in Vietnam, the assassinations of Martin Luther King, Jr. and Robert Kennedy, and the police/protestor violence at the Chicago Democratic Convention, even some dedicated activists became discouraged about the prospects for peace abroad and social change at home. The counterculture beckoned, with its liberated lifestyle and its messages about turning inward, discovering yourself, and learning to live simply on the Earth, in harmony with nature and your fellow human beings. Several years earlier, drug researcher and guru Timothy Leary had suggested that the young "turn on" (to hallucinogenic drugs and the search for personal enlightenment), "tune in" (accept that you weren't going to change the power structure and start looking for higher realities), and "drop out" (of school, jobs, protest movements, and all of ordinary society). Increasingly, young people thought he had a point.

What was the counterculture? Most people associate it with the "hippie" lifestyle: long hair, eccentric clothing, free love, drugs, rock and roll, and psychedelic art. Linked with the student movement and sympathetic for the most part to the anti-war movement, the counterculture began as an attempt to live a different kind of American life, to create an alternative to materialism, selfishness, and conformity. Young people who embraced the counterculture were the spiritual offspring of the Beat Generation of the 1950s. They first began to appear in the mid-1960s in urban enclaves—Haight Ashbury in San Francisco, Greenwich Village and the Lower East Side in New York City, Cambridge, Massachusetts, and Old Town in Chicago. The streets of their neighborhoods sprouted free stores, free clinics, free kitchens, "crash pads" (where the homeless or itinerant could stay for a few days), food cooperatives, and shops selling incense, drug paraphernalia, mystical books, pop records, "underground" newspapers, posters, and exotic dresses. Idealistic groups like the Diggers in San Francisco tried to live as much as possible without money, giving food and clothing to the community and sponsoring free concerts and theater.

Young adults, teenagers, school dropouts, as well as the merely curious, flocked to urban hippie enclaves between 1966 and 1969, and the style if not the substance of the counterculture began to catch on around the country. By the early 1970s, long hair was everywhere, even on lawyers; trousers had flared legs (or "bell bottoms," as they were popularly called); many people experimented with drugs; young couples began living together without the benefit of marriage. Americans found it pleasant and increasingly acceptable to graft elements of counterculture style onto conventional careers and lives. Meanwhile, many of the earliest advocates of "flower power," peace, and enlightenment drifted away from the cities. They felt that their earnest efforts to create loving, non-materialist communities had been doomed by the influx of underage runaways and social derelicts, people who had come for the freedom and the free stuff but brought with them desperation or violence, thereby killing the dream.

Some of the true believers moved to the country, bought or squatted on land, and tried to create alternative communities that would be self-sufficient. By and large, they were hoping to recapture what they assumed were the rhythms and values of a simpler, pre-industrial time. The "back-to-the-land" movement gave rise to some successful rural communes, such as The Farm in Tennessee and Twin Oaks in Virginia, that thrived by imposing structure, choosing leaders, and setting limitations on personal freedom. Unlike these intentional communities, places like Morningstar and the Wheeler Ranch in Northern California were haphazard settlements of idealistic but inexperienced young urban refugees. The landscape at these communes became littered with shacks, tents, old school buses, and derelict cars. There was no electricity and no plumbing, and there were no rules.

Communes dedicated on principle to anarchy and hedonism frequently made their members insecure. Free love, which sounded like a grand escape from inhibitions and outworn morality, actually led to jealousy and possessiveness and the exploitation of women. When work went undone and freeloaders drained communal resources, many of the unstructured communes failed. However, some groups successfully experimented with different forms of the family—same-sex partnerships, extended families, and parenting shared within the group. In addition, the back-to-the-land movement helped to raise the nation's consciousness about the environment and the need for alternative energy sources. Back-to-the-land practitioners became the pioneers of movements for recycling, organic farming, and sustainable agriculture.

Drugs were a significant aspect of youth counterculture, pervading the lives of students, urban hippies, and rural pioneers. Young people all over the country smoked marijuana, which produced a relatively mild intoxication somewhat comparable to the effects of alcohol. Some sought more intense drug experiences by sampling the potent hallucinogens psilocybin, mescaline, and lysergic acid diethylamide (LSD). These drugs were either plant products derived from mushrooms and cacti or laboratory-synthesized chemical compounds. Many users believed that LSD and other drugs would expand their minds, leading to spiritual enlightenment, an awareness of universal harmony, and freedom from attachment to material things. In 1966, Timothy Leary went so far as to found a religion, the League for Spiritual Discovery, which regarded drugs as sacramental substances.

Smoking marijuana was referred to as "getting high," while taking more powerful drugs such as LSD was called "tripping." Many drug users described "mind-blowing" trips full of color and light; some felt they had traveled to a new level of consciousness, solving the mysteries of life. Sometimes, in the cold light of day, after the drug's effects had worn off, the "answers" disappeared. Drug-induced visions inspired psychedelic art, a new form reminiscent of *art nouveau* but characterized by swirling, neon-bright colors and exaggerated organic forms. Certain types of rock music (for example, songs by The Grateful Dead, Jefferson Airplane, and Pink Floyd) were also characterized as "psychedelic."

Some drug takers experienced "bad trips," hours filled with paranoid visions and sickness. Because the drugs were illegal and often purchased from shady street "dealers," there was no guarantee of their purity or content, and there was never any guarantee about the effect of any particular drug on an individual consumer. The use of hallucinogenic drugs was highly controversial, even among people who took them. Many worried that continued use of LSD and other substances could cause permanent mental or emotional damage. As early as 1967, fears surfaced that LSD could cause chromosomal damage or birth defects. Those who used marijuana and hallucinogens usually condemned "uppers"—methedrine and amphetamines, commonly called "speed." The slogan "Speed Kills" began appearing on posters, buttons, and urban graffiti. "Meth reduces you to your lowest self," wrote editor Wayne M. Hansen in the August 18, 1967, issue of Boston's underground paper, *Avatar*, " . . . and you'll babble the rest of your worthless life away, until your nervous system and your mind have rotted, your synapses have quit, and your soul is sealed off and you're a walking, blabbering, slobbering, lifeless, deathless, feelingless, nothingness shell of a man."

By the late 1970s, with the "War on Drugs" in full swing, most members of the Sixties generation had outgrown their interest in "mind altering" substances, especially psychedelic drugs. Not many people had time for "tripping" in the world of careers and families. A few discovered that the deleterious effects of prolonged drug use had made it impossible for them to function normally; others simply moved on.

For a number of young Americans of the Sixties and Seventies, the search for enlightenment led beyond "tripping" and other forms of hedonism. Disillusioned with drugs, or determined to avoid them, but still eager to distance themselves from conventional values and established authority figures, thousands of young people rejected mainstream religion and sought alternative spiritual paths. For some, the quest meant a generalized interest in what came to be known as New Age spirituality, which often involved reverence for nature and visions of universal peace and brotherhood, combined with the use of astrology, numerology, Tarot cards, the *I Ching* (an ancient Chinese book of divination), and other mystical techniques for predicting the future or delving into one's inner being.

However, some people sought more formal, structured religious experiences by joining the many groups that proliferated on the spiritual fringes of society. Participation in these groups often involved living communally with other members and severing ties with family and friends in the outside world. Some groups lasted only a short time and disappeared, leaving few records; others were highly secretive or tended to exaggerate their membership numbers.

Often described pejoratively as "cults," these alternative religions ranged from obscure groups virtually unknown outside one city or region of the country to such high-profile organizations as the Unification Church (often called the "Moonies," a reference to its leader, South Korean preacher Sun Myung Moon) and the International Society for Krishna Consciousness (nicknamed "Hare Krishnas"), whose saffron-robed devotees attracted attention by dancing, chanting, and soliciting donations on street corners, in airports, or in other public places.

Some so-called cults of the Sixties were offshoots or variant forms of long-established faiths. For example, Unification Church members hailed Reverend Moon, a former Presbyterian, as a new messiah carrying on the work that Jesus began. The Krishna Consciousness movement, brought to the United States by a businessman-turned-swami from India, had its roots in Hinduism, as did transcendental meditation, a practice promoted by the Indian spiritual teacher Maharishi Mahesh Yogi and practiced, at least briefly, by the Beatles and other celebrities. The Nation of Islam (also known as the Black Muslims), popularized under the leadership of Elijah Muhammad, adopted many features of orthodox Islam, such as prohibitions on eating pork and drinking alcohol, but also incorporated a black separatist political agenda. The Way, founded by Victor Paul Wierwille, and the Children of God, founded by David Brandt Berg (known to his disciples as Moses David), described themselves as Bible-based organizations, but both groups alienated many mainstream Christians by their behavior and their deviations from standard theology. Young people from these loosely controlled organizations were religious fundamentalists but not social conservatives, so their lives often included drugs, alcohol, and sex outside marriage. They proudly referred to themselves as "Jesus Freaks."

Many fringe spiritual groups did exercise rigid control over the lives of their members, requiring followers to eat restricted diets, abstain from drugs and sexual intercourse, and observe periods of fasting and other penitential disciplines. Some groups pushed members to prayer, meditation, and religious study, even to marry spouses chosen for them by cult leaders. Members worked for little or no pay in church-run businesses or spent hours on the streets raising money by selling incense, candles, religious literature, and other items. Some cults were organized as strict hierarchies, with lower-ranking members expected to take orders unquestioningly and to show great deference to their superiors.

Alternative religions often faced charges that they employed psychological manipulation techniques to control their followers' minds. Alleging that their children had been "brainwashed" by fringe religious movements, some parents hired controversial figures known as "deprogrammers," who specialized in persuading young people to abandon cult membership—sometimes abducting, confining, and haranguing them until they gave up their cult allegiance. Critics of deprogramming maintained that the practice was a violent and illegal infringement on individual religious freedom.

Most of the smaller Sixties and Seventies-era cults have disappeared. A few have by now survived long enough that they may be poised to move beyond fringe cult status and establish places for themselves within the nation's diverse religious mainstream.

In the decades that have passed since the 1960s, some Americans have come to regard the legacy of the counterculture as destructive to the American way of life. With its spiritual detours, drugs, rootlessness, and sexual freedom, the counterculture, along with women's liberation and gay liberation, is held responsible by some for destroying traditional family structures, undermining the authority of churches and government leaders, and degrading the entertainment industry. Those who argue against this perspective point to different legacies of the counterculture, including environmentalism, organic farming, health foods, blended families, and increased tolerance of religious and sexual differences. However we view the long-term impact of the counterculture, it may be important to realize that the young people who embraced it were participating in a search for utopia, and that similar quests have cycled in and out of American history since the very beginning.

The five authors of the stories in this section struggle to explain what set them on the paths they followed in the 1960s and 1970s. They tell us that so much of what looks, in hindsight, like conscious choice may have been accident, impulse, curiosity, or pain avoidance at the time. For each of them, altruism—wanting, in some way, to be of help—played a part in their decision making, but some of them also describe directionlessness or disillusionment with the other choices available to them. Middle-class and well educated, they had the luxury of time for experimentation and the idealism that characterized many young members of the Great Society.

R. Thomas Collins' story, "Hope House," takes place when he is still a teenager in secondary school. Somewhat self-conscious about his privileged background, Collins was inspired by the bravery of civil rights activists and troubled by the violence in America's cities. He felt a sense of obligation to help make the world a better place. In 1964, when liberal teachers and social reformers at his Midwestern preparatory school created a program for tutoring inner-city African American boys, he signed on to help. His involvement with the tutoring program led him to join the staff of one of the first Upward Bound summer programs in the country.

Upward Bound was a creation of the Economic Opportunity Act of 1964. Along with the preschool program, Head Start, Upward Bound formed part of the educational battlefront in the Johnson administration's War on Poverty. Selected high schools around the country would identify bright but poor students underserved by their school systems, students who might be able to attend college on scholarships if they had proper preparation. These students spent the summer living on university or boarding school campuses, attended special classes, received individual tutoring and counseling, and participated in cultural and recreational activities. Many of them moved on to universities in the fall or during the next year. Upward Bound gave middle-class college students an opportunity to share the educational gifts they had been given with less fortunate students only a few years younger than themselves. In that sense, the program benefited two social classes. Upward Bound still exists and is now part of TRIO, an expanded government program supporting college preparation and success.

When R. Thomas Collins encountered Upward Bound in the spring of 1966, it was in its second year and still in the experimental stages. As a tutor in training, collins was sent into Cleveland's inner city to spend a weekend working with a grant-funded housing rehabilitation program, Hope, Inc., or HOPE, which stood for "Housing Our People Economically." Looking back on his encounter with poverty and its consequences, Collins later wondered about his own desire to help, measuring it as naive against the seeming intractability of poverty and racism in 1960s America.

John Manners ("The Peace Corps: Kenya 1968–1972") begins his story with his graduation from college in 1968, just in time to be eligible for the draft. Like many of his generation, Manners was opposed to his country's involvement in the war in Southeast Asia and had no intention of becoming part of it. He chose the Peace Corps as an alternative form of national service and requested a posting to Kenya, the African country where he had spent a year of his childhood. Manners describes his life as a teacher and sports coach in a boys' secondary school, the connections he made with local people, and his frequent get-togethers with other Peace Corps volunteers scattered across a country as large as the state of Texas. He shares his perspective on the difference between the British colonial Kenya he had known as a child and the post-colonial Kenya of 1969, which was struggling to educate its children and lift its people out of poverty. Manners describes his discomfort with the deference paid to whites and with whites' racist attitudes in Kenya, but says he did little to challenge the prevailing system. He explains that he finally found his niche in defending his students' rights, getting to know their families, and coaching young athletes to national victory. Manners' story, told with irony and self-deprecation, offers an insider's view of the Peace Corps experience and an outside view of U.S. international policy in the late 1960s.

James Fadiman's story ("Opening the Doors of Perception") takes place during his years as a graduate student and teaching assistant in psychology at Stanford University. Already acquainted with the work of Timothy Leary and Richard Alpert, Harvard professors notorious for their experimentation with the drug LSD, Fadiman helped to run a foundation-sponsored psychology experiment that utilized LSD, one of many such programs of the mid-1960s. Intrigued by the results he saw in laboratory situations, Fadiman also used the drug informally. He became involved with the community around Ken Kesey, the best-selling author of *One Flew Over the Cuckoo's Nest* and leader of a group of young Palo Alto people experimenting with drugs and alternative lifestyles. It was through Kesey that Fadiman met his future wife. When the U.S. government called a halt to experiments with LSD, Fadiman experienced deep disappointment, feeling that an important tool for understanding human potential had been lost.

Author Steve Diamond ("Back to the Land") was about to graduate from Columbia University in New York City in the tumultuous spring of 1968. A student of journalism, Diamond had already begun to pursue his own brand of radical activism outside the university, working as an editor at the Liberation News Service (LNS), a left-wing news agency founded in 1967 by Raymond Mungo and Marshall Bloom. Based in Washington, D. C., and New York during its two most active years, LNS sent hundreds of subscribers (mostly college and "underground" newspapers) twice-weekly news packets with stories and photographs documenting the progressive movements and counterculture of the late 1960s. This news tended to emphasize anti-war protests, the Civil Rights and women's liberation movements, and youth culture. Because LNS staffers had worldwide contacts among radical groups and Third World liberation movements, the news service was able to provide the underground press with a global perspective.

Diamond opens his story just as LNS is breaking apart into two opposing factions. He describes the inspiration that led him to bring the Beatles' movie *Magical Mystery Tour* to New York City for its U.S. premiere. The screening was to be a benefit to raise operating funds for LNS. Diamond and his colleagues used the money to move themselves and the press to a farm in western Massachusetts, where they planned to continue their work while learning to farm organically and live off the land. The rest of the story describes the demise of LNS and Diamond's own deepening spiritual connection with the natural world and the members of his communal household. Diamond's personal experiences are part of a larger shift in youth political culture during 1968, a response to the country's failure to end the war in Vietnam or to create a fair and just society at home. Although many young Americans continued their political activity, some, like Diamond and his friends, turned inward, hoping to change themselves and then change the world, one human microcosm at a time.

Karen Smith ("The Process") explains that she was searching for community and adventure when she began her spiritual quest in the summer of 1969. Unable to settle into an "ordinary" life after college, Smith joined a small group of seekers who traveled the United States in search of enlightenment. A trip to England led them to become members of The Process, Church of the Final Judgment, a "New Age" religious cult whose complex theology combined elements of Eastern mysticism, psychotherapeutic practice, and Judeo-Christian tradition. Smith experienced both the restrictions and the excitement of cult life. She endured the long, hard hours of work, the physical privation, and the subservience to hierarchical superiors but thrived on the companionship of charismatic people and the opportunity for personal growth. She also loved the challenges involved in building an organization. However, when the organization suffered a schismatic rupture, she had to make up her mind whether to stay or leave.

HOPE HOUSE
R. Thomas Collins, Jr.

There was a time when I believed good intentions were what mattered. I learned otherwise when I was 18 in Hough, Cleveland, where I went to find out what living in poverty meant to the people trapped in it. The idea that someone like me could drop in and out of a place like Hough as a learning "experience" was typical of many wrongheaded fantasies of that time. What the experience taught me is that good intentions are only a beginning, and that willful innocence, particularly when combined with arrogance, means trouble.

Everybody who passed through that time has a story. The journey that led me to militia duty in one of the War on Poverty's minor skirmishes began in 1962 when I enrolled in Western Reserve Academy, a boys' preparatory school in Hudson, a small village 35 miles southeast of Cleveland, Ohio. For me, Reserve became a calm sanctuary; I was a 14-year-old refugee from a family torn beyond repair by alcoholism and a disintegrating marriage.

Reserve took its name from the late 18th century, when northern Ohio was called Connecticut's Western Reserve. The Western Reserve was settlement territory under the Northwest Ordinance of 1787, and a favored locale of Connecticut veterans who had yet to receive pay or pension for Revolutionary War service. Hudson was settled by Yankee farmers and tradesmen, and the Academy was established in 1826 by Yale graduates to bring God to the frontier.

In time, Ohio became a state and the college moved to Cleveland, where its successor institution today is called Case-Western Reserve University. The brick buildings in Hudson, including the oldest still-standing astronomical observatory in America, were taken over by others who established a school to prepare boys for college. Visitors who come to Hudson still can see the influence of its New England founders on the village and grounds. There is still a common green, a band gazebo, and white clapboard homes with picket fences, giant elm trees, and ivy-covered brick buildings with huge windows.

Reserve students came primarily from the families of industrialists and professionals from Cleveland and Akron and the other river and lake towns of the industrial Midwest. My father was an executive with General Motors' Delco Products Division in Dayton, where we had moved from Connecticut three years before. When I entered Reserve in the fall of 1962, my awareness of public issues was limited. I was more interested in a private calm. As far as civil rights was concerned, my understanding focused around the Civil War and the abolition of slavery. My great-grandfather, Henry E. Savage, served in the Union Army. His photograph, showing him in his chin beard and sergeant's uniform from Company G, 16th Connecticut Volunteers, stood on my dresser as a source of pride. I understood that segregation was illegal, or so I thought, and that discrimination was wrong. The fact that there was only one black student among my classmates didn't seem unusual or affect my thinking one way or the other.

My first year at Reserve I was preoccupied with football, wrestling, Latin, and attending dances at girls' schools nearby. There were a few students who considered themselves civil rights activists. To be an activist then was to wear a button of one sort or another on the lapel of your suit jacket, to listen to the music of Joan Baez on your mono record player in your dorm room. Perhaps it meant wearing a black turtle neck sweater on off hours when regulation suit jacket and tie weren't required. To the adventuresome, a trip to nearby Kent, home of Kent State University, offered darkened coffee houses where musicians played folk songs on guitars. On free Saturdays, I enjoyed sneaking over to a place called The Blind Owl, where the dark interior allowed me to smoke cigarettes without fear of being caught by a master or prefect from Reserve.

Before I had been at Reserve for many months, civil rights became part of the sermons at Sunday mass, and at morning chapel services on campus. Rev. Dr. Martin Luther King, Jr. captured national attention over the course of several spring weeks in 1963, when a civil rights dispute in Birmingham grew in intensity. On Good Friday, April 12, Rev. King led a protest march. After eight blocks, he was arrested and jailed. The marchers met with fire hoses and dogs. Television networks carried the news and vivid images in detail. In May and June, as if it had spread through the air via television, a virulent fever took hold of the nation, as more than 700 demonstrations erupted across the country, each of them meeting violent response. Police in southern cities made more than 13,000 arrests. The National Guard was called out in Cambridge, Maryland. Authorities in Jacksonville tear-gassed the crowds. Violence plagued Memphis, Baton Rouge, and Charlottesville. There were mass street demonstrations in Detroit, New York, Philadelphia, and Chicago.

In June, 1963, President Kennedy submitted the Civil Rights Bill to Congress. The debate, so simple on TV, grew in complexity in Congress. Meanwhile, politics was on the airwaves and in the streets. Television as an instrument of current events came into its own. Once TV news had been a daily newsreel, little different from the shorts before the movies. But now it joined the nation together, conveying information, permitting a sharing of emotion and, at times, revulsion. All you had to do to be part of daily events was tune in and feel. You could watch a police dog tear the shirt off a black Alabama protester; you could see a woman turned over and over on the ground by a jet of water from a fire hose; and, in August 1963, you could hear Dr. King on the steps of the Lincoln Memorial say "I have a dream . . . "

Experiencing the impact of those images became a political event. On the gray screen of television, subtlety and reflection were erased. Events took on a new kind of reality, in which the world became divided into forces of good and evil. Lines were drawn. The segregationists were wrong and represented values that had to be crushed. Fundamental moral issues appeared at stake. I had grown up with values taught by nuns in Sunday school and I was an Eagle Scout. I believed in the Boy Scout Oath and Scout Law. Ancestors on my mother's side had fought in the American Revolution and in the Civil War. In my frame of reference, discrimination was wrong. These were the values I held. Equal rights was something I wanted to see realized. The details of how this would be done never crossed my mind, and I had no idea how I would become caught up in the painful struggle.

In June and July of 1963, the academy let out for the summer and I was sent to summer school at St. George's School in Newport, Rhode Island. As my folks' marriage deteriorated and I grew older, living away from home was a fine arrangement to me, so I didn't mind summer school. I had a little spending money, and

I could fall asleep each night without wondering whether I'd be awakened by the sounds of shouting I couldn't control and which did not stop no matter how hard I prayed.

Newport was home to the U.S. Navy, huge mansions once called cottages by the New York rich, a famous tennis club, a famous yacht race, and the Newport Jazz Festival. In the early years, the Newport Jazz Festival was for jazz aficionados. Now, however, the commercial laws of the recording industry were changing that. In 1963, the festival departed from its purist jazz tradition and showcased several popular folk singers whose music and lyrics had become a kind of political poetry to preach about social inequities.

Music was the medium of choice for many contemporary poets. Where in earlier times such poets might be confined to the printed word and a small circulation, now their imagery in songs was produced by record companies and broadcast nationwide. The simple traditions of folk music and the primal drive of rock and roll fused. Politics was not only being conducted through television news, it was in popular music, which became a new language to communicate feelings and frustrations.

Along with other summer students and music fans from the east coast, I went to the festival several times over its four-day course. One of the performers was a new singer-song writer, Bob Dylan, who wrote what was then the best-selling song, "Blowin' in the Wind." I had a seat in the middle of the audience the night Dylan performed. From my wooden folding chair, I saw a runty fellow with unkempt hair, wearing worn blue denims. As he played his guitar, a harmonica was suspended inches from his mouth by some contraption around his neck. Like a modern Elijah warning his congregation to repent, Dylan sang songs that would later become standards, among them "Hard Rain's Gonna Fall," and "The Times They Are a Changin'," and, of course, "Blowin' in the Wind." "How many roads must a man walk down, before he is called a man . . . " No one who heard that song thought it was about anything but civil rights.

The following November, when I was back at Reserve, I heard the news of President Kennedy's murder on a day when my uncle and aunt from Connecticut were visiting. My uncle, James F. Collins, a professional politician, was a Republican Party operative in Connecticut. In 1962, he had been the GOP candidate for U.S. Congress from Hartford, a race he lost, as he would again in 1964. Uncle Jim, who went on to become a Connecticut Superior Court Judge two years before his death in 1975, was from the Rockefeller wing of the GOP, a pragmatic politician, not an ideologue. On that overcast November 22, he stood with his wife, Connie, before the television set in my dormitory common room. He said, over and over, "This'll change everything . . . "

After Uncle Jim and Aunt Connie left later that afternoon, I went to wrestling practice. We were subdued as we went through our warm-ups, waiting for practice to begin. Our coach, still dressed in his street clothes, came into the wrestling room late. He called us over. "I am in no mood to conduct practice today," he said as we gathered around. "I don't know about you, but I don't feel up to it . . . "

A number of us later wandered over to one of the basketball courts to get a pick-up game going. A few of us leaned against the whitewashed cinder block wall, talking about Kennedy's murder. "Something is screwed up with the country," someone said. That night I called home. My father got on the line. "I didn't agree with the guy," he said, "but this is tragic. No way to do, no way at all . . . "

But it had happened. Suddenly things seemed changed, as if with Kennedy's death, the country had been shoved over a boundary line. Not that I was particularly caught up in any Kennedy mystique, such as it was then; not at all. My uncle was a Republican candidate, my father a GM executive, all in my family, both the Irish side and the Yankees, were Republicans. Rather, I got caught up with everyone else in Kennedy's death; the suddenness of it; the unfairness of it. Something was wrong. There was a survivor's guilt to it all. Those evils clearly visible had to be crushed, such as the discrimination we believed Kennedy had fought against. Within months, the new president, Lyndon Johnson, had joined the crusade against discrimination, and had begun his war on one of the country's great visible evils—poverty.

I signed up the following year. My opportunity came in a Community Action Program called the Akron/Summit Tutorial Project. It was launched by a Reserve graduate who had taken a student leave from Yale to start an education program for poor children in his home county in Ohio. He came to Reserve one evening early in 1965 and spoke about his dreams. He was ambitious and idealistic. The project he outlined was simplicity itself: Here at Reserve was an island of learning and privilege within a few miles of communities of great poverty. Why not bring the communities together so that students could give of their learning to those who didn't have it and who could use it to better themselves? Once a week we would go to the poor community and teach children assigned to us. He had already done some preliminary work with the federal government, had the endorsement of the school administration, and within weeks would have the blessing of the appropriate local governments and school boards. Several teachers from Reserve volunteered as administrators. I was among the 20 students to sign up as tutors.

One Tuesday, a few weeks later, we climbed into a van after dinner. It was dark by the time we arrived at Twinsburg Heights, a town on the southeast periphery of Cleveland. The Heights was a hardscrabble ghetto of small tarpaper and wooden homes. The section was laid out on a grid of narrow streets criss-crossing a flat terrain. Our van bounced in the ruts and potholes. Small shacks stood behind some homes. Inside lived hundreds of black families whose breadwinners worked in nearby factories, or as day laborers, or not at all. A few of the buildings on street corners were lighted with neon signs advertising beer and soft drinks. There was a saloon. Some older men milled around a fire burning in a barrel. As we drove past, they watched in silence.

We arrived at a small, newly constructed prefabricated building. The parking lot was unpaved and grooved from truck tires. Pockets of ice cracked under our feet as we walked to the front door. The building had aluminum sides, a poured concrete slab floor, and numerous fluorescent lights suspended from the ceiling, giving the inside a white-light clarity similar to a hospital. There was a newness to the smell of the interior, combined with a musty smell of moisture and dust.

It was here that I met Carl, a sturdy black boy of 11 years with a sweet temper. We were introduced and within a few minutes we found a place at one of the new school tables and began a relationship that lasted nearly two years. Carl was shy. His face had a few deep scars from childhood mishaps. At first he tended to look away when we spoke. Often in response to questions Carl would simply shrug his shoulders.

I spent 90 minutes a week with Carl for the rest of the year and all the following year. We soon moved beyond simply going over his schoolwork. He seemed to know it well enough much of the time. We both came to prefer talking instead. Carl was content to defer to me. For one thing, I was much older and bigger. For another, I was in the driver's seat; a well-off white guy volunteering to help him. What Carl really thought I don't know. He had been recommended for the tutorial project by his teacher. Our relationship became one of big brother/little brother. I knew stuff and I was happy to give him tips about schoolwork and getting along with his pals.

Some evenings we would have our lessons in homes in the Heights, perhaps to satisfy the curiosity of the neighborhood residents. One home we visited had an uneven floor covered by a cracked sheet of yellowed linoleum. The windows were sealed tight against the winter wind. The air was saturated with the smell of coal oil. The temperature inside must have been in the 90s. Carl and I sat on a sofa in the main room and talked through his lesson under the eye of an elderly woman who rocked back and forth on her well-worn easy chair.

In time, the tutorial project grew. More Reserve students signed up and more kids like Carl enrolled. We eventually moved the evening sessions to a nearby public school, which provided Carl and me with large grounds to walk around and a country stream to skip rocks on.

In early 1966, after mid-winter break of my senior year, a chaplain from Wesleyan University in Middletown, Connecticut, moved on campus with the intention of organizing a program called Upward Bound. We soon learned that the Reserve's Board of Trustees had agreed the previous summer to have an on-campus program for inner-city boys in the summer of 1966. The boys were to be instructed by Reserve teachers with Reserve students acting as counselors. Essentially, Upward Bound would be a summer school for the boys. It was hoped that their educational levels would rise significantly and that some would go on to college.

After the Reserve student-counselors were selected, we would meet to discuss plans. The meetings took place amidst the various other activities involved in finishing four years at Reserve: last minute essays, sending late information to colleges, prom dance plans, and sports events. As part of our preparation, outside speakers came to our meetings in the athletic building's common room. They explained to us the nature of poverty, the effects of racism and the role programs like Upward Bound could play in ridding the country of the effects of discrimination. We read Michael Harrington's *The Other America,* among other books favored by Great Society administrators and like-minded academics and activists.

One weekend we went to a camp near Hudson. We slept in cabins and ate food cooked over campfires. During the days and evenings, speakers from various area anti-poverty groups instructed us in the organizing principles of fighting poverty. Among the non-Reserve people who showed up were artists, writers, a political cartoonist, and a few musicians who played Depression-era ballads on guitars. How they came to be part of the orientation effort I don't know. However, at those meetings we met full-time, dedicated soldiers who, for a variety of reasons, had made the War on Poverty a profession.

FIGURE 3.1　In this photograph of an Upward Bound classroom in 1966, a high school student works on an assignment while others receive instruction from their tutor. Upward Bound was part of President Lyndon Johnson's War on Poverty, a set of ambitious social programs providing education and employment opportunities for disadvantaged Americans. Upward Bound selected talented youth from rural or inner-city schools for an accelerated instruction program that would help them gain acceptance to college. The tutors for the program were usually college students, who spent their summers teaching other young people what they themselves had recently learned.

Source: DuPont & Company

The message throughout our training was that we counselors should be sensitive to the day-to-day reality of the youngsters we would be dealing with in Upward Bound. To further our understanding, we were to spend some time in the Hough section of Cleveland, and work with neighborhood anti-poverty organizers to get an idea of what life in an urban ghetto was like.

The day we got into station wagons for the drive to Hough was the first warm Friday in May. It was beautiful in Hudson that day. The tulips and daffodils were up, the yellow forsythia in full bloom. The sky was blue, and sun bright. The spring wind swept across campus the rich fragrance of the purple laurel that lined the athletic fields.

We arrived in Hough at about 4:30 p.m. It was crowded and paved. We pulled in front of a yellow, wood frame three-story dwelling on Hough Avenue, across the street from a large red brick church. We walked up a long stoop of perhaps 15 steps at a steep incline to reach the front door. On either side of the cement stairway were small patches of grass about 10 feet below the walkway's stone banister. In the middle of one of the patches of grass was a large painted sign that said: HOPE House.

Underneath, smaller letters explained that HOPE stood for "Housing Our People Economically."

HOPE House was operated by a white minister in his late 40s who was affiliated with the church across Hough Avenue. He lived in the house on the third floor, along with other anti-poverty activists. Inside we found a few people talking over coffee and cigarettes. The atmosphere was friendly. Dinner was an hour or so away. The minister who ran HOPE House was not there. We had some time to kill. Our chaplain suggested that we walk around the neighborhood to get a feel of the place.

There were about a dozen of us from Reserve that day. Among them were Morris, my red-headed room mate; Anderson, a Harvard-bound intellectual who would become a physician; Paddock, now a judge, who we called Tweety after the cartoon bird because of his slight stature; and Bill Swan, one of the few black students at Reserve, who was among the elite of Providence, Rhode Island, possessing a rare combination of grace, intelligence, and personal presence. All of us joined the pedestrians on Hough Avenue, a commercial thoroughfare alive with Friday afternoon traffic.

We crossed the street and passed a laundromat and a diner and came to a small grocery store on the corner. A few in our group wanted a bottle of soda to drink away the heat. While they went inside, the rest of us stood on the corner waiting.

The several dozen residents moving around us were black, as was nearly everybody along Hough Avenue. A few walked in and out of the grocery, pausing slightly to give us a look. One middle-aged woman of some size ushered her two boys past without seeming to notice us, moving as quickly as possible to get out of the way. Standing several steps away was a group of black men, some wearing nylon do-rags around their heads holding their conks in place. One of these guys started at me directly, his look that of challenged cool.

Soon my friends came out of the store commenting on the goods for sale. The candy bars they had purchased were smaller than a dime Hershey bar or Snickers, and were some off-brand confection that cost a quarter. The soft drinks were also a brand we'd never seen and tasted too sweet and watered down. They cost 30 cents for a 10-ounce bottle.

The chaplain gathered us together. He suggested we get off the commercial avenue and go back into the neighborhood to see the people's living conditions. There was no time to consider consequences, only time to go along. We stayed in a reasonably close group as we walked down the sidewalk of the side street. The sidewalk was broken apart here and there, and we had to watch our step. Several cars lay abandoned at curbside, some burned out, and others stripped of seats, lights, chrome and other valuables.

The frame homes along the side street were tired. Cracked and peeling paint slashed scars across the rotting clapboards. Wooden front porches were out of trim and sloping on crumbling pilings of cinder block and stone. We came to the end of the block and turned left. The front yards of the homes were dirt not grass. Discarded balls and aged tricycles and wagons lay about. A few dogs of indistinct pedigree sniffed here and there. One little boy dressed in soiled underwear played in the dirt with a spoon. The chaplain was speaking to a few of the boys in the front of our group, explaining this or that. I wasn't paying attention. I was too distracted by the stares we were provoking from the people on their front porches. There was no pedestrian traffic on the street except us. Several in our group still had on their jackets and ties. I had a sweater draped over my shoulders, as though I was on my way to the golf course for a quick nine.

As we proceeded down the block our conversation slowed and finally stopped. I don't remember him walking up, but suddenly a tall, well-muscled black man in his mid-30s was in our midst asking questions. He wore a clean T-shirt, which pulled across his chest and back. On his head was a wool stocking cap. His clean brown pants were torn at the ankles and pockets. His lizard skin shoes were fashioned with narrow toes. His language was unbelievably hostile, laced with obscenities and racist slanders.

The chaplain quickly engaged the angry man in conversation hoping, he told us later, that keeping him talking would prevent an assault. "Keep moving," I heard somebody in our group whisper, "just keep moving . . . "

No one needed to be told. Our pace quickened. The angry man stayed in conversation with the chaplain. First a few children came alongside riding bicycles, then a group of four, then 10, now 20 youngsters, teenagers and young men. Soon it was as if all unattached men in the neighborhood were now drawn to us, like sharks to chum. At first there was laughing and taunting. One boy at the rear of our group felt his ears being tweaked from behind. His hands swatted at the teasing fingers as though they were bothersome bees. The crowd around us kept growing. Now more than one hundred people surrounded us. The teasing was over. The yelling started. The refrain had several variations, most of them obscene. The message: Who do you think you are coming into our neighborhood like this? We didn't ask you here and we don't want you here. My heart was racing. Images of the fires at Watts and the National Guard silhouetted against a burning building flashed in my mind. A side street leading back to Hough Avenue was near. We turned the corner as if in close-order drill. The chaplain kept talking to the angry man, holding his arm, earnestly explaining the unexplainable.

Anderson, who was in the back of our group, stumbled. Someone had stepped on the back of his heel, and his shoe was slipping off. He had lost his balance struggling to keep his shoe and continue. The jeering from the crowd grew more intense. Ahead I could see Hough Avenue, just a few dozen yards away.

Then it happened. At the corner of Hough Avenue and the side street was a saloon with its front door open. In the doorway sat a small dog, just a skinny street dog. It sensed the crowd approaching and became confused which way to run. The dog's confusion caught the attention of the angry man with the pointed shoes. Suddenly, the angry man broke away from the chaplain, ran to the corner and kicked the dog in the ribs. The dog's body went into the air, emitting the strangest sound; not a bark or yelp, more like a scream. The dog's body fell silent 20 feet away on the other side of a fence out of sight.

Fear shot through us like a lightening strike. Raw violence was set free. This wasn't television. This was real. Each of us knew we were on our own. Safety was possible only inside HOPE House—if there—and if we could reach that destination two blocks away.

We headed straight for the center of Hough Avenue, ignoring the heavy Friday afternoon traffic. The crowd surged around us. There was no way to run now.

We were enveloped in a circle with only just enough distance left to enable us to make our way slowly. Motor traffic slowed to a crawl. Horns sounded.

Then came the brick. It fell against the head of the boy next to me. He dropped five feet in front of me. I leaned over to grab his arm. He was still conscious and struggling to stay on his feet. The brick had opened a jagged wound on his cheek. Then another brick fell behind me, hitting Tweety in the center of his back. The brick hit with a dull thud, like the sound of a muffled drum. Tweety's wind was knocked out. Despite his stature, he kept his balance, gasping for his breath as he struggled to continue.

I turned to see Anderson separated from the rest of us alone on the sidewalk to the right. Several teenagers were running up behind him, slapping his head, others trying to trip him with their feet. His shoe was now missing. Suddenly a teenager holding a cut-off broom handle with soft metal wrapped around its end appeared. He ran up to Anderson. Someone called to Anderson to watch out. He turned just as the teenager brought the weapon down with full force. Anderson had moved just enough so that the blow missed his skull, slamming instead on his neck and shoulder. The force of the blow knocked Anderson away from the sidewalk. He stumbled into the street where one of our group grabbed him before he fell, holding him upright so he could keep walking.

Then in front of me I saw Morris, crawling into a ball on the street, having just been struck on the back by a ball bat. I leaned over and picked him up by his waist. He was dazed.

"Walk," I said into his ear, "walk." Slowly he was able to carry his weight and continue.

In a moment I saw Swan. I didn't even think about the sensitivities. I pulled him over to me as close as I could get him. He looked at me. His eyes showed as much fear as mine. "Holy Jesus," he said.

We had a half a block to go. I wasn't touched throughout. Perhaps it was blind luck. Perhaps it was because I was over six feet, 175 pounds and in shape. Perhaps, toward the last few yards, it was because I was so close to Swan. HOPE House was only a short distance away now. We aimed for it, each from our widely separate spots on Hough Avenue. The crowd swirled around us, chanting, shouting, jostling and shoving. Like leaves caught in a river rapid as the water approached the rush of a sluice, Swan and I stepped onto the sidewalk, up the stairs of the long stoop leading to the front door of HOPE House.

Some in the mob were on the upper steps preventing our progress. Others in our group hoisted themselves up onto the lawn next to the sign and climbed onto the front porch over the railings. Swan and I stopped just five steps from the front door, unable to move any closer. At the base of the steps the chaplain was still engaged with the angry man. They were pointing fingers at each other, shouting. Now the chaplain was shaking his head. Suddenly, the angry man looked up the stairway of the front stoop and pointed at Bill and me.

"Hey you," he shouted. "What are you doing there?"

It seemed that the eyes of the entire crowd were focused on me.

Confused, I said, "Who, me?"

"You'll do."

It was only then that I realized my mistake. He had meant Swan, my companion. The angry man ran up the steps, two at a time, ignored Swan, and stopped directly in front of me, pushing his face within inches of mine.

"And what are you doing here? Just come down to nigger town to see us ignorant niggers . . . trying to help us poor niggers . . . just look at my face . . . it's ugly, tell me it's ugly . . . That's a nigger face . . . "

I tried to stammer out an explanation. By that time, I was against the edge of the walkway, the stone banister at the middle of my backside. The angry man was leaning so that I had to back up to keep his face from touching mine.

"Come on now, white boy, tell me what you see." He pointed to his face. He had several deep scars, and patches of acne. His teeth were uncared for. His breath was rancid. "You're not talking white boy . . . come on."

I was beginning to teeter over. Behind the angry man, teenagers were jumping up and down. Sensing my lack of balance, the angry man shoved me hard.

My arms went out in an attempt to regain my balance. But his push was too hard. I was falling back out of control, teetering over the banister like a seesaw. I struggled to catch onto something to prevent myself from falling backwards onto the ground 10 feet below. My legs came up with some force. By chance, my right foot caught one of the jumping teenagers in the crotch. There was nothing to do but keep my right foot moving with all the power I could muster. The teenager was light and my kick was enough to propel him up. He jumped over the banister onto the ground below.

I was recovering and raising myself back upright, certain that I would be attacked. As I tried to gain my vision and protect myself, I heard the scream of auto tires and the blast of a police siren. The angry man in front of me looked toward Hough Avenue below. He was turning now, stepping over the side of the other stone banister, and jumping away.

Below me I saw the flashing red light of the unmarked car. A burly plainclothes cop jumped out of the front on the passenger side, his .38 caliber Smith & Wesson in his hand. His partner emerged from the other side and the two cops stood with their revolvers hoisted in their right hands. They were shouting orders and waving to the crowd to disburse. There were shouts and screams as other police cars arrived. The crowd scattered in all directions, across Hough Avenue, down side streets, between buildings. In a moment, it was over.

We went inside and collected around the dining room table, too stunned to talk above a whisper. Wounds were dabbed with cold water and bandaged. Bruises were left to throb. The nightmares would come later.

In a few minutes, a white man in his mid-40s ran into the dining room, shouting.

"Just what in hell do you think you were doing?" he said to no one in particular. "Don't you know this place is about to blow?" The man, who we learned later was the rector of HOPE House, shouted at our chaplain. "You could have started a riot this afternoon. All we have worked for finished; I can't believe this . . . "

Our chaplain led the rector out of the room. When they reappeared a few minutes later, the rector had calmed down, but for the rest of the weekend he retained his air of arrogance and anger.

We slept that night and the next on army cots in the earth and stone basement of HOPE House. Saturday we worked at the church across the street cleaning up the yard of debris and trash. What we really did, though, was not leave Hough, which the rector and chaplain agreed was the most important thing we could do. They reasoned we had to prove our commitment to good works and demonstrate that lawlessness and violence could not scare us off. On Sunday morning we went to the church across the street. There was gospel singing. When the preacher spoke, it was to a chorus of " . . . That's right! Praise the Lord! Hallelujah!" At one point the preacher asked the congregation to recognize the visitors in the community, which they did with applause. We later learned that the police had appeared because several residents, among them those seated near us in the church, had seen the mob and called for help.

We returned to the Academy that afternoon. Several of us spoke about our experiences at a chapel service later that week. We soft-pedaled the mob's attack out of fear that the trustees might call off the Upward Bound project.

As it turned out, the riot feared by the rector of HOPE House occurred eight weeks later. The worst rioting in the nation that year erupted in Hough between July 18 and 23, 1966. Four residents were killed, and more than 50 others were injured in the disorders, which included fire bombings, looting, and gunfire between snipers and police. Nearly 250 fires destroyed property throughout Hough. Police arrested 164 persons, the majority for looting. The Hough riots reportedly started because a white saloonkeeper refused to serve a glass of water to a black man. It took more than 300 police to put down the rioting the first night. The next day, Governor Rhodes dispatched 1,600 National Guardsmen to Hough at the request of Cleveland's mayor, who the following day asked for 400 more.

The Upward Bound summer program was by most standards a success. It continues today. That first year we hosted it, 1966, nearly 60 boys lived in Reserve dorms for two months. The days were similar to a regular school day at Reserve. In the morning there were formal classes in the traditional three Rs. The program's academic goal was to make the students aware of their environment, to improve their ability to communicate and to make the boys want to learn more. Afternoons alternated various other activities—art, music, canoeing, chemistry, wood shop, photography and geography. Students also participated daily in either a team or individual sport for athletic competitions. On Sundays each boy visited the home of a local family, who had volunteered to act as companions for church, Sunday dinner, and family outings.

I was one of the 12 Reserve grads who held the position of counselor that first summer. I was assigned classroom duties in the drama section. During one drama session, a co-counselor named Joe and I engaged in a mock tug-of-war. Joe and I got so into pulling our imaginary rope that it in fact became a test of wills—with each of us exerting real energy into our imaginary pulling to and fro. We became so involved we turned red from exertion and began to perspire from the workout. It was all in our heads, but our play-acting showed just what the drama teacher was looking for—helping the boys tap into reserves of imagination that would turn an act of fantasy into something concrete.

These lessons were among the many, but in fact, what the entire program did that year was offer a regular structured environment for personal growth—including eating three square meals a day and sleeping in clean, comfortable beds. There was class work, sports, several outings, music and theater. Many also learned for the first time about toothbrushes, reliable plumbing, telephones, and table utensils.

With another Reserve grad my age, I was assigned a dozen students and served as supervisor, confessor, and big brother to each of the boys, among them Carl. One in my group later went on to get a scholarship to Western Reserve Academy itself, where he did well, eventually becoming captain of his varsity basketball team. He later graduated from an Ivy League college and today is a dentist in the Midwest. He is mainstream. I lost track of Carl.

QUESTIONS FOR DISCUSSION

1. R. Thomas Collins witnessed a number of early Sixties events that shaped his thinking about what was going on in the country and influenced his decision to join those trying to make a difference. What were the most significant of those events for Collins?

2. How would you describe Collins' feeling about his private school, Western Reserve Academy? Can you connect his strong involvement at his school and his desire to help others with the problems his family was having? In what ways does he express an awareness of his privilege as a well-to-do white American? (Look again at his physical descriptions of the academy, Twinsburg Heights, and Hough.)

3. How does Collins react when he first encounters poverty and poor people in the Akron/Summit tutorial program in the winter of 1965? Why do you think his instructors insist that the Western Reserve students witness poverty first-hand? What is the effect of this "immersion?" Collins uses the term "wrongheaded fantasies" in the opening paragraph of his story. Do you think he is applying that judgment to the trip to Hough, the tutoring program, or something larger?

4. Discuss the mixed reactions of the African American residents of Hough to the arrival of the prep school boys in their neighborhood. What do they assume the boys are there to do? Why are they angry at the boys? Who is not angry at the boys? Why do you think neighborhoods like Hough were such powder kegs in the mid-1960s? Consider the multiple meanings of the words "HOPE House" as they play out through Collins' story.

5. Collins ends his story with the flat statement, "I lost track of Carl." How do you interpret that statement? Looking back on his experience, would you say that Collins thinks Upward Bound was effective in helping poor inner-city kids in the 1960s? Do you think the experience had any lasting effect on Collins?

6. Can you identify with Collins? If you had been in his position in the 1960s, would you have wanted to be an Upward Bound tutor? If not, but if you still wanted to help those less fortunate than you, what other choices were available at the time? (Review the introduction to the "Pathways" section of this book.) What would you choose today?

THE PEACE CORPS: KENYA, 1968–1972
John H. Manners

I joined the Peace Corps to dodge the draft. I won't say I was entirely without nobler motives, but in the spring of 1968, when I was about to graduate from college, the Peace Corps looked like my only deferrable option, and that was the overriding consideration.

In fact, while I'm sure many of my fellow PCVs (Peace Corps Volunteers) were stirred by idealistic notions of service and sacrifice, I'd guess that a healthy majority of the draftable males in my training group that fall saw the Peace Corps, above all, as a comparatively painless and honorable way to escape a tour in Vietnam. This lent a faint air of cynicism to the otherwise conscientious preparations we went through for three months, before being shipped off to become secondary school teachers for two years in Kenya.

There were about 100 of us in the training group, Kenya Education IV, plus about 40 Kenya-bound nurses who joined us for "total immersion" language instruction for the first four weeks. This initial phase of the training, which began in early October, was conducted in a run-down Catskill resort called the Monte Carlo, about 50 miles northwest of New York City. The dilapidated hotel sprawled over ragged grounds that boasted a couple of cracked asphalt tennis courts and an empty swimming pool. Single PCVs like me bunked four to a room; married couples had rooms to themselves.

We met two or three times a day in small classes for Swahili lessons, taught entirely in Swahili by Kenyan and Tanzanian graduate students who lived with us in the hotel. Most evenings were given over to orientation and acculturation classes about Kenya. Meals were served in the hotel dining room and I remember them being of an unusually low standard, even for institution food. But the most onerous part of language training was the prohibition against speaking anything but Swahili until after supper. For twelve hours a day, we were supposed to communicate with one another and our instructors using what little we could recall from our lessons and vocabulary lists. No doubt this was an effective pedagogic technique, and most of us were willing to make the effort, but by the end of the day we felt the strain, and backsliders were not subject to any great condemnation.

The whole experience that first month—the rural setting, busy schedule, crowded bunks, bad food, and petty restrictions—savored much more of summer camp than college. And that camp atmosphere appears to have been something of a holdover from the early days of the Peace Corps in 1961 and '62, when the agency felt its *in loco parentis* responsibilities keenly, and training groups were put through bed checks and daily calisthenics. Some evolution had taken place by 1968, of course, but the Peace Corps still held to its original conception as a wholesome outlet for youthful exuberance. The idea still seemed to be to bring together recent college graduates, put them through preparations that combined a benign version of military basic training with some rudimentary instruction in the skills they were expected to employ, and then send them off to charm the Third World with their naive enthusiasm.

Much of this was soon to change. In 1969, the incoming Nixon administration would try to put its stamp on this quintessentially Kennedy program by professionalizing it. Nixon's Peace Corps would recruit older volunteers with proven skills, as opposed to wide-eyed "B.A. generalists" like us. In hindsight, you might imagine that as the presidential election approached in the fall of 1968, we Kennedy-era idealists would have done all we could to elect the candidate most likely to preserve what was left of the Kennedy legacy. But that's not what I remember. There may have been some eager Humphrey supporters among us, but most of us felt so disillusioned over Vietnam and the fiasco of the Chicago Democratic Convention that we saw little to choose between the major party candidates, and no prospect for positive change anywhere within "the system." I took more interest that October in the Mexico City Olympics than the presidential contest, and although the 1968 election was the first in which I was old enough, I didn't bother to vote.

Training moved to New York City in November, based at Columbia University's Teachers College. We were housed about 20 blocks away in the Hotel Paris, which in the late '60s had acquired a reputation as a low-rent hookers' hangout, though I never spotted any goings on. Our instruction in basic teaching methods was disrupted by a strike in the New York City public schools, which sent our training program directors scrambling to find Catholic high schools that would accommodate us as student teachers. I wound up someplace in the Bronx and taught, as I remember, all of two practice classes.

The program directors also had trouble finding home stays for all of us. The intention was to house each PCV with a low-income family for a few weeks so as to give the overwhelmingly middle-class volunteers a taste of material deprivation and as close to a cross-cultural experience as could be found in the New York area. Some kids wound up in pretty rough circumstances—unheated tenements and such. But there was a shortage of true hardship postings, and we were asked to come up with our own if we could. As it happened, my father had an old friend who, out of political conviction, chose to live in a Brooklyn slum. I stayed with him for three weeks. It was scarcely a cross-cultural experience, but the building did smell bad, and the neighborhood was genuinely shabby.

Part of the purpose of the home stays was to assess our adaptability to unfamiliar circumstances. Training, along with preparing us for what we were supposed to do in Kenya, was also intended to weed out those who might not be up to the job. A few kids had washed out in the first two months for various personal reasons, but the home stay was the big test. I don't remember anyone clearly failing, but I do recall pressure being put on several people to drop out in the last two weeks of training to spare themselves the humiliation of being "deselected," as the directors so delicately put it. Some of us were concerned about the possibility of being dropped for our politics. We had all passed perfunctory FBI checks, which mainly involved agents interviewing our college roommates to determine if we were dope fiends or bomb-throwing anarchists. But one friend of mine was summoned two or three times by the Peace Corps brass, who were concerned about his having turned in his draft card during an anti-war demonstration. In the end, they let him through.

We flew to Kenya on New Year's Day, 1969. The Kenyan school year follows the calendar year, and we were supposed to arrive at our posts in time for the start of the first term. After a couple of days' further orientation in the capital, Nairobi, those of

FIGURE 3.2   Walking on a woodland path in Togo, West Africa, in the mid–1960s, a Peace Corps volunteer teacher holds the hands of two of his pupils. Volunteering for the Peace Corps meant training in the United States for several months, learning the language and culture of your destination country, and then serving two years abroad. Many volunteers taught school, others worked in agricultural programs or medical clinics. They lived simply and received a monthly stipend rather than a salary. Many returning Peace Corps volunteers felt that the two-year stint had been one of the most rewarding experiences in their lives.

Source: Corbis/Bettmann

us whose postings had been confirmed boarded various forms of public transport and headed "upcountry" to our schools.

Kenya sits directly on the equator on Africa's east coast. It's about the size of Texas and much of it is arid scrub land, but three-quarters of the population—then about 12 million—is concentrated in the southwestern quarter of the country, where the altitude ranges upwards of 5,000 feet, the climate is wonderfully temperate, and the landscape green and lush. The country had been a British colony for 60 years before winning independence in 1963, and the 60,000 white settlers who farmed the fertile highlands during the colonial period had made homes in Kenya and intended to stay. By 1969, however, most whites had pulled up stakes, preferring not to live under "black rule." The infrastructure they left behind was among the most developed in tropical Africa: a network of serviceable roads and railways, dozens of tidy market towns, a reliable postal system, a disciplined military and police force, and a competent civil service.

What the colonial regime had neglected was education beyond the primary level, and that had become one of independent Kenya's top governmental priorities. We Peace Corps Volunteers had been enlisted as part of the all-out effort to make secondary education widely available. The government had established scores of secondary schools in the first several years after independence, but to meet the overwhelming demand—in 1969 there was only one place at a government-supported secondary school for every seven kids finishing primary school—the government also encouraged local communities to start their own schools, with a view to the government eventually taking them over. This approach was very much in the spirit of the national motto, "*Harambee,*" which means "pull together" and implies communal self-help. Many of the volunteers in my group were assigned to struggling little *harambee* schools.

My school, Kaplong Boys Secondary, had started out as a *harambee* school, founded by a Catholic mission, but it had been taken over by the government in 1967 and was fairly well established by the time I arrived. It had a classroom building, a separate science lab and six teachers' houses, all constructed of concrete-block with corrugated iron roofs. Like most Kenyan schools, Kaplong was set in the middle of the agrarian countryside. About half the 140 students lived at home and walked as much as five or six miles to school; the rest, whose homes were farther away, lived in a make-shift dormitory converted from one of the mission's storage sheds and took their meals in a large, open lean-to that also incorporated a kitchen. As postings went for the volunteers in my group, Kaplong was about average in terms of comfort and amenities but for me it was ideal in a way I should now explain.

I had lived in Kenya for a year with my family when I was 12. My father had been doing anthropological fieldwork among a tribe called the Kipsigis, and I had spent all my time with local Kipsigis boys, tagging along when they went to their mission-run primary school and on weekends joining them as they herded their families' cattle and goats. I developed a strong attachment to the area and the people. Kenya was thus an obvious choice for me when I filled in the "country preference" blank on my Peace Corps application and during training, when we volunteers were asked if we had any thoughts about where in Kenya we'd like to work, I said, "Anywhere in Kipsigis territory." When we reached Nairobi and I saw "Kaplong" next to my name on the assignment list, I recognized it immediately. It was three miles from where I had lived as a kid and on the same Catholic mission compound as the primary school I had gone to with my friends.

My 200-mile bus journey up-country to Kaplong was thus a kind of homecoming, and I started to feel sentimental as each familiar vista came into view. The last 30 miles of the trip passed through rolling hills blanketed with a tidy patchwork of green crops and pastures—views that might have put most visitors in mind of rural England. But to me, this was the Kipsigis country of my childhood memory, almost unchanged in the ten years since I had last seen it.

I climbed off the bus opposite the Kaplong mission hospital and collected my duffel bag from the overflowing roof rack. As I walked along the road that ran beside the mission compound, I was quickly attended by a troop of giggling children, none of whom was bold enough to say anything directly to me. But several summoned friends with word of the new attraction: "*Mzungu!*"—meaning "white man." It wasn't that whites were so rare in the area—there were several on the mission compound, and a few old colonials still hanging on—but it was unusual to see one walking rather than driving along the road. I soon reached the short driveway leading to the secondary school and walked in; my young followers peeled off at the gate.

I stood by the flagpole in front of the classroom building, and within seconds a white man in his late 30s bounded awkwardly out of a nearby house, waving and shouting, "Hoy, hoy!" which turned out not to be some unfamiliar Swahili exclamation but northern English argot, roughly the equivalent of "Yo!"

"You must be our Peace Corps man," he said as he came up to me. He introduced himself as Father Wild, the headmaster, and immediately led me to my house at the top of a row of teachers' houses at the far end of the campus. It was newly built, with three bedrooms, a fireplace, and what Father Wild described, with just a hint of irony, as "all the mod cons:" a kitchen with running water, a stainless steel sink and a propane gas stove. It also had a bathroom with a sit-down flush toilet, sink, tub and gas-fired hot water. This was more than I had hoped for. No electricity, but gas lamps would provide plenty of light and the short-wave radio I'd brought ran on batteries. If I could find a kerosene-powered refrigerator, I'd be all set.

I thanked Father Wild for my unexpected comforts, and he confided that he had saved the new house for me. Another new teacher, Mr. Mwangi, had arrived the day before and had been given a smaller, older house at the bottom of the row, because, as Father Wild explained, an African wouldn't have known what to do with all the amenities in the new place.

I was dumbstruck. I was perfectly familiar with the racial segregation and rigid hierarchy of the colonial period but this was independent Kenya. White privilege was supposed to have gone out with the British flag. I was soon to learn, however, that the egalitarian revolution I had imagined was slow in coming, and I confess I didn't do as much as I might have to advance it. I didn't protest being given the new house, for example, and the next morning when I woke up to find a row of job seekers lined up outside my front door, I followed Father Wild's advice and hired a cook.

Household help was a delicate issue for the Peace Corps. In general, volunteers were supposed to mix with the common folk. We were not allowed to own cars, for example, so we'd have to travel the way the locals did, by public transportation. And we were paid just $100 a month (it was called a "living allowance"—we were volunteers, after all). This topped the average Kenyan monthly income by a good deal but it was thought to be the bare minimum necessary to sustain a modest Western lifestyle. We had been told in training that we were likely to be approached by people eager to work for us and that we had to make up our own minds—provide a much-needed job or maintain our PCV purity and fend for ourselves. Most volunteers who chose to become employers seemed appropriately uncomfortable in the role—there was a lot of euphemizing about "the man who helps out around the house" and the like, though I remember one kid registering his distaste for such squeamishness by baldly referring to "my servant." At Kaplong, it was taken for granted that any *mzungu* had to have at least one servant. Father Wild suggested that if I wanted to eat something other than sandwiches and not spend several hours a week hand washing my laundry, I had better employ somebody. I took his point. But rather than choose among the guys lined up at my door, I decided to look for somebody I knew. That morning, Father Wild drove me to buy supplies in the nearby town of Sotik, which was where I'd lived as a boy. The place still looked much as I remembered it—a frontier outpost with a single street of tall-fronted stores and raised sidewalks—but now there were more cars, fewer Asian shopkeepers and almost no white settlers. In the biggest of the shops, a kind of general store that had once catered to the settlers, an old clerk remembered my family and offered to help look up a couple of people I hoped to find. One was the man who had cooked for my family ten years before.

There are no street addresses in rural Kenya. You find somebody by knowing a name, a village, and perhaps a neighborhood, and asking around. It seems a hopelessly hit-or-miss method, but it works surprisingly well. The morning after I enquired in Sotik, the man in question, Kipsang arap Mursi, turned up on my doorstep eager for work. We agreed that I'd pay him 100 shillings a month, one-seventh of my allowance, which seems appallingly stingy to me now, but it was the going rate, and arap Mursi seemed pleased to have the cash and free meals to supplement what he made on his small farm, which his wife ran while he was away.

I wasn't so lucky in trying to reconnect with my childhood friends. Arap Mursi asked around on my behalf and learned that my best friend had died ("His stomach got big and he died," was all I could find out) and that most of the rest had scattered in search of work. The only one we were able to find was doing odd jobs around Sotik, and after a few awkward meetings, the two of us came to an unspoken understanding that there wasn't much point in trying to recapture our preadolescent camaraderie.

Classes were to begin at Kaplong soon after I arrived, and Father Wild called a staff meeting to apportion duties. There I met my colleagues: Mr. Ogola and Mr. Odumba, respectively the school's history and math specialists; Erica Murray, the science teacher, a hearty Englishwoman a couple of years older than I was; and Mr. Mwangi, fresh out of teacher training college, who by rights should have been given my house. I was assigned English and geography in Forms I and II (roughly eighth and ninth grades) and, because I was the only one who didn't express an active distaste for the job, I was named games master, which meant I was in charge of daily after-school sports.

I concluded pretty quickly that I didn't have much in common with my fellow teachers. Mr. Ogola and Mr. Odumba were both experienced professionals in their mid-30s, married with children, though Mr. Ogola's family lived in his home village some 70 miles from Kaplong. Both came from a neighboring tribe and seemed to regard their tenure at Kaplong as a kind of penance among the hicks—dues they had to pay before they could secure assignments to schools in their home area, where students were thought to be more sophisticated and academically adept. Both were *kali* (fierce) disciplinarians, and Mr. Odumba was particularly quick to apply the stick to confused or inattentive students.

Mr. Mwangi was also a long way from home, and I suspect rather lonely. He was my age, and I imagine we might have been friends, but he was too shy to take the initiative, and I guess I was too.

Initially, I spent most of my free time with Erica or Father Wild. Both were perfectly amiable and Father Wild was well-read with an eager, wide-ranging curiosity, but he was often tied up with mission duties and Erica liked to socialize with the remnants of Sotik's settler community, whose company I found generally disagreeable.

Most of the expatriate teachers in Kenya at that time were, like Erica, trained British professionals serving under contract to the British Ministry of Overseas Development. Some of them had a genuine interest in Kenya or in Africa, and some even showed glimmerings of idealistic commitment to nation-building. But most were just there for the money—quite a bit more than they'd be making at home—and the privileges that accrued to whites with First World incomes living in tropical countries. Many had brought sizable families, which they supported with the help of generous government allowances.

Most British contract teachers seemed not to share the common PCV confusion about what their role should be in the rapidly changing society of post-colonial Kenya. Few had any reservations about hiring servants or treating them with peremptory disdain. All the ones I knew owned cars and laughed at the holier-than-thou restrictions imposed on Peace Corps volunteers. They had no time for what they saw as the Peace Corps' self-righteousness or the volunteers' deluded idealism. Most seemed either contemptuous or amused at typical PCV earnestness. They viewed themselves, by contrast, as cold-eyed realists about Africa and "the African." I met none who were as nakedly racist as the departing settlers, many of whom were headed for apartheid South Africa, but few showed anything like the racial sensitivity that was already second-nature to young Americans who had grown up with the Civil Rights Movement. A key indicator, I found, was the use of the pronoun "they" with reference to the local people, or Africans in general. Few of the British contract teachers I knew hesitated to make sweeping generalizations about the way "they" lived or thought or behaved. Most PCVs, on the other hand, were scrupulous in qualifying even the most casual observations about local habits and practices.

Quite apart from matters of political correctness, though, there was a more fundamental difference between the British contract teachers and the PCVs. The Brits tended to see themselves, rightly, as grownups, whereas most of us thought of ourselves as kids. There was thus a kind of generational divide that stood in the way of close personal ties, with the result that most PCVs tended to socialize with other PCVs, even if it meant traveling several hundred miles in a weekend to do it.

I remember going as far as Nairobi as often as two or three times in a month just to join a little gathering or see a movie with a couple of other volunteers. Nairobi at that time was an attractive destination in itself—a model post-colonial metropolis, with fragrant jacaranda trees lining its broad avenues, bustling shops full of Western goods, half a dozen world-class tourist hotels, a range of moderately fancy restaurants, and a couple of theaters playing Hollywood movies only about six months out of date. I remember running into PCVs there on vacation from elsewhere in Africa. (Peace Corps policy at the time required that volunteers stick to the Third World for their holidays as well as their work.) One who had come from some forlorn West African outpost marveled at Nairobi's comforts and was convinced that Kenya should be giving foreign aid to his place.

The big city enticements notwithstanding, what really got volunteers moving on weekends was news of a Peace Corps party. Word would arrive either by written invitation or by word of mouth from a passing volunteer (phones were very rare): so-and-so is having a party on Saturday night at such-and-such a school in such-and-such a remote spot; come if you can. If you didn't know the host well, you'd try to find out who else was going, but otherwise you'd just set out on Saturday morning and expect to spend most of the day on the road. It was seldom necessary to pay for public transportation. If you were white, hitchhiking was absurdly easy; you rarely had to watch more than a few cars go by. It seemed that Kenyan drivers, regardless of ethnicity—African, Asian, or European—were happy to stop for a *mzungu*, while they'd leave Africans to wait for buses or shared taxis. Black PCVs (there were half a dozen in my group) hitchhiked, too, but with not quite the same ease. One guy who lived not far from me would dress up in his Sunday best and hang a large camera from his neck. He said he had pretty good luck that way, so I suppose a charitable interpretation might be that Kenyan drivers were not strictly racist; they were simply extending a courtesy to people they perceived to be overseas visitors.

For all the time it took to get to them, the parties I went to were generally pretty tame. There was beer, of course (usually warm for lack of refrigeration), and often marijuana, which, though illegal, was readily available in most parts of Kenya. Sometimes there was dancing, but that normally required electricity, because few battery-powered tape or record players could generate enough volume. Mostly, there was talk, and for volunteers in isolated locations, that was attraction enough. After weeks of struggling to make yourself understood with a few hundred words of care-fully enunciated English and rudimentary Swahili, it was almost thrilling to be able to lapse into colloquial American laced with casual references and jokes you didn't have to explain. Partygoers brought sleeping bags, and hosts provided beds or floor space for most, with spillover going to fellow teachers or nearby PCVs. In spite of the informality of these arrangements and the licentious, late-'60s *zeitgeist*, if there was lots of casual sex at these parties, it managed to escape my notice.

Back at Kaplong, I found myself keeping uncharacteristically to myself. I taught my classes, coached football (soccer) in the afternoon and then retreated to my house. My closest personal contact was with arap Mursi, who departed for his own home late every afternoon. Weekends I was often away for sports matches or Peace Corps gatherings, but most of the time I was on my own, and after a few weeks I had begun to adjust to the solitude. I read a lot and became an avid listener to the BBC World Service, and I was not altogether happy to hear from Peace Corps head-quarters in Nairobi that I would soon be sharing my house with another volunteer who had just been reassigned to the fledgling girls' secondary school on the Kaplong mission compound.

I knew the guy, Steve, fairly well from training, and I liked him. He was a laid-back Californian with an agreeably lax attitude toward just about everything. So I managed to suppress my disappointment at the loss of my reclusive self-sufficiency, and we got along very well. Steve had initially trained to be a Kenya agri-cultural ("ag") volunteer, but for reasons I no longer remember, he was reassigned to my training group just as his ag group was about to leave for Kenya. He knew sev-eral of the ag volunteers in the Sotik area, and we wound up spending quite a bit of time with them.

I'm not sure I was ever very clear on what most ag volunteers were supposed to be doing. I'm not sure they were either. Almost all males, they made up perhaps a quarter of the 300-some PCVs in Kenya at the time, practically all the rest being teachers. Some of the ag guys worked on water projects (piping water from streams to villages), some on cattle dips and inoculations, and some on agricultural exten-sion, whatever that was. In any event, they seemed to have more time on their hands than teachers did, and I would often see them on their lightweight, Peace

Corps-issue *pikipikis* (motorcycles) just cruising around the countryside, which looked like a lot of fun. A few of them might have had agricultural backgrounds, but most, like the teachers, were just B.A. generalists from the suburbs. Because of the bikes, though, they tended to adopt a kind of macho "outlaw" posture with implicit disdain for us strait-laced chalk pushers.

For the most part, this routine was perfectly harmless. Ag volunteers were perhaps more uniformly cynical than teachers about Peace Corps and Kenya Government policies. They dressed more shabbily than those of us confined to post-colonial British-style campuses, they lived in grungier quarters, and they smoked a little more dope. Sadly, this last had unfortunate consequences for Steve.

A month or two after he arrived at Kaplong, Steve came down with a pretty severe case of malaria. The symptoms are like a bad flu, and can last as long as a week. The disease is endemic in most parts of Kenya and in spite of the Peace Corps issuing us chloroquine pills to take once a week to ward it off, many volunteers experienced a bout or two. Steve was treated at Kaplong Hospital with a large injection of chloroquine, to be followed by several tablets of the stuff each day for a week. After a few days, he was pretty well recovered and accepted an invitation to a Friday night gathering at an ag volunteer's house. When one of the ag guys brought Steve home the next morning, he was acting strangely. He talked rapidly and incoherently and complained that his mind was racing uncontrollably.

It seems they'd made a pizza at the party and sprinkled it with marijuana instead of oregano, and Steve had eaten a lot. Normally, it wouldn't have been a problem, but there appeared to be a powerful interaction with the chloroquine, and as he had eaten the dope instead of smoking it, generous amounts of both were still in his blood stream.

He couldn't sleep and couldn't stop talking, and his hyperactivity continued through the weekend. When it hadn't let up by Sunday evening, a couple of the ag guys and I persuaded him to go to Kaplong Hospital for a sedative. The nurse who treated him naturally wanted to know what was wrong, and Steve told her. She advised calling Peace Corps in Nairobi (the hospital had a phone), but we balked, having been told repeatedly that being caught with drugs meant instant dismissal. When the sedative wore off the next morning, however, Steve's antic behavior resumed, and it was clear he wouldn't be able to teach his classes. Eventually, he became so frightened by his condition that he called Peace Corps headquarters, and they told him to come to Nairobi immediately. Two days later he was on his way home. The last I heard, he had fully recovered, both from the effects of the drugs and from being kicked out of the Peace Corps. I seem to remember that the drug thing also kept him out of the draft.

Steve wasn't replaced, and I was on my own again. For the most part, I enjoyed teaching my classes, but it took me a while to adjust to the rigidity of the curriculum. We had been told in training that Kenyan secondary schools were still run on a British model, with all instructions geared to a single, national exam at the end of the fourth year, and that deviating from the prescribed path was generally frowned upon—something I soon learned first hand. The syllabus for my Form 2 geography class was largely confined to physical geography—ocean currents, trade winds, floodplains, ox-bow lakes, westward littorals, and the like—which kids would be expected to know for their exam in a couple of years. I found this stuff impossibly boring, and I thought it far less relevant to the students' lives than rudimentary political geography of places outside Kenya, of which they knew next to nothing. So for several weeks I devised my own lessons on the various continents and major countries, sketching in a little history and ethnography along with prominent geographical features. The kids seemed quite engaged. Our liveliest discussions were about race in America; the students were especially curious about "Red Indians," imagining them still to be the majority population confined to reservations by the white minority, as had been the case in Kenya.

But for all their interest in the material I presented, the students were growing quietly restless to get on with what they knew was supposed to be the principal business of the class. I'm sure a few of them must have politely mentioned this to me once or twice, but I chose to continue with my own lessons until one day the kids simply sat mute in class, refusing to open their notebooks or respond to my questions. I got the message, and we went back to the regular syllabus, and the next term I switched classes with Father Wild, taking over his Form 3 English, where I was quite happy teaching the literature syllabus's "set books," such as *Cry, the Beloved Country* and *Lord of the Flies.*

The passive resistance I experienced in the geography class was a common tactic in Kenyan secondary schools, often taking the form of all-out strikes, in which students completely boycotted classes. Grievances varied and were not always well-articulated, so there was often little in the way of productive negotiation, but the protests, in those days, were always peaceful and orderly. Sometimes exasperated headmasters sent striking students home to be disciplined by their parents, who were only too aware of the sacrifices they were making to pay for the privilege the students seemed to be disregarding.

In my second year at Kaplong, we had a short-lived strike. One morning, instead of standing by the flagpole for the opening assembly, all the students sat down calmly in the middle of the football field. The teachers gathered in Father Wild's office, where I learned that no one was quite sure what the kids were striking about. I volunteered to find out. I felt comfortable as a mediator; I had gotten to know a number of the older kids pretty well through sports coaching and was actually a lot closer to them in age and attitude than I was to my fellow teachers. I took my typewriter out onto the field and told the students I was there to draft a list of their grievances.

I don't remember most of what was on the list, but I do recall that it took a while to elicit from the kids. Like most Kenyans in my experience, the students were reluctant to state their complaints with enough specificity to make clear who they felt was responsible. Eventually it emerged that the principal concern was Mr. Odumba's harsh discipline. I've mentioned that he would routinely thrash kids with a ruler for a moment's inattention or confusion in class. What upset the students about this was not the physical pain or public embarrassment. It was the indignity of having to passively accept arbitrary beatings. By Kipsigis tradition, Kaplong's students were adults, warriors. They had passed through arduous initiation rites at about age 14 and were now expected to conduct themselves like grownups and to be treated accordingly. Tribal custom laid down elaborate rules governing appropriate behavior between adults and most certainly did not countenance one whacking another with a ruler. Anyone dealt with in this way would be entitled by custom to exact revenge. Of course, the school situation overrode custom to some extent, but Odumba's excesses were deeply offensive. The students felt no Kipsigis teacher would have abused them so, which heightened their sense of injustice.

By the time I finished drawing up the list, the teachers had dispersed, and I was relieved to be able to give the document to Father Wild alone. He agreed to talk to Odumba, and to let me tell the strikers he was doing so. He also found one or two of the other demands reasonable, and I explained to the kids what he would and wouldn't do about each. That seemed to satisfy them, and they were back in class by midday. I was naturally pleased with my role in the business, though I remained a little baffled at a system so rigidly hierarchical that it took a walkout by the whole school to air a few grievances.

I mentioned sports. After-school sports were supposed to be an integral component of the curriculum, but there were no sports exams at the end of four years, so at Kaplong, as at many newly-established schools, the sports part of the curriculum had always been followed rather casually. Participation was effectively optional. The kids who were interested had organized their own teams and had taken part in one or two inter-school competitions each term with little success. When I accepted the job of games master, I had no idea how the school's sports were organized, and I entertained no ambition of overhauling the program, much less of turning Kaplong into a mini-powerhouse. But that's more or less what happened.

We competed in four sports—football (soccer), volleyball, cross country, and athletics (track and field)—mainly against the schools in our district, of which there were seven or eight, half of them twice our size or bigger. My first year there, Kaplong finished a close second in the district in both football and track. The next year we moved beyond the district in track and cross country, performing creditably in regional invitational meets and placing second in the provincial cross country championships. And the year after that we hosted and won the provincial cross country and three Kaplong kids won medals in the national secondary school track championships. One of them was later selected for Kenya's 1976 Olympic team.

My contribution to all this was simple: enthusiasm. I certainly had no expertise; I had done a little running in high school and played a little soccer in college, but that experience was barely enough to make me halfway credible as a coach. What mattered was that although I occupied a position of dignity and authority, I was quite happy not to behave in a manner befitting my stature. My willingness to make a fool of myself, together with my transparently sincere interest in the kids and the teams, seems to have been something the students hadn't encountered before and it clearly had a galvanizing effect. And once the newly inspirited teams began winning, the usual factors of pride and dedication kicked in. As often happens, the teams' successes also lifted general morale; the students and the staff took more pride in the school, which made it a more congenial place to live and work.

An additional benefit for me was the strengthening of my connection to the kids, and ultimately to Kenya. The informality and close contact of the sports setting normally fosters comradeship, and this was no exception. The older students were about my age (it was common in many parts of Kenya to start school late), and though we were never quite peers, we were—in a sense—friends. I was regularly invited to students' homes on weekends, and I went quite often, for the most part enjoying the fuss that was made over me by their families and villagers. I suppose my childhood experience among the Kipsigis made it easier for me to feel comfortable sitting in what were usually dark and smoky thatched huts eating the local staple, *ugali* (a kind of stiff corn meal mush, served in tightly woven baskets and eaten with the fingers), or sucking home-brewed beer through a six-foot straw from a communal pot in the middle of the room. I also knew some of the tribal language and was familiar with a few of the more recondite local customs, so I had no trouble impressing the highly receptive audience that would inevitably gather.

But, in general, my cross-cultural experiences of this type weren't substantially different from those of a number of volunteers I knew. The Peace Corps attracted kids who were open to such things and whose demeanor showed them to be approachable and receptive, especially when compared with authority figures in the stiff-backed British mold. So while a shared activity like sports might have helped foster personal connections, it was ultimately the volunteers' humility and curiosity that animated these off-the-job contacts—contacts that the Peace Corps' founders no doubt intended to be a large part of the volunteers' role as cultural ambassadors.

One of the rare occasions when I became vaguely conscious of my ambassadorial function occurred as I was on my way to a student's home deep in the most traditional, un-Westernized part of Kipsigis territory. It was late July of 1969. I was walking along a dirt road at dusk and came up behind an old man walking in the same direction. He had long, distended earlobes hung with small copper ornaments and was wearing only a blanket. I asked him for directions and we walked along together, chatting in Swahili. At some point I identified myself as an American, which made the old man stop. "*Kumbe!*" he said, pointing to the newly risen moon. "*Watu yako natembea uko mwezi,*" that is, loosely translated, "Wow! Your people are up there walking on the moon." News of the Apollo 11 landing had been on the radio that morning. I hadn't paid much attention but it had clearly made a big impression on the old man. Indeed, it must have seemed absurdly impossible to him. I hadn't really thought about it until that moment, but as I looked up at the moon, it seemed absurdly impossible to me, too.

The news from home that I paid most attention to had to do with the emerging phenomenon of youth culture. Reports about Woodstock, which happened a few weeks after the moon landing, and various campus upheavals gave me the sense that I was missing my generation's revolution as I whiled my time away in bucolic Kenya. If I had drawn a high number in the draft lottery, which was introduced in the fall of 1969, I might well have gone home—to do I don't know what. But as it turned out, my number was too low for safety, so I stayed. In fact, I re-upped at the end of my second year and spent another 12 months in Kenya, which took me past my 26th birthday and out of reach of the draft.

It's a testament to my own poor judgment that it took the draft to get me into the Peace Corps and to keep me there. The years I spent in Kenya were among the most enjoyable and formative of my life. I often wish now that I'd stayed longer, but I was plagued by the notion that I had to go home to get my life off the ground. Still, in my three years I developed a deep attachment to the country and the people, and I've been back a dozen times (to date), mainly as a journalist, usually covering the extraordinary runners I used to coach. Recently, I've helped set up a program that recruits and tutors exceptional Kenyan high school students who want to attend highly competitive American colleges and universities. That program takes me back to Kenya at least twice a year.

My post-Peace Corps involvement with my "host country" may not be typical of most ex-PCVs, but I'm confident most of the 70,000 kids who became volunteers in the 1960s—and for that matter, the 100,000 who have served since—have been profoundly affected by their experience. To what extent they fulfilled the Corps' founding aims with respect to winning friends for the U.S. among host country governments and citizens, I have no idea, though on balance I suspect the record is positive. Perhaps it is less so with respect to accomplishing whatever explicit development goals the volunteers were supposed to be working toward— leaving aside the question of whether those goals were always the right ones for promoting the host country's long-term prosperity. But the effect of Peace Corps service on the volunteers themselves has, I believe, been of significant benefit to them and to the people they come in contact with. Given the likely predispositions of kids inclined to join the Peace Corps in the first place, I suspect few were turned around politically, but on-the-ground experience of Third World realities is always a salutary thing for comfortable Westerners, and the fact that there are now upwards of 170,000 additional Americans with two years or more of that kind of experience has got to be a good thing for the country.

QUESTIONS FOR DISCUSSION

1. Opposition to the Vietnam War and strategies to avoid the draft were frequent topics of conversation in the divided America of the 1960s. John Manners starts his story by stating, "I joined the Peace Corps to dodge the draft." What effect does this statement have on the reader? Does its frankness surprise you? Can you detect any irony in this statement?

2. What is the purpose of training Peace Corps volunteers in primitive conditions in the United States and having them stay with families in poor neighborhoods? In what ways does this kind of "immersion" experience remind you of the training that R. Thomas Collins went through for Upward Bound?

3. What is Manners looking for in Kenya, besides the opportunity to teach Kenyan school children as a Peace Corps volunteer? What are the results of his search for old friends? What is your impression of his fellow Peace Corps volunteers? In adjusting to their jobs and the new environment, they faced language barriers, cultural differences, and climate issues. What were some of the ways they tried to cope?

4. Manners supplies a brief background on Kenyan history and geography. He also shares a fairly negative picture of black–white race relations in this post-colonial African country. Do you find any similarity to racial strife in the United States of the same period? What is different? What does the student strike at Kaplong demonstrate about relations between Kenyans of different tribal groups and ages?

5. Manners makes friends with his students and visits their homes, where he politely eats some very strange foods. What does his willingness to make these connections tell you about him? What is the effect of his enthusiasm on his students and young runners?

6. Why does Manners tell the story of his conversation with the old man on the day of the moonwalk? What does the incident tell us about the quality of his immersion in his life halfway around the world? What can it tell us about the way the United States was viewed by outsiders during the Sixties era?

7. Towards the end of his story, Manners says, "It's a testament to my own poor judgment that it took the draft to get me into the Peace Corps and to keep me there." What does he mean? Do you think the work Manners did in Africa made a difference? What circumstances (or beliefs) might lead you to join an organization like the Peace Corps in today's world?

OPENING THE DOORS OF PERCEPTION
James Fadiman

The date is early in 1966. Four of us are seated around a table, called out from the session room for a moment to respond to the contents of a special delivery letter. Back in the room, four men are lying on couches and cushions, eyeshades blocking out the daylight, hearing a Beethoven string quartet on stereo headphones. Each man, a senior scientist, took 25 micrograms of LSD-25—a very low dose—about two hours earlier. Two of these men are working on different projects for Stanford Research Institute, another for Hewlett Packard, the last is an architect. They are highly qualified, highly respected, and highly motivated to solve technical problems. Each one brought to this session several problems that he had been working on for at least the past three months and had been unable to solve. None had any prior experience with psychedelics. In another two hours, we plan to lift their eyeshades, take off their headphones, turn off the music, and offer them finger food, which they will probably not touch. We will help them focus on the problems they came in to solve. They are the fifth or sixth group we have run. The federal government has approved of this study. It is an experimental use of a "new drug," a drug still under review and not available commercially.

In 1966 there were about 60 projects around the country actively investigating LSD–25. Some were therapeutic studies: one at UCLA showed remarkable success in getting autistic children to communicate again; others were working with animals from monkeys to rats to fish, even with insects. Spiders, it turned out, make radically different web designs when given different psychedelics. A year or two earlier there had been a disastrous experiment when psychiatrist Jolly West gave an elephant enough LSD, it is fair to say, to kill an elephant. It did. The dose was several hundred thousand times what any human had taken or would ever take. While it made a brief media splash, the disaster did not seem to stop the research going on worldwide. Sandoz Pharmaceuticals in Basel Switzerland, the developer of LSD-25, had recently made available summaries of the first 1000 human studies. LSD-25 was the most studied psychoactive drug in the world. It was remarkable in two ways. One, it was effective in micrograms (millionth of a gram doses). This made it one of the most potent substances ever discovered. Two, it seemed to have the effect of radically changing perception, awareness, and cognition but not in any predictable way. These results seemed to be dependent not only on the drug effects, but equally so on the situation of the subject—what they'd been told about what they were going to experience under the drug—and, even more interesting to science, the mind-set of the researcher, whether or not he or she had communicated a point of view to the subjects in any given study.

In short, here was a substance whose effects depended in part on the mental expectations of both subject and researcher. Often people in the studies had experiences that appeared to be deeply therapeutic, blissful and life changing, religious in content or mystical, but they also might have experiences that were profoundly disturbing, confusing or terrifying. The after-effects of the experience looked more like learning than simply the passage of a chemical through the brain and body.

LSD was the genie in the bottle and there were bottles of it all over the country and a growing number outside laboratories and research institutions as well.

When that special delivery letter came from the Food and Drug Administration, none of us yet knew that many of the early conferences of LSD researchers had been sponsored by foundations that were covertly funded by the CIA, or that the United States Army had been giving psychoactive substances to unsuspecting members of the military, prisoners, even some of their own staff. Nor did we know that every project in the country, except those run by the military or intelligence agencies, had received a similar letter on the same day.

Sitting in Menlo Park, in the offices of the International Foundation for Advanced Study, we four plus a small support staff were running the only study designed to test the hypothesis that this material could improve the functioning of the rational and the analytical parts of the mind. We were trying to find out if, instead of being diverted into the amazing inner landscape of colors and forms or into the adventures of mystical exploration or psychopathological terror, LSD-25 might be used to enhance personal creativity in ways that could be measured.

There had been a string of very successful studies in Canada showing that LSD administered in a safe and supportive setting led to a high rate of curbing long-term alcoholics' drinking. Other studies conducted in Southern California by Oscar Janniger showed that artists' work changed radically during an LSD session and often was changed thereafter. However, it was an argument in the art world, and in the science world, if that art was "better."

Our team wanted to see if another aspect of the creative—technical problem solving—could be helped by the use of these agents.

The answer thus far in our study was a resounding "yes." We were amazed, as were our participants, at how many novel and effective solutions came out of our sessions. Client companies and research institutions were satisfied with the results (if not fully informed of how they occurred). Members of other research groups about were asking to be included in the study. It was a deeply satisfying time.

The letter from the FDA was brief. It advised us that as of the receipt of this letter, our permission to use these materials, our research protocol, and our capacity to work with these materials in any way, shape, or form was terminated.

I was by far the youngest member of the research team, a graduate student at Stanford in a psychology department that I'd not informed about this research. Two of the others were full professors of engineering at Stanford in two different departments, and the fourth was the founder and director of the foundation, a scientist in his own right who'd retired early and set up a nonprofit institute to better understand the interplay between consciousness, deep personal and spiritual experiences, and these substances.

Very soon we would need to go back into that room where the four men lay, their minds literally expanding. I said, "I think we need to agree that we got this letter tomorrow." We went to our subjects, now the last group of people who would be allowed the privilege of working with these materials on problems of their choosing with legal government support and supervision for at least the next 40 years.

One example of the kinds of results we were seeing did come out of that last session. The architect had bought in a project to build a small shopping center. The client had not liked his earlier designs and he was stuck. In the session, he saw the project, completed, and in his mind was able not merely to envision it but to walk around inside it, to see the size and shapes of bolts, to count the number of parking spaces, etc. The design he came up with was approved by his client and he spent the next few weeks doing the drawings that corresponded to the project he had already seen in its finished state.

How did I come to be in that room at the International Foundation for Advanced Study when only a few years before I'd been a writer, living in Paris in a sixth floor walk-up, living on as little as possible, sleeping in train stations and hostels when I traveled and staying with whoever would put me up and feed me?

As was said of many of our lives then, it was a long strange trip.

What sent me from Paris to Stanford and headlong into psychedelic research was not just a visit from my favorite college professor, Richard Alpert (later known as Ram Dass) and his friend, Timothy Leary, but also a cordial note from my draft board asking about my whereabouts. I realized that there was an M-1 waiting for me to cradle it across my elbows while crawling through mud and dank vegetation in Vietnam while overhead shots were being fired in both directions, giving me the chance of dying by enemy or friendly fire. In my mind, neither of those choices made sense, so I returned to the United States to the draft deferment haven of graduate school.

For the good of the military and for the nation, I was sure then and am now that keeping me out was the better alternative. When you have a long history in junior high and high school of being picked last for team sports, you don't assume that you will thrive in the infantry, let alone rise to the higher level of competence needed in actual combat. I saw my government fellowship to study psychology as the government saying that it was better to keep me out than to deal with any potential hazards to others and myself it risked by inducting me.

Why I plunged into psychedelic research, however, did begin with that visit from Alpert and the first night we spent together.

Paris, 1961. I'm sitting at night in a cafe on the Boulevard St. Michael, watching all the people who in turn are watching me. I'm twenty-one and have just taken psilocybin for the first time, and I've no idea what it is or does, but I know that the man sitting next to me is my favorite professor, Dr. Richard Alpert, who has given it to me as a gift. The colors are getting brighter, peoples' eyes are flashing light when they look at me, the noise is playing inside me like a multi-channel broadcast. I say, as evenly as my quavering voice allows, "It's a little too much for me." Richard Alpert grins at me from across the tiny round glass table. "Me too, and I've not taken anything."

We return to my walk-up a few blocks away. The hotel has a plaque to the side of the front door that says that Freud stayed there. I am writing a novel and sometimes imagine that in the future, they will add a second plaque. But not tonight.

I lie down on my bed, Alpert takes the chair. (That about uses up the space in the room.) I watch my mind discovering new aspects of itself. Alpert keeps letting me know that whatever my mind is doing is safe and all right. Part of me is not sure what he is even talking about, another part knows how deeply right he is, another part of me hopes he is.

One week later, I left Paris and followed Alpert and Leary to Amsterdam, where they joined Aldous Huxley to jointly present a paper to an international congress. Leary and Alpert were working together teaching psychology at Harvard and were already in the midst of controversy over giving psychedelics to graduate students and other members of the academic community. Six weeks after their conference, I was flying to California to begin graduate work in psychology.

While at Stanford, I led three lives. In life one, I wore a sport coat and tie, and made sure I showed up every day in the psychology department, visibly a student doing what he could to learn from the lips of the masters. In my second life, two days a week, I was a research assistant at the off-campus International Foundation for Advanced Study. There I sat in on daylong, high-dose (and legal) LSD therapy sessions. Each client had at least two people supporting their experience during the day. A man and a woman stayed with every client (male and female energy seemed helpful), plus there was a physician who checked into the session now and then, and was there if needed. I can't recall when we ever had any simple medical needs but it added to the feeling of total support and reassurance that made the LSD sessions more beneficial. In addition, a Freudian psychoanalyst had met with each client when he or she first volunteered for our program to determine if each person selected was likely to benefit and unlikely to run into problems beyond their ability to cope. Given the government's skittish stance at the time, the analyst told us we needed to have close to a 100% cure rate, something not demanded nor achieved by any other therapy.

My third life was spent with the people who revolved around Ken Kesey. They used psychedelics of all sorts, as well as uppers, downers, marijuana, even alcohol and cigarettes. One member worked for a pharmaceutical chain and arrived at any event with his pockets stuffed with samples.

It was a group of outlaws, but not lawbreakers—more like paradigm breakers. LSD and many of the other drugs were not illegal in the early 1960s, but their use, especially outside any research or medical setting, was not socially acceptable. These explorers of inner space were doing field research, exploring what it was like to have free access to these drugs outside of any control or restraint except self-preservation. During these times, when these drugs were opening doors all over one's mind, the Kesey group used psychedelics while playing, singing, drawing, watching TV, cooking, eating, making love, watching the stars spin and dance, and asking aloud the sorts of questions their experiences brought up:

- Who are we, really?
- Is the soul mortal or immortal?
- What did Blake or Van Gogh or Plato really experience?
- Is my identity inside my body or does it interpenetrate my body and yours?
- What is common between my mind and the nearest redwood tree?
- Were time and space subjective?
- What was fixed? What moved?
- What stayed constant from session to session (that is, what was remembered)?
- What happened in a group where all the minds were opened, loosely linked, and apparently in telepathic communication with one another? When someone in such a group becomes terrified, do the rest get sucked into the down draft? Or can the combined weight of the other minds lift the one who has fallen away?

These questions and more were at the heart of the Kesey group's experience. Not outlaws, but outliers. Better to think of them not as the cultural icons they eventually became but as people who had outgrown the limitations of the laws and were furiously developing a bigger set of laws to bring order to their own larger sphere of behavior and experience. It sounds philosophical and it was, but it also had all the raw immediacy of putting your arm across the throat of a drowning swimmer so he or she doesn't panic, drag you underwater, and kill you both.

For me, a critical moment happened one morning at the edge of the Pescadero town dump. Pescadero is a tiny town two miles from the California coast about 15 miles from Stanford. The dump is a hillside, the bottom of which was littered but the top and sides were covered with vines sporting small patches of wildflowers. One dawn I went there with Ken Kesey and his girlfriend at the time, Dorothy, a woman who would later become my wife (after 40 years of marriage, we think it will probably last). The night before, she'd taken some LSD ("dropped acid," to say it the way it was) and was in a state of delighted wonder at the personal discoveries she was making about her own consciousness and how it shaped and reshaped her world.

Ken had taken us to Pescadero because it was a wonderful place to meet the dawn. It is correct to say he took Dorothy there, but because I had been guiding her through parts of the night, she wanted me along.

I was not in the inner circle of the Kesey world. I was too straight and too unwilling to take drugs with everyone. None of the women in the group were interested in me, and I had not much in common with any of the men. However, as I worked with LSD by day and legally, I was welcome as an odd ornament, as one might want to have someone around who trained tigers or who could chew broken glass.

Dorothy recalled that the defining moment of that dawn came when she was about to step on a small flower. Instead, she lay down on the path and stared at it. I suggested she let the flower do the communicating. What she saw—not thought or contemplated but saw, such was LSD's curious power—was the flower fully open up, go through its cycle and wither, but also she watched the flower reverse this same flow, recovering from its dried state, re-flowering and returning to being a bud. She could see it go in both directions, forward and backward in time, dancing its own birth and its own death. When she said what she was seeing, I confirmed that her experience was one others had shared. Relieved, she returned to her plant contemplation.

She looked up at Ken—handsome, rugged, talented, a natural leader, possessed of enormous energy and power. Also married. Ken had two kids; he was fully committed to the marriage and also to having it open to other partners as well. Dorothy looked at me. I was engaged, but my fiancée was 6000 miles away in Scotland. What she did see was that I seemed very knowledgeable, even comfortable, about her newly discovered inner world. From the moment of the encounter with the flower, her gyroscope began to spin away from Ken and turn toward me.

Our courtship and marriage is outside this moment in time but as one can trace a river back to a small spring coming from a cleft in a rock on a mountainside, our three lives shifted that day through the lessons that arose from Dorothy's encounter with a single flower.

FIGURE 3.3 An artist drew this sketch while under the influence of Lysergic Acid Diethylamide (LSD), a powerful drug known to cause hallucinations. LSD was first synthesized in a laboratory in the 1940s. Proponents believed the drug had psychotherapeutic and spiritual value. The U.S. government briefly experimented with LSD as a tool for interrogation, but in the end decided the drug was unpredictable and dangerous. Though many who used LSD informally reported "mind-expanding" experiences, others had "bad trips." LSD became a controlled substance (i.e. illegal drug) in 1966. The fierce energy of the sketch in this illustration suggests the drug's power to influence perception and experience.

Source: AP Wide World Photos

What about my legal research? What was it like to do legal drug research? Since the Sixties, on most college campuses, it is no trick to find a psychedelic drug, take it, have a wild ride, and to wonder about it all. To give it to people in a setting so supportive that 80% of our subjects reported that it was the single most important event of their lives—ah, that was a different time. For more than two years while the experiments were going on, I'd slip away from Stanford classes when I could and sit with people who were having their introduction to psychedelics and, through psychedelics, to other levels of consciousness, and perhaps to other levels of reality.

Since I was usually introduced as "a graduate student who will be with us today," I was not primarily responsible for conducting the session. I was truly a sitter and could watch, sometimes help, and sometimes record what people reported as they went through the events of the day. Sometimes I would only appear in the late afternoon, and take a person home for the evening. We found that while the effects of the LSD would have worn off after 8 hours, a person's newly found capacity to move in and out of different realities diminished, but did not stop until the client was too tired to stay awake. I often had the treat of being with people as they puzzled out the major events or insights of the day. I also helped them deal with their families, who were usually baffled by the combination of tales of bizarre inner experiences and the sense of being with someone, a husband or wife, who was so totally open and loving and caring that it often brought the spouse to joyful tears.

By day, in my graduate studies, I was being taught a psychology that seemed to me to cover only a small fragment of the mind. I felt as if I were studying physics with teachers who had no idea that electricity, atomic power, and television existed. I would listen, take notes, ask appropriate questions, and would try to appear as if I were not dumbfounded by the tiny little nibbles my instructors seemed to assume was the whole of the apple of knowledge. By night, having completed my school assignments, I would read books that helped me to piece together the larger world I'd been opened to: *The Book of the Dead*, the *I Ching*, the works of William Blake, Christian mystics, and Buddhist teachings, especially those of the Zen masters whose cutting-through-it-all clarity was wonderfully refreshing. I also struggled with Tibetan texts that were hard to comprehend, but clearly had been written by people who knew about what I was discovering. I would sit and read those books wrapped in plain covers the way one had wrapped dirty comics in *Look* magazine in high school to hide pictures of women with amazingly large breasts from one's teachers.

When I could no longer follow the texts I would sit, cross-legged, on the bare linoleum floor of my graduate student "office," which was in a trailer turned temporary classroom. The space was even smaller than my bedroom in Paris. I'd look through the sliding glass door at a small pine tree planted to deny the fact that we were in a temporary trailer in a large parking lot. I would breathe and stare, breathe and stare until the tree began to breathe with me. It would not move or sway, but would begin to shine with an invisible illumination, the fact of it extremely alive. It would grow and shrink before my eye, a very tiny movement, but reminiscent of the flower at the Pescadero dump. I'd attune to that tree until I felt balanced again and then go home to bed.

A Moment of Reflection

A few months after we ended our research program, California passed a law declaring the possession or distribution of LSD to be a crime. Federal policy concerning LSD was later consolidated with the enactment of the Comprehensive Drug Abuse Prevention and Control Act of 1970.

Why did our drug research frighten the establishment so profoundly? Why does it still frighten them? Perhaps, because we were able to step off (or were tossed off) the treadmill of daily stuff and saw the whole system of life-death-life. We said that we had discovered that love is the fundamental energy of the universe and we wouldn't shut up about it.

Christianity, for example, says come to the Father through Me, and be forgiven sins (even those you had not committed) and be loved without reservation. FREE. FREE. FREE! (as if that alone wouldn't make you look underneath to see where the price tag has been hidden).

Once you have declared yourself to be a Christian, however, you find church authorities saying that the actual price of being forgiven includes admitting that you are not only unworthy, but you are very, very unworthy and there is no way you will ever get to worthy on your own hook.

What we found out was that the love is there, the forgiveness is there, and the understanding and compassion are there. But like water to a fish or air to a bird, it is there all around and without any effort on our part. No need for the Father, the Son, the Buddha, the Saints, the Torah, the books, the bells, the candles, the priests, the rituals, or even the wisdom. Just there—so pervasive and so unending that it is impossible to see as long as you are in the smaller world of people separated from one another. No wonder Enlightenment is always a crime.

QUESTIONS FOR DISCUSSION

1. How did James Fadiman become involved in psychological research using LSD? Given the information he provides, how would you evaluate the results of the LSD studies on personal creativity?

2. Fadiman was acquainted with a number of well-known Sixties personalities: Timothy Leary, Richard Alpert, and Ken Kesey. What is his connection with each of these people, and how does each influence his life? What else do you know about Leary, Alpert, or Kesey?

3. In what ways does Fadiman compare LSD experience with religious experience? How does he evaluate the relevance or truth of all the world's major religions, and what conclusions does he draw? What effect does this evaluation have on the reader?

4. James Fadiman lists the questions that people like Ken Kesey and his friends were asking under the influence of mind-altering drugs. What kinds of questions are these? Are they important? Universal? Can they be answered? Do you ever find yourself asking questions like these?

5. Why does Fadiman think the government stopped LDS research? Why do you think the research was terminated? Do you think the government was right or wrong to terminate the research? In the 40 years that have passed since the time when drug experiments were legal and received funding, what has happened to the national attitude toward drug use? How do Americans generally regard drug use today?

BACK TO THE LAND
Steve Diamond

Sometime in the mid-1980s, I was sitting in my apartment on De La Vina St., in Santa Barbara, California, leafing through a magazine when I came across a cartoon showing an aged hippie, headband covering bald head, long gray hair flying every which way, sitting under a tree with a guitar. A bunch of five- and six-year-olds were sitting in a circle around him. The caption read: "Tell us another one about the Sixties, Grampa Windsong . . . "

Well, it was hilarious to me at the time, but now, more than years later, perhaps I'm not laughing so hard. But anyway, here's another one about the Sixties. . . .

There was a war on in Southeast Asia, a war at home, and a war raging in our offices in the basement on Claremont Avenue in uptown New York City.

We were a ragtag band of anti-war college students who had started a news agency. Officially we were known as the Liberation News Service, unofficially as LNS, the "underground press syndicate." Journalists and photographers from the United States and around the world would send us stories and images documenting the progressive movements and counterculture, and, two or three times a week, we would prepare packets of anti-war news articles, photos, artwork and poetry, plus assorted features to send to our subscribers. We wrote about everything from campus demonstrations—of which there were many, most notably at Columbia University (my alma mater), Berkeley, Kent State, Boston University, and Indiana University—to interviews with the outrageous personalities of the day like Timothy Leary or Allen Ginsberg. Twice a month we published columns by black activist Julius Lester, and we syndicated Anne Koedt's pathbreaking piece, "On the Myth of Vaginal Orgasm," and similar radical writings. Not exactly the kind of stuff you'd find in America's family newspapers of 1968, but certainly the meat of most underground and many college newspapers of the day. Our subscribers, publications like the *Berkeley Barb*, Atlanta's *Great Speckled Bird*, Austin's *Rag*, San Francisco's *Oracle*, New York's *East Village Other*, and four hundred others around the country happily printed our articles, photos, and commentaries—all with the letters LNS at the start of each article. For this service, our subscribing newspapers paid a nominal fee of $15 a week—when they could. In addition, we operated on small grants and loans floated from wealthy, older liberals who were opposed to the Vietnam War and who were only too happy to make a donation to an organization of young, passionate people willing to take on the "Establishment."

LNS was launched in the culturally and politically tumultuous year of 1967, birthed in the nation's capital by Marshall Bloom, Ray Mungo, Harvey Wasserman, and Allen Young, as well as several others, to serve as a voice of the anti-war movement. Since the Establishment "controlled" the media, including the press syndicates UPI, AP and Knight-Ridder (of that we had no doubt), we "media freak" pioneers thought it necessary that our side also had a voice. As the great American journalist A.J. Liebling once commented, "Freedom of the press belongs to those who own one." Made sense to us. (Many is the time since then I've thought, "Man, if we'd had computers and the Internet back in the day, wow, what we could have done.") Occasionally, after our move to New York City, we held benefits to raise funds, which leads me to the current memoir, but more about this in a moment.

What is important to realize is the overview—that America was polarized, divided in two, politically, culturally, and psychically, between the forces fighting to maintain the status quo and those of us fighting for change. And of course it was right in this atmosphere of dynamic division that folksinger Bob Dylan released "The Times They Are a-Changing," which concretized in song what was happening throughout the land in a way no news report ever could.

And this polarization all across America was occurring at every level of society. The Civil Rights movement of the '60s, led by the Rev. Martin Luther King, Jr., Stokeley Carmichael, Fannie Lou Hamer and others, was demanding equality and an end to the racist policies of segregation; the women's movement, in its infancy, staged outrageous public demonstrations, sometimes burning brassieres in public as symbols of women's oppression, and sending shock waves through not only the apparel industry, but the schools and churches as well. Scorning materialism, Abbie Hoffman and comrades tossed wads of single dollar bills from the balcony in the New York Stock Exchange, and watched in delight as the brokers on the floor scurried to capture them. But most of all, the Vietnam War sliced America right down the middle—you were either for it or against it, there was no middle ground. An old labor song, revived by protest groups of the Sixties, asked the rhetorical question: "Which side are you on?"

In homes all across the nation, fathers and sons fought the war vociferously at the dinner table, while in the background Walter Cronkite and Dan Rather tallied the scores of the latest casualties, American youth dying on battlefields in far away places with names like Da Nang, Long Bin, or the DMZ.

So in the midst of all this national and international upheaval, there we were in our basement offices (literally and figuratively "underground") a few blocks from Columbia University, pumping out our LNS packets and mailing them to our subscribing papers, when, much to our surprise, the news service itself began to split into two warring camps. One half emerged as the hardcore political leftists, the other half, the "cultural revolutionaries." The hardcore leftists—with Lenin and Marx as their idols—believed it was necessary to overthrow the government, to change America from a capitalist to a socialist country. The cultural revolutionaries (the side I was on)—with (John) Lennon and (Groucho) Marx as our heroes—believed in rock and roll, marijuana, LSD, free love, and individual freedom to explore. We believed in The Beatles' magical theorem: "All You Need Is Love." In short, one side wanted to change the government, the other wanted to change people's minds, their ways of thinking, and their hearts.

The latter group, ours, was called the "Virtuous Caucus" by my friend and colleague at the time, author Ray Mungo. The other side he termed "the Vulgar Marxists." (This story is in Ray's 1969 book, *Famous Long Ago: My Life and Hard Times with Liberation News Service*.) As it happened, several cadres—small groups—of political leftists had joined our organization as volunteers, with the single idea of taking it over, controlling the news service so they could control the flow and the flavor of the news that was going out in those LNS packets, making it more politically left-leaning. And because we had a loose, more or less democratic structure—one person, one vote—by packing the outfit with their volunteers they quickly outnumbered the original group and were able to out-vote the rest of us. It was sort of a stealth campaign at first, but as the spring and summer of 1968 wore on, with the assassinations of Martin Luther King and Robert F. Kennedy, the student rebellion at Columbia, and worsening news from Vietnam, their campaign to take over the news service became apparent. Whenever there were meetings that led to a vote, the "new" members had the majority and could turn it to the direction of their agenda.

In the midst of this internal (and external) upheaval, something magical occurred. One day, while I was sitting at a lunch counter having my morning coffee, a small article in the *New York Times* caught my eye—down at the bottom of an inside page was a report that The Beatles had made a short documentary film, *Magical Mystery Tour,* as a Christmas special for television, but it seemed that the sponsor, Singer Sewing Machines, had found the finished product too "freaky," and had cancelled its airing on NBC-TV. The movie, as it turned out, was a precursor for what would become known as music videos, but at the time, the format was unknown. The film had no "story-line" in the classic sense of a beginning, middle, and end. A band, in psychedelic costumes, boards a tour bus and travels the countryside playing songs from a newly released recording. With its swirling colors, rapid cuts, and flashing images, *Magical Mystery Tour* was just too radical (culturally speaking) for Singer Sewing Machine to want to have their name attached to it on national television.

At that moment, sitting and munching on a donut, I heard a little voice whispering in my ear: "Call them up, maybe you can get the film to show as a benefit to raise funds for LNS." (Now, more than thirty-five years later, I've come to regard such "messages" as voices of spirit, the influence of the Invisible World on our daily lives, but that's the subject for yet another essay.) The *Times'* article on *Magical Mystery Tour'*s sudden cancellation quoted the manager of The Beatles' New York office, one Nat Weiss of Nemperor Productions, as saying he was "sincerely disappointed" by the show being scratched. So I had a clue, suddenly, as to how to get in touch with them.

I went to a nearby payphone, dialed information, and got the number for Nemperor Productions' office in Times Square. When I called, a young man answered.

"Hi, my name's Steve Diamond," I said, "and I'm calling from a group called Liberation News Service. I'm wondering if we could arrange to show *Magical Mystery Tour* as a benefit for our organization."

There was a pause at the other end of the line, then, "Why don't you come down to our office and talk to Mr. Weiss about it?" The young man gave me a time the following day and when I hung up the phone, I had the sense that my life was about to change. I was twenty-three years old, more than halfway through my senior year in college, but about to begin a magical mystery tour of my own which would run for the rest of my life—though of course at the time I didn't know it.

Mr. Nat Weiss was jolly, clean-shaven, smoking a cigar, and an essential New Yorker. He welcomed me into his office high atop Times Square in midtown Manhattan, a pearl pinkie-ring gleaming as he motioned me to sit in a leather chair on the other side of his polished desk.

I explained briefly what Liberation News Service was and why I thought we should be allowed to show *Magical Mystery Tour* for a benefit. We talked for maybe ten or fifteen minutes, the specifics of which I can't fully recall (the whole thing happened so fast, that now, as I look back on it all those years ago, it has a slightly dreamlike quality), and then he reached for the phone, saying to his assistant in the other room, "Andre, get me George Harrison on the line."

I took a deep breath.

Mr. Weiss clicked on the speakerphone, and we sat there listening to the tone as it rang a number of times over in London.

Finally, a voice through the speakerphone, "Hullo, this is George."

"Nat Weiss here. George, I'm sitting here with Steve Diamond from an underground press group called Liberation News Service," Mr. Weiss eyed me as he spoke into the device on his desk, "and he's wondering about showing the movie for a benefit."

"Liberation News Service?" I heard George say, "Oh, I know those blokes. One of them, Richard something or other, from *International Times* here in London interviewed me last week. They're good chaps, sure, let them have it."

"Good, George," replied Nat Weiss, "I'll take care of all the arrangements."

And that was that. Well, not exactly.

Earlier that spring, Bill Graham of the Fillmore West in San Francisco had launched the Fillmore East on St. Mark's Place in Greenwich Village. I'd been there to see Janis Joplin perform with her band, Big Brother and the Holding Company, and I thought it would be the perfect venue for our *Magical Mystery Tour* benefit. So I called Bill Graham up and made an appointment to see him.

"What night are you closed?" I asked Bill at our first meeting. "I'd like to rent the theatre for one night to show *Magical Mystery Tour.*"

As it turned out, he hadn't booked anyone for Saturday night, August 11, 1968, less than two months away. For a flat fee of $1,000 he would also provide the ushers and theater personnel for that night. And since the film was only fifty minutes long, we'd be able to have two showings, 8 and 10 p.m. Graham was happy that I'd come to see him, as he also was aware that The Beatles film hadn't yet been seen by anyone in America, so it would definitely be a premiere showing, and his new East Coast venue would get some additional publicity from it.

When I got back to the LNS office the next day with the good news, quite exciting I thought, there was less than the enthusiastic response I'd anticipated. The internal war between the Vulgar Marxists and the Virtuous Caucus had gone into high gear. A big meeting of all concerned had been scheduled for the end of the week, clearly aimed at ousting the main founder and director of the news service, Marshall Irving Bloom, known fondly as "Mad Marshall" or "The Incredible Freak." And, while it could be said that Marshall was "mad," it was a brilliant kind of madness, more like that of a wily fox; Marshall, at 25, was much "older" than the rest of us, more worldly. And he was unstoppable.

A thin, wiry fellow ("It's just that I have an awfully high metabolism!"), Mad Marshall was an Amherst College graduate. At the 1966 graduation ceremony he had led a walkout in protest of America's involvement in the Vietnam War. He later attended the London School of Economics, where he also incited a major protest, leading to a front page editorial in the London *Times* with the blaring headline, "Bloom, Go Home!"

I have no doubt that, as LNS grew and gave encouragement to the nationwide anti-war movement, J. Edgar Hoover and his F.B.I. troops must have kept several antennae focused on this madcap "troublemaker." (In later years, rumors abounded that perhaps even the split in our organization might have been engineered by undercover FBI agents. Who knows? In those tempestuous years, anything was certainly possible.) In truth, the members of our little band, the Virtuous Caucus, loved Mad Marshall, "our fearless leader," even though Marshall could also be exasperating, being a master at pulling people's chains to get them to do what he wanted.

As June turned into July, I was busy drumming up excitement for the LNS *Magical Mystery Tour* benefit. I'd taken out some ads in the *Village Voice* and other publications, plus a few on New York's rock and roll radio stations (FM radio had only recently become widely available). Advance ticket sales were bringing in some cash, so I opened an account at a small Polish-American bank on the Lower East Side where the funds continued to accrue.

At night, the Virtuous Caucus would have secret meetings to figure out how we would thwart this "democratic"—so to speak—takeover of our organization. Simultaneously, the other side was also having secret meetings to oust Bloom and his band. Ray Mungo had already announced that he and some friends, including a poet named Verandah Porche, and Marty Jezer, a radical anti-war writer (and a close friend and comrade of Abbie Hoffman), as well as a few others, had bought a farm in a southern Vermont village called Packers Corners. They would soon be leaving New York and leaving us to deal with the whole roiling LNS scenario.

"I think we should just take the whole news service out from under them," Bloom said at one of our night meetings in an uptown Manhattan apartment, "and move it up to a farm in the country, maybe somewhere in western Massachusetts."

"A farm?" I replied, somewhat in disbelief. "No, it's better to be in a city, like Boston, maybe, where at least we'd be connected to things and have a pool of volunteers and activists from the big student population there. Doesn't that make more sense?"

"Yes, it does Steve," Marshall replied, diplomatically weighing his words, "but in the coming New Age of information, with electronics and everything, it really doesn't matter where the news service is based, be it New York City or a farm in Timbuktu." He smiled at me through his perpetually lopsided glasses, stroked the ends of his Fu Manchu mustache, then added, "Moving to a farm is the right thing to do at the right time, now. The movement's going through a lot of changes, and our living communally and growing our own food organically, if you want my opinion, is the best thing we could do for all our brothers and sisters, by setting an example."

As I said, Bloom was wild and crazy, but he was also a visionary. No doubt his desire to stay geographically close to his friends Ray and Verandah in Vermont had a lot to do with his plan, and, as it ended up, the farm we bought was only about forty-five minutes away from theirs. But to live communally and farm organically (a very new concept at the time) and put out a twice-weekly national and international news service was a radical notion. The environmental movement had not yet been born; Earth Day would not be conceived for another couple of years. The routine recycling of metal, glass, and paper had not yet been imagined, and, believe it or not, health food stores as we know them today barely existed in 1968. The very concept of organic gardening, which at the time was being promoted by a little-known magazine published by J.I. Rodale and his family, was roundly derided by the mass media and mainstream agricultural authorities. "How could you think you could grow food without pesticides and chemical fertilizers?" was the prevailing opinion. But after a brief discussion amongst the crew that night, Marshall won the point, and we were headed for a farm in Massachusetts.

To encapsulate for you what happened next: Marshall and I quietly took some trips up to western Massachusetts looking for farms. In fairly short order we located a beautiful, forty-odd acre place in Montague, just north of Amherst, with a two-story, eleven-room farmhouse and huge barn—the perfect place for one of the first modern-era communes in New England. Without anyone knowing it, we used money I'd collected from advance ticket sales for The Beatles' movie benefit for the down payment, and after the screening on August 11th, we put down another chunk on the purchase price.

The Beatles benefit was a smash. Both 8 and 10 p.m. showings were sold out. Since most of the ticket sales came at the last minute, on August 11 we were flooded with cash at the box office. One of our crew, Al, had an apartment only a few blocks from the theatre, so we decided to wrap the stacks of greenback dollars into aluminum foil bricks and then walk them over to his place and stash them in the freezer. If anyone did break in, we reasoned, that was the last place they would look. You could say we put the funds "on ice."

On August 12th, a bright Sunday morning, while our opponents lay sleeping, our crew, the Virtuous Caucus, removed everything from the basement offices—printing press, files, desks, etc.—and loaded them onto U-Haul trucks for the big move to Massachusetts. (As one writer for the *Village Voice*, Steve Lerner, put it so aptly, we "performed a unique change of address.") On Monday morning, the Vulgar Marxists discovered they'd been had, found out where we'd gone, and came roaring up to Montague to try and wrestle back what they thought was theirs.

Unfortunately for them, Bloom was too sly a fox for that to happen. Since he was officially the director of the Liberation News Service, he had all legal authority to own both the presses and the property. After holding our side hostage for the better part of a whole night, and roughing up Bloom a bit, the Vulgar Marxists went back to New York City and regrouped, planning to start their own version of LNS. When we cranked up the press in the barn for the first issue we produced from Montague Farm, Bloom insisted that we use the subhead, "Accept No Substitutes."

So the Vulgar Marxists in Manhattan had to call their news service LNS-NY and put out their version on white paper with thick black ink. Bloom had always insisted on using bright, multi-colored mimeo paper for our releases. I recall thinking to myself that this small indicator was symbolic of the two factions. We saw the world in colors, and wanted to add colors to the menu (Day-Glo), while they had a need for everything to be seen (and understood) in black and white.

For a couple of months that fall, the two news services went head-to-head in an intramural campaign to keep subscribers, and, where possible, to add new ones.

As it turned out, the rigors of a New England winter and the duties of surviving on the land called our attention louder than the reality of keeping LNS going. The inks froze in "Little Johnny," our small mimeo-printing machine, since the garage where we'd installed it had minimal, and I do mean minimal, heat. Since Marshall had named me Editor-in-Chief, it fell to me to tell him that the news service, in my humble opinion, had to be laid to rest. Although we had no idea what the future held in store, living (I should say "surviving") on the land as an organic communal family had to take precedence over pumping out the latest political blat from far-flung regions of the country.

Several of the others were instantly upset with my take on the subject, my decision to stop printing. "Why, then, we'll just be farmers!" one person commented, quite dismayed by the prospect. "No," I remember replying, "we'll be people. Let's be a new kind of human on a different kind of mission. Instead of trying to change the world, let's change ourselves."

Much has been written about the remarkable Marshall Bloom, including my own book, *What The Trees Said: Life on a New Age Farm*, because Marshall didn't just have far-out ideas, he lived most of them, no matter how wild other people might have thought them at the time. Marshall's commitment to anti-war protest led to a walkout at the Amherst College commencement in 1966; Marshall's determination to publish material ignored by the mainstream media led to LNS; Marshall's idea about communal organic farming led us to become pioneers on the East Coast of what was to be called the "back-to-the-land" movement.

But there were one or two secret fantasies deep in Marshall's soul that the rest of us at the farm didn't know about. On November 1, 1969, "All Saints Day," after we'd survived our first four seasons on the land, Marshall Irving Bloom committed suicide by sitting in the woods in his small Triumph sports car, hose attached to the exhaust, and letting it fill up with carbon monoxide. There was no suicide note to speak of, just a loving "Jiffy Memo" (as he'd written at the top of his final document the night before he died), leaving his personal possessions to assorted individuals and requesting that the remaining seven of us inherit the property. The mortgage for the farm was in Marshall's name alone, since he was the only one of us who had been able to qualify for a loan at the Amherst Savings Bank (now defunct—through no doing of ours, I have to add).

Several months before Marshall's passing, sitting around the long kitchen table, which in its earlier incarnation had been a barn door, we had been brainstorming about creating an organization—on paper, at least—to give the Farm an official sounding name. We'd been referring to it and to ourselves as "Pretty Boy Floyd Associates," because we considered ourselves at the time outlaws in the eyes of the Establishment, but now that we'd survived that first and difficult winter on primitive (to us) wood heat, we thought we'd better have a "straight" name that would come in handy when needed in the legal system. (In the *I Ching*, the Chinese book of divination, which became sort of my bible at the time, I found an important corroborating line: "The superior man veils his light." We assumed this meant us.)

"What about . . . The Fellowship of Religious Youth?" I remember suggesting. "That sounds pretty straight, and sure to confuse 'em."

"Hey, not bad, Stevie," someone else chimed in, and somehow it stuck, but the place was always known simply as Montague Farm. Thus, after Marshall's death, the seven of us created the Fellowship of Religious Youth Realty Trust (not believing, of course, that we would ever grow up, or grow old), and we had the property officially 'conveyed' into that paper housing, with the seven of us as trustees duly registered with the State of Massachusetts.

FIGURE 3.4 Gathered outside their farmhouse in western Massachusetts in the fall of 1971, members of the Montague commune pose with their children and pets. Author Steve Diamond ("Back to the Land") is in the back row on the right, wearing a wide-brimmed hat. The members of this intentional "family" sought personal freedom and meaningful connection with one another. They raised organically grown vegetables, milked cows, and heated the huge farmhouse with wood they harvested themselves. Originally founded by the publishers of the alternative press syndicate, Liberation News Service, Montague Farm outlived the death of its leader, Marshall Bloom, and lasted until the early twenty-first century.

Source: Peter Simon Photo

No one ever satisfactorily figured out the reason for Marshall's suicide. Rumors abounded. Did he die at the hands of sinister government agents? Did he die because of some lost love? A sense of failure, of one kind or another? To this day, no one can say for sure.

Bloom died, but in his wake, as often happens, some of the things he worked for, organic farming and environmentally balanced living, came to pass—and not just for those of us who had been his colleagues. They moved right on into the mainstream of American life.

At the time we established the organic communal farm in Montague, there were no other hippie groups for miles. Conservative farmers of Polish and Irish ancestry owned the local land and ran the local towns. Today, Franklin County, Massachusetts, is as much a bastion of New Age consciousness (though they probably wouldn't use that term) as Mt. Shasta and Bolinas in California, or the Twin Oaks Commune in Virginia, or other such communities around the country.

Life on the "hippie farm," as the local people in Montague called it, was quite conventional in some ways, though definitely not conventional in others. Like a lot of other Americans, we earned our living by hard work, we struggled to keep warm, we ate and sang and listened to music together, there were children and pets. Since we thought of ourselves principally as "revolutionaries, cultural and otherwise," there was a revolutionary spirit that pervaded our lives together. In addition, those were the earliest years of the women's movement, and I can say unequivocally that the women of our community were in the front lines of that revolution, too. There was also the little matter of our revolutionary attitude towards certain customs and laws, especially when it came to smoking marijuana and enjoying sexual freedom and nudity. When we all swam nude at a pond in some neighboring woods the local citizens were outraged, and even though we started wearing swimsuits to keep the peace, we found the road to the pond chained off one brutally hot day and a big NO TRESPASSING sign. We later heard that the property owner did not want to contribute to "your-way-of-life."

(At least once afterwards, late at night, when only the stars were awake, we stole back into the pond in the woods, the water soft and dark, laughing voices amid the sounds of splashing and happy dog yaps, all the bodies swimming and one with the water, no witnesses to the crime save the warm summer moon.)

We never hurt anybody (except ourselves, inadvertently) or cheated anybody; we weren't un-neighborly. But we were different, and we meant to be. We were trying to live in a new way, trying to see if we could truly cooperate and truly live in harmony with each other and with the Earth and keep our material needs very basic.

There were unforeseen pressures on couples within a communal set-up. Even the most committed couples had difficulty surviving the communal lifestyle. Certainly single people had the freedom to make love when and with whom they chose—but when couples strayed, and often it was the woman first, it almost always meant the end of the relationship. Some couples tried to incorporate a kind of sexual freedom into their relationships—but, regardless of all the things you hear about hippie lifestyles, it never worked. As young people in our twenties (and in the grip of raging hormones), we knew a constant sexual charge in the air, in the kitchen, and on the land. So it was absolutely inevitable and really only a matter of time before people found themselves turned on and in the arms of someone else, thus bringing to an end whatever youthful pairing they'd started out with. Yes, hearts got broken—but, surprisingly, they mended, and managed to fall in love again, and again. In some ways, this was my greatest lesson at Montague Farm, and one I'm still learning, the resiliency of the human heart and how it goes on.

When our first spring on the land finally arrived and it was time to plant our organic garden, there were a few dissenters, most notably Ira, who thought we should grow a cash crop using pesticides. He quickly gave in to the majority opinion. We went organic.

That first summer, we grew tomatoes like crazy, cucumbers, zucchini, broccoli, and corn—though the tomatoes are what stick in my mind. In the fall we canned and froze enough of those saucy red fruits to feed a small army. So the following winter, it was tomato soup, tomato bread, tomato pancakes (I kid you not), and of course a multitude of spaghetti dinners with tomato sauce. So much tomato-themed food came out of our kitchen that for ten years after I left the farm, I couldn't bring myself to eat a single tomato—raw, cooked, in sauce, or in salads. And only after twenty years, have I come back to be able to enjoy those delicious red fruits again.

Another notable "farming" factor, was our first year's marijuana crop. The plants grew well enough, but the THC content was so low that you had to smoke at least ten joints to get the slightest "buzz." And even then, you weren't sure if you were high or just dizzy from inhaling too much.

Over the years we learned to grow every conceivable variety of organic vegetable and grains. If we had a surplus we sold it. We cut our own firewood to heat the house. We kept chickens for eggs and meat, and we acquired Dolly and Delilah, two dairy cows who gave us all our milk and the butter we churned ourselves. Some of us had outside jobs, because even though we shared everything, it was impossible for the group to live without some cash. Mostly, though, we farmed.

But it's funny, now in retrospect, how important our effort to grow organic food, to live organically with the Earth, would become. I recall that Marshall Bloom was insistent on the subject, whenever anyone suggested we use pesticides. And in some ways, the farm at Montague began to radiate out the need for organic, sustainable agriculture to the larger community and region. It's an impact that is invisible, can't be measured really, and yet was as real as day. If you go to a farmers' market nowadays, in the Montague area or, really, almost anywhere in the country, you'll find about three quarters of the food for sale is organically grown. Look at the success of the Whole Foods supermarket chain! Almost every town in America now has a recycling program. So, we made a difference. We radiated news even without a news service.

In one sense, I grew up at the farm, though whether I've actually matured (in my 50s as I write this), is of course debatable, depending on which of my friends you speak to. I lived at the communal hippie farm for ten years, off and on, and after I left it to "go out into the world," I thought about the place and the people for another ten years or more, like the initial longing for an old lover after you've split up. In my heart and psyche, the farm remained alive as a "free zone" where you could be yourself, bumping, of course, into other free souls also being themselves. Imagine twelve or thirteen or fourteen twenty-somethings, living together, sharing the load and the love—with no "adults" around, with no rules, figuring it out (i.e. how to live) on a day-to-day basis.

On that hillside in Western Massachusetts, I learned about Nature, about Love and Heartbreak, about myself, as well as some early inklings about God. I learned about birth (a little girl named Sequoyah was born at the farm) and Death (Marshall's, and that of Burmie, the steer we lovingly fed only to one day shoot him in the head and turn him into beef), and I learned about human nature by interacting with my fellow communards. I also learned about the Invisible (Spirit) World that we can't see or feel but which nevertheless interacts with us on a daily basis. I had my first psychedelic experience there—on mescaline—at age 24, during which time the trees spoke to me, saying, very simply, "You'll never get past the trees." To me, it meant, "In life, you'll never get past Nature."

Growing up at the farm made me into a strange breed of human. I grew up believing in sharing the world's wealth and helping people in need, and what a shame it was that in the U.S.A., the richest country in the world, less than half the population has medical insurance. It was at the farm that I learned the true secrets of Einstein's "Theory of Relativity," namely that all people and all things are related. Given that we live in a "closed system," i.e. our atmosphere, the breath I inhale and exhale on the side of a rural hill in New England will some day find its way into the lungs of someone halfway around the world in China, let's say, and that person will breathe it in and out and over time those same air molecules will travel to the next continent, to the next human.

It's the Gaia hypothesis come to life—the Earth as one big body, and each of us humans as 6 billion cells (and counting) of that terrestrial body. There were times at the commune where I felt like we were a microcosm of the world—and if we couldn't get along with each other, then the world of nations never would either.

Most of all, I learned that Nature is God, and God is Nature. For it is in Nature, including us humans, that God resides, and it is there, inside ourselves, that we must go to look for God. Happy hunting! And may all your dreams come true.

QUESTIONS FOR DISCUSSION

1. Steve Diamond describes the Liberation News Service at the height of its effectiveness and on the eve of its destruction. What factors contributed to the organization's success and its downfall? If you are familiar with the problems encountered by other left-wing groups of the Sixties era—for example, SDS or the Black Power movement—how would you say the split at LNS reflects or resembles the fracturing of those radical groups?

2. Why do you think the Beatles would surrender the U.S. premiere of their film, a potential moneymaker, to a small group of young, radical journalists? Diamond explains that the television premiere was canceled but, beyond that, what does this gesture tell us about the Beatles in particular, and about the 1968 cultural and political climate in general?

3. Why does the group stop publishing the LNS with such minimal struggle to keep it alive? What has become more important to them? Historically, how would you account for the switch from outwardly directed activism to inwardly directed rural communalism in mid-1968? Is the change solely attributable to the influence of a charismatic leader or are other factors at work? How do the residents of Montague Farm justify their choice?

4. Diamond describes his group as "cultural revolutionaries" and later as "hippies." What does he want his readers to understand by these terms? Does Diamond's picture of hippies coincide with your previous ideas about hippies? If not, what is the difference? What is your opinion of their lifestyle? Do you think it would be difficult to live in a group with few rules? According to this story, what kind of challenges—internal as well as external—did members of communal groups face in this period?

5. Diamond claims that rural communes like the Montague Farm started the movement for organic farming, recycling, and sustainable living. Do you see any connection between the way you live now and the work accomplished by these new agricultural pioneers? Do you or members of your family recycle, celebrate Earth Day, or eat organically grown foods? In what ways has modern life benefited from the discoveries of Diamond's generation?

6. Do you think Diamond's story conveys nostalgia for his days on the farm? What did he discover spiritually during those days? What did he mean by saying, "You can never get past the trees?"

THE PROCESS
Karen Manners Smith

My poor father. He only wanted me to have what so many suburban fathers wanted for their daughters: a happy childhood and a superb education, followed by marriage to some successful man who would take care of me and give him grandchildren. But I kept disappointing him. I kept looking for a community to be part of, and I thought maybe I would find it in a church. This was a real dilemma for my Jewish atheist father. When I was eight I joined an Episcopal choir my little girlfriends sang in. At fifteen I joined the youth fellowship of a local Congregational church, and tried to join the church as well. That was too much for Dad. He went to the pastor and demanded that I be withdrawn from the indoctrination classes. And that was it for the moment. I went to college and had friends who never went to church or temple. I encountered religion only in art and history classes.

College was a community, and I was happy there, but graduate school was cold and professional. I dropped out in the spring of 1969. I became a hippie and hung out with a group of hippies in a house in Central Square in Cambridge, Massachusetts. Unlike my friends, I wasn't very good at taking drugs; marijuana made me cough and hurt my throat; I thought hallucinogens like mescaline were pretty silly—why, anybody could see that the walls weren't really moving, that was just an illusion caused by the blood pulsing through the small blood vessels in our eyes. My friends said I was a downer and stopped inviting me. I had a lot of boyfriends. I got engaged. I got unengaged. I went to a therapist. He found me so boring he fell asleep during our sessions.

I rallied and marched against the Vietnam War, took buses to New York and D.C. for the big demonstrations, and finally quit when I saw some people carrying severed pigs' heads on poles above the marching crowds. I think I missed the point of the anti-war/anti-violence metaphors, and was just supremely grossed out. My roommate was very committed. She went to jail a couple of times for her anti-war protests, and she joined a building takeover during a famous student strike at Harvard in 1969. I didn't seem to have the degree of idealism it took to stand up for my beliefs or put my body on the line. I felt inferior to the activists I met every day. Boston and Cambridge seethed with them. They would stop the war, end racism and poverty—I just knew it!—and I would not be part of it.

I had tried graduate school. I had tried a job helping people—at least that was my intention—by working with poor families in the Roxbury section of Boston. But the Boston Welfare Department, which hired me as a social worker, wasn't able to help the city's poor people do much more than survive. A lot of us—idealistic young social workers—felt we were never going to make a dent in what Michael Harrington had called the "culture of poverty." My own brother had joined the Peace Crops and become a teacher in Africa, but I didn"t feel brave enough to tackle proverty in the Third World.

I really was sick of everything, and it was becoming increasingly clear that no Prince Charming was going to come along and solve all my problems, deliver me a perfect life wrapped up in a white picket fence. It was what I'd been raised to expect and it just wasn't happening. Maybe if there was a Prince Charming he had already been killed in Vietnam and I would never get to know him.

So when my friends, Bob and Gerry Miller, a couple in the hippie house, started talking about this wonderful English religious group they were going to join—The Process (pronounced Prōcess)—I thought why not try it? I've tried everything else. By that time I was more or less living with my boyfriend, a brilliant guy named Rhodes, who had dropped out of Harvard. We shared the house with Bob and Gerry and several other people, including, until he got caught, a soldier named Mike who was AWOL from the army because he didn't want to go to Vietnam.

Rhodes wanted to explore some other religious options before checking out The Process, and Bob and Gerry liked the idea. So we all piled into Bob and Gerry's VW bus, Rhodes and I and a guy named Steve, Bob and Gerry and three huge dogs—two German Shepherds and a St. Bernard, and drove across the country to San Francisco. Driving across the country was cool. It was what people our age did, or they hitchhiked.

It was July 1969. We were on the road when American astronauts walked on the moon. We were hippies, and even in 1969 we looked weird to a lot of Americans. The guys wore jeans and long hair and Gerry and I wore long skirts and long earrings and hair parted in the middle and falling halfway down our backs. We all wore beads and bandanas. We said "Peace!," and "Far out!" and "Outta sight!" to each other a lot. Bob had been scrupulous about banning drugs from the car, but after we made a detour to see the Canadian side of Niagara Falls the U.S. customs took one look at us trying to reenter our country and tore the minibus apart. All they found was ginseng and I can remember Gerry, in her sweet, patient way, explaining to the customs cops that it was a natural supplement that you bought at the health food store.

In Vernal, Utah, we stopped at a roadside café and a crowd of local men—we'd call them rednecks now—followed us out to the parking lot after we ate. I was sure they were going to beat up the three hippie boys and do God-knew-what to us girls. When the crowd saw our three huge dogs sticking their heads out the open windows of the minibus, they took off. We decided it was a good idea to travel with dogs.

We stayed with Bob's parents in San Mateo, just south of San Francisco, and drove into the city every day to explore the alternative religious scene and hippie culture. People who looked like us were everywhere. People told us the Haight Ashbury scene was dead, but we went to have a look anyway. All the head shops and free clinics and kitchens and used clothing stores were still there, but people kept telling us it just wasn't the same as '67, man, the Summer of Love. We hung out in Golden Gate Park, visited the Aquarium and spent hours in the streets and coffee houses and bookstores of North Beach, which had been the headquarters of the Beat Generation. We all went to services and breakfast at the Krishna Consciousness Society's temple, sang "Hare Krishna," and danced with the devotees in their orange robes through long, long records of Indian music. One day Rhodes and I visited the Church of Satan and talked with its founder, Anton LaVey. LaVey explained his version of Satanism with a twinkle in his eye, and we left with some literature. We later discovered that LaVey's *Satanic Bible* was dedicated to W.C. Fields and P.T. Barnum, among others. In the end we thought the Satanic Church was something of a scam: hedonism and self-indulgence tricked up with spooky symbols and theatrical rituals. Maybe there was something more to it, but it certainly wasn't frightening, or even very interesting.

We had a much better time driving down to Big Sur, running on the beach, and then inching our car down the steep canyon roads in the Los Padres National Forest

FIGURE 3.5 Ecstatic followers of Guru Maharaj Ji at a mass gathering at the Houston Astrodome in 1972. Maharaj Ji was 13 when he first came to the United States from India, seeking a following for his Hindu-based religious cult. His "Divine Light Mission" was one of a score of sects that flourished in the late 1960s and early 1970s, among them the Unification Church, the Children of God, and the International Society for Krishna Consciousness. Most cults had charismatic leaders who expected adherents to follow strict regimens of discipline and devotion, forsaking their normal lives. In general, Americans found the era's religious cults merely bizarre, but some feared that they were dangerous for the naïve young people who joined them.

Source: Peter Simon Photo

to reach the Zen Center at Tassajara Hot Springs. Rhodes had a friend who had become a monk there. The friend fed us grains and vegetables, we attended some kind of worship service, and then, because it was too scary to drive back up the canyon road, we spent the night on the library floor. It was peaceful and beautiful, but not what we were looking for. On the other hand, I've never forgotten it, or the face of Rhodes' friend Glen, who was truly and serenely happy as a Zen Buddhist.

It was August and time to leave California. It had been a summer full of California earthquake fears and rumors and my friends were convinced they felt portents of doom. Bob and Gerry and Rhodes and Steve had each had an earthquake nightmare, but mine waited until we were on the road. I woke up terrified and fell off my seat onto the dogs. I realized my earthquake nightmare was nothing more than a response to the bumpy road we were driving over. My rational side had asserted itself again; it looked as if I wasn't going to be any better at "vibes" and premonitions and psychic awareness than I was at taking drugs.

Back in Cambridge, we pooled our savings and bought tickets to England on the ocean liner *Bremen*. Hard to believe nowadays, but in 1969 tourist-class transatlantic passage cost about the same as airfare. It would take five days, they'd feed us royally, and we could transport a lot of stuff, including the three dogs, who would have to spend six months in quarantine in England. We weren't planning to come back. My father wasn't happy about my chasing spiritual enlightenment overseas, but he didn't try to stop me.

A few days before we were set to leave, my cousin Bruce dropped by on his way to a big music festival in Woodstock, New York. Did Rhodes and I want to go? No thanks, we said, we were going to see Baba Ram Dass, formerly a Harvard psychology department colleague of LSD researcher Timothy Leary, and formerly called Richard Alpert. Dr. Alpert had become a Hindu and was revered as a guru. So we went to Ram Dass' place in the New Hampshire countryside and didn't go to Woodstock, and didn't participate in one of the great events of the twentieth century.

However, we had not wasted our time. Ram Dass was a wise and gentle man. We sat cross-legged for two days under the trees, listening to him tell stories of his abandonment of hallucinogenic drugs, his travels to India, and his struggles towards enlightenment. Then, on Sunday morning, we had a private interview, a chance to ask a single question. Should we go to England and check out this new religious group? Ram Dass looked at us, looked inside us, it seemed, and then said he knew nothing about the spiritual qualities of the group, had never heard of it. But, he added, "At least you'll meet some interesting people."

And that was confirmation enough that we were on the right spiritual path. In the last week of August we loaded the trunks onto the *Bremen* in New York harbor, and sought our tiny third-class staterooms. On September 1st we landed in Plymouth, and then a few hours later we were in London, in the heart of elegant Mayfair, knocking on the door of The Process' coffee house.

We entered below street level through the basement door of a narrow six-story town house. In the hallway stood a very tall, very slender man all in black, with a plain silver cross around his neck. On his chest he wore a little black and red triangular badge with what looked like a goat's head in the middle. He introduced himself as Brother Micah. He was genial and handsome, with shoulder length blonde hair, perfectly groomed. We asked about the cross and the goat's head and were told they were symbols for Christ and Sátan.

We bought membership cards—you couldn't enter a "club" in this posh residential section of London without them—and walked into a dark room with tables and chairs and banquettes and a second tier of seating in a gallery accessed by a narrow wooden stairway. It didn't look like a basement at all; it looked like a very cool club, dimly lit by red votive candles on all the tables, their light glittering off the gold and red and silver dragon murals on the black walls. The menu offered coffees, herbal teas, fruit and vegetable drinks, sandwiches, and a variety of vegetarian dishes. More people in black with crosses and goat-headed triangles served us, all of them—it seemed to me—just vibrating with charm and self-confidence.

Suddenly a small man with bright brown eyes appeared in front of us. He said he'd heard we were new American arrivals looking to join The Process. It was

Brother Matthew, an American from Long Island. I'm sure my mouth dropped open. I felt an instant connection to this man. Surely I must know him from somewhere? But, no, we quickly established that I didn't. I don't know if it was the familiarity— he looked like all the guys I'd gone to college with—but I felt I had known him for years. I immediately adored him. (A few days later, after I got up the courage to tell him I felt I had known him before, he would tell me that we had all known each other before, through many past lives. In this incarnation we were coming back together, and I had been drawn to London and to The Process because it was time for me to rejoin my brothers and sisters. Powerful stuff. It's hard not to believe some divine purpose is guiding you when an impressive somebody says you were drawn away from your family and across an ocean to join a more mystical family for a predestined purpose.)

Mother Cassandra came to our table. She was English and one of the original members of the group—which is why she had the rank of Mother rather than Sister. Mother Cassandra seemed to be in her late twenties, with dark curly hair, and though she was not classically beautiful, she had tremendous warmth and a great laugh. I remember she was carrying around her dog, a miniature Yorkshire Terrier absurdly named Big Daddy.

Mother Cassandra wanted to make sure we could find a place to live in London, and some jobs, while we were working towards becoming members of the inner circle of The Process. We would have to support ourselves. It would take many months, she explained. They didn't accept just anybody; in that respect they were very different from a normal church. You had to go through a period as an Acolyte, then an Initiate. If you abstained from sex, alcohol, cigarettes, and drugs for many months, if you attended all the classes and religious services ("Sabbath Assemblies" and "Midnight Meditations"), and you spent every spare minute doing some kind of work for The Process, you could attain the rank of "Messenger" and receive a new name. The name would be chosen for you by the Oracle and the Teacher, the two founders of the group. Mother Cassandra urged us not to rush into anything. We might find we didn't want to join the group at all. That, of course, clinched it for me. I would work my way in and prove to these dynamic people that I could be one of them. I had very little idea what the religion was, or what the group was really about, and already I wanted in.

Over time, I learned the group's history and religious beliefs. Not all the information was public. Like most cults and religions, The Process had plenty of secrets, information that would be doled out to you piecemeal as you climbed up the hierarchy. Bob Miller had already told us about the group's origins as a spin-off of Scientology. The Teacher and the Oracle, a married couple whose names were Robert and Mary Ann de Grimston, had left Scientology and adopted some of that group's techniques to start a therapy practice called Compulsions Analysis. The core group of young London professionals and artists who gathered around Robert and Mary Ann at Compulsions Analysis felt drawn to discovering the spiritual meaning of their bond. In 1966, they traveled to the Yucatan peninsula in Mexico to experiment with privation. Miraculously, they survived a hurricane while sheltering in the foundations of an abandoned sugarcane mill. As a result of that experience they decided they had been chosen to found a new religion. The group became "The Process, Church of the Final Judgment." Robertde Grimston, whose dreams and visions had generated much of the spiritual quest, became the chief theologian—the Teacher. Mary Ann, intuitive and analytical, focused on the human relationships of the group. She was the Oracle, a source of revelation, fully Robert's equal in power and authority. Everyone else abandoned their birth names and took new "sacred" names prefixed by "brother" or "sister," "mother" or "father," depending on how long they had been with the group.

During a brief attempt to establish chapter houses in San Francisco and New Orleans the group was joined by several young Americans, including Brother Matthew, who went with them when they returned to Europe to begin a period of proselytizing. Dressed in long black cloaks and accompanied, always, by enormous German shepherd dogs, the Processeans hitchhiked in pairs around Europe, preaching to those who would listen, totally dependent on the kindness of strangers for food and shelter.

My friends and I had come upon the group in a settled phase, with nobody out on the road. In 1969 there were chapters in London and Paris offering classes and programs that were a mixture of spirituality and therapy. The London Chapter also ran a coffee house and conducted a weekly Sabbath Assembly. They sold Process books and psychedelic-colored magazines on the city streets, and on Sundays some of the men preached on soapboxes at Speakers' Corner in Hyde Park. Seeing a pair of Processeans striding down a London street, long hair flying, cross and goat symbols flashing, eyes intense, black cloaks swirling around them, was a sight to take your breath away. No wonder young Londoners were attracted and older ones appalled. No wonder the British tabloid press dubbed them "The Mindbenders of Mayfair." The French have a saying: "*Il faût épater les bourgeois*," meaning let's shock the middle classes. Well, The Process had great shock value.

Like Scientology, which started with an alternative system of psychological analysis and later added religious trappings, The Process had developed its theological beliefs based on theories about human personality. The Teacher's writings described four deities, Jehovah, Lucifer, Satan, and Christ, who were aspects of a single Supreme Being, and whose separate traits were reflected in human behavior with all its mental and emotional conflicts. Jehovah represented authority, duty, self-sacrifice, and paternal love. He was also the god of wrath and vengeance. Processeans did not consider Lucifer just another name for Satan. On the contrary, Lucifer was, as his Latin name implied, the light bearer; he represented harmony, enjoyment, success, worldliness. Satan had positive and negative traits, representing on the lower end lust, violence, and excess—destruction—and on the upper end detachment, mysticism and aestheticism. Christ was the fourth figure, the unifier, representing the gods' link with the human race. These four gods, we learned, were reuniting into one, coming together for the end of the world, an end brought about by the greedy and unloving acts of the human race throughout history. So humanity was God's enemy, not Satan, who merely had the terrible role of destroyer. In the end Christ would overcome evil with love, and even Satan would be redeemed.

All this made a kind of sense to me. The Christ/Satan thing was kind of like the Buddhist concept of yin and yang. I knew every human being was complex, two-sided; I knew everyone had the capacity for both good and evil. I hoped good would triumph in me and in the rest of the world, because there was an awful lot of evil out there, including the atomic bomb and the Vietnam War, the assassinations and the urban riots, the hatred and bigotry I had left behind in the U.S., along with the problems of poverty I had felt so powerless to heal. If the end of all this was inevitable, then maybe I didn't have to feel so guilty about bailing out on the good fight of my generation.

Still, I didn't like the idea of the world ending, though no Processean would give me a precise date when it would happen. I knew I'd be OK because I was in The Process, but what would happen to my family, my parents, my sweet little brother and sister? I worried about them a lot. Processeans didn't really dwell on "The End," however; living in the present was too exciting. I suspect a lot of them didn't want to believe in it either.

People were encouraged to figure out which of the gods they most identified with. Our personal "god patterns" worked a lot like astrological signs. If you were a "Jehovian," you might be an authority figure, you might be austere, easily angered, blameful, guilt-ridden. You would also be honest and generous and loving. If you were "Luciferian," you would love the good things in life, cherish nature and beauty; you might be an artist, but you might also be lazy and irresponsible. If your personality was "Satanic," you could either be cerebral, intellectual, an ascetic, or you might be a lowlife, a glutton, an alcoholic, a sex fiend. "Christians" were loving and gentle, self-sacrificing, but they could also be bland and ineffectual. To make things more complicated, as the body of Process religious theory changed and developed, personalities, too, became more complex. Everyone had one characteristic from the Jehovah/Lucifer pair, and one from the Christ/Satan pair. In ourselves, we expressed the binary nature of the universe. I figured out I was probably a Jehovian-Christian, a "J-C," mostly because, even though I felt guilty a lot of the time, I really did care about helping people. Rhodes was a J-C, too, mostly because he was searching for a powerful religious authority, but Gerry was clearly Luciferian-Christian, an L-C, so light and spiritual and gentle and harmless. Bob Miller, if I remember correctly, was a J-S. He had tremendous leadership abilities, but he had had disastrous periods of self-destructiveness, too, spending some part of his adolescence in a mental clinic. Steve—I don't remember what god pattern Steve was. He left after about a month and went back to Boston. So, The Process clearly wasn't for everybody.

The god pattern game was endlessly fascinating, and it was a good motivator in the search for self-awareness. You could spend hours talking about each other's god patterns, or using their many meanings in group sessions to try to understand yourself and other people. A lot of the analytical work we did in groups was embarrassing or painful; but it was always also thrilling to learn about ourselves. It didn't kill us and it did make us stronger, or at least it did me. I am actually quite grateful for the self-awareness I acquired in The Process, though I no longer relate any of it to "god patterns."

Anyway, not to get too far ahead of the story, Bob and Gerry and Rhodes and I found an apartment in a section of west London called Hammersmith. We were joined there by a number of other new recruits, people who had met charismatic

Processeans on the street, come to the coffee house, and decided to make a real commitment to join. We all found jobs in small retail establishments where the employers weren't too fussy about work permits for non-citizens. My job was in a dry cleaning shop. We worked evenings in The Process coffee house or we did laundry, sewing, food preparation, layout work for the magazine, any job that needed doing. By November 1st we were Initiates and sometime around Christmas the four of us, plus an eighteen-year-old girl named Ruth who had joined us, had become Messengers. My new name was Sister Meredith. Rhodes became Brother Alexander, Gerry was Sister Bethany and Ruth became Sister Hagar. Bob was called Brother Simon. In April of 1970, we were invited to become "inside" Processeans, and we moved into the house in Mayfair.

We were the lowest people in the hierarchy. It was our job to serve the Priests and the Masters, make their beds, clean their rooms, cook and serve their food. Their job was to give us spiritual guidance and training. We quit our day jobs and learned to sell magazines on the street, scrupulously handing in all the money at the end of the day. We had no money of our own, and nothing to spend it on. Our black uniforms and cloaks were provided; if we needed underwear or shampoo or toothpaste, the group bought it for us. If relatives sent money, we handed it right to the chapter treasurer, and it went into the general coffers. We learned that some members had given entire inheritances to The Process. If relatives sent clothing or birthday presents, we were encouraged to give them away immediately to someone higher in the hierarchy. I remember feeling very bitter when warm pajamas and a warm coat I had especially requested from my parents had to be given to Sister Maia and Mother Ophelia. I also felt guilty about feeling bitter. Sister Hagar loved to give things away, and fully understood the religious axiom that if you give materially you will be rewarded spiritually. Material sacrifice for the sake of spiritual enrichment. In The Process, we were also told that people at the upper end of the hierarchy were more detached than we were, therefore better able to handle worldly possessions than we were. I felt that having a pair of flannel pajamas would not seriously impede the course of my enlightenment, especially as I was sleeping on couch cushions spread out on the floor at that time.

Every minute of our day was scheduled for us with military precision. And every waking minute we were under somebody's control. We lived dormitory-style on the upper floors of the vast house, where no members of the public ever visited. Compared to the opulence of the coffee house and the elegance of the public meeting rooms on the lower floors, the living space was unfurnished and spartan. We started each day in silence until after a brief morning religious service, and ended the day with a meeting of the whole group, sometimes lasting until 1:00 or 2:00 a.m., where we sat around in a circle, told everyone about our days, and listened to the latest theological writings by the Teacher.

We never had any privacy and we were never alone. It was total intimacy and total strangeness at the same time, because the lowest-ranking people were never on confidential terms with those at the upper end of the hierarchy, and there were many, many secrets we were not allowed to know. (I later discovered how mundane most of those "secrets" were: things about finances, expenditures, and general gossip about everyone beneath them in the hierarchy.) The Teacher and the Oracle were deeply sequestered, always living separately from the chapters. In five years I never saw either one of them, though Robert's picture was prominently displayed in the coffee house and featured in the books and magazines. Robert was bearded and long haired and was always photographed in soft focus. People often commented that he looked like Jesus Christ. There was never a picture of Mary Ann. To this day I have no idea what she looks like.

We continued to attend our classes—"Progresses"—where we practiced Scientology-type communication exercises to learn self-control, make ourselves impervious to insult, and improve our contact with other people. On Friday nights we had regular Telepathy Developing Circles, which cost a couple of British pounds for the general public to attend and where we insiders practiced opening our awareness to other people's "realities." It was surprisingly easy to "read" other people if you kind of got yourself out of the way and really focused on what they were telling you, not just in words but in body language. I doubt we really were telepathic, but we certainly were good at tuning into other people. In time, I started to hear that newcomers to these circles were impressed with my telepathic abilities! Amazing. Sister Seraphine told me that one day I would be leading Telepathy Developing Circles, and, a few years later, that turned out to be the truth.

Above all, we were told to feel and not think; it was through feeling and not through intellect that both spiritual and personal enlightenment would come. Over-intellectualizing things was a Process crime; Mary Ann, the Oracle, was said to despise "pissy intellectuals." Since I was a pissy intellectual (meaning I had had a college education) that always made me uneasy.

Rhodes and I had ended our relationship because of the celibacy rules, but also because we kept getting crushes on upper-level Process people. We remained good friends, and that was important to both of us. I fell in and out of love with Brother Matthew, then Brother Lars, then Brother Phineas, Father Mendes, and Father Dominic. It didn't make any difference; everyone treated me just the same, like a long-lost sister learning how to be part of the family again. I think they knew how I felt, but were convinced almost as a matter of doctrine that sexual attraction that never went beyond attraction was just a useful way to bind people to the group. I was also completely in awe of the women at the top of the hierarchy, and even some at the mid-level rank of "Prophet." Mother Hathor and Mother Cassandra seemed both clairvoyant and wise; I felt they knew more about me than I would ever know myself. Sister Seraphine was beautiful, with auburn hair and brown eyes. She was fun and kind. Sister Diana was beautiful in a totally English, delicate blonde way, but she had a flaming temper and I was terrified of her.

The no drink, no drugs rule was strictly enforced, as was the celibacy rule. That seemed hard for outsiders to believe, since society was in the middle of the "sexual revolution," and unmarried sex was practically routine, and here were all these young people living communally. I remember one guy who visited the coffee house looking around at all the beautiful Process brothers and sisters. "What a waste!" he said, shaking his head. There were a few married couples in the group, but almost nobody was married to person they had been with when they joined. In 1969, no new marriages were allowed; the following year that rule changed and several couples did marry, including our little friend Hagar, who married the man of her dreams, the tow-headed, lighthearted Father Christian.

In the spring of 1970, the Process leaders decided it was time to expand the religious mission and go back to the United States. Within a few weeks, small groups of Processeans sent to Boston and Chicago had established Process chapters. Alexander, Hagar, Simon, and Bethany were all sent to the Boston Chapter, which was actually in Cambridge, just a few blocks from where we had lived, and only a few miles from my parents' suburban Boston home. So much for never coming back to the U.S.!

In July, I was sent to Chicago, where we had a coffee house/church set up on Wells Street in Old Town. The group's residence was separate, way down the South Shore on E. 72nd Place. Every day Father Lucius would drive a station wagon full of Messengers and Prophets into the city and drop us off in the Loop, where we would sell magazines and collect donations until well after 5:00 p.m. In the evening we did more of the same, though the scene shifted to Rush Street and other places where the night streets were lively. I was usually paired with Brother Reuben, who was a nice guy. He kept encouraging me to do better. I had been a total failure at street sales in London, but in Chicago, for some reason, I blossomed. Businessmen, tourists, shoppers—it seemed they couldn't wait to give a donation to Sister Meredith. In fact, I achieved a certain celebrity around the chapters when I became the first person ever to make $100.00 in a single day of fund raising—the equivalent of about $500.00 in today's money. (We called the funding activity "donating," since we believed that we "donated" something—spiritual contact, friendliness in the unfriendly city, whatever—and people bought a magazine or gave us a "donation" in return.) I think, really, I just felt comfortable in an American city asking Americans for money. In any case, my celebrity lasted exactly two days; after that Father Christian and Sister Bernadette easily surpassed me.

Ask anybody who lived in Boston, New York, Chicago, Miami, New Orleans, or Toronto between 1970 and 1975 if they remember the kids in black cloaks selling magazines on the streets. They will. We made quite a spectacle. Of course, some people might have seen us as panhandlers, but we scorned that comparison. We felt we had so much more class. We were always dressed in clean uniforms, we had shining, well-cut hair, we were polite, and we had items for sale—we were not asking for "spare change!" Plus, we could honestly claim to be doing good work. We weren't only a church, we were also a social service agency. All the American chapters (in time there were five), as well as the one Canadian chapter, ran coffee houses, soup kitchens, and free clothing stores; the brothers and sisters regularly visited nursing homes and schools for the disabled. The Toronto chapter had an active prison ministry and even received a Canadian government grant for social service. In the coffee houses we frequently counseled young people who came to us with a variety of problems. We saw a lot of runaways, and a lot of kids with drug problems. In New Orleans, year after year, Processeans saw the same faces every February—ragged, exhausted, hippie kids on the yearly circuit, hitch-hiking to New Orleans for Mardi-Gras, then maybe to Boston or New York for the summer, then, when the cold weather started to set in, west to California for the winter.

Winters were bitter on the streets. The winter of 1970–71 in Chicago was brutal. I remember the leaders said they wouldn't send us out if the temperature went below 10 degrees Fahrenheit. But they did. Every chapter had a weekly financial quota to make, so the work went on. That winter we took more frequent breaks than usual, ducking into the vestibules of banks and office buildings for a few minutes, or even, sometimes, the lobby of a posh hotel. Nobody begrudged us warm air, though we got a lot of odd looks. I got chilblains that Chicago winter; they still act up sometimes.

I was sent to New Orleans late in February of 1971. New Orleans was where I spent the longest part of my five years in The Process, and it was the place I liked best. Well, for one thing, it was New Orleans! And it was warm; there were magnolia trees in bloom in February! And we lived in the French Quarter, and we sold magazines in Jackson Square and on Bourbon Street (until the city fathers got fed up with us buttonholing tourists and insisted we confine our magazine sales to the business district).

In New Orleans I spent only half my time on the streets selling magazines. The other days I spent running the domestic apparatus of the chapter, kind of like a glorified housekeeper. I ordered the shopping (or I did it), arranged the rotation for cleaning jobs, supervised the Messengers and Initiates who were assigned to chapter chores during the day, and was responsible for running the coffee house, free clothing store, and soup kitchen. We did everything on a shoestring. I can remember I had to try to feed about twelve "inside" Processeans, including three or four Masters and Priests, about eight of the "Brethren" (men and women) and several babies, on a food budget of $120.00 a week.

What we ate was very simple, and it was supplemented by loaves of stale French bread salvaged from the trash cans outside French Quarter restaurants. ("Really, it's OK," I explained to my father when he visited. "The loaves are wrapped when they throw them away!") Our poverty might have horrified others, but we took it in stride. And besides, it was very lopsided poverty. We ate badly, but we were all required to take expensive vitamin supplements and swallow a daily protein drink at breakfast. We had several changes of uniforms, an ample supply of soap and towels, and we all had our hair cut at professional salons. The leaders had some odd ideas about what mattered, but image was central. They'd spend money on keeping us healthy, but not on nourishing food we could enjoy. And, of course, if we looked clean cut and wholesome, we made more money donating. We each had a dollar a day to spend as we pleased. Unless you were crazy, you spent that dollar on some kind of lunch or snack to get you through the long donating day between breakfast and dinner. The Process did not do lunch.

None of our food budget went into the free kitchen. For that we relied on donations from retailers and wholesalers: unsold vegetables from the French Market, dented cans, bags of grain. There was never anything coherent that looked like a meal, though I remember one year we did actually pay for and cook a Thanksgiving dinner for the odd assortment of hippies, street kids, winos, and homeless men who came our way. The free store was easier. It's easy to acquire used clothing from suburban donors. We collected it by the carload. We'd wash it and hang it up and people would come in and take what they liked. Sometimes they'd leave their own filthy garments in exchange, and we'd either toss them out or wash them if they were salvageable, and hang them up for the next comers. It was very New Age.

I remember one day I was making a soup in the free kitchen with whatever ingredients we had—probably something like turnips and oatmeal—some horrible mush, anyway, and I was cutting up the vegetables when I got called away. A moment later I heard the sounds of a fight breaking out among the racks in the free store, and some poor old wino calling "Sister! Sister! Come quick! He's got a knife!" I ran in, took one look at the kitchen sink and realized that somebody had seized my one and only cooking knife. I was so furious I marched right up to the swaying drunk who was waving the knife in his friend's face, and snatched it away from him. The guys were dumbstruck. So was Father Lucius, when I told him about it later. I hadn't even considered the danger; I was so pre-occupied with shortages and making do, and the fact that that was the only knife we had! When I told my own children that story years later they thought I was heroic. I know I was just stupid.

In an odd sort of way, the free store introduced me to Brother Jerome. Jerome was a new Messenger, sent down from the Toronto Chapter in exchange for one of the English brothers whose visa had run out. (Toronto functioned as a kind of bolt hole for the English Brethren: when their visas ran out they would go to Canada—a British Commonwealth nation—and then after a while apply to come back into the U.S. Visa hopping was not a good long-term solution for The Process, if they wanted any stability. I think this is one reason they started to allow marriages within the group. A lot of British Processeans married American Processeans between 1971 and 1974, and several of those were clearly marriages of "green card" convenience.)

The first day Jerome was there Mother Diana assigned him to help me in the free kitchen, which he did with great good humor. He was kind to the homeless men and seemed happy to cook mush. He had been the eldest of eight children growing up and was from the same big Boston suburb I had come from, though we had never known each other. He had dark blonde hair and blue eyes. He was smart and witty. By the time he rolled up his sleeves to wash the dishes I was hooked. A year later we were married.

The most fun I had in The Process has to have been the road trips. Every second Sunday night we'd pile six or seven of the Brethren and several cartons of magazines into one of those huge late-'60s station wagons and drive all night to some big southern city, like Atlanta, or Memphis, or Houston, or Birmingham. We'd spend all week on the streets of the new city, telling people about our religion and raising money for the chapter back in New Orleans. Processeans in other chapters were doing the same, making expeditions to Cleveland and Cincinnati and Newark and Providence from bases in Chicago and Boston and New York. If you were in the Toronto Chapter, you drove to Ottawa or Hamilton to sell magazines. The rule was, you took no money for anything except gas for the car. Everything else had to be donated by strangers. Towards the end of each day, we'd start asking people who seemed friendly if they would let us stay at their place for the night. We had bedrolls and towels, any piece of floor would be fine, we said. It's amazing how many people agreed to it. Imagine inviting seven strangers to sleep in your house after talking to one of them for a few minutes on the street!

People usually let us take showers in the morning and sometimes gave us breakfast, too. Or, if they didn't have food for breakfast, we could get a breakfast of eggs, grits, toast, and coffee for thirty-nine cents at a McClellan's or a McCrory's or a Kresge's lunch counter almost anywhere in the South in 1972. We always tried to get dinner donated, if we could, though some nights we did have to spend some money on McDonald's. One night, I remember, in Underground Atlanta, a thriving district of shops and bars and restaurants, we got a meal donated by a restaurant called Dante's. Unfortunately, what they gave us was cheese fondue, which was made with wine. Even though we were starving hungry by that time, several of the Brethren refused to eat until I called Father Lucius and got permission for us to break the "no alcohol" rule. I am still astonished at our obedience and our innocence.

When I look back on those road trips I tend to forget the exhaustion of driving five hundred miles and working all the next day without sleep, and the long hours on icy or sunstruck street corners, and the anxiety about finding food and a place to stay at night. We were told it was a test of our faith, and a test of our ability to give enough, spiritually, in those momentary street conversations, so that strangers would respond with Christian charity. The Bible passage we used as a reference was Matthew 10, verses 5–15, where Jesus sends the Disciples out into the world to preach and heal the sick. He tells them not to take any money with them, but to expect to receive sustenance from those who respond to their teaching. I was always very proud of the fact that in all the trips I led nobody ever had to sleep in the car. We always found accommodation. Other trips were not so lucky. Sometimes their days ended with seven people sleeping upright in a car, which had a terrible effect on morale and fundraising the next day. Eventually, the chapters grew wealthy enough to acquire second-hand RVs, which we called P-Cars (for Process cars), and we used those for travel, thus removing a great deal of uncertainty from these trips. As for me, I missed the challenge and the magic of the Matthew 10 trips.

In June of 1973 I was transferred to the Toronto Chapter, for no good reason except that the leaders felt it was time to separate me from my husband, to whom I had been married for just seven months. Although The Process sanctioned some marriages, they didn't really approve of them. It's not good communal practice to create dyads within the group. Your allegiance, your energies are supposed to be focused on the group as a whole, not on another individual. And by this time, The Process needed all the concentrated focus it could get. The group was involved in a lawsuit against an author who had published a book accusing The Process of inspiring the Manson murders. The lawsuit, which The Process easily won, since the charges had been ludicrous, cost money. So did the PR campaign we launched to shore up our image as a good Christian cult. Among other things, we abandoned the dramatic black cloaks and uniforms for innocuous gray ones, and later for navy blue—a costly re-outfitting. Also expensive were the spending habits of the Teacher and the Oracle, Robert and Mary Ann de Grimston, who had rented a country estate in Pound Ridge, N.Y., and needed constant infusions of cash from the chapters.

I remember one season we had to go out on the streets ten or fifteen extra hours every week to earn the money to buy the Teacher and the Oracle a Lincoln Continental they wanted. I remember I resented it. I think it was then that I started to question what I was doing.

I had my birthday while I was in Toronto, and Jerome sent me a shoebox full of soaps and scented bath salts and colognes and trinkets. He had saved his daily dollars for weeks, going without any kind of sustenance from breakfast to dinner, to buy me those little luxuries. Like I said, you had to be crazy not to spend that dollar on food every day. I was awed by his crazy devotion.

I had set myself a goal to become a Priest, to become Mother Meredith. That happened right after I was transferred to the New York Chapter in February of 1974 to be the fulltime assistant to the editor of *Process* magazine. I was thrilled. No more street sales, I thought, and a chance to use my education. As it turned out, becoming a Priest made almost no difference. I did the editorial assistant job and I also worked in the New York Chapter's coffee house, and I also went out donating many evenings.

Things were getting tight. The Process closed the Boston and Miami Chapters, partly because fund-raising had dried up. A lot of the newer, younger members were leaving. It was hard for them to leave. Most often, they'd disappear during the night, not wanting anyone to try to stop them, but also ashamed of not being tough enough to live with all the rules and all the deprivation. And after the person left, the waves of gossip—"he just wasn't strong enough," "he broke one of the rules," "he was too quarrelsome, independent, disobedient"—would wash over the person's memory and he would be gone. Unless he came back. A few people did do that, worked their way back in, took a new name, and tried it all again. My friend Barbara was one of those. Headstrong and independent, she started out as Sister Christie, left, came back, and became Sister Deborah. She also changed her name several times while she was "in," becoming Sister Veronica, then Sister Pythia, then Sister Deborah again. As Deborah, she married Brother Reuben, but, in the end, they both left, separately. She got a divorce and raised their child, Jacob, by herself.

Shortly after I arrived in New York, my old friend Brother Alexander (Rhodes) was sent there as well. In all the years we had been in The Process, we had never been assigned to the same chapter. It was great to see him again. He was ordained a Priest at the same time I was. Jerome was transferred up to New York a few weeks later.

In April 1974 the whole thing fell apart. Robert and Mary Ann's marriage came to a disastrous end as a result of Robert's love affair with one of the Priests, an American woman who had joined the group in 1967. When the Council of Masters learned of this relationship, they sided with the Mary Ann against Robert and expelled him from The Process. This left them in a difficult position, since Robert's name and picture were attached to all of the organization's published teachings. Mary Ann and the Council quickly cobbled together a new religion called the Foundation Faith of the Millennium, complete with new doctrines, new rituals, new insignia for our uniforms, and new names for the ranks. Messengers, Prophets, Priests, and Masters became Witnesses, Mentors, Superiors, and Luminaries. Same people, same structure, new religion. While Mary Ann remained in seclusion, her top-ranked lieutenants traveled from chapter to chapter breaking the news, telling us that we were now devotees only of Jehovah, and that Lucifer, Satan, and Christ were no longer parts of the religion. As they explained it to us, our founders' divorce was just the iceberg tip of a vast religious schism, a sign that the church was meant to seek a new spiritual direction.

Jerome, like a lot of members who left the group over the next few months, was disgusted. "If they can just make up a new set of beliefs," he told me privately, "that means they never cared about real spiritual enlightenment or real psychological insight. It's just a cult of personality." To me, the community, the challenge, the service, had mattered much more than the Process religion, so I might have been willing to go along with the Foundation. However, I could see another problem heading my way. It was becoming obvious to me that Jerome, who had been writing articles for *Process* magazine while in New Orleans, had been brought to New York, not to rejoin his wife, but to take her place on the staff of the magazine (renamed *Foundation*). I would probably be sent to Chicago. I was not willing to be separated from my husband again. And what about a family? I was almost thirty! The more I thought about it, the less I wanted to raise children in the cult.

We made plans to leave. Such collusion, in itself, was an act of rebellion. We called my father to tell him we were leaving. He didn't say "I told you so," but I could hear the long sigh of relief over the phone. We decided that Jerome would leave first, in early September. We called his parents in Amherst, Massachusetts, and asked if they would put us up until we found work. We arranged for them to mail us bus tickets and a small amount of cash, since we had no money and neither of us would have dreamed of stealing any donating money. (I later found out from Barbara that lots of people stole from the donating receipts to buy cigarettes or extra snacks, little things. I was amazed that I never thought of it; it could have softened the hard edges of Process life.)

Jerome made an appointment with the chapter director, announced his resignation, turned in all his regalia, and departed for the Port Authority bus terminal. I knew the usual disparaging talk about an ex-member would begin to circulate as soon as he was gone. But I was deeply moved by Mother Rebecca, who was crying as she and I watched him go. She thought he was leaving not just the group, but me, and she didn't want him to abandon his wife. I felt terrible that I couldn't tell her I would soon be following him. I thought she was brave to confess sentiments so far from the party line.

Two weeks later I formally announced my intention to leave. I said I would spend a week wrapping up my work at the magazine and do whatever else they wanted me to do to finish cycles. It was unusual for anyone of my rank to leave, so they pulled out all the stops to make me change my mind. I had to have an audience with Father Aaron, who told me he always thought I was a little strange, a little aloof. (A little less credulous than you would have liked, I privately thought.)

The day I was scheduled to leave, Mother Cassandra was sent to stop me. She talked very earnestly for hours; I think I missed four buses talking with her. She asked if I knew that I would fail out in the world, that my husband would leave me, that he had no talents anyway, that all the talents I had before I joined the group would be taken away from me; that I was abandoning the one, true family? It was very much the kind of thing I had said myself to wavering members in the past, and, I now know, very much the line all cults and communes spin to their members—you are meant to be here, without the group you are—and you will be—nothing. And, for a lot of kids, this was true: they had rushed into the era's religious cults very young, dropping out of high school, escaping from their parents, seeking community and purpose, and losing out on education. If they left the group, for whatever reason, it would take a long time and a lot of work to put together a reasonable life in mainstream society. If they stayed in the cult or the commune, and the group survived, then that would be their life. I'm not saying it wasn't a good life—many people thrive in communes—but by that morning I was certain that life in a religious cult was not for me.

I stuck it out through Cassandra's long harangue. I reminded myself I had a loving family and a husband, who also had a loving family, and that I had an education I could put to good use. I simply did not believe I would fall apart. I didn't regret my five years of spiritual searching and communal life, and I have never since regretted it. I just knew that it was over.

Cassandra gave up, I got my bags. Alexander was waiting for me in the front hallway. He called me a cab and put me into it, and it's my memory that he said "Good for you!" He had been with me in 1969 when I first met The Process, and his was the last Process face I saw.

Three hours later I stepped off the bus in Amherst and into an enormous hug. Jerome had met four earlier buses from New York, and was beginning to worry that I wasn't coming. He picked up my bags and we walked off in the direction of his parents' house and whatever the rest of life had in store for us.

QUESTIONS FOR DISCUSSION

1. Why do you think Karen Manners Smith ignores opportunities for graduate education and professional success and becomes a hippie? What do you think she and other "dropouts" of the period are searching for? Can you relate their activities to the events of the Sixties era and the "temper of the times?" Are there people like Smith and her friends today?

2. Why do you think the leaders of religious cults keep secrets from new members? Why would the top leaders isolate themselves from the group's rank-and-file members? How and why would a cult represent itself as a surrogate—and better—family than the one the new recruit has left behind? What effect might that have on someone who was insecure or immature?

3. What is your impression of the lifestyle Smith leads while in the group? Why would somebody choose to give up all personal possessions, sleep on floors, go short on food, and work long hours with no pay? Are there any circumstances under which you would consider such a life? What does Smith find exciting about life in The Process?

4. Why do you think strangers in American cities would give money to The Process or other religious groups on the street? Why would some people even invite them to stay in their houses? Would people do that today? Do you think the world has changed since the 1970s in ways that make us more suspicious of one another? What changes can you cite?

5. Smith does not talk much about her religious connection to The Process. Although she discusses the group's theology, she never really says what it is she believes and never gives any indication that she has found religious faith. Why would she stay in a religious group if the religion was not that important to her?

6. Smith and her husband, Jerome, leave The Process in 1974 after many years of total commitment. Why do they feel it is time to go? What has happened to them and to the group as a whole to make them change their minds? What has happened in "the world" by 1974 that might make living in isolated groups seem less attractive or less necessary to young people? Are there any risks in leaving the group? The people who stayed behind in the group thought Smith and her husband were deserters in a time of crisis. What is your opinion of their departure?

Conservative Currents

Introduction

For many Americans, "The Sixties" conjures a set of images: liberalism triumphant in national politics (Lyndon Johnson's "Great Society," and the landmark Civil Rights Act of 1964 and Voting Rights Act of 1965); the hard-fought battles of the Civil Rights Movement, where people risked injury and death for social justice; radicalism on college campuses and elsewhere (massive demonstrations against the war in Vietnam, new liberation movements for women and homosexuals); and a rebellious youth culture characterized by drug use, sexual freedom, and other departures from mainstream American life. Relevant though they are, these images, and the realities behind them, do not tell the whole Sixties story. No picture of this revolutionary era would be complete unless it included the conservative counter-revolution and its far-reaching effects.

Conservatism in the 1960s had come a long way from its pre-World War II base in isolationism. In some ways, it was a reaction against the bipartisan liberal consensus of the post-war period. But Sixties conservatism also had a newly youthful appeal. Many young right-wingers of the period were economic and political conservatives who favored free-market capitalism and low taxes and opposed government regulation of corporations. Some were libertarians, whose political philosophy held that individuals should be free to do whatever they wished without government interference, as long as they respected the rights of other individuals. Libertarian ideas were shaped by Barry Goldwater's landmark 1960 book

The Conscience of a Conservative; by the novels of Ayn Rand, an apostle of individualism; and by the political thinking of right-wing intellectual William F. Buckley, Jr., founder of the influential journal *The National Review*.

Some individuals, such as members of the hard-line John Birch Society, saw opposition to Communism as the most important piece of any conservative agenda. Others supported the politics of segregation and its leaders, such as South Carolina senator Strom Thurmond and Alabama governor George Wallace, who resisted desegregation orders and other forms of "interference" from the federal government in the name of states' rights and local control. Still other young conservatives shared the traditional religious views and moral sentiments of their socially conservative parents and grandparents, who felt that America was losing its way, becoming an immoral and degenerate society. As it turned out, the social and political upheavals of the period—from the "sex and drugs and rock 'n' roll" of popular culture to Supreme Court decisions that recognized a constitutional right to personal privacy and overturned laws against contraception and abortion—spawned a vigorous conservative backlash that brought moral traditionalism and evangelical Christianity to the forefront of U.S. politics in the late twentieth and early twenty-first centuries.

One example of the far-reaching effects of Sixties conservatism can be seen in the political career of Republican Richard Nixon, who appealed to conservative Americans with his strong anti-Communist crusade in the 1940s and 1950s but lost the 1960 presidential election to Democrat John F. Kennedy. Nixon returned later in the decade to defeat liberal Democrat Hubert Humphrey in the 1968 election and, in 1972, won a landslide victory over another liberal Democrat, George McGovern. Another and perhaps even more significant example of long-term effects was the impact of ultra-conservative Republican Barry Goldwater, who suffered a resounding defeat in his 1964 presidential campaign against Democrat Lyndon Johnson. Yet Goldwater's candidacy and his ideas helped to energize a new wave of conservative political activism that led, a decade and a half later, to the election of Ronald Reagan in 1980 and then to Republican control of Congress in the 1990s. It is not surprising that many historians today regard the 1960s as the cradle of modern American conservatism, just as much as it was, more obviously, the cradle of the New Left and its radicalism.

At colleges and universities around the country, the anti-establishment Free Speech Movement and the left-wing Students for a Democratic Society (SDS) may have defined Sixties campus life in the eyes of many observers, but the right-wing Young Americans for Freedom (YAF) and Young Republican clubs were also a strong activist presence at most of the same institutions. Using many of the same tactics as SDS—meetings, marches, demonstrations, get-out-the-vote (for conservative candidates) campaigns—the New Right was as visible on many campuses as organizations in the student left. Short-haired, coat-and-tie-wearing, young right-wingers may not have looked like their radical counterparts, but their political style was a close relative. Groups from both sides frequently confronted each other at campus demonstrations.

The American right, like the American left, has never been a monolithic phenomenon. The stories in this section show how four young adults came to follow a variety of conservative paths during the Sixties and Seventies, from anti-Communism to libertarianism, to Republican Party politics, to participation in the "War on Drugs." With one exception, these writers have remained connected to conservative ideas they first encountered as young men, and those ideas have shaped their life choices and careers.

John Werlich, now a Los Angeles attorney, tells the story of his all-American boyhood, his underage stint in the U.S. Army, and his delayed education. Born on the Fourth of July, he grew up in a time when many Americans celebrated patriotism and revered the servicemen who had fought for the United States in World War II. These same Americans experienced massive anxiety caused by the Cold War—the decades-long geopolitical and ideological struggle between the United States and the Soviet Union that began after the end of World War II. During the Cold War, the threat of nuclear annihilation hovered over the entire globe, and Soviet-inspired Communist revolutions seemed to be spreading across the eastern and southern hemispheres. Although an outright war between the United States and the Soviet Union never happened, every U.S. government of the period promoted the "arms race" (competing for weapons supremacy) and practiced a policy of "containment" (trying to keep Communism from spreading throughout Asia and Africa). Both sides had nuclear weapons and "the bomb" was a dread possibility all children lived with daily. Schools in the 1950s conducted air raid drills nearly as often as they held fire drills. Children were marched to the school basement or told to duck under their desks and cover their heads, as if that would protect them from the nuclear blast and radiation. For a brief period in the late 1950s, suburban families were encouraged to build fallout shelters in their backyards. Fallout shelters resembled air raid shelters used by the British during World War II but they were deeper, stronger, and designed for longer stays. People who opposed fallout shelters felt they represented a dismal fatalism and provided a false sense of security, which might even make nuclear war more likely.

John Werlich begins his story with descriptions of childhood patriotism. His adolescence was characterized by a series of pranks that got him into trouble with the police and forced his early entry into the Army. After completing his service, Werlich began his education in the early years of American involvement in Vietnam, which he saw as a necessary action to "contain" the spread of Communism in Southeast Asia. Everything Werlich learned both in and out of the classroom in college and law school, combined with his reading, helped to confirm his deep suspicion of Communism and his faith in U.S. anti-Communist policy, especially with regard to the war in Vietnam. A strong supporter of individual liberties, he read about untrammeled individualism in the works of Ayn Rand and refreshed his belief that totalitarian governments are the "death of the individual mind and death of anything good in society." He devoured courses on politics, government, and economics. When it came to studying the U.S. Constitution and laws, he discovered that he believed in a very strict and limited interpretation of the Bill of Rights and in a minimum of government interference in the workings of society and the economy. When his legal work began to include the prosecution of anti-Vietnam War protestors, Werlich acted as a strict constitutionalist: the protestors could have complete freedom to say what they wished, but if they trespassed on private property in any way, then they were liable to prosecution. Werlich frames his story with the narrative of a visit to an "Iron Curtain" country in the late 1970s, an episode that, at the time, he imagined would be the culmination of all his fears. The outcome was not entirely what he expected.

Robert Poole describes his path to libertarianism through his leadership in a college chapter of YAF and his work for the election of Barry Goldwater in 1964. YAF was founded in 1960 during a meeting of about 90 young people, mostly college students, at the Sharon, Connecticut, estate of conservative journalist William F. Buckley, Jr. The group's manifesto, the Sharon Statement, set out the organization's goals to preserve individual freedoms and free enterprise and to work against the spread of international Communism. YAF recruited thousands of members on college campuses around the country and, by 1962, had grown so large that a membership rally filled New York City's Madison Square Garden. Sometimes allied with campus Young Republicans, YAF members were more conservative and less partisan than the Young Republicans, though members might belong to both groups. A number of YAF members, those on the libertarian end of the spectrum, supported the legalization of marijuana and opposed the draft. They argued that drug laws and military conscription represented government violation of individual rights.

In 1964, YAF members worked hard to defeat the liberal Republican, Nelson Rockefeller, and gain the presidential nomination for Barry Goldwater, whose conservative ideology more nearly resembled their own. Though Goldwater won the nomination, he lost the election; however, his ideas laid the foundation for the conservative revolution of the 1980s. Many of today's leading conservatives first entered politics through YAF and Young Republican clubs of the 1960s.

Robert Poole describes his disillusionment with some factions of YAF, whose position on states' rights led them to embrace segregationists and extremists. He moved further into the libertarian camp, formally resigning from YAF and joining another campus conservative organization at MIT, the Radicals for Capitalism. Libertarians who shared Poole's reservations about YAF left that organization *en masse* during a faction fight at the 1969 convention; a few years later, some of them founded a new political organization, the Libertarian Party.

Poole carries his story forward a number of years to illustrate the growth of his libertarian ideals and their application to his choice of profession. Initially an aeronautical engineer, Poole turned part-time to journalism and, through his writing on privatization and the free market, helped to shape thinking that resulted in the deregulation of the airline industry. Poole and libertarian colleagues later organized the Reason Foundation, a public policy think tank that exists to this day.

Ron McCoy grew up in Arizona and, while still in high school, traveled the country promoting conservative politics in speeches to young audiences. His speeches brought him to the attention of the Republican Party. Highly idealistic, McCoy believed in working within the existing political system to address problems in American life. In the summer of 1967, impressed by Richard Nixon's promise to end the war in Vietnam, McCoy accepted a position as Youth Coordinator for Nixon's presidential election campaign.

Richard Nixon had made his reputation in the U.S. Congress as a militant anti-Communist. He became Dwight Eisenhower's vice president in the 1950s and lost his own bid for the presidency to John F. Kennedy in 1960. While out of office, he built a successful legal career and a strong political base, surrounding himself with aggressive supporters willing to take many risks for their leader. The 1968 election was Nixon's chance to capture the presidency. He appealed to what he called the "silent majority" of socially conservative Americans, people who resented anti-war demonstrators and the loosened morality represented by "hippie" culture. He had a great deal of enthusiastic support among conservative college students, who campaigned for him under the slogan "Nixon's the One!" Nixon also promised to find the United States an honorable way to exit the Vietnam War and leave peace in its wake, though he did not provide details of his plan.

Ironically, despite his support from conservatives, Nixon is remembered today as the last liberal Republican president of the twentieth century. His administration initiated a number of progressive domestic policies, including major environmental protection legislation and dramatic increases in spending for social programs. Even though anti-Communism had been a central theme of his political career, Nixon took the bold foreign policy step of making a state visit to China and opening diplomatic and trade relations with that Communist country. Nixon's two-term presidency was ultimately destroyed when authorities arrested people in his employ who were engaging in illegal surveillance activities. In the aftermath of the arrest, the president obstructed the investigation to cover up his own complicity. The ensuing "Watergate" scandal and the threat of impeachment led to Nixon's resignation in 1974.

Ron McCoy's story takes place during Nixon's run for the presidency in 1967–1968. It introduces most of the president's top aides and provides an insider's view of party politics at the presidential level. Immersed in political life, McCoy met a variety of people who shaped his ideas but found that his personal evolution was leading him to question the motivations of those he was working with. Early in 1968, stunned by the cynicism of the politicians and concerned about his interrupted education, McCoy left the Nixon campaign and returned to college at Arizona State University. As the late Sixties and early Seventies unrolled, he pondered the pros and cons of trying to work within the system.

Inspired by a desire to serve his country in law enforcement, Missourian Gerald Scott joined the "War on Drugs" in 1971, becoming an agent of the Bureau of Narcotics and Dangerous Drugs (BNDD). In less than three years, the BNDD had merged with several other government programs to form the Drug Enforcement Administration (DEA), a major new agency within the Department of Justice.

Although the U.S. government had attempted drug prohibition in piecemeal fashion ever since the first anti-opium legislation in the 1880s, it was Richard Nixon who initiated the country's "War on Drugs" in 1971. The War on Drugs was an "all-out offensive" against the non-medical use of certain prohibited substances. High on the list of dangerous and illegal drugs were heroin, cocaine, and amphetamines, but the new drug warriors also hoped to stamp out the use of marijuana and a variety of hallucinogenic drugs, such as LSD (lysergic acid diethylamide, a substance made in laboratories and first designated illegal in 1966), as well as mescaline, peyote, psilocybin, and similar "organic" substances. Because the international trafficking of heroin and cocaine was a billion dollar opportunity for organized crime, most of the agency's energies were directed toward control of these "hard" drugs. Agents like Gerald Scott risked their lives daily in the attempt to break up hard drug trade and distribution rings.

Gerald Scott's story covers his years in the BNDD and its successor, the DEA. Writing with both humor and intensity, Scott describes several of his undercover operations in the Kansas City area, his pride in his work, and the terrible emotional price he had to pay to carry out his country's drug enforcement policies. Scott found that undercover work required him to fully inhabit the characters he invented to infiltrate drug rings. In the end, impersonation and its consequences led him to make a career-altering decision.

The DEA is still fighting a war on drugs. Many Americans, including people on both the liberal and conservative ends of the political spectrum, feel the war must be continued to protect the health of the nation's young people, though enforcement is costly and the country's prisons are overcrowded with people convicted of drug-related offenses. Others feel that some drugs should be legalized so that their purity and price can be controlled by government authorities—much as alcohol and tobacco are now controlled—and criminals would no longer be able to profit from illegal sales. Barry Goldwater, conservative icon of the Sixties, came to believe late in his life that some drugs ought to be legalized, especially if they had medical uses. Still other people, including many libertarian conservatives, feel the government should not violate the civil liberties of adults by telling them what substances they can or cannot use in their private lives. Like all wars, the war on drugs exacts a high price no matter how we regard it. Gerald Scott's story explores some of those costs first-hand.

BORN ON THE FOURTH OF JULY
John M. Werlich

In September 1972, my wife Valerie and I ventured to Europe. Our mission: to visit the cobblestone-studded streets of the 1000-year-old city of Nuremberg, Germany. Valerie was born in Belfast, Northern Ireland. As a teenager she accepted an offer to work in West Germany. After four years as an executive secretary for two large German companies, she spoke fluent German and had made many European friends. We were both excited.

Upon our arrival in Europe, Valerie surprised me with two tickets for a one-week bus tour to Budapest, Hungary—one of the first opportunities for foreigners to visit the Communist-controlled country. She was elated. Though I tried not to reveal it, I was stunned. The two things I feared most were snakes and Communists.

A sense of discomfort shadowed me as I boarded the German tour bus, loaded with forty Germans and us—one Brit and one Yank. The closer to Hungary we rode, the more apprehensive I became. I convinced myself that as we approached the border, we would be able to see the Iron Curtain. I envisioned it as a massive drape, following the contours of the borders of the Eastern Bloc nations, something like the aurora borealis, but gray.

At dusk we approached the border from Austria, less than a hundred miles from Budapest. A mile from border control, almost on cue, the German chatter subsided after shushes prevailed. Light drizzle dampened everything. All I could hear was the droning of the diesel engine, the clicking of windshield wipers, and the pounding of my heart. I stopped breathing.

Suddenly, the bus halted at the crossing gate, rocking. To the right and left of the bus were perfectly straight lines of forty-foot-high telephone poles at fifty-foot intervals, laced on both sides with chain link, capped with thick piles of cascading barbed wire. Vegetation had been cleared for a hundred feet on each side, stopping only at the dark green pine forest. No birds or any evidence of animal life were apparent. Every hundred yards a massive tower straddled the huge barrier, each tower topped with a gun turret.

As the guards beckoned us into Hungary, a pall of gloom blanched my face. The bus coasted two hundred yards, stopping at a series of single-story green-gray buildings. A green-uniformed officer wearing a cap with a red band and gold star boarded and collected the passports, previously retrieved from us by our guide. The officer disappeared into the approaching darkness. Time stood still.

Fifteen minutes later the officer, now accompanied by two grim-faced machine-gun-toting soldiers, boarded the bus. A slight breeze wafted in the smells of the dew-laden forest. The officer eyed us all as he strode ten feet down the aisle of the bus, then barked in German, *"Wo ist der Amerikaner?"* I couldn't speak. He continued down the aisle and pointed, at me, *"Sie sind der Amerikaner!"* I was dumbfounded and meekly raised my right hand. *"Kommen Sie mit mir,"* he ordered. You, come with me. I could hear my wife pleading in German to accompany me since I spoke little German and no Hungarian. I'm not sure if she was given permission, but she followed me anyway as I guardedly stepped off the bus.

The Communist soldiers directed us towards the buildings now lit with blaring spotlights. I was nauseous. Though outside was cool, my palms were damp. Nightmares were becoming reality. I pinched myself, no change in the script. Surely, we were doomed. As we approached the largest building, I stumbled. Each soldier swung the barrel of his gun facing me. I then . . .

*****

Fears are often self-fulfilling. My apprehensions of Communism almost immobilized me. Life's lessons contributed. This story recounts a few of my life experiences that likely contributed to this foreboding view.

*****

Had I orchestrated it myself, I couldn't have dreamed of a better day to be born: the 4th of July, 1945. My earliest memories are yearly parades of bright red fire trucks and cars decorated in red, white, and blue crepe paper, proudly cruising up Georgia Street along with young girls in sequin-laced costumes, tossing their batons high in the bright blue sky, all timed to the deafening drums and tubas of the Vallejo High School marching band. And tiny towhead me, circling in and out of the flag-waving crowd of well-dressed women and well-behaved children, gawking at the Navy men wearing red and sometimes gold chevrons on their neatly-pressed uniforms, all waving at the spectacle. Yes, Vallejo, California was a Navy town, home to the Mare Island Naval Shipyard, the first shipyard on the West Coast. In those heady days of the 1950s, it seemed like all of us loved America and were deeply patriotic. It wasn't a matter of "my country, right or wrong," there was no notion that our country could possibly be wrong. Life was good during these formative years merging into the 1960s. It was indeed, for me, "America the Beautiful."

Few families owned television sets and most of those sets were black and white. Yet none of the kids I knew watched television that much anyway—maybe *The Mickey Mouse Club,* but they certainly did not watch alone. It was a family event. On Saturday nights, some of us kids, on one pretext or another, would drop in at the house of one of our fortunate neighbors who just happened to own a color T.V. After a brief "how are you?" and "what beautiful weather," we'd find ourselves sitting in the front room of this accommodating neighbor, watching *The Ed Sullivan Show* or *The Lawrence Welk Show,* sipping hot chocolate and munching homemade cookies.

All public schools supported recreational centers that were open on Saturdays. Any kid could just pop by one of the converted classrooms and sign up to challenge the ping-pong table or engage in arts and crafts. Whether swimming, hiking, or playing pickup games of baseball, basketball or football, most kids were very active. My Saturday routine was to read the sports section of the *Vallejo Times* to determine what organized events might be scheduled at one of the local school grounds that day. Usually some event for kids was taking place. Then I'd find myself on a public bus (a nickel each way for students) or walking to a tetherball, flag football or marbles tournament. Although there were the customary first, second and third place ribbons, all entrants received a round or square or triangular patch that signified their participation. We'd have our moms sew the colorful patches on our jackets and proudly wear them to the next tournament. And yet, just maybe, all was not perfect in paradise.

Okay. I admit it. Once I cast away my self-protective filters and try to focus objectively on what is reflected in the mirror of the past, I can see that I was an inveterate mischief-maker. No challenge, big or small, was turned down. I'll gloss over the little ones: loading my dad's shampoo bottle with something other than golden shampoo; stuffing tailpipes with potatoes; placing dead bluegill, caught three days earlier in Lake Chabot, on the front porch of a family who slighted one of my friends. Of course, engaging in fisticuffs (not started by me, just responses to challenges), or running away from home, didn't help.

At twelve years old, along with a couple of friends, I threw rocks at a sign advertising the sale of a vacant parcel of property across from our home. The sign was in pieces when we were finished. I have no idea why we did this. Perhaps an early sign of my environmentalist bent—a plea for more open space. Nevertheless, a neighbor turned me in. For the next six weeks, I wheeled the family push lawnmower over to the realtor's house and mowed his front and back lawns. It was a fair sentence. The lemonade generously furnished by the realtor's smiling wife almost made it worthwhile. Similar incidents were common over the next few years, but I'll go right to the last one that took place just as I turned sixteen.

A year earlier, just before I dropped out of high school, while playing a noontime game of baseball, I broke two windows on the second floor of the school gymnasium by hitting a baseball about three hundred feet from home plate. The vice principal, not a bit pleased, was positive that I'd done it intentionally. He was right. Heck, I was trying to, we all were. Rather than call an agent and arrange for me to be signed with the Yankees, he treated me to a public paddling inside the same gymnasium. The three swats from an oversized oar didn't really hurt. But having it administered before a throng of five hundred fellow students made it humiliating.

In the late summer of 1961 I found an opportunity to get even. A block from where the vice principal lived, a new-fangled drive-through market had just opened for business, selling milk, bread, candy and similar items. As we cruised down Springs Road in a friend's old truck (probably one of the same friends who helped me destroy the For Sale sign), we beheld a beautiful sight. Beaming down at us from the rooftop of the single-story building was a beautiful, life-sized, black-and-white cow. Eureka! We couldn't resist. We returned at 11:00 p.m. with a ladder and tools in hand. We removed the four bolts and hoisted the surprisingly light "Bessie" down the ladder and into the bed of the truck. Voila! Two minutes later, Bessie was strategically plunked on the front lawn of the vice principal's home with a large sign around her neck announcing "Lost Cow For Sale."

A squad car was in front of the vice principal's home the next morning, friends informed me. While no one was charged, fingers were pointing in my direction. After conferring with the local authorities, my mother, also a teacher, came to me a week later with the bad news. I had been labeled "incorrigible," an unfamiliar term to me at the time. "Something has to be done." Well, that something was a Hobson's choice. I could either go "up river" where incorrigible little boys go for retraining (actually it would have been about 40 miles up the Sacramento River) or join the Army. What? This is a Navy town! "But I'm too young!" I protested. But everything was already arranged. A letter had been written to the Army recruiter on Florida Street explaining that my birth records were lost because I was adopted and that I was 17. I had aged a year overnight. All I had to do was take a simple test. I had two weeks to choose.

A few days later, as fate would have it, I visited a friend at his home. It transpired that his older brother, Jim, was just home from Army boot camp at Fort Ord, near Carmel, California. He was all decked out in his uniform, wearing a shiny sharpshooter medal, a shiny brass belt buckle, and other military paraphernalia. I knew next to nothing about war matters. In the early '50s my friends' fathers spun stories of World War II encounters with "Japs" and "Krauts," and in the late '50s I remember hearing on the radio about an uprising in Hungary and a revolution on some island named Cuba.

Jim and I spoke animatedly for an hour. I left, absolutely gung-ho, wondering when I would get some of those chevrons I had coveted as a little tot. Three days later I was in the recruiter's office.

On October 25, 1961, I was officially sworn in to the United States Army as a Private E-1 at a processing center in Oakland. That evening, fifty new recruits were scooted aboard a Greyhound bus, sent for basic training to their new home for the next couple of months, Fort Ord. I learned from others on the bus that one-half of the recruits, mostly in their twenties, had been drafted in response to the events of the Berlin Crisis (the Soviet Union's threat to cut off Western access to Berlin, an important Western European city that was completely surrounded by Soviet-dominated East Germany).

Boot camp was heaven. I blossomed. It seemed that I could run faster, perform more sit-ups and more pull-ups, shoot straighter, assemble and reassemble my M-1 faster, remember and recite my General Orders more accurately, and salute better than most of the other recruits. I even ate more than anyone else did; thirds were not uncommon. Indeed, most of my fellow recruits were convinced that I had a tapeworm.

Naturally there were some glitches. In the second week of boot camp, during a 5:30 a.m. inspection (always before chow), a lieutenant approached me while I was standing at attention and barked, "Werlich, did you shave this morning?" My cocksure answer, "Sir, I don't have to shave." A true answer, the only hair I had on my face was blonde peach fuzz. The lieutenant saw it differently. He turned to the sergeant, "Werlich is on trap duty for three days and take him right now and teach him how to shave."

It was the death of a thousand cuts. And the sergeant wasn't finished. He led me to the kitchen and introduced me to the mess hall sergeant. I had a dozen tiny pieces of red-soaked white tissue dangling from my face. After he finished laughing at my predicament, the mess hall sergeant explained to me the unpleasantness of "trap duty." For the next three days, before I could eat, I spent an hour per day removing the five circular grates located on the kitchen floor and then spooning out the smelly grease and lard (and other muck) that had accumulated in the traps after the floors had been hosed down the night before. Clearly the Army diet was not fat free in the 1960s. But even this gray cloud had a silver lining. Because I was in the kitchen I could eat all of the food my still developing belly could hold. And, even better,

FIGURE 4.1   Crowds in Moscow's Red Square gather in 1965 to watch a military parade celebrating the twentieth anniversary of the end of World War II. The parade includes this massive Intercontinental Ballistic Missile (ICBM), capable of delivering a nuclear bomb to a target 5000 miles away. ICBMs, developed in both the United States and the Soviet Union, were the most significant by-products of the Cold War. Both superpowers had thousands of these weapons stockpiled in remote "silos," ready to be launched at each other at a moment's notice. It was enough nuclear might to destroy the world many times over. The threat of "mutual assured destruction" affected almost every international political and military decision either nation made, and the planet hovered near the brink of nuclear war for decades.

Source: Getty Images Inc. —Hulton Archive Photos

because I raved so loudly about the great food, the mess hall sergeant became an ally. From then on, I had access to food day and night. Paradise!

After eight weeks of boot camp most of us were cut orders for our next assignment. That assignment depended on how well one performed in boot camp, individual requests, and test results. My newfound friends, who had taught me how to tie a Windsor knot and how to order "Cutty on the rocks" during a weekend pass to North Beach in San Francisco, were now leaving. They were ordered to report to European assignments in France or West Germany, or for further military training at U.S. installations in such places as Ft. Sims, Alabama (artillery training), Ft. Benning, Georgia (paratrooper training), and Ft. Ord (advanced infantry training). My assignment was different. I was ordered to remain at Ft. Ord for further testing.

After three weeks I was classified as a clerk typist. Now I just had to wait and see what they were going to do with me. I spent another week at the camp, trying to avoid pulling guard duty, before a sergeant handed me my orders—a quarter page of all upper case, bold-typed, elusive words. To me, the encrypted-like document was indecipherable. My fellow soldiers were not helpful. The speculation as to what it said was almost comical: somewhere in France; or Sweden; perhaps Germany; someone even speculated Baghdad (I'd known a girl whose father was in the Foreign Service there). Guess I'd learn when I got there. By the end of the week I found myself in a window seat of a jet plane leaving the airport at Oakland, California, listening to the popular song "Soldier Boy" by the Shirelles, on my way to: OBERAMMERGAU.

Life was sweet during the next few months. No sixteen-year-old army private was ever treated better. The army base at Oberammergau, West Germany, turned out to be a NATO officer training school with relatively few non-officers stationed there. As a result, I had my own room and was allowed to eat in the officers' mess. I worked as clerk typist for the lieutenant colonel who was in charge of organizing the classes and keeping track of records. My sole responsibility was to respond to inquiries from universities seeking confirmation of class attendance and grades of former officers at the school. Otherwise, I did just about what I wanted, including skiing, playing baseball and drinking beer and eating sausages in the local German taverns. I even dabbled at being a Little League umpire (after going to umpires' school in Munich) and driving the American kids and some of their mothers to the games in huge army buses (after taking a driving test, of course). By late spring, however, I was becoming restless. Two events occurred, changing my assumption that the Army would become my permanent home.

First, a mentor, a staff sergeant to whom I looked up proudly, was nabbed for selling cigarettes on the black market. American cigarettes were expensive in the German marketplace. The Army rationed us a carton per week. As I did not smoke, I gave the staff sergeant my ration tickets; apparently, others did the same. Unbeknownst to us, he bought cartons of cigarettes from the canteen for $1 and then sold them in the black market for $10, pocketing the difference. His punishment: two weeks in the brig and the loss of all of his stripes, which had taken him fourteen years to earn. It was sad to see him stroll around the base wearing faded olive green Army fatigues that contained contrasting dark green patches where his chevrons had once been sewn. Any lingering notion that the Army was a secure place for me to stay quickly evaporated. Second, disillusioned by this turn of events, that Sunday I attended church.

The thrust of the sermon was that each of us was capable of doing much more with our lives and that we invented far too many excuses, "false hurdles." As proof, the Army chaplain (a captain) informed us about a very special blind person who had written a massive book called *Paradise Lost*. Much later I learned that the author was John Milton. I was astounded. Here I was already sixteen; not only had I never written a book, I had never even read a book. And I wasn't blind. I had an epiphany: education was the key to security and success. What was I doing in the Army? At the end of the service, I introduced myself to the chaplain and scheduled a meeting for the next day.

Over the course of the next week, I opened my heart, including telling the chaplain of my dream to return to school. But I did not want to wait two years until I would be eligible for discharge. The chaplain conferred with an Army lawyer and informed me that there was a way out. If I could prove that I was actually only sixteen years old, the Army would be forced to grant me an honorable discharge. It took a month, but after writing to the appropriate authorities in California, I received the requisite court records and achieved my wish. I would receive my honorable discharge, but not until I first went to Fort Hamilton, New York.

After boarding the train to the West German port city of Bremerhaven, I embarked on a ship bound for New York City. The ship was an old troop transport from World War II, and it was a claustrophobic's nightmare. A small contingent of us who weren't sick enough to be glued to our beds below paced around on the deck day and night, staring at the horizon, praying to hear the words "Land Ho!" On the seventh day the fog started to brighten. A partial dark image appeared. I shuffled toward the ship's railings to get a closer look. And then, simultaneously, the sun shone and fog parted just where the image had been. I could only blurt out "Oh . . . wow!" I recognized it instantly, the gorgeous turquoise-green lady wearing her crown of hope, beaming down just on me—the Statue of Liberty. I, a natural born citizen, felt like a refugee, overwhelmed by the magnanimousness of this dear nineteenth-century gift from France. Fortunately it was still misty, as were my eyes.

On July 10, 1962, at noon, the major at Fort Hamilton handed me a DD-214 form (my honorable discharge) and nonchalantly turned around, heading back to his office. "Wait," I said, "what about transportation? How do I get back home?" He swung around, "Oh, I almost forgot," and handed me an envelope, "The cab's downstairs, better hurry." Inside were two vouchers, one for a taxicab, the other for a 1:00 p.m. TWA non-stop flight to Oakland—leaving in less than one hour! As I clutched the duffel bag which contained my known life's possessions, the oldest lady in the office (she must have been at least forty) wished me good luck and handed me another small envelope, saying, "The major forgot to give you this." Inside was a five-dollar bill and five ones, a godsend considering I was down to less than a dollar's change. Somehow, the cabby got me to LaGuardia Airport on time.

The TWA jet arrived in Oakland late in the afternoon. In anticipation, I phoned home. I had already sent a long letter explaining my new plans in life. "Call your father at work," was my mom's response. I did. As dad worked in Oakland at the time, we met for a sandwich nearby. At the conclusion of our meeting, it was agreed that it would be best if I got away from bad influences in Vallejo and relocated to San Francisco, across the Bay Bridge. The thirty dollars cash my dad handed me helped with the consensus.

I rented a room just off Market Street for $14.50 a week and found a series of odd jobs that paid about $1.30 an hour. I enrolled in San Francisco's Polytechnic High School. A year and a half later, when I graduated, I was accepted to Long Beach State College.

Upon arrival at college, I was a naïve sponge. My appetite for knowledge was voracious. Though I could protect myself on the streets of San Francisco, I was oblivious to intellectual battles. I still hadn't read a book cover to cover. My book reports at Poly were frequently based on the *Classic Comics Illustrated* version. The reading list for my first college class, "History of the United States, Part I," taught by a Harvard-educated professor, quickly revealed that all would be different. Thirteen books had to be read during the next few months, including *Life on the Mississippi, Huckleberry Finn, Leaves of Grass,* and *Walden Pond,* not including the two reference texts. I cracked open *Huckleberry Finn.* I was mesmerized, enthralled. Two days later I proudly finished my first book. I had come a long way, but I had a long way to go.

I had to choose a major. At some point I heard that my hero, John F. Kennedy, had majored in political science at Harvard, so political science became my choice.

I took courses relating to government, history, economics, and politics: "American Political Thought," "The Constitutional History of the United States," "Political Theory," "Economic History," "Constitutional Law," "Capitalism v. Communism," etc. In the process, I was introduced to an array of previously unknown authors and philosophers (including Aristotle, Socrates, Jeremy Bentham, Hume, Berkley, John Locke, Montesquieu, Rousseau, Voltaire, Thomas Hobbes, Karl Marx, Friedrich Engles, Lenin); and books (including *Wealth of Nations, The Communist Manifesto,* and *Brave New World*); and political leaders (including Stalin, Nikita Khrushchev, and Barry Goldwater and his 1960 book, *Conscience of a Conservative*). I began to think about things other than what I would do on Saturday night or how much money I would make in my life.

For the next three years, four of us students met constantly on campus under "our" pepper tree. We discussed and argued for hours a day about our courses and current events, and engaged in conversations that were far more engrossing and revealing than those that took place in the classroom.

Among other things, we talked about broad, sweeping constitutional changes taking place under an exceedingly activist United States Supreme Court. The original Bill of Rights, adopted in 1791, specifically only applies to actions of the federal government. The Supreme Court began to "incorporate" its protections (via the "due process" and "equal protection" clauses of the Fourteenth Amendment, adopted after the Civil War) to apply to the conduct of state and local authorities. During the 1960s, the Supreme Court held that many of the safeguards contained in the Bill of Rights applied to state authorities. Such safeguards included the right to be protected from unreasonable searches and seizures and cruel and unusual punishments, the right to counsel in criminal cases, the right against self-incrimination, the right to trial by an impartial jury, and protection from double jeopardy (being tried twice for the same charge). Moreover, the "exclusionary rule" (which precluded the use of evidence obtained in violation of the Constitution) was implemented, forbidding the police from using evidence obtained in an unreasonable search, or in violation of a person's Miranda rights (the warning police must give when they arrest a suspected criminal, advising him of his right to a lawyer, and warning him against self-incrimination).

Most students certainly did not complain that they now had more rights. But when I moved on to Loyola Law School in Los Angeles in 1967, I saw that some students were concerned—for purely intellectual reasons—that the Supreme Court appeared to be doing more than "interpreting" the Constitution. The most vocal groups were horrified that "states, rights" were being nullified, and that guilty criminals were now actually going free because of the exclusionary rule. For some years, the words "Impeach Earl Warren" (Chief Justice of the Supreme Court 1953–1969) were emblazoned on billboards throughout the country.

On another front, the Supreme Court began to uphold limitations imposed by federal and state governments on the actions of private parties that were perceived to violate the civil rights of others (mostly minority groups), including discrimination in housing and employment. States began to adopt protective legislation. In 1964, one such law, Proposition 14, came before the voters in California.

The essence of Proposition 14 was that landlords in California would be prohibited from discriminating on the basis of race regarding to whom they chose to rent. I was against Proposition 14, but not for racial reasons. Rather, I was against it because in my view at the time the government should not tell property owners how they should operate their businesses; the market place should make that decision. I remember giving a speech in one of my courses in opposition to Proposition 14. I altered part of John F. Kennedy's Inaugural Speech to fit my purpose. Rather than "ask not what your country can do for you, ask what you can do for your country," I wrote, "ask not what your state can do for you, ask what you can do for yourself." I received an A+. I have since changed my mind. Having handled a number of antitrust matters following law school, I now consider landlords as having monopolistic power when it comes to making decisions about tenants. That monopolistic power should be restrained.

Naturally, Vietnam was a popular discussion topic among us students, particularly after Congress passed the Tonkin Gulf Resolution in 1964. President Johnson's speech detailing the specifics of naval incidents in which North Vietnamese craft dared to attack a U.S. vessel is still vivid. Now we could fight back. Though years later the idea was raised that the administration may have misrepresented aspects of the Tonkin Gulf incident, this possibility was not considered in the early stages of the Vietnam War and later became blurred.

At least in the early years of the war, most students appeared to favor taking some action against North Vietnam. It wasn't a matter of being in favor of war (no sane person wants war); it was more a matter of "if we don't do something now, all of Southeast Asia will be infected by Communism." Most of us accepted the "Domino Theory" (a term originally used by President Dwight Eisenhower to predict the way nation after nation in Asia would fall under Communist rule, unless the spread of Communism could be halted).

Personally, I was certain that Communism was a horrible idea that led only to a totalitarian-type government. One had only to look at the Soviet Union. Wasn't it Lenin's and Stalin's implementation of Marx's romantic vision of "from each according to their deeds, to each according to their needs" that resulted in the death of millions of Russians in their version of utopia? Didn't a Communist country shoot down Gary Powers in 1960? Wasn't it Nikita Khrushchev, the president of a Communist government, who in 1960 banged his shoe on a table in the United Nations and shouted "We will bury you!"? Wasn't it a Communist government that constructed the Berlin Wall, dividing a city? Wasn't it a Communist government that set the stage for the Cuban Missile Crisis?

Popular literature was full of examples of what a totalitarian government could do. *Brave New World,* a 1932 novel by Aldous Huxley, portrayed a totalitarian welfare state created in an effort to make everyone happy. A world with no war, no poverty and no crime; yet, at the same time, there are no individuals, no ideas, and no creativity—only benign conformism; or, put another way, Communism run amok. George Orwell's *1984* pictured a nightmarish vision of totalitarianism in which Big Brother is everywhere and the individual is nowhere. *We the Living* by Ayn Rand had the most profound effect on me; after all, Rand had been born in Russia and experienced Communism first hand. Her novel, set in Russia just after the Communist Revolution of 1917, is a romantic story of three idealistic individuals who struggle bitterly to maintain their individuality in the face of a totalitarian system. The book's sad ending impressed upon me that Communism can have but one result: death of the individual mind and death of anything good in society.

Certainly, towards the end of the Vietnam War, sentiment was gathering toward pulling our troops out of Vietnam. I thought that daily death tolls, reported on the evening news, had proved to be too much for many people. To me the mismanagement of the war and the failure of our country to continue to prosecute it spawned this sentiment; I did not think that the original purpose of containing Communism was wrong.

Some critics have argued that the credibility of students' opinions during this time was tainted because they received student deferments from the draft. Though I do not recall direct evidence, I think the point has some merit. In 1970, I almost had an opportunity to see if such a change in status would affect my viewpoints. I was drafted.

When I turned eighteen in July 1963, with little thought, and even though I had already done my service, I dutifully registered for the draft. Thereafter, because I was in college, I received a series of student deferments, even during law school. I lost my student deferment in my last year of law school. Without a student deferment, I was ordered to report for a medical exam; if I passed I would be officially drafted. In October 1969, I did as requested, with my DD-214 form (honorable discharge) tucked securely in my pocket; my plan was to show it to someone at the end of the examination.

At the end of the examination, a sergeant held his hand out to welcome me and inform me that I passed. I reached in my pocket and smiled. Before I could remove my hand, the sergeant exclaimed, "Oh no, we can't take you, not with that metal in your mouth." I had completely forgotten that a couple weeks before, in the process of closing a small gap between my two front teeth, an orthodontist had secured one thin piece of silver metal in the front. It was to come off in two weeks. When I smiled, the sergeant caught the glint of metal. After informing me that the Army did not have the facilities to take care of such dental conditions, he ordered me to return in ninety days. As it turned out, I did not return.

To resolve the uncertainty as to "when" a male might be drafted (i.e., anywhere from eighteen to twenty-six), Congress adopted a random lottery system. Once the lottery was instituted, men would be drafted on the basis of their birth date. On December 1, 1969, the first random selection took place. July Fourth, my birthday, was chosen on the 279th draw. As only the first half of the dates selected were actually going to be drafted, the possibility that I might be reintroduced into the Army was, practically speaking, over.

In January 1971, I passed the California Bar Exam. I was hired by the Los Angeles City Attorney's Office to prosecute crimes within the City of Los Angeles. While assigned to the West Los Angeles division, for a short period of time during 1972–73, part of my time was spent assisting with the prosecution of anti-Vietnam War demonstrators at UCLA. The charges primarily related to criminal trespass and failure to disperse after an unlawful assembly had been declared by the police.

For most of my life, the notions of free speech have been paramount to me. Dissenters (even those who hold views fundamentally different from mine) should be able legally to present their views to the public, unabridged in most instances. For the good of us all, hopefully, such individuals will not just harbor their thoughts, but will actually take the next step and express their views. To me, it is better that the differences be reconciled in the "marketplace of ideas," rather than by a government censor. Thus, my feelings were fairly mixed about participating in these prosecutions. Yet, once the protesters crossed the line from speech to violence, I had and still have no qualms about their being prevented from doing so, even if this means their going to jail.

Back to Hungary

*****

I got hold of myself, straightened up proudly (after all, I was an American) and told myself, as others had informed me, that nothing is either as bad or as good as one first thinks it is. We were directed through the doors of the dank building and a series of hallways and into a room, and told to wait. Thirty seconds later, another Hungarian officer, wearing a star-studded cap, appeared and engaged us with a broad smile. Then started a series of questions, in English. Where do you come from? Is there really a Grand Canyon? Have you been there? What does it look like? It was clear after the first few questions that this Hungarian officer merely wanted to practice his English and learn something about America!

*****

The lesson? People around the world are pretty much the same. It is their governmental systems that can be dramatically and harmfully different.

As I write today, I still believe, as strongly as ever, that America's efforts at containing Communism in Southeast Asia were correct, perhaps even mandatory. The killing fields in Cambodia, the 60,000 executions of South Vietnamese by the North Vietnamese following America's departure, and the one million Vietnamese "boat people" who took to the seas in desperation in the late 1970s prove that the "Domino Theory" was right. Moreover, the collapse of the Eastern Bloc and the Soviet Union in 1989 have finally demonstrated that the Communist method of searching for a utopian society is a failure.

QUESTIONS FOR DISCUSSION

1. What aspects of John Werlich's childhood seem typical for the 1950s? Which ones seem atypical? Were you surprised that his family gave him a choice between joining the military and a sentence in a boys' reformatory? Do you think his treatment was fair? What might happen to a boy like Werlich today?

2. Compare Werlich's life in boot camp with that described by Paul Thomas Coe in the "Vietnam" section of this book. Does it make any difference that Coe is drafted during wartime and Werlich signs up in peacetime?

3. What effect does Army life have on Werlich? Despite his enjoyment of Army life and his comfortable situation while stationed in Germany, he decides to leave. What causes him to realize that he won't become a career Army man? What is the nature of his "epiphany?"

4. When Werlich finally seeks an education, he takes it very seriously. In what ways do his education and, in particular, his reading shape his views of American law and politics? How would you describe Werlich's views of the role of government? What about his view of the role of law? Do you think those views remained constant or changed over time?

5. Do you agree or disagree with Werlich's version of Vietnam-era history? Why does he appear to have little sympathy for anti-war protestors? Do you know any adults who share Werlich's political views today?

6. What is the effect of the framing story, the 1972 visit to an Iron Curtain country? Does the visit to Hungary change Werlich's view of Communism or just his view of individual Communists?

LIBERTARIAN AWAKENING
Robert W. Poole, Jr.

In January 2001, I stepped down as president of The Reason Foundation, a public policy think tank I launched in 1978. Begun on a shoestring, it had grown to a $5 million annual budget and a staff of 30. Our monthly magazine, *Reason,* had won journalism awards and kudos from scholars such as Milton Friedman and advocates ranging from Nadine Strossen of the ACLU to Rush Limbaugh. Our policy work had put the concept of privatization into the U.S. mainstream.

Running a libertarian think tank was the last thing I could have imagined when I went off to college at the Massachusetts Institute of Technology (MIT) in the fall of 1962. A child of the Sputnik era, I'd been tracked as promising material for science and engineering, and, with my love of trains, planes, and automobiles as well as space, MIT seemed a natural choice. When I won a good-sized scholarship, there was no question that that was where I would go to school.

Yet the seeds of what would become my passion for libertarian ideas had already been planted, and would be nourished by my years at MIT. Part of the tracking in my large, mostly working-class Hialeah (Fla.) High School was a senior class in "Math Analysis" for the 30 of us who appeared most promising. Supplementing the standard college-track trigonometry and solid geometry class, Math Analysis taught things like set theory and some of what later became New Math (though, surprisingly, it omitted calculus, which would have been far more helpful at MIT).

Math Analysis was taught by Daryl W. Johnson, who was also the school's debate coach. Because we were all honor students, Mr. Johnson got away with devoting one class per month to political economy instead of math. His own views were apparently conservative/libertarian, for he had quotations posted above the blackboards from people like Lord Acton, Santayana, and Milton Friedman (though I didn't know who these people were, at that point). I got very interested in political philosophy and economics, perhaps because what I heard in Mr. Johnson's lectures seemed consistent with my budding anti-Communist views and the views of my moderate Republican parents, who favored a reduction in the size of the government. And when I left for MIT, I went with brand-new subscriptions to *National Review* and *The Freeman.* The latter was a little digest magazine put out by the Foundation for Economic Education.

The other publication I discovered as a result of Mr. Johnson's class was Barry Goldwater's *The Conscience of a Conservative,* which was published in 1960 and was an extremely popular book. I read it cover to cover, and was particularly struck by the concluding paragraph of Chapter 2, in which Goldwater called for public officials who would campaign along the following lines:

> *I have little interest in streamlining government or in making it more efficient, for I mean to reduce its size. I do not undertake to promote welfare, for I propose to extend freedom. My aim is not to pass laws, but to repeal them. It is not to inaugurate new programs, but to cancel old ones that do violence to the Constitution, or that have failed in their purpose, or that impose on the people an unwarranted financial burden. I will not attempt to discover legislation is*

*'needed' before I have first discovered whether it is constitutionally permissible.
And if I should later be attacked for neglecting my constituents' 'interests,' I shall
reply that I was informed that their main interest is liberty and that in that cause
I am doing the very best I can.*

Those words remained with me, and stir my passions to this day. But they were
far from my concerns as I adjusted to the reality of competing with hundreds of other
valedictorians, many of them smarter than I, at MIT. The shock of flunking my first
freshman physics quiz turned me into a super-nerd, afraid of losing my scholarship
and determined to master course-work that was much harder than I'd imagined it
would be, after coasting through 12 years of public school.

By my sophomore year, I'd regained my confidence and was getting mostly A's
(this was before grade inflation). MIT's two-year required sequence of "Modern
Western Ideas and Values" had introduced me to Aristotle, Hume, Locke, Smith, and
Mill, among others, rekindling my interest in politics and economics. And as it
became clear that, despite the political strength of the incumbent president, Lyndon
Johnson, Barry Goldwater would make his promised run for the presidency in 1964,
I decided that I had to play a part in that historic effort.

The initial focal point of my political activity was the MIT chapter of Young
Americans for Freedom, a relatively new campus conservative group that had been
launched at William Buckley's estate in Sharon, Connecticut, several years before. I
joined the group and enjoyed lively debates and discussions among what was already a
group with both traditionalist and libertarian factions. Nearly all were solidly for
Goldwater, but leaders of the libertarian faction decided that a separate Goldwater
group was advisable. David F. Nolan launched MIT Students for Goldwater, and I
volunteered to be its literature director. In the '63–'64 school year, we staffed a regular
literature table in the lobby under MIT's Great Dome. With something like 200 members, our group topped all other campus Goldwater groups in New England by a large
margin. (I think the Harvard group had about a dozen members.)

One of our successful projects was to "take over" the statewide group,
Massachusetts Young Republicans, on behalf of Barry Goldwater, to ensure that it
would support him rather than the hated Nelson Rockefeller, at the GOP nominating
convention. We all joined Massachusetts Young Republicans and ended up packing
its nominating convention. By sheer strength in numbers we converted the state
organization from Rockefeller supporters to Goldwater supporters, to the shock of
the national Young Republican leadership.

In working on the campaign with my campus colleagues, most of those
I befriended, and those who seemed to have the better arguments in our endless
political debates, were devotees of Ayn Rand's philosophy, objectivism. [Objectivism
holds that reality is objective and exists independent from the human mind.
Objectivists believe that the exercise of reason is the only way humans can understand that reality. Objectivists also believe that individual human beings should
pursue their own self-interests and that government should provide police and a
military to protect the people but maintain a complete separation of state and economics.] My colleagues chided me for never having read Rand's books, despite my
seeming to have more in common with the libertarians than the traditionalists. So in

FIGURE 4.2   Handsome, silver-haired Arizona Senator Barry Goldwater ran for president on the Republican ticket in 1964, having defeated his liberal Republican competitor, Nelson Rockefeller, in the primary. Goldwater appealed to Americans with conservative political and economic values, though he was not, himself, a social conservative. He campaigned as an opponent of the federal government and the welfare state. Although he lost the election to the incumbent president Lyndon Johnson, Goldwater is credited with the conservative political resurgence that started with his campaign and came to fruition nearly 20 years later during the presidency of Ronald Reagan.

Source: Prentice Hall High School

the summer of '64, while working a summer job at Southern Bell Telephone Co. in Miami, I lugged around a paperback copy of *Atlas Shrugged* and read all 1,084 pages of it. It made a tremendous impact. All my previous reading and thinking about politics and economics, as well as values, had prepped me for Rand's rugged individualist philosophy. My only previous hesitation about reading her books was my religious faith, which had been eroding after reading skeptics like David Hume in any case. I went back to MIT that fall a confirmed objectivist, ready for the final push in the Goldwater campaign.

Alas, the first meeting of the Students for Goldwater leadership brought heartbreaking news. First, the national campaign was foreswearing a hard-edged antibig-government campaign in favor of the feel-good slogan, "In your heart you know he's right." For us newly-minted radical rationalists, that was a bitter pill to swallow. But even worse was the official word from the national committee: we're going to lose, but we must persevere to make as good a showing as possible, to build a base for the future.

Like most of my colleagues, I soldiered on, even though my heart wasn't in it. We welcomed Goldwater to Boston with a motorcade to Fenway Park (the only time I set foot in that famed stadium during five years in the Boston area). And on election day I joined many colleagues in serving as a poll watcher in Back Bay. We were told (though I don't know if it's true) that in many precincts of traditionally Democratic Boston, this was the first time anyone could recall Republican poll watchers ever being there.

Goldwater lost big, and many of my friends dropped out of political activity, leaving a large void in the MIT chapter of Young Americans for Freedom. I decided to stick with it, and in the spring of 1965 found myself elected president of the chapter. As the new president, I decided it was up to me to revitalize the chapter, and in furtherance of that cause, I registered to attend the YAF national convention that summer in Washington, D.C.

The convention was a major event, despite the recent defeat of Goldwater. I attended sessions all day for several days, and looked forward to the closing banquet. The guest of honor turned out to be South Carolina senator, Strom Thurmond, who had left the Democratic Party during the Goldwater campaign to become a Republican. I was uncomfortable about YAF's decision to put him in the spotlight. This was 1965, remember, and Thurmond was still seen as a defender of racial segregation and an opponent of civil rights. When he walked into the banquet hall and got a standing ovation, I remained seated (earning a lot of nasty looks). I don't recall what he said in his speech, but he said nothing that dispelled my concerns that he was the wrong man to honor if we were going to build a majority movement.

And that episode led me to reflect on the previous summer. In addition to reading *Atlas Shrugged* during lunch hours and weekends, I had spent many evenings going door to door in Miami for Dade Youth for Goldwater. Our handler was an old southerner with a big air-conditioned Cadillac (which I got to drive). In addition to handing out Goldwater fliers, we were given boxes of John Stormer's right-wing conspiracy book, *None Dare Call It Treason*, to hand out. Recalling bits and pieces of conversation from that summer, my hindsight guess was that our handler was probably (1) a member of the John Birch Society, and (2) a segregationist like Thurmond.

Going to school in the 1950s in South Florida, I'd attended legally segregated public schools. I had clear memories of "colored" and "white" drinking fountains in supermarkets, and "colored" and "white" rest rooms at gas stations. For a junior high civics class, I did a research project on "colored schools," riding my bike to nearby black areas and taking photos. I was shocked to see how old and shabby the buildings were, compared to the clean, modern schools I'd gone to. My parents had always taught us that all people are individuals with dignity, who should be treated as such regardless of race or color. My sisters and I never said "nigger," despite its being commonly used by classmates.

There was no question in my mind that racial segregation was wrong. And I had no desire to associate with people who tolerated it, or who cheered on its champions. So at the end of summer 1965, I decided to quit YAF. I sent a letter to national headquarters telling them why, and said they would have to find a new president for the MIT chapter, since the position was now vacant. It felt very good to wash my hands of the organization. (Five years later, there was a historic split at the

YAF national convention in St. Louis. After Dave Schumacher, a libertarian, burned his draft card, the large remaining libertarian faction walked out, many of them to launch a competing student organization, the Society for Individual Liberty.)

****

Like most of my libertarian/objectivist friends, I pretty much ignored politics in the wake of the Goldwater debacle. Our assessment was that his overwhelming defeat showed that our radical critique of the status quo was not yet politically saleable, and that (as Ayn Rand wrote) much more work was needed at the intellectual level before a libertarian-type political effort would be viable.

On campus, that sort of thought led to the creation of a group we called MIT Radicals for Capitalism. I was not one of the founders, but my friend and roommate Jim Weigl and I joined it, and we organized a campus showing of the movie version of Rand's popular novel, *The Fountainhead*, which was a big success. "RadCaps" went on, after I'd graduated, to launch an alternative student newspaper, *Ergo*, which was published for 15 or 20 years at MIT.

The only political issue that got my attention during my last years at MIT was the growing war in Vietnam. During my YAF days, I had gone along with the YAF party line: the Communists were invading South Vietnam, Communism was evil, and therefore the United States had to fight back. But as LBJ kept pouring in troops and the death toll kept mounting, I began to question whether the war was really worth the cost in lives and taxes. And the fact that upon graduation I would be subject to the draft suddenly made the issue of vital personal importance to me.

Until that point, I hadn't given much thought to the draft. I had had a student deferment all through my undergraduate years, and, since I was majoring in mechanical engineering, I'd assumed I'd probably be going to work for an aerospace or other transportation-related company when I graduated. But now I learned that only defense-related companies could offer a draft deferment. I had an enjoyable summer job at Ford Motor Co. in Dearborn, Michigan, the summer of '66, and, then, after a year of grad school, ended up with job offers from both Ford and General Motors, as well as from several aerospace firms. The job offer that tempted me most was from Southern Pacific Railroad; their management trainee program would have given me six-month stints in a half-dozen aspects of their operations. Even though the work wasn't engineering, per se, it sounded the most interesting of the bunch. But there was no way they (or the auto companies) could provide a draft deferment. So I ended up accepting an offer from Sikorsky Aircraft in Connecticut, a defense-related industry that manufactured helicopters for the "helicopter war" that was going on in Vietnam.

Out in the real world, cut off from my whole circle of political and intellectual friends (except for snail-mail), I was starved for political discussion and intellectual stimulation. So I eagerly went to taped lecture courses on objectivism offered by the Nathaniel Branden Institute. Alas, I didn't find any new friends this way; the people seemed very rigid and not interested in really exploring the ideas handed down by Rand and her associates. So I had to create my own circle of freethinkers, and I turned to my new engineering colleagues at Sikorsky. A whole group of us had been hired in 1967, fresh out of school, and I was able to engage three or four of them in regular political and economic discussions. One, who had just arrived from England, had been brought up an ardent socialist in a Labor Party family. I actually got him to read Robert Heilbroner's *The Worldly Philosophers* (a very accessible overview of the greatest economic thinkers and their ideas), after which he was very engaged in debating socialism vs. capitalism. Reading Rand then brought him over largely to the capitalist side.

We young couples (I'd gotten married in 1968) got together for dinner at each other's houses, listening to rock music, experimenting with marijuana, and discussing politics and economics. Though we males all worked for a defense contractor and had draft deferments, we increasingly opposed the war, even to the point of wearing black armbands on a national day of protest. Needless to say, this did not endear us to the management (nor did my refusing to participate in their drive for 100% employee enrollment in a savings bond payroll deduction plan). Increasingly, I chafed at being part of a huge corporate bureaucracy, and concluded that this was not where I would enjoy a productive career.

The big break came in 1969 when the draft lottery was launched. (I'd briefly campaigned for Richard Nixon for president in 1968, largely on the basis of his Milton Friedman-inspired promise to abolish the draft.) When my number came up, it was at the far end of the scale, making it highly unlikely that I'd be selected. I was free!

Having ruled out aerospace, the next question was what to do with my career? I still thought of myself as an engineer, especially valuing the quantitative approach and rigorous analytical thinking I'd learned how to do. And I'd actually enjoyed the kind of cost-effectiveness analysis that I'd done in some of my assignments at Sikorsky, analyzing whether various proposed helicopter design changes would do enough good (in terms of mission accomplishments) to make it worth the cost of building and maintaining them. But I didn't want to get locked into learning more and more about a narrower and narrower area of engineering. I wanted to work on big-picture issues.

What I decided to focus on was the think tank industry. In the course of my work, I'd run across studies from RAND Corporation, Stanford Research Institute, GE Tempo, and others. Most of them were branching out into non-defense work (e.g., RAND had done a devastating critique of rent controls in New York City). And best of all, they were nearly all located in California. After five winters in Boston and two more in Connecticut, this Florida boy had concluded he would never get used to ice and snow, and never wanted to live through another such winter. So in the summer of '69 I sent out resumes and was delighted to get a good offer from General Research Corp. in Santa Barbara. GRC was a relatively low-profile think tank, set up by some people from the Advanced Research Projects Agency (ARPA). Though mostly defense-related, like RAND, it too had just launched a civil division, which was where the job offer had come from. I was sold before they flew me out to Santa Barbara for a final interview, and even more sold thereafter. So in January 1970, I left freezing Connecticut for good, driving across the country to bucolic Santa Barbara.

Before leaving Connecticut, however, I'd had a life-changing experience. Back in the summer of '65, while doing endlessly boring work at a summer job at Eastern

Airlines, I had spent many hours daydreaming about writing articles on political economy subjects. As I was manually plotting hundreds of data points from jet-engine test runs, I thought about issues like government regulation of airlines, social security, the postal monopoly, and many others—and how satisfying it would be to write about them, presenting free-market alternatives to the conventional wisdom. I thought vaguely about publishing a newsletter or magazine where I could write such commentaries. I had no plan to do any such thing, only an unformed sense of excitement about the possibilities.

Four years later, while working at Sikorsky and reading *Aviation Week* regularly, I thought more and more about what seemed to me to be the rather flimsy rationale for government regulation of the airlines. As a child, I became aware of the Civil Aeronautics Board's role in handing out route awards. My father worked for Eastern Airlines, and my uncle, who lived up the street, worked for National. So my family flew on company passes on Eastern, and my cousin Tom flew on company passes on National. In 1955, both airlines applied for a new route from Miami to Los Angeles, where Disneyland had recently opened. National won the award—which meant that Tom and his family went to Disneyland but my family and I did not. I resented that ever after.

So I took advantage of the Sikorsky library to read up on the history of commercial aviation and its regulation. And I discovered the emerging economic writings on the low fares brought about by real competition, in those markets within a single state (California and Texas) that were therefore exempt from federal regulation by the Civil Aeronautics Board. After much work, I ended up writing a long article arguing the case for airline deregulation (and, for good measure, privatization of airports and air traffic control).

I sent the article to a start-up libertarian periodical called *Reason*. Published in mimeograph, it was the creation of an objectivist journalism student in Boston named Lanny Friedlander. I'd discovered it in its second issue and, being starved for libertarian/objectivist stimulation, immediately subscribed. Despite its amateurish format, *Reason* was pretty well written. Several months before sending in the article, I'd driven up to Boston to meet Lanny, thinking I might offer to get involved with the publication. He seemed so disorganized that I decided against it. But he did encourage me to write for the magazine, which rekindled my musings from the summer of '65.

Lanny didn't tell me, when he accepted the article, that he was about to switch to typesetting and offset printing. Or that he was making my article the cover story of the first issue to appear in the new format. So when the new issue arrived, with "Fly the Frenzied Skies" on the cover, I was completely blown away. It was so amazing to see my thoughts in print, and in a respectable-looking publication! But the bigger thrill was still to come. A short time later, *The Freeman* (my economics life-line through college) wrote asking to reprint the article. And when it hit their pages and became available to 40,000 subscribers (compared to *Reason*'s few hundred), I started getting letters—from fans, from academics, even from people in government. Getting published really does make a difference, I concluded.

Hence, after getting settled in Santa Barbara, I decided to continue writing articles for *Reason*. I did a piece on natural gas price deregulation, another on ocean mining, and a third on the new topic of ecology. And via the *Reason* connection, I met a fellow contributing writer, Tibor Machan, a Hungarian refugee then working on his Ph.D. in philosophy at UC Santa Barbara. Through Tibor I got plugged into a number of other libertarian individuals and semi-underground publications in California.

By 1970, the anti-war movement had become a major political force, and riots and demonstrations were taking place around the country. I recall being horrified by the killing of students by National Guard troops at Kent State. And, closer to home, I listened to live radio coverage of the riots in Isla Vista, when a police–student confrontation led to a branch of the Bank of America being burned to the ground.

While most libertarians were not directly involved in anti-war activities, the government's heavy-handed actions against those activities led to considerable paranoia among California libertarians. Many of those who wrote for a semi-underground 'zine called *Libertarian Connection* used "movement names" in print. One of those I knew personally was a research scientist at TRW (a defense contractor), who held a Secret clearance. He was concerned that if his real name appeared in the pages of *Libertarian Connection,* he might lose his clearance and hence his job. (He subsequently achieved fame under his real name as a longevity expert, co-authoring a national bestseller and appearing on TV talk shows.)

That was the climate of opinion the summer of 1970, as Tibor and I discussed the impending demise of *Reason* magazine. Lanny had run out of money; numbers and business had never been his strong suit (as opposed to writing, editing, and graphic design). Instead of acceding to his pleas to send money, Tibor and I had a different idea: we would buy *Reason* from him and hire him back to continue editing the magazine. Tibor and I drafted a business plan (hopelessly naïve, but better than nothing, which was what Lanny had), and our new friend and partner, libertarian attorney Manny Klausner, drafted both a partnership agreement and an acquisition contract. After some negotiating, Lanny agreed to the deal, and at the end of 1970, Reason Enterprises was launched.

The Reason Enterprises years, from 1971 through mid-1978, are a tale best told another time. For most of that period, it was a garage business, operated out of my various houses and apartments. We partners all had full-time jobs, so we published *Reason* every month as a kind of hobby business. Despite having begun with all of a couple thousand dollars, we bootstrapped the business, growing the circulation from an initial 400 to about 12,000 over those seven years. Two marriages and one friendship from within the partnership broke up, but Reason Enterprises survived.

Finally, at the start of 1978, I told Tibor and Manny that we could not continue as a glorified hobby business, with the brunt of the responsibilities on me and the office in my apartment. Having gone on from General Research Corporation to become a consultant on government operations and efficiency, my ability to accept consulting assignments was conflicting with the demands of a monthly magazine production cycle. I could do one or the other, but not both.

We decided to take a gamble on turning the organization into a real business, which our research showed would make the most sense as a non-profit. That especially appealed to me because such an entity could also do policy studies and publish books in areas like government regulation and privatization, in which I was even more interested as time went on. Those plans culminated in the creation of Reason

Foundation, for which I went to work full-time as president on July 1, 1978 (with two other employees). How we survived those first few years is, again, a story for another time.

Looking back, I still marvel at the inflection points along the way. Had Daryl Johnson not taught political economy in my high school Math Analysis class, had I not read Barry Goldwater's book, had I shielded myself from Ayn Rand's writings, had I not received a draft deferment, had I not taken the time to write that first article, had we lost our initial investment in Reason Enterprises (which we gambled on a test mailing to new subscribers, and won) . . . there would likely be no Reason Foundation or *Reason* magazine today.

QUESTIONS FOR DISCUSSION

1. What elements in Robert Poole's background and education lead him to admire conservative philosophers and theorists? How do we know from Poole's college days that he has leadership abilities?

2. Why do Poole and his friends in YAF and the Massachusetts Young Republicans favor Barry Goldwater over the "liberal" Republican, Nelson Rockefeller? Why might Goldwater's "liberty" rhetoric and his plans to cut down the size of government seem so appealing in the era of Lyndon Johnson's Great Society and all its social programs?

3. What causes Poole to break with YAF? What causes his disillusionment? Does Poole's repudiation of Strom Thurmond and the John Birch Society help to define or limit his conservatism in any particular way? How does it make us feel about him?

4. Describe further steps in the evolution of Poole's libertarian conservatism. How does his intellectual growth in conservatism compare to that of John Werlich in the previous chapter? What readings seem to be particularly influential for both men?

5. How does Poole's response to the military draft compare to other responses to the draft that you have read about in this book? In what specific areas having to do with personal freedom might libertarians resemble radicals such as draft resisters? Does this surprise you? Can you see some ways in which libertarian conservatives differ from social conservatives?

6. What do you think of the quotation from Barry Goldwater? Does it echo any of your own political passions? How does knowing about the nature of Sixties conservatism help you to better understand the political struggles that we see today?

IT AIN'T ME, BABE: WORKING FOR RICHARD NIXON
Ron McCoy

> *You say you're lookin' for someone*
> *Never weak but always strong,*
> *To protect you an' defend you*
> *Whether you are right or wrong,*
> *Someone to open each and every door,*
> *But it ain't me, babe,*
> *No, no, no, it ain't me, babe,*
> *It ain't me you're lookin' for, babe.*

"It Ain't Me, Babe" Words and music by Bob Dylan
1964 Warner Bros., Inc. Renewed 1992 Special Rider Music
Used by permission

In June 1967, at the age of nineteen, I joined Richard Nixon's presidential campaign staff in Washington, D.C. Defeats in the 1960 presidential election and 1962 California governor's race saddled Nixon with the image of a loser, and knowledgeable observers put long odds on his chances for winning the Republican nomination and beating President Lyndon Johnson. Almost four decades later, I'm a university history professor. The only trace of Nixon in my office is his visage surmounting a half-foot-tall plaster gargoyle perched precariously on the edge of a bookcase. Looking at that gargoyle, I pose the same question I always ask when I recall working for Richard Nixon: Just what in the hell was I thinking about?

I was recruited to work for Nixon in February 1967. I lived in a freshman dorm at Arizona State University, attended classes I liked, ignored those I didn't, and avoided compulsory Reserve Officer Training Corps drills whenever possible. ASU's sprawling campus lay almost two hundred miles north of my family's home in the high desert outside a town called Nogales, separated from a Mexican city of the same name by the international border's wire fence.

Until 1962, we had lived in suburban Southern California. My father, Tim McCoy, born during Benjamin Harrison's presidency, was a Wyoming cowboy who became the reel hero in about a hundred Hollywood westerns. My mother, Inga Arvad, was a Danish journalist whose pre-war interviews with Adolph Hitler brought so much unwelcome attention from the FBI—surveillance, bugging, a break-in at her Washington, D.C., apartment—that she advised me to "avoid getting your name on any lists." In the early fifties, my dad hosted a live television program in L.A. about the history of the American West. During summers, my mother, younger brother Terry, and I joined him on three-ring circuses as he performed feats of marksmanship and trick roping. My nascent political aspirations and later career in academe were undoubtedly informed by my experience as a circus clown and sideshow barker.

(One summer Terry worked as an elephant trainer, contending with a five-foot-tall calf named Susie who seemed to take particular delight in swinging her trunk and knocking him out. As an observer, I learned to be wary of elephants. But

I should have paid more attention, given my subsequent encounters with those of the political sort.)

In 1962 we moved to Nogales, where I attended high school. Time spent on the Mexican border was crucial to my formative years. *Piñatas,* conga lines, singing mariachis, bullfights, *quinceañeras,* celebrating friends' name-days—I received a healthy dose of multiculturalism long before the word came into vogue. (Our high school cheerleaders led crowds in chanting, "Two bits, four bits, six bits, a peso—All for Nogales, stand up and stay so!")

Some good teachers helped me overcome a stutter and success in speech competitions instilled confidence, as did acting in plays and working as a disc jockey at the local 250-watt radio station. I attended the American Legion's Boys State, went to Boys Nation, and was elected president. The next year I won the Legion's national oratorical contest. My senior year served as a kind of victory lap as I drove around Arizona and flew across the country delivering speeches at high schools and conventions.

I graduated from high school in 1966 and enrolled at Arizona State University, where I majored in political science in the naïve belief that "poli-sci" as taught in the classroom is directly related to its practice in the real world. I wanted to become a lawyer and enter politics. In the movies, I'd seen the kind of lawyer I wanted to be: Spencer Tracy in *Inherit the Wind* and Gregory Peck in *To Kill a Mockingbird.*

Such was the state of affairs one morning in February 1967, when Don Johnson, a former head of the American Legion, whom I had met at the Legion's national convention in 1965, rang me on the phone in my dorm room.

"Who do you want to get the Republican nomination in '68?" he asked after some pleasantries.

"Percy, I guess," meaning Senator Charles Percy of Illinois. It seems laughable today, but back then the GOP boasted a fair number of liberals and moderates who favored social justice. They took a drubbing when archconservative Senator Barry Goldwater of Arizona captured the Republican presidential nomination in 1964, only to suffer a catastrophic defeat in November at the hands of Lyndon Johnson. LBJ won a mandate in that election, but Goldwater's acolytes took the long view and sowed the seeds that blossomed into today's Republican Party. (Indeed, Ronald Reagan's political star began its real ascent after he gave a nationally televised speech on Goldwater's behalf on October 27, 1964.) As for me, I came from a politically mixed marriage. My conservative dad believed America's decline and fall began with Franklin D. Roosevelt. My mom was an old-line liberal. I was nineteen, at a time when nineteen year-olds could not vote in the United States, and more enamored of vague ideas about basic fairness than wedded to an ideology.

"Who do you think will actually be the nominee?" Johnson queried.

"Nixon."

"How would you like to work for him?" There was a pause, then: "Look, if you're interested call this number." He reeled off the number for the Nixon, Mudge, Rose, Guthrie, Alexander & Mitchell law firm (known in verbal shorthand as Nixon-Mudge) at 20 Broad Street in New York. "Ask for Tom Evans."

Nixon-Mudge attorney Evans and I had met the previous summer at the American Legion's 1966 national convention in Washington, D.C. Nixon had addressed the convention, delivering a warning that if the U.S. wasn't out of Vietnam within five years there could be a world war. After the speech, I joined about twenty others for lunch with Nixon, shook hands and exchanged a few words. Afterwards, Evans introduced himself, said he'd heard a speech I delivered at the convention and liked it. It was a pretty liberal one for that audience. I'd said something along the lines of: "The System" must respond to the concerns of youth; if it didn't, my generation might lose faith and become further radicalized.

"As you probably know, Mr. Nixon is not a candidate at this time," Evans explained when I telephoned him at Nixon-Mudge. "Some people are attempting to convince him to seek the Republican nomination in 1968. As I said, the former vice president is not a candidate; he hasn't made up his mind; he's got to be convinced . . . " You'd have thought it was necessary to put Nixon in a hammerlock and hold his feet to a fire to get him to run.

Then Evans cut to the chase. "We'd like you to come to work for us. You'd organize youth support for a much-maligned statesman who is actually quite progressive." This was the first time I encountered a key concept in the 1968 presidential campaign: the New Nixon whose heart was in the right place.

We agreed I'd work at the Nixon for President Committee in Washington, D.C., from mid-June until mid-September for a bit over $700 a month. (It was pretty good pay. In those days the median annual household income was $7000; a new Volkswagen bug ran $1500; and a first-class postage stamp or a Hershey chocolate bar set you back a nickel.)

In June 1967, a week after the Six-Day War left Israel in possession of the Gaza Strip, Sinai, East Jerusalem, and the Golan Heights, I flew to Washington, D.C. For a couple of months I lived with the chairman of the Nixon for President Committee, Dr. Gaylord Parkinson, in a spacious home the committee rented in Georgetown. (Later, I leased a tiny garret apartment above a Georgetown restaurant.)

Parkinson was the former head of California's Republican Party. His claim to fame lay in issuing the Eleventh Commandment—"Thou Shalt Not Speak Ill of Any Other Republican"—to avert bloodletting in GOP primaries. Parkinson displayed a high regard for his own abilities as chairman, but the magic wasn't working—the Nixon campaign was still a small operation, plagued by money problems, lacking coordination and organization.

While I was on board, there were never more than fifteen or twenty of us full-time staff. Some worked out of Nixon-Mudge in New York; others (like me) at 1726, the Pennsylvania Avenue address of the campaign's Washington, D.C., headquarters, located one hopeful block from the White House. Across the building's three-story white façade, a larger than life, faux-wooden gold eagle hovered above red, white, and blue letters spelling "NIXON." Inside, photomurals of Nixon with Chiang Kai-Shek, Willy Brandt, Arnold Palmer, Jack Nicklaus, and Korean orphans adorned white walls. The reception area, carpeted bright blue, was dominated by the campaign's logo: a white, N-shaped lightning bolt inside a rectangle, bordered red at the bottom and blue at the top. Because the building was owned by the husband of pop culture astrologer-psychic Jeanne Dixon, the black humor joke when a negative story about the candidate appeared in the press was, "Well, at least Dixon's for Nixon."

I got my orientation tour by seeking out colleagues at Nixon-Mudge and 1726 for a crash course in *realpolitik* and Nixonian corporate culture. Staffers called Nixon "the former Vice President" until it was decided the phrase lacked the cachet of now-ness. So we called him "RN" (the moniker he used signing off on memoranda), "The Old Man," and "The Boss." Our first objective was to stay alive until January, when Nixon publicly revealed his intentions. The presidential election was almost a year-and-a-half off and a lot could happen between now and then. More immediate hurdles lay closer at hand, in primaries and state conventions. For the nomination to be worth anything, it must be won without alienating GOP voters on the left, right, or in the middle.

California governor Ronald Reagan posed the biggest potential threat to Nixon's plans and needed to be held in check. Although he did not seem to have sufficient fire in his belly for a run in 1968, Reagan merited careful monitoring and placation. Nixon might lay claim to Reagan's rightwing base, but conservatives' love for Reagan was matched by their suspicion of Nixon, known since his days in Congress as "Tricky Dick." That unflattering nickname was a byproduct of California's 1950 U.S. Senate race, a bitter contest which pitted Nixon against Democratic Congresswoman Helen Gahagan Douglas. Snapshots from that battle include: Nixon asking radio listeners why Douglas was "refusing to tell you which side she is on in this conflict" (the Korean War); Nixon standing up in front of an audience at San Francisco's Press Club and reading a letter of support from Eleanor Roosevelt (not the widow of Democratic President Franklin D. Roosevelt but another woman of the same name); and Nixon's office distributing information about Helen Douglas's voting record printed on pink paper, "pink" at that time connoting sympathy for "the Reds," or Communists.

Nixon also wanted former Michigan governor George Romney's campaign for the nomination to survive long enough to hamstring New York governor Nelson Rockefeller's chances. Rockefeller and Romney relied on the same middle-to-left voter base, and it was assumed Rockefeller wouldn't announce as long as Romney stayed in the running. We assumed it was only a matter of time before Romney committed a fatal gaffe, which he did in early September 1967. Attempting to distance himself from his prior support for the Vietnam War, Romney told a journalist that the U.S. military had "brainwashed" him into supporting the war effort during a tour of Southeast Asia two years earlier. "Brainwashing" was the explanation U.S. officials offered to account for American P.O.W.s who, during the Korean War, made anti-American statements while in Chinese and North Korean captivity. It implied sophisticated manipulation of a person's psyche and destruction of their will and ability to act independently. Romney knocked himself out of the race by unburdening himself of this howler and becoming an object of ridicule, but the presence of too many presidential wannabes kept the GOP's progressive wing hopelessly divided.

Working for Nixon, even as a bit player, felt like swimming in shark-infested waters. (I thought so at the time, and when, years later, I actually did swim in shark-infested waters the comparison held up well.) The jockeying for position around the candidate, the depressing cynicism, the tendency to think everybody played a particularly nasty brand of hardball (paranoid staff members regularly had 1726 swept for "bugs") did little to kindle the warm fires of idealism. I retained an interest in politics and followed developments closely even afterwards, but my days at campaign head-quarters left me wondering whether trying to effect change by working within The System made sense.

What I encountered within "The System" was the very worst of corporate cul-ture. The truly pathetic yes-men hadn't taken over yet. (They would do so later, when the campaign swung into high gear, and they would come to the fore during Nixon's presidency.) Careerism, callousness, and cynicism negated the possibility of compassion playing much of a role. I'd never believed I would find a community of ascetics modeling themselves after St. Francis of Assisi, but I had hoped passion about social justice, about putting an end to the Vietnam War—about, in other words, some of the things the candidate professed to believe in—might play a role in the equation.

It became clear that results were important to Nixon's people; means weren't. Substance received short shrift, because appearance was all. So we could spend days debating what length Nixon's sideburns should be trimmed so his face appeared thinner. And it was not much of a surprise that when a young African American woman was finally hired to work at 1726, she was told to position herself at the receptionist's desk like a display of multiracial inclusiveness for visitors and passersby.

The campaign was very much a male environment. (I never met a woman who worked in any capacity other than secretary or office manager.) The testosterone stream ran swift and strong. "The Old Man likes to set staffers against one another," one of Parkinson's aides explained. "They cut each other up and the fittest survive." I would not have been surprised to hear the sound of young rams' horns crashing in the building, as members of the herd jockeyed for position.

During the time I worked on the campaign I met and worsked with people whose names would later figure prominently in news stories, especially stories detailing the Nixon Administration's demise: John Mitchell, Nixon's crusty but nev-ertheless likeable law partner who became Attorney General and later went to prison for conspiracy, perjury and obstruction of justice; money raiser Maurice Stans, who became Secretary of Commerce and beat major federal charges of conspiracy, obstruction of justice, and perjury; Dwight Chapin, Nixon's buttoned-down personal assistant ("My job is taking care of The Body"), whose involvement with "dirty tricks" led to a perjury conviction; Pat Buchanan, an affable speechwriter; Tom Charles Huston, who in 1970 devised the notorious "Huston Plan" for bringing the weight of the FBI, CIA, and Defense Intelligence Agency to bear against Nixon's domestic "enemies" through illegal mail intercepts, wiretaps, and break-ins.

The staffer to whom I most easily gravitated was John Sears, a 27-year-old Nixon-Mudge attorney. He occupied a tiny office at the top of the narrow stairway leading to 1726's third floor. Sears had attended Notre Dame and graduated from Georgetown Law School by the time he was twenty-two. During the 1966 congres-sional campaign he and Pat Buchanan traveled with Nixon, who wasn't running for office that year but piled up political I.O.U.s speaking on behalf of Republican candidates. Sears told me that during the campaign he stopped at home to see his wife when she was about to have a baby, but left before the child arrived because "it wasn't in Mr. Nixon's schedule."

Searss' owlishly wise face usually bore the trace of a sardonic smile, and his long eyelashes often concealed whatever might otherwise have been discerned in his large, all-seeing eyes. Len Garment, another Nixon-Mudge attorney who knew him well, later wrote that Sears was "widely read, from Aristotle to current politics, and full of Catholic metaphysics and Irish charm." Working under tremendous pressure, Sears was a heavy smoker and a connoisseur of Scotch whiskey. Uptight, on edge, blindingly smart, working without notes and relying on a photographic memory, he could dictate ten-page memoranda about gossip, strategy, and tactics that were models of insight, logic, canniness, and political savvy. He experienced no difficulty reciting the name of every county party chairman in targeted states, or analyzing the faintest signals picked up on his political radar and consistently getting it right. John claimed his talent lay in knowing "where the bodies are buried." He once put that talent to work while attending a party at Nixon's apartment in New York, where he introduced the mistress of one of the law firm's partners to the partner's wife, stepped back and watched the sparks fly. I would come to the belief that this incident, requiring more than a dose of insouciance on Searss' part, served as but one example of the connoisseurship of *Schadenfreude* that runs like a mother lode through the political field. (*Schadenfreude* is the enjoyment of another person's misfortune.)

Sears was one of the few people on the staff with whom you could talk about any number of subjects beyond politics. He was, for instance, not in the least interested in ever running for office. "I'd make a lousy candidate, young McCoy," he once admitted. "Couldn't put up with all the bullshit." (I was always "young McCoy" to John, who was all of eight years my senior. Perhaps he'd been "young Sears" once, and saw an opportunity to pass the unwelcome handle on to someone else.) John's powers of reasoning were positively Jesuitical; the scope of his interests utterly catholic. Whether lunching alone with him and or listening to his elegant discourses during our staff meetings, spending time with John Sears was always an illuminating experience.

I was responsible for the Youth Section, an empty desk and bare filing cabinet on the ground floor at 1726. After sending Parkinson, Evans, and Sears a memo about my perception of the general mood of young people—"Richard Nixon is viewed with great apathy and disdain by the youth"—I started laying some plans. But nobody was spending any money or taking responsibility for giving me a go-ahead signal.

By late July, 1967, as staffers at 1726 and Nixon-Mudge worked the phones, mulling over the situation, a consensus developed: Gaylord Parkinson had to go. He could not be fired from the chairmanship of the Nixon for President Committee—it might look like the campaign was in trouble—so his job was made as pointless and unbearable as possible. His instructions were ignored, directives circumvented, access to Nixon curtailed. By September he left.

The morning Parkinson departed for California, Bob Ellsworth, a former congressman from Kansas, arrived on the scene, called the staff together and fired everyone. (One of Parkinson's aides, in the hospital with pneumonia, got the word via a telephone call.) A few minutes later, Ellsworth called those of us who hadn't been in Parkinson's clique and rehired us.

That evening, as I sat at my desk mulling over the day's weirdness, John Sears appeared, carrying a bottle of Scotch and two glasses. "Sooner or later," he observed over drinks, referring to the purge. "It was bound to happen sooner or later."

We made our way out of the office, down Pennsylvania Avenue, walked over to the White House, and leaned against the metal fence.

"Yeah, young McCoy, sooner or later everybody gets it," Sears mused. "In this business, everyone gets canned. You make one mistake and that's it. You're only allowed one."

"Don't you think that's a little harsh, John?"

"Sure, but that's because it's a crappy business." He gazed at the White House, lights illuminating the landmark against the night. "I'll make it to this place if the Old Man pulls it off. Then I'll be in for a while and out for a lot."

As usual, John was right. He got to the White House but fell victim to the endemic infighting. (It appears John Mitchell got the impression Sears thought he was a fool and exacted his revenge.) I saw Sears when I visited Washington at the end of the summer of 1969. He inhabited space near storage rooms in the Executive Office Building, seemed relaxed and said he didn't mind that not many people—"old friends," he sardonically called them—found their way to his lair. Sears was a casualty of the political wars; many associates, acting as if his was a highly contagious type of misfortune, sought to inoculate themselves from a similar fate by shunning him. Though Sears was still on the White House payroll, his fate was sealed and his name soon disappeared from the list of employees.

As I left John's office, I noticed a stack of pictures recently removed from the walls. On top of the pile was one of Nixon, autographed with an inscription expressing thanks to John for a job well done. (Later, John was instrumental in managing Ronald Reagan's presidential efforts in 1976 and 1980.)

In 2000, Len Garment, a campaign operative and one of Nixon's lawyers during the Watergate mess, published a book called *In Search of Deep Throat*. "Deep Throat" was the *nom de guerre* of an anonymous informant who provided reporters Carl Bernstein and Bob Woodward of *The Washington Post* with invaluable inside-government information during the Watergate scandal. Deep Throat has long been credited with playing a major role in blowing the whole Watergate mess wide open. Hal Holbrook played the role in *All the President's Men*, the movie adaptation of Woodward and Bernstein's 1974 book of the same name. In the movie, Deep Throat tells the investigators how not to get sidetracked: "Follow the money."

In their book, Woodward and Bernstein described Deep Throat: "He was, incongruously, an incurable gossip, careful to label rumor for what it was, but fascinated by it . . . He could be rowdy, drink too much, overreach. He was not good at concealing his feelings, hardly ideal for a man in his position." Over the years, something of a cottage industry arose involving speculation about who Deep Throat was. In 2000 Len Garment weighed in with his conclusion in his book *In Search of Deep Throat*: John Sears was Deep Throat.

Sears scoffed at Garment's theory and both Woodward and Bernstein backed Sears up. In 2005 we discovered that the real Deep Throat was Mark Felt, former assistant director of the FBI, who finally confessed to his role after suffering a stroke

FIGURE 4.3   An exultant Richard Nixon gives his trademark " 'V' for Victory" sign after receiving the presidential nomination at the Republican National Convention in Miami, Florida, in 1968. Nixon, a former California congressman and two-term Vice President under Dwight Eisenhower, returned from private life with a message that appealed to conservative and moderate Americans and a whole new cohort of young voters. Part of Nixon's youth appeal stemmed from his support for lowering the voting age to 18 and his promise to end the war in Vietnam. These factors, in addition to a well-orchestrated campaign in the traditionally Democratic South, brought Nixon the victory in November.

Source: Getty Images Inc.—Hulton Archive Photos

at age 91. I was almost sorry to hear about Felt's confession, because John Sears had struck me as perfect for the part.

Working without a job description, I spent my time visiting with other staffers and operatives about progress in early primary states like New Hampshire; giving speeches at colleges and to financial contributors; monitoring the development of mock conventions at universities; consulting politicians on Capitol Hill who had experience in working with youth groups; drafting the occasional statement in Nixon's name (I especially remember speechwriter Pat Buchanan insisting my phrase "greatest welfare" in one be replaced with "greatest benefit" because "welfare" smacked of left-wing views); that sort of thing.

The lack of a job description for me, or much in the way of direction, combined with the campaign's nascent state provided me with an opportunity to feel out the possibilities. I drew up lists of universities as possible venues for Nixon speeches, helped organize the unannounced candidate's forces at college and university mock political conventions (we won the first, held at tiny, unaccredited Rio Grande College in Rio Grande, Ohio), worked up and fought for a budget for outreach efforts to mobilize young people. (Nixon favored giving 18-year-olds the vote.) In attempting to identify possible supporters, I obtained several years' worth of Boys Nation mailing lists from a contact at the American Legion's national headquarters. From a girl Buchanan met at a party we got the National Student Association's campus coordinator list. The NSA was a hotbed of anti-establishment sentiment and the list proved almost completely worthless for the Nixon campaign. Typical comments we received from NSA members in response to written invitations to help Nixon ran along the lines of "Are you kidding?" and "Fuck Nixon!"

I helped Tom Huston to draft a letter for soliciting student involvement in Nixon's campaign. Huston was then an intelligence officer in the U.S. Army and somewhat leery of being identified with the Nixon for President Committee. ("The government takes a dim view of its employees' involvement in partisan politics," he dryly observed.) However, he agreed to write the letter, and in it he said that 25,000 American soldiers had died in Vietnam.

"But, Tom," I protested while we edited the missive, "twenty-five thousand soldiers haven't died in Vietnam. The total is less than that."

"Don't worry," Huston replied grimly. "I've seen the figures and there's a certain predictability to this stuff. By the time this letter gets printed it'll be accurate enough."

And it was.

As time went by, I grew increasingly edgy about the Vietnam War. Early in 1967 a Gallup poll found that 52% of Americans supported the war, while 32% didn't. By the end of that year more than 18,000 U.S. troops had died in Vietnam, 486,000 found themselves immersed in that quagmire, and 46% of Americans felt that the war was a "mistake." By the end of that year, more than 16,000 U.S. troops had died in Vietnam, and 486,000 found themselves immersed in that quagmire, The mainstream *Life* magazine renounced its earlier support for LBJ's Southeast Asia policies, Robert McNamara resigned as Secretary of Defense, and in-country commander General William Westmoreland was blathering on in *Time* magazine about how he hoped the enemy would "try something because we are looking for a fight."

One day, New York corporate attorney and veteran of Nixon's vice presidential staff, Charlie McWhorter, visited 1726. Charlie was quick, intense, simply could not sit still. A jazz fan and connoisseur of abstract art, he maintained contacts with people who wouldn't vote for Nixon if you put a gun to their heads. We quickly struck up a friendship.

One weekend, visiting Charlie at his Greenwich Village apartment, I met David Hawk. David was a divinity student and major league organizer of the anti-war movement who later worked with Amnesty International and the United Nations. Friendly and committed, he presented arguments against the war. I found David's combination of passion and logic both attractive and irrefutable.

In October, on a plane returning from New Hampshire, I met Washington attorney James W. Barco. He'd worked with the U.S. delegation to the U.N. during Eisenhower's administration. Barco can be seen in a famous Cold War photograph from 1960, sitting just behind U.N. ambassador Henry Cabot Lodge (Nixon's running mate that year), who displayed a two-foot-tall wooden carving of a United States seal the Soviets had presented to the American ambassador in Moscow, complete with a bugging device enclosed.

Barco was concerned about youthful attitudes to the Vietnam War, too. He and I tried to map out a strategy for impressing the weight of anti-war sentiment on Nixon, but we failed because a meeting could not be arranged with the candidate. Bob Ellsworth said such activities were "too long range" and should be put on hold until "later." I thought I was starting to understand some of the lyrics Stephen Stills wrote for a song of the time, Buffalo Springfield's hit "For What It's Worth"—"There's something happening here/What it is ain't exactly clear." As with so many of my generation, Vietnam was beginning to weigh heavily on my mind. It served as the nexus for a web of discontents with American society and "business as usual."

Around that time I was reminded of the 1950s CBS television series "You Are There," in which anchorman Walter Cronkite concluded re-creations of historical events by delivering an Olympian peroration: "What sort of a day was it? A day like all days, filled with those events that alter and illuminate our times . . . and you were there!"

Saturday, October 21, 1967, a pleasant enough autumn day in Washington, D.C., was certainly all of that. More than 70,000 people gathered at the Lincoln Memorial for the largest anti-Vietnam War rally up to that time. (David Hawk was one of the organizers.) After listening to speeches on the Mall, at least 50,000 of them marched across the bridge over the Potomac and flowed onto the grounds of the Pentagon. A secretary at the Nixon committee offered me a ride in her car to the demonstration, where we found twenty-five hundred troops and two hundred U.S. marshals warily observing the crowd. There were some Old Lefties, for whom the Spanish Civil War of the 1930s remained a burning issue. Then there were the Yippies, a coterie of ebullient street theatre aficionados who flocked to the banner of the Youth International Party—hence the name: "YIP" became "Yippie," much as "hip" evolved into "hippie"—founded in 1967 by Abbie Hoffman and Jerry Rubin. Already steeped in the drug culture—spiced with a bit of Eastern mysticism—they planned to surround the Pentagon and exorcise the evils of war by chanting mantras until the whole building levitated, wobbled a bit and turned orange. (As Abbie Hoffman, the closest thing to a leader the Yippies ever had, pointed out: "Sacred cows make the best hamburger.") But most of the people there seemed to be students, eager, earnest, and confident in the efficacy of working within The System to profoundly affect the hearts and minds of their nation's leaders.

As I roamed through the throng people seemed determined but still cheerful, the atmosphere practically festive. The gaps, fissures, and schisms so characteristic of the late Sixties were then only just forming. I watched, transfixed, as young women placed flowers in the barrels of rifles held by soldiers no older than themselves. Late that afternoon some hardliners rushed the Pentagon, hurling themselves like kamikazes at soldiers blocking the entrance. Tear gas poisoned the air and I decided to call it a day.

Potomac Fever had taken hold of me, the excitement of finding oneself near the center of something important. I decided I'd take time off from school. Caught up in the 12-hour days of a presidential campaign, I had little opportunity to do anything other than work.

(Indeed, for a long time I owned only one suit, a gray pinstripe, because there was no chance to shop for another. When it needed dry cleaning I marched from 1726 to the "One Hour Martinizing" establishment next door, entered a dressing room, took off my suit, waited until it was cleaned, pressed, and ready for public display, got dressed and returned to work. After I wore the ass-end out of that suit a coworker told me where I could buy a couple more at a discount haberdashery allegedly favored by Dwight D. Eisenhower.)

I'd forgotten about an important element of 1960s life: young males not enrolled in college were ineligible for a student deferment from the draft. Which is why, soon after the March on the Pentagon, my draft notice arrived in the mail. This was not a trifling matter—only recently Muhammad Ali, heavyweight-boxing champion of the world, had had his title taken away and found himself facing five years in jail and a $10,000 fine for not submitting to the draft.

John Sears told me to call Tom Evans, who promised to check things out with a young attorney at Nixon-Mudge who had succeeded in getting some other draft-eligible guys off the hook. But Evans didn't call back and each day was like the Chinese water torture, until I finally tracked him down.

"Oh, yes, well . . . " he said when I called him, "the fellow I had in mind, you know, the one who handled draft cases? I just found out: he's been drafted."

I was numb. "So what do you recommend I do?"

"Look, Ron," he answered, lapsing into a low baritone voice that nearly matched Nixon's, "if worst comes to worst you can enlist in the Marines and become part of the greatest fighting force the world has ever known."

I never knew whether Tom meant to be sarcastic or deadly serious (potentially literally so). In either case, the bottom line remained the same: I'm washing my hands of this and now it's your problem, kid.

On a chilly November morning I joined an unhappy, mostly African American crowd of young men milling uneasily outside a recruiting station in downtown D.C. A couple of buses delivered us to Fort Holabird, Maryland, for physical exams and intelligence tests. I handed the Air Force physician a letter from our family doctor attesting to knee damage from high school football.

The Air Force physician was recently inducted himself. "It's a close call," he murmured, examining my knee. "Do you want to go to Vietnam?"

"No," I replied. "Absolutely not."

I got a temporary deferment and joined the handful of those who boarded the buses for the return trip that afternoon. The others, a much larger group, could not leave the base: they were slated for induction. Some of them, profoundly angry and shouting curses, threw rocks at the vehicles as they pulled out of Fort Holabird. That visit to Fort Holabird convinced me it was time to return to Arizona and reclaim my status as a student—which I did, about three weeks after attending Richard Nixon's Christmas party a few days before the holiday.

It was snowing when I flew to New York and took a cab to Nixon's apartment building on Park Avenue. The elevator shot me up to the Old Man's floor—it seemed to be entirely taken up by his spacious, posh abode—and when the door slid open there he was, the candidate, sporting a brown smoking jacket and green tie.

"Oh, yes, Ron McCoy," he said, giving me a handshake. Nixon was renowned for memorizing facts about people he was about to meet. "Aren't you the one from Arizona?"

"Yes, that's right."

"You're doing the youth work." He smiled. "I've heard a lot about you, Ron."

"Well, I've heard a lot about you, too, Mr. Nixon."

Nixon regularly held a couple of Christmas bashes, and this was the one for the political operatives. Virtually the entire campaign staff attended, as did others who came aboard later. John Mitchell, Nixon's law partner, whose life collapsed a few years later when the president attempted to make him the fall guy for Watergate, appeared to be feeling no pain. He kept asking me why I was leaving and would I come back.

John Sears and I stood together in a corner. Sears muttered something about me going to the bathroom.

"No, perfectly all right, John," I replied. "I can wait."

"No, I mean you really ought to go to the bathroom," he said with a mischievous grin.

Weaving through the crowded apartment, I came to the bathroom door, opened it, and ducked inside. And there it was, a toilet the likes of which I had never seen before and have not seen since: a wicker throne that reminded me of an unfolding lotus and bore an uncanny resemblance to the magnificent chair Black Panther leader Huey Newton was photographed sitting in. In that picture, Newton was wearing a black leather jacket and black beret, with a rifle clasped in his right hand and a spear clutched in his left.

Go figure.

A couple of weeks after I left Washington, the Tet Offensive shattered Lyndon Johnson's presidency. At the end of March, Johnson announced he would not run again. After he stepped aside, Nixon won the GOP nomination and squared off against Vice President Hubert Humphrey, who bore the war's weight on his shoulders. During the fall 1968 campaign I made some speeches for Nixon in Arizona, stressing his stance in favor of ending the draft by creating a volunteer army, providing "a dividend" (as he called the beginnings of affirmative action) for those trapped in urban ghettos, and ending the Vietnam War with a "secret plan." Although my working experience in Washington left me somewhat skeptical, I still hoped—with what now seems an almost hopeless naïveté—that Nixon offered the best chance for working within The System.

Nixon won the election, and I stayed in school. After the election, I drifted farther and farther away from contact with my former associates in the Nixon campaign. The university campus was heavily charged with the atmosphere of nearly apocalyptic transformation, rampant with societal change, heady with possibilities, increasingly radicalized and more and more falling under the watchful eye of the government's illegal domestic intelligence activities. It was a restless, confrontational time. There was a good fight ahead and it was worth fighting. It was as if the barricades beckoned to many of us, with our attitude of "If not now, when?" The Nixon answer to Vietnam was "Vietnamization," the gradual drawing down of American forces. During that torturously slow process nearly half of all the Americans who died in Vietnam were killed. My days under the GOP's elephant logo came to an end. There was simply nothing left for me and my former associates to talk about.

A year and a half later, in the spring of 1970, Nixon ordered the invasion of Cambodia and all hell broke loose on college campuses across the nation. In early May the Ohio National Guard shot students dead at Kent State University, and a few days later police and state troopers at Jackson State College in Mississippi killed more students.

I was the student body president at Arizona State University in the aftermath, when three federal Justice Department lawyers visited the campus. As we sat in my office, it occurred to me that the four of us lived in different worlds. Shorthaired, they sat there primly, swathed in coats and choked by ties, models of icy lawyerly dispassion. My hair was long, I wore the college radical's uniform: blue work shirt, jeans, and sandals. Their leader, his face dominated by massive glasses that seemed oddly askew and desperately in need of straightening, repeatedly pursed his lips and maintained that he and his colleagues were there to "improve communications" between students and the government. He seemed to believe that all the tension, anger, confusion, and violence triggered by the war and systemic problems in American society could be diffused by talk, talk, and more talk.

We chatted a few minutes, maintaining a somewhat amiable distance, until the subject turned to politics. The spokesman asked me what I thought of the Nixon administration.

"Well, I used to work for Nixon," I explained. "I don't think there's a sincere bone in his body. As for the White House staff, they're cold, cut off from people, concerned only with kissing The Boss's ass."

"But don't you see that the source of the disagreement you people have with us is simply a matter of differing opinions?" he asked.

You people?

"Sure," I replied, "but can't you see that some people are driven practically out of their minds differing with you guys?"

"How so?" he inquired, sitting back, slowly moving his head back and elongating his words as if trying to impersonate conservative pundit William F. Buckley.

"It's your attitude," I explained.

"Yeah," he agreed. "But you'll be in one of these days."

In other words, you do what you want when you're in a position of power; those on the outside should wait until it's their turn. So much for the utility of improved communications. When I look back on the Justice Department lawyer's remarks I see them as the coda for any ideas I might still have retained about working within The System.

By the way, the sage with whom I engaged in this nonproductive discussion was William Rehnquist. About a year later, Nixon appointed him to the United States Supreme Court; fifteen years after that, Ronald Reagan made him Chief Justice of the United States, a position he held until his death in 2005.

At Christmas time, 1970, families of Arizona servicemen listed as Prisoners Of War and Missing In Action (POW and MIA) in the Vietnam War sent me to Paris along with a local television executive and commentator and the most recent Democratic candidate for Arizona governor. By then, I was speaking out regularly at anti-war demonstrations (while my brother served with the Air Force in Vietnam). These desperate families gambled that an anti-war student might have some luck learning about their missing loved ones from representatives of the North Vietnamese government and the National Liberation Front, the Viet Cong's political wing. But our hopes never panned out, and our mission was unsuccessful.

I might have been working within The System, but I was doing my best to rattle it in ongoing fights with Eugene Pulliam, ultraconservative owner of *The Arizona Republic* (the state's largest newspaper) and Jack Williams, Arizona's retro governor, who told me he would rather have students shot than lower the flag in memory of those killed at Kent State.

The sun was rising one morning in the spring of 1971 when I returned to my apartment in Tempe after spending the evening with friends. As I entered the apartment, I felt uneasy—I'd left the lights off, but now they were on. Something else seemed wrong, but I wasn't sure exactly what. Then I saw it: a hole, big enough to put a hand through, cut in one of the windows. Carefully done, it was obviously the work of someone who knew what they were doing. My desk drawers lay on the floor and papers were scattered everywhere. Bills, cancelled checks, letters, memos and notes. I'd been getting ready to take a trip and left $300 in cash—equivalent to more than $1500 today—in plain sight on a table in the middle of the room. Oddly, it was still there. Whoever burglarized my apartment rifled through my papers and ignored the money. That did not fit my understanding of the standard burglar profile. I'll probably never know what that was about. But then, more so later, I started wondering just how deep some of my former colleagues' efforts to gather intelligence on people with whom they disagreed really ran.

To say that the Sixties began on January 1, 1960 and ended on December 31, 1969 is just a matter of dates and calendars. When it comes to *zeitgeist*, the Sixties—like the Renaissance, Reformation, Gilded Age, the Twenties, Great Depression, World War II, and the Fifties—commenced and concluded at different times for different people. The Sixties didn't start winding down for me until August 8, 1974, the day Richard Nixon resigned the presidency in disgrace. Nearly four decades have passed since I went to work for him in the summer of 1967, and I still ask myself: Just what in the hell was I thinking about?

I hoped to help develop a political career of my own. I also believed it might be possible to bring about positive changes in this country by working within The System. I operated less from an ideological perspective than from a sense of what was good and what was bad, what was right and what was wrong.

In 1967, when I started working for Nixon, the first microwave ovens appeared. The first heart transplant took place. The *Jimi Hendrix Experience* was introduced to America at the Monterey Pop Festival. The Green Bay Packers defeated the Kansas City Chiefs in Super Bowl I. Thurgood Marshall became the first African American nominated to the Supreme Court. Woody Guthrie, Carl Sandberg, and Langston Hughes died. Harry Connick, Jr., Nicole Kidman, Laura Dern, Mira Sorvino, Julia Roberts, Kurt Cobain, and Moon Unit Zappa were born. Martin Luther King, Jr., labeled the U.S. "the greatest purveyor of violence in the world." Nearly half a million young Americans served in Vietnam, and scores of our cities served as battlegrounds for devastating race riots.

In order to see Nixon as he was seen in 1967, one must erase all memories of him unleashing his vice president Spiro Agnew (whose own hubris had its eventual reckoning) on the opposition. One must remember that Nixon campaigned as an anti-war candidate, but one would also have to forget about the unimaginable tragedy of the Vietnam War—in which nearly half the Americans who died did so on Richard Nixon's four-and-a-half year watch. Forget, also, the "secret" bombing of Cambodia, the 1970 U.S. invasion of that nation, and the killings at Kent and Jackson States. And, of course, there's the matter of Watergate. You'd have to forget a lot to see Nixon as he was seen in 1967.

It's almost embarrassingly easy today to look back on Nixon's life and perceive the all but inevitable course of its arc. Few today experience much difficulty discerning about that life the gaping maw of a psychic black hole, home for monumental personal failings that contributed so much to such a stunning, tail spinning denouement. (Pressed about the illegalities with which his name will always be associated, Nixon told an interviewer, "Well, when the president does it that means that it is not illegal.") Watergate and a tarnishing of the presidential office few of his successors have done much to burnish—all that lay in the future.

Working for Richard Nixon did not rob me of idealism. But I learned that "working within The System" is reminiscent of the old saw about a fellow who's advised he shouldn't get into a card game because it's crooked. "Yeah," he replies, "but it's the only game in town."

I leave the final words to Nixon. They are revealing words, spoken to his staff on August 9, 1974, as he prepared to leave the White House and go into exile. It's a pity they didn't come to him earlier: "Always give your best. Never get discouraged. Never be petty. Always remember, others may hate you, but those who hate you don't win unless you hate them, and then you destroy yourself."

QUESTIONS FOR DISCUSSION

1. What specifically motivated Ron McCoy, at the age of 19, to work for the election of Richard Nixon? Would you say McCoy, who describes himself as a naïve idealist, was a progressive or a conservative Republican at the time? Does it seem to you that he was or was not ever a true conservative?

2. How would you describe the political maneuvering and interpersonal dynamics at Nixon's campaign headquarters in Washington, D.C.? What kind of politics do you feel Nixon's staff members represent? Compare the Republican Party leaders you meet in this story to Barry Goldwater and the young Republicans portrayed in Robert Poole's story. Do they have any ideas or beliefs in common?

3. Richard Nixon appears in person only once in this story, yet we learn a great deal about him from McCoy's encounters with his supporters. Has McCoy's story changed or expanded your perception of Nixon in any way? Where would you place Nixon on the Sixties-era political spectrum between radical and conservative?

4. McCoy's tone is frequently ironic. How does this tone help or hinder your understanding of his personal and political development while in Washington?

5. What makes McCoy finally change his mind about working for Richard Nixon? Is it a single event or a set of circumstances? What does he do instead? What has the Nixon campaign lost in the defection of somebody like McCoy? Why does McCoy turn down his chance to rejoin what he calls "The System?"

6. McCoy is telling his own story here but he is also a working, professional historian. What aspects of this piece demonstrate his concerns to communicate the larger historical context of his memoir?

WAR ON DRUGS, 1971–1978: A VIEW FROM THE TRENCHES

Gerald J. Scott

Washington D.C.'s cherry trees were spectacular in the spring of 1971. As I stood beneath this living peace symbol, absorbing the sight and scent of countless blossoms, the bloody war in Vietnam seemed infinitely more than half a world away. Focusing on the fiery caldera of racial and political civil war which had begun erupting through America's thinning cultural crust with increasing frequency over the past decade was equally impossible in the presence of such beauty.

Or at least that's the way it seemed. Reality was far more complex. Reality was my being in Washington that spring as a member of the Bureau of Narcotics and Dangerous Drugs Basic Agent Class 16. We were being readied—as our instructors constantly reminded us—to become front-line troops in a war that was costing many times more American lives than was Vietnam. We would fight this war armed with only a badge, a handgun and our wits. For most of us, the battleground would be within the borders of the United States.

Under both the best and worst definitions of the term, BNDD Class 16 was a "pride" of America's fiercest young lions. Although we varied in size, color, intelligence and cultural background, each of us believed in his or her invincibility. That a few of us would die and that many of us would be physically or emotionally crippled was, to us, absurd.

Even in retrospect, I believe we received the best training possible. In the gym, a rugged physical exercise program hardened our muscles and provided a sense of discipline. On the range, we practiced with handguns, shotguns, and submachine guns. In the classroom, we covered subjects designed to make us experts on developing prosecutable cases under the new Controlled Substances Act, which was to take effect a few days before we graduated. Then, armed with cap guns, we practiced what we'd learned through role playing exercises conducted on the streets of Washington.

I was in excellent physical condition and an expert marksman when I arrived in Washington. On the other hand, federal law enforcement was a brand new world. I was very determined to absorb everything the classroom instructors presented. Nevertheless, as the weeks went by, I became more and more convinced that this particular type of police work could only be learned beyond the walls of the training center, out in that ephemeral world called "the street."

As it turned out, the streets of Washington D.C. had something to teach us before we had received our badges and pistols. Thousands of young men and women gathered in Washington in the spring of 1971 to protest the Vietnam War. Whether we agreed with their politics or not—and more than a few of us did—my compatriots and I could see that the protestors, like ourselves, were people who were ready to step up and take risks for what they believed was right.

Furthermore, we understood that their jeans, medallions, and sandals were a uniform worn with as much pride as any soldier's or police officer's. We, of course, wouldn't be wearing clothing that could identify our profession once we reached our duty stations. However, while the protestors were in town, we were ordered to dress in suits and ties whenever we were outside of our hotel. One morning soon after this order was issued, several of us were standing on Thomas Circle, waiting for the light to change. We were joined by a man about our age. His hair was shoulder-length, and he was wearing jeans and a sleeveless sweatshirt.

Suddenly, three marked police cars slid to a stop in front us, blocking all avenues of escape. Uniformed officers grabbed the young man and roughly forced him into one of the cars. They then sped away, presumably to deliver their prize to a sports stadium that had been pressed into service as a detention center. Breaking the shocked silence that followed, one of my classmates said, "My God, what have we signed up for?"

That question—and the memory of the stark terror in the young man's eyes— was unsettling to me personally. My father, a World War II veteran, a lifelong Democrat and a true patriot by any definition of the term, had begun marching in anti-war demonstrations during the Johnson administration. He had no intention of being part of Nixon's "silent majority" after the 1968 elections. I wondered if that decision would earn him a ride in a police car some day.

The thought terrified me, because in a way I would have been responsible. Dad had assured me that if I decided to move to Canada to avoid the draft, he and my mother would go with me. I had no such powerful feelings either for or against the war. However, Dad's passion led me to alter my plans to become a pilot in the Air Force in favor of serving my country in civilian law enforcement.

I reported to BNDD's Kansas City Regional Office in early June 1971. The first morning, I stood before a federal judge and took the appropriate variation of the same oath taken by every federal officer from the president on down. In it, I swore to defend the "Constitution of the United States against all enemies foreign and domestic." I'm not the least bit ashamed to admit that I was awed by the sheer enormity of my promise to uphold the entire Constitution—not just those parts I liked or those parts that didn't hinder my duties as a Special Agent.

Call my reaction naïve if you must, but that oath meant something to me then and it still does today. As a direct result, I'm very proud to say that all of my investigations were conducted within the boundaries set by the law. What's more, the subjects of my investigations were treated with as much human dignity as they themselves would allow. Did it work? I was the lead agent in dozens of cases over an eight-year span, but I've never heard a jury say, "Not guilty."

Remember my theory that undercover police work could only be learned on the street? In the 1960s and '70s, each Special Agent was expected to initiate and develop his own investigations. More often than not, the agent first learned about the existence of the subject drug trafficking organization from a confidential informant (CI). Experienced agents obtained the CI for their next case from among the defendants in their last case. But how could a new agent find that all-important first CI?

For me, the answer was the Kansas City Missouri Police Department's Special Weapons and Tactics Unit (SWAT.) I wasn't privy to the negotiations between my Group Supervisor and the SWAT commanding officer, but the result

FIGURE 4.4 Agents of the federal Drug Enforcement Administration (DEA) display packets of cocaine seized in a raid on a drug ring in New York City. The DEA was created by executive order in 1973 to consolidate all federal drug control agencies and bureaus under a single command in the Department of Justice. Raids such as the one whose aftermath is depicted here took months of preparation and the work of many undercover agents, who often risked their lives gathering information that could lead to arrests. Long hair and casual clothing on some of the officers pictured here suggest that they may have been undercover agents.

Source: AP Wide World Photos

was a 20-something "speed freak" (amphetamine addict) named Billy. Let the record reflect that Billy and I were equally convinced that the other would be the cause of his death.

My assignment was to penetrate a group of burglars and strong-arm robbers on Kansas City's east side. Among many other crimes, this group robbed pharmacies in small towns within a 200-mile radius of Kansas City in order to augment their sales of marijuana, heroin, cocaine and amphetamines. Billy's description of the group made them sound like the "real deal," a supposition that was confirmed by several SWAT officers.

The time had come for me to play "cops and robbers" with real bullets, but that didn't worry me nearly as much as did the fact I'd be driving a 4-door Chevrolet that couldn't have looked more like a cop's car if it had a light bar. My Group Supervisor drove a new Dodge Charger. When I asked to borrow the vehicle for use during my first undercover buy, he refused, but added, "Show me you can be an undercover agent in your car, and I'll assign mine to you permanently."

An experienced agent had warned me that Kansas City's drug dealers thought that anybody new they saw with a revolver had to be a cop, despite the fact that many of them carried revolvers themselves. For my undercover debut, I traded my issue .38 special for a 9 mm semi-auto Walther PPK. Not only was it easy to conceal inside my waistband, but it was the same type of pistol James Bond favored.

I'll bet James Bond never had an experience like mine. Billy's story that I'd stolen the car I was driving got us inside Big Bubba's front door. As we engaged in the criminal version of small talk, my confidence rose with each passing moment. This man whose life and livelihood depended on his ability to sense danger obviously believed I was one of the good (bad?) guys.

Billy was dismissed to the back of the house, and Big Bubba and I stood up to "take care of business." It was then I felt the Walther begin to slip down my pant leg. It hit the wood floor with a clunk that was heard in New York City. I bent down, picked it up and mumbled some incoherent something about needing protection from other people, not Big Bubba.

He laughed and said, "Don't ever apologize for protecting yourself, but if you're going to carry a gun, carry a gun." Then he reached under his sweatshirt and produced the biggest handgun I'd ever seen. Big Bubba showed me how he wrapped several rubber bands around its grip. This, he explained, provided enough friction to keep the weapon from sliding down his pant leg as mine had.

Big Bubba sold me the drugs I wanted. I collected Billy and drove away from the house, confident I'd learned my lesson for the day. It was about then that the car behind me turned on its red lights. A few seconds later, Billy and I were unceremoniously removed from the car and had "assumed the position" with our hands on the car's roof and our legs spread.

I recognized the plainclothes officers as SWAT members I'd met earlier. Assuming they also recognized me I said I was green and I took my hands off the car and turned around. The next thing I knew I was on the ground ineffectively warding off a blizzard of kicks and blows. An eternity later (i.e. a few seconds), one of them heard me saying I was a cop, and I was pulled back to my feet.

It was then that purely by instinct I did something that opened the door into the strangely intertwined worlds of cop and crook. I said, "That was perfect. They were watching me leave, and what you did should have them convinced I'm on the level."

What I said was literally true. More important, the SWAT team knew I was really saying, "I know the beating was my fault, and everything's cool between us."

As a very broad general rule, a Special Agent's first undercover experience was cathartic. Most novice agents developed an instant determination to avoid repeating the experience. Conversely, a few became instant adrenalin junkies. I was one of the latter. The following morning, I marched into my Group Supervisor's office and, with a flourish, tossed the bag of amphetamines on his desk. Then, doing my best John Paul Jones imitation, I declared, "Now give me a fast ship, for I intend to sail in harm's way." I walked out with the keys to the Dodge in my pocket.

In the 1960s and '70s, "recreational" use of illegal drugs was relatively commonplace in all levels of society. Therefore, it was only natural that "civilians" (our term for anyone who was neither an agent nor a criminal) tended to have romanticized views of drug trafficking and of drug traffickers. Many, perhaps most, civilians believed drug trafficking was, at worst, a minor crime, and a few sincerely believed the war on drugs was a war on their civil liberties.

Meanwhile, those of us who worked undercover were sitting around tables with drug dealers who discussed murder, rape and torture with no more concern than a civilian would exhibit when planning next week's dinner party. The people we dealt with and had to pretend to be like cared about nothing except money and their own survival. They held drug users in contempt. Ironically, they were even more contemptuous of society in general, because it, however unwittingly, helped their businesses flourish.

Given the circumstances, it was only natural that those of us who sought to enforce the nation's drug laws were haunted by a sense of isolation. Most agents closed ranks and socialized only with other law enforcement officers and, occasionally, with CIs or even with criminals involved in crimes other than dealing drugs. The plain ugly truth was, in the '60s and '70s, many police officers felt their treatment by society left them with more in common with prostitutes than with the neighbors to whom they rarely spoke.

I tried to avoid that trap by developing civilian friendships, but my efforts were only partially successful even at first, and the gulf widened with time. There were many reasons why this was so. High among them was that, in my undercover world, everybody had guns, and everybody knew the rules of underworld etiquette. In the civilian world, my ever-present pistol was the unspoken "elephant in the corner," fueling the imaginations of one and all.

There's no more apropos descriptive phrase for undercover narcotics work than "the theater of the absurd." Obviously, no undercover agent can ever forget that he is a law enforcement officer doing his job, in this case gathering evidence of criminal activity. At the same time, he must immerse himself so completely in his undercover persona that his responses to any given situation are as immediate and as natural as his alter ego's should be. That sounds like an actor "getting into character," and it is. The only difference is perfection is the minimally accepted standard for each and every live performance, and there are no rehearsals.

Like most undercover agents of the period, my first undercover double was a long-haired, bearded petty criminal who dreamed the drug traffic would take him to the big time. The previously described rough beginning notwithstanding, "Tom" was a quick learner and was readily accepted by the criminal element.

The same could not be said for hotel desk clerks and maitre de's, and therein lay a potentially serious problem. To say I had little tolerance for insult was an understatement. In fact, a particularly snotty hotel desk clerk in New Orleans has no idea how slender the thread of his life became when he refused my new bride and me a room.

A couple of years later, Tom died, and "Joe" rose from his ashes. Joe was clean shaven except for the mustache, which made me bulletproof. He had his hair styled in an upscale salon patronized by many of the city's biggest cocaine importers and distributors. He dressed well, but not so well that he couldn't blend into a crowd if he so desired. Joe never made overt threats or boasts, but everyone he met instantly recognized that death lurked behind his eyes.

Petty drug dealers often robbed and murdered each other for no reason, but professional traffickers fully expected both the amount and quality of the drugs sold and the amount of money paid to be "right" every time. "Rip-offs" (robberies) at the professional level were rare, primarily because punishment for shorting either buyer or seller was swift and severe. Joe's constantly honed persona, which was aided by input from numerous CIs, was that of a man who was willing and able to "take care of business" in both senses of the term. As such, he became a trusted member of drug rings whose reach stretched from Kansas and Missouri to Illinois, California, and Mexico.

At this point I want to stress that I had a very supportive wife, two children, and several civilian friends. I also attended church regularly. Despite all that, Joe's persona and personality inexorably began to overwhelm my own, until, by 1977, I wasn't completely sure whether I was Gerald pretending to be Joe or Joe pretending to be Gerald. It's impossible for anyone who hasn't "been there" to fully understand this phenomenon, but perhaps the following story, which I'll tell from Joe's perspective, will help illustrate how an agent with a splitting personality might react to a potentially dangerous undercover situation.

Joe had penetrated the lower level of an international cartel that was selling the purest heroin being found anywhere in the United States at that time. An infusion of cash from DEA headquarters allowed him to purchase drugs in large enough quantities to convince the cartel's next level of operation that he was a legitimate buyer.

A wiretap was the next logical step in the investigation, but the Kansas City Regional Office lacked the manpower resources to conduct one without outside assistance. Additional buys were put on hold while my supervisor negotiated with headquarters. Several weeks passed, and Joe finally won permission to make another substantial purchase to relieve the cartel's growing suspicions.

This group of traffickers was the most thoroughly professional Joe dealt with during his career. Drug transactions were completed in seconds at the exact pre-arranged time and place. If there were any problems with either the drugs or the money—which, up to now, there hadn't been—arrangements would have been made later to discuss the matter. This system worked, because the cartel demanded absolute trustworthiness of each of its members. Those who were worthy of that trust prospered. Those who weren't, were summarily executed.

Joe made the usual arrangements to coordinate the surveillance activities of his fellow agents and a number of local police officers. Joe then contacted his source, "Jim," and placed an order for four ounces of uncut heroin. Jim said he'd have to call his boss and would get back to Joe. About a half hour later—far longer than any previous order had taken—Jim called back and said he would sell Joe two ounces of heroin and three ounces of cocaine for the same price as four ounces of heroin. When Joe realized that further arguing would be pointless, he agreed to meet Jim at their regular spot (a public park) at 1:00 p.m.

Jim didn't show up at the appointed time and place. Surveillance agents advised that he had not left his residence. Joe called Jim, who agreed to meet at a different location in one hour. To this day, I don't know whether it was Joe or myself who took complete charge at this point. Both were convinced that the cartel intended to rob and probably kill Joe. Perhaps I still held sway and was determined to see the investigation to the end. Or perhaps Joe simply refused to allow this challenge to his hard-worn image to go unanswered.

In any event, Joe contacted a local police officer he knew he could trust. He told him about the change in location and about what he thought would happen there. He also gave him some instructions on what he wanted him and his fellow officers to do "when things get exciting."

Joe arrived at the location and backed his car up to a concrete wall at one end of the parking lot. Jim pulled into the lot a few minutes later and backed his car into the space on Joe's passenger side. Jim asked Joe to get into his car, which he did.

For the first time in their dealings together, Jim demanded to see and count the money before producing the drugs. After commenting, "What's the matter? Why don't you trust me all of a sudden?" Joe handed Jim a large roll of one hundred dollar bills.

Joe looked up while Jim was counting and saw a vehicle coming toward them across the parking lot. He immediately reached for his pistol. Jim noticed the gun just as it was clearing Joe's back. He screamed, "No! No! That's just Laura (Jim's number one hooker) bringing your stuff."

Laura pulled her car in front of Jim's and stopped. Joe told Jim to have Laura park on the opposite side of Joe's car and then get in the passenger's side of Joe's car with the drugs. Jim agreed. When Laura was in Joe's car, Joe looked Jim in the eye and said, "If something's not right here, give me my money back, and we'll start fresh tomorrow. If I get in my car and find out the drugs are turkey (not real) or if you start your engine before I tell you to, I'll kill you both."

Jim returned my look with an equally steady gaze and said, "I understand."

This story has a happy ending. The drugs were just as advertised, and all three of us left the parking lot alive and well. The next day, I called Jim and admitted that I was afraid he intended to rip me off. He replied that his boss had thought that I was a cop, but after Jim told him what had happened in the parking lot, he didn't think so now.

Obviously, no one can sustain that level of tension indefinitely. Every once in a while, I couldn't resist trying to inject a little humor into the danger. Here's an example.

At the conclusion of a major investigation, standard operating procedure called for serving all of the arrest and/or search warrants as close to simultaneously as possible. Warrants were passed out to every streetwise agent regardless of his previous participation in the investigation or lack thereof.

On one such occasion, I was handed several warrants, among which was one for Martin—a.k.a. "Inky"—Fountaine. Inky didn't just think he was tough; he really was tough. Half of his 40 years had been spent in prison for crimes up to and including shooting a police officer. The word on the street was that he'd "go down shooting" before letting himself be arrested again. Lucky me.

The street address printed on the warrant didn't make me feel any better. It was a nearly new multistory apartment building with solid doors and narrow hallways. Worse yet, Inky's apartment was at the end of the hall, making providing cover for an arrest team impossible.

The teams of DEA agents and local police officers were to begin making arrests at 5:30 a.m., and putting Inky's warrant on top of my stack was a no-brainer. However, to this day I have no idea why I decided finding a funny way to arrest Inky was the thing to do. I do know that my plot was fully developed by the time my fellow officers and I arrived at Inky's door.

I held my index finger to my lips to signal my desire for complete silence, and then motioned one officer to each side of the hallway about six feet away from the door. I drew my Colt .45 semi-auto, knocked fairly softly on the door and then placed my left thumb over the peephole. After a second series of knocks, I heard Inky on the other side of the door. I then mumbled a few deliberately unintelligible words I hoped would be interpreted as an acquaintance asking for admittance.

As I had hoped, the fact that he couldn't see through his door's peephole didn't register on Inky's sleep-befuddled brain. He opened the door just far enough to stick his head out into the hall. I shoved the barrel of the .45 under his chin, snapped off the safety and said, "Guess who?"

Except for his eyes, which rolled down to stare at my finger on the half-depressed trigger, Inky froze. After a few seconds, he croaked, "I sure hope you the police."

Talk about an ice breaker! I laughed. Then the two officers laughed. Finally, Inky began laughing. I removed my pistol from his Adam's apple—although its muzzle never strayed from Inky's torso—and all four of us entered the apartment. Inky and I sat down in the living room, while the two officers conducted a quick search for other occupants, visible weapons, drugs, etc. One of them brought Inky some clothes.

"Man, you one cold dude," Inky said wryly. "I got a whole shitload of guns in here, and you never gave me a chance to do nothin'. You never said who you was neither."

"Maybe not," I replied. "But you guessed on the very first try. Besides now we've both got a great story to tell, and we're both alive to tell it."

To his credit, Inky did tell it. The war between Kansas City's mostly white narcs and mostly black heroin dealers went on apace, make no mistake about that. Even so, I'd like to think that the incident helped build our side's street reputation and thus reduced the danger we faced for some—albeit brief—moment in time.

So why would anyone, in particular me, decide to leave a job which made him a 20th century badge-toting gunslinger? I'm not sure I can explain it fully, but I'll try.

The "official answer" I give most people is I was unwilling to accept the soon-to-be-inevitable transfer to a larger metropolitan area. In addition, while I truly loved police work, I loathed intra- and inter-office politics. It was easy to see that not only did political talent outweigh police talent, but that the higher one rose in the organization, the more time he must devote to politics.

The official answer is true enough, but it isn't the real answer. I loved my wife and children, and I could see that no matter how hard we tried to avoid it, me being a drug agent would eventually drive us apart. For me, choosing my family over my career wasn't all that difficult.

Finally, I was becoming increasing afraid that I would become Joe. Not that Joe's utter lack of feeling for anyone, including himself, wasn't tempting at times, because it was. But I didn't want to live that way, and I knew of no other way to survive in either the drug world or the drug enforcement world.

So after eight years, seven years longer than most soldiers spent in Vietnam and four years longer than my father fought in WWII, I returned to civilian life. Except for nightmares and occasional flashbacks, I thought I had beaten the game. Then, on September 25, 1999, my mental world came apart. I'm still under treatment for post-traumatic stress and may be for the rest of my life. As I told my doctor, "I wouldn't have put my head so deeply into the lion's mouth, if I had known he could bite so hard so many years later."

QUESTIONS FOR DISCUSSION

1. Gerald Scott chooses to become an agent in the BNDD in preference to joining the U.S. Air Force in 1971. What factors contribute to his decision? Does he give any clues to his own feelings about the Vietnam War?

2. What does undercover life do to Scott? How does it affect his friendships, his family life, his daily interactions, and his sanity? Why does he fear that he will become Joe? Do you think he feels proud of his service? If you had to guess, what would you say is Scott's own attitude about drug use?

3. Do you think Scott's life was exciting? How does his story compare to the law-enforcement dramas that are so popular in the movies and on television? What is your opinion of today's "War on Drugs?" What is your opinion of the way that "war" is depicted in the media?

4. Scott tells his story in a series of vignettes. Wayne Coe, the Vietnam helicopter pilot whose story appears in another section of this book, tells his story in a similar fashion. Compare the two stories of American "warriors" of the 1960s and 1970s. What do they have in common in terms of drama, self-presentation, and writing style? What are some crucial differences?

5. Why is a story about law enforcement located in a section of this book called "Conservative Currents?" Is law enforcement the responsibility of conservative elements in U.S. society? If so, what might be a broad definition of "conservatism"—one that reaches beyond political conservatism? What aspect of American life do you think the War on Drugs represents?

6. Compare Scott's version of the drug world he inhabits in the 1970s with the world of LSD users portrayed in James Fadiman's story of the mid-1960s, "Opening the Doors of Perception," in another section of this book. Have the social and legal attitudes toward drug use changed in the course of a decade or so? Or is it the drugs and the consumers that have changed?

5

Landmark Events

Introduction

Our collective memory of the Sixties era tends to focus on dramatic episodes or events: the assassination of John Fitzgerald Kennedy; the 1963 March on Washington; the 1965 March on Selma, Alabama; race riots in major cities; the Chicago Democratic Convention; the assassinations of Martin Luther King, Jr., and Robert F. Kennedy; the My Lai massacre; or the Kent State and Jackson State shootings. Violent episodes, in particular, seem to have a way of clinging to our historical imagination. So, too, do moments of great triumph—Martin Luther King's "I have a dream" speech in Washington, D.C., in 1963; students protesting on behalf of free speech in California in 1964; an outdoor music festival in 1969 that turned a rainy weekend into an extended demonstration of fellowship and goodwill. In this section, we have included the stories of people directly involved in some of these events. We asked our storytellers to convey what it felt like to be inside a landmark event in history.

The middle years of the 1960s witnessed a series of destructive riots in the country's largest cities. Almost all the disturbances took place during the summer months, when temperatures were hot and tempers short. At base, the cause of the riots—or rebellions, as some historians have come to call them—was racism and poverty. The spark that set them off was usually a racially charged incident, perhaps an accusation that a white police officer or business owner had mistreated or brutalized a black person. Local residents took to the streets of their decaying inner-city

315

neighborhoods, shouting and throwing bricks and bottles, firing guns, and clashing with local, state, and federal law enforcement. Arsonists and looters targeted specific businesses for destruction and pillage, usually those owned by nonresident whites. Most urban rebellions lasted several days, and some went on for more than a week, with the worst rioting occurring at night. In the most serious disturbances, local officials called in state and national guards to help restore order. Damage estimates were in millions of dollars; whole blocks burned or were rendered uninhabitable. Many people were injured and, in almost every riot, people died.

There were hundreds of riots in a five-year period between 1965 and 1970; in 1967 alone, there were 164 eruptions in 128 U.S. cities. Some of the worst rioting took place in Watts, a predominantly black section of Los Angeles, where, after six days of street violence in August 1965, more than 34 people had died, at least 1,000 were injured, 600 buildings were damaged or destroyed, and an estimated $200 million in property was lost. As many as 10,000 people may have taken part in the rebellion, which required thousands of National Guardsmen, county deputies, and city police to quell. In 1967, the streets of Newark, New Jersey, and Detroit, Michigan, erupted, leaving 66 people dead and nearly 2,000 injured. More than 8,500 suspected rioters were arrested.

The political, economic, and social factors contributing to the disturbances in Los Angeles, Newark, and Detroit, as well as those in Cleveland, Chicago, and many other places, were remarkably consistent. They included police brutality, political exclusion of African Americans from city government, inadequate housing (partly caused by urban renewal projects), and unemployment, as well as racism and poverty. Prior to the "Long Hot Summers," as the violent seasons were called, the race riots of 1919 had been the worst period of urban unrest in U.S. history. Historians believe the disturbances of the 1960s had their roots in the 1950s, when many whites left the inner cites of the North and West for life in the suburbs, and industries also relocated outside major urban areas, taking the jobs with them. Suburbs routinely blocked residential access for African Americans; even middle-class professionals who could afford to buy houses were excluded by racist real estate practices that prevailed all over the country. That left the inner cities to African Americans and other nonwhite minorities. Jobs were scarce, and, over the years, city officials invested fewer and fewer dollars in maintaining the infrastructure (streets, housing, schools, businesses, public transportation) of the urban neighborhoods. While the rest of the country was enjoying unprecedented prosperity in the 1960s, young black job seekers became demoralized by the racial discrimination that ruled their lives and limited their opportunities in northern cities. Their boredom and despair turned to anger.

It was obvious to most Americans that the Civil Rights Movement was making progress in ending legal segregation in the South. But poverty and *de facto* segregation in northern and western cities seemed permanently entrenched. In Watts, for example, where the 1965 riot took place, there was 30 percent unemployment and 60 percent of the people were surviving on public assistance. Throughout the mid-1960s, as part of the War on Poverty, the Johnson administration attempted to address the problems by establishing programs specifically geared to help inner city dwellers. The programs included the Community Action Program (CAP), 1964; the

Housing and Urban Development Act, 1965; and the Model Cities Program, 1966. In many cities, however, these programs faltered because they were under-funded. In other places, federally funded programs ran into conflict with mayors and local officials, who feared they were going to lose control of their cities. Saddest of all, the federal programs may have been inadequate to address deep-seated, longstanding problems. When Richard Nixon took office in 1969, he declared the programs a failure and moved federal funds into block grants for states and cities. Block grants returned fiscal control to mayors, governors, and (mostly white) state legislatures.

Urban riots continued into the 1970s and have arisen sporadically ever since. American cities underwent a partial renaissance when wealthy young white professionals began moving back in during the 1980s, but many cities still contain depressed areas. Television coverage of Hurricane Katrina, which devastated New Orleans in 2005, made it clear that poor neighborhoods are very much a part of American urban life today.

A different kind of uprising took place at the Democratic Party Convention in Chicago in August of 1968, when crowds of anti-Vietnam War protestors surged through the city's streets and parks, attempting to influence convention delegates and hoping to bring about the selection of an anti-war candidate for president. Many remember the three days of chaos as a "police riot" because so much of the news coverage depicted Chicago police clubbing and tear gassing unarmed protestors.

When President Johnson announced at the end of March 1968 that he would not run for reelection, the front-runners for the Democratic presidential nomination became Robert Kennedy and Minnesota senator Eugene McCarthy, who were opposed to the war in Vietnam and wanted to end it. Hubert Humphrey, a traditional Democrat then serving as vice president, became the candidate pledged to continue both Johnson's domestic programs and the war. Outraged by the country's deepening involvement in Vietnam after the Tet Offensive, the student anti-war movement went into high gear. In the spring, campuses around the country erupted in strikes. Students became increasingly militant, occupying buildings or blocking access to them, damaging files and property, and hurling insults at administrators. Their strikes were usually multi-issue, demanding that the government end the Vietnam War and bring about racial justice at home. Students also railed against their own universities, angered about university investments in companies that made napalm and other deadly weapons. Some striking students demanded that the universities establish black studies programs and scholarships for underserved youth. Students around the world staged demonstrations as well, protesting the policies of their own nations and universities, but also demanding American withdrawal from Vietnam. In France, student demonstrations led to a general strike throughout the country.

The assassination of Martin Luther King, Jr., on April 4, touched off urban rebellions all over the country, reminding everyone that progress on racial matters had slowed down after the mid-1960s. In June, Robert Kennedy was killed, also by an assassin. The two deaths were heartbreaking disappointments for millions of young Americans. The Democratic nominating convention would have to choose between Hubert Humphrey and Eugene McCarthy. Members of a nonviolent organization, the National Mobilization to End the War in Vietnam (nicknamed "MOBE"), along with members of Students for a Democratic Society (SDS) and a newer left-wing group, the Youth International Party (or "Yippies"), began making plans for massive anti-war demonstrations at the August convention, inviting participants to join from all over the country. Founded by Abbie Hoffman and Jerry Rubin, the Yippies were highly theatrical and confrontational free speech and anti-war activists. They promised to stage a "Festival of Life," to contrast with the "Convention of Death" that they expected to see in Chicago. They threatened Chicago's Mayor Daley with their plans for outrageous mischief. Daley responded by refusing all protest or marching permits and forbade any camping in Chicago's parks.

The protestors began to converge on Chicago the weekend before the convention. The Yippies introduced their own candidate for president, "Pigasus," an enormous live pig. Thousands of protestors staked out Grant Park and Lincoln Park, despite the ban. When the convention started, on Monday, August 26, supporters of Eugene McCarthy failed in their attempt to insert a peace plank in the party's platform. The Democratic Party was bitterly divided over the war. In the streets, Yippies and other protestors with signs opposing the war, racism, and Hubert Humphrey's nomination encountered brutal repression, as police openly attacked them with clubs. The worst attacks came on Wednesday the 28th, after the convention nominated Hubert Humphrey on the first ballot. A peaceful rally, followed by an attempt to march to the convention center, met frenzied police and Illinois National Guardsmen, who indiscriminately clubbed and maced marchers, tourists, bystanders, and even convention delegates. Television cameras caught it all.

The arrest count for the entire convention week was 668. Hundreds of demonstrators sustained injuries. The level of violence brought to bear against unarmed citizens shocked many Americans. However, the majority of U.S. citizens did not sympathize with the protestors. Frightened by the increasing level of militancy and disorder in the country, and reluctant to fully condemn a war in which American men were dying, many sympathized with those who wanted to maintain order.

In the aftermath of the convention, eight of the protest leaders, including Hoffman and Rubin, SDS leader Tom Hayden, and Black Panther leader Bobby Seale, were charged with conspiracy to cross state lines "with the intent to incite, organize, promote, encourage, participate in, and carry out a riot." They became the notorious "Chicago Eight" (later, seven; Seale had been chained and gagged in the courtroom because the judge's order because the judge felt his attempts to defend himself were disruptive, and he was subsequently tried separately). The trials and appeals of the Chicago Seven were a national spectacle. Eventually, all were acquitted of conspiracy charges. The courts did not convict any Chicago police for assaults during the protests.

A year after the Chicago Convention, Richard Nixon was president, and the war in Vietnam seemed no nearer to concluding than it had in the summer of 1968. More and more young people were angry about the war, and more and more were experimenting with the counterculture. Sometimes "politicos" and "hippies" were the same people, or at least they shared the same dress code and some of the same ideals. Almost all young Americans were deeply and enthusiastically attached to their generation's music.

Hoping to capitalize on youth's passion for rock concerts, four entrepreneurs in their twenties planned the largest outdoor rock festival of all time, scheduling it for

August 15–17, 1969. They decided that the upstate New York town of Woodstock, near the home of folk-rock star Bob Dylan, would be the perfect place. But there was no appropriate site in Woodstock, a well-known artists' colony. Instead, the entrepreneurs settled for the nearby town of Bethel, where they rented the use of a meadow shaped like a natural amphitheater from a farmer named Max Yasgur. The concert itself was called the Woodstock Music and Art Fair. The promoters advertised it all over the country with the carefully chosen slogan, "Three Days of Peace and Music," assuming that the word "peace" would link anti-war sentiment to the rock concert. They also reasoned that a slogan with "peace" in it would help keep order.

Woodstock's organizers planned to accommodate 100,000 concertgoers, who would camp out on the grounds and listen to music for three solid days. By offering huge fees, they enticed some of the best bands and vocalists of the decade, everyone from the famous Jefferson Airplane, the Grateful Dead, and The Who to blues artist Janis Joplin, folksinger Joan Baez, and guitarist Jimi Hendrix, who was the hottest act in the country in 1969. Bob Dylan had a prior commitment and did not attend. Crowd control was left to some very relaxed off-duty police officers—who tacitly agreed to ignore drug use—and to members of the Hog Farm, a New Mexico commune informally directed by a man named Hugh Romney, much better known as "Wavy Gravy." The Hog Farmers also helped construct fences and concession stands in advance of the concert. They prepared free food for thousands and ran a medical tent. Most importantly, the members of the Hog Farm set the tone for Woodstock. People behaved calmly and cooperatively, shared food and water with smiling generosity, and laughed at the rain and the mud—largely because that was the example set for them by the Hog Farmers.

The concert was more popular than anyone could have dreamed. The cars of more than 450,000 eager concertgoers overwhelmed the access highways, causing the biggest traffic jam in U.S. history. Most people arrived at the site after leaving their cars behind and walking several miles. The performers had to be delivered to the stage by helicopter. Crowds pressed so hard that fences came down and people surged past the ticket booths. Except for those who had bought the $18 tickets in advance, it became a free concert. Richie Havens opened the concert on Friday night and Jimi Hendrix closed it on Monday morning with a spine-tingling electric rendition of "The Star Spangled Banner." In between, concertgoers sat in the rain and the sun listening to music, slept rolled up in blankets and sleeping bags on the hillside, camped in the woods, went swimming nude in the pond, shared what food there was, and got high on drugs and wine. There were a few bad drug experiences, handled with care by medical staff and Hog Farmers, and there was at least one vehicle-related death.

As news reports filtered back to people in the world outside of Woodstock, many assumed that the concertgoers were having a miserable time, given the overcrowding, the lack of sanitation, and the rainy weather. But those who were there, and people who have written about the festival since then, remember much more vividly the spirit of camaraderie, the total absence of violence, and the disappearance of selfishness. Together, they had shared a great deal of discomfort and a great deal of enjoyment. Woodstock seemed to realize the promise of the counterculture; it was a demonstration of the possibilities of peace. For a moment, human community seemed attainable and, in the end, that seemed to matter more than the music, and certainly much more than the mud.

Peace, however, proved elusive to members of the Woodstock "nation" and to the rest of the country. An attempt to re-create the "vibration" failed miserably later that year, when members of the Hell's Angels motorcycle gang, who had been hired as a security force for a Rolling Stones concert at Altamont, California, near San Francisco, attacked concertgoers, stabbing one man to death.

Politically, little had changed. In late April of 1970, President Nixon announced that he had expanded the Vietnam War into Cambodia, an independent nation on Vietnam's western border. Nixon had promised during his election campaign two years earlier that he would end the war. Student protestors felt, if possible, more betrayed by the U.S. government than ever before. Angry demonstrations broke out on campuses all across the country, though most remained non-violent. On the campus of the University of Kansas, however, after a week of racial tension and vandalism in the surrounding community, arsonists set fire to the Student Union, causing extensive damage. Many students around the country focused their anger on campus branches of the Reserve Officers Training Corps (ROTC), which they felt was little more than a recruiting tool for the war machine.

At Kent State University in Ohio, anger against the war mounted in the first week of May, leading to rioting in the town streets of Kent and several attempts to burn down a campus building holding ROTC equipment. Outraged at the damage and the continued protests roiling the campus, the state's governor called in the Ohio National Guard. Troops occupied the campus and, at about midday on May 4th, responded to incessant student taunts with gunfire, killing four young people and wounding another nine. Ten days later, in Jackson, Mississippi, in an incident related to racial issues rather than anti-war protests, police fired into a dormitory at traditionally black Jackson State College, killing two students and wounding 12 others. The two incidents in which unarmed young Americans were shot by the country's own guardians horrified the nation.

The shootings intensified the polarization of sentiment about the war. Many colleges and universities, unable to cope with campus unrest, simply ended their spring semesters early, canceling final exams and urging everyone to go home. Some citizens interviewed at the time said they thought the Kent State and Jackson State students got what they deserved. In New York City, some 60,000 trade unionists wearing hard hats demonstrated in the streets in support of the president's war aims. They carried signs saying, "America—love it or leave it!" Both anti-war protestors and those who resented them claimed the mantle of patriotism.

Although the pro- and anti-war quarrel continued, critical opinion in the United States was powerfully affected by the shootings at Kent State and Jackson State. More and more people turned against the war in Vietnam. Polls taken in the fall of 1970 showed the war's approval rating had plummeted to below 35 percent. The country was nearly three years away from the official withdrawal of American troops from Vietnam, and more than four years from the fall of Saigon and the departure of the last remaining American soldiers, but May 1970 changed a lot of minds.

Pat Royse's story takes place during her years as a reporter for the *Cleveland Press* in the mid-1960s. Eager to tackle "real" news and avoid being stuck on the paper's women's page, Royse accepted an assignment to a newsbeat in Cleveland's Hough neighborhood. She came to know the neighborhood, its problems and personalities, the ministers of the local churches, and the people who ran the area's social service agencies. Among her friends were a dozen young men she called the "bench sitters." Largely unemployed, the "bench sitters" typified the lost black youth of America's inner cities of the period. But they liked and trusted Royse, a white woman, because she was young, nonjudgmental, and generous. The "bench sitters" gave Royse insights into neighborhood dynamics that lent a valuable perspective to her reporting. When the rioting started, Royse's long acquaintance with Hough and her contacts with people on the street enabled her to get inside the event in ways that made her coverage of the riot especially vivid and accurate. Royse's story, illustrated with quotations from her 1966 articles, makes it clear that she understood both the short- and long-term causes of the riot far better than either the mayor or her own boss, who headed a committee of dignitaries appointed to investigate it.

In the summer of 1968, Tara Collins Gordon was a graduate student in New York, pursuing her studies and trying to decide what she was supposed to do with her life, while also working actively in the anti-war movement. Concerned about her two younger brothers, Gordon enrolled in a draft counseling class so she could teach them how to avoid being drafted. At a Quaker counseling center, she met and became attracted to a young man who urged her to accompany him to the anti-war demonstration at the Chicago Democratic Convention in August. Even though she supported the protests planned for the convention, Gordon went to Chicago because her boyfriend was going, not because it was her idea. However, as she discovered when she arrived, she also wanted her voice to be heard. She was completely unprepared for the violence she met outside the convention center. Her anger—at the war, at the police violence, at her own powerlessness—was captured in a *Life* magazine photograph that has since become an iconic image of the Chicago riots.

In telling her story, Tara Collins Gordon is able to access her feelings from many decades ago and express them openly. She combines her personal history and identity struggles with the political issues of the time. In that sense, her story captures more than just the events at the Chicago Convention; it reflects the fullness of a single human experience within any historical episode; there is a self one brings to the event and a self one takes away from it. For Gordon, the trip to Chicago was life changing.

Sheila Lennon, a veteran of the Woodstock festival, is today an editor at the *Providence (RI) Journal.* In 1989, for the twentieth anniversary of Woodstock, she ran a notice in the *Journal,* asking other Rhode Island Woodstock veterans to contribute their memories of the event to a three-part feature article. The result is the story we have included here, the only previously published piece in this collection. The contributors' combined memories of getting to Woodstock, living outdoors for three days in the sun and rain, and listening to a rich variety of music provide a sustained narrative of the entire concert, highlighted with individual perspectives and commentary. Sheila Lennon's own words supply the background, linking everything together. On the whole, the memories of Woodstock in this story are positive. Most participants recalled the music and the performers with great clarity; many expressed astonishment at their own youthful tolerance of discomfort and the wide acceptance of nudity, eccentricity, and drug use they observed during the three-day concert. No one regretted having been there.

The Kent State shootings took place less than a year after Woodstock but seem a world away from that weekend of peace and music. Yet Carole Barbato and Laura Davis, who tell the Kent State story, could easily have been at Woodstock. That is to say that, like the kids from Rhode Island who went to the concert, Barbato and Davis were ordinary young Americans. Ordinary Americans do not expect to be shot at by their own soldiers while conducting a constitutionally protected demonstration on a college campus. After Kent State, many people were saying the war had come "home." For Barbato and Davis, it seemed like the end of ordinary life.

Barbato and Davis have chosen to structure their memoir in alternating paragraphs, as if swapping anecdotes. The life stories build from their conventional childhoods in the Midwest, punctuated by memories of landmark events from the 1950s and 1960s—Civil Rights marches, the Kennedy assassinations—to the time when they both enrolled at Kent State University and became involved in campus civil rights and anti-war activities. Campus culture of the period comes alive, complete with personalities. Step by step, we see how young people on college campuses became politically engaged, deepened their commitment, and moved on to higher risk activism. The story slows and becomes intensely focused as it describes the events that led up to May 4, 1970, and the shootings on the day itself. It unrolls into the aftermath of Kent State and raises questions that remain unsettled to this day.

Davis and Barbato are still at Kent State, though now as professors. Together they teach a course called "May 4, 1970, and Its Aftermath," which is a semester-long history of Sixties-era events leading up to the big event of May 4th and its legacy. Sometimes they invite one or another of the wounded survivors of the shootings to speak to their class.

FIRE IN THE STREETS
Pat Royse

In 1965, when the editors of the *Cleveland Press* assigned me to report on community news in Cleveland's poor, black inner city, I jumped at the chance. My motivations were not notably altruistic, although I did believe I might be able to do some good things there. My acceptance was mostly selfish. The assignment was my opportunity to get out of the women's department, where I had labored for most of the previous four years covering softer so-called "women's news" of school events, teen activities, PTAs, social events, and food. I had finally convinced those who made such decisions that I was both "tough" enough and a good enough reporter to handle city-side assignments. I think they were surprised that I took this one.

Journalism at the *Cleveland Press,* when I joined in the fall of 1961, was largely a man's world. Of the nearly ninety editorial staff members, only nine were women, and they were usually steered to the Women's Page department. Only one woman was a reporter on city desk assignment and, although she was exceptional at her job, her example had not prompted a rush to move women reporters to more significant beats.

So I was paying my dues in the women's department but had been pushing for a couple of years to move to the city room staff. I had argued that it was an issue of fairness.

Fairness was a factor in the way I approached my coverage of news in the poor, black communities of Hough and Central and the "moving up" community of Glenville. I believed it was unfair to judge people on the basis of race or religion or gender stereotypes, especially since I fell into one of those groups. I had signed petitions in college supporting the student sit-ins at five-and-dime lunch counters in the South and voting rights efforts and I was a charter member of a group supporting civil rights at Miami University in Oxford, Ohio. That group, a couple of years after I graduated, would send bus loads of students to register black voters in the South during Freedom Summer.

It didn't take long on the job, however, for me to learn it was going to take more than writing about unfair treatment for things in Cleveland's black ghetto to change. It was much more complex—the prejudice of whites was deep and the resulting social and economic problems that the prejudice created so pervasive that, 40 years later, we still have not solved it.

My job in 1965 through early 1967 was not to solve these problems but to cover and write about community news, which included reporting on meetings of the various neighborhood councils, writing features on kids' programs, stories on efforts to improve housing and job training, profiles on the dedicated folks working every day to try to make life more bearable in the slums, and covering a push by residents to control nascent gang growth and its resulting violence and mischief in Glenville.

I didn't do many stories on Glenville's young men between 16 and 22 years, a large number with no jobs, no skills, and no hope of a change anytime soon. They were not at the meetings I covered and didn't hang out at the neighborhood centers.

They fell though the cracks of most social programs and they would be the group most involved in the destruction wrought in the July 1966 race riot.

The black inner-city neighborhoods of Cleveland were all east of the Cuyahoga River, which divides the city into east and west segments. For the most part, Cleveland's numbered streets run north and south and named streets run east–west. The neighborhoods were colloquially named for the most-used streets that ran through them. Hough Avenue began at E. 55th Street and ran east until it ended at 101st Street at what was then Mt. Sinai Hospital and Rockefeller Park. The Hough neighborhood was roughly bounded by Euclid Avenue on the south, a distance ranging from three to nine blocks south of Hough Avenue. The northern boundaries were harder to pinpoint, but varied between 8 and 20 blocks north of Hough Avenue.

The so-called Central area was well south of the Hough area by a dozen blocks or so. In 1965, it began at E. 14th Street and extended east to E. 86th Street. The housing in the Central area was better the farther east on the avenue it was. The Central neighborhood closest to downtown was an area of manufacturing buildings, warehouses, and other industrial structures with poorer housing mixed in here or there. Central also had housing projects, with their adherent social problems. Cleveland did not have much of a hard drug problem, but when heroin was to be found, it was usually in the projects or near there. (In 1965, hard drugs meant heroin—this was before crack cocaine or designer drugs.) The poverty and poor housing in the Central area was enough of a concern to the federal government that they sent in VISTA (Volunteers in Service to America) workers, part of Lyndon Johnson's War on Poverty program, to help.

The Glenville area was northeast of Hough and had the most varied economic base of the three black areas. Some housing was poor, some was working class, and some was middle class. In places, the large homes around Rockefeller Park that had once belonged to industrialists, oil magnates, bankers, automobile builders, and assorted robber barons had been broken up into apartments. This area began south of the Lake Erie shoreline west of Rockefeller Park and ended near the eastern boundary of Cleveland. It extended about 30 blocks south of Glenville Avenue to an area near University Circle and the Italian neighborhood of Murray Hill, whose residents made no secret of not wanting blacks in their community or their schools.

As I began covering area council and assorted community meetings, I was surprised at the low expectations of community members. Leaders would be talking about discrimination on a lofty plain, and residents just wanted to be respected enough to get the garbage picked up every week and have the police respond quickly when they called. The lesson was: discussions, of which there were many, were fine, but what mattered were concrete results.

Covering my new beat, I got a tremendous boost through an accidental friendship with a varying group of street people who took up residence most days on a bench across the street from the Hough Opportunity Center, at 7612 Hough Ave. The Opportunity Center was a combined services organization supported by the Office of Economic Opportunity. When I first pulled my Chevrolet convertible into a parking space of the small lot next to the Center, someone on the bench called to me. "Hey, girl!" he said. I thought they were waiting to talk to someone inside the Center. I walked over to them and told them they couldn't call me girl unless I could call them boys. It never crossed my mind that maybe I should be afraid of them. They took it with good grace. I learned the bench-sitters were not waiting for anything particular. They were, in fact, passing around a wine bottle. They wanted to know what I was doing and why. I answered but asked questions of my own. After a bit, someone asked if I had enough money to pay for a McDonald's; they were hungry. I said, "No. I never carry cash much because I keep losing my purse." But I promised to bring them some sandwiches on Friday, which was my next payday. I did go by McDonald's Friday and carried a bag of cheeseburgers to the bench.

I believe it was the McDonald's and the fact that I kept my word that protected me and my soft-top car for the next year and a half of reporting on Hough. Eventually I got to know about a dozen of these young men. Most of them were not nice guys by everyday standards. I would learn, a little at a time over the year, that the bench-sitters were composed of a mugger, at least one wino, a sometime pimp, and a bank robber, among other things. But they had enough influence to put the word out on the street that I was okay—that the toughs were to leave me, a white outsider, and the car that I loved, alone. When the group eventually learned the *Cleveland Press* had some influence with City Hall, they would tip me to such things as upcoming housing inspections, or programs or people they thought were interesting. And they would feed me tales of police corruption that I could never prove.

In the year before the riots, I would also learn from my bench sitters just how much profound poverty limits life choices.

One of the original bench-sitters was a 23-year-old who had spent a couple of years in prison on an armed robbery charge. I talked to him once about his childhood. His family had been large and poor, he said. Sometimes there was not enough money for food or clothes that fit. The worst time, he said, was when one of his shoe strings broke and there was no money to buy a new pair. He traded off with his brother every other day; he went to school one day with shoes tied, and stayed home the next so his brother could go. (It was way before anyone could imagine untied sneakers as a fashion statement.) He was not surprised when he was caught in his bank robbery attempt. He said his hand was shaking so much, he was just glad he didn't kill anyone. In prison he learned to box and would have tried to fight professionally if he had been able to afford the training at the gym.

Another man was an artist who was earning some money teaching drawing and painting at Karamu House, a non-profit community arts and education center in the Central neighborhood. He talked once of his school days as a child. He never had breakfast, he said, and came home at noon for a lunch of corn flakes and milk nearly every day. He seemed surprised that I thought this unusual.

I had always classified myself as poor because, in my small town, middle class people owned houses. My parents did not own a house until I was out of college. I lived in eight different homes by the time I entered high school. But we always had food, and plenty of it, and we always had clothes and school supplies, a car to take us to school if we missed the bus, and a big Christmas with presents for all. I upgraded my own growing up status to lower-middle class after listening to many of the folks in Hough.

When I was doing a story on a children's program at the Bell Neighborhood Center off Hough Avenue at E. 81st Street, the director mentioned a grant he got from Case-Western Reserve University that had something to do with the number of times children's eyes would blink during certain activities. I asked the purpose of the study and he confessed that he was not remotely interested in the premise of the study. What he wanted was attention for his kids. They get so little, he said. Parents are so busy struggling to make ends meet, so tired when they get home, that they have little time to give to their children. Unless they have an extended family member, like a grandmother, who thinks they are terrific and praises their accomplishments, he said, these kids have little self-esteem and low expectations. They accept society's label.

I compared my own family situation to those. All of the Royse kids (there were five of us) were the center of our parents' lives. We all had different personalities but my mother, in particular, made each of us feel special. We all turned out pretty confident. So, at the age of seventeen, I had no qualms taking the $375 I had saved and the promise of a job in the dorm that paid for my room and board and going off to college. I expected to succeed and was sure it would work out.

Once when I asked someone in a story interview what success meant to him, he said, "We all want a house in the suburbs with a picket fence and a regular job that pays the bills." In a society that values a man by his job or financial success, it is particularly damning not to be able to get a job that pays the bills. Although not all men in Hough were without jobs, it was hard for those with no training, no education to speak of, no transportation, no clothes, and no interview presence to get a job. Cleveland was a union town and unions had to be pressured into opening their apprentice programs to blacks. In 1966, African Americans and sympathizers were still picketing construction sites downtown because there were no blacks in the union or on the job. Two years before, a white minister who lay down in front of a bulldozer was killed in one of those protests.

The resentment and frustration, prompted by job and poverty issues in particular, erupted in Cleveland's poor neighborhoods on the hot Monday night of July 18, 1966, and went on for four days. The riot was not unexpected by anyone in Cleveland who had thought it through. There were plenty of warning signs.

Two years before, in January of 1964, Cleveland whites had staged a small race riot of their own in the Italian Murray-Hill community when blacks approached to picket a public school where bused-in black students were in classrooms segregated from the white students. There had been bad feelings between the Murray-Hill and Glenville neighborhoods for years, largely over racial matters. Even though Martin Luther King, Jr., put racial equality on a moral plain at the March on Washington in August of 1963, Cleveland's blacks told me later it boosted their spirits but made little difference in the attitudes of whites. Racial tensions were escalating all over the country. There had been race riots in New York, New Jersey, Pennsylvania, and Chicago in the summer of 1964. In the summer of 1965, angry black residents in the Watts area of Los Angeles rioted for six days, and many buildings were burned to the ground.

A small riot also took place in the Superior Street area of Cleveland's Central neighborhood in June of 1966, over a minor racial incident. Those who wanted to blame outside extremists for the July race riot would later call the Superior incident a "dry run" for the much larger Hough riots.

FIGURE 5.1 Police wearing riot gear and angry residents face off during the Detroit riots in July 1967. The police sealed off this block of 12th Street, the heart of the predominantly black area where the earliest incidents occurred. The disorder soon spread to surrounding streets. In the background of this photo are a number of wrecked vehicles, just visible in the smoke from one of the multiple fires that eventually destroyed the neighborhood. On the right is the Chit Chat Lounge, a club frequented in the 1960s by jazz musicians and Motown's best-known recording artists. Forty-three people died in this riot, one of the worst urban riots of the era. In its aftermath, the city of Detroit renamed a long stretch of 12th Street Rosa Parks Boulevard.
Source: AP Wide World Photos

A number of people in Cleveland did know a disturbance was likely but hoped it would bypass the city. Three weeks before the riot "jumped off," the Glenville Area Community Council got together neighborhood street clubs to brainstorm on remedies for roving bands of restless and angry young men and street violence. The next week the Superior Area Community Action Program met to try to work out how to improve relations between white and Negro sections of the city. This meeting was called following the June racial incident. On July 6, 1966, Father Albert Koklowsky, pastor of Our Lady of Fatima on Lexington Avenue in Hough, held a fundraiser to help pay for rehabbing housing for needy families. He was part of the interdenominational group that formed Hope, Inc., a housing rehabilitation program. A local subcommittee of the Ohio State Advisory Committee of the U.S. Commission on Civil Rights, according to the Cleveland *Plain Dealer* of July 8, issued a 47-page report calling for citizen advisory committees to work with schools and police relations. They also called for officials to work with Negro employment issues, using help from the AFL-CIO. They requested help from the

Academy of Medicine to provide health care to inner-city, low-income families. They recommended a watchdog program for housing, as well as twice weekly garbage pick-ups in crowded neighborhoods, and they made a number of other suggestions.

But for the frustrated, unemployed young black men, who wandered the streets of the Hough area on a July night in 1966, all of these efforts were too little too late.

That July week was hot. People were on the street because there were few places with air conditioners in Hough. If people were not roaming the streets, they were sitting on porches and elsewhere, hoping to catch a breeze. The heat factored in the story I covered on how the riot began. I quoted a 25-year-old man near the Bell Center who said he was in the bar where it all had started. "I heard the owner say, 'Don't serve no niggers no water.' Then he (the owner) put a sign on the front door saying, 'No ice water.'" Word spread around the neighborhood quickly and people just got mad, he said.

Someone had been treated badly—a story probably embellished as it moved on. Then everyone knew someone who had treated them badly. As recounted later, some of the young toughs took it very personally and decided to do something about it. Rocks, bottles, bricks and anything else that was handy were thrown first. A few knew how to make a firebomb.

By the time I got there the next day, after being delayed at the office by my overly cautious editors, and delayed in Hough by police barriers, I found people were still milling around in the streets. Adults were trying to round up kids and keep them out of trouble. Various social-program personnel were trying to talk folks down and warn against looting. I walked a few blocks down Hough with some of the staff from the Hough Opportunity Center and it became obvious that while only a few were vandalizing places or setting fires, a whole lot more of the residents could not resist taking merchandise from neighborhood stores once the windows and doors were gone. As one young man put it, "If the grocery store was broken into, all the neighbors had a good meal. If a shoe store was looted, everybody in Hough had on a new pair of shoes."

In a news story that appeared in *The Cleveland Press* following the second night of rioting, I reported on encountering a number of people near the Bell Neighborhood Center on E. 81 Street. In spite of the fact that I was sticking close to the Center, several young teens approached me and tried to sell me looted items. "Most of these boys are young. No place to go; no place to play. No gyms. Can't go to Rockefeller Park because they get in fights with the white boys," a neighborhood resident adult told me. "There's only one gym—Fairfax Recreation Center. But it can't hold all the boys in town."

It appeared that wary police, who had set up a mobile center at 73rd and Hough, had been attacked by young men throwing things at them and had to shoot out the streetlights so they could move about without getting hit. They were, at this time of day, just protecting firemen who were being called out constantly. Most fires were small, a number were false alarms, and a great many involved abandoned buildings, but alarms kept fire trucks on the run, nevertheless.

Even with the frenetic activity, officials thought the area had calmed down by Tuesday evening, the 19th. However, 67 fire alarms were turned in overnight.

My editors decided I should go interview a firebomber. Not an easy task, I told them. They wanted to get a picture, as well. Impossible, I thought. Most of the street people I knew would not let their picture be taken except for the most banal of reasons. And it was impossible. The photographer gave up after a couple of blocks strolling down Hough Avenue.

The day before, I had talked to most of the neighborhood people I knew about the firebombing, including my bench sitters, although I had in mind a softer approach than my editors wanted. I had promised no one would be named. But no one would give me a looter or a firebomber's name or nickname or admit to any wrongdoing themselves. They would not put someone they might know in a position of danger from authorities or others, they said.

I finally got someone to point out three youths who "might have had something to do with fires." Even with assurances, all I got from the three youths was a "maybe I did and maybe not." I talked and listened to the banter and, as they relaxed, I asked them, "If you did throw a firebomb, why would you do it?" They all jumped in and gave me the short angry answers that would appear in the newspaper later. When they saw me taking a few notes—I tried to take as few as I could—I had to practically promise them my first-born child to keep them from bolting. And I was a little leery about this "maybe I did, maybe I didn't do anything" stuff. Newspapers of the day were very black and white in their coverage. Naming names was part of the work. My plan was to get views from a bunch of young men who were likely involved in the looting and firebombing for a news story. I needed more talking time to add the personal background information that would flesh out their anger, because the window from which people look out on the world frames their view and subsequent actions, particularly at 18 or 19 years of age.

But after the photographer and I came up empty on names and faces, I told the editors about my conversation with the "maybe I did and maybe I didn't" firebombers of the day before. They hurried me over to a re-write man (daily newspapers used to have writers available on staff to help reporters quickly translate their notes to news stories in order to make the deadline). The rewrite man helped me to work out a quick story that would hide the identities of the young men and still display their anger. I changed the new shirts of my interviewees to new shoes, made up a name no one would connect to any of the three, and used quotes mainly from one young man but also a couple on which they all gave a "that's right" response. The story, "Niles Hurled a Fire Bomb, Tells Why" ran that day.

The "Niles" story was filled with the young men's frustration. One of the firebombers said, "All my life, people been calling me Nigger." Another explained his attitude towards firebombing, "White man own the place. Prices too high. Like to see it burn."

When things did not calm down in Hough by the end of the second day, Cleveland Mayor Ralph Locher called out the Ohio National Guard, of which some units included reservists just back from Vietnam. Then, after two days confined mostly to Hough Avenue, the rioting spread to the Glenville and Central areas. Ultimately, 1700 National Guard troops were backing up police, blocking streets, and protecting firemen. The rioting ended on July 24. A Cuyahoga County grand jury was convened two days later to investigate the causes of the riots. Their report appeared on August 9.

On August 11, I filed a news story about a meeting at the Hough Opportunity Center where residents confronted city officials and presented a letter composed by Hough residents. Responding to the grand jury report, the letter began with a denial that the riots were caused by extremists and outside Marxist agitators, a charge that had been made by police chief Richard Wagner shortly after the riot began. The letter listed positive steps they thought should be taken to prevent future disturbances. They wanted more Negro policemen, more and better recreation for the young people, better jobs and fewer handouts, better schooling, improved city services, and better and fairer business practices.

A month later, the story that the riot started at the 79er's Bar over a denial of a drink of water was confirmed for me in more detail by another source.

The grand jury report was particularly troublesome for me because my boss, the Cleveland *Press's* editor, Louis B. Seltzer, was the jury foreman. He had apparently not read my stories, or he preferred to believe Chief Wagner instead. Wagner had told the Cleveland *Plain Dealer* in the middle of the rioting that a small band of extremists had plotted and organized selected bombings in a "get whitey" campaign. But further into that same story, *Plain Dealer* reporter Doris O'Donnell quoted some residents who told her that some white businesses were spared because they understood the community's plight. One white owner was called a soul sister at heart. Black businesses were sometimes looted because their owners didn't understand any better than the whites, the story said.

My own story in response to the grand jury report communicated the outrage of Hough citizens: "Why can't the Negro be smart? Don't they realize we read the papers? Most of that report is a lie." Another said, "On this street we know everybody. We'd know if a stranger came in here trying to tell us what to do."

The report from a special session of the grand jury singled out the Jomo Freedom Kenyatta (JFK) House, run by Lewis G. Robinson, described by some as a firebombing training school, and the W. E. B. DuBois Club, which was alleged to have Marxist and Communist ties. Robinson testified to the grand jury, denying the firebombing charges and said Chief Wagner lied. "What can you expect of a fool like that? He has cobwebs in his head."

The Reverend Charles Rawlings, a local minister and community activist, called Wagner's accusation a dangerous simplification. Supporters of the JFK House testified that the storefront recreation center for youth had been under intense investigation for the past 18 months but nothing had been found. Rawlings said, "It is incredible that widespread rioting can be reduced to a storefront recreation center." In the end, no indictments were brought and nothing further was done about the JFK House or W. E. B. DuBois Club. Conspiracy rumors faded from the news.

In the days after the riot, the Hough area was minus several stores, including a much-needed pharmacy, as well as a lot of dilapidated buildings that had been set afire. Rumors were rife that some white business owners who lived elsewhere and could not sell their businesses had had their structures burned intentionally to collect the insurance and rid themselves of a nuisance. Most of the burned buildings were on the edges of the central Hough neighborhood and fires also were set in numerous buildings in Central and Glenville. On Euclid Avenue, a main thoroughfare from downtown Cleveland, a number of older buildings, many of them abandoned, were firebombed. For years after the riots, many of the lots remained vacant. The most unfortunate loss was the Hope House building that was being rehabilitated for low-income families. The street talk was that those working on Hope House were often patronizing, an attitude that breeds resentment at any economic level. But the project continued after the riots in spite of the loss of one building that had to be mostly rebuilt.

Four people died in the riots, including a mother who was frantically trying to get home to her children in Hough. She was shot attempting to enter a blocked-off area. The police also shot up a car containing a whole family. They had been trying to drive around the barriers so they could leave town. Newspaper accounts differed on the number of fires but they agreed that more than 200 were set in the four days of active rioting. More than 100 people were arrested for looting or lesser charges and over 50 were injured, some seriously.

Many of the bench-sitters who befriended me initially became members of the Hough Young Adults that formed after the riot cooled down. One of the more centered members of the group became its president. The Young Adults learned to use the newspaper for its purposes, calling the housing inspector out to a Hough building and telling him they also had called *The Press*. They would usually let me know also. The problem was, of course, that after a couple of these incidents, my editor said we had run enough of the same story.

Civil rights groups, Martin Luther King, Jr., and other such leaders came to the area to talk to the young men in particular, telling them to stay in school and to press intelligently for change. King, who came with a cadre of staff including Jessie Jackson, would not let me attend his meetings with the community males. I was, after all, a white woman. Ralph Bessie and several prominent business leaders held a five-hour meeting with black leaders at the Hough Opportunity Center, offering inner city residents help in finding jobs. I wrote stories on social issues, one of them a series on the problems of finding adoptive parents for minority children.

Although I maintain I was right all along in my explanation of the riot's roots, and historical accounts of the riots all cite the incident at the 79er's Bar as the flash point, Louis Seltzer did not really forget that I had run a story that countered his grand jury's preliminary conclusion. My story appeared in the newspaper the same day as the grand jury report, chaired by him.

As an afternoon newspaper, the *Cleveland Press* was rapidly losing circulation and one of the efforts to save it was zoned pages. I was shifted to coverage of suburban city councils, zoning boards, and community meetings from Euclid and Mayfield Heights all the way out to Geauga County. When I was reassigned, I was given certificates by the Hough Opportunity Center, The Hough Young Men's Group, and Cuyahoga County for my service to the community through my news stories. One of the bench-sitters also called Seltzer on my behalf. Seltzer was not impressed.

I didn't name any of the bench-sitters I knew well and I have to say that I don't remember the names of all of them. They were never in the news clips, preferring to give the tips and drop into the background, and most used nicknames. They all had their own brand of problems to overcome; some had police records, some had alcohol addictions and others had less than respectable pasts. But my hope for them all is that they managed to get to a better place in their lives.

Late in 1967, I married a reporter I met during the riot coverage and moved with him to Washington, D.C. I was there during the rioting in 1968 in response to the death of Martin Luther King, Jr. I did not cover those riots, but I understood what drove the anger. And I wasn't even near the worst of it, though a dry cleaning establishment about a block away from where we lived on Capitol Hill was burned, as was the grocery store a couple of blocks away.

As for the complex social and racial equality issues I covered and reported on in the mid-1960s, change has been slower than I would ever have imagined when I was in my 20s. I still think we are moving in the right direction. It's just that sometimes and in some places the progress can only be measured in millimeters rather than the miles I would have expected 40 years ago.

QUESTIONS FOR DISCUSSION

1. Why does Pat Royse eagerly accept her new assignment to cover community news in Cleveland's poor black neighborhoods? Why do you think Royse and women like her were limited to writing for the "Women's Page" in the early 1960s? Are the same limitations in place today?

2. Many people would have found Royse's assignment to the inner-city beat somewhat frightening. By her account, the neighborhoods were depressed, unemployment was high, and people were seething with resentment against whites. What personal qualities does Royse possess that make the work safer and easier for her? How important is it that she befriends the "bench sitters?"

3. Royse describes her encounter with true poverty and revises her estimation of her own modest childhood. What do you think of the childhood stories contributed by her "bench sitters?" What circumstances might make it almost impossible for the young men to escape the life situations they are in? Do you know anyone who has experienced any of the problems Royse's contacts share with her?

4. Royse's story may remind you of the final incident in R. Thomas Collins' story in another section of this volume. Both Royse and Collins found themselves involved in inner-city violence in Cleveland in 1966. How are their experiences similar? In what ways are they different?

5. Looting and firebombing are frequent aspects of urban rioting. Royse attributes these activities to systemic poverty and the racism that causes chronic unemployment. Do you agree with her assessment? How does Royse's story make you feel about inner-city poverty? About riots and looting? Can you connect this 1966 event with urban problems of your own time?

6. One of the most puzzling things to outside observers of urban rebellions is that people seem to be destroying their own homes and neighborhoods. Can you think of any reasons why people would do this? What circumstances might lead a person to think there was something to gain from destroying buildings and businesses?

CHICAGO '68

Tara Collins Gordon

Going to Chicago's Democratic Convention in the summer of 1968 was all about my anger at America for all its false promises and failures. But it was also about a guy from Brooklyn who couldn't make up his mind about me . . . because I wasn't Jewish.

I had just graduated from the New School for Social Research in New York City. I had been in a wonderful interdisciplinary program in the humanities and arts at the Eugene Lang College. That summer, I had to leave my apartment on Manhattan's upper West Side and move downtown. I had decided to do graduate work in American Studies at New York University, which was down in Greenwich Village, and I was broke and would need a cheaper place to live.

I also wanted to change the world. And I was young and arrogant enough to think I could.

So instead of just moving into the West Village near NYU I moved all the way over to the poorest part of the Lower East Side. If I was going to change the world, I'd have to learn to live the way poor people lived. A group of us shared a shabby top-floor apartment. The bathtub was in the kitchen, covered with a board that did double duty as a countertop. With my roommates, I joined the NYU chapter of the Students for a Democratic Society (SDS), and went to countless meetings and protests, involving myself deeper and deeper in the anti-war movement. We painted a North Vietnamese flag on the wall in our kitchen because we felt the men running our government were more against our interests than the North Vietnamese. To make some money while maintaining my ideals, I took a job as circulation manager of a radical newspaper. I remember we organized concerts at the Fillmore East to benefit anti-war causes.

I probably should have thought about my safety, living in that lower-Manhattan neighborhood. But I didn't. I guess my determination to change the world gave off a "don't mess with me" attitude that helped me as I walked from the subway station home at night through winos and drug addicts, gangs, kids, and pan-handlers on the street.

And, as scared as I should have felt in one of the toughest neighborhoods in New York City, I was more scared for my brothers than for myself. 1968 was a full war year in Vietnam. My brothers, two and five years younger than I was, would be eligible for the draft and had a good chance of being drafted. I had heard about a draft-counseling course being offered at the Quaker Meeting House on 15th Street near 2nd Avenue . . . so I decided I would teach my brothers how to become conscientious objectors. I would learn from the Quakers. I had to save someone, so I would try and save my brothers.

I walked to my first draft-counseling meeting in bright orange and red satin bell-bottoms and a puffy-sleeved paisley see-through blouse. There were about six people at the meeting and there, sitting across from me, was Joe Levin—a not particularly attractive man, but with a sweet smile, darting, anxious eyes and a kind of stalling interest in me. He was very smart, I discovered. He was getting his doctorate in psychology from Brooklyn College, and, somewhere behind the brain and those thick glasses, he had a heart, with real feeling.

I was a rich kid but the product of an alcoholic home with a violent father. I felt enormously guilty that with all their money, all my parents did was drink, fall apart, and almost kill each other. Now the whole world was falling apart. From my point of view I was a victim of all of them, not just my parents, but the politicians and generals who had gotten us into Vietnam, the police and their dogs in Mississippi, the subtle racism and the anti-Semitism in West Hartford, Connecticut, where I was from—anything that kept the world from being human. Our family employed African-American maids who helped raise me and who performed other household chores. I found I often identified more with them than I did with my own parents. My mother was raised as a Protestant, but my father was a Catholic. We kids were raised as Catholics, but somehow the Protestants' typical prejudice against Catholics found a place in our home. We knew Catholics were not part of the respectable establishment, which in the neighborhood where we lived was dominated by the descendants of the original New England settlers. And in that world, no one was equal to the WASPs. Catholics co-existed, Jews were always outside of our community, and blacks were "the help." My mother was always complaining she couldn't ever find "good help" or "keep them." And the one thing my mother feared was for me to look "Jewish."

My parents' generation had messed things up for everyone. But I was going to save them all—the North Vietnamese, the African-Americans, the Jews, my brothers, and any men who thought they might want to go to Vietnam. I had a mission.

It got confusing though. My best friend from college, Karen Snow, had married a Marxist who was kicked out of the University of Wisconsin. And he beat her. But somehow, even though he was like my father, we thought his behavior was understandable because he didn't drink, he was an intellectual, and he was "right" and concerned about society and changing it. Somehow I could connect with Karen's pain, and her intellectual rationalizations about being a member of the women's movement even though her husband beat her and the women's liberationists were pushing women to leave those kinds of men. She was going to save him and thus stayed with him. And I identified with his pain and her pain; with his rage and her subservience, which mirrored my own father and mother in a very cracked mirror. I was caught in these spider webs of confusing connections that would brush against me and hold onto me.

But there, in the Quaker Meeting House, sat Joe Levin, not violent like Karen's husband or my father, but interested in me, somehow, interested in my Irish blue eyes and real soul that kept spilling out inappropriately in a kind of quasi-needy way. Joe and I studied conscientious objection together. Somehow, as we talked after the meetings, his Jewishness and my Irishness seemed to connect and he definitely liked me and wanted to see me, but at an intellectual distance—which I really liked for a while because I couldn't keep anyone or anything at a distance. Joe seemed, somehow, to understand all this, and he stayed interested and kept me interested. He talked to me a lot about the anti-war movement, and, later in the summer, about "getting ready for the big protest demonstration at the Chicago Convention" and that it was going to be a "bloodbath" and did I want to go?

Protest, revolution, stopping the war whatever it took—even a "bloodbath"— these were words to me. Even though I was politically active they were still just ideas. They weren't real. But the world I came from—rich, conservative, mainstream, "in charge"—that wasn't me either. Who were these guys who were running the country and the war and where did they come from? They did not represent me. I was on the outside. Looking at them, my friends and I saw an American dream that wasn't working. I was a satin hippie with long brown hair and these men in crew cuts with tight suits were sending young, vibrant men to war. Plus they wanted my two brothers to die. And if my brothers didn't want to die, they would be sent to jail.

So I identified with Joe, the draft resister, the anti-war activist. And I drew closer. Joe had an apartment in Brooklyn, near his mother's place. I visited his home, met his mother and met his friends and went to the Jewish bakery to get mandel bread, a kind of Jewish cookie. Joe had a friend, Hank. And they were always planning what they would do in the coming "bloodbath." Now Hank was a real hood, scary and angry . . . very quiet and quick to temper. And the girls found him sexy because of that. He had a girlfriend, a teacher named Sharon, who didn't understand him, never questioned him, and thought he was so sexy, in a kind of James Dean sort of way.

Joe's eyes really darted and dashed when he was with Hank. And they would go off together to "plan" and Sharon and I, women, were left alone to talk. Then they'd come back and Joe and I would sleep in his bed in Brooklyn and he wouldn't touch me, he'd just hold me and talk. He was sweet and intellectual and gentle and I really liked him. He would talk about "guns" and his eyes would dart and dash the way they did around Hank and I would like him. And I would listen to his words, but I wasn't listening to what they could really mean. . . . I was listening to the feeling inside him. And he felt safe to me.

Still, I waffled about going to the convention. I didn't like Hank but I liked Sharon. She needed me to be her friend so she could be free to be sexy. She wanted me to go with her and be a friend because she'd told Hank she'd follow him anywhere but she didn't want to go without a girlfriend.

So, in the last week of August, a thug with a leftist and girls following boys all got into a beat-up Ford and drove from New York City to Chicago listening to The Doors, Steppenwolf's "Born To Be Wild," and "Time Has Come Today" by the Chambers Brothers. They had marijuana, but I couldn't smoke it with them; it made me more paranoid than I already was. We hung out and sang and slept and I remember feeling happy and free as we hit Lake Shore Drive. The whole thing was an adventure. The demonstration would be fun, just like all the others I had been to.

But Joe definitely was not into relaxing with me. He was nervous all the time now. We got to the Quaker Meeting House on Chicago's near north side where we were staying with many other people coming from all over the country. It was Tuesday night, August 27. The Democratic National Convention had opened the day before, but the protests had been building for five days. Our sleeping bags on the floor, we sacked out hard until the next morning.

When I woke up Sharon was there but Joe and Hank were gone. She and I talked and she told me the guys were going off to do "their thing" and she and I would be together. I was perfectly OK with that. Hank and Joe came back later in the day and told us that "we girls" should stick together. They gave us hardhats and bandanas. We had to protect ourselves; they were not going to protect us or even be with us for that matter.

I was feeling insecure, unsure with Joe. He was not acting like we were together. He was uneasy and he hung with Hank the hunk, not me, and I was uncomfortable. But I wanted my voice to be heard, too. So Sharon and I set off, hitching a ride down to the site where the protest was gathering near the Convention Hall.

But what was in store for me on those streets would change me; change how I felt about Joe and Hank and Sharon and how I felt about demonstrating.

From the moment we got out of our ride, I saw police attack, without provocation. I saw groups of these men dressed in helmets and light blue short sleeve crisp-looking shirts, working together, hitting with sticks, together, thick sticks; and I put my helmet on. The police were really coordinated, attacking and hitting grungy, long haired, dirty kids, some with flowers in their hands. They would pick one straggly looking kid out of the crowd and beat him up, hard, to make an example of him and then drag him into a wagon. Then they would pick another and charge and everyone around that kid would scatter in panic. All I could think of was getting out of their way. For one moment it looked as though I was the next person they had picked to hit. I ran with fear, with panic, with a charge I had never felt before in my life. I turned a corner and got away from the crowd as fast as I could.

They didn't see me. I stood against a wall below some stairs watching them rush after the people I had been with, pick off the guy who had been next to me and crack his head. He fell to the ground, bleeding. They left him and got the next guy. I couldn't move. I could hear my breathing sounding like a jet engine. There was so much bustle and cracking and screaming and yelling. I felt like I was in a movie. My heart raced. I crouched down in the stairwell and waited. I was shivering in fear.

Slowly, in a few minutes or so, I inched my way up. No one was near me. I couldn't find Sharon. I had no idea how much time had gone by. It was warm and it was now completely dark. Lights were on everywhere. I saw kids coming back again, without cops in pursuit. I started walking toward a hotel where more crowds were gathered. And then out of nowhere again, kids were running and I was part of them and I was running. And then I felt the mace. I had never felt mace. My skin burned. I crouched down and took my bandana and wiped my skin. I was lucky. My eyes had been shut. But kids were rolling beside me in pain, screaming "My eyes, my eyes!" And then, out of nowhere, Sharon was pulling me up, asking me if I was all right. She had my hand and we were moving toward a crowd who were screaming.

The dynamic was different now. The bright lights I saw everywhere were television lights and television and photographers had changed the demonstration. The cops were now in a disciplined row. They were not hitting or kicking or dragging us, they were standing in rows with the sticks, looking straight ahead. Some of them were really mad. One or two would strike out in anger, and then someone would order them to get back in line and they would. When they were watched, they acted differently. But we were mad and frightened and hurt and scared to death and those of us in front of those lights suddenly knew we could finally act or demonstrate without being hurt. And we did. Theater groups danced around, a couple of crazy kids took their shirts off and gave the cops the finger and Sharon and I stood by Sometimes I put my fist in the air and shouted "Hell no, we won't go!" Light bulbs popped, people inside the hotel were on their balconies or leaning out the window screaming, "We're with you!"

FIGURE 5.2 Angry protestors face the cameras near the Democratic National Convention center on the night of Wednesday, August 28, 1968. Some of them have just been clubbed and sprayed with mace by Chicago police. Thousands of young people had converged on Chicago to demand that the Democrats nominate an anti-war candidate for president. They met with fierce police opposition throughout the convention. In three days of street confrontations, hundreds of demonstrators were injured and hundreds arrested. Wearing a white helmet and a handkerchief mask, and standing behind the shirtless, gesturing young man, is Tara Collins Gordon, the author of "Chicago '68." Perry C. Riddle took this picture for the Chicago *Sun Times*, and LIFE magazine featured it in a retrospective collection.

Source: Chicago Sun-Times

Sharon was tired. She said "Let's go" and we went. We hitched to the Quaker Meeting House. We went to get a soda. She and I sat and told our stories. Hers were very similar to mine. She was scared and shattered and so was I. It was late. She and I fell asleep. We were really tired. I woke up as Joe and Hank came in. They told us it was a "bloodbath" and they sat up whispering and talking. Sharon snuggled next to Hank, glad he hadn't been hurt. I went to sleep, glad I hadn't been hurt. I wasn't interested in darting-eyed Joe, or sexy Sharon or hunky Hank. I was interested in tired Tara.

The next morning I woke up first. The others were asleep. I felt removed. I didn't know why exactly. I just wanted to get back to New York City. I rolled my sleeping bag, got my duffle packed, washed and took a shower. When I got out of the shower, they were getting up. Joe asked me how I was and I said fine and asked when we'd be leaving. They were all set to go. We got in the car, got a McDonald's and started driving. Joe and Hank were in the front seat talking. Sharon slept in the back and I looked out the window. I felt dazed and uncomprehending. And didn't know much of much other than that I wanted to get home.

I got back to my apartment on the Lower East Side in the dangerous part of town. But I was so glad to be there. Joe gave me a kiss good bye and said he'd call me. And he did and I wasn't interested. I later found out from Sharon that his mother didn't like me because I wasn't Jewish. So he wasn't ever really going to be interested in me. Now that was a switch. I was used to fighting against my own mother for being anti-Semitic, but Joe had gone into agreement with his. I heard from him and it was all friendly enough and he invited me out and I think I may have gone, but I wasn't interested in him and he already had another girl who was Jewish.

I started my life again. Chicago had changed things. And, without realizing it, I began to change things. I started and then dropped out of graduate school and began squirreling away money to save for something else. I stopped going to protest meetings. After Chicago, a lot of people felt defeated. Some friends of mine, the really radical ones, disappeared into the "Underground." Some of them ended up in jail.

Someone told me my picture was in *Life* magazine and I looked and there I was. With Sharon, my hand in the air. My face covered after the mace. My helmet on. Someone told me that because I was in the photo, the FBI would have a file on me. And you know what? I believed them. I suddenly began noticing self-defense classes offered everywhere.

And decided I wasn't going to do it. I wasn't going to another demonstration and I wasn't going to learn self-defense. I didn't want to think that way about my life. I didn't want to prepare myself for violence or revolution. I wanted to make love not war. And I would never put myself in that kind of situation again.

I quit my job at the political paper and began searching for an entry job anywhere. I needed to find myself, and I knew it.

QUESTIONS FOR DISCUSSION

1. How would you describe Tara Collins Gordon in the summer of 1968? How has she been shaped by her family background, her education, and her own self-consciousness? She is very involved in the anti-war movement, to the extent of working for a radical newspaper and studying draft resistance, but is she politically naïve or politically sophisticated?

2. What social and racial issues typical of the 1950s and 1960s can you find in Gordon's story about her family? Why does Joe date her but keep his distance from her? Discuss the social relationships between whites, African Americans, Catholics, Protestants, and Jews as she experienced them growing up. Do you think those prejudices still exist today?

3. Gordon never explains the reason for the demonstrations at the Chicago Convention or who organized them. She assumes we will know. What do you know about that event? What can you learn about the event from Gordon's story that you did not know before?

4. What is your opinion of Hank and Joe and the way they treat the two young women who accompany them to the demonstration? Are they being protective or are they being neglectful? Does it seem that they know more about what is going on than they are willing to share?

5. Can you identify with Gordon's revulsion about the violence in the streets of Chicago? Gordon says that many of her activist friends felt defeated after Chicago. Why would they feel defeated? Why would some go "Underground?"

6. Gordon herself loses interest in "preparing for violence and revolution" and has no tolerance for people like Joe and Hank. She quits the anti-war movement and pursues her own life goals. Why does she do this? Compare Gordon's story to Steve Diamond's story of going back to the land, in another section of this book. Diamond's decision to leave "the movement" also takes place in the summer of 1968. What has happened during this particular year that makes some people feel they cannot do anything more to solve the country's problems?

WOODSTOCK NATION
Sheila Lennon

The rain of Friday night had turned Max Yasgur's dairy farm to cow dung mud, and now the August sun was pumping it back up as steam. In little puffs it rose to meet the cloud of marijuana smoke hovering over the sweaty people drawn here by the promise of three days of peace and music.

"The sun was beating and beating with the rhythm of the 'copters," says Dottie Clark, one of the many from southeastern New England who answered the call. "It had a jungle look." Since the night before, tiny helicopters had been dropping musicians and their instruments behind the stage. The drone was familiar. But now big green Army choppers, the same Hueys that strafed Vietnam on the nightly news, were sweeping in behind our backs, loud and low.

"Nixon could wipe out the anti-war movement in one fell swoop here," murmured a voice behind me, setting off a nervous ripple in our neighborhood. "Paranoia from the sky," recalls Jim Edwards. A rustle spread over the peaceable hillside, a wrinkle of bad vibes.

"Everybody looked up. I was just gripped with fear," remembers Mel Ash. "I was 16, but I was actually thinking about my death."

From the stage, the deep velvet voice of emcee Chip Monck boomed, "Ladies and gentlemen, the U.S. Army . . . Medical Corps," as the choppers' red crosses came into view.

All weekend, the National Guard would drop sandwiches and blankets and performers and instruments, evacuate casualties and laboring mothers, and assault us with fire hoses to cool us off. Sunday, as we stood 6 inches deep in mud, a tiny private plane swooped down to spray us with daisies, a gift from Festival organizers.

Welcome to Woodstock. These are our war stories.

Rumors of the Woodstock Music & Art Fair had been in the air all summer. Joe Landry ran a folk club in Cleveland at the time, and hung out with musicians. "Everyone was hyping it as the happening of the century. They were gonna make it as big as they possibly could," he remembers. "Of course they succeeded beyond their wildest expectations."

By late July, bright posters with a whimsical logo of a dove perched on the neck of a guitar began popping up on telephone poles throughout the East. The magic words were "3 Days of Peace and Music." It was like broadcasting a radio signal, and anybody tuned in would get it. Somehow they'd find White Lake, N.Y.

This festival was fielding a band list that read like the course description of Rock 'n' Roll 101. If we were typed by the music we liked, all kinds of people would show up here: fans of Joan Baez, Arlo Guthrie, Tim Hardin, Richie Havens, The Incredible String Band, Ravi Shankar, Sweetwater, Keef Hartley, Canned Heat, Creedence Clearwater Revival, The Grateful Dead, Janis Joplin, Jefferson Airplane, Mountain, Santana, The Who, The Band, Jeff Beck, Blood, Sweat and Tears, Joe Cocker, Crosby, Stills and Nash, Jimi Hendrix, Iron Butterfly, The Moody Blues or Johnny Winter. With a lineup like this going on in his backyard, it seemed likely that

Bob Dylan would drop by and sit in. What the heck, maybe The Beatles and the Rolling Stones, too.

By surrounding the music with an art show, music and craft workshops, a bazaar, food booths and hundreds of acres for camping, festival organizers guaranteed that nearly everybody under 30 except Tricia Nixon would want to be there. Coming together seemed long overdue.

Rhode Island's "Beats"

"Woodstock Nation felt like pre-Vietnam," says David DelBonis. "There was a beatnik culture on Thayer Street. The guy who lived next door to me in Johnston—Richard Carbone—used to take me to the Tete à Tete coffee house, to Jone Pasha's. He bought me e.e. cummings' poems, at 7, 8 years old. That changed my whole life. I knew there was an alternative."

Jack Kerouac explained the "beat" attitude as "a weariness with all the forms, all the conventions of the world."

"They were nice people," DelBonis said of Rhode Island's beats. "They had their own little business and their own little community and they played music. They were much more sensitive than the people I knew in Johnston. They didn't want any part of the 'commercial' world. They were interesting, and they were interested in art; they traveled and enjoyed the things of the world. Everybody can't be that way or we couldn't function, but I saw a whole other world."

Pop art, Eastern religious ideas, John Kennedy's Peace Corps and Bobby's idealism, Dylan and The Beatles, anthropology courses on cultures that ate "magic mushrooms" and peyote buttons for spiritual visions were absorbed along with Buddy Holly, Betty Friedan's *The Feminine Mystique*, Percy Sledge, and Hermann Hesse's mystical novel, *Steppenwolf*.

At Hope High, Shelly Lynch decided a beatnik was something to be. She went to NYU's theater department in Greenwich Village. "We were gonna grow up and live in a little white house," she says. "Then the '60s happened."

Beginnings

When the ads appeared in the underground press and the New York Sunday *Times* Arts section July 27, the response was overwhelming. At $7 a day and a pricey $18 for the weekend, the official expectation was a crowd of 150,000. But before the festival opened, Woodstock Ventures had sold 200,000 tickets, and had requests—but no more printed tickets—for 100,000 more.

The festival was almost held in the ominously named Wallkill, but the town balked. Less than a month before the festival was to happen, Yasgur, a prominent citizen of Bethel, agreed to rent his cow pasture, a natural amphitheater, for $60,000 for three days. In Hebrew, Bethel means a holy or consecrated spot. A good omen. With the help of 80 people from the Hog Farm Commune in New Mexico, and a staff who were into the music and into the lifestyle, Woodstock Ventures began to build a city.

By Wednesday night, 50,000 people had already come to Bethel. In Providence, WBRU was announcing that Woodstock would be a free concert. There hadn't been time to build the gates.

The Road to Woodstock

Hope High senior Joseph Caffey and his friends took the bus to New York City, planning to catch a bus to the festival. There was no bus, but there were 250 kids. They improvised:

"We rented U-Haul trucks and hired bus drivers to drive them," said Caffey, now director of rental rehabilitation for the City of Providence. "We chipped in, collected from everybody and headed up to Woodstock." The trip was a metaphor for what was to come, physically uncomfortable but high-spirited. At one point they were stopped by police for having the back doors open, and had to finish the trip in the hot, stuffy darkness of the box.

"The water pump went and the truck broke down 20 miles away," says Mike Kaprielian, who had joined the navy two months earlier rather than be drafted. "We knew something special was happening, because when we piled out of that truck and stuck out our thumbs, 50 cars must have lined up to pick us up." They couldn't get closer than 10 miles, "so we walked in the rest of the way. I had just finished basic so I was in shape," Mike recalls, "but Joe was huffing." Five minutes after getting to the field, they got separated and didn't see each other again for 19 years.

By Friday, thousands of people had converged on New York's Port Authority terminal at Eighth Avenue and 42nd Street, lining up under signs that read "Woodstock Festival Load Here." Among them was John Rossi, who had seen an ad for the Aquarian Exposition in Providence's underground newspaper, *Extra*. Rossi, 38, now works for the Department of Defense in Washington, D.C., as a computer systems software specialist, devising ways to ensure the security of top-secret information, but at the time he had just graduated from Mount Pleasant High School. The atmosphere of the "party bus" set the tone for the weekend: he recalls a camaraderie never experienced before or since. Rossi's bus stopped within a mile of the field.

After the festival, the Short Line bus company ran ads featuring pictures of the drivers who manned the party buses, along with little quotes such as: "We have a lot to learn from them about getting along together;" "They don't look at the public the way the public looks at them;" "I don't understand why they wear long hair but now I don't care" . . . and "They're the most no-griping, no-complaining, patient and generous, respectful kids I've ever met. Come on kids and ride with me. It's a pleasure driving you."

A bit later in the day, the bus carrying Dena Quilici of Providence, then 19, gave up three miles away. Meanwhile, her future husband, Jim Edwards, who worked at India Imports of Rhode Island, was driving the company van toward Woodstock, accompanied by anybody he knew who needed a ride. He didn't know Dena.

He found a dirt road and followed it. It led directly to the festival grounds.

"The Endless Vans"

Friday morning, the New York State Thruway was jammed with cars, long hair streaming out of every window, peace sign decals on back windows and "Make Love Not War" bumper stickers. Most amazing were the psychedelically painted vans and school buses with faraway license plates—California, New Mexico. The communes had come east flying their colors.

"The endless vans," said Dottie Clark, "were kitchens, bedrooms, dance floors."

Near the site, traffic slowed, and people with guitars, bongos, flutes, pan pipes, whistles or bells clambered up on hoods and trunks, serenading the bumper-to-bumper traffic. There was dancing on van roofs, and anticipation in the air. People tired of walking hopped on your hood and rode with you for a while. These were, as John Haerry of West Greenwich put it, "the days of high hippiedom."

At the White Lake exit, one lone policeman had closed the ramp, but cars crossed the median strip and exited from the southbound lane onto the gridlock of Route 17. Complicating the mess was a junkyard of overheated cars by the side of the road. Amateur mechanics swarmed over them. If they couldn't be restarted, their passengers were scooped into any vehicle still moving, and the beat went on.

Michelle Keir of Warwick recalls tossing a deli pickle to the car behind her, never dreaming how precious that pickle would seem the next hungry day. Chris Heinzmann of Pawtucket, who had piled into his father's International Travelall with his two older brothers and five friends, remembers that "everybody was yelling back and forth, having a good time."

Cheri Light spent Friday night in the woods 10 miles away. Saturday she walked and rode to the site on the hood of a car behind a giant moving van. When traffic jammed, the back doors opened up and four bikers zoomed down a ramp and up the road. John Sousa of Rumford remembers that "when cars got stuck (on the already wet dirt roads), people would literally lift them up. We were spontaneously working together."

The traffic jam was fun.

Cars were ditched at whatever point their drivers decided this was as close as they were getting. These pioneers circled the wagons and cordoned themselves off in the center of a parking lot with a 10-mile radius. Dennis Lemoine parked in a field where he could hear the music. "A farmer came up on a John Deere with a shotgun," he says. They moved, and the woman who owned the second field came out and said, "Please don't make a mess, and don't keep us up all night."

By Friday night, police blockaded the main roads. Most people who heard what was happening Friday and tried to crash the big party were just too late. David DelBonis, who arrived in Bethel on Wednesday to pitch in, watched the crowd swell. "If all the people who were blocked out had gotten in, you would've had a mess, from sheer numbers and from the partiers who were trying to get there," he said. "The people who came early enough to get in were a different kind of people. The authorities did a great job. They blocked it at the right time.

"You had a good balance. The people who were there ahead of time had already gotten into the feeling of the whole thing and the helping and the sharing, and then enough people came to give you the masses. So the powers that ran it had already set the tone, and that's why it never got out of hand. Security was just to keep people mellow," he added.

For those who did make it, the long walk in the company of thousands made an indelible impression. Dottie Clark, who had parked about 5 miles away, thought the road "looked like an old movie of refugees leaving Berlin." Friday, the people who lived by the roadside couldn't help enough. One middle-aged woman urged me to take oranges and drink from her hose. There had been radio reports that residents were charging a dollar for a drink of water, and she was outraged. "We're not that kind of people," she said.

John Sousa remembers families on the lawn flashing peace signs and, amazingly, police doing it, too. "It was the first reassuring element," he said. Others would follow: a farmer who milked his cows and gave away milk, and hoses that ran constantly.

Six or so abreast, we streamed up a country road lined with streetwise types quietly muttering the menu, "Acid, hash, grass . . . Owsley acid . . . Afghani, gold weed . . . sunshine, blotter . . . red Colombian . . . Vietnamese . . . Thai stick." ("New Yorkers," says David DelBonis disgustedly. "Hard-core New York City people came up and that's where all the drugs came from.")

We exchanged sidelong glances. The dealers were being discreet only in the volume of their voices. The police were directing traffic, discussing crowd control, returning peace signs, accepting flowers, smiling, and being polite.

We weren't in Richard Nixon's America anymore.

Colors on Top of a Mountain

Blue and brown were the colors of Woodstock. Blue jeans and sky, tanned skin and mud and bare stage. Coming up the road and over the hill behind the stage, the first view of the festival field was stunning. Many of our brains could not process what our eyes saw.

The hillside was seething with moving bumps as far as I could see. Cheryl Godek Curran saw colors on top of a mountain. We each asked our friends, "What's that?" "That" was rows of densely packed heads stretching to the horizon.

How many of us? The respectable conservative estimate is 400,000. Ty Davis, who was at both Watkins Glen (which officially drew between 600,000 and 650,000) and at Woodstock, says Woodstock was bigger. There was no way to know. Little festivals were going on wherever the traffic stopped. Some people who never heard a note report having a wonderful time.

To Phil Kukielski, it was like "walking onto the set of a Fellini film. I had a sense of what the world would be like if it were run by people 18 to 25."

Freedom in the Air

The concert that came to be called Woodstock began a few minutes after 5 p.m. Friday, August 15, 1969. Black folksinger Richie Havens was tapped, simply because he was available and no other bands were. Woodstock Ventures had rented every helicopter they could book, but the ferrying process was way behind schedule. When the helicopter came for Havens, he was the only performer available who didn't come with complex equipment that would demand a time-consuming sound check. Havens' acoustic guitar set could be the sound check for the evening.

The crowd, growing by the minute, was happy it was finally underway. There had been a false start earlier when Swami Satchidananda took the stage and talked about peace, but that had merely been the invocation.

Havens sang every song he knew, including "Here Comes the Sun" and "The Universal Soldier," which drew cheers from this group who were facing a test of their core philosophy: make love, not war. Then he made up "Freedom," the song on the album, on the spot, because he felt freedom in the air, and nobody was ready to follow him. Woodstock, the concert, was off to a fine start.

"What's It Spell?"

Country Joe McDonald was near the stage when Havens came off. McDonald's band, The Fish, wasn't around, but one of the concert organizers asked Joe to kill time with an acoustic set. What happened next is one of the few Woodstock moments everybody who was there remembers. Everybody. It was called the Fish Cheer.

After a lackluster 20 minutes, Country Joe (nobody called him McDonald) was dying out there. With nothing to lose, he called out, "Give me an F . . . " Well trained by football cheerleaders, the crowd came to its feet and followed along through four letters that don't spell "fish."

Then "What's it spell? . . . What's it spell? . . . What's it spell? . . . What's it spell? . . . What's it spell? . . . What's it spell?"

"Country Joe, like Abbie Hoffman, seemed to understand we had a tendency to take ourselves too seriously," said Jim Edwards. Chris Heinzmann recalls, "Half a million people didn't say that word in public at the same time."

John Sousa, a member of the Rhode Island National Guard at the time, remembers, "It felt great. I felt free. The F word is horrifying for some people to hear. This was freedom of speech." Besides, "The F word was common in basic training."

With the sound of the liberated word still vibrating in the air, Country Joe segued right into the catchy little ditty called "I-Feel-Like-I'm-Fixin'-to-Die Rag." The audience picked it up, singing along and dancing merrily. It was fun.

If there's a collective memory for our deathbeds, a song that took permanent root in the consciousness of a generation, this is it. This ditty became the de facto anthem of Woodstock:

> *Now come on mothers throughout the land,*
> *Pack your boys off to Vietnam.*
> *Come on fathers, don't hesitate,*

Send your sons off before it's too late.
Be the first one on your block
To have your boy come home in a box
[Awright]
And it's one, two, three,
What are we fighting for?
Don't ask me, I don't give a damn,
Next stop is Vietnam;
And it's five, six, seven,
Open up the pearly gates,
Well, there ain't no time to wonder why,
Whoopee! We're all gonna die.

The cheers and whistles rocked the night. For a moment, time had stopped for me. I was stunned. Looking around in mid-chorus, I realized that some of these joyous, vital young men around me would indeed come home in a box, as had so many before them. The horror of war usually brings the message home, but war had never seemed so senseless to me as at that lighthearted, macabre moment.

Country Joe soon found it hard to get bookings, perhaps because booking him was not only political, the Fish Cheer might be part of the package. The IRS audited him. He suspected his phone was tapped. His career stalled. He had become identified with one song that summed up an era people would soon try to forget. The veteran whose Woodstock performance is burned in our brains says he never said they wouldn't fight; he just wanted to know—and still does—"What are we fighting for?"

John Sebastian followed Country Joe. He had just left the Lovin' Spoonful— the San Francisco band that sang "The magic's in the music and the music's in me"—but was not booked for Woodstock. He had just come to hear the show, but couldn't resist the chance to play this crowd, despite having just swallowed God knows what chemical compound. He wore tie-dye from head to toe, and sounded spaced out and hokey—hippie-dippie—to me. But Cheryl Godek Curran felt the combination of Country Joe and John Sebastian left the crowd feeling unified against the war.

Tim Hardin, who wrote "If I Were a Carpenter" and "Reason to Believe," seemed too fragile for this population. I liked his songs, but he played a disappointing set. Chris DeLuca especially wanted to hear the Incredible String Band, a Scottish band whose work is described as avant-garde folk. They had played at Newport, opened for Judy Collins and Tom Paxton, and were riding a crest after a lovely album entitled *The Hangman's Beautiful Daughter*. But "the audience was unresponsive to them," says a disappointed DeLuca, who heard rude comments about their performance in his neighborhood.

Nobody seems to remember Bert Sommer, a folksinger who had been in the Broadway musical *Hair*, which introduced the notions of the Age of Aquarius and hippie nudity to the masses in 1968.

Skinny-Dipping

The long road to the stage passed by a pond full of unself-conscious skinny-dippers. Most of this multitude of middle-class kids had never seen groups of people of both sexes take their clothes off together. It was apparent that we were about to examine our taboos.

Most of the nudity that so shocked the older generation about Woodstock came as a result of being mud-crusted and ripe-smelling, hot and miserable. Bathing in their birthday suits became, for many, the lesser evil.

Several people we talked to volunteered that they were among the nude bathers. But the 1980s, like the 1880s, are Victorian enough that we present their comments without attribution, to spare them both their good names and obscene phone calls:

"I remember going swimming, washing up. I took my clothes off to wash up and cool off. No one watched. Everyone did things at their own pace," said one woman.

"I was taking a bath. That's all it was. I would rather be nude than dirty," said a practical man.

"I was naked, or maybe wore just underpants. I felt completely at ease—as if skinny-dipping with best friends. I didn't feel I was naked among half a million strangers. It was truly wonderful."

One festival worker had been standing all day in the hot sun, and was getting sunstroke. She was ordered by a festival honcho to get cooled off. "You took your clothes off and went in the pond because you didn't want to get your clothes totally wet. That was basically the nudity, except for isolated incidents. When the sun came out, some women took their blouses off, but it wasn't craziness. We didn't even pay attention to it. It didn't mean anything."

Although it seemed important to passers-by to be nonchalant, different things were going on inside them.

"I didn't see anybody getting intimate together, but I did see a little bit of nudity," Chris Heinzmann says. "Being 14, I thought it was great. I wasn't gonna take off my clothes, but I thought it was neat. There weren't that many people doing it."

Phil Kukielski wasn't shocked. "It wasn't lewd. There was a gentle, non-predatory ambiance to it," he recalls. "It was a celebration, an expression of being comfortable enough to take off your clothes without embarrassment, like brothers and sisters."

Susan Vogler saw some bare-breasted women, and remembers walking over people making love. "I was embarrassed, but I thought 'Good for them.' I couldn't do it but look at them—that's what everything was about. Be free, don't worry about what the future brings."

John Haerry's first response was, " 'Wow, naked women!' But after a while," he says, "it was 'Hey, nice pond, chuck your clothes and go swimming.' "

Al Puerini says he "felt like a voyeur. We'd look in amazement, shake our heads and say 'This is unbelievable.' They were totally self-unconscious."

John Sousa remembers "one guy doing cartwheels in the nude all the way down to the stage." His was perhaps the only way to get all the way from the back of the crowd to front, and quickly, too. He was roundly cheered.

"Friendly People"

All this freedom didn't really lead to "Why don't we do it in the road?" It depended on who you were, how old you were and with whom you had come. Certainly, lovers who had been intimate at home probably found a way to be so at Woodstock, but without a tent it wasn't easy. Maybe on the West Coast people were freer, but making love in the mud surrounded by a half-million people trying not to step on you was not most people's idea of a good time.

Joe Landry was 29. He spent a lot of time at Woodstock with the people from New Mexico's Hog Farm Commune, who were older and much less conventional than the college students still living at home. David DelBonis, who also hung out at the Hog Farm, said "The Hog Farm people were totally outrageous. They were in another universe."

"There was a lot of love going on," says Landry. But "free love" didn't mean a free lunch.

"I got turned down by more women at that time," DelBonis chuckles. "I don't think the '60s were as wild as everyone thought they were. People made easier attractions, maybe. I never thought of it as a sexual revolution."

Mike Kaprielian, who was 19, says, "I went to Woodstock a virgin, and I left a virgin."

"It wasn't the type of environment that was conducive to forming really close personal bonds," said John Haerry. "A lot of people came with a group they were hanging out with, and they tended to stay together and keep an eye on each other. Other contacts were just ships passing in the night."

People were constantly roaming, all day, all night. "Everyone was so friendly to each other. It was a constant movement of people, hooking up with a group of people for a while, sharing with them, then moving on," says Dena Quilici.

Cheri Light remembers, "There was never a pass the whole weekend, not even a suggestion of it. Men walked up and talked to me, but it was just friendly people making conversation."

A Soaking

Friday night, Woodstock almost felt like a pretty normal outdoor concert. Jim Edwards remembers actually buying a hamburger (from an ad hoc group of New Yorkers misnamed Food For Love who, the day before the concert, threatened to pull out unless they could keep all their profits, and threatened the promoters enough that they called in the FBI. By Saturday, their staff was trading burgers for anything useful, then giving them away.)

Then it began to rain hard during Ravi Shankar's set. Phil Kukielski, who had come with his future wife just for "folk night," was holding a wool blanket over their heads as an umbrella. As the rain soaked in, "the blanket got heavier and the smell of wet wool got stronger, to the point of misery," he remembers. The rains whipped for about 15 minutes, and then died. The concert resumed, with everyone wet and a mountain chill in the air.

Then Arlo Guthrie came on, and his cheerful good humor changed the vibes. He goofed on how many freaks there were, on how the New York Thruway was closed—something most of us didn't know. We were unaware of the million or so people trying desperately to get to the exact spot where we shivered miserably.

"Arlo made the crowd totally relax. It was like, 'Thank God, he's funny, we can relax.' If all those people ran, you knew you'd get trampled," said Dena Quilici.

Troubles Went Away

"All those troubles kind of went away once you just settled down and started listening to the music," Ty Davis says.

Sweetwater came and went, leaving no mark on the memory of anyone we spoke with. About midnight, Kukielski, who lived not far away in Newburgh, N.Y., left the festival. During the long walk to his car, the mud sucked his shoes off his feet. He drove barefoot, taking whatever passable road seemed to lead away from the site.

He pulled into a field and slept in the car with his girlfriend under an airplane beacon that revolved all night with a bright white light, and went home in the morning. After hearing the news reports, his parents hadn't expected to see him for days.

A New Kind of Freedom

The only real taboo at Woodstock was violence. Hundreds of thousands of people roaming the woods at night could have meant real trouble. Despite an atmosphere which John Haerry describes as, "The only rule was that there were no rules other than what people established for themselves," there was no real trouble. The announcers, the bands, all said, "We're in this together. It's up to us to make it work."

"You knew you really had to cooperate with the people next to you," says Dena Quilici.

Kathleen McDevitt remembers, "It was a little bit frightening to have such freedom, like another world where you could do anything, say anything, be anyone, nobody would stop you. It was hard on all of us having that much freedom; it could have gone the other way and been really dangerous. The balance was unnerving, and everybody at the end said, 'We did it.'"

"It would be so embarrassing to (be violent) in a sheer crowd that was obviously enjoying itself and full of good feelings. There was a feeling that you were among a select group of people who could gather in such huge numbers without any problems," said Stephen Shechtman. "We probably thought that half a million of our parents couldn't get together and do as good a job with it."

"I knew something could go wrong, but I didn't feel that it would," said Chris Heinzmann, and about a dozen others.

Points of Light

From the stage, announcer John Morris asked us each to light a match, just so we could see how many of us there were. At first, the response was slow but then little lights appeared, far, far away, and we began to get the idea. The cynicism faded. Your light was a gift to everybody else, and marked your place in the big picture. All along the hillside and into the woods as far as you could see were tiny fires. Michael Craper lit his match and just watched in awe. "I had never seen anything like it," he reports. "I was mesmerized for about an hour."

Melanie was on stage next, and all this incendiary business went on during her set. She later wrote a song about Woodstock called "Candles in the Rain," and audiences lit matches whenever she sang it. Now, flicking one's Bic is a polite way to request an encore. Joan Baez finished it all off, pregnant and sweet.

Dawn Jabari-Zhou had earlier met someone who knew of an empty chicken coop she and her friends could sleep in. They followed him into the woods, where there was an abandoned coop that didn't smell. Rain poured in. She rolled her bag out on a plank that was probably a former chicken roost. "Back then, we trusted each other completely," she says.

Woodstock, Day One, was over. Bid goodnight from the stage with a solemn reminder that the person next to us was our brother, hundreds of thousands of wet, tired people crept off to the woods, under or into vans, or stayed on the field, sleeping where they had roosted. Tens of thousands of others, too keyed up to sleep, milled all night by firelight. This convention of the unconventional had just begun.

There were easily 500,000 points of light in Woodstock Nation that night.

The Music Went on for 24 Hours

The first of the "3 Days of Peace and Music"—and mud—had been just a prelude to Rock 'n' Roll Survival Weekend. By the time Carlos Santana finished playing "Soul Sacrifice" Saturday at Woodstock, he was a major star.

"Every band changed the vibes," recalls Dena Quilici, one of the many there from southeastern New England. And the crowd came alive for Santana. The by-now broiling sun, the hunger and thirst and mud, the army helicopters intermittently turning fire hoses on us full-force to cool us off—"all those troubles kind of went away once you just settled down and started listening to the music," says Ty Davis.

Santana was a salsa band without a contract, who came at The Grateful Dead's insistence. "Santana came out and just blew everyone away," says Ron Gamache. "We kept saying, 'Who are these guys?' We'd never heard such rhythms."

Quill had opened Saturday's show about noon. Only Ty Davis seems to remember them "as one of the totally unimportant bands. But they were one of the first Boston bands to get any notice." Michele Keir had a tremendous time at Woodstock, even though she heard only one band and doesn't recall which one. Many of us who were there don't individually remember much of the music for which Woodstock has become a synonym.

The quality of the sound was fantastic near the stage, deteriorating to terrible at about half the depth of the crowd and beyond. And the bands were faraway specks to many, competing with the human kaleidoscope around us. Musicians had to touch and amplify some powerful human chord just to get our attention. "You knew you were there more for the experience than for the music," says Dennis Lemoine.

There were bubbles and banners and weirdly dressed people. Many of Ken Kesey's Merry Pranksters were evolving into the Hog Farmers, those members of the New Mexico commune who cooked, and counseled and taught survival skills. Both groups were at Woodstock.

Mel Ash didn't know who the Pranksters were then, but he later read Tom Wolfe's chronicle of their bus trip across America playing theatrical cosmic jokes, *The Electric Kool-Aid Acid Test*. "The next year," I said, "These are famous people."

The experience was intensely visual. The Hell's Angels arrived, and started ferrying medical supplies. "I remember one guy with an American flag headband and a flag cape, going around with some sign about 'If we all coordinate our energies, we can end the war this weekend'—a very intense wired cat," remembers John Haerry.

"We were next to a blanket containing a really huge guy dressed only in athletic shorts," Tom Mulligan recalls, "getting his body painted by his girlfriend. That was my first exposure to body-painting."

"I don't remember the music so much as the people, but it was a background," says Dena Quilici.

"It got so big the music was just a little part of it," says Walter Williams.

Food Lines

We seemed to be spending as much time searching for food as our ancestors had. Joe Caffey lined up to buy overpriced tomatoes. "You knew you were gonna get ripped off, but you're starving. And the guy had a 10-gallon can of tuna fish. Then a guy comes out of nowhere, naked, sticks his hand into the pot, grabs a handful and goes off into the woods."

"Somebody came in with a soda truck and started selling cans for a buck," David DelBonis recalls. "Everybody got really ticked off, and kind of confiscated the truck, passed out the soda. But they started handing the guy what he should have been selling it for—a quarter, at that time. They just starting throwing the money at him, saying

'This is what the can's worth, you got it.' He tried to scalp everybody . . . but they didn't steal it."

I had a half-full bottle of Vin Rouge Superieur left from Friday night, and I desperately wished for a miracle that would turn the wine into water. When the water truck arrived, I dumped out the wine. For two days that empty bottle was my most precious possession.

"There was a premium on cold things," Tom Mulligan remembers. "People with beer and soft drinks were held in high esteem. Someone nearby had a basket with raw carrots and shared it, but nothing went very far."

Mel Ash of Providence, a vegetarian, had the foresight to bring about 21 cans of sardines to barter with. "I hated fish, but they could be opened with keys, so they were convenient. We traded for watermelons."

At the Hog Farm, across a road from the music area, where street signs read High Way, Groovy Way, and Peaceful Way, Woodstock Stew was on the menu. It was a sticky vegetable and grain glop that tasted strange to those of us raised on canned soup casseroles, but was very filling. They served free brown rice and vegetables all weekend, and more.

When Ash went there looking for food, "They were handing out cones of granola, and Wavy Gravy (the commune's leader) was saying some Zen saying, 'A day without work is a day without eating.' So we volunteered to clean the pots. Then we went closer to the crowd at the stage and said, 'Free food this way, eat all you can, if you can't eat it, give it away,' over and over again for a couple of hours."

Demand for Pay

We settled in to wait for Bob Dylan. With every helicopter that landed behind the stage, rumors spread that it was Dylan, who lived in Woodstock—the town, not the nation—50 miles away. He never came. He was scheduled to play the Isle of Wight on the English Channel for $87,000, a booking he had before the Woodstock organizers asked him to play.

Jimi Hendrix, the highest-paid act at Woodstock, got $18,000. Santana earned less than $2500. The Who ($6250) and The Grateful Dead got nervous about the free concert and refused to play unless they were paid in cash. A local banker was roused after midnight and whisked by helicopter to the bank in his pajamas to get $25,000 cash.

The performers didn't share our physical hardships. Helicopters were delivering delicacies and champagne to the performers' area. David's Potbelly Restaurant from New York City catered and offered to ferry them back to the hotel and the party in the bar. But they had to face the biggest, most distracted crowd in rock history and were looking at major flop sweats.

If other bands griped about facing a crowd too big to reach, Creedence had a different problem. They followed The Grateful Dead at 3:30 a.m. and the biggest crowd in rock history was dead asleep. John Fogerty has said he saw one guy flash his lighter, and played the whole set to that one person.

Power Acts

Rock's power lineup was on Saturday night's bill, but by then many of us were exhausted. "The music was 24 hours, so you had to pick and choose," says Mel Ash. "My friend and I took turns waking each other up. There was a lot of sharing of blankets and what not." Still, with all the distractions wrenching our attention from the music, among us we have a composite memory good enough to reconstruct most of the action.

To many, Janis Joplin was the only woman really out there on the edge alone. The reigning folk and rock women—Baez, Grace Slick, Joni Mitchell, Michelle Phillips of the Mama and Papas, Judy Collins—were romantic figures, and Mama Cass was a 300-pound hot ticket in a quartet. But Janis was beyond the pale, a brazen hussy singing her soul out as she swigged Southern Comfort. A lot of us were rooting for her, but the woman who wailed, "I'm gonna show you that a woman can be tough," seemed born too soon and too alone.

She is reported to have said, "Me, I was brought up in a middle-class family; I could have had anything. But you need something more in your gut, man." Her emptiness seemed bottomless, and the more she battled the blues with hard liquor, heroin and one-night stands, the deeper she seemed to sink.

Woodstock isn't generally considered one of her great performances. She seemed genuinely distraught as she wailed and sobbed in a skimpy dress with spangles instead of her customary feathers. Her band—neither Big Brother and the Holding Company nor Full Tilt Boogie but the Cosmic Blues Band with saxes and trombones—didn't seem to work with her.

To some it didn't matter.

"When Janis sang 'Ball and Chain' . . . we all felt tied down like that," says Carmino Scaglione.

David Weinrebe had plopped down in a ditch to sleep. "I woke up to Janis Joplin shrieking. She was a goddess. To be waking out of a dead sleep to Janis . . . "

When Sly Stone followed, he did something with "I Want to Take You Higher" that had the entire crowd on its feet shouting "higher" for 45 minutes. Dawn Jabari-Zhou remembers Sly for the "enthusiasm and energy he created in concert. Everybody was up, paying attention, shouting and clapping, Sly in a bright white outfit, an Indian jacket with tassels along the sleeves. He almost looked like he was a bird and like he was gonna take off and fly."

The Who and Abbie

The Who played at 2 in the morning. What everybody remembers is Pete Townshend bashing Abbie Hoffman with his guitar. Abbie had seized the mike to urge the crowd smoking flowers so freely to mobilize on behalf of John Sinclair, head of the White Panther Party, who was serving a 10-year sentence for having passed a joint to a narcotics officer. Somebody turned the mike off and Townshend made like a bayonet with the guitar and jabbed Abbie in the head and off the stage.

In *Soon to be a Major Motion Picture,* Abbie wrote, "Townshend, who had been tuning up, turned around and bumped me. A non-incident." But Townshend told *Rolling Stone* magazine, "I kicked him off the stage. I deeply regret that. If I was given that opportunity again I would stop the show. Because I don't think rock and roll is that important. Then I did. The show had to go on."

Rico Topazio of Bristol, who now plays in a band called the Pink Cadillacs in Los Angeles, says, "I liked Abbie, but it was the wrong time for Abbie to be on stage. As a guitar player, I knew that. Pete didn't know who Abbie was. Woodstock wasn't political in that way. It was as if Bob Hope were at a USO show, time to get away from all that, to see how many of us were together."

The crowd seemed to agree with Pete that Abbie was out of line. There were no boos or shouts, and The Who continued playing. "The Who were in their prime, not like they are now," Haerry recalls. "Roger Daltrey still had his voice, and Pete Townshend still had his voice, and they did a hell of a show."

It's unfair that Abbie is remembered for a stupid act at Woodstock. Abbie had organized the medical tent, worked in the bad trips tent, and been an extraordinarily competent man to have around. His death by suicide earlier this year (1989), so close to the Woodstock anniversary, seems to mark the end of yet another era. Wavy Gravy, the man on the record saying, "There's a little bit of heaven in every disaster area," suggested to me this week that if we cared, it would be fitting to "do something for the Yipper."

Just as dawn broke, the Jefferson Airplane took the stage. They had been waiting to play since 10:30 the night before, and Grace Slick played with her eyes closed.

"I remember waking up at about 5 in the morning," said Haerry, "and all of a sudden hearing Grace Slick out of nowhere, 'Good morning, people, it's time to wake up,' (BOINGGGGGGGG, Whoa, yeah!) and going down to the stage, treading my way through what looked like the aftermath of a battlefield, all these bodies and getting right down to the front of the stage and there was Jefferson Airplane, 25 or 30 feet away."

"I had to see Grace Slick," Mel Ash says, "because I was in love with Grace Slick and I thought the Airplane represented at that moment everything the culture stood for." Grace Slick in a white-fringed minidress in the blue dawn is an image burned in many brains.

"The sun was coming up over the hills," recalls Carmino Scaglione, "over the campfires of the people who'd been up all night," and she sang "White Rabbit," the song that let the East know what the West had been up to in the summer of '67. "Do You Want Somebody to Love?" sent ripples up spines; hearing only "Volunteers" on the concert tape is one reason to have been at Woodstock.

It was Sunday morning. Time enough to sleep.

We Had Pulled It Off

Despite two days of uncomfortable conditions, peace and music are both holding out. Sunday is the acid test.

The storm bore down on us, all hard rain and whipping wind, just after Joe Cocker ended the set that opened Woodstock, Day 3. "The ground was slippery red clay, and then it really looked like Baghdad," remembers Dottie Clark. "People selling the junk of the time were packing up, my friends were crying, and I was laughing. I thought it was funny. I said, 'Someday you'll see that this was something.' "

Cocker had finished his set with what may have been the best ever live performance of "With a Little Help From My Friends." "I ran into a friend from school standing at the stage when Joe Cocker was performing," says Stephen Schechtman, "and I just remember tears in his eyes, this guy just standing there crying. He was really moved by it."

The storm that followed, with clouds straight out of a Hollywood epic, "was almost like a test from some god," says Kathleen McDevitt. "That was really hard to get through. But I remember being exhilarated. People on stage were saying 'hang in there,' and everybody did."

These people had been too long wet, hungry, hot and cold. Spontaneously, the rain chant began—"No rain, no rain, no rain . . . " When the hour-long deluge stopped, the field was a giant mud puddle. But the Woodstock attitude held: another bad situation was turned around. With a slight shift of perspective, any kid could see a perfect hill for sliding. The long coast to the stage was fun.

"It looked like a picture from the World War II archives, the refugees after a town had been blitzed or invaded," says John Haerry. "Here were all these people, cold, wet, miserable, hungry, thirsty, but still keeping it together."

"I remember people walking around quietly asking, 'Do you have any spare food, or anything to drink?' At the same time, if people had anything, it was 'Well, we've got a bag of potato chips, here, have some of our potato chips.' "

"To the media it was a catastrophe, but to us, it was the very best life," says Carmino Scaglione.

"There were enormous garbage bags and people sitting all around them," remembers Dottie Clark. "It was Felliniesque."

"It stunk on Sunday," Rico Topazio recalls. "People were burning clothes to keep warm. Then a helicopter came over the field and started dropping things. It was scary, people freaked out, until they saw they were flowers."

"It was like a reward for just being there, and staying," says Kathleen McDevitt. "There was someone somewhere concerned about us."

Lee Blumer, assistant to the security director then, said that the gesture had been arranged by Michael Lang, the man who thought up the whole idea of a festival that would bring together the counterculture so we could see how many of us there really were.

A Recent Reminder

Dawn Jabari-Zhou, who was forced to leave China last month after teaching there two years, said the students in Tiananmen Square in June reminded her of Woodstock. "In Beijing, people did make that analogy: They hadn't seen these many people since Woodstock. People were orderly, friendly, and shared food and shelter. There was a tent city at Tiananmen."

Woodstock also had shadows. At least two deaths were reported. A 17-year-old who slept Friday night under a tractor was killed when the driver started it up and ran over him. Another young man died, but it is not clear whether it was from a heroin overdose or a heart attack.

I suspect that Margaret Chevian speaks for many when she says, "At the time people were sucked into being liberal; what you were then and are now is not the same. We went along with the crowd. I don't know why we didn't die from bad sanitation."

And others would agree with Ed Dalton's statement that "Woodstock was a promise unfulfilled because I don't think my generation accomplished what they set out to accomplish: change the world. When we saw all of us, we knew we had force and power. I think the whole generation has sold out, and I hope the kids turn out better than we did."

Most of us who were at Woodstock also know somebody who tried to stay there no matter where they were later, and became casualties of drugs and alcohol. Tom of Providence was 14 at Woodstock, doing drugs. "I regret that Woodstock set me on this path. I wish I'd spent more time studying, learning a trade. Because I was so young and doing drugs, I didn't have a chance to have a real adolescence, to grow up." He's been in AA for two years.

One caller from North Kingstown wouldn't identify herself but wanted to say that her parents didn't let her go to Woodstock, and her friends who did all developed serious addiction problems.

Three births and four miscarriages were reported at the festival, but, so far, no one has come forward waving a birth certificate to prove, "I was born at Woodstock."

No Unknown Garage Band

Crosby, Stills and Nash had only played one concert—in Chicago—before Woodstock, but this was no unknown garage band. David Crosby had been a founding member of the Byrds; Stephen Stills played in Buffalo Springfield with Neil Young; and Graham Nash was stolen from the Hollies. Their first album together, *Crosby, Stills and Nash*, would stay on the charts for 107 weeks. But that night at Woodstock, Graham Nash sheepishly greeted the crowd with, "We'd like to a do a medley of our hit."

Several people named them as a favorite memory, but on "Suite: Judy Blue Eyes" the harmonies were so badly off key that the tracks would be redubbed for the album. It didn't matter, except to festival-goers who swore later they were off key but couldn't prove it by the movie.

Neil Young joined CSN at Woodstock, and again two weeks later at the Big Sur Festival at the Esalen Institute, where Joni Mitchell first sang "Woodstock," the anthem she wrote for the festival without ever having been there. Mitchell was living with Graham Nash at the time, but spent the festival weekend in New York City with her manager, David Geffen. Geffen convinced her she might not be able to get out of Bethel, N.Y., in time to make a TV appearance on *The Dick Cavett Show.*

Bulletin Board of the Air

The stage announcements were sometimes witty, often humorous, and excessive. The bulletin board of the air was full of lost people, headlines about what the world thought was happening to us, happy news, call your mother, come get your medicine, and colorful—if meaningless—warnings about specific colors of bad acid. There were probably fifty shades of green acid, and if anybody had just taken some, this was no time to hear it was polluted.

Cheryl Godek Curran knew people who had taken green acid. "They said, 'Take us to the doctor,' so we went to the bad trips tent. There they said, 'If you took it and you're having a good trip, just go back and enjoy the festival.' And they did."

David DelBonis had helped build the children's playground, the hospital tent (which Abbie Hoffman ran) and the kitchens. During the festival, he roamed the crowd, bringing people whose mental circuits had crossed back to the bad trips tent. Rick Danko of The Band and John Sebastian dropped in to play a sort of mellow rock for people who weren't digesting mind-altering substances well.

DelBonis explains a bad trip as "being with too many people and thinking you can party on LSD. Your brain can't sort it quick enough. You feel scared and paranoid." A good trip: "It's searching; it's kind of like looking for yourself. It's a very spiritual thing."

From his observations, "The drug thing was totally overblown. Certainly there was marijuana used, but not as many drugs as people imagine."

"Not everybody at Woodstock used drugs," Phil Kukielski says, "and people didn't drink much. A little wine, maybe. But this was a place you could safely smoke grass."

For some, the novelty of being able to take a social puff in public was the big thrill. A joint lit up in the crowd got passed all over. "It was nice not to feel worried about the police," said one Rhode Islander. "That was very liberating."

Although there were dealers, most people were wary of what they might be selling. Street drugs could be anything. "LSD is more dangerous for anybody to experiment with now," says Dennis Lemoine, now a Corrections Officer at the Rhode Island Training School for Youth. "Then it was made by chemists in universities and people with real knowledge of it. People now make it in cellars from a book in the library. They use strychnine (a favorite poison in old murder mysteries) to get a physical effect.

"Back then, the marijuana was less strong than what it is now. The grade has accelerated. People got stoned, laughed, sang and got happy. Now kids smoke it, sit back and nod and that's it. The old Mexican was destroyed with Paraquat.

This stuff they're importing has a higher THC content. And they don't stick with pot anymore.

"I know people who did heavy drugs for years on the streets, then crack and freebasing got them in a year. They're chasing that first big high from then on.

"We did drugs, but not the dangerous drugs. We were a whole different generation who cared for each other. We were against war, we had goals . . . "

I asked Wavy Gravy, who ran the bad trips tent, what he thinks of drugs now. "You need to differentiate between smack, crack and smoking flowers," Wavy said. "Cocaine is horrible. It's nature's way of telling people they have too much money. It makes them mean to their friends and their kids. Psychotropic stuff in moderation can lead to extraordinary results. I like to say, 'My father's mush has many rooms.' "

Wiring Repairs Halt Show

There was music through the night, but the sound system was shut off during the storm, which soaked some dangerously tattered wiring. While repairs were made and new wires were laid, the show did not go on.

So the Sunday bands played too late to too few still awake. And the movie crew slept at night, which is why so many great sets are missing. Sha-Na-Na made it into the film only because the crews were getting up to shoot Jimi Hendrix.

"We tried to book Roy Rogers to sing 'Happy Trails' as the closing number for the festival," Michael Lang told Joel Makower in *The Oral History of Woodstock.* "His agent declined." Instead, Hendrix insisted on closing the show with the national anthem.

"Obviously, he got the meaning of this thing sufficiently enough to know to play 'The Star Spangled Banner' at the very end," Lee Blumer told *Rockfax,* a small music paper published in Norwich, Conn. ". . . He saw Woodstock come from out of dust to a nation and he played an anthem." But not before he tossed off what was probably the strangest line of that long strange weekend: "Maybe the new day might give us a chance, blah-blah, woof-woof."

It was 8:30 Monday morning when Hendrix started to play. He was in lavender fringe with a head band, "letting his freak flag fly," as one member of the group would write. There were fewer than half a hundred thousand left when he did it. Most people had gone.

Hendrix played in the early morning sun with garbage all over, and he was loud. Too loud, I remember, for my frazzled nerve endings. His guitar seemed to frizz my brain, but I was finally next to the stage, 10 feet from Jimi, and I had to watch his face. It seemed illuminated from within.

I could hear Vietnam in this anthem, bombs bursting on guitar. It flew and dived and made brand new a song that had always seemed to me a war chant. The anthem of Woodstock Nation was the anthem of America loosened, freed of its rigid measures. It was okay to be different.

The song ended at 10 a.m., 65 hours after Richie Havens began it. We had pulled it off. It was over, and we left on whatever roads have brought us to where we are now.

FIGURE 5.3 Exhausted after the Woodstock concert in August 1969, a couple sleeps on the trunk of their car in the midst of a huge traffic jam leading away from the concert site. Thousands of people packed up their tents and blanket rolls and walked miles to reach their cars or the buses that would carry them home from this history-making event. Estimates are that over half a million people attended the concert, billed as "Three Days of Peace and Music," where many of the most famous bands and solo artists of the 1960s performed night and day, in rain and sun, entertaining an audience spread out over 37 acres.
Source: Corbis/Bettmann

An Invitation to Dinner

"On the way home," remembers Tom Mulligan, "we were slogging to the car and noticed some people standing around a house. We walked over and they invited us to dinner. They were making a huge meal for anybody who wanted to come by." Phil Kukielski and David DelBonis both remember being handed flyers as they left. They read, "Come to Chicago" for the radical Weathermen's Days of Rage.

People stayed for weeks, reluctant to leave, cleaning up Yasgur's Farm. "On the way back I was bummed out and didn't know why, because I'd had a good time," says Jim Edwards. "At first I thought, 'Every high has a crash,' but then I really felt like I had just attended an Irish wake."

Woodstock's promoters flew to New York to explain to the bankers and lawyers why they threw a free festival and spent the bank's money to drop flowers on the crowd.

So what came out of all that mud and music 20 years ago? Joe Landry, a Providence native who at 29 was one of the oldest people at the festival, seemed to sum it up: "That it's no good for me if it's not good for everybody."

QUESTIONS FOR DISCUSSION

1. If you have heard of the Woodstock concert before reading this story, does this story challenge any of your preconceived notions of the event? Does it add anything? Do you know anyone who went to Woodstock? If so, how would you compare their experience to those described here?

2. Some students today may assume that Woodstock was an anti-war rally. Was it? Among the young people who attended the concert, there were a few soldiers and guardsmen on leave, yet it appears from the story that a majority of the people who attended the concert were opposed to the war in Vietnam. What does this tell you about how Americans felt about the war in 1969?

3. Discuss the widespread use of drugs at Woodstock. Why do you think the authorities opted to look the other way? How could this happen in a country where drugs are illegal? Would it happen today, or were there special circumstances at Woodstock? If so, what were they? Can you tell from the story if anyone regretted drug use at Woodstock?

4. What is your reaction to learning about the physical stresses of Woodstock—the weather, the lack of sanitation, scarcity of food, and so on? Was it worse or better than you had previously thought? Why do you think people stayed? To what would you attribute the successes of this mass event: i.e. the fact that there was no violence and there was great deal of sharing and cooperation? What were the conditions that unified the crowd? Do you think those conditions could be replicated today, or were they limited to the era of the late Sixties?

5. If you had to plan a rock concert today, what would you do differently? What equipment and technology would you have today that was not available in 1969? How would those items make a difference in organizing and publicizing the concert, or in providing concessions and amenities for the crowds?

6. What is the "meaning" of Woodstock in American history? In Sixties history? Was Woodstock just a long outdoor concert or does it represent a high point of Sixties culture or freedom? Some people in the story mention the "promise" of Woodstock. What was that? (Look back at Sheila Lennon's description of Jimi Hendrix playing "The Star Spangled Banner.") Was the promise fulfilled? Some people mention outgrowing Woodstock. What do you think they mean by that?

ORDINARY LIVES: KENT STATE, MAY 4, 1970
Carole Barbato and Laura Davis

"These students want disruption. They seek to prove that this system of ours, when faced with crisis, does not work. If it takes a bloodbath, let's get it over with!"
California governor Ronald Reagan (*San Francisco Chronicle,* May 15, 1969)

CAROLE: I grew up at a time when butter, cottage cheese, and milk in glass bottles were delivered to your doorstep, when Charles Potato Chips came neatly packed and delivered in the familiar gold and brown round can, when parents and children all ate dinner together (for us it was 4:30 p.m.), and you could tell what day it was by what your mother was cooking, when she was cleaning, or when she was washing and hanging out clothes to dry. All the girls had to wear skirts or dresses with hems no more than an inch above their knees—no slacks or blue jeans. If you wore blue jeans, the kids felt sorry for you because it meant your family couldn't afford to buy you regular pants that might not have lasted as long as jeans.

LAURA: Sometimes the milkman would let us hitch a ride on his truck and we'd suck the milk from the chunks of ice that kept the bottles cold. While we thrilled to the arrival of the Charles Chips man, my mother preferred the diversion of the Fuller brush man's sample case, which she pored over before making her selection. Tuesday was spaghetti night. Friday was fish. Even my father, who was rarely home, returned every evening at 6:00 p.m. for dinner. Sunday nights of my childhood were marked by drives back from my grandparents' house on the west side of Cleveland, past the fire and sulphur mills of the Flats. Along this route I remember the pleasure of being able to read for the first time something that I had seen before many times on the side of a building, it not making much difference that I was reading the phase backwards: "OVER IS WAR THE." Later I could only guess—was it the most recent Korean War, or was it the war more centrally of my parents' generation? According to the family story, my father, a singer, but not to become famous, served with Tony Bennett and drove a jeep for a general in Italy in World War II. Parents of the friends I would make in junior high had survived concentration camps.

Our own first war was the Cold War. Kindergarten on the industrial east side of Cleveland was punctuated as often by air raid drills as fire drills. We executed these in two variations, carefully getting our heads all the way under our desks as we crouched in the classroom or kneeling facing the lockers in the hallway, our school-issued, military-style dog tags dangling to the floor or tucked inside our shirts.

In fourth grade we chose sides for the school's mock Nixon-Kennedy election. Nixon supporters signaled their allegiance by penning over the first letter on their big pink Dixon erasers. Not choosing, as my classmates did, to vote my parents' political preference (despite my father's Catholic connections, they were Nixon supporters), I was vindicated when Kennedy won the real election.

CAROLE: Growing up in Youngstown, Ohio, I really wasn't politically savvy nor concerned that much about politics. Almost everyone I knew voted Democrat in Youngstown. This is true even today. There was a strong blue-collar working class who immigrated to the area to work in the steel mills in order to make a better life for their families. The Democrats had the best interests of the working class and poor at heart and the Republicans were for big business, and by definition, against the working class. In Youngstown, any self-respecting, working class, union person voted for any candidate with a "D" following their name on the ballot, regardless of their qualifications.

When John F. Kennedy was running for president in 1960 one of his stops was, of course, "Steeltown, USA." I remember my Uncle Ralph piling us in his car and driving us to the town square to catch a glimpse of this young, handsome, energetic candidate, who was not only a Democrat, but a Catholic too! You could feel change in the air. President Eisenhower represented the older generation—old ideas, and worn out policies. John F. Kennedy represented youth, liberation from the ideas of the older generation, and hope for a brighter future. Kennedy would not have let the Russians beat us into space. When I heard that Kennedy won the election, I felt the times were really changing.

LAURA: The Cold War flared up during Kennedy's administration with the Bay of Pigs invasion in April 1961. I reacted viscerally to the language of the invasion: I equated the enemy, the other, with the place that named the event.

October 1962 brought the Cuban Missile Crisis. My ex-Marine sixth-grade teacher, who, like our school's other sixth-grade teacher had undoubtedly received his education through the G.I. Bill, recounted the evening news to us and assured us (and himself) that his uniform still fit. He made it clear that the Cold War would soon become a hot one, the only way to protect democracy and prevent the spread of Communism.

CAROLE: In Youngstown, in the fall of 1962, I felt the fear of war for the first time. Would the Russians be so cruel as to kill innocent women and children with their missiles? Could the Russians send missiles as far north as Ohio from Cuba? Because we made steel in our area, would Youngstown be one of the first targets for the Russians? My family debated these questions. Would our fathers have to go off to war again, this time to fight the Russians and Communists? I remember wishing that we had an air raid shelter in our backyard. I thought how safe the folks who had them must feel now that war was imminent. But as quickly as the crisis came it also went away, and it vanished from my consciousness.

LAURA: The need for constant vigilance against the spread of Communism, embodied during the '50s and '60s in our hatred and suspicion of the Soviet Union, seemed to transfer readily for our parents' generation to Communist North Vietnam. I remember it started with the Gulf of Tonkin event in 1964. While the Cold War had tangibly permeated my existence, America's entry into the war in Vietnam played at first in the background, in a continuous, but somewhat dim, reel in the black and white images of men, stretchers, and helicopters on the six o'clock news narrated by Walter Cronkite.

More vivid was the changing social climate of the Civil Rights Movement. I remember we were visiting the New York World's Fair in the summer of 1964 when Goodman, Cheney, and Schwerner, three civil rights workers, were murdered in Mississippi and the news was announced on the futuristic electronic crawl screen mounted high over the fair. "Black is Beautiful" became embodied in Angela Davis's "Afro" hair and "Black Power" in the raised fists of the black athletes in the 1968 Summer Olympics. I tried in vain to update my mother's vocabulary from "Negro" to "black." I questioned whether my two best high school guy friends had actually been able to see the July 1966 disturbances in Hough, Cleveland's inner city, from the safe distance of segregated Murray Hill as they had claimed.

CAROLE: Segregation was not just part of the South; we experienced it in Youngstown. There were two high schools on the south side of the city where I grew up. On the one side of the tracks was a predominantly black high school and on the other was a predominantly white high school. I happened to live on the "white side of the tracks." Growing up Catholic, we were taught to treat others as equals and as we would like to be treated. Yet when busing was introduced as an answer to the segregation entrenched in the neighborhoods of the city, it was met with resistance. I can remember neighbors talking about others fleeing to the suburbs to avoid having Negroes move in next door. I didn't understand how or why they feared that would change the neighborhood or property values. I believed the vision of the Civil Rights Movement, believed in Martin Luther King, Jr.'s dream. Reading John Howard Griffin's *Black Like Me* had the most profound influence on me. I felt that we needed to treat each other as brothers. It was wrong that Negroes were denied the right to vote. The images of the black protesters being chased and clubbed by white police officers were startling to me. I was going to go to college to become a teacher and I would teach in the inner city and make a difference.

LAURA: Against this backdrop, we lost the leaders that we admired, who we believed could change the world, each assassination delivering a stunning, disheartening blow. I was in last-period, seventh-grade science class when the voice of our principal announced the death of John F. Kennedy. We filed, numb, some girls crying, into the lobby; school closed early for the first time in our lives. When Martin Luther King, Jr., was shot I sat alone on the family room couch staring at the scenes of the Memphis motel balcony, feeling both hollowed out and filled with a dead weight at the same time. I went to sleep on the night of June 5, 1968 thinking it wasn't possible that Bobby Kennedy wouldn't be alive when I got up in the morning.

CAROLE: When I came to Kent State University in 1967 most of the female students wore skirts or dresses to class and the guys wore pants and loafers. I really can't say that I recall seeing very long hair on the guys. The "surfer cut" was in for the guys, with hair right below the ears. The girls were still wearing bouffant hairdos with just a slight upturned flip at the ends. I can remember one of the first projects of our dorm was "Vittles for Vietnam." After the cafeteria closed, girls in the dorm would go downstairs, bake cookies, and make packages for Vietnam soldiers. I only knew one person who was fighting in Vietnam. He was a Marine and we corresponded for the two years he was in Danang. Most of my other high school friends had college deferments. At this time, I bought most of the rhetoric of the "hawks." Without question, I accepted the fact that we needed to be in Vietnam. We were assisting the South Vietnamese in liberating themselves from the Communists in the north. As the year progressed and I read and saw more pictures about the effects of the war, those thoughts changed.

LAURA: I arrived at Kent State at 17 in 1969, happy to have escaped the oppressive cliquishness of high school. Afraid that how little I knew would be revealed, I sat up all night in a desk chair discussing race riots and social oppression with my new friend Julie. On "Moratorium Day" in October, I pinned on a black armband and marched down Main Street in line behind the KSU chapter of Vietnam Veterans Against the War. One spring afternoon, our longish-haired, grad student poetry instructor sent us in pairs to walk around campus with bags of popcorn. We were supposed to register people's reactions as we offered it to them. Not a radical act, it nonetheless strained the boundaries of social convention in Ohio of the late 1960s. And it reflected the unspoken, but growing mandate among students at Kent State that we should reach out to one another, across whatever lines of class, race, gender, and sexual mores that might divide us.

Alison Krause exuded that spirit. It was difficult to be in a room with Alison and not notice her. I used to get to Professor Glenn Frank's super-sized geology class early freshman year, to get a seat in the first row of the second section back, a good place to stretch one's legs and to watch the other students piling into the auditorium. One day, Alison Krause came bounding in, like a deer or a puppy, went up to Kenny with the Beach Boys blond hair and started licking his face. She seemed so unembarrassed, so sure of what she was doing, so exuberant.

CAROLE: At Kent State, I began reading and thinking about things that I never thought about before. I was living with thousands of other young people all around my age, with different religions, different colors, and different belief systems. It was time to test out the ideas of my youth. The black students on campus began to join a group called Black United Students—BUS. "Say it loud, I'm Black and I'm Proud!" was the phrase you could hear. Some were saying that the Civil Rights Movement supported by Dr. King got them nowhere. They were taken with the rhetoric of Stokely Carmichael and Malcolm X. It was time for a "marvelous new militancy." I supported the ideas and ideals of Martin Luther King, Jr., and it was difficult for me to understand why some of the black kids at the university felt they had to separate themselves from the white students. Those who were supporting the Civil Rights Movement seemed to also be the ones protesting the war. A fact few remember about the early stages of the Vietnam War was that the black soldiers were fighting in combat and dying at a disproportionate rate.

During the summer of 1967, the tumult of 1968, and especially after Woodstock in August 1969, it seemed that everything changed. The "Summer of Love" and the "Hippie" movement were coming to Kent State—the middle of the country. We could see and hear it in the change in clothing, the disappearance of the bouffant hairdos, and the continued anti-war sentiment in the music. Even "soul" music was declaring "War! What is it good for? Absolutely nothing!" War protestors were being beaten by police outside the Democratic National Convention in Chicago for seemingly no reason. Kent State University became part of the Hippie/Yippie movement. There were protests outside the student union, which was called the "Hub." What affected me most during this time was talking with Dave, a former soldier who had joined the Vietnam Veterans Against the War. Dave told me about his time in

Vietnam as a conscientious objector. He realized once he was over in Vietnam that he could not kill—that "they" were not the enemy. His platoon sergeant would send him out on reconnaissance as a human decoy. He lived to tell the story.

LAURA: 1969–1970 was a time when change seemed not only possible but a social responsibility—we had to bring about an end to social inequality and to the war, which many had begun to perceive as an intrusion of the U.S. as a military-industrial superpower into a simple, non-industrial country. The U.S. was the superpower aggressor, a message driven home in a series of demonstrations at Kent State in front of the student union. I remember one demonstration where organizers threatened to napalm a dog, another at which unseasoned pumpkin soup was served from a large kettle to illustrate the simplicity of the Vietnamese diet and, thus, the lives of these people who were up against the juggernaut of the West.

May 4, 1970. The war our country was fighting to stave off the domino effect of the spread of Communism reached a crisis point for the Kent State campus in May 1970. Thursday night, April 30, the voice of Richard Nixon replaced Walter Cronkite's to announce that planes had been sent over the South Vietnamese border into Cambodia. In the context of promises to wind down U.S. involvement according to Nixon's official plan of Vietnamization—withdrawing American troops and turning the war effort over to the South Vietnamese army—this action was understood as an escalation of the war, a betrayal.

Friday afternoon, May 1, we watched as a group of graduate students from the history department buried a copy of the Constitution and I worried for the student who burned his draft card. That night, the first magically warm spring night, I went for a ride on the back of a motorcycle with a sweet guy named John. We sat on the far riverbank across from the downtown bars, kissing a little under streetlights and the moon.

CAROLE: There was a great divide in our country and on our campus. There were those who supported the efforts in Vietnam and those who opposed the war. It seemed, however, that many students were becoming more sympathetic to the fact that we had to get out of this war before many more young Americans came home in body bags. Martin Luther King, Jr., and Robert F. Kennedy were against the war and we had looked to them for leadership and guidance; however, they were both now gone, gunned down in cold blood and with them the dreams they—and we—held dear. Richard Nixon had won the 1968 election with the promise of sending the troops home. On Thursday, April 30, 1970, his lie was exposed.

It was with this behind me that I attended the rally on campus Friday, May 1, 1970. We were all very angry at the betrayal of Richard Nixon. How many more young people have to die before something is done? I watched the members of WHORE (World Historians Opposed to Racism and Exploitation) bury the U.S. Constitution near the Victory Bell on the Commons. The Black United Students were to hold a rally at Rockwell Hall (the library) at 3:00 p.m., and we were invited to attend. At the end of the protest it was decided that we all would meet at the same place at noon on Monday, May 4, for a major protest against the escalation of the war.

May 1 was a warm spring night in Kent. A favorite pastime of students and area young people was to go to the strip of bars on Water Street and this night was no different. There was a real party atmosphere as my roommate and I walked downtown from our house on Depeyster. She went drinking at the Loft and I went to dance and listen to music at a place called the Kove, which was located below ground level on Water Street. Someone said that a motorcycle gang was outside having some fun so some of us went upstairs to see what was going on. People had blocked off Water Street and the motorcycles were running up and down the street. People were cheering and laughing. Someone dumped a trashcan and started a fire in the middle of the street. It was still playful at this time. However, a car tried to break the barriers and was pelted with beer bottles. Then, someone said that the Highway Patrol was coming. When you heard this you wanted to get out of the way—they meant business. People were pouring out of the bars by this time—police had gone in around midnight, turned on the lights, and yelled for everyone to get out—and the crowd was really getting large and out of control. Many were unhappy at missing the end of the Lakers-Knicks playoff game. Later we would know that Kent Mayor Leroy Satrom had called a state of emergency and ordered all the bars closed.

Suddenly, some people started shouting anti-war slogans, which surprised me because this wasn't an anti-war protest by any stretch of the imagination. People started throwing beer bottles at the bank and at the offices of the Ohio Bell telephone company—an emblem of the world's largest corporation. I remember trying to hold back the arm of one person and I asked why he was throwing things. He replied, "Fuck the establishment."

I found a friend in all this confusion and he drove four of us home in his small sports car, somehow missing the police. The news the next day showed the windows smashed and the damage done to the downtown area. I was living at the time in a residential area and heard that our neighbors were not very happy with us students. I tried to explain that I had seen what went on downtown and that not all of the rioters were student protesters. People were convinced that there were outside agitators going from college campus to college campus to cause trouble. I suppose I didn't help this perception.

LAURA: Saturday night, May 2nd, a line of protestors marched past my dorm. I joined them as they made their way to the large field called the Commons in the center of campus. I was dismayed when they set fire to the small shed that held archery equipment. As I watched the fire spread to the tall tree standing over it, I more clearly understood that they were attempting, ineptly, to set fire to the ROTC building. While someone did manage to catch some curtains on fire, and some damage was done to the fire hoses when the city fire crew arrived, the ROTC building was intact and little damaged when students left the area. One student who left in the direction of the old front campus reported that he saw the Ohio National Guard coming up Hilltop Drive. The Guard had been put on alert earlier on Saturday by the city mayor in response to the trash fires and breaking of bank and utility company windows in downtown Kent Friday night. Later that evening, the ROTC building did burn down while it was being guarded by the Guard and local police.

CAROLE: After Saturday night, my roommates and I decided to go to a house party rather than risk any chance of getting arrested. Besides, there was a curfew in the city declared by the mayor. Ironically, the curfew on campus was several hours later. My mother called to see if I was part of the protest. I told her everything was fine and that people were exaggerating the damage done to the storefronts. The part about exaggerating the damage was true but everything was not fine. That evening we heard that the ROTC building had been burned to the ground. I wondered who would care? The building was old and was about to be torn down anyway. Hours later we could hear helicopters with searchlights flying over the city moving toward the campus.

LAURA: Sunday afternoon, May 3, had an atmosphere both ominous and carnival-like, with students walking around taking pictures of the Guard and their equipment and the ROTC building. We later heard the story of Alison Krause sticking a lilac in the gun barrel of a guardsman and saying, "Flowers are better than bullets." On Sunday night, the Guard ringed the buildings on front campus as students demonstrated by sitting in the intersection of Main Street and Lincoln. Helicopters hovered frighteningly low overhead as we sang "All we are saying, is give peace a chance" and held up hands overhead in the bright lights, flashing fingers or the peace sign. Students were coaxed out of the intersection with the promise that we would be able to talk to the KSU president and the mayor of the city of Kent but it was soon apparent we had been lied to, betrayed. Some students, we heard, were bayoneted as they ran across campus. Arriving at Julie's dorm room, I saw Paul sitting cross-legged on the floor, picking off the cross in white medical tape that he'd put on the back of his brown vinyl jacket. Running from Lincoln and Main, he had been told by a guardsman, "I bet that cross'll make a good target." I returned to my dorm and put up signs on notebook paper in the bathrooms before I went to bed: "Rally at Noon on the Commons Monday."

CAROLE: On Sunday, May 3rd, I had to work at the cafeteria in the Hub. It was eerie walking to campus and seeing armed guardsmen in clusters. As I walked toward the student union I could see personnel carriers that looked like armored tanks, jeeps, fatigue-clad soldiers, and tents. My campus looked like an armed camp. I became angrier and angrier at this sight as I moved closer to my destination. When I finally got to the Hub I saw for the first time the burned-down ROTC building. It was roped off and guarded by weekend soldiers. I thought it was stupid to guard a bunch of ashes of a building that was not worth the trouble. But this building was a symbol—this was an attack against our government said my boss. He told me to give the guardsmen some hamburgers to eat, but I refused to give them any food because they had no business being on our campus.

During my break I went outside and started to talk with one of the guardsmen. I asked him why he was carrying a gun on a college campus. He said that it was standard procedure. I asked him if the gun was loaded and he replied that he had "ammunition on his person" but the weapon was not loaded. I somehow felt a bit relieved to hear that. That evening a friend of mine was having a party at the Glen Morris Apartments near campus. We had to go through the fields and dodge the searchlights of the helicopters overhead to get there that night. Our friends said that they were drinking with some of the guardsmen that afternoon and they said that they didn't want to be on campus either.

Some of us thought the guardsmen were just like us. They didn't want to be doing what they were assigned to do. Hell, weren't they dodging the draft by joining the National Guard? As we walked by, some of the guardsmen even gave us the peace sign. Just because they have a uniform on, we thought, doesn't mean they are necessarily against those who protest the war. These were actually dangerous thoughts. Although this peaceable attitude might represent some of the National Guard sent to Kent State, there was a hard-core group of men who hated college students and echoed the sentiments of President Nixon that they were nothing but "bums."

LAURA: Monday, May 4, was brilliantly sunny—unusual for Kent—with a cool breeze blowing. While I wore my slicker to block the wind, others celebrated the day by going out in just their shirts. Students gathered in the usual spot, by the Victory Bell on the Commons. The protest against the war took on a new dimension as students asserted their rights to speech and assembly by refusing to leave the Commons when ordered to do so. Soon after the gathering began at noon, the Guard threw tear gas to disperse the students gathered at the bell. Most moved out of range by walking up between Taylor and Johnson Halls at the top of the hill on the east side of the Commons. Some tear-gas canisters and stones were thrown in the direction of the Guard as they followed the students. Bayonets raised, the Guard marched past Taylor Hall, down a hill, and across a practice football field where they huddled and then gestured with their weapons. They marched back toward Taylor Hall, toward the Commons.

They reached the top of Blanket Hill, near the sculpture called the Pagoda. Then, in what seemed like slow motion, like birds, or dancers delivering a Greek prophecy, the Guard wheeled, together. Some lowered down. They all lifted their rifles, then they fired down the hill into the Prentice Hall parking lot.

I was doubled over and screaming, "They're shooting their guns, they're shooting their guns!" Linda pulled me away and into nearby Lake Hall. Safe in the lobby, I clung to her and sobbed, "Why did they shoot?" Someone ran in right away and said that people had been shot. As we walked out, I noticed that down the hallway to our right drops of blood divided the floor in a neat line up to the drinking fountain.

A body lay in the drive. We glanced at it, keeping a distance because it seemed more respectful. Later I would learn it was Jeff Miller, easy to spot in photos in his burgundy and white cowboy shirt, shot through the mouth, the back of his head blown away. Another student lay on his back on a little slope. We

FIGURE 5.4 May 4, 1970: Kent State photojournalism student, John Darnell, captured this shot of Ohio National Guardsmen firing on protesting students. The soldiers fired more than 60 rounds over the course of 13 seconds, killing four students and injuring nine others. When Darnell left the campus after the shootings, he thought the roll of film containing this picture might be confiscated, so he hid it in his sock and surrendered a blank roll when challenged by the authorities. In court hearings after the event, the guardsmen claimed that they had been afraid for their lives and fired spontaneously. Other accounts insisted that the soldiers had received an order to fire.

Source: John Darnell

gathered over him for a moment. His legs, clad in orange pinwale corduroy pants, were propped up, his knees slowly wove back and forth. Bill Schroeder. We looked across the parking lot where there were more clusters of people around what we knew must be other fallen bodies. Sandy Scheuer, Alison Krause, dying. Nine others who were wounded would live: Alan Canfora, John Cleary, Tom Grace, Donald MacKenzie, Joe Lewis, Jim Russell, Robby Stamps, Doug Wrentmore, and Dean Kahler, who will spend the rest of his life in a wheelchair.

We gathered again in protest on the Commons, this time to signify with our bodies our outrage at the unprovoked, unjustified, unjust assault that had just been committed. Bonnie from geology class walked up to me and said, "Alison's been shot."

We sat on a small slope along the edge of the Commons, a concession to the National Guard: we no longer occupied our original territory. Glenn Frank, one of our professors, paced in front of us, lecturing, pleading, crying. He made us believe we might be killed. Friends I was sitting near and some others made a plan. Quietly,

FIGURE 5.5 Mary Ann Vecchio screams in anguish as she kneels by the body of Jeffrey Miller, one of four students killed by members of the Ohio National Guard during anti-war demonstrations at Kent State University on May 4, 1970. Rioting off campus and the burning of a campus ROTC building fed tensions throughout the first days of May. On the 4th, students threw rocks at the guardsmen, and guardsmen lobbed tear gas canisters at the students. The confrontation culminated in the shootings that erupted at about 12:30 p.m. on the 4th. Photojournalism student John Filo took this picture, which later won a Pulitzer Prize and became an enduring symbol of the era. At Kent State today, memorials mark the spots where each of the four fatally injured students fell.

Source: Getty Images Inc.—Hulton Archive Photos

we followed Glenn Frank toward the lilac lane that edged the only open side of the Commons, the only side not closed in by buildings or the Guard. When we reached the other side, we scattered, thinking that if we ran in different directions, they couldn't shoot all of us.

CAROLE: Monday, May 4, started out to be a picture perfect day. In the morning there was a bit of a chill in the air. I put on my hand-knitted cape over my blue jeans and top and headed for my first class in the Music and Speech Building on the east side of campus. My first class was Rhetoric of Nonviolence—talk about irony. I remember our professor encouraging us to attend the noon rally. I had every intention of doing so, especially after that weekend. I wanted to let people know that the Guard had to leave our campus! Others felt as I did. My next class was Advanced Public Speaking, taught by the head of the department. He took the whole class time to plead with us not to attend the rally at noon. He literally begged us not to go. He said that something terrible was going to happen. I don't know why, but I believed him. So instead of going to the noon rally as I had planned I went to the office building behind the Newman Center to get my roommate. She had a car and she drove us home to have lunch. I had a sociology class after lunch so my roommate dropped me off at Bowman Hall.

It seemed a bit strange that not too many people were at the 250-seat lecture hall that day. The professor came running down the aisle and when she got to the front of the room she said that students had been shot, perhaps killed, and we needed to leave the campus immediately. My first instinct was to run toward the shooting sight. As I crossed the grassy area toward Stopher Hall, I was stopped by the Guard. They told me to go back and leave the campus. I remember being on a campus bus sitting in a daze. When we got to College Street, a guy came on the bus with a flag that was draped in blood. He said it was from the blood of our brothers and sisters. I immediately got off the bus and just walked around for what must have been a couple of hours. I eventually ended up at my house on Depeyster. All but one of our roommates was already there and no one knew where the missing roommate was. I had told her I was going to the rally at noon but I never made it there. Could she have gone? Could she have been among the wounded or killed? We tried to call our friends but the lines were jammed. Eventually, our roommate appeared and we all spent the next hours glued to the radio. It was first reported that guardsmen were killed on the Kent State campus and students were shot. But I knew that students were killed because of the young man on the bus and my professor.

LAURA: As I ran from the Commons, I retraced my route in reverse order from Sunday night. Meeting back in Julie's room, we were somber and in shock, but thankful to be reunited with Jeffrey and David, whom we hadn't seen since the shooting started. Luckier than Jeff Miller, they dove for cover behind the slope along the drive where he was killed. We were ordered to evacuate the campus. The phones were turned off or lines jammed. We couldn't call. I left with Jeffrey. A solid line of cars clogged Route 43 coming into Kent from the suburbs of Cleveland. My mother, meeting friends for lunch, was asked when she arrived at the restaurant what she thought about the shootings at Kent. She and Betty Lou jumped in the car, which broke down just before she tried to turn onto 43. By the time it was fixed, 43 was sealed off. She drove to the next town and came into Kent the back way.

CAROLE: My mother heard that students were shot and some killed. She tried desperately to reach my house in Kent. After not being able to reach me by phone she got in the car and drove the 50 miles from our home in Youngstown. I still don't know how she ended up in Kent as they sealed off all the roads leading in and out.

She told me no one was going to stop her from getting to me. She didn't care how many roadblocks she had to cross. The drive home that night was endless. I was still worried about who was shot. Did I know them? It could have been me. What would have happened if I had attended that noon rally as planned? The possibilities were too horrible to imagine.

LAURA: At six o'clock, I sat at the kitchen table. My father walked in the back door. His hand still on the doorknob, he looked at me across the family room and said, "They should have shot all of them." I answered, "Don't you know, then, that one of them would have been me?" He passed into the back room.

CAROLE: We heard on the news that a local girl was shot and killed in the Kent State riots—Sandra Scheuer. We knew Sandy from when she was five years old. I couldn't believe it was her, of all people. She wasn't an anti-war activist. This must be a mistake. It wasn't. My mother went to the pantry and got out the gold and brown Charles Chip can where she stored her bread flour. Whenever anyone would die, my mother would bake buns to take to the family. Without saying a word, she started to measure the flour with her ceramic cup. The sound of that cup hitting against the tin can is a sound I will forever associate with May 4, 1970.

LAURA: The Library of Congress Subject Index classifies May 4, 1970, as a "riot." If the events of that afternoon had conformed to what we think of as a riot, May 4 would be more understandable. The four days of May 1–4 blur in public accounts—muddling the truth about Kent State, yet, in another way, making the shootings comprehensible. The elements of Friday evening, May 1—the street fire, great numbers of people emptying onto the street at one time, and broken windows—did constitute a "riot."

In an interview on May 4, 1980, the tenth anniversary of the shootings, Lucius Lyman, Jr., a local car dealer, related the common perception of Friday night and offered an explanation of the community's reaction. Told that "there had been a riot and a lot of property damage," he recalled that when he went to take a look, "the amount of damage I saw at that time—and this was probably eleven o'clock in the morning—was not as great as I anticipated it to be, as it had been painted to me by my colleagues." Lyman added, "But you have to understand, in a way that maybe you don't, how important property is in the mentality of those of us who are in the system. You see, it's life, liberty, and property. And the deprecation of property as part of this process still astounds me, because from the time I was born, I and all my peers aspired to be property owners" (Bills, 1990, p. 70).

The destruction of property continued on Saturday night with the burning of the ROTC building. President Nixon's postscript on May 5, 1970, was typical in eliding the activities of Friday and Saturday nights with Monday, May 4: "When dissent turns to violence it invites tragedy" (Semple, 1970).

The Justice Department's summary report of an FBI investigation begun May 5 states that "of the 13 Kent State students shot, none, so far as we know, were associated with either the disruption in Kent on Friday night, May 1, 1970, or the burning of the ROTC building on Saturday, May 2, 1970" (Stone, 1970, p. 99). While condemning the National Guard's firing as "inexcusable" (p. 289), the President's Commission on Campus Unrest asserted, "Those who wrought havoc on the town of Kent, those who burned the ROTC building, those who attacked and stoned National Guardsmen, and all those who urged them on and applauded their deeds share the responsibility for the deaths and injuries of May 4. The widespread student opposition to the Cambodian action and their general resentment of the National Guard's presence on the campus cannot justify the violent and irresponsible actions of many students during the long weekend" (p. 287).

While certainly following a long weekend of political protests, the gathering at noon on Monday, May 4th, was not a riot, but a demonstration, a planned protest announced in advance—a continued expression of dissent with Nixon's escalation of the war, layered with objection to the presence of the Ohio National Guard. Admittedly the language used on Monday, May 4, was elevated: "Pigs off campus," "One, two, three, four, we don't want your fucking war." Stones were thrown. Middle fingers and anti-establishment power fists were raised. Two black flags were lofted. Tear gas canisters were lobbed back at the Guard. But even when the tear gas was being fired, many students could simply walk away from it on the cool, windy day. Many walked out of the path of the Guard, either moving to the sides or getting far enough out in front to be at, they thought, a safe distance. The Guard were walking back to where they had come from. There was no line of students in front of them blocking their way to the Commons, to which they seemed to be returning. The air was clear. Students stood and watched the Guard walk up the hill; others walked through the area on their way to class. There was undoubtedly some yelling, perhaps some stones thrown in the direction of the guardsmen, at least one raised finger, but not a roaring crowd, not a moving mass of people. The Guard reached the top of Blanket Hill. They turned 180 degrees, lifted their rifles, and—without warning—fired, the motion so synchronous as to suggest preplanning or a response to a command.

The truth of that moment is too dark to seem real. Instead, picturing the violence of destroyed property, picturing the moment of the shootings as chaotic, smoky, noisy, makes the event readable. The Guard were nothing more than kids, people said; they were tired, they were poorly trained, they felt their lives were in danger. No wonder they fired.

CAROLE: It is important to realize that the Guard were at the peak of Blanket Hill on campus and in order to kill students they had to aim down the hill at them. Most of the students who were wounded or killed were in the Prentice Hall parking lot. This was the site where the most vocal demonstrators had mocked the Guard and thrown stones at them while they were on the football practice field moments before.

It was admitted in court that the Guard did have considerable riot training (Kelner & Munves, 1980). The FBI reported that the shooters had received some level of riot training and none were novices. The range of riot training was between 16 and 62 hours. Most had 4–5 years of service in the National Guard. Most of the shooters came from Troop G, which was made up of predominantly blue-collar workers in their late 20s and early 30s. Members of Troop G were among the first to arrive on campus to guard the ROTC building on Saturday night. Eight guardsmen were reported hit by rocks and flying glass with one requiring medical attention that Saturday evening (Kelner & Munves, 1980).

According to the President's Commission on Campus Unrest (1970), 28 guardsmen fired 61 shots over a 13-second period of time. Photographs show that nine members came from Troop G. Although students admitted to throwing rocks when the Guard were on the football practice field minutes before the fatal volley of shots, at the time of the shootings no rocks were reportedly thrown. The Justice Department's Civil Rights Division of the Federal Bureau of Investigation concluded in its summary report, "Six Guardsmen, including two sergeants and Captain Srp (correct spelling) of Troop G stated pointedly that the lives of the members of the Guard were not in danger and that it was not a shooting situation" (Stone, 1970, p. 84). The President's Commission concluded in its investigation that "the indiscriminate firing of rifles into a crowd of students and the deaths that followed were unnecessary, unwarranted, and inexcusable" (President's Commission on Campus Unrest, 1970, p. 289).

All 13 young people who were wounded or killed on May 4, 1970, were students enrolled at Kent State University. No guardsmen sustained serious injury during the time of the shootings. None were hospitalized for any injuries they received (one guardsman was hospitalized for heat exhaustion). No students were "charging" the guard at the time of the shootings as claimed by the guardsmen who fired. Photographic evidence proves that the nearest student to the Guard was 20 yards away. Of those killed or wounded, the closest was 60 feet away and the furthest was 730 feet away.

I often wonder what the guardsmen were thinking when they looked into their scopes and pulled their triggers. Did they not see the young women and men with books and notebooks in their arms? Were they so angry at the vocal protesters that they just wanted to "make them pay?" Did they agree with their commander-in-chief, President Richard M. Nixon, who called the students on college campuses "bums?" Did they hear Governor James A. Rhodes's speech at the firehouse on Sunday, May 3rd, in which he proclaimed: "I think we're up against the strongest, well-trained, militant revolutionary group that has ever assembled in America . . . We are going to eradicate the problem, we're not going to treat the symptoms" (Davies, 1973, p. 22). Did they realize that the bullets from their M-1 rifles could travel a mile or more? Did they see the students running behind cars, diving for cover behind trees, and falling to the ground? How did they feel when they were done shooting and they marched back to the ROTC site from where they started? Did they think about those wounded and dying? Did they think about the parents of those students they just killed? How could they live with the fact that they killed another human being—and for what?

WORKS CITED

Bills, Scott. *Kent State/May 4: Echoes Through a Decade*. Kent, Ohio: Kent State University Press, 1990.

Davies, Peter. *The Truth about Kent State: A Challenge to the American Conscience*. New York: Farrar Straus & Giroux, 1973.

Kelner, Joseph, and James Munves. *The Kent State Coverup*. New York: Harper and Row, 1980.

President's Commission on Campus Unrest. *The Report of the President's Commission on Campus Unrest*. Washington, D.C.: U.S. Government Printing Office, 1970.

Semple, Jr., Robert. "Nixon Says Violence Invites Tragedy." *New York Times*, 5 May 1970, A17.

Stone, I. F. *The Killings at Kent State: How Murder Went Unpunished*. New York: New York Review Books, 1970.

QUESTIONS FOR DISCUSSION

1. In how many ways does this essay illustrate a phrase often used to describe the Sixties—the "generation gap?"

2. In the lives of young Americans who came of age in the 1960s, the issue of Communism loomed very large. Is there an equivalent in the experience of young people today?

3. What role did public figures play in the events of May 4, 1970?

4. How did the townspeople of Kent react to the events of Friday evening? How did the values of the townspeople conflict with those of the students? How did Barbato and Davis's parents respond to the shootings at Kent State? Why did each respond as they did? How would your parents respond in a similar situation?

5. What happened at the moment that the National Guard opened fire on Kent State students? Why did the Guard shoot? They fired on unarmed Kent State students for 13 seconds. Count out loud to 13: one (one thousand), two (one thousand), three (one thousand), and so on. What is your impression of the length of time? Does that change your opinion about the Guard shooting?

6. Why is it difficult to understand "the truth about Kent State?" For example, why does Barbato feel it is dangerous to think of the guardsmen as "just like us?" Nixon called college students "bums." Does that judgment seem to apply to the actual lives of the students killed? What role did judgments like these play in this long weekend at Kent State? How are they central to the Kent State tragedy?

7. Every true story is affected by the author's memory to a certain degree. Are there any differences between the stories told by Barbato and Davis?

SECTION

6

Speaking Out

Introduction

The protest movements of the Sixties era dealt with issues specific to that period in the nation's history—civil rights, racism and poverty, the war in Vietnam, the proliferation of nuclear power, and mid-twentieth-century campus and workplace conditions. However, the protestors who confronted those issues were the heirs to a long-standing American tradition of speaking out against established custom and authority.

The First Amendment to the U.S. Constitution protects "freedom of speech" and "the right of the people peaceably to assemble and to petition the government for a redress of grievances," thereby safeguarding the right to protest. By the time those constitutional provisions were adopted in 1791, political protest already held a distinguished place in American history. The 1776 Declaration of Independence was a protest document enumerating injustices that the British Crown had inflicted on its American colonies. The 1773 Boston Tea Party was an act of civil disobedience, a deliberate violation of the law committed as a political protest.

Every generation of Americans has witnessed antigovernment protests in the form of speeches, petitions, parades or other symbolic actions. In addition, the growth of the labor movement in the nineteenth century saw workers organizing strikes and boycotts against the companies that employed them. Organized protests have usually taken the form of demands for political, social, or economic justice. The demands can be written, spoken, or acted, as in a strike or a protest march. However, because civil society does impose limitations on even protected behavior, protestors risk arrest if they trespass, impede traffic, destroy property, or incite violence.

Protest marches, in particular the tradition of marching on Washington, D.C., to demand human rights or draw attention to political or social problems, started in 1894 with Coxey's Army, a band of unemployed men seeking government relief during a depression. The Washington police arrested Jacob Coxey, the protest leader, and dispersed his followers, but subsequent peaceful marches became common occurrences in the nation's capitol. Among the most notable of these were the August 1963, Civil Rights March on Washington, where Martin Luther King, Jr., gave his "I have a dream" speech. A November, 1969, Vietnam War protest—one of many—brought nearly half a million marchers to Washington.

Members of labor unions staged the first major sit-down strikes in the 1930s. They stopped their work and took over factory space, halting production until their demands were met. Sit-down strikes were the ancestors of both civil rights lunch counter sit-ins and campus strike actions of the 1960s, including the occupation of administration offices at the University of California at Berkeley in 1964 and Columbia University in 1968.

Acts of civil disobedience, such as destroying property, trespassing, refusing to pay your taxes, or refusing the draft, involve deliberate lawbreaking to draw attention to something felt to be a greater evil. Such acts go back as far as the ancient world. In the United States in the 1840s, writer Henry David Thoreau refused to pay a tax that would support the Mexican War, which he opposed. Thoreau went to jail, the ancestor of many war protestors jailed during subsequent conflicts. In the Sixties era, in addition to their legal picketing and marching, anti-war activists took over buildings, organized strikes, burned draft cards, and vandalized draft induction centers, as well as committing other acts of civil disobedience. Civil rights activists organized bi-racial sit-ins at segregated lunch counters and train stations, and rode in the "whites only" seats on Jim Crow buses—acts in violation of southern laws. They stood their ground until dragged away by the police. Going limp, refusing to fight back or protect themselves against arrest, they practiced passive resistance.

Protest movements that employed nonviolent direct action and passive resistance owed their inspiration to the Indian leader, Gandhi, whose mass movement for independence had freed India from the British Empire in 1947. Ultimately, almost every protest movement of the Sixties era owed its tactics, if not its ideology, to earlier confrontations with authority. And because every protest action was also a kind of performance, its drama, its message, and the reputation and comportment of its "actors" influenced its reception by the public and the authorities.

Historians now believe that more than two million protestors were involved in the Civil Rights Movement throughout the 1950s and 1960s. Hundreds of thousands of others took part in local and national protests against the Vietnam War, opposing the draft and questioning the morality of U.S. involvement in another country's civil war, even though the stated objective of that involvement was to halt the spread of Communism. Opposition to the war was spearheaded by students and by student organizations such as the Students for a Democratic Society (SDS) and the National Mobilization to End the War in Vietnam (MOBE). After 1970, many Vietnam veterans joined or sponsored anti-war protests.

On university campuses, students engaged in a variety of protest actions, some in support of civil rights activity, others in opposition to the war, and still others involving specific group interests or concerns, such as women's rights and gay liberation. Less well known were the early Sixties protests against college or university authority, where students protested rules that restricted their personal freedom and choices. Arguing that they were 18 and therefore adults, students protested the universities' imposition of curfews, restrictions on travel off campus, and enforcement of "parietal" hours, which limited visits in single-sex dormitories by members of the opposite sex. Universities had instituted these rules to reassure parents that they were acting *in loco parentis* (in the place of parents), a promise that sons and daughters would be cared for as they were at home. Student resentment of such oversight inspired protests of many kinds. Sometimes these protests were linked to other demands for academic freedom or civil rights. By the end of the 1960s, most coeducational colleges and universities had abandoned parietal rules and curfews and relaxed their supervision of students' personal lives. Late in the era, some campus protests, building on the discoveries of the civil rights and other liberation movements, took the form of demands for black and ethnic studies programs and for increased hiring of African American, Latino, and female faculty.

The stories in this section deal with three different types of protest action in the Sixties era, three different examples of "speaking out." One is an early campus protest in defense of free speech, the second is a strike by agricultural workers, and the third is an individual act of civil disobedience on behalf of an environmental cause.

The Free Speech Movement at the University of California at Berkeley took place in 1964, in the immediate aftermath of Mississippi Freedom Summer, and it lasted into the following year. Students at Berkeley were accustomed to stationing themselves on a sidewalk on the campus periphery to pass out pamphlets and flyers, recruit volunteers, and collect donations for a variety of causes, some university related, others related to political causes and the Civil Rights Movement. When the university administrators, pressured by conservative citizens, withdrew permission for students to use the area, the students protested that their rights to free speech had been violated. Several groups refused to obey the ban. The university suspended eight student leaders and then ordered the arrest of a civil rights volunteer, one of a number of students who had set up tables with literature right outside Sproul Hall, the university administration building. The spontaneous outrage of thousands of students in response to the suspensions and the arrest launched the Free Speech Movement.

Notwithstanding the disapproval of their parents and the hostility of the California Board of Regents and most of the state's government officials, hundreds of students from conservative to radical engaged in continuous protests for several months. At one point, they seized and occupied Sproul Hall, an action that led to the arrest of more than 750 people. Eventually, the university conceded the students' right to political speech on campus and the protests came to an end. The Free Speech Movement led Sixties-era students to understand that they had political power. Inspired by the Civil Rights Movement, the Free Speech Movement in turn set the stage for a wide range of campus and community protests in the decade that followed, including the embrace of issues that were far less clear-cut than freedom of speech.

Jackie Goldberg was already politically active in the civil rights, labor, and anti-nuclear weapons movements when she became a student at Berkeley in the mid-1960s. Beginning her story with a series of events that "radicalized" her, including an arrest at a pro-labor sit-in, she explains how she came to assume a leadership role in the Free Speech Movement in the fall of 1964. Sometimes leading the charge, sometimes functioning as a voice of moderation, Goldberg was involved throughout the long student campaign, surviving threats of expulsion from the university, a brutal arrest and jailing, and, for a time, the mistrust and suspicion of the movement's leader, Mario Savio. Goldberg was awed by the freshness, energy, and courage of her fellow students. She was astonished at the broad, almost campus-wide appeal of the Free Speech cause and proud of its final outcome. She emerged from the struggle for free speech as a confirmed, lifelong activist.

College students were not the only ones to learn tactics and the power of moral suasion from Gandhi and the American Civil Rights Movement. César Chávez, a Mexican American migrant farm laborer, studied Gandhi's philosophy as a young man and taught nonviolence when building a union of California farm workers to fight for fair pay and decent working conditions. After spending ten years working in the migrant workers' Community Service Organization, where he received training as an organizer and gained confidence in his own abilities as a leader, Chávez joined forces with Dolores Huerta and several other leaders to found the National Farm Workers Association (NFWA), which would later change its name to the United Farm Workers (UFW).

In 1965, joining a walkout by Filipino American members of another agricultural workers' union, the largely Latino NFWA began a five-year strike against grape growers. The workers had many issues, including backbreaking labor conditions, low wages, and the total lack of basic amenities such as access to water and toilets during their long days in the fields. When word of the strike made the news, the plight of the striking workers, who had risked their bare-bones livelihood to fight for better wages and working conditions, attracted the attention of other labor unions, gaining their support. Further support came from churches and civil rights and political leaders, including Martin Luther King, Jr., and Robert F. Kennedy.

In the spring of 1966, carrying signs that read *"Huelga!"* ("Strike!"), Chávez and a band of strikers embarked upon a 340-mile protest march from their headquarters at Delano to the steps of the California state capitol in Sacramento to draw national attention to the farm workers' cause. After a four-month boycott, the Schenley Company, a major grower of wine grapes, negotiated an agreement with the workers. Moving quickly in pursuit of their next goals, the farm workers took on other major growers, DiGiorgio Fruit Company and Giumarra Vineyards, California's largest table-grape grower. Although the strikers were frequently subjected to brutal attacks by the growers' hired thugs, and sometimes to arrest by local officials who sided with the growers, Chávez held them to a policy of non-retaliation, even undertaking a 25-day fast to underline the need to stick to nonviolence and the principles of Gandhi and Martin Luther King.

Between 1967 and 1970, hundreds of grape strikers and volunteer supporters traveled across the United States and Canada to organize an international grape boycott. Millions of consumers rallied to the farm workers' cause, refusing to buy grapes, and eventually the growers were forced to accept the union. To symbolize their victory, workers stamped the union insignia—a black eagle with spread wings—on every box of fruit and produce shipped from a company that had accepted the union.

In the years that followed, farm workers carried their strikes to flower and vegetable growers, and Chávez, choosing the most widely popular of salad vegetables, declared a national boycott of lettuce. By 1972, the United Farm Workers had over 70,000 dues-paying members and hundreds of thousands of supporters and sympathizers all over the country. They continued, and continue, to use strikes and boycotts in ongoing conflicts with growers over working conditions, protection from pesticides, and many other issues. Chávez died in 1993 and was posthumously awarded the Medal of Freedom, America's highest civilian honor.

Maria and Antonia Saludado, whose story appears in this section, were among the earliest supporters of César Chávez and the newly formed union. Chávez recruited them with the force of his personality and the righteousness of his cause. He did not minimize the toughness of the struggle or the danger inherent in opposing the powerful, and he asked great things of them. In the late 1990s, the sisters told their story to Kent Kirkton and Jorge Garcia, professors at California State University at Northridge, who were conducting a project to tape the stories of veterans of the early days of the United Farm Workers. In this selection from the project's archives, Professor Kirkton has blended the voices of the two sisters as they tell their stories. Kirkton's italicized interjections supply the background information.

The sisters' story begins in their teenage years, which they spent in the fields alongside their father, working to help support younger siblings and sacrificing their own education to keep the family fed. (Although Maria and Antonia were born in Mexico, their father was American-born and so able to bring his family to live in California while his oldest daughters were young.) The sisters describe working in plums and beets and peas, the crippling pain of cultivating crops with the short-handled hoe, the pitiful wages they earned, the scorn with which they were treated, and their father's heartbreak at being unable to provide for his children— even with their help. Persuaded to action by César Chávez, and with the firm support of their parents, they chose to quit their jobs to become full-time union organizers, trying to learn to speak and write English as they went along. Despite their youth and inexperience, they became part of Chávez's cadre of organizers, involved in the first great march on Sacramento and later in city-by-city organizing for the international grape boycott, where they struggled to speak out in a language not their own.

The Saludado sisters are modest about their accomplishments and about their own courage in sustaining without vengefulness attacks that could have left them disabled or dead. In retrospect, they find humor in much of what they endured. And they revere the memory of César Chávez. As Kent Kirkton says about them and the other contributors to his oral history project, "The workers have the greatest respect for César Chávez because he was a transforming agent in their lives. However, the movement is still alive and it rests on the shoulders of thousands of people."

During the Free Speech Movement, student leader Mario Savio memorably said, "There is a time when the operation of the machine becomes so odious, makes you so sick at heart, that you can't take part, you can't even tacitly take part, and you've got to put your bodies upon the gears, and upon the wheels, upon the levers, upon all the apparatus. And you've got to make it stop." The last story in this section is about a man who did, literally, throw his body on the machine to make it stop. Samuel Lovejoy confronted the powerful nuclear energy industry and, at the risk of injury and imprisonment, destroyed property to save lives.

The story of the anti-nuclear power movement really begins in the 1950s with the international movement to halt nuclear weapons testing. People opposed weapons testing for two reasons: one, because of what they saw as the insanity of countries competing with each other to build more and more weapons of mass destruction, and two, because the testing released radiation into the atmosphere. Scientists had known for decades that radiation was linked to birth defects, cancer, and other diseases.

Many people all over the world engaged in protests of nuclear tests, some even trespassed at atomic weapons test sites. In 1957, the National Committee for a Sane Nuclear Policy (SANE) was founded and within a year had 25,000 members in 130 chapters. In the early 1960s, a Student Peace Union founded in the United States adopted the symbol used by the British Campaign for Nuclear Disarmament (CND), which later became the universally accepted peace symbol. Members of Women's Strike for Peace testified in Congress about their fears for the nation's future generations should nuclear testing continue.

Governments worldwide and many citizens in the 1950s and 1960s thought there ought to be a peaceful use for atomic energy. Surely, they argued, this great discovery must have applications beyond war and destruction. Technological development of the "peaceful uses of atomic energy" led to the building of nuclear reactor plants to generate electricity. Reactor designers insisted their structures posed no threat to people or to the environment and did not release radiation into the atmosphere. The powerful nuclear industry claimed it could manufacture electricity so efficiently that it would be "too cheap to meter." That promise had a strong appeal to people who already found their energy bills too high and were aware that fossil fuels would eventually run out. Nuclear plants were constructed around the country throughout the 1950s and 1960s.

Skeptics who doubted the safety of atomic energy in any form mounted studies that demonstrated potential problems if nuclear plants should malfunction. An explosion, a "meltdown," or a release of radioactively contaminated water or steam would cause irreparable damage to the environment, poisoning the area around the plant for thousands of years to come and making it uninhabitable for people. If a plant had an accident, people in a 100-mile radius would have to be evacuated to protect them from radiation. Many would never be able to return to their homes. In short, people opposed to nuclear plants foresaw unimaginable horrors. People who supported the plants insisted they were safe.

Concerns about nuclear power plants became linked to the growing environmental movement in the United States and Europe. The first protests against the plants took place in France and West Germany in 1971, and in the United States a growing anti-nuclear power movement began attacking the industry giants with lawsuits about safety concerns. Nuclear power became a subject for serious debate.

Sam Lovejoy was an organic farmer who entered the debate about nuclear power because of his concern for the environment in the small western Massachusetts town of Montague, where he lived. Plans to build a twin-towered nuclear power plant in the town set him off on a crusade to learn as much as he could about the nuclear power industry and to see what he could do to thwart the building of the plant.

Lovejoy's story begins with his childhood in western Massachusetts, where he was the neighbor of an elderly fruit farmer whose routine use of pesticides led to his illness and eventual death. Lovejoy grew up, won a scholarship to a nearby college, and became involved in SDS and campus protests against the Vietnam War and the college's investment in war industries. He discovered his aptitude for leadership.

After college, Lovejoy decided that creating a serene and purposeful life by living on the land was what mattered most to him, and he joined the organic farming commune in Montague started by Steve Diamond and his friends from the Liberation News Service (see Diamond's story, "Back to the Land" in another section of this book). Unlike the city kids, Lovejoy was an experienced countryman, and was additionally deft at creating good relationships with his rural neighbors, whom he came to care about.

In 1973, when Northeast Utilities built a 500-foot tower to test weather conditions for their planned nuclear plant in Montague, Lovejoy decided he had to act. His housemates agreed that something must be done to stop the building of the plant, which they felt carried with it the potential to poison their organic farm and the lives and health of their children—in fact, the health of all the children in the county. Lovejoy, however, was reluctant to involve others in his illegal assault on the weather tower. His story develops around his solo act of civil disobedience and his court case, and ends with his leadership in the anti-nuclear power movement that surged into action in New England and California in the mid-1970s.

Widespread protests of nuclear-energy generating plants stopped or delayed their construction throughout the late 1970s and early 1980s. Today, there are 104 nuclear power plants in operation in the United States. The Montague plant was never built.

So did Sam Lovejoy commit a heroic act or an act of vandalism? Is it ever any use to stand up to an industrial giant or the government or a war or a longstanding social tradition or some other element of a vast power structure? Could a single individual make a difference in something that was important to thousands of people beyond himself? Like many of the other Sixties-era activists in this book—conservatives, radicals, those with special interests, those who worked alone, and those who worked with others—Sam Lovejoy reached a point where he felt he had both the right and the obligation to protest.

SIT DOWN! SIT DOWN!
Jackie Goldberg

I grew up Jewish in Inglewood, California. To say that I didn't fit in at my high school was an understatement. Kids at school would burn people's pictures on crosses in their lockers. Boys wore German pith helmets and there were swastikas all over the school. Luckily, the University of Southern California opened a program in 1961 called the Residence Honors Program for High School Seniors and my counselor got me into it.

While at USC, I went to downtown Los Angeles on November 1st, 1961, for the one day Women's Strike for Peace and met some of the most remarkable women I'd ever met in my life: Mary Clarke and Gail Eaby, who had a storefront on Pico Boulevard. Along with other women, they were protesting the American and Russian build-up of nuclear arsenals, the resumption of aboveground nuclear weapons testing, and the risk to children from fallout—especially strontium-90. I was just so impressed with them. When I went back to my dorm room I found that my conservative Orange County roommate had locked me out because she knew where I had been. That made me realize that USC wasn't too different from Inglewood, and that I should look for another school where I fit in a little better.

I applied to the University of California in Berkeley, and happily got in, but couldn't get into university housing or the co-op as they were full. I felt I was too young to take care of an apartment and ended up trying to rush a sorority (which I had thought was the last thing in the world I'd ever want to do).

I met some women from San Francisco who were rushing Pi Beta Phi, the big name sorority and told them, "You know, there's a lot of anti-Semitism here." They said, "Oh no, no, no." I bet them five dollars for each house that dropped me on the first day. I was dropped by 24 of 28 sororities because my name was Goldberg and they didn't take Jews. That money paid for my expenses for quite a while. I finally ended up in Delta Phi Epsilon and planned to stay only a year, but I really enjoyed it and stayed in the house the whole three years I was at Cal.

I stayed involved in Women's Strike for Peace, and was a nominal member of male-dominated SLATE, a campus left-wing political organization. (SLATE was connected with the movement to end the nuclear arms race and other off-campus issues. They had originally picked their named because they wanted to field a slate of candidates.) I wasn't heavily involved in SLATE as there were Communists in the organization, and I wasn't sure I was comfortable with that at this point in my life, but also because SLATE wouldn't vote on issues until the end of the meetings. Women who lived in dorms or sororities had a curfew, so we could listen to the debate, but they waited for us to leave before they voted.

A year later ('63–'64), my brother Art transferred up to Cal. He identified himself as a radical left-winger, or a socialist at least. I was a little more cautious. I would have described myself as a left-wing liberal but certainly not a radical.

That year the Ad Hoc Committee to End Discrimination, led by Tracy Sims, became a very important group in San Francisco. Tracy was a dynamic, inspiring young African-American working-class woman who managed to get a black civil rights movement, a white liberal-left student movement, and the Longshoremen's

Union together for a variety of actions. I got involved in the one at the Sheraton Palace Hotel.

The Sheraton Palace had black and Chinese employees, but not in positions that could be seen by the public. They were employed as maids, butlers, and valets, but they weren't allowed to be desk clerks or even restaurant servers. They had no hope of getting into management and they were poorly paid. Tracy decided the Sheraton Palace should be a target for the Ad Hoc Committee to End Discrimination, and for many weeks everyone on our side of the Bay trekked over the Oakland Bay Bridge to picket the Sheraton Palace on Friday nights, Saturdays, and Sundays. Eventually Tracy decided the picketing wasn't working and in March of '63 she called for a sit-in. We knew there were going to be arrests, and I was a little nervous, but decided to do it anyway. We were sitting in the hotel library and when the police came they told us "This is an unlawful assembly, go home." Of course we didn't go home, and I was scared to death—not just of the police, but I had planned on becoming a teacher and I thought my teaching career would be over if I went to jail.

The police really hurt people. They grabbed us and carried us to the paddy wagon and just threw us in on top of each other. This was where I learned a lot about how the system worked. I was very naïve. I really thought that the criminal justice system worked like it should (or at least that it did for white people—I wasn't naïve about racism). But when I was arraigned for the first time, the officer on the stand lied when he identified me. He was not somebody I'd ever seen before in my life. I told that to my attorney, and he said, "Oh yeah, they used your picture; there were 167 of you so they don't know who they arrested." I said, "You mean he's going to say that he arrested me and he didn't, and there's nothing we can do about this?" He said, "Yeah, pretty much."

We were divided into groups of 10, and we all presented the same case. In some courtrooms every single person in that courtroom was convicted. In some, everybody was acquitted. In others everyone got hung juries. Since the facts of the case didn't change, it was clear the judge, the instructions to the jury, and the facts each judge allowed made a big difference. Who was actually guilty and who was innocent had nothing to do with it.

I was just devastated; this was big news to me. If you have 167 people arrested for the same action and the verdicts differed depending on the judge, then what the hell is the system about? It's obviously meaningless as it isn't a system of justice that relies on presenting a fact. Everybody who still believes that should be arrested one time. Just be arrested one time as a demonstrator and it will change you forever. It changed me forever. If someone were to ask me "When did you become radical-ized?" I'd say it was my arrest at the Sheraton Palace.

In my junior year at Berkeley there was a lot of fear of nuclear war, and fallout shelters began appearing everywhere on campus and in the city. The shelters had gold and black signs and a number that told you how many it would hold, and that there were cookies and water somewhere nearby. A group of us from Campus Women for Peace went to the Oakland Civil Defense office and said that we thought we should have a fallout shelter test. We didn't say we were from Women for Peace, we just said we were students and we wanted to do a test. They were intrigued by the idea, so they agreed to participate. We were going to test whether or not the shelter had its supplies there, and if it would work. We picked a narrow office used by three graduate students in the lower level of Cal's Dwinell Hall. The fallout shelter sign said that the shelter could hold something ridiculous like 212 people. We had a couple of Nobel Laureates help us out by calculating how long we would be able to breathe the air in the shelter. We also had them calculate the size of a weapon the building would provide protection from and the amount of heat generated. We got considerable help from some of the senior faculty and distinguished scientists like Linus Pauling, who were pro-peace. Then we sent out press releases saying we were going to have a test of a fallout shelter and recruited about 500 students to try to get into the shelter (because if there's an attack, everybody was going to try to get in). The Oakland Civil Defense department had let us include them in the press release, so it was a big press event.

We squeezed in less than half the number of people stipulated by the sign. As we proceeded, we sent two people out for water and wafers because there was no water in the shelter and there were no wafers in Dwinell Hall at all. We told the two people we sent out that they wouldn't be allowed back in since they were sacrificing themselves for the greater good. They never found stored water, but they finally found rancid wafers that had been stored for years in the basement of the administration building of Sproul Hall. To keep radiation out of the fallout shelter the windows had to be closed, so unfortunately a young woman in the shelter passed out from the god-awful heat. We were using up all the available oxygen and she just plopped over. So we had to end it. And of course we said the point was that "our only real shelter is peace."

In the summer of '63, the Women's International Democratic Federation (WIDF) put on "The World Women's Congress" in Moscow. Women from the Soviet Union, the United States, England, France, and other nations had founded the WIDF after World War II to deal with refugee and women's issues. Every three or four years, they'd have an international conference, and the Soviet block, China, and the socialist nations would send official delegations, while the rest sent unofficial peace delegations as their governments didn't participate. The U.S. government didn't say we couldn't go, so we went "unofficially." I was made a delegate to the statewide convention of Women's Strike for Peace, and then in June of 1963 became the Northern California delegate to go to Moscow, while Mary Clarke was selected from Southern California.

The Sino-Soviet split was visible publicly for the first time at that convention. The Chinese attacked the Soviets bitterly in several of the debates on the floor about their "reactionary stance" and their unwillingness to support liberation movements. It was really fascinating and I got an opportunity to examine what I thought of Communism while in a Communist country.

Moscow is a very big city, but nobody was out begging and no one lived on the street. Anyone could get medical treatment. And free public education through the university level was available to anyone who qualified. Retirement was meager, because your wages were meager, but you retired with 100% of your final salary. Housing was hard to come by and small, and large numbers of people lived in tiny spaces, but the rents were cheap. On the economic side, I was blown away. But politically, I would ask questions about Stalin and it was like turning on a tape recorder. It didn't matter who I talked to in what walk of life, I got the exact same answer. That scared the shit out of me.

I sat for seven days at the conference and saw almost every country in the world condemn the United States and its role in the world. They also condemned England, France, Germany, and some socialist countries, but not as much. I didn't even know where these places were that they were talking about or that we had bases here and troops there. That was just an astonishing education.

At night I'd go back to my room and talk to Jane McManus, who was with the *National Guardian* newspaper, and another wonderful woman who ran cooperative nursery schools in Great Neck, New York. They were both politically very knowledgeable and I was completely politically naïve. They didn't tell me what to think. They kept telling me: here are places to go to look; here are questions to ask; and here are things to take and things to learn. I'm very grateful for that because they made me figure out what I believed instead of just accepting what someone else believed and then living with that until something contradicted it. It was a great lesson for me.

While there I met the women from Vietnam who told me that there was a war going on there. I said, "No, the French lost," and they said, "No, no, it's not the French, it's your country." I said, "No! How can our country be in a war in Vietnam and nobody's heard about it?" After I came back to Cal I talked with SLATE and the Women for Peace and said, "Do you know there's a war going on in Vietnam?" They didn't know that. Then, in the next school year, Ngo Dinh Diem and Madame Nhu were invited to come to campus, and we heard about American military "advisors." Sure enough, what the Vietnamese women had told me about what was going on turned out to be true. I wasn't ahead of anybody on any issue at this point, but for the first time I knew more about an issue than most of the guys did. I had brought material back from the conference and I showed it to them, and they had said, "No, not true." But it turned out to be true.

The Sheraton Palace arrest was one of the biggest events in my life. The other was this trip to the World Women's Congress, where I gained a notion of the world and a notion of women in the world. I found powerful American women friends who didn't try to shove anything down my throat. And I realized that people outside this country thought that America's role wasn't at all about helping women and children in their nations. Those events affected my work, really almost everything I think about and do.

That brings me up to September of 1964. I had started to become more active in SLATE; I ran for sorority representative in SLATE, and lost. I did represent Campus Women for Peace and my brother Art was the chair of SLATE.

We weren't supposed to advocate political organizations or causes on campus. But there was a sidewalk area just outside of campus where Telegraph Avenue ended at Bancroft Way that the City of Berkeley had agreed would be a free speech area. It was a small area, just between the street and the poles that the school put up to keep cars from driving onto campus, and the University didn't bother us as long as we stayed in front of those poles. Everybody thought that this area belonged to the City of Berkeley.

The previous year we had organized demonstrations against the Oakland *Tribune's* discriminatory practices. William Knowland, who was the owner and publisher of the *Tribune,* didn't like what we were doing. Knowland had been a U.S. senator and the California campaign manager for Barry Goldwater. He told the University of California Regents that if they didn't do something about "those damn kids," that the Oakland *Tribune* would work with the legislature to undermine the university's funding.

Then Chancellor Strong noticed the little plaques on the sidewalk at Bancroft and Telegraph that said, "Property of the Regents of the University of California." That meant that our little area was really on campus and didn't belong to the City of Berkeley at all. So on September 14th, Dean of Students Kathryn Towle was directed to write to all the heads of the "off campus" organizations telling them that political activity was not allowed on campus. She said that since the area at Bancroft and Telegraph was on the campus, we couldn't have tables, distribute pamphlets, give speeches, or recruit members there anymore. We thought . . . "Oh my God, what the hell is wrong with these people? We've been there for years and years! This can't be!"

Dean Kathryn Towle and I had become very good friends that previous spring. There was overt racism at the sororities and fraternities at Cal and she was under orders from the state legislature to get them all to sign a non-discrimination pledge for their houses. I was the pan-Hellenic council representative and Dean Towle and I devised a plan. We figured out that no one at Cal liked to think that they were part of a racist institution, but many couldn't sign the non-discrimination pledges because southern campus chapters controlled their charters. Our plan was to try to show the young women and young men in the various houses what racism really looked like. So we organized a meeting where each house brought a representative from their national organization to talk about the non-discrimination pledges. You can't imagine what came out of the national reps' mouths, and it was made worse by their southern accents. These were West Coast kids in the room and they had never heard anybody talk like that before. When the national reps left the room, jaws dropped, mouths opened, and everybody said, "I don't want to have anything to do with those people. I don't know who they are, but they ain't us." Every sorority and fraternity signed. Kathryn Towle was grateful that I helped her engineer this and we became fast friends.

Art and I talked to each other on the night the sidewalk ban went into effect and he said, "I'll call the Left, you call the Right," and we got everybody together at his apartment on College Avenue that next day. It wasn't just about politics; no student groups were going to be able to use that location to promote their causes, so we even had religious groups at the meeting.

It was a national election year and the Young Democrats were upset because they couldn't show their support for Johnson. The Young Republicans were upset as well because they couldn't show their support for Goldwater. Centrist groups were every bit as confounded by all of this as everybody else. We were all in the same boat and the university's action had brought us all together.

We formed a group called the United Front and had to pick someone to be the spokesperson. That was a big fight. The Young Democrats didn't want the Young

Republicans, and the Young Republicans didn't want the Young Dems. Finally the right gave in and supported me, because I was in a sorority and just couldn't be all bad. I did tell people about my relationship with the Dean and they thought that would be useful. (Nobody really knew it, but we got a lot of information from her throughout the entire Free Speech Movement about what was going on in the administration and what they were planning.)

We then had a series of meetings with Dean Towle, and eventually with Chancellor Strong. The Dean was very sympathetic and really wanted this to go away. None of us thought it would blow up to what it was, though we knew it was not going to be pleasant for anybody.

After a couple of weeks of picketing and meetings, it became clear that nothing was going to change. We then decided to up the ante. If it was illegal to have our tables at Bancroft and Telegraph, then why not put them right on campus? The discussions were extraordinary. The California College Republicans, California Young Republicans, and the Young Americans for Freedom (YAF) struggled with what they thought about civil disobedience, as they didn't approve of it. At the same time we had Civil Rights Movement veterans for whom civil disobedience was the first option. And we had everything in between.

We agreed to move the tables onto campus at Sather Gate. And one of the things that I am most proud of is that before we did all of that, we put out a joint press statement about why we were going to set the tables on campus. The three prominent Republican groups all agreed to say that while they didn't support civil disobedience and they weren't going to participate, they understood that other people had a different point of view, and that "the United Front still stands." That was the last phrase in the press release. It was very important because there had been an attempt to break the center and the right off from the rest. But they were very courageous and their support was really important.

School started and for a couple of weeks we had tables set up at Sather Gate. The Assistant Dean came and started taking down the names of the people sitting at the tables. As soon as he took a name down, that person would get up and another person would sit down and say, "Whatever you're going to do to him, you gotta do to me." They took down 50 or 60 names until they reached a point where they realized that they weren't getting anywhere and decided instead to take disciplinary action against Mario Savio, my brother, Art, Sidney Stapleton, and a few others.

When the time came for those designated for discipline to meet with Dean Towle, I led about 150 people to her office for the meeting because it was about all of us. But the staff shut the door after the first few people entered and didn't let anybody else inside. I decided that if they weren't going to let us in, we weren't going to let them out and we sat against the door to block their exit. At about midnight Chancellor Strong announced that eight students were indefinitely suspended. We sat there till about 3:00 or 4:00 in the morning. The university threatened us with felony kidnap for sitting outside the door, and the eventual negotiation was that we would leave and there would be no arrests or disciplinary action. The compromise we negotiated was that the Chancellor would convene a faculty committee on student conduct to hear the cases of the students who had been charged with illegally sitting at tables at Sather Gate. After the compromise we all went home.

A few more days at Sather Gate and nothing happened. Mario Savio and Jack Weinberg and others now pressed for us to move our tables in front of the Sproul Hall steps on Parents Weekend, the first weekend in October. We figured that the parents would be at Cal for the Saturday football game and we'd have maximum visibility.

On the morning of October 1st we put our tables up at Sproul Hall Plaza where the food places are located. I had an 11:00 class and planned to come at noon, but my class was on the north end of campus and I didn't get to Sproul Hall plaza till about 12:10 or 12:15. It was lunchtime, so thousands of students hurried downhill to the plaza to eat and there they found a campus police car and cops right in the middle of the Plaza (a surprise, as no one had seen a police car on the Plaza before). The cops arrested Jack Weinberg while he sat at the Congress of Racial Equality (C.O.R.E.) table passing out civil rights literature. They had picked him out because he looked a little older and therefore must have been an "outside agitator." It turned out Jack was a graduate student, but they didn't know that. And he was a bad choice because almost everybody on the campus supported CORE. You couldn't have picked a group that was friendlier and better liked by everybody than the Congress of Racial Equality.

Jack was an experienced civil rights activist and went limp. The cops just dragged him from the table and put him into a police car. They did this right in front of all the students—the ones who had nothing to do with us, didn't care about the issues, who thought that all the leaflets we handed out were annoying. The students then just sat down around the car. I've never seen anything like it in my life—not before or since. The reaction was immediate: "What are you doing? You can't just drag somebody off into a police car! He didn't do anything. He wasn't fighting anybody and he didn't shoot a gun off. He was just sitting at a table!" A few people said "Sit down, sit down!" Hundreds and then thousands of people who had never before been part of a demonstration just sat down. They weren't part of any of the campus political organizations. If you put together all of the organizations up to that point, they probably only had five or six hundred members combined. Now there were several thousand people involved and we had no idea who they were. These students just happened to be going to lunch when they saw Jack get dragged across the plaza. Whether they ever wanted to be in a political group in their whole lives or not, their sense of justice was offended. And that's why they just spontaneously surrounded a police car in the middle of Sproul Plaza and sat down!

The campus cops were always very friendly with kids, so they weren't anxious to move anybody. They didn't threaten us; they just hung around and chatted. I approached them and said, "If we take our shoes off, can we stand on the roof of the car?" They said sure. So that's why in the photographs we're all in stocking feet. We were trying not to hurt the car. We had a rally to talk about what to do and it was just remarkable. We set up a microphone and a sound system on the car, and anyone who wanted to could speak. It was a very interesting discussion; there was really a debate about what to do. Nobody felt like they were in charge, certainly not our little United Front.

Charlie Powell, who was ASUC (Associated Students of the University of California, the student government) president, came down and said, "Oh, this is embarrassing, this is Parents Weekend, go home, go home please." ASUC Congressman Mel Levine came and said, "This is a bad thing. I support your cause but this isn't the way to get it." We stayed. That night, some of the fraternity guys came down out of the hills. They were drunk and stood up on the steps above Sproul Plaza to throw lit cigarettes and eggs into the crowd. Everybody was tired by this time, so there were some tense moments. Then a minister appeared, an adult not from the campus ministry, and he just told the fraternity boys to go home and they did. We have no idea why they listened to him. He said, "I don't care who you are or what you want to do. You can disagree all you want, but you're putting people in danger, go home." And they left.

The first speakers had been people like me who immediately had something to say. But then the people who were listening to us decided that they had something to say. It was a completely free forum. You could just get up there on the car and speak. People who had never done anything like this or been involved politically in any way would say: "I think we should do this," or "we should negotiate with the police," or "I think we should negotiate with the university." They never stopped speaking from the top of the car; it went on all day and all night.

Through all of this we had to feed people, so we organized a group to put together cheese sandwiches and Kool-Aid. When you don't have any money that's what you do. We also had logistics to deal with. We set up notifications so that the women who were in dorms got notifications so that they wouldn't be locked out of their dorms if they went home. That was the beginning of when we knew that we had to get serious, because we were no longer a little ragtag band. There were now a lot more of us, and we needed to decide how to organize all these people and determine who would speak for them. There were all kinds of questions: Did anybody speak for them? What the hell was going on? Who were these folks? Were they going to stay involved? What does all this mean?

Mario spoke several times and Art spoke several times. All this time Jack Weinberg was in the car, and when he had to go he went in a Coke bottle, which everybody talked about for about thirty years. About 3:00 in the afternoon of the second day we got a note from University President Clark Kerr's office that he would like to see the leaders of this demonstration. That raised a pretty interesting question. Who were the leaders? This was spontaneous. But there were leaders who had set out the Sproul Hall tables and we had a meeting of the United Front. So we picked someone from SLATE, me (cause I was the "spokesperson" still), Mario, a couple of people from the Young Republicans, from Young Americans for Freedom, from the Democrats, etc. We tried to have a wide spectrum of representation.

That evening we went to President Clark Kerr's office on University Avenue, about a good six-minute walk away. While there we heard sirens. The Oakland police had been called and they brought in hundreds of police in riot gear, hundreds of police vans, and a "V" wedge of probably 30 big Harley motorcycles that the police kept revving up. We could hear the roars in Clark Kerr's office. They'd turn them off for a while, and then they would turn them on again and rev them up. The whole thing just made the Sheraton Palace look like a lawn party. We were worried about all those kids out on the concrete plaza, and we kept asking Clark Kerr for assurances that nothing would happen as long as we were negotiating. We weren't going to sit in his office while all those people got the crap beat out of them. So he assured us over and over and started negotiating with us.

One of our demands was for the reinstatement of the students who had been suspended a few days earlier. Then negotiations turned to "time, place, and manner." They were about where we could have our tables and how to deal with free speech issues for students of all stripes (that's why we decided to take representatives from each group up to Kerr's office). Then we debated about how much we could accept before we left to end the demonstration. At some point we got what Kerr said was his final offer, which was to immediately convene the Faculty Senate Committee on Student Conduct. We found out after the demonstration was over that the committee didn't exist, but we didn't know that at the time. He said he would immediately convene them and have them adjudicate the suspensions so the students would get hearings and there wouldn't be any indefinite suspensions. He also said he would immediately put together a faculty, administration, and student group to discuss how to solve the issues of student activism on campus.

We then debated whether this was enough or not. Meanwhile, every few minutes Kerr's secretary would run in and audibly whisper, "The police don't know how much longer they can hold before they arrest." He'd whisper back, "Tell them to wait, we're working on this." She'd reply, "They're not sure how long they're going to wait for you, sir."

We then asked him to let us use his conference room. We had a huge row in which the California College Republicans and I argued that this was enough, that we should end this demonstration and fight another day. That was because we didn't know who the people were out there. This was spontaneous; they had not signed on to be a part of a "revolution." It was dark and they were unprotected in the middle of a cement plaza. It was possible that nobody would be killed, but it was also possible that somebody would be killed. It was a certainty that a lot of people were going to be hurt. The police weren't there just to arrest us, I can assure you. It was very clear by the way they were equipped that they were just going to haul ass on us. So I said, "Frankly, I'm afraid I don't feel like I can take responsibility for voting to put people in danger. I think someone's going to die and that other people are going to be seriously hurt." Sandra Fuchs, a dear buddy and SLATE representative supported me, as well as a couple of the more conservative groups. Mario and a couple of others on the left were furious with me. Mario said, "This is not the right time to give in. We can't give in now. We'll get what we want. They're not going to kill anybody out there. It would be bad publicity for them because it's Parents Weekend." We fought and fought, then took a vote and my side won. We agreed that Mario would be the person who would tell the crowd that this was over. Then we raced out because we could hear engines revving. We got there and it was just the most horrifying thing you've ever seen. It looked like a police state and the motorcycle cops were ready to run over anybody who was in their path.

Mario got up and explained the negotiations. He said, "It's not a good deal, but it's the best deal we could get. We think you should take it. Go home." There was some discussion and a few more people came up to speak. But finally everybody went home.

Mario was just livid. He thought that this was just the worst thing we could have possibly done. Then the YAF representative denounced us all in front of President Kerr and said, "You should have them all arrested and throw them all out of school." He said, "I'm not a part of this, I'm going to go get my people and get out of here." And he left. That made us nervous because we thought the California College Republicans or the California Young Republicans might go with him, but they didn't. Their students weren't at the demonstration and they weren't sitting around the car, but their representatives still supported us. They didn't even threaten to leave, they stayed right with us.

So after 32 hours Jack finally got to leave the car. He was arrested and booked, but released and the charges were dropped. We didn't go home. We went to Stiles Hall and began setting up. That was the birth of the Free Speech Movement. We first established a Steering Committee that included a representative from each campus organization, a representative from each dormitory that wanted to participate, a representative from the co-ops, one from the graduate students' union, and a representative from each of the various religious groups. Altogether there were 65 to 70 of us. I was elected to the Executive Committee of about ten representatives that also included Bettina Aptheker, Mario, Jack, Art, and Sid Stapleton.

We began developing an organizational structure and everything was "central." We had communications central, food central, security central, people in charge of getting paper, distributing leaflets, etc. We had several thousand people who wanted something to do, to be involved. We had volunteers to make calls on the phones, put out leaflets, make sandwiches and Kool-Aid, communicate with the press and within the organization, write, print, do graphics, purchasing, etc. The organization got everybody's phone number and address, and then developed a mailing and phone list. It was an extraordinary organization.

Mario and Bettina and a couple of others were selected to be on the larger committee to put together the Faculty, Administration, and Student Committees. I saw my star fading, but I didn't mind. The press singled out Mario as the leader. He was fiery. They thought he wasn't a student, as he had come from Mississippi and he hadn't been in Berkeley long. They were looking for the "outside agitator" angle. But Mario *was* a student and he was clearly an extraordinary spokesperson; there was no doubt about it at all.

By this time, we were so big that it didn't matter if a few groups broke off into smaller committees. Mario and I were nominated to the Steering Committee and in the first meeting Mario denounced me and said that I had tried to ingratiate myself with Clark Kerr, that he saw me do it, that I was a sellout, and I couldn't be trusted. He used my association with Dean Towle as proof that I should be thrown off the Steering Committee and just be on the Executive Committee. That caused my brother Art to want have a fistfight with Mario, but instead he threatened to take SLATE out of the Free Speech Movement. SLATE was the best-organized, largest group, the one that had real depth, so therefore the only one that had to be there. So they didn't take any action against me.

After a couple of weeks the Executive Committee reconstituted the Steering Committee to better reflect the "breadth and depth" of the group. Somehow, not only was I no longer on the committee, but I also stopped getting phone calls from Communication Central (which I had set up) for meetings, even of the Executive Committee. Art and several others tried to get me to bring this before the Executive Committee, but I refused. I really believed that because I had a following, particularly with the centrists and the liberals, that a lot of people would feel that this would be divisive and the press would have a field day. So nobody at the time (or today) knew that I was "purged." I would attend every rally and I would stand on the stage, but I was never a speaker again. What I did then was "living group" speaking—I went to the sororities, fraternities, and dormitories to explain why they needed to be involved in this movement and what was in it for them.

This all happened between September and December. All the students who had been suspended were reinstated. The university had finally lightened up, or so we thought. Just before Thanksgiving, the Faculty and Student Committee (over the objections of the Free Speech Movement) proposed the following: tables would be allowed around the fountain at Sproul Plaza; students would be able to sell buttons, T-shirts etc.; and they could hand out literature. There would be some time restrictions (for example they couldn't interfere with classes), but advocacy of "unlawful actions" would still lead to university discipline. Everybody from the liberal democrats to the right was covered. That left out the civil rights groups, the socialists, the Communists, and the radicals that weren't socialist or Communist, because they were the ones who used civil disobedience.

We went home for Thanksgiving, thinking, "They finally figured it out. They take care of the bulk of the people, and they screw us." We thought that it was over. We got something, which was better than nothing, but we were thinking about going back and doing one last stand. Art and I told my parents that we'd probably be thrown out of school and that I wouldn't graduate that year, but it'd be all right. The radicals and lefties were preparing their parents as well. We were going to have one big event, one big act of civil disobedience and we'd all get disciplined, thrown out of school, and that would be that. We just didn't know what the issue was going to be. While we were home Mario, Brian Turner, Art, and I were sent letters saying that we were going to be disciplined for our roles. Before those letters went out the university had won, I swear to God, they had won. Then they sent us letters saying they were going to throw four of the leaders out.

Of course, Mario had to apologize to me because if I had been "ingratiating myself to the administration" I had done a pretty poor job of it.

We planned a protest demonstration in front of Sproul Hall for December 2nd. Mario gave the speech that no one who heard it will ever forget, "There is a time when the operation of the machine becomes so odious, makes you so sick at heart, that you can't take part; you can't even tacitly take part. And you've got to put your bodies upon the gears and upon the wheels, upon the levers, upon all the apparatus, and you've got to make it stop. And you've got to indicate to the people who run it, to the people who own it, that unless you're free, the machine will be prevented from working at all!" I had decided not to sit-in. But then I heard that fabulous speech and decided that I was going in. There were 6000 people at the rally and about a thousand of us entered the administration building. I really believed that the rally would be small. I thought that people felt defeated and that even though the four of us got the hatchet it would not change anything. But I was completely wrong! The students were just outraged.

A lot of people who had not been seriously involved went in, joined the sit-in and stayed all night. Each of us had different floors. On the first floor we had a big Hanukkah party and a little film festival with François Truffaut films. On the second floor we had a "free university" where graduate students taught courses about current issues. The fourth floor was a study hall. Throughout the building everybody made sure to stay out of the offices.

We did pretty well. We had a food arrangement set up, and even had some contingency arrangements if they blocked the doors. The student union was on the second floor, so we set up a pulley system so that if they tried to starve us out by

FIGURE 6.1 Mario Savio, a leader of the Free Speech Movement, addresses a large crowd at the University of California at Berkeley on December 2, 1964. The Free Speech Movement began when university officials denied students access to campus space that they had traditionally used to distribute literature and promote their clubs and political causes. The call to restore "free speech" galvanized students across the political spectrum, uniting activists, moderates, and conservatives. Following Savio's December speech, 814 students occupied the administration building, Sproul Hall, and remained there until they were arrested the next day. Supporters called a campus-wide strike and raised bail for the arrested students. The university reinstated the "free speech" area the following year.

Source: Corbis/Bettmann

blocking the doors we could still bring in food. I was pledge mother of my sorority, and my pledges were having their dance and had to rehearse. I made them come into the building because I wasn't going to leave. They didn't stay, but they came in and rehearsed their skit, I gave them the OK, and they went home. I told them, "If I'm not there, you just go on without me."

About one or two in the morning on the second day the local radio station broadcast that Governor Brown had decided to send in troops to get the 800 or so of us out of there. We didn't have the radio on and nobody told us, but students from all over the Berkeley hills heard it. We looked out the windows from the upper floors and saw hundreds of students running down out of the hills toward the building. It was remarkable.

The Steering Committee and the Executive Committee had a quick meeting and we drew straws to see who would leave the building to organize what would happen in the aftermath. Because if everybody in the leadership were arrested, there wouldn't be anyone left to organize a response. A few people drew short straws and left the building to get ministers, rabbis and priests, the ACLU, and other people to be observers.

The Oakland police, the Highway Patrol, and the Alameda County Sheriff's Department arrived. The first thing they did was to kick the observers out by telling them that if they stayed they would be arrested. A few stayed and got arrested, but most of them left. Then the cops systematically covered all the windows with newspapers and masking tape so that the press could not see what was going on inside. That scared the shit out of all of us. There were no observers and no press to watch what was going on. Then the police came in and started taking people away floor by floor. We heard people screaming on the first floor, then on the second floor, but we didn't know what was going on.

The police had learned from other demonstrations. The officer who arrested you held up a number in front of you, stood next to you, and they took a picture so that they knew exactly which officer arrested you. They wanted to match you exactly, your number, your picture, and the arresting cop so that they wouldn't screw this one up. It was a civil rights movement and we had all agreed to go limp, so it took them well over 12 hours to arrest all of us. They dragged each of us into the elevator, took us down to the basement, and out into the paddy wagons. They filled up the Oakland jail, the Berkeley jail, and the Alameda County Sheriff's jail, and there were still more of us. Then they started taking us out to the state prison out at Santa Rita, which we later renamed as the University of California at Santa Rita or UC Santa Rita. When they filled up Santa Rita they took us to the Oakland Armory.

My treatment was bad. Most of the time when people went limp the police picked them up. Instead of taking me right to the paddy wagon, they took me down to the basement and isolated me. They put me in a room and interrogated me for at least an hour or hour and a half. They tried to get me to identify people in the leadership by threatening me with arrest for felony conspiracy. I just did what we were all taught to say, "I have nothing to say to you except my name and address, and I want to see an attorney before I talk to you about anything." They got really angry, threatened me, menaced me, and finally said, "OK, let's go, we'll take you out to the paddy wagon." Of course I didn't get up. Then a very big guy grabbed me by the hair and dragged me on my back all the way up a flight of stairs and out of the building. The base of my back hit each stair. Then he threw me in the bus, and when the bus was full, they took me out to Santa Rita. By the end of that evening I had a huge ball of swelling on my back and I was in a lot of pain.

There were a lot of women arrested. About a hundred of us were packed into visitor cages. We literally sat on top of each other. I got on one of the stools and stood on it for five or six hours. A lot of women were quite frightened because it was their first arrest, but also because they thought that bail would be set too high and we'd never get out of there. I remembered my first arrest and how frightened I had been, so we did a variety of things to keep them occupied. We decided to determine the most "radical" street in Berkeley. Everybody said what street they lived on and we kept tallies to figure that out. After we picked the most radical street, we figured out which camps everybody went to and which camp songs they knew, and we sang songs. Then a few women had to go to the bathroom, which was our first emergency because we could not get anybody to come to the cage. It wasn't like a cell because there was no bathroom in the cage. After a while it got to be an emergency, so we screamed, made noises, and yelled until finally they did take a couple of us to the bathroom. From then on they took us for regular bathroom breaks and that went on for many hours.

People finally calmed down, but nobody knew what was going to happen. I reminded everybody that we had drawn straws and there were people outside who knew that we were there, and that I was sure that the entire world had seen the pictures of us being arrested because there were a lot of cameras there. I told them that we were not going to be forgotten, that we were going to get out, but it would not be quick. I told them that it took 15 or 16 hours to process the 160 of us in the Sheraton arrest, and this would be slower than that. It would take time, but we would get out. I told them to not worry about it, that they were going to be all right, that we were all there together and it was going to be okay.

As I finished this little reassuring speech for about the 14th time that evening, they came and said, "Goldberg!" Two matrons grabbed me and took me out of there. They put me alone in a room, locked the door, and left. What had happened was that there were four females with the name Goldberg arrested that night, and they didn't know which one of them was the leader. Three hours went by before they put me back in the cage again because they thought I was the wrong Goldberg.

They finally decided that they should feed us and took us all out together to the dining hall. There we could hear other people's voices, but we had no way of knowing whether they were regular inmates or Free Speech Movement inmates. Then the people at my little table and I heard somebody crying pretty heavily. Two of us decided to walk towards the sound and found one of the Goldbergs who had been interrogated. She was terrified. She had been arrested, held, and interrogated just because of her name. So we took her back to the dining hall with us and put her with people far away from me.

They kept telling us that we wouldn't be arraigned if we gave them more information. They also said that bail would be set at $25,000 each and that no one would ever raise all the bail, so we'd be there forever. It was psychological warfare.

We finally began to get called in groups of ten or twelve to be formally booked. People were beginning to get bailed out and on their way out had to pass the area where we were penned up. One woman told us that she had looked out the window and that there was a five-mile line of cars waiting to come get us and take us home.

It was unbelievable. The cars carried faculty, parents, students, and friends. They had raised over half a million dollars in bail in something like ten hours. People all over the state, all over the country had seen the arrests. To the press it had looked pretty awful. There were photographs on all the TV stations of the police covering the windows and it looked bad. People were beaten up and injured. There were no brutal, savage beatings, but nonetheless there were injuries. We were not well treated.

This was all after the university had already won. They had snatched defeat out of the mouth of victory! It was just phenomenal. There was no way in the world that we could have ever gotten our movement to get that kind of support without the university coming after the four of us. What brainiac figured that move out, I don't know.

It took a day and a half, but eventually we all got out. Afterwards there was a student strike, which was effective because a lot of students didn't go to class and a lot of professors cancelled classes. The press said "Strike Fails," yet there wasn't anyone on campus. That was another big change in my life. I would never again believe the newspapers about any account of protests. Whatever they wrote, I just assumed it was a lie.

I have a copy of a newspaper with the headline, "Strike Fails," but of course the strike didn't fail. It went on and the faculty began to get their act together. They were horrified that the police had been brought onto campus to arrest all those students in a relatively brutal fashion. No one had any idea what was going on during the arrests because the police had kicked out the observers and blocked the windows, but they heard the screams. And that really brought the faculty to our side and they voted to support us.

At the trial we made a huge, stupid mistake because we agreed to one trial for all of us. We should have done exactly what we did in the Sheraton Palace arrest and asked for trials of ten people or five, or however many they wanted and tied the court system up forever until it became more expensive than they cared to accept. What was worse was that the case made terrible law because for the first time in California going limp was declared to be "resisting arrest," so we were all convicted of resisting arrest.

I was the witness that the defense used to do the bulk of the narrative of the Free Speech Movement. I was on the witness stand for three days on direct, three days on cross-examination, and a day on redirect. Our attorneys had me do the narrative because they wanted the prosecutor to ask, "What were all of your affiliations?" Of course I could say that I was pledge mother of a social sorority.

I was charged with three felony assaults. They knew they had hurt me, but the deal was that they would drop the three felony assaults if I wouldn't charge them with police brutality. Stan Golde, my lovely attorney, said, "Of course you're going to sign a waiver that you were not injured by them and they will drop these charges." I said, "I will not!" And he said, "Yes you will." I asked why and he said, "Who's going to believe that three officers dragged you by the hair and hurt you in the way that you were hurt, and you did nothing to cause it? Nobody will believe that. There's nobody in the world that will believe it. If you were a jury member and you hadn't ever been arrested, you wouldn't believe it." So I said okay. With the several misdemeanors I had by now, it was possible that I could still teach. But with a felony on my record, teaching was unlikely. I also had to consider that a felony assault on a police officer would get me jail time. So I signed the waiver saying that nothing bad had happened to me and released them from all responsibility for any injuries that may have occurred. They dropped the felony charges and I was convicted of misdemeanor charges of trespassing on public property and resisting arrest.

We were all convicted and then they started to sentence us. They couldn't sentence people in groups and therefore had to sentence us one at a time. I had a problem because I had just been accepted for graduate school at the University of Chicago. I was afraid I'd get a probation where I'd have to report to a California probation officer and wouldn't be able to leave the state. Unfortunately my pre-probation report suggested that I be given probation, no jail time, and a fine. Since that would keep me from going to graduate school I requested that I be given a fine and jail time, but no probation. Only about 40 people had been sentenced before me, and the court was completely paranoid. When they got to me I said, "Your Honor, I've read the pre-probation report, but I would like to respectfully ask for straight jail time." I told him that I was going out of state to the University of Chicago and didn't want to be forced to stay in California. The judge said, "You want to go to jail today?" And I said, "Yes, I'd actually like to go right now, if I could." I thought I'd get maybe a few months and would be able to go to the University of Chicago when I got out. The judge said, "We'll take a twenty minute recess. Golde, I want to see you in my chambers immediately." And he ran out of the courtroom. Stan went in and when he came back out he said, "The judge doesn't want you to go to jail." I said, "Well, I'm sorry, he should just not sentence me to any jail time if he doesn't want me to go to jail." The judge had decided that if I went to jail, then everybody after me would ask for jail time, and they would never have enough room for everybody. He thought that it was a trick. When he came back out on the bench, he asked, "You still want to go to jail?" I told him I did and was really clear as to why, that there was no game here. The judge went back in his chambers and called in my attorney. When Stan came out he said, "You won't believe this. You can take a big fine and three years probation. If you refuse that you'll get jail time, a big fine, and three years probation." I took the fine and the probation, because I certainly wasn't going to take all three if I could take two.

The fine was $3,000, and in the Sixties that was a lot of money—enough to buy a new car. I got probation, but the judge did hear me and gave me summary court probation so that I didn't have to report and could leave the state. It took me two and a half years of monthly installments to pay that fine. The terms of the probation were that I couldn't "sit-in, sleep-in, lie-in, walk-in, bathe-in, etc." during that time. Of course the following year I took part in a sit-in.

That school year I was initiated into Phi Beta Kappa. At the dinner there were five tables with ten kids at each table. And of the five tables, three of them were all veterans of the Free Speech Movement.

I applied to be a graduation speaker, went through the full process, and was one of the three final candidates. While I was waiting to give my speech in front of the faculty committee, one of the members came out and said, "Are you ready to go?" I said, "Just about." "You must be getting pretty tired of all of this." "Tired of all of what?" "Well, don't people confuse you with that other Jackie Goldberg?" I said, "Nooo, actually they don't. I am that other Jackie Goldberg."

I didn't get to speak because they weren't sure what I'd say.

QUESTIONS FOR DISCUSSION

1. Jackie Goldberg describes several personal encounters with racism and prejudice. What are they? How do they affect her and how does she deal with them? How are these experiences different from those of Ray Hubbard, Gwendolyn Zoharah Simmons, Toby Marotta, or Yolanda Retter? How are they the same?

2. Goldberg describes women who had an impact on the way she thinks and how she views life. Who are these women? What did they do or say that made them role models? Goldberg discovers that women's freedoms on campus are limited by regulations, and that women are sometimes left out of decision making in student organizations. How is life for women different on today's college campuses? To what would you attribute those changes?

3. There is a point early in Goldberg's college career where she is no longer merely a participant in protest actions but becomes an organizer. In which actions is she a participant and which does she organize? Which of Goldberg's organized actions do you find most imaginative or effective?

4. Review the events that lead up to the Free Speech Movement. Do you sympathize with the actions of the "United Front" or with the university? Are you surprised that young conservatives, Republicans, Democrats, radicals, and religious groups could get together and agree on a common course of action? Do you think that could happen today?

5. There are points in this story where it is apparent that the students have achieved what they wanted and others where the university has won, and yet the confrontations continue to escalate. What has happened? Who is responsible for the escalation?

6. Does it seem odd to you that college students would have to fight for free speech? Do you think colleges or universities should have the right to tell students what they can say on campus? Do you think that free speech is a good thing or are there circumstances under which it should be limited? Why?

7. What do you think of the actions of the police? What about the justice system? Do you think it worked the way it should? What about the tactics that Goldberg and others used—do you think that they should have taken another approach? Goldberg says to her readers, "Just be arrested one time as a demonstrator. It will change you forever. It changed me forever." What does she mean by that? What does she hope people will learn?

STANDING WITH CÉSAR
Maria and Antonia Saludado, with Kent Kirkton

Antonia and Maria de Los Angeles Saludado squeezed into a car with four other young huel-guistas in August 1967 and headed to Chicago to stop the sale of grapes. They had no idea what lay ahead of them, no real idea even where Chicago was. They just knew that César had chosen them to go.

He said, "You guys are going to go to Chicago because you're good workers." We didn't know we were good. But anyway, he sent us—my sister and me, one other girl, and three boys.

This was not the beginning of their journey, either literally or metaphorically. The Saludado sisters were born in Michoacanejo, Jalisco, Mexico where they lived with their mother and siblings. Their father, Lorenzo, was working for a steel company in Los Angeles and when he returned in 1957 to visit his family they decided it was time to move the whole family north. Lorenzo had been born in Morenci, Arizona, so there was no problem with citizenship. But he didn't want his girls to grow up in Los Angeles. The family settled in Earlimart, California, near Lorenzo's brother, and went to work in the fields.

When people come to the United States, this is the only way we can do it, you see. It wasn't easy. It was hard work. But you could get a job anywhere. Because it was like Mexican people were only good for the fields. So everywhere you go it was, "Oh, yeah, you can have a job." Nobody said no. They especially liked you younger. This is the only way you can do it. But there is no—there is no hope for a farm worker.

Antonia, Maria, and their sister Dora were soon working alongside their father. At first they worked on weekends and summers but soon they left school. There were too many mouths to feed on such small salaries for them to stay in school for long and there was little or no opportunity for other work. Maria and Antonia wanted to bolster the family income so that their younger sisters and brother could stay in school.

When we came to Earlimart, California, we started working then in *chicharo* (sweet peas). So, we do *chicharo* and it was piecework. We fill it up by the basket and we went to trade them for the money. We make like 70 cents per basket, sometimes 80 cents, sometimes less.

This is the thing that was very sad because it was *pochos* (Americanized Mexicans) around us. And that's why I was very upset, because the communication with *pochos* wasn't very good. And so I didn't have friends until I was in my twenties. I didn't date anybody from seventeen to twenty because I was very afraid of those people. They don't like us because we don't speak any English.

Most of the time the family could find work within driving distance of their little house in Earlimart but sometimes they had to follow the crops.

When we were going, everybody was crying because we didn't want to go over there (over to Santa Rosa to pick plums), but at the same time we were happy because we knew that coming back, we had money. We used to go in this little car. I guess it was about a 1955 Chevy. I don't know how all nine of us fit in there. But we carried flour, and we carried potatoes, we carried . . . the most important thing a Mexican eats, you know . . . beans. We didn't have to worry about corn, or chiles, or tomatoes because in those places over there, the grower already grew up their chiles, their tomatoes because they know that the Mexicans liked that. They had squash already growing over there. When they had cows, they give us some milk over there. In a way, we were happy.

Everyone, including my little sisters, worked at picking plums. My father and another person, they shake the trees and all the fruit came down. So we pick it up and we fill up the boxes and they took it to the dryer to make prunes. We stopped going over there because it was just taking chances if we were going to go to work or not.

The girls' father, Lorenzo, quickly learned the work-flow in crops in the Central Valley and was able to locate enough work to stay busy without driving to the coast to work in the plums.

When we started going to work for hourly wages, we started going to the cotton fields. And it was very hard for us. We started getting heat problems. There was a lot of heat. There was no water in the fields. There was no toilets. We were sweating and no water. If you were carrying water, you carry it in. But, if you didn't carry it, there was no way for us to drink water.

But my God! I didn't like to pick cotton at all. I didn't. I'd sit and cry. I didn't like it. We were going and picking cotton on the weekends. And my daddy used to tell us, if you get a lot of cotton, we might be able to go and buy something else. You know, they always give us moral support. Wow! Yeah! Yes! We want to do it!

One year, we were chopping sugar beets in the wintertime. That sugar beet. It was the hardest thing in my life! My feet, they were so blistered up it was coming blood from my feet. I do remember the labor contractor turned around and he told my daddy, if she doesn't get into the [wage] line, she is not going to get paid. She has to come and stand up in the line. And I couldn't hardly make it up myself because it was so hard for me. I was crying.

I told my daddy, "That little bastard. He's going to make me stand up in the line? Can't he give you the money for me?" He say, "No. You have to come . . . I'll hold you up." He took me over there and got my pay. It took three days to finish the corner they gave us. And do you know how much they paid us? Nine dollars for all, my dad and my two sisters and me.

One day we went into this potato area. We were picking potatoes, and they didn't have no potatoes. . . . (it was the 3rd pass through the field) . . . there were about six of us picking potatoes. And we didn't even make $5.00 in the whole day, from 3 o'clock in the morning till about 5 o'clock in the afternoon.

We used to stop by the little store and buy soda. Kids, you know, they just get satisfied with a soda because, you know, it's just a kid. And we were satisfied just with a soda or little cookies or something. That's it for us. But that day, we couldn't stop by. We just looked at the store. And we just passed it by because we couldn't even go and buy a soda. And my daddy . . . I saw my daddy. He just looked at the store, and he looked at us, and we were just like laying down in the car. He got really sad. He got really sad. He had tears in his eyes. He said this is not one of the days that it worked for us.

So, this is how it is, you know? Migrants move from one area to another then come back and stay in a place if they got a place to stay. So, they stay. Since we came over here, we had a place to stay because my uncle owned two little houses. That's why we always came back to Earlimart.

Grapes had become the primary crop in the Central Valley by the early 1960s and there was a lot of work in the vineyards. Maria and Antonia worked in the grapes when they were in season and the rest of the year they worked at different jobs such as chopping cotton and picking potatoes.

We were working in wine grapes. It was different than picking grapes for the table. And during those years, you need to be working hard because you have trays that are very big. You fill it up with grapes and dump it in the big gondolas. So you need to be—not be careful with all that, because if you're very careful then you're not going to make your quota. You're scared. "I'm going to get covered with fungicide dust. I'm going to get stung [by a bee]." But you need to forget about those things. So, when you finish, you have dust all over and juice and all—even your body is so sweet with all the grapes. This is the difference. Because with table grapes you are picking and [grading them] number one, number two, and you're more careful with that kind of grape because they go to the market.

The Saludados seemed to be destined to spend their lives struggling to eke out a living in the fields. For Maria and Antonia, the only relief from the long hours and back breaking work was the Saturday night dances in Delano. Then one Saturday in April 1964 even the dance was interrupted. Instead, Lorenzo took the girls to his compadre, *Leandro Gutierrez's house for a meeting on Saturday. Leandro had told him,*

"We have this guy. He really is a good organizer. Find all your friends and bring them over to my house because we're going to have a meeting. We're going to have a union. *Vamos a tener union. Vamos a hacer esto.*" ("We are going to have a union. We are going to do this.")

Lorenzo knew from his experience in the steel mills in Los Angeles that a union was the workers' only hope. He was ready to unionize. When Maria and Antonia asked their father who this organizer was, he told them that he heard it was César Chávez. And they said OK, let's go.

Maria and Antonia were the last to enter the house because they had gone to gather their friends for the meeting and they couldn't even see Chávez because there were so many people in the small house. But they were very taken by what he said.

It was talking like a big dream. That dream was very nice, and I liked the dream because I felt like all my body had those words that he said. We are the workers. We make and raise the food for this country. And we are paid less and we live on less than anybody. Why? We need to do something. We need to get together. And it was so quiet, so slow. Like every word that he said was so strong.

Later when Antonia and Maria questioned their father about whether these union people could be trusted, whether they would do anything but collect their dues and disappear as others had done in the past, they discovered that their father had belonged to a union when he was working in Los Angeles.

So see, we didn't know until that time. He said, "I used to belong to the union, to the steelworkers union in Los Angeles. I didn't work for this [kind of] money. I didn't bring you guys over here to be squeezed. If these people are trying to do something, let's help. Let's help. Let's get together. Let's see what's going on. Let's see if we can do it. But, let's try it. Let's not stop trying to do something." And my dad always believed in the union because I think his father was in a big strike in Arizona. My dad was very strong. He knows the union is the best thing for people.

The Saludados continued to work over the next 18 months and to pay their dues to the National Farm Workers Association (later to become the United Farm Workers). Every week or two César Chávez or Dolores Huerta would stop by their house to visit and to pick up their dues. And while the sisters wondered whether any good would come of this new organization, Lorenzo began attending house meetings and organizing his friends. The girls remained interested but somewhat uncommitted. However, as the months passed and Lorenzo pointed out the inequities in the fields, their commitment to the Farm Workers Association grew. As they became more and more aware of the tricks the ranchers and the labor contractors employed to cheat them out of wages, they became more convinced that they had to stand up for themselves.

Then in September of 1965, the Filipino members of the Agricultural Workers Organizing Committee (AWOC) sat down in the vineyards. Chávez then called for a meeting at the Guadalupe Church Hall in Delano. The hall was so packed with farm workers that many had to gather on the lawn.

This hall is a humongous hall. We didn't expect that we were going to see so many people. They were outside, the people!

César said, "Do you guys think that we are ready to go on strike?"

My goodness! That strike started! They started it!

Maria and Antonia threw themselves wholeheartedly into the strike. The day after the vote at Guadalupe Church Hall, they returned to work with their father so that they could organize the rest of the people they were working with. Their father said,

"We're going to go like it's regular work. We're going to go dressed for work. We're going to take a lunch, but remember, we're going to be sure that everybody in our crew walks out in a strike."

So I (Maria) was almost 25-years old, but I think I was looking like 18, like a teenager because I was very skinny. I weighed 110. So, I said OKAY. I went talking to everybody, Let's go. We're going to go on strike. We're going in a *huelga*.

Yeah. We're going to go on strike. We're going to make more money. So, we organized all the crew. Everybody went on strike in our crew.

Life became extremely difficult for everyone as the strike wore on.

The people that were outside [on the picket lines] were suffering a lot. But, I think the people that were organizing inside . . . I think it was worse [for them] because the companies, they were hitting us. All this time they were saying, these people [the strike organizers] . . . look at how much damage they did [in the fields].

And, we turn around and say to the people, that's not true. They did it. They paid these other guys to do it. So we were having people against us . . .

Finally, it came to the time for the pruning. In the pruning, we were suffering too because we were organizing. And the foreman there used to ask us, "Are you for them or are you against them? They are a bunch of lazy people there. They go to the welfare."

We used to tell them that there were lots of families that we knew. We used to mention this family, and that other, and this other one. They are not supported by the welfare. They're workers, and they are out there [on strike] because they are doing something good.

The foreman told me, "I think you are one of them." And, I said, "So what if I am one of them? What are you going to do about it?"

She said, "Well there is nothing I can do about it."

I said, "What are you going to do, fire me? I am already fired. I'm gone."

She didn't fire us. We quit.

The Saludados joined the picket lines and got up very early so that they could drive a scout car. The scout car was something peculiar to the grape strike. Since the ranches were so big and the workers could be picking anywhere on the ranch at any time, the union had to find them before they could set up their picket lines and try to call the workers out of the fields. There was no factory entrance in this strike. So, Antonia and Maria would get out well before sun-up and start searching for the workers. But even this seemingly innocuous chore had its dangers.

There was one time, it was myself, my sister Maria, and the one who was driving the station wagon was Mike Vasquez. In that car was another lady, Amelia Cardena, my aunt. What happened is that we were coming and there were 2 stop signs. We were coming straight, right there on county line. And they were supposed to make stops, both cars. So what they did, they hit us in the middle of the station wagon. It was so exact the way they worked it out. And they hit us from one side and the other side. And we were not able to get out.

Fortunately, for the scouting team they had a citizen's band radio in the car and were able to call union headquarters to come and get them. Nobody was injured but the union was down one station wagon and there were no pickets at the DiGiorgio ranch that day.

The huelguistas *(strikers) were undaunted though. They continued to throw up their picket lines and they had a lot of success calling the workers out of the fields. The workers were often very sympathetic with the* huelguistas *once they learned that there was a strike. As often as not, they would walk out of the fields. But they rarely joined the union, rather they would just move on to find work elsewhere.*

It was an exciting time for Maria and Antonia. They were quickly learning how to work on the picket lines and their successes were very encouraging.

It was very exciting to see everybody on the picket line and everyone yelling, "Come on! Come on! Come on! Join the strike. *En huelga!* We're going to win this strike. More money."

And that was good, speaking to the people. I started thinking about how to talk to the people. From my experience in the field I said, you know, we're working so hard and we're making so little money. Come on, and things like that. So, I started talking to the people. And people listen. I think I became an organizer. I don't know if I'm a good organizer or—but I feel like I am a good organizer.

I wanted to be strong. I wanted to win the strike. And I started getting stronger and stronger. Let's go. We are going to win. We are going to win. If we stay right, you know we can stop everybody in the fields. We are going to win the strike. And everybody started getting stronger and stronger.

It was late October 1965 when we started thinking that we were not going to win the strike because we started to see all those people coming that wanted to break the strike. There were undocumented [workers] they were bringing from different areas [of Mexico], from Tijuana and Juarez and Mexicali in buses, not only cars, but buses. Where Helen Chávez was working in Sierra Vista Ranch, that company was

DiGiorgio, it was like 27 buses. It was 1500 people a day that was working in that company. There was a lot of people. And they replaced them with the undocumented people.

Oh, I hear in some areas [where] the picket lines were working, the [company] would bring some [replacement workers]. "Let's go over there and talk to them." And so we went into that area and we'd say, "We're on strike. You're not supposed to cross our picket line. We're brothers! Come on!"

And we pulled so many people out. And then the next day, they bring some more people. It was like a crazy thing. I think the growers started feeling we were really very strong. And then they started to fight us a lot with the police.

And they started to do all kinds of things to our cars. Like one day after the picket line I was coming out and this guy, I think it was one of those who favored the growers. They pushed us and they mashed my car, the car I was in. And I was bleeding. And they took me to Delano Hospital and they don't do nothing because we were strikers. They don't give us attention.

We started thinking that we're not going to win the strike like this because we have already had so many big strikes in different areas. So, César called us to a meeting. He said we're going to send farm workers to San Francisco and to L.A., to the main brokers. And we're going to picket. We're going to make picket lines over there because the season is almost finished in the table grapes. It's going to be the end of the harvest. So, we need to go to the stores.

So we went to San Francisco and we started picketing because there was a ship that was ready to move grapes to all the different countries, to Europe. And we had a big victory because the longshoremen refused to handle the grapes, you know to load them. And so it was a very good, very good response from them.

When we came back to Delano, we told the people, "You know what? We stopped the grapes. They don't put them in the *barco*, in the ship."

The once reluctant Saludado sisters had by this time made a real commitment to the union.

I think it was—it was something. We wanted to do it. We started getting so into, into this movement . . . There was something for us. Something . . . this is mine. This is my job and I want to fight for my job. No one is going to take my job out. And I think I'm going to fight it in the way, the nice way. Not respond to anger. And I feel, like I said before, I don't feel angry.

So we started to feel like it was our jobs and we are going to fight for them. And César was so, so involved in the non-violence. I think, I think for the way my dad always told us not to respond bad to people. And I think it was easy for me to accept when César started to tell us, don't be angry. I'm not angry.

Then, we went into the march (the 300-mile march from Delano to Sacramento made by the farm workers in March, 1966) and we see so many supporters, we see so many things that we never seen before. There were a lot of farm workers outside [on strike]. They didn't care too much if they were going to lose cars, they were going to lose their homes, they were going to lose . . . They could care less. They just quit and went. So, that's why we did too.

So, we got Schenley. (Schenley Corporation, one of the largest grape growers in California, signed a contract with the union.) Some of people that had a lot of family,

FIGURE 6.2 César Chávez (center), founder of the National Farm Workers Association (later called the United Farm Workers), leads a group of workers and their families on a 250-mile march from Delano, California, to Sacramento to bring state and national attention to their strike against California grape growers. Chávez timed the march for the weeks of Lent in 1966, describing it to his followers as both a pilgrimage and a revolution. "But," he added, "it is also the pilgrimage of a cultural minority who have suffered from a hostile environment, and a minority who mean business." By the time the marchers reached the state capitol, on Easter Sunday, one of the large Delano grape growers had signed a union contract guaranteeing its laborers better pay and working conditions. The UFW continues its work today.

Source: Take Stock—Images of Change

they went back to work for Schenley. My father was one of the persons. He went to work for Schenley. He started making money so he could support our sisters. He was an irrigator, so he was full-time, year around.

We stayed out of the fields, me and my sister. We told him, you go to work and we'll stay out. We are just going to have to help them, help ourselves to see what we can do. We came back from the [1966] march and then César said, "You know what? The second head we are going to get is DiGiorgio Corporation."

We started organizing and getting people. We just barely organized a hundred people and by the following day they [the company] bring people from Mexico. And then César said, "Let's do a boycott. Hurt them again."

Yup, they went to a grape boycott. We started doing boycotts in L.A., San Francisco, everywhere. Every city you can name, we had people. We were going to those boycotts, me and my sister. We went to organize. They taught us for organizers. Fred Ross came and gave us classes for organizing, to see if we would be able to do it because we were so ignorant. We were not ignorant [but] we didn't read. I didn't spoke the language.

At that time I started to learn how to speak English and I started learning how to read and write. . . . I knew a few words but not for a conversation, not to explain myself.

The Saludados had made a transition from a life of struggle and deprivation in the fields to a life of struggle and deprivation in the union. The sisters had been on strike and without income since September, 1965. They, along with the rest of the union members, had to rely on donations of food and clothing from supporters, and they endured long hours, cold weather, and abuse on the picket lines.

As the union began to engage in boycotting grapes at markets in Los Angeles and San Francisco, the support for their cause increased but the anger and recalcitrance on the part of the growers increased as well. Picketers had to bear up to verbal attacks, people spitting on them, police harassment and violence, and attempts by company employees to hit them with pick-up trucks.

They used to come and throw things at us, water; spit on us, try to run over us, and all kinds of things. My mom used to be there almost day and night. She was on the picket line there. They would try to make us angry, but César told us it was the non-violence. He was the one that teaches us how to do that. He said, if you ever feel angry don't think about it. Ignore that. Try to get out. Ignore the stuff or walk out. Don't listen to it. And that is the way we did it.

There were certain days that we were so angry, we were so mad that we were just ready to go and fight. But [he would say] "You know what? We've been all these years working on *La Causa*—to lose it in five minutes? Is it worth it? Just think about that. Just think about what you are going to lose. There are so many years that you have been working so hard, and to lose it in that time . . . Let's just go like Ghandhi."

Ghandhi used to see all of this fighting and everything. He just kept ignoring things. He would just keep going and going. He knew they were killing people. But he knew he was doing something good for his people.

César had a lot of ideas from Ghandhi. I think it was part of the classes we got from him. He gave us some classes. He used to sit down and see us so tired. And he used to say, "I know you guys are tired, but let's not give it up."

One day . . . I guess it was the worst thing that the companies did. There was a picket line and one truck came over. There was a whole bunch of people in the line and that truck had to get out of the road in order to try to run over all of these people.

César came up and said, "Girls, I don't know how to say it, but didn't you feel what they did to us?"

"Yes."

"How do you feel?"

"We feel that we have to fight. We're going to stay. If they think they are going to get rid of us like that, no way. We are just going to have to do it."

And the following day there was more people than you ever thought were going to come out. Our cause is going to be on and on. And we might not finish it, but somebody will.

The transition from trying to stop the work in the fields to boycotting the sale of grapes was effective but limited. The union had to expand its boycott if it was to be successful, so Chávez began to make plans to include the large eastern cities in the struggle.

In August 1967, César said, "OK, let's send a group to Chicago." He made three groups: to Chicago, to New York, to Florida. He said, "You guys are going to go to Chicago because you're good workers." We didn't know we were good. I didn't know. But anyway, he sent us to Chicago, six of us, three girls and three boys. Eliseo Medina was the coordinator for our group. He said, "OK people. This is it. We are just going like an army. We are going to have to find out how good we are, to organize."

We got to Chicago. In one block, we got lost.

We didn't have any idea how cold Chicago was going to be. In August here in California, especially in Arvin and Bakersfield it is so hot. So, I have little sandals and a pair of pants. I have two pairs of pants and very light clothes. And this is all my things. There was no luggage at all. I had a bag. And my sister did the same thing.

And we get there and we started working and it was the hardest days in organizing because we went from Delano area and it's a very little town. And to be in Chicago . . . it was hard and it was exciting. The harder thing was because we were singles, and in those days, they don't trust very good Hispanic people, and younger.

So it was very difficult because [the people back in] Delano sent each of us $5 a week. They sent us $30 a week for the six of us. That was for food. So then we—they decided, because I was—we call it *metiche* (when you always try to do, organizing in the kitchen or something). I was a *metiche* so I was in charge for the food. And with those $30, I buy the cheapest things like bread, eggs and I told my—my other friends, we're going to eat only one time a day because we don't have—there is no way we can eat three times a day or two times a day because it's very little money. We're going to try to make it on only one meal a day and that's going to be between 1:00 and 2:00. So we can go in the mornings to the brokerage house, to the grapes.

Now we have three plates. We have three spoons. We have three glasses. And I say, three are going to eat first and when you finish, the rest are going to eat. Okay. So we—we do it that way. Well, one day we don't have anything to eat. But we had a little time, you know. We know most of the area and who's going to be good to us and who's not going to be friendly. So then we asked, "Who's going to be the best organizer to find the food for today?" I saw a Spanish Catholic church and I said, "Well, okay. I'm going to try to be a good organizer. I'm going to go over there."

And so I went over there and I knocked on the door and the priest come over and it was Spanish, a priest from Spain. He was a very nice person. And he says, "Where you come from?" I said, "Well, I'm Mexican and I'm a farm worker. I'm from California." So I told him all my—you know, all my message. And I said, "To tell the truth, we don't have anything to eat today."

He said, "Okay, okay, don't worry. Let me see, maybe I have some money in my pocket." So he found out he had $7 and he said, "Okay. I'm going to give it to you. Okay."

So I stop in the store, the Casa Del Pueblo, and there was three bags of bread for a dollar. So I get bread. I get eggs. I don't remember how much the eggs were. But with the money they give to me, I get two bags of food. So I came and I was very excited. "I am the best organizer because I bring the food for today and for a few days more." And everybody was laughing, good, good, good.

And then—then it started snowing and it was so cold. We don't have any clothes for the cold. But our job was to make a picket line and to talk to the brokers every Mondays because it's a big market. Monday and Tuesday and Thursdays. So we always got up at 5:00 o'clock in the morning . . . making a picket line or talking to people. We started talking to the workers and sometimes they would listen to us. And sometimes they made fun of us. But we don't care. We tried to ignore it when they made fun of us.

And this particular day was very bad, it was a very cold day. And there was a bunch of nuns that come over and they stopped. One went to the broker and the broker was so mad and saying bad things. And then the nun said, "What's wrong?" and he said, "Well, those guys, you know, they stop all my business. They cut my business." The nuns came over and asked us why we try to do that kind of thing. We said, "Well, we are farm workers," and we gave them the whole message from the California strike. And then they say, "OK. Well, we're not going to buy anything from him. And we're going to tell him that if they don't stop handling those grapes we're not going to buy anything." And that was the nuns that make all the purchases for the convent. So the broker gets so mad because it was good business for him.

I was so cold that day. Eliseo has a very tiny sweater, and I have only a little sweater. We were jumping up and down, trying to stay warm you know. And we're getting close together. Eliseo and I said, "Let's sing. Let's do something. So then we can feel much better." So we started singing, "We Shall Overcome" and "De Colores," all the things that we sing in the union. And so we started making lots of attention from the public. Everybody was stopping and asking what's going on?

The broker was so mad, he called the police. . . . And so the police came over and said, "You guys not supposed to be to singing." And we say, "We know our rights and we have a right to make a picket line." And so the police told him, "They have a right to be there. There is nothing we can do." So the broker said, "Well, tell them I don't want to listen to the singing. They make me sick." So the police came over and said, "The broker says he doesn't want you guys to sing." "OKAY, we're not going to sing."

Then we started whistling. Because we're whistling, people started getting more excited. So, the police came over and say, "I told you guys not to sing." Eliseo answered very serious and very honest, "We're not singing. We're whistling."

So that way we make a lot of friends. Dark people started getting more friendly; people started coming with us, and the church, of course, the church started coming because we were very honest and very quiet. We don't get angry. We started making more picket lines and winning more friends. Then we started to get more excited.

They called us in November from Delano and they say, "César wants to have a meeting with you guys in Chicago. He's on the way to New York and he's going to stop in Chicago for two hours. And he wants you guys to be there so he can talk to you."

When César came into the airport we were very skinny and very dark because it was cold. I think we look so bad. César was happy to see us, but I think not the way he saw us. So he immediately started talking about business. And then, and when he saw us, he had two big drops from his eyes. And he said, "Do you guys see yourselves? Are you guys eating?" And I said, "Of course we eating." He said, "You guys look very skinny, very thin. It looks like you guys haven't eaten for days." And I said, "Don't worry," and Eliseo answered, tried to joke with him. He said, "Don't worry. We want to show the people how much we need them."

And César said, "Yeah, but I don't want to find out that you guys got sick." I will always remember what he said to us, you know. And the way . . . the reaction, the tears coming from his eyes.

But soon things began to get better. There was a girl who volunteered in the office that we had. She had a boyfriend, a professor in Chicago University. And he had a Spanish class for people that want to learn Spanish. So she came over and she told me, "You know what? My boyfriend said if you guys can make a tape for his classes, he can help in another way." So then the boyfriend came over and we said, "Yeah, we can do that. But we need to negotiate."

He said, "What kind of negotiation?"

We said, "We are very short with food." And he said, "OK. I can give you $25 of food every week. All right." So we can have more food. So every week, and in return for helping with the tape, he give us $25 worth of food. And that was a big help. And then like I said, we started making more, bigger picket lines because people started getting interested and they started coming to help us.

After a long, cold, difficult winter, Maria, Antonia and the four other boycotters began to be invited to speak to unions, service organizations, churches, and schools. They enlisted volunteers and organized them as pickets at grocery stores all over the city.

I was so demanding of myself. I wanted to win the strike. It was my goal, mine. Everybody has their own goals. But my goal was I want to win the strike. I forget everything about everything. Except my mom, my mom I'm pretty sure my mom pray a lot for me. But it was my work. I worked, I don't know how many hours. Twelve, 14 hours a day. Everywhere I went, I spoke only about farm workers, the struggle, what happened in Delano. I don't even told my parents about how hard it was, "Oh, no, the people are so nice." And they was nice but, you know, between the nice we find some people that are mean. But I always, "No, no, no. Don't worry. People are very nice."

Eventually, their efforts effectively stopped the sale of grapes in Chicago. Chávez then asked the Saludado sister to go to New York to help organize a boycott there because they had learned so much and became so good at their jobs in Chicago. While Antonia stayed in New York for some time, Maria returned to Chicago and then went to Indianapolis by herself to set up an organization there.

I had a boycott committee for the supporters of farm workers in Indianapolis, and I tell them, "We need to do something so we can put pressure to that company." I told them I knew something, something to really let people know how we feel. "I want to fast." Some did not really agree with me. And some, they agree. So I say, "Well, you agree or not agree, I got to do it. I'm going to do my job and you guys are going to do your job and really support the farm workers." I make a fast for ten days.

I think it was easy. It was only ten days. It was not 20 days like César or 25 days. But ten days, it's not very—it's like you get—you really want something and, I think—you get your strength from yourself. And not to think about food. And after a few days, I didn't even feel like to eating. I feel cramps, little cramps. I think I lost a few pounds. I don't remember exactly, like ten or 12 pounds. And then I started eating crackers and . . . drinking apple juice and tea. All kind of teas. And I started feeling good. After one week, recuperation, I started to feel OKAY.

And the people were marching in front of the store. And some very nice people, you know, African Americans from the Southern Christian Leadership Council. They have a group over there in Indianapolis so they come in every day. Sometimes ten or 15 people. Sometimes more. But they always helped me in those days. There was some really nice people. I met Jesse Jackson over there, too.

And we hurt the company. We stopped the grapes!

Antonia also spent some time in Toronto, where the union mounted one of its most successful boycotts.

They transferred me to Toronto, Canada. Canada is the same as Chicago. It was real cold. Well, me and Marion Moses, we stopped the grapes there. It was so strong a boycott in Canada that we stopped the grapes. The car loads from the train. They were canceled out.

John Giumarra, Jr. (an owner of Giumarra Vineyards Corporation and a spokesman for the table grape growers) even came to Canada and tried to tell everyone there was no such strike. That there were no such workers that were involved in the strike. That all of the workers were working. We had a panel discussion in a big hall. They were asking questions to him and they were asking questions to me. And I told him, "John, you cannot tell me that you do not recognize me," I said, "because I am one of your workers."

And this is how we worked. That time we stopped 15 carloads of grapes in a train in one of the biggest markets for grapes. We had so many community people that were boycotting those grapes! At least one day at that time there was no grapes in Toronto, Canada!

I see it in my way. There are a lot of things . . . have been changed . . . good not just for the farm workers or the Mexicans but for all of us, for black people because black people were also in the farm workers. White people are also in the farming system. I think this is good for everybody. It wasn't exclusive to the Mexican people. It's for everybody.

I really liked it, in a way I learned a lot. Not by books, by seeing and by living it. It was incredible. We felt like we were doing good. But at the same time they make us sad because of the way they were treating people . . . I thought many times, should I go on? Or am I doing something wrong? But then I had my parents. They were very strong for the union and they were the ones that were saying we have to keep on going even though we have seen so many things. We have to go ahead and do it. You cannot sit in the middle of the road and stay there. Nobody is going to come and pick you up. We have to go on and get to the end if we are able. We don't know. Maybe we're (not) going to get to the end. But we are going to have to do it.

And César always worked real close to us. César . . . kept us so close. He didn't want to do anything until he talked to all the crew. He'd say, "Come on *raza*. I'm going to talk to you guys . . . I want your opinion." He didn't do anything until he got all the crew together and said, "This is what's going to happen. What do you guys think? With the majority of the vote, this is how we are going to go. If you want to."

We always had a democratic way to do it. He used to say, "You are the union. I'm just the leader but you are the union. You are the ones. If I go and talk to somebody over there, I am going to tell him I need this. But I know that I got somebody backing me up. I cannot go by myself and say that I am going to do this."

And still right now, a lot of people [today] stand up and they say, "You can't do that to me."

"And why not?"

"Because the union said that you cannot do this to me."

This old man did this for me, and this is how it is. There are many people that can tell you that.

QUESTIONS FOR DISCUSSION

1. What are some specific hardships that Maria and Antonia Saludado experience while working in California's fields and orchards? What is your opinion of the conditions under which they labor? Are you surprised to learn what they are paid?

2. Why do you think Mexican American migrant laborers would endure terrible working conditions for so many years before the advent of the union? How is their situation similar to that of laborers elsewhere in the United States? How is it different?

3. What is it about the union and Chávez that attracts the Saludado sisters and leads them to dedicate their lives to union work? Do you think Chávez has special qualities of leadership? What are some of his qualities? When Maria and Antonia look back on their days as strike leaders, their biggest source of pride is their own strength. How has Chávez helped them to find that strength?

4. How does Chávez respond when the growers' hired thugs hurt the sisters and other workers? Is he able to protect them? How does he advise workers to respond to threats

and violence? Where in the story do we see that César Chávez cares about his young boy-cott leaders?

5. Maria and Antonia believe so fervently in the union cause that they nearly freeze and starve to death in Chicago, where they are sent to run a boycott even though they speak almost no English. Why do you think they are so dedicated? Does this story of the early days of the United Farm Workers help you to understand how labor unions work? How do you think labor unions are generally perceived in the United States today?

6. Maria and Antonia are American citizens, though born in Mexico. What makes them citizens? The sisters are angry about the undocumented workers that the growers bring in from Mexico to take over striking workers' jobs. Why would a worker agree to take a job with a company whose regular workers are on strike? What causes people to be "scabs?" Do you feel sympathy for the scabs? For the striking workers? For the growers? What is César Chávez's solution to scab labor?

7. In recording and transcribing this oral history, Professor Kirkton has made no attempt to standardize the Saludado sisters' English. He reproduces exactly what they say. What is the purpose of not "cleaning up" the language? What is its effect on you as a reader? Do you feel the sisters' speech patterns enrich their story? How does their language help you to see them and their lives more clearly?

SOMEBODY'S GOT TO DO IT
Samuel Lovejoy

My father was a U.S. Army captain and the commandant of the Springfield (Mass.) Armory. He died when I was four. I was raised by two people: my mother, Olive Lovejoy, a nurse and a very strong woman, and an old guy named Harold Porter, an apple and peach farmer.

My family knew Harold before I was born, and when my father died, Harold read about it in the newspaper and called up my mother and said, "Could I help, do you need a place to live?" So he gave us a house for very low rent and he became kind of a surrogate father. I worked for him in the orchard from the time I was six.

I think my first taste of "environmentalism" took place when I was about ten. I had just come home from a Cub Scout camp when I ran into Harold in the backyard of the house. His farm operation was attached to the house that we were living in and he lived next door. There was an open pasture and a hillside pasture with junipers, and then the orchard was farther up. Harold was parked right out back with his old pesticide-spraying rig. The truck had a big wooden tank on it, and Harold had just poured all these chemicals into it.

My mother is in the kitchen, sort of looking out the window at this scene, Harold on his rig, me coming home from the Cub Scout camp.

"How was camp?" Harold asked. And I said, "Great! The only trouble is I got athlete's foot."

"No problem, climb up here!" He picks me up, almost like a rag doll, I'm this little guy, remember, he's a monster of a guy, he picks me up and dunks my feet up to my knees in the pesticide spray tank. Then he pulls me back out and drops me on the ground. My mother's watching this from the kitchen, and it's the only time I ever saw my mother flip out.

"What are you doing to Sam?!! You can't do that!!" My mother screams as she comes flying out of the kitchen.

Harold looks up at her and says, "I guarantee he won't get athlete's foot anymore!"

Mom looks at Harold, then at me, and says, "Sammy, get in here and wash those feet right now!"

Somehow, my mother knew that the chemicals were dangerous. But for Harold, who would spray his orchards ten times a year for hours at a time, getting bombarded by the mist because he sprayed every tree by hand, for him there was nothing wrong with it. And that was certainly the prevailing attitude toward pesticides in America in the 1950s. Quit spraying them for even one month, and every bug in the world gets on the phone and says, "Harold's orchard hasn't been sprayed in a month!" And that's the end of the orchard.

In those days, the sprays consisted of arsenic, lead, and God knows what else. Later, right before he died, Harold got a buildup of either lead or arsenic in his body. One day, my mother was in her kitchen and she thought she saw something moving in the pasture—she looked again, and finally she realized it was Harold. He was crawling on his hands and knees down the hillside from the orchard. He had passed out while spraying, and then he sort of came to, but couldn't actually stand up, so there he was crawling down the hill. They put him in the hospital and got him back to half decent, but that was really the end of his career. He died a while later of a heart attack.

I went to Wilbraham Academy for my high school years, as a day student. At this prep school, there was a tension between the day students, called "dayhops," and the boarders. I would say that probably 20% of the school was day students. I realized in junior year that no day students were on the student council, because the student council meetings and votes were always at night—so even though the day-hops were 20% of the school, we had no seats on the student council.

So right at the beginning of senior year, I wrote up a note and I stuck it under the headmaster's bell because special announcements were always put under the bell to be read at the end of lunch. And it said, "All the day students are to meet downstairs in the recreation room for ten minutes after lunch." You know, like something the dean would write. And the headmaster read it, and because he didn't know what it was about, he just assumed one of the masters had written it.

So I went downstairs and told everybody, "Tomorrow, strike! There are no seats for day students on the student council, and until we have day students on the student council, nobody goes to class. Is everybody agreed?"

And most of the kids were nervous, and saying, "Wow, you can't do that!" But some of them said, "Hey, that's kind of cool." But this was a good educational moment for me, because what happened was they had spies, there was a teacher there or whatever. And by the end of the afternoon, I got approached. I can't remember by whom, but you know, Sam, please check in with the dean. So I showed up at the dean's office and he says, "You have to go down and see the headmaster." Oh dear. So I go down to see the headmaster with the dean and he gives me a dressing down that you just wouldn't believe, something about there's no strikes here at Wilbraham Academy, and this and that. And we're going to write a note to your mom.

The next morning, I come to school, and the headmaster and the dean had called up a couple of the trustees of the school and they had rewritten the constitution. From now on the Student Council would have one day-student representative for each class—freshman, sophomore, junior, and senior year. And by the way Sam, you're it for the senior year. Pah! So much for democracy.

The revolution came to town the easy way.

At Amherst College, I got involved with radical politics and the anti-war movement by joining Students for a Democratic Society, SDS. In a short time, I sort of became the head of our SDS chapter. I was the guy who would travel around to the other schools, and go to the New England-wide meetings, partly because I had a motorcycle and not a lot of kids had cars in those days. I ended up getting appointed to the SDS New England Coordinating Committee.

In April 1969, about a year after the Columbia University student strike, I said to myself, "We've gotta shut Amherst down, It's absolutely nuts the way the college and its board of trustees are so intimately involved in making the Vietnam War happen, while the students are so against it. We'll just take over the administration building. Enough of us can do it really easily."

I got some chain and thought, "We'll cut up the chain, get some locks and just lock the doors of the campus buildings from the inside. I'll call up the cops and tell them to stay out," because we all knew the campus cops were all unarmed, and they were nice guys.

So we devised a little plan for the next morning. We would work at night setting up the occupation of the buildings, get all our food and gear together for the occupation, print pamphlets in advance with our demands—which included turning Amherst co-ed—and we'd just shut down the buildings until our demands were met.

I remember that we planned to go on the air, because the little campus radio station was in one of the buildings, and we'd just tell everybody, "School's closed! Until the administration or trustees come out against the war and let women in," plus the rest of our demands, "this place is shut down!"

But around seven or eight o'clock at night, I got a phone call from a faculty guy; he was phoning me because word had gotten back to him from one of the kids that were at our meeting. And the reason the kid talked to him is that he thought maybe the faculty would join us. Now there's a joke. So of course, the faculty guy immediately called up the administration, and the next thing you know, I'm over at this faculty guy's house, and he's saying, "I've already talked to the president and school's closed tomorrow. How long do you want it closed?"

I said, "I don't know, a week." And he said, "Fine. School will be closed for four days. We're going to organize workshops, we'll have position papers and . . . "

"No, no, no," I told him. "One thing we gotta have is like a big mass meeting where people get to say why this is all happening. This is not going to be totally co-opted by Amherst College." Because I could already feel that they were pulling the rug out from under us beautifully.

So the first thing that happens at the mass meeting was that the president of the college stands up and says that he has written a letter to the board of trustees which he read and which had this incredible anti-war tone.

(Meanwhile, the board of trustees of Amherst College was filled with members of the Council on Foreign Relations and other heavyweight war hawks.) I was sitting right up front, and I burst out laughing. And because everybody's sort of looking at me, I stood up and took the microphone.

"I'm laughing," I said, "because look at this slick shit. President Plimpton tells us he's written this nice letter to the trustees about our demands, our desire to end the war—but these trustees are the very same pigs who are orchestrating the war!"

"We don't want a stupid letter read to us from the president of this college, telling us he's submitting this letter to the trustees. This is the end of all classes and everything until they vote unanimously to approve our demands!" Students started cheering, and I could feel a kind of nervousness coming over the president and the other administration people present.

"I think now we should break up into these groups that the faculty has organized, and go do our thing, but basically this college is closed as far as I'm concerned, until they get back to us.

"By the way, what happened to all of our other demands, like women at Amherst College? Let's clean up the sexism and a few other things at the same time."

The week ended with resolutions announcing that the college was coming out against the war in Vietnam; some of the trustees refused to sign, but the majority of them did.

They also said they would start bringing women into Amherst College, and they did, but not until 1975.

Basically what did they do? They thwarted us from taking over any buildings. Naturally, that made the administration very happy. We got most of what we wanted. But we also got taught another good lesson about quick action and quick subversion and being co-opted.

In the winter of my senior year at college, a friend of mine, Ira Karasick, shows up one day, and tells me he's been living at a communal farm north of Amherst, in the town of Montague. Ira came to my room and it was the dead of winter, and he says, "You know, those guys that are up there at the commune Marshall Bloom started are really having a hard time. They're just barely eating, and they got no heat, and they're out of money, and—this is a disaster—they haven't paid their mortgage. We need some money for the mortgage, or these guys are gonna get thrown out." I gave Ira some money. I think I paid more than one mortgage payment at the farm, but I think what I cared about at the time was to keep the anti-war Liberation News Service going, which they were publishing from the farm.

And then, a little while later, Ira shows up in my room again, and since he knew that I grew up on a farm, he says, "Now it's spring, and I'm doing a fundraiser to buy a tractor for the commune." At least he knew that they had to turn over a piece of the field to make a garden. He'd hit up all the people he could think of, and he had raised like three hundred of the five hundred needed, so I helped him find the rest of the money, and he bought the tractor. But I didn't actually go to the farm for the first time until late April or May of '69. I certainly had no idea I would end up living there, or that it would have such an important impact on my life.

The farm on Chestnut Hill Road in Montague was one of the first communes in the country. When it started, Marshall and Ira had had a big argument about organic versus chemical farming. Ira was quite emphatic that you needed pesticides, but in the end Marshall and the others won the day, and the farm went strictly organic.

I think it's fair to say that it was the women at the farm who were the first people who got educated and pushed the organic farming thing. And don't forget, this was before the environmental movement got off the ground, before there were organic health food stores; there were only a few farmers around the country who were growing organically, i.e. without chemicals or pesticides.

The farm was also organic in that it was always changing, new things were being tried, it was like a free place where you could experiment—and all sorts of dietary efforts went on, like there was a period where brewer's yeast was in fashion, or at one point, it was "no dairy products." But vegetables were constant, and brown rice and tofu, long before it became available at your local supermarkets like it is nowadays. Tofu was like an exotic product.

I started living at the farm in 1970, a year and a half after they started. I think that it took about two or three years to make everything work. You know, the tractors worked, the pastures worked, the timing worked, we got the wood to heat the house, piled up the leaves from the garden to insulate things. Tighten up the windows, pay the bills, organize everything, get the barn fixed, get the animal care figured out. We bought a hay baler, got the water line running, and figured out what to do when the well went dry. We fixed the septic system, and all that sort of infrastructure stuff. It sure seemed like a long time when we were doing it, but by '72, '73, the garden didn't have a million weeds in it anymore, and we knew that in April you get the manure out in the garden so that by May you can plant, and you get the greenhouse built so that in February you can start the tomatoes and pepper plants and all that kind of stuff. So everything started to get the rhythm that it needed.

One of the things that I did when I first got to the farm was to get the commune kids to start opening up to the larger farming community around Montague. Back in those days, coming out of the '60s and into the '70s, there was this incredible paranoia of not wanting to connect with people outside of the farm, paranoia probably, because they'd all just come from the anti-Vietnam War movement to their commune and felt like everyone was against them. Certainly the majority of the folks in the rural farming area were, at that time, way more conservative politically than they are now. But they were the greater community and, like it or not, we were part of that. I was always saying, "Oh no, you gotta get to know the gas station guy, the Agway guy, and this guy, and the parts guy, and the woman who runs the store. You gotta know all these folks, this is the way you get to know your community."

It's true that at that time there was this disgusting tourist thing—where local people would love to drive by the hippie farm, especially on weekends, sort of to gawk. Chestnut Hill Road went right between the farmhouse and the barn, so people could drive by slowly, stick their heads out the window, and try to "sight-see" what was happening at the hippie farm. In 1969–'70, we were more or less the only commune in a fifty-mile radius, something of an oddity. And the sightseers, particularly on summer weekends, would drive up the road, and they'd often just stop right in your front yard and stare at the longhairs. Or they'd ask you some question that was so inane simply because they're trying to come up with an excuse for why they're parking there. And, of course, it was to see the hippies! Maybe they hoped to see people naked, which certainly was the case on more than one occasion.

Also, occasionally, the F.B.I. would show up at the farm. They came from nearby Springfield, in an army-green Ford. They'd drive up with these two guys, one leaning out the car window saying, "Hey, I just want to talk to you."

And for us there was always a tension because of our belief that you should never talk to an F.B.I. guy, because of course they knew we were political and cultural radicals, and because you were afraid you might say something you shouldn't say.

In 1973, I went to Seattle for a visit. I read in the Seattle papers about a massive leak of about one hundred thousand gallons of radioactive wastes from a storage tank at a nuclear power plant in Hanford, in the eastern part of Washington State. The company, Atlantic Richfield, wasn't going to mention it, and neither was the Atomic Energy Commission, until some investigative reporters found out about it. So then the AEC said the radioactive liquid wouldn't make it through to the Columbia River (which would destroy the river) before the year 2700. Until then, the Commission assured us, everything would be fine.

That did it for me. I started reading everything I could get my hands on about atomic energy. The more I read the more I realized that nuclear power plants were, as somebody said, "the most horrendous development our community has ever faced." And the AEC seemed like a kangaroo court—a panel that acted as promoter and regulator, judge, jury, and thief all rolled into one.

I flew back from Seattle in the summer of 1973, and Dan Keller, who had started another organic commune in the nearby town of Wendell, picked me up at Bradley Airport in Hartford. And as I got in the car with him, he said, "You will not believe what's happening in Montague." But that's all he would say.

Finally, as we get onto Route 47, right on the south end of Montague, just coming over the town line, he says, "Oh man, just you hang on, you're not gonna believe what they've built!" And there's a little bluff that the road wiggles around, a sort of double S, and then you jump up onto this blip of a rise in the road for a second.

"You ready for this?" says Dan.

And there, straight ahead, in these beautiful hills leading to a flat plain, even though it's nighttime, I can make out this enormous needle of a tower. The tower is sticking up and it's got strobe lights blinking on and off. And I say something like, "What the fuck is that?" and Dan says, "That's the weather tower for the twin nuclear plant they're gonna build here on the Montague Plains." (The AEC had a regulation that before you applied for a license to build a new nuclear plant, you had to have one full year of meteorological information, which was what these testing towers did.)

A twin nuclear power plant on the Montague Plains, not more than three miles from the farm? It blew my mind. Something would have to be done. "Someone's gotta knock that thing down," were first words out of my mouth. But I never in a million years thought it would be me. It seemed like such an obvious target, such a romantic target. I just thought, hell, we live at this commune, we're very focused on living organically, naturally. We're also doing a million other things. And now here's this thing that could end it all.

Anyway, there are two key timings at this point in the story: One of them has to do with the farm, and me at the farm, and the fact that the farm was together. I had sunk roots there. The farm had become a place where you could say, "The milk didn't spoil, the roof is fixed, we're definitely gonna survive."

There's a second timing, and that is the political reality of what was going on in America. The war was still on, but anybody with half a brain knew it was winding down. And some of us had moved from that '60s political thing to getting a base, a community, and making a commitment to each other and the land. And once we got that established, it really became a question of what's going to happen now? Or, what's going to be the next battle?

What's funny is that we didn't have to answer the question—they gave us the answer: a nuclear energy plant. So the environment was definitely going to be the next thing, the next big, political, theoretical battle (not excluding the women's and gay movements, which appeared sort of right before that).

Some people thought it was too hard to understand nuclear energy. And I think it's fair to say that 99.99% of the country when you said nuclear power, they kinda went, "Uhhhh, it makes juice. It's too cheap to meter." And of course, back then, nukes were "automatic power." The promoters just said, "We're gonna build a nuke. It'll bring jobs into the community. Electricity will be very, very cheap. You'll love it."

Of course it was all a propaganda campaign. Not enough people were saying, "What if there's an accident? What about radiation? What happens to the people near the nuke?" I thought we oughtta be asking those questions.

I was a double physics and math major in college, so I had a facility with science. I didn't have a problem reading something that was "technical" so I understood atoms and nuclei and isotopes, and what radiation does to you. Learning about the nuke took me no time, in terms of its science. What did take the time was the politics, the regulatory stuff, the why-did-they-choose-our-town? the corporation stuff. So while everyone else is reading, "How does a nuke work?" I'm reading, "Who's on the board of directors for Northeast Utilities," and other corporations. So I'm learning all this other political stuff just like we had to as anti-war people in the late '60s.

When I would talk to local people, longtime residents of Franklin County, I'd talk about the safety of the nuke. And do we need it? And do you know how big it is? And what's the community impact? And the pro-nuclear people would always answer that the tax rate in Montague would go down to one percent of what it was, so you would get jobs and lower taxes. That was their main argument. Well, the taxes thing sort of blew up in their face because we went campaigning in communities all around and said, "The town of Wendell isn't gonna get a dime. Greenfield isn't going to get a tax break. Montague is gonna keep it all." And we'd get people so pissed off at Montague, you wouldn't believe it. The way taxes are collected in Massachusetts, they could go ahead and build on this selfish design. But radiation doesn't stop at the town boundary.

So, what I'm focused on is the weather-testing tower. I would bring up the subject nonchalantly at the Farm, suggesting we ought to get going against the nuke at this stage, before they could start building it, and people would say, "Oh yeah, let's get together and knock over the tower." And nothing happened. But, more and more people were starting to see that something direct had to happen, something straight out of the tradition that we were coming from. There was no difference between the big Washington marches in '68 and '69, or shutting down colleges in May, 1970, and seizing the moment with a nuke. And what do you do? Wait until the nuke is built to protest against it? Occupy Northeast Utilities headquarters? No, that's in Connecticut. No. You do something—direct action—where it's actually happening, which in this case is in our backyard, on the Montague Plains.

FIGURE 6.3   The Three Mile Island nuclear plant near Harrisburg, Pennsylvania, sits idle after a notorious 1979 nuclear disaster—the partial meltdown of its nuclear reactor core. Children and pregnant women were evacuated from the surrounding area until the accident was contained and families learned that their homes were safe to reoccupy. When scientists and engineers first designed and built nuclear power plants in the 1950s, they assumed they had found a safe use for nuclear energy and a replacement for the planet's disappearing fossil fuels. Fears about nuclear plant safety soon arose, however, focusing on the possibilities that an accident might spew radioactive contamination over an area as wide as 100 miles in every direction. Three Mile Island seemed to confirm these fears. The accident led to a sharp increase in anti-nuclear-power activity in the late 1970s.

Source: Getty Images, Inc.-Hulton Archives

There are two attitudes towards organizing. One of them is that you're supposed to build everybody up equally and get everybody on the same page and everybody has to get there at the same time. And that's OK, it sounds rational and everything, but, you know, a lot of the time, you can get everybody to the same place real fast, and you can do a lot of education real quickly if you can do one clear, symbolic bang. You can ring a really loud bell once. Not hurt anybody, but you can get a lot done.

There was already an anti-nuclear effort of sorts in the country. It was made up of people who'd been fighting nukes from the beginning, but they were doing it by raising a hundred grand, hiring a lawyer, trying to get a nuclear plant pipe moved from here to here, trying to get that smaller and this different, and manipulating details, but basically conceding to the building of plants. We wanted to make it clear that the plants themselves had to go.

We started by organizing meetings, and we got together an anti-nuke coalition called Nuclear Objectors for a Pure Environment (NOPE). By 1974, there was at least one little group of politically active people or an organic farming commune in almost every town in western Massachusetts, and all over Vermont. We knew a ton of people in Vermont, New Hampshire, southern Maine, eastern Massachusetts. The issue just sort of went "doink!" and that "doink!" created hundreds, thousands of interested people in no time, people who instantly got it and knew that having a twin nuclear plant in their neighborhood—meaning within a 100-mile radius—was not something they were in favor of.

I started reading like a maniac, a lot of us did; we started getting our hands on all kinds of literature. First we learned about the science—including the fact that they had no real waste disposal for these nuclear infernos—and then we did the corporate analysis, and then the government analysis. So then we asked ourselves: do you commit some act against the nuke and send some statement to the press or the cops or whoever and not turn yourself in? Don't say who it was, just say this was sabotage in the name of God? Then the question became, is anonymity really the right message? Because, we do have to know who we are; we do have to communicate with our neighbors; and we do have to start an organization that is actually going to defeat the plant in the end.

It would have flipped people out and they wouldn't have gotten the message if I anonymously knocked over the tower and mailed in an anonymous statement. Everybody would have become all hung up over the idea that this was some sabotage. So the more I thought about it, and the more I read Thoreau and Gandhi, and passive resistance stuff, I came to the conclusion that the trick was to knock over the tower and turn myself in. And then let them put me on trial, because first you get publicity from the tower, and that would energize round one, and then you get the obvious publicity from the trial. So, right there were two huge, grandstanding events that a person could create by turning himself in.

The planning went pretty simple. I'm living at a politically oriented commune, and everybody knew about everything, there weren't too many secrets. I had to tell everybody at the farm, because I thought it was critical that they all knew about it. But I couldn't tell them when it was going to happen, and I had to give them the inkling that maybe I might not do it. Probably I would, but I might not. Because the problem was, if it was just a straight sabotage, the worst they could do to me was a five-year felony for destruction of personal property. But if there was a "conspiracy," and other people were involved, then it immediately would become a twenty-year felony, and I'd spend a lot of time in jail and other people would go to jail, too. I was willing to do the tower, but I didn't want to sweat twenty years, and I sure didn't want to put other people in jail, just because they knew it was going to happen.

Then, in terms of planning, I decided that I didn't want to get caught at the site. I wanted to be able to knock the tower over, and get away. And that was part of the theater of it. It would be way better if I turned myself in, rather than having someone catch me at the site. Because then the evidence would be completely different, and the cops could testify only to what they had seen. So, number one it had to be late at night. Number two it would be nice if it was dark, so we had to time it to the moon a little. And then, it was just a question of what tools to use, and what to wear.

I did come up with this funny idea that they might be quicker than I anticipated in bringing people in to hunt for me, to hunt for whoever knocked over the tower. They might actually arrive at the scene, and they might have dogs. So I bought a brand new pair of sneakers, and I kept them in box. I bought two brand new pairs of wool socks, and then some plastic garbage bags. And it was wet out, so the plastic bags served two functions. Number one, there would be very little smell of me on the sneakers, because I used gloves when I put them on. So I put on a pair of socks, plastic bags, another pair of socks, brand new sneakers, tied 'em up. I'd be waterproof, warm, and emit the least amount of my smell. That was the only thing I did to avoid the dog problem.

And another question became, do I knock it over on Valentine's Day or on George Washington's birthday, because February looked like the right month. So, I checked with someone who was into astrology at the time, and they said George Washington's birthday, "I cannot tell a lie, I cut down the cherry tree," and there were all those little red lights on the thing, I mean it was just too beautiful. The new moon also began on February 22, at like 12:30 a.m. So later at night would be just fine.

And then, a person who, until I ask him, should remain nameless, until he decides whether he wants to reveal himself, actually agreed at like two o'clock in the morning to drive me to the general vicinity of the site.

It was a crystal clear night, probably not quite ten degrees out. You could see every star in the sky. You could see anything that you needed to see, you didn't need a flashlight or anything. There were a couple inches of snow on the ground. It had rained a day or two before, you had those crunchy puddles, so when I walked in there, if I hit a puddle, it made so much noise, or at least that's how it seemed to me. Meanwhile, it's like 2:30 or 3:00 in the morning and no one is waking up, and anyways, the closest house is like a mile or half mile away. My main paranoia was that two teenagers would be out having their little love-'em-ups out in the road there, and I didn't want the tower to come down on some teenagers and really screw up this political action. This is the last thing you need.

I had to walk around the tower on two little roads that went in there, to make sure no one was on the roads. And then it was set to work. My initial estimate was that it would take me about a half hour to knock it over. But it did take a little longer, about an hour. My initial plan was to undo the bolts at the bottom of the tower. That would destabilize the base. And then I would undo the turnbuckles that were holding the cables that kept the tower up.

But the wrenches I had under the turnbuckles didn't work, and I ended up having to use this big crowbar. And there was a lot more tension on the cables than I expected. But there was no way to figure that out except to get in there and turn the buckles. The turnbuckles were about three feet long, and when I first started turning them, the tension was really enormous, so I had to really grrrrr on it. It took a long time. And my theory had been that there was so much tension on the first turnbuckle, that when I undid the first one the tower would probably just break, by releasing the first one.

The tower is 500 feet tall, and there's seven turnbuckles, so essentially every 70 feet there was a guy wire, a big support wire. And the tower is triangular, if you undo one side, the other two vectors are pulling away from you, and it's going to pull itself over. I undid the first turnbuckle, and I gotta tell you, when that first cable let go, I had to be really careful, because there was thousands of pounds of tension on the guy wire, and I didn't know whether the thing would break. If one of them broke, and one of the cables let go, of course it would backlash and would cut me in half in a second. I had to be careful. As the thing started to let go, or get close to letting go, I was putting the crowbar in at an angle, and turning it and hoping that it would let go and take off. It was so crystal clear that night, and so still, and sharp, cold, and just perfect, and when the first guy wire let go, it made so much noise, I couldn't believe it. Five hundred feet of solid steel, sticking up, and this big piece of guy wire with a turnbuckle on it was going "wang, wang," spinning around the goddamn tower, bouncing off of it, and making this incredible racket. I was completely spellbound and I thought, "Oh my God, everybody in Montague is gonna hear this." And it didn't fall down. And I'm thinking to myself, "Shit, I've made so much noise that everybody in the world is gonna be awake. I'm gonna get caught."

I just bolted off into the woods and hung out there for like five minutes, just waiting. Because I figured, the cops are gonna come, this is ridiculous. The lights are gonna go on, people are going to report it, whatever the hell. But nothing happened. So I undid the second turnbuckle, it let go, made the same noise, crash bang. And it recoiled into the tower. I mean it was like a guitar string, but with a weight on the end. And it didn't have a soundboard made out of wood, it had a soundboard made out of steel. Anyway, when I undid the second one, same thing happened, tower didn't go down. And nobody comes. Third one I undid, damn thing made the same noise, and the tower still didn't go down, because the three-sided tower had so much superstructure in it, triangulation and steel in it, that the damn thing actually stayed up. Then I undid the fourth one, and when the fourth one let go, the tower just crumpled, and came right down.

I remember watching the thing coming down, and the lights flickered and went out, and this incredible cloud of ozone just burst out, because you're short-circuiting an enormous amount of electricity running up in this tower. So there was an incredible smell of ozone all around the area of the tower.

Lights went out, tower comes down, and I remember looking up, and the whole thing had not fallen down, there was still this little finger of the damn thing still up. And I was really disappointed that I didn't knock the whole thing down. But afterwards, I sort of realized that it actually was all to the good, because it made it look like such a wreck with that little piece left standing. I climbed around the tower, and I bolted north, through the Montague Plains.

My plan was to get myself all the way to the police station and turn myself in. So I ran about a mile through the woods towards the power lines and then followed the power lines out to the road that headed towards where the police station was. And I got two, two and a half miles north, then down onto the road, and I was just going to walk down to the police station along the road.

There's a sportsman's club on the road headed out that way. And just as I came to where the sportsman's club driveway was, the Montague police cruiser comes out of the sportsman's club. And they were probably down there sleeping. As a matter of fact I'm positive they were sleeping. And the cruiser pulls up, and there are two cops in the car. The cop that's driving pulls up next to me, and says, "What's up, where you going?" And I said, "I'm going to the police station." This guy was such a space shot, that he says, "Oh, we're going down that way, we'll give you a lift. Jump in!" And the guy in the passenger seat, also a cop, was sleeping. I mean, he was out cold. So, dig this, they drive me to the next town, Turners Falls, to the traffic lights, two blocks from the police station.

The only thing the guy said to me was, "What's your name?" I said, "Sam Lovejoy." Then he said, "What were you doing at 3.30 in the morning?" So I said, "Out for a walk." And we get to the lights, and I don't know if you've ever been in a police cruiser, but once you get in the back of the cruiser, you can't get back out again. There's no handles. You can't get out unless someone's opening the door from the outside. So the guy driving the car actually has to wake up the cop in the passenger seat, "Wake up man! Let this guy out." He's mumbly grumbly, gets out of the passenger seat, opens the door, and I said, "Thanks an awful lot!"

I walk down to the police station and the sergeant on duty is a guy named Sergeant Cade. I walk in, he looks up at me, he's met me a couple of times before. And I said, "Sergeant Cade! I'm here to report that the tower's not there. I was just walking down the road!" Because what I wanted to do was have him confirm that the tower was down, and then I would hand him the statement.

He looks at me totally mystified; he can't believe it. You know, 3:30 in the morning, Gonzo me standing there, probably completely lit, I'm sure that I was in complete seventh heaven. I was totally energized, and I said, "I was just taking a walk and the tower's not there." So he gets on the radio to the cruiser and says, "Hey, I got a report that the lights on the tower are out." And the cruiser radios back immediately and says, "Oh no, the lights are fine, we were just up there." And I look at him, and I said, "Uhhh, Sergeant Cade, I think you better check." Very dead serious. And he says, "Look, I got a really strong report here, you better go check."

About ten minutes later, this is what you hear: suddenly the radio goes on and you hear this heavy breathing noise, and, "Good God, Jesus Christ!!!! Sergeant! Looks like an airplane hit the tower about halfway up!"

And I look at Cade, and I say, "Well Sergeant, you know and I know that there ain't any airplane in the world that can fly into a steel structure like that and fly away. Right?"

So Cade says to the guys, "Check and see what's going on. If it was an airplane, there's gotta be a crash somewhere." That's when I said, "It wasn't an airplane." And I hand him my statement taking full responsibility for knocking down the tower.

He didn't read the whole statement at once, he read it, sentence by sentence, slowly, probably the entire first page. Then the rest of it he sort of glanced through. But he would read a sentence, and he'd look up at me. Then he'd read another sentence, and then he'd look at me again, as if in disbelief. And this ritual went on for five or ten minutes. He did not say a word to me. He would look at it, look at me, look at it, and look at me. Shake his head, read it, and shake his head some more.

"As a farmer concerned about the organic and the natural," I had written, "I find irradiated fruit, vegetables and meat to be inorganic; and I can find no natural balance with a nuclear plant in this or any community.

"There seems to be no way for our children to be born or raised safely in our community in the very near future. No children? No edible food? What will there be?

"While my purpose is not to provoke fear, I believe that we must act; positive action is the only option left open to us. Communities have the same rights as individuals. We must seize back control of our own community.

"The nuclear energy industry and its support elements in government are practicing actively a form of despotism. They have selected the less populated rural countryside to answer the energy needs of the cities. While not denying the urban need for electrical energy (perhaps addiction is more appropriate), why cannot reactors be built near those they are intended to serve? Is it not more efficient? Or are we witnessing a corrupt balance between population and risk?

"It is my firm conviction that if a jury of twelve impartial scientists was empanelled, and following normal legal procedure they were given all pertinent data and arguments, then this jury would never give a unanimous vote for deployment of nuclear reactors amongst the civilian population. Rather, I believe they would call for the complete shutdown of all the commercially operated nuclear plants.

"Through positive action and a sense of moral outrage, I seek to test my convictions."

Cade finished reading the statement. Then he said, "Well Jesus, I'm gonna have to arrest you. And I'm gonna have to make some phone calls. But it says here, and you signed it, didn't you? This is your signature," and I said, "Yup, that's my signature on the back page." And he says, "I'm gonna have to arrest you, I'm gonna have to put you in the cell." And I said, "Well do I get to make a call?" He says, "Yup."

I call up this lawyer friend of mine, Tom Lesser, and I say, "Thomas, I'm in the Montague jail, I've been arrested, and you're my phone call. But you gotta do me a favor. Before you come over here, or you can wait till the morning, don't worry about it. But you gotta call up my brother in Wilbraham and you gotta tell him what's happened so that he goes down and tells my mother." Because my mother was a nurse, and she worked the 6:00 a.m. to 2:00 p.m. shift, and she always left about five o'clock in the morning. What scared me to death was that my mother would be driving to work, little Olive, driving slow into Springfield, early in the morning, and listening to the radio news, and at 5:30 in the morning, she might suddenly hear, "Sam Lovejoy of Montague arrested for knocking down this giant tower." And I could just see my mother gasping and driving off the road or something. I didn't want her to have a conniption. So I wanted Tom to tell my brother, who could drive down and tell my mother, "Don't worry about it, Sam's fine, if you hear anything, it's cool." So Tom called my brother Tony and he was cool, he went down and talked to my mom.

I'm in the cell, and Tom comes, and we talk in the little lawyer room, and, as my attorney, he reads the statement, and says to me, "You know, this is a really good statement you wrote, Sam." So then Tom says that he'll meet me at the courthouse later that morning. I wanted him to do the bail hearing, but I told him flat out, if and when I get to court, I'm gonna defend myself. Tom wasn't into that. He was giving me the formal advice, "Any idiot who defends himself has a fool for a client." But I told him, "Forget that, this is civil disobedience, I should defend myself. Don't worry about it. I'm not relying on anybody else."

So Chief Hughes gets there about 6:00, and he yanks me out of the cell, and tells me that they're going to charge me with this five-year felony, and he puts handcuffs on me, and he sticks me in the back of the cruiser to go over to the courthouse. But they don't even leave for the courthouse until like 8:30. So I sat in the back of the cruiser, in handcuffs, for two hours, and it was uncomfortable; he knew what he was doing. It hurt.

Finally, we drive over to the courthouse, and he's livid. He's railing at me all the way. He's really pissed. And I think the only thing I remember him saying other than being pissed off, was that I was never going to get out on bail.

Two weeks before I knocked over the tower, Patty Hearst had been kidnapped. The word "terrorism" was now out in public. So the question was, would the Patty Hearst thing and bad vibes and everything, affect my trial?

We go to the bail hearing, and Tom did the whole litany about me: born in Springfield, father was career Army, commandant of the Springfield armory, and he died during the Korean War, and I lived in Wilbraham, and I graduated valedictorian in high school, and graduated from Amherst College, and I'd lived in the Pioneer Valley my entire life. Tom made me out to be the most honorable citizen to ever walk the face of the earth.

There was this new judge in District Court, Judge Ball, and he was really pissed, too. By coincidence, he also had graduated from Amherst College. So when Tom said I was a graduate of Amherst College, Judge Ball said, "You graduated from there?!" He just burst out, I'll never forget it. And the judge then said that he was going to have to take this question under advisement. Because everybody knew that this was a big thing.

So the judge says that he's got to consider this question of release on my own recognizance, and go in the chambers, and be back in a couple minutes. He ends up staying for like forty-five minutes in chambers. He was gone a really long time. And there are all these prisoners from the county court, the county jail, your normal people waiting for their hearings. But there were a lot of media people there, too, and a lot of people who knew me from the area, a lot of supporters and stuff. They were all crowded into the courtroom. And it turns out that the judge made like 15 or 20 phone calls, including calling up Amherst College and finding out if I actually went there. It turned out he was also calling politicians and the district attorney's office, and other judges, asking them, "What the hell do we do here?"

Because they were flipped out that this was political, like, "Uh-oh, this political commune, maybe they've re-activated." That was one of the things I think was really going on. The anti-war people at the farm had been pretty quiet for a while. But the authorities knew that there was an activist past that these people came from.

But after all these phone calls, Judge Ball comes out and says he's going to have to release me on personal recognizance, because that's what the statute says. We would have won the appeal of any bail ruling. So after all this incredible lengthy consideration of everything, they had to let me go without putting up bail money.

The next step was a grand jury hearing in order to re-indict me with all the formalities. And I knew that they were bringing in other people to talk about the crime, so I appeared at the grand jury. I stood outside the door and kept saying, "Are you gonna let me in?"

"Oh, no, we don't want you in there."

"Come on! Let me in! I want to meet with the grand jury!" And they wouldn't let me in the grand jury because they were scared that somehow I'd be able to talk the grand jury into not indicting me. The local community was furious with me. The Greenfield *Recorder* denounced me; one of the columnists compared me to John Wilkes Booth, Sirhan Sirhan, Lee Harvey Oswald, and Adolph Hitler. Somebody suggested that people opposed to the plant should leave town.

But I got lots of support, too. People began to realize that the nuclear plant was an issue that affected them and their families. In the spring town meetings in our neighboring towns of Shutesbury, Leverett, and Wendell people went on record against the plant. Amherst town meeting raised but did not pass a nuclear moratorium resolution. Montague, however, still favored the nuke in town.

The trial got delayed until September. By the end of the summer we had national media attention, we had collected more than 3800 signatures, and we had two referendums on the local ballot. Our blue-and-white "No Nukes" bumper stickers were selling like hotcakes.

The trial was great, an unbelievable trial, went along for two weeks. The jury selection took a day, and the courthouse was completely full of people. Right off the top, the judge (Judge Smith) had a giant argument with me about whether I was going to have a lawyer—he really wanted me to have a lawyer, and said to me, "Don't you realize you could go to jail for five years?" that kind of thing. I said, "Yes, your honor, I realize the potential danger, but I have Tom Lesser as my attorney, even though he's sitting in the audience. The only time I'm going to use Tom Lesser is when I take the stand, so he can ask me questions, because I'm announcing now that I'm going to take the witness stand. The defendant is definitely going to testify in this case."

And I got Dr. John Gofman, who's the nuclear expert, totally great educator and analyst and a lot of government credentials, to testify about the harmful effects of radiation. Howard Zinn, the historian, was there to talk about civil disobedience, the historical importance of all that stuff. (At first Howard didn't really know what to make of me. I went down to Boston University before the trial, talked to him, and he said he'd be glad to testify, but didn't know anything about nuclear power. I told him about it, gave him all the corporate analysis and the rest of it, and he saw right through it, and he said he'd be glad to testify.)

The trick is, how do you get the court to allow you to bring these witnesses in for you as evidence, since they weren't anywhere near the event?

You see, I wasn't trying to make a thing of me—I was trying to make a thing of the nuke. I didn't want people to get so focused on the idea of property destruction and all that shit. So turning myself in, I thought, would mitigate that notion. But Gofman and Zinn had to testify for me; they were my witnesses about the issues.

The judge got really hung up over the question: had I ever met Gofman before I knocked over the tower? No, I had never met Gofman, but I had read his books, I'd seen him in anti-nuclear movies and other kinds of stuff, but I had never actually physically met Gofman beforehand.

The judge asked me, "Well, did you speak to him?" And I said, "Well, don't you 'speak' to Oliver Wendell Holmes when you read his Supreme Court decisions? Aren't you 'speaking' to him?" That really threw the judge for a loop. I remember him looking at me like, "What?" But the argument came down to: did I know these people, had they influenced me before I knocked over the tower? And I said, "Yes, they had influenced me in all their writings and stuff. I can't put Thoreau on the stand, but I should."

So that got to be a real hang-up. What the judge decided to do was to allow them to testify, for the record, but with the jury out of the room, so that if I lost, I could bring the record forward on appeal.

Gofman went first. He did the science and economics stuff. He raised the issue of a reactor meltdown, which could destroy hundreds of thousands of lives and do billions of dollars worth of damage. An area hundreds of miles in every direction would be desolated for centuries. Pro-nukers always claimed that the chances of a meltdown were almost nil, but Gofman said: "I find when we're talking about a mass of a hundred tons of material at five-thousand degrees Fahrenheit, with water around there, with hydrogen being generated, burning explosively, melting through concrete into the soil, when somebody tells me, 'We're sure it isn't going to go far away,' I look at them as a chemist and I say, 'I've heard various forms of insanity, but hardly this form.' "

"I don't really know whether the chance is one in ten, or one in a hundred, or one in ten thousand. I just ask myself in view of the fact that we have so much easier ways to generate energy needs, why do it this way?"

Gofman talked about his research on plutonium. He even quoted the AEC as saying plutonium is "the most fiendishly toxic substance ever known." Each nuclear plant creates thousands of pounds of waste plutonium, and what do you do with it? "The proliferation of nuclear power carries with it the obligation to guard the radioactive garbage . . . not only for our generation but for the next thousand or several thousand." Gofman said he knew there was a lot of money invested in uranium and the future of atomic power. "And unfortunately their view is, 'We've got to recover our investment, no matter what the cost to the public.'"

Now, dig this, Howard Zinn is on the stand, probably one of the world's foremost authorities on civil disobedience, and I'm asking him a bunch of questions, and he's answering them beautifully, historically and poetically. He's telling the court that the tower-toppling was in the tradition of Gandhi, Thoreau, and the Abolitionists, including (of course) my distant cousin Elijah P. Lovejoy, who ran an abolitionist newspaper and was hanged by a proslavery mob in southern Illinois in 1837. The judge interrupts to ask if true civil disobedience did not have to be strictly non-violent. Zinn replies that the destruction of property is not violent when life is at stake. "Violence," he says, "has to do with human beings, not property." Zinn also points out that I had turned myself in, whereas many people who commit civil disobedience just disappear.

It took days to get through the prosecution's case. Then, when we got to my case, I was on the stand for two days. That's where my attorney, Tom Lesser, was great. When I got on the stand, Tom basically spent a day and a half running through my entire life, and how I got to be sitting on the stand. It was really quite amazing. Then I talked to the jury about my life and my conversion to direct action, and I told them about Sequoyah, a child who lived at the farm. I said, I acted, taking down the tower, not out of malice, but because I had fallen in love with a little four-year-old girl named Sequoyah. I asked myself, who am I to do this thing, to take on the role of judge? But then I thought about this little girl who couldn't defend herself, and I knew I had to act.

I thought that the prosecution did not win the jury, but in the end it didn't matter because the indictment said "destruction of personal property," but all the tax records and tax officials in Montague testified that the tower had been assessed (at $42,500) as "real" property, and Northeast Utilities had even paid the tax under the category as real property. We had a technicality the court couldn't get around. The judge threw out the charge, dismissed the jury and that was it. I practically pleaded with the judge to go on, so we could air the issue, but he banged his gavel, said, "Not guilty" and it was over. I didn't even get six months for destroying "real" property.

As far as the trial was concerned, the anti-nuclear argument was totally compelling. The corporate greed analysis was totally obvious. The governmental corruption, and the inability to do anything within the governmental rules at that time was perfectly clear. I mean, there was supposed to be this "intervention process." And the intervention process was: you don't want the nuke, so you hire a lawyer, pay him fifty to seventy-five thousand dollars, he goes to the Atomic Energy Commission, which was, at that time, legislatively mandated to promote nuclear power and regulate it. You pay them a bunch of money to file some sort of administrative legal action. Basically, to do what? Make it safer. Not to stop it. It was impossible to stop the building of a nuclear plant if you followed the government rules.

The final ending of the twin nuclear plants planned for the Montague Plains took a long time. In 1976, they announced that there was a one-year delay. In '77 they announced a two-year delay, and then a four-year delay. And sometime in late '77 or '78, they finally announced that it was cancelled, once and for all.

I would say it played out this way: we rang a big bell in Montague and then we immediately focused on anti-nuclear organizing outside of Montague. I spent a lot of time in New Hampshire, and I traveled all over the country throughout '75 and '76. And when the company announced the licensing of the Seabrook, New Hampshire nuke, probably mid-June of '76, we had this meeting of 40 or 50 people and called ourselves the Clamshell Alliance. The statement of purpose of the organization and the organization itself, the coordinating committee, and consensus decision-making, and the first occupation, and everything was designed all in the space of a couple weeks.

That Clamshell model of attacking a nuclear plant by occupying the building site then spread to other states. I was involved in organizing the Abalone alliance, which was the first big one in California. And then we put together a whole bunch of other ones all over the United States. I probably was involved with doing civil disobedience training for like 15 or 20 organizations. But it brought in everybody. All the anti-war people, you know, American Friends Service Committee, and all sorts of people who knew about civil disobedience, they were all brought in to help with the training. And we were educating them about nuclear power, and they were educating people about civil disobedience. There was an incredible amount of outreach to other kinds of groups, like women's groups, like Native Americans, for example, because most of the uranium mines were on Native American land. I mean, there were all sorts of interconnections that you could make.

Montague was about the last plant that was proposed but never built. That was the last announced one. They got to a hundred and one nuclear plants, and now there's maybe just a couple more. They're slowly closing them down. Maine Yankee plant is closed. They're talking about Pilgrim; Connecticut Yankee is going down; Indian Point, they've already closed one or two units there. Yankee Rowe is decommissioned. They're starting to hit the diminishing returns syndrome.

And you know, all the technological stuff that we talked about 30 years ago is all coming to pass. Chernobyl. Three Mile Island. The cracked containment vessels. And just the other day one of the nukes had a hole in the top of the containment, some acid dripping on the top of the thing. I mean, what can go wrong, will go wrong.

What I did was, I became the lightning rod for the radical anti-nuke people. When you do a radical act, you give instant credibility to all the more moderate people who looked like they were radicals before. So all these people that used to be hated, the anti-nuclear proponents, suddenly they're raising way more money for their lawyers, and they're totally credible, and they're showing up in every newspaper article, and even the governor is calling them up, and everybody is looking at them like, "What credibility!" when, a month before, they were the radicals, they were the people no one would talk to. And then people started listening to them.

EDITORS' NOTE

The courtroom testimony quoted above was accessed by a western Massachusetts reporter and published in WIN magazine shortly after the conclusion of Samuel Lovejoy's trial: reporter and published in WIN magazine shortly after the conclusion of Samuel Lovejoy's trial: Harvey Wasserman, "Nuke Developers on the Defensive," WIN 10, no. 41 (5 December 1974): 4–9.

QUESTIONS FOR DISCUSSION

1. Sam Lovejoy's story is based on a tape-recorded interview. In that sense, it is an oral history and the language is informal. In what ways do the tone and language of this story convey Lovejoy's personality? What is your opinion of Sam Lovejoy as a person and as an activist?

2. Sam Lovejoy first becomes involved in campus political issues at Wilbraham Academy and later at Amherst College. What are those issues? How is Lovejoy similar to the other students and what makes him different? What events in the late 1960s make Lovejoy an activist and organizer?

3. Compare the way Amherst College administrators respond to student activism with responses at the University of California four years earlier, as described in Jackie Goldberg's chapter, "Sit Down! Sit Down!". What has changed? What is still the same? What would you say accounts for the similarities and differences?

4. How does Sam Lovejoy become involved in "environmentalism?" Why does he make a commitment to organic farming and who influences that commitment? How does Lovejoy's commitment to the environment and organic farming affect his later decision to oppose the Montague nuclear power plant?

5. Why is Lovejoy already considering opposition to nuclear power plants when Northeast Utilities constructs the tower near his farm? What sort of background research does he do? What does he find that leads him to oppose the plant?

6. What do you think of Sam Lovejoy's trial? How is the justice system Lovejoy experiences different from the one portrayed in Jackie Goldberg's chapter? How important are the judge and the press to the outcome?

7. What do you think of Lovejoy's decision to bring down the tower? Do you agree or disagree with his decision or his action? Wouldn't Lovejoy's deed be considered a terrorist act today? What do you think would happen to Sam Lovejoy if this were a recent event? What has changed?

The Contributors

CAROLE BARBATO

A year after the May 4, 1970, killings at Kent State, Carole graduated from the university with a bachelor's degree in speech education. She began her career at Newfield High School in Centerreach, New York, where she taught English and Speech and coached Forensic Speech Teams. The following year, she married Patrick Barbato. Carole received a master's degree in communication in 1975 and a Ph.D. from Kent State in 1994. She is now Associate Professor of Communication Studies at Kent State University's East Liverpool Campus. Carole and Patrick's daughter, Alissa, also a Kent State graduate, is now pursuing a master's degree in counseling. In 2001, because of her special connection to the Kent State shootings, Carole Barbato was asked to co-teach a Kent State course about the May 4th tragedy. She continues to teach the lessons of those shootings today.

WAYNE "CRASH" COE

After leaving the army and completing college, Wayne "Crash" Coe became a commercial pilot. He also worked as a chemical engineer and for some time owned a chemical company in Utah. For several years in the 1980s, he was the Port Engineer for a tugboat company in San Francisco. He has five children and he and his second wife, Judy, live in Florida, where they are raising their daughter, Haley. Now retired, Wayne spends much of his time fishing in the Gulf, and he is currently building a house designed to withstand hurricanes. He still suffers from post-traumatic stress disorder, a consequence of Vietnam combat, but feels that with the help of his wife, who has training in psychology, he is slowly healing from damage incurred 40 years ago. Wayne says that he does not re-read the Vietnam stories he writes, and he cannot bear to read the letters he sent home from Vietnam, as they remind him too sharply of the loss of his brother and many comrades in the war. However, he is planting a lot of trees these days, a sign, he says, of his belief in tomorrow.

R. THOMAS COLLINS, Jr.

Tom Collins earned a B.A. in government from Boston University in 1970 and an M.S.J. from Columbia University's School of Journalism in 1974. He worked as a reporter for newspapers in New England, then as a reporter, rewrite man, and editor with *The New York Daily News*. He moved to Mobil Oil, where he was the public relations manager for their U.S. marketing and refining unit and later for their worldwide exploration and producing unit. Tom's work focused on Nigeria, Indonesia, Qatar, and Vietnam. After retirement from Mobil, Tom worked as a Washington, D.C., lobbyist for an Australian oil company. He then founded and managed RavensYard, a print-on-demand publishing company. Tom's own books include *Newswalker: A Story for Sweeney* (2001), *White Monkey: A Journey Upstream* (2003), and *Just Business, Just War* (2004). Tom married Sun Ok Kim in 1971. Their daughter, Lee, is a radiologist in New York and their son, Micah, is product manager for a semiconductor company in Oregon. Tom was diagnosed with leukemia in 2005 and died on May 24, 2006, at the age of 58.

LAURA DAVIS

Laura Davis was graduated from Kent State with her bachelor's degree in English and American studies in 1973 and a master's emphasizing comparative literature in 1976, when her first child with husband Tom Clapper was born. That son, Jeffrey, is now married to Kelly Dietrick and they have two children. Tom and Laura's second son, Jesse, was born in 1979 and graduated from Kent State. After completing a Ph.D. in English at Kent State, Laura taught at Kent State's East Liverpool Campus for nine years. She is now Associate Provost at Kent State, with responsibility for the academic budget and all manner of planning—strategic, facilities, and technology. With Carole Barbato, she teaches the university's May 4th course and in other ways supports understanding the May 4, 1970, legacy. In 2006, Laura and Carole helped create the text for a campus marker from the Ohio Historical Society. At home, Laura and Tom spend time with their grandchildren, Lucy and Finn.

STEVE DIAMOND

In 1971, Steve Diamond wrote *What the Trees Said: Life on a New Age Farm*, the story of the Liberation News Service (LNS) and its move from New York City to rural Montague, Massachusetts. Steve himself spent many years on the farm. In the late 1970s, he was the editor of the *Valley Advocate*, an alternative newspaper based in Amherst, Massachusetts, and in 1979 he published *Panama Red*, a novel. He and his former wife, Judith, raised two daughters, Crescent and Maia. Steve wrote for the *Atlantic Monthly*, the San Francisco *Chronicle*, the *L.A. Weekly*, the *International Times of London*, the New Orleans *Times Picayune,* and *The Village Voice.* He also worked with Green Mountain Post Films, scripting and narrating two films: *Voices of Spirit* and *Save the Planet.* In 2004, he completed *Citizen Bloom!,* a screenplay for a documentary on the life of Marshall Bloom, LNS, and the Montague Farm. Steve was co-author of *One Day in Peace, January 1, 2000,* which was translated into 18 languages. His work with the United Nations resulted in a resolution for a "One Day in Peace" holiday. Steve died February 4, 2006, in Santa Barbara, California, while waiting for a heart transplant.

SARA M. EVANS

Sara Evans completed her Ph.D. in women's history at the University of North Carolina in 1976. She joined the faculty at the University of Minnesota that same year and helped to found the university's pioneering Department of Women's Studies. In 2004, she was named Regents Professor, the highest honor the University of Minnesota bestows. She is the author of a number of books, including *Personal Politics: The Roots of Women's Liberation in the Civil Rights Movement and the New Left* (1979), *Born for Liberty: A History of Women in America* (1996), and *Tidal Wave: How Women Changed America at Century's End* (2003). Sara Evans has two children: son Craig, now an Internet specialist in an advertising firm, and daughter Jae, who serves in the Coast Guard. In a new marriage since 2002, Sara Evans continues her political activism on feminist, environmental, and social justice issues, and she anticipates an active and adventurous life in retirement.

JAMES FADIMAN

James Fadiman completed his Ph.D. and taught psychology at San Francisco State University and Brandeis University, and Design Engineering at Stanford. In 1976, he co-founded the Institute for Transpersonal Psychology, where he still teaches. In 1974, Jim wrote a psychology textbook (now in its sixth edition) and subsequently edited six books on topics including madness, holistic health, and Sufism. He has also published a self-help book and a "Sixties" novel, *The Other Side of Haight.* He continues to present his ideas internationally through speeches, workshops, and consulting. His life and work are the subject of a 2005 documentary film, *Transpersonal Conversations: James Fadiman, Ph.D.* Jim has been married for over 40 years to Dorothy Fadiman, a social-activist filmmaker. Jim and Dorothy still miss the open inquiry of the 1960s.

JOHNNY FLYNN

In 1974, Johnny Flynn moved to California, where he became involved in American Indian employment and Indian Education programs in the public schools. Between 1978 and 1980, Johnny and others protested—and ultimately halted—the construction of a dangerous liquefied natural gas off-loading facility near Point Conception, California. In 1984, Johnny graduated with honors in history from the University of California at Santa Barbara. He earned an M.A. in religious studies in 1987, and a Ph.D. in Native American religions in 1991. He taught Native American studies and religious studies in Arizona and Oklahoma. Dr. Flynn is now a faculty member in the Department of Religious Studies at Indiana University in Indianapolis. He remains active in Native American education and cultural and language preservation. He is writing a book about Native American religions.

JACKIE GOLDBERG

Jackie Goldberg became a community activist. After earning an M.A.T. from the University of Chicago, she began a 20-year teaching career. In Compton, California, she developed a model cross-disciplinary reading program for low-income and English-language learners. In 1983, she was elected to the Los Angeles Unified School Board, where she worked to create on-campus health clinics, improve curriculum, and attain higher salaries for teachers. In 1993, Jackie became the first openly lesbian woman on the Los Angeles City Council. Her city council legacy includes instituting a "Living Wage" ordinance for city employees, banning "Saturday Night Specials," and developing a successful "Slum Abatement" program. Since 1979, Jackie has lived in Los Angeles with her lifelong partner, Sharon Stricker. Their son, Brian Stricker Goldberg, recently married Carmen McDonald. Jackie Goldberg was elected to the California State Assembly in 2000. During three terms in office, she championed legislation in education, civil rights, labor, and election reform and she continues to work on behalf of the disenfranchised and the underrepresented.

TARA COLLINS GORDON

Tara went on to receive her M.A. in art history from Queens College and worked on a doctorate at the City University of New York (CUNY). She has published articles in *Arts Magazine,* the *New York Art Journal,* and *East Village Eye,* and she taught design history at a number of New York City schools, including Parsons School of Design, the School of Visual Arts, the Fashion Institute of Technology, and Pratt Institute. With her husband, David Gordon, she founded Mata Ortiz Pots (www.mataortizpots.com) to bring fine art ceramics from Mexico to the American market. Both Tara and her husband have lectured at the Museum of Latin American Art, Long Beach, and the University of California at Fullerton. Tara's book, *E. McKnight Kauffer: American Designer between the European World Wars,* was recently published. Tara Gordon, her husband, and their daughter, Samantha, now reside in Solana Beach, California, where Tara is active in Girl Scouts (she led a troop for 10 years) and in the Solana Beach Public Arts Commission, recently leading an Arts Alive Banners fundraiser.

RAYMOND HUBBARD

Ray Hubbard graduated from Texas Southern University with a B.S. in mathematics. He interrupted his graduate work in mathematics for a two-year stint in the U.S. Army in Colorado. After this tour of duty, Ray moved to California in late 1963 where he met his wife, Geneva (Gean), on a blind date. They married four months later. While working for the IBM Corporation in various capacities for 28 years, Ray was able to continue his education and to support Gean in continuing her own education. Ray received his M.B.A. in 1976 and Gean became an RN in 1979. Before his recent retirement, Ray worked for Multimax, Inc., telecommuting to that Herndon, Virginia, company from his home. Ray and Gean have two children, Sybil and Eric, who are both college graduates; Sybil received her master's degree in social work in 2006.

TIM KOSTER

Tim Koster received his B.A. in international relations from the University of Minnesota in 1976. He began his career as a planner for the Minneapolis Housing and

Redevelopment Authority, then for the Twin Cities Agency on Aging. Tim served as a board member for charitable institutions and was a member of the Twin Cities Area Health Planning Board. In 1984, he moved to Southern California and in 1989, founded Search Systems, a research company that is now a successful corporation with a popular public records website at www.searchsystems.net. Tim's wife, Prudence, is his business partner, his son, Darryl, is the company's I.T. Director, and his daughter, Dana, is in graduate school at Cornell.

SHEILA LENNON

Sheila Lennon holds a B.A. in English and American history from Wellesley College. In 1969, she dropped out of a Ph.D. program at Brown University to work for Bangladesh relief at India Imports of Rhode Island, where she also started a food coop. She married in 1971 and, with her husband and another couple, established a clothing factory in Gambia, West Africa. In Gambia, she learned Woloff, an unwritten language. After 18 months, she and her husband returned to the States the long way: they crossed the Sahara (in the back of a Peugeot pickup truck and atop an open boxcar full of iron ore), lived in a cave in the Canary Islands, and traveled through Spain, France, and Luxembourg. In 1976, Sheila gave birth to a daughter, Casey. Divorced, she waitressed, headed a library circulation department, and edited a literary magazine. A features editor at *The Providence Journal* (R.I.) since 1985, Sheila now produces the projo.com website and writes the Subterranean Homepage News blog. In 2003, she married Joe Landry, whom she interviewed for the Woodstock stories, and they live with two cats in an 1835 house. Sheila's daughter and her nine-year-old grandson, Dylan, live around the corner.

SAMUEL LOVEJOY

After defeating the Montague nuclear plant in 1975, Sam Lovejoy helped to found many nonviolent, direct action groups all over the United States, including Clamshell Alliance in New Hampshire, where over 1,800 protesters were arrested opposing the Seabrook nuclear plant. Sam raised over $1 million for safe energy groups in 1979–1980 by organizing the Madison Square Garden No Nukes Concerts. The concerts became the subject of an album and a documentary film, both called *No Nukes*. Sam graduated law school in 1988, and now primarily practices conservation law and advises the indigent in civil and criminal matters. Sam remains committed to Montague, Massachusetts, his hometown since 1970, though he no longer lives at the farm. He has held many town political offices including Selectman, and has served on both town and county Planning Boards, spending five years as Franklin County Commissioner.

RON McCOY

Ron McCoy graduated from college in 1971. He spent time in the Yucatan, Big Sur, and the Southwest before marrying in 1976. Entering graduate school at Northern Arizona University in 1979, he earned a master's degree in anthropology and a doctorate in history. In 1989, after living on the Navajo Reservation and working as a teacher and freelance writer, he joined the faculty at Emporia State University in Kansas. Recognition for his books and articles—most dealing with American Indian art and culture—include a Wrangler Award from the National Cowboy and Western Heritage Center and the American Association of Museums' Award of Distinction. Ron's wife works in the special education field and their son is a professional scuba instructor in the Florida Keys.

JOHN H. MANNERS

After leaving Kenya in 1972, John Manners earned a master's degree in journalism from Columbia and held a series of jobs in the field, including an 18-year stint as a writer and editor in various branches of Time, Inc. He kept up his connection with Kenya by covering the exploits of Kenyan runners in competitions around the world. Since 1994, he has worked freelance and has returned to Kenya more than a dozen times, most often for magazine and television projects. Lately, he has initiated a program that helps place outstanding Kenyan high school students in first-rank universities in the United States. John lives in Montclair, New Jersey, with his wife, Suzanne, a teaching assistant. Their oldest daughter is in law school, their youngest is a 2007 college graduate, and their son works in Ohio.

TOBY MAROTTA

Toby Marotta began his writing career by illustrating why the Stonewall Riots were a historic watershed. *The Politics of Homosexuality* (1981) shows how Stonewall-inspired activists forged a Gay, Lesbian, Bisexual, and Transgender movement that led to globe-spanning counterparts. *Sons of Harvard* (1982) details a number of post-Stonewall personal transformations by profiling the lives of some of Toby's Harvard College classmates. Even as these complementary books were being published, Toby applied their lessons in his federally-funded research on behavioral approaches to preventing HIV infections and AIDS. Concerned that AIDS policymakers and service-providers were not making connections with many of the people who needed their help, he tried to help them find ways to accommodate the psyches and sensibilities of people occupying every sexual, social, and economic niche in American life. Contemporary offshoots of all this work can be found at Toby's Community-Roots Archive at www.RootsArchive.com. Toby and his longtime partner, Rusty Kothavala, now reside in Tucson, Arizona.

HUỲNH QUANG NGỌC

Huỳnh Quang Ngọc taught for five years at Appalachian State University and then earned a Ph.D. from Cardiff University. His most recent novel is *The Family Wound* (2004), and he is currently working on another novel and translating a collection of Vietnamese poetry. Ngọc teaches creative nonfiction and Asian American literature at St. Lawrence University in Canton, New York, where he lives with his wife, Maxine, and two daughters, Natasha and Alexandra. In the summer of 2006, under a Freeman Foundation grant, Ngọc took a group of students from St. Lawrence University to Vietnam. It was his first visit after 30 years living in exile. He stayed with his parents and two older brothers and went back to his childhood home. Ngọc reports that little remains of the rural Vietnam he knew before the war, and says that in some ways he felt foreign to his home, his village, and his country of origin. He found that his former countrymen now consider him a tourist. Ngọc's experience of contemporary Vietnam will be documented in his next book project, a second memoir.

LEAH O'LEARY

Leah O'Leary earned an M.S.W. at Boston College Graduate School of Social Work. She also pursued doctoral studies in Social Welfare Policy at Brandeis University's Heller School. In 1972, she met her future husband, Paul Plato, who was a Roman Catholic priest. After Paul left the priesthood in 1976, Paul and Leah married in 1977 and worked in human services in the Boston area for over 35 years. Both were active in their Norwood, Massachusetts, community around diversity issues. They have three children, Russell, Katharine, and Dennis. Leah is the Founder and Executive Director of A Red Thread Adoption Services, Inc., where she helps families adopt children from all over the world. The agency takes its name from an ancient Chinese belief that there are some people destined to come together in this lifetime and that those people are connected by an invisible red thread. In 2006, Leah decided to pursue her activism in the political arena, and ran for the State House of Representatives in Boston.

ROBERT W. POOLE, Jr.

Bob Poole served as President of the Reason Foundation from July 1978 through December 2000, when he handed the presidency over to Lynn Scarlett, who later became Deputy Secretary of the Interior in the George W. Bush administration. Bob stepped back in temporarily as acting president but soon became Director of Reason's Transportation Studies program. His ongoing transportation policy work addresses urban traffic congestion, highway finance, airport security, and air traffic control reform. In 2003, Bob and his second wife moved to South Florida, where they were able to find a house large enough to build Bob's ultimate model railroad layout, which has its own 30' by 50' room.

YOLANDA RETTER

Yolanda Retter currently manages the UCLA Chicano Studies Research Center Library and Archive. She continues to work on behalf of lesbian and women's issues and has co-edited two anthologies on Lesbian, Gay, Bisexual, Transgendered, and Intersex (LGBTI) history: *Queers in Space: Communities, Public Places, Sites of Resistance* (1997) and *Gay and Lesbian Rights in the United States: A Documentary History* (2003). She also writes about subjects such as ethnicity, gender, sexual orientation, and photography history. She and her partner, Leslie, live near Los Angeles. When she retires, Yolanda plans to live in a spiritual women's community and volunteer for short-term social justice projects in the United States and other countries.

PAT ROYSE

Pat Royse married a *Wall Street Journal* reporter she met covering the 1966 Hough riots, and they moved to Washington, D.C. Pat and her husband purchased a weekly newspaper in Morro Bay, California, sold it two years later, and returned to D.C. The marriage did not last, but Pat continued in journalism. She contributed regular stories to *The Washington Post,* and served as one of the *Post*'s on-call editors, soon joining a chain of weekly newspapers in Maryland as managing editor and reporter at the state-house in Annapolis. She was a charter member of Washington Independent Writers. When her son and daughter were grown, she returned to Ohio, where she is now managing editor of the *Daily Standard* in the city of Celina. Pat's son David is a screen-writer and editor in Los Angeles, and her daughter, a recent graduate of Kent State University, is pursuing a career in theater.

MARIA SALUDADO AND ANTONIA SALUDADO, AND KENT KIRKTON

The Saludado sisters still live in central California. Maria has been employed in the office of the UFW AFL/CIO in various capacities since the grape boycott ended. She is married and her children have all gone to school and entered the professions. Antonia is working as a health care provider and continues to serve others. She is divorced and her children are grown; her youngest child is now in college. In their stories, the sisters both explained that they went into the fields so that their younger siblings would not have to perform agricultural labor and could attend school. The strategy proved very successful. Five of the Saludado siblings are now teachers or administrators in the California public school system.

Kent Kirkton is a professor of journalism at California State University, Northridge. For the past 15 years, he and his colleague, Jorge Garcia, have been inter-viewing the earliest UFW members. Much of the story of the Saludado sisters was drawn from their oral histories.

GERALD J. SCOTT

Gerald J. Scott left the DEA in October 1978. After retreating to an Ozark farm for eight years, he returned to "The World" and began a tri-vocational career as a freelance writer, the owner of a private investigative agency, and, as of 2005, a member of the adjunct faculty of State Fair Community College in Sedalia, Missouri. Medication keeps his chronic PTSD more or less manageable. Gerald's wife, Amber, is the Executive Director of Citizens Against Spouse Abuse in Sedalia. His son, Aaron, a mechanic, lives near Memphis, Tennessee. After obtaining a B.A. in musical theater, his daughter, Susan, spent five years as a firefighter with the U.S. Forest Service. She is now preparing for a career in nursing.

GWENDOLYN ZOHARAH (ROBINSON) SIMMONS

Gwen Robinson continued her civil rights work for several years as a SNCC organizer in Atlanta and Alabama. During that period, she married Michael Simmons, a fellow SNCC organizer. They have one daughter, Aishah Shahidah, who is now a documen-tary filmmaker. In 1972, Gwen was given the name Zoharah by her Sufi master, Sheikh M.R. Bawa Muhaiyaddeen, with whom she studied for 17 years. For 23 years, Zoharah worked as a program officer and later as director of institutional giving for the American Friends Service Committee. She became reconciled with her beloved grandmother and other family members and completed the college career she had given up decades before to work in the Civil Rights Movement. She earned her B.A. at Antioch College, an M.A. in religious studies, and a Ph.D. in Islamic studies at Temple University. The recipient of both Fulbright and USAID Fellowships, Zoharah conducted extensive fieldwork in the Middle East. She accepted a position at the University of Florida in Gainesville, where she is now Assistant Professor of Religion and the author of a forthcoming book, *Muslim Feminism: A Call for Reform.*

KAREN MANNERS SMITH

After leaving The Process, Karen Manners Smith and her husband lived in western Massachusetts from 1974 to 1995. They raised two sons, Noah, now a playwright, and Abe, an actor, and Karen earned a doctorate from the University of Massachusetts in Amherst. Since 1995, she has taught history and women's studies at Emporia State University in Kansas. In 2006 she became the director of Emporia's Ethnic and Gender Studies Program. Her husband pursues a freelance career as a writer, actor, and stand-up comedian. Karen is the author or co-author of several books. She and Tim Koster began work on *Time It Was* in 2002.

JOHN M. WERLICH

John Werlich received his Juris Doctorate from Loyola Law School, Los Angeles, in 1970. As a Los Angeles City Attorney, John served as a prosecutor for four years and then transferred to Los Angeles International Airport, where he is an Assistant City Attorney. He has published law review articles, lectured throughout the country, appeared before numerous courts throughout the United States, and was American Bar Association Chair of the Airport Law Committee for five years. John lives with his wife Valerie in Southern California. Their daughter, Katja Fried, a writer and graduate of Stanford and Columbia, is an editor with an independent American publishing company.